WITCHCRAFT AND DEMONOLOGY
IN SCOTT'S FICTION

WITCHCRAFT AND DEMONOLOGY IN SCOTT'S FICTION

With chapters on the
Supernatural in Scottish Literature

COLEMAN O. PARSONS

1964

OLIVER & BOYD
EDINBURGH AND LONDON

OLIVER AND BOYD LTD
Tweeddale Court
14 High Street
Edinburgh 1

39a Welbeck Street
London W.1

First published 1964

PREFACE

SCOTT'S place in the Romantic movement and in world literature, both as a poet and as the Author of Waverley, has often been discussed by critics and literary historians. His firm bedding in the tradition and culture of his own land has received less consideration. It is my purpose in this study to take up one important aspect of Scott's fictional world, the use of the supernatural in poetry and prose, and to relate it to the attitudes of fellow Scots and to the rich store of Scottish literature and folk-lore which was at his disposal. The supernatural is traced in Scottish narrative poetry from Barbour to Burns and in prose fiction from Sir Walter's contemporaries, Hogg and Galt, to our own contemporaries, Gunn and Linklater. Within this larger framework, the supernatural in Scott's work is related to his knowledge and experience and to his critical theory and practice. The term "supernatural" refers to those unearthly agents, forces, and phenomena which men envisage but cannot understand and which operate, for the most part, outside religion.[1]

Throughout this work, my greatest debt has been to my wife, June L. Parsons, who shares a taste for Scottish fiction—read aloud. I have had the privilege of discussing Scott with Frederick A. Pottle of Yale and with my friend William M. Parker. I owe thanks to Mordecai Grossman for reading and commenting on an earlier draft. Death has removed scholars whose helpfulness is still vividly present to me: Chauncey B. Tinker, of Yale; George L. Kittredge, of Harvard; Henry N. MacCracken and Christabel F. Fiske, of Vassar; Sir Henry Meikle, of the National Library of Scotland; Sir Herbert Grierson; and Lewis Spence. My regret at completing this monograph too soon to use the forthcoming life of Scott by my colleague, Edgar Johnson, is hardly lessened by the assurance that it contains no new material with a significant bearing on Scott's use of the supernatural. Finally, I must thank Miss Mary Ross who prepared the index.

C.O.P.

New York
20 October 1962

[1] For religion, see Klaas Bos, *Religious Creeds and Philosophies as Represented by Characters in Sir Walter Scott's Works and Biography*, Amsterdam 1932.

CONTENTS

ABBREVIATIONS

See Bibliography for the complete details

Allardyce	= *Letters from and to Charles Kirkpatrick Sharpe*, ed. Alexander Allardyce.
B.E.M.	= *Blackwood's Edinburgh Magazine.*
B.M.	= British Museum.
Demonology	= Scott, *Letters on Demonology and Witchcraft, addressed to J. G. Lockhart, Esq.*
Domestic Manners	= James Hogg, *Domestic Manners of Sir Walter Scott.*
E.E.T.S.	= Early English Text Society.
E.U.L.	= Edinburgh University Library.
F.Q.R.	= *The Foreign Quarterly Review.*
G.M.	= *The Gentleman's Magazine.*
Grandfather	= Scott, *Tales of a Grandfather; being Stories taken from Scottish History.*
Grierson, *Scott*	= Sir Herbert Grierson, *Sir Walter Scott, Bart.*
Hughes, Mrs	= Mary Ann Hughes, *Letters and Recollections of Sir Walter Scott.*
Irving, *Abbotsford*	= Washington Irving, *Abbotsford and Newstead Abbey.*
Journal	= *Journal of Sir Walter Scott*, ed. J. G. Tait.
Lay	= Scott, *Lay of the Last Minstrel.*
Letters	= Scott, *The Letters of Sir Walter Scott*, ed. H. J. C. Grierson.
Literary Life	= John Galt, *The Literary Life and Miscellanies of John Galt.*
Lives	= Scott, *Lives of Eminent Novelists and Dramatists.*
Lockhart	= John G. Lockhart, *Memoirs of the Life of Sir Walter Scott.*
Minstrelsy	= Scott, *Minstrelsy of the Scottish Border*, ed. Thomas F. Henderson.
M.L.Q.	= *Modern Language Quarterly.*
M.L.R.	= *Modern Language Review.*
N. & Q.	= *Notes and Queries.*
N.L.S.	= National Library of Scotland.
Partington, Letter-Books	= Wilfred Partington, *The Private Letter-Books of Sir Walter Scott.*
Partington, *Post-Bag*	= Wilfred Partington, *Sir Walter's Post-Bag.*

Peveril	=	Scott, *Peveril of the Peak.*
P.M.L.A.	=	*Publications of the Modern Language Association of America.*
Q.R.	=	*The Quarterly Review.*
Select Remains	=	David Laing, *Select Remains of the Ancient Popular and Romance Poetry of Scotland.*
Sinclair	=	George Sinclair, *Satan's Invisible World Discovered*, ed. T. G. Stevenson.
S.T.S.	=	Scottish Text Society.
Walpole	=	MS. Letters to Sir Walter Scott, acquired by Hugh Walpole.

Chapter I

DIVERSITY OF BELIEF AND UNBELIEF

IN religious and philosophical controversy, as well as in literature and popular lore, attitudes toward the supernatural are dynamic. There are periods of intensity and of languor; intellect dispels and imagination recreates the shadow world; opinions constantly modify each other. Storied faith is not so much destroyed by enlightenment as displaced, so that it moves from the centre of belief to its periphery, where it takes up a position in folklore and literature and awaits its chance to invade religion and philosophy once more.

Arising as it did in part from unrest, insecurity, and suspicion, the hysteria of witch-hunting and extermination in the seventeenth century relaxed into a more critical attitude toward divine or diabolical intervention in human affairs. Fear of Catholic and civil plots gave way to complacency about the social order and man's place in the firmly linked chain of being. Eighteenth-century thinkers interpreted phenomena in relation to logical patterns in whose discovery or creation they took pride. Reason, however, could lead men into predicaments when applied to the past or directed from the particular to the general. Addison's avoidance of the latter dilemma was acceptable to many Scotsmen and Englishmen:

> There are some opinions in which a man should stand neuter, without engaging his assent to one side or the other. . . . When I consider the question, whether there are such persons in the world as those we call witches? my mind is divided between the two opposite opinions; or rather (to speak my thoughts freely) I believe in general that there is, and has been such a thing as witchcraft; but at the same time can give no credit to any particular instance of it.[1]

When Biblical events were scrutinised by eighteenth-century reason, a temporal boundary was drawn between bygone supernaturalism and the unbroken operation of known laws of nature. In the debate on miracles, for instance, extremists like Thomas Woolston and Peter Annet argue that

---

[1] *Spectator*, No. 117 (14 Jul. 1711). Also see Sir William Blackstone, *Commentaries on the Laws of England*, ch. iv. 6.

miracles are to be interpreted either as pure allegory or as deliberate Apostolic deception. Defenders of the faith like Bishop Smalbroke, Thomas Sherlock, and Zachary Pearce accept all miracles, consider the disinterestedness of the evangelical witnesses, or concentrate on the credibility of the resurrection. After declaring that "no testimony for any kind of miracle has ever amounted to a probability, much less to a proof" (*An Enquiry concerning Human Understanding*), David Hume takes the middle of the road by exempting the Christian religion—as rooted in faith—from the consequences of his reasoning. Wary of the prestige which their acceptance would confer on Catholicism, Conyers Middleton denies the miracles attested by the Church Fathers and leaves the reader free to apply objections against post-Apostolic miracles to earlier instances. And Bishop Douglas, resenting Hume's brand of rationalism, sets out to disprove ancient pagan as well as modern Papist miracles, and concludes that "the age of Christian miracles must have ceased with the age of Christian inspiration," *c.* 100 A.D. (*The Criterion*). Indeed, this acceptance of early Christian supernatural intervention and disbelief in its continuance became practically an eighteenth-century commonplace.

It would scarcely be warrantable to assume that the opinions of theologians and philosophers articulate common thought. When Hugh Farmer contends that it is mere superstition to suppose that devils cause disease, he departs from majority notions. And the English Nonconformist, John Wesley, is perhaps more all-inclusive than the average man when he expresses belief in ghosts, witches, and visions, in devils as the root of disease, and in demoniacal possession as the cause of most cases of lunacy.

In the early decades of the nineteenth century, the supernatural—the world of ghosts and unearthly powers which was thought to intervene between man and the hierarchies of gods and devils—enjoyed a general revival. The "intellectual chaos"[2] which Sir Leslie Stephen sees at the end of the eighteenth century was accentuated by various movements and upheavals which were groping, violent, and emotional rather than securely rational. It has been observed that political unrest, augmented by fear, usually re-animates belief in the grosser superstitions. The general apprehension of danger in England and Scotland was evident in discussions of the reality of evil spirits and in occasional re-awakening of folk creeds and practices. To many orthodox minds, Napoleon's meteoric career suggested the frenzy of Satan because his time was short. Thus Granville Sharp writes of "the present awful crisis" in which "the malicious rage of

[2] Stephen, *History of English Thought in the Eighteenth Century*, 3rd edn, New York 1927, II. 456.

these *spiritual Enemies* will undoubtedly be excited to the utmost exertion of diabolical mischief (in Suicides, Duels, Murders, &c. &c. besides the horrible National Wars and Public Slaughters in all parts of the world!) during the short remaining time that they will be permitted to assail all unguarded persons."[3] No less hysterical are Scott's own remarks on Napoleon:

> God forgive me! But I think some evil demon has been permitted, in the shape of this tyrannical monster whom God has sent on the nations visited in his anger. I am confident he is proof against lead and steel, and have only hopes that he may be shot with a silver bullet, or drowned in the torrents of blood which he delights to shed. Oh for True Thomas and Lord Soulis's cauldron![4]

> Besides, distant and secure as is Napoleon's present place of exile, we have but scotched the snake, not killed him; and while life lasts, especially after his extraordinary return from Elba, there will not be wanting many to rely upon a third *avatar* of this singular emanation of the Evil Principle.[5]

Seeing God's judgment in contemporary events, religious persons realised that their faith had been undermined by what Lecky calls the "gradual, insensible, yet profound modification of thought prevailing in Europe."[6] Refusal to accept infernal spirits and their activity was indirectly a denial of good spirits and an attack on God. Therefore, the more rigid Christians defended their faith by avowing the theoretical possibility of witchcraft. In the last of five articles "On the Rise and Progress of Witchcraft," a writer who signs himself I.P. refers to cases as special instances of Providence, "for thereby a strong confirmation of the truth of the sacred

[3] Sharp, *The Case of Saul, shewing that his Disorder was a real Spiritual Possession*, London 1807, pp. iii–iv. For the increase of visions and apparitions in World War I, see Forbes Phillips and R. Thurston Hopkins, *War and the Weird*, London 1916.

[4] Letter to [George Ellis], 13 Dec. 1808, in *The Letters of Sir Walter Scott*, ed. H. J. C. Grierson [=Letters], London 1932–7, II. 135–6. Also see Scott's letter to [J. B. S. Morritt], 29 Nov. 1812, *op. cit.*, III. 202; [Morritt], 19 Sep. 1813, and [Joanna Baillie], 3 Feb. 1814, in Mss. Letters to Sir Walter Scott, 1796–1831, acquired by Hugh Walpole [=Walpole], N.L.S.; Thomas Hardy, *The Trumpet Major*, ch. i: "At this time there were two arch-enemies of mankind—Satan as usual, and Buonaparte, who had sprung up and eclipsed his elder rival altogether."

[5] Scott, *Paul's Letters to his Kinsfolk*, Edinburgh 1816, p. 446 (quoting *Macbeth*, III. ii). See also Scott, *Life of Napoleon*, Philadelphia 1827, I. 22, 516; III. 86, 355: Wilfred Partingon, *Sir Walter's Post-Bag* [=Partington, *Post-Bag*], London 1932, pp. 27, 106: [Joanna Baillie] 3 Feb. 1816 (E.U.L., Letters to Sir Walter Scott). J. G. Lockhart, *Memoirs of the Life of Sir Walter Scott, Bart.* [=Lockhart], Edinburgh and London 1837–8, III. 115; VII. 31: H. J. C. Grierson, *Sir Walter Scott, Bart.* [=Grierson, *Scott*], New York 1938, p. 113. For Boney's infernal counsellor, "l'Homme Rouge," see *Paul's Letters to his Kinsfolk*, pp. 418–19, and *G.M.*, 1815, PT I, pp. 122–3. Cp. William Hone's travesty on anti-Napoleonic malisons appearing in the press of 1815, *Buonapartephobia*, 10th edn, London 1820, pp. 8, 10, 14.

[6] W. E. H. Lecky, *History of the Rise and Influence of the Spirit of Rationalism in Europe*, New York 1866, I. 35. See also, I. 114–15.

volume is afforded."[7] The comfortable compromise of Blackstone and Addison also strikes I. P. as convenient.

No tacit admission of the absurdity of the grosser tenets of witchcraft was necessary in theological discussions of the Witch of Endor and the demoniacs of the New Testament, the usual inference being that like phenomena could still appear. The debate on the Witch of Endor concentrated on the problem whether the vision of Samuel was a messenger of God, a delusion of the sorceress, or a cheat of Satan. The interpretation generally accepted was that Samuel's spirit actually appeared to Saul.[8] Demoniacs were explained by fundamentalists as men possessed by veritable devils, and by realists as men afflicted by known diseases.[9]

Although the average man was not deeply interested in the continuity of beliefs from Scriptural times, he did more or less instinctively cling to those forms of superstition which gave him assurance of life after death. The controversy over ghosts, which were commonly accepted as links to the unseen world, may best be summarised in the titles of six slight volumes. The first three are chapbooks, and all but the last are attempts to alter widespread belief:

> An Antidote to Superstition: Or, A Cure for those Weak Minds which are Troubled with the Fear of Ghosts & Witches, or who Tremble at the Consequences of Inauspicious Dreams or Bad Omens [Dunbar n.d.]

[7] G.M., 1830, PT I, p. 109. Historical and entertaining articles on the subject had already appeared in The Retrospective Review, V (1822), 86–136 (seventeenth-century witchcraft), and in The London Magazine, V (1822), 205–15, 376–87, 472–80 (origin, progress, and decay of witchcraft, with allusions to modern survivals in North Wales). George Moir's criticism of G. C. Horst's Zauber-Bibliothek, Maintz 1826, for the F.Q.R., 1830, turns into a summary of dramatic witchcraft trials, with a reference to the forthcoming "History of Daemonology and Witchcraft, for Murray's Family Library, by the person best qualified perhaps in Europe for the task—Sir Walter Scott." (VI. 25 n.) The essay was published separately as Magic and Witchcraft, London 1852, some of the Scottish materials being supplied by Moir's friend Robert Pitcairn, who also gave Scott valuable assistance.

[8] See Thomas Stackhouse, A History of the Holy Bible, ed. George Gleig, London 1817, II. 133, 162–71; The London Christian Instructor, I (1818), 641–8. Scott cautiously asserts that the vision was either Samuel or "some good being." Letters on Demonology and Witchcraft [=Demonology], London 1830, pp. 59–60.

[9] See particularly Hugh Farmer, An Essay on the Demoniacs of the New Testament, 2nd edn, London 1805, p. 96, (1st edn, 1775); James Macknight, The Truth of the Gospel History Shewed, London 1763, pp. 169–70; and William Carlisle, An Essay on Evil Spirits; or, Reasons to Prove their Existence, 2nd edn, London 1825. According to Scott, possession was "a dreadful disorder, of a kind not merely natural" (Demonology, p. 70). It is not, however, an affliction to be suffered in modern times, for miracles ceased after Christ's passion. Sir Walter probably forgot a strange instance of nineteenth-century belief in demoniacs contained in a letter from Joseph Wolff, "Apostle of Jesus Christ," Convent Stauros, Island of Cyprus, 31 Jul. 182 [9], Walpole. The missionary's exorcism of a Devil which tormented a Bedouin Arab was performed at Aboolmayim on 24 Dec. 1828 (Journal of the Rev. Joseph Wolff, London 1839, pp. 188–9).

Visits from the World of Spirits, being a Collection of Facts relating to the Appearances of Ghosts, Spectres, and Apparitions: To which is prefixed, the Best Cure for Imaginary Terrors [Glasgow n.d.]

An Account of Some Imaginary Apparitions, the Effects of Fear or Fraud [Stirling 1801]

Joseph Taylor, *Apparitions; or, the Mystery of Ghosts, Hobgoblins, and Haunted Houses, Developed,* 2nd edn., enlarged [London 1815]

Ghost-Stories: collected with a particular View to Counteract the Vulgar Belief in Ghosts and Apparitions, and to Promote a rational Estimate of the Nature of Phenomena commonly considered as Supernatural [London 1823]

T. M. Jarvis, *Accredited Ghost Stories* [London 1823][10]

Popular notions of the supernatural were complicated between 1811 and 1825 by the appearance of several books which related spectral illusion to bodily or mental disorder. Even as late as 15 March 1825, when requesting permission to dedicate the second edition of his ghost treatise to Scott as President of the Royal Society, Dr Samuel Hibbert explains that the newness of his speculations and the uncertainty as to how the public would receive them kept him from seeking Sir Walter's countenance for the first edition.[11] Hibbert's title is self-explanatory: *Sketches of the Philosophy of Apparitions: or, an Attempt to Trace such Illusions to their Physical Causes* (Edinburgh, 1824). But if the scientific approach was new in 1824, it must have been because of general imperviousness to such books as John Alderson's *An Essay on Apparitions, in which their Appearance is Accounted for by Causes wholly Independent of Preternatural Agency* (Hull, 1811, and London, 1823) and John Ferriar's *An Essay towards a Theory of Apparitions* (London, 1813). Perhaps, the ghosts themselves refused to be laid. Such is the view of two contributors to *Blackwood's*, both of whom attack Ferriar

[10] To this list may be added a volume projected, but apparently not published, by M. I. Horne, who writes to [Scott] on 18 Dec. 1829, for extensive bibliographical aid in performing "what I consider a moral duty in expressing the cause of undoubted Truth." The title is to be *Apparitiana.—Or Evidence of the Actual Appearance to human Perception, on certain Occasions, of Supernatural Visitants, deduced from the Authority of the Sacred Writings, & Historical Records; & containing upwards of 100 rare & well authenticated Instances of modern Data,* Walpole.

[11] Walpole. Hibbert adds that Scott's "successful illustrations of the ancient superstitions of Europe . . . have had no small share in inducing me to consider the subject of many popular illusions with much attention; the result of which has been an attempt to explain some of the important mental laws to which they may be considered as attributable." Also see the dedication of Sir David Brewster, *Letters on Natural Magic addressed to Sir Walter Scott, Bart.,* London 1832, pp. 1–2. In Letter 1 of *Demonology,* Scott ascribes certain experiences to sensory "delusions," "a depraved State of the bodily Organs," and insanity. The emphasis of twentieth-century rationalism may be noted in Henry C. McComas, *Ghosts I Have Talked With,* Baltimore 1935, pp. 178–92.

and Hibbert for asserting that the age of ghosts and hobgoblins has fled.[12]

What beliefs the common folk still clung to may be surmised from fragmentary evidence. We are told that in Scott's homeland Boston's encounters with Auld Nick, which always ended with the latter's discomfited retreat in an effulgence of hellish fire, were popularly received. In order to destroy the craft in which witches sailed to Flanders, gudewives crushed eggshells. William Mabon, who died about 1836 at the age of ninety-three, used red thread, rowan-tree pegs, and circles of hempen rope to protect his cows from evil hags, and boiled pins in the threatened animal's blood. He also thought that witches and warlocks could do harm in the form of "bummers [bees]."[13] When aged Margaret Girvan died about 1811, it was happily reported that the malignant and numerous succession of Edencraw witches had come to an end. Her lonely departure was attended by an exceedingly high wind, which blew down a house near her smoky hut.[14] The fairies were still carefree enough to cut capers and strong enough to transport mortals through the air. Allan Cunningham is remarkably positive and inclusive in affirming in 1828:

> That evil spirits trouble the earth, that good spirits protect it, and that families and persons are under their influence, is a belief consistent with human nature; and, what is more to the purpose, current amongst mankind. That Fairies lived among our pastoral hills, that Brownies frequented our hearths, that Witches wrought their spells, that the dead came from the grave to admonish or alarm the living, that Mermaids haunted our bays and isles, and that Spirits appeared as Satan did of old among the children of men, are beliefs yet current in our country, and not likely to die with an imaginative people dwelling on wild hills and in lonely vallies.[15]

[12] Review of *Phantasmagoriana* and "The Spectral Dog—an Illusion," *B.E.M.*, III (1818), 589–92; XXVIII (1830), 784–6. While other writers are adding fuel to the blaze of superstition or filling controversial fire buckets, Charles Lamb admits the logical strength of orthodoxy in his essay, "Witches, and Other Night-Fears": "That the intercourse was opened at all between both worlds was perhaps the mistake—but that once assumed, I see no reason for disbelieving one attested story of this nature more than another on the score of absurdity." *The London Magazine*, IV (1821), 385.

[13] T. Craig-Brown, *The History of Selkirkshire*, Edinburgh 1886, I. 285; II. 154–5, 100–01. Also see William Henderson, *Notes on the Folk-lore of the Northern Counties of England and the Borders*, 2nd edn, London 1879, pp. 14–15; Allan Cunningham, *Traditional Tales of the English and Scottish Peasantry*, London 1822, II. 90–1, 110, 116–17.

[14] G. Henderson, "The Proverbs and Popular Sayings of Berwickshire," *History of the Berwickshire Naturalists' Club*, I. (1834), 123.

[15] Cunningham, *Sir Michael Scott*, London 1828, I. vi–vii. The author once believed in fairies, "and would to God I could do so still! for the woodland and the moor have lost for me a great portion of their romance, since my faith in their existence has departed." David Hogg, *Life of Allan Cunningham*, Dumfries 1875, p. 234. Cp. *The Sale-Room* (14 Jun. 1817), p. 189: After recalling his boyhood dread of twilight "ghosts and fairies," "J" remarks that "the superstition of the retired cottagers of Scotland, is hinged upon virtue. . . . Why should we attempt to destroy that which . . . is actually conducive to good?"

In extending his survey to Scotsmen in general, Cunningham has put the belief in the present, the creatures and acts in the past. The fading of faith suggested here is rather pompously lamented by Christopher North in *Noctes Ambrosianae* of March 1829: "I fear there is less superstition now, James, in the peasant's heart than of old—that the understanding has invaded the glimmering realms of the imagination." Scott's testimony, in a letter to Thomas Crofton Croker of 27 April 1825, is that of a man well versed "on the subject of elves ghosts visions &c": "I think . . . that the progress of philosophy has not even yet entirely 'pulld the old woman out our hearts' as Addison expresses it. Witches are still held in reasonable detestation although we no longer burn or even *score above the breath*."[16] Moralising for the sake of his grandson, Scott writes in a different spirit of the three witchcs in *Macbeth*: "Nobody would believe such folly now-a-days, except low and ignorant creatures, such as those who consult gipsies in order to have their fortunes told."[17]

In his informal, belated study of the supernatural, *Letters on Demonology and Witchcraft*, Scott is less dogmatic. About 1806, he had a *Daemonology* in mind.[18] Then, in 1809 and 1812, he suggested to his friends, Robert Surtees and Charles Kirkpatrick Sharpe, a joint work on unearthly lore. Between 1812 and 1823, he put together in dialogue form part of a book on superstition. This he considered revising and completing, but Constable's offer of 1823 was inadequate. The small volume was finally published in John Murray's five-shilling Family Library on 21 September 1830. The reception of this work will suggest the temper and state of belief of a public about which Sir Walter was always concerned.

When news of the project got abroad, collectors and anecdotalists came to Scott's assistance with rare pamphlets, transcripts of records, and ghost tales. Sir Francis Freeling sent a list of 202 items in his "Collection of Diablerie which you may desire to consult in the progress of your Work," but the tired writer seems not to have used any of the "Ghost books."[19] On 3 September 1830, Allan Cunningham writes to Lockhart:

> I am glad to see that Sir Walter is in the land of 'Gramarye'—he will charm us all when he comes out of it. The belief in witchcraft is still strong in the northern land. A shepherds wife in my younger days whom I

[16] *Letters*, IX. 94–5. For scoring above the breath, see J. G. Dalyell, *The Darker Superstitions of Scotland*, Glasgow 1835, pp. 631–2.
[17] Scott, *Tales of a Grandfather* [= *Grandfather*], First Series, London and Glasgow 1923, p. 12. As for fortunes, see *The Trial of Joseph Powell, the Fortune-Teller*, London 1808.
[18] Grierson, *Scott*, p. 83, n. 1.
[19] Abbotsford Mss., N.L.S. Scott may have felt that the witch nook of his own library was adequately filled. "He had long possessed ample materials in his thorough mastery of perhaps the most curious library of *diablerie* that ever man collected." Lockhart, v. 280.

caught churning imagined to my great advantage that I had ill or unsonsie een: and to appease them and obtain butter she made the owner an offering—at that moment a welcome one, of butter and scone and cream. I supped and the butter made its appearance rich and yellow. Many a curious look the woman took at me whenever she saw me, but I never could catch her at the churn again. My wife too when a gilpie of a lassie was a witness to the preparation of a charm in the good town of Dumfries which was to remove the witchcraft from a milk-cow and moreover retaliate upon the witch herself. It was nigh twelve at night—the doors were barred the windows fastened, a clear fire burned in the grate when one of the women who undertook to manage the whole put a brass saucepan on the fire with some of the cows milk and pins and needles and nails. 'Now said she Mr^s. Robertson—that was the name I believe—will come flying like a demented creature whenever the milk begins to boil— but dinna for the soul of ye let her in.' As the milk heated a noise was heard—the woman cried 'Lord what will become of me' & snatching the pan from the fire undid the charm.[20]

Once Scott's book was in print, acquaintances and reviewers volunteered corrections, comment, and additions, often with an eye to future changes by the author. Of these many suggestions, however, only two, made by W. S. Rose, were given effect in the second edition, which was published about 24 December and postdated 1831. We find Lady Louisa Stuart writing to Scott on October 25 that she has been "feasting upon the Demonology and Witchcraft; yet some stories freshly rung in my ears, and I am sure fully equal to any of those you tell, give me a longing to attack you for civilly supposing the present *enlightened age* rejects the superstitions of our forefathers because they were absurd, though I grant it has dropped them because they are out of fashion." A recent story of animal magnetism is instanced as being every bit as miraculous as any supernatural exploit credited to fairy or devil. "My dear Sir Walter, it is not for you to toad-eat the March of Intellect when it can counter-march in such a manner." She then regales her friend with the experience of David Middleton's widow, who, when past fourscore, was haunted by spectres for three days. Bleeding conduced to her recovery.[21] In his reply

[20] Letters to J. G. Lockhart, N.L.S., IX. 66. For "the way of restoring milk to the udders of a cow bewitched," which involves a young virgin, pins, rusty nails, and a rowan wand, see Cunningham in R. H. Cromek, *Remains of Nithsdale and Galloway Song*, Paisley 1880, pp. 233–4 (1st edn, London 1810) and Hogg, *Life of Allan Cunningham*, pp. 131–2.
[21] *Lady Louisa Stuart: Selections from Her Manuscripts*, ed. J. A. Home, Edinburgh 1899, pp. 259–62; *The Letters of Lady Louisa Stuart*, ed. R. B. Johnson, London 1926, pp. 235–8. Cp. *Letters of Lady Louisa Stuart to Miss Louisa Clinton*, Second Series, ed. J. A. Home, Edinburgh 1903, pp. 204, 206, 243. For an early satirical treatment of animal magnetism, see *The Lounger* (23 Dec. 1786) in *The Works of Henry Mackenzie*, Edinburgh, 1808, VII. 1–19.

of 31 October Scott pleads not guilty to the charge: "The inference was pretty plain that the same reasons which explode the machinery of witches and ghosts proper to our ancestors must be destructive of the supernatural nonsense of our own days."[22]

One of the most appreciative readers of the *Letters on Demonology and Witchcraft* was the wife of a canon of St Paul's Cathedral, Mrs Mary Ann Hughes. In a long chatty epistle of 26 October, she accepts Scott's challenge (p. 360): "But who has heard or seen an authentic account from Earl St Vincent, or from his 'companion of the watch,' or from his lordship's sister?" The famous watch of John Jervis, who was elevated to the peerage in 1797 as Earl St Vincent, and of Captain Luttrell was kept on Tuesday night, 6 August 1771. When not yet ten years old, Mary Ann Watts heard the version of Mrs Gwynn, the most intimate friend of Jervis's sister, Mrs Ricketts, who occupied the haunted house.

> I remember the sort of hysterical smile with which my Aunts endeavoured to carry off their fears in order to quiet me. . . . If the deception was caused by Ventriloquism it must have been performed by an able hand (or rather voice,) & by one who had the tact to dove tail it with the hideous story connected with the house: its former occupant (a Mr Stawell to the best of my recollection) was a libertine of no common degree had been more than suspected of having seduced a beautiful girl, sister to his wife; a child was born & as the story went, was made away with by the butler an old man of the vilest character the abetter and pander to his masters vices: this man had a singularly harsh voice & those who knew the parties naturally identified the ghostly dialogue with the lady pleading for her child to the unnatural father & the wicked destroyer: the old butler I remember came to an untimely end . . . it was the practice of Mrs Ricketts to write the occurrence of each night in a large journal book . . . the Duchess of Buckingham . . . says the mystery has never been cleared up, tho' the most probable account is that the Diablerie was acted for the purpose of smuggling. . . . When we meet (when will that pleasant time come?) I have a capital ghost story I heard since I saw you from a friend who had it from a Ghost seer.[23]

While regretting the "thrill that attended the influence of these tales," Scott finds compensation in the legal and psychological approach. The

[22] *Letters*, XI. 403. Through confusing the second with the first edition of the *Demonology*, Lockhart misinterprets this reply as an explanation of "the forthcoming Letters," which were "not published until Christmas." Lockhart, VII. 228.

[23] Walpole. We learn from Mary Ricketts's *poltergeist* journal that the disturbances at Hinton Ampner manor-house lasted from the first year of her lease, 1765, to 1772. The explanation of the voices given by Mrs Hughes of Uffington is hinted, but not developed in the additional narrative of Mrs Ricketts's granddaughter, Martha H. G. Jervis, 10 Jul. 1818. See "A Hampshire Ghost Story," *G.M.*, CCXXXIII (1872), 547-59, 666-78. The guess that haunting may be the ruse of smugglers is, of course, highly conventional.

poet, to use Henry A. Beers' phrase, has become "a student of *Cultur
geschichte*."[24]

> It winna believe for me. . . . The story is never told the same way though
> there is a kind of general resemblance. . . . In short the facts are all different
> and yet the same and hence my disbelief in apparition evidence. I do not
> believe my own experience would convert me though I might tremble I
> would reverse the part playd by the devils and certainly *not* believe. I wish
> you would write down Mr[s]. Rickets story as well as you remember it.
> Every such story on respectable foundation is a chapter in the history of
> the human mind.[25]

Among Scott's feminine critics, Mrs Anne MacVicar Grant of Laggan
does not send her best comment to the author. Instead, she writes Mrs
Smith on 17 November that the incidents in Sir Walter's new book are to
her mind well told, but very revolting.

> There is so much gross folly and deliberate cruelty on the part of the per-
> secutors, and on the part of the persecuted so many distinct and connected
> circumstances in their confessions, that one is at a loss how to keep down
> one's credulity. . . . I knew personally the granddaughter of a reputed
> witch who was burnt at Inverness at a later period than that which Sir
> Walter mentions as the latest. She was a woman of great powers and strong
> passions, and a notorious scold. The Provost of that day, Macintosh by
> name, was a very good-natured man, and popular. The culprit was
> believed in the town to possess supernatural powers, and rather boasted of
> the evil she could do, and particularly threatened the life of the provost:
> he was seized with a lingering illness, probably increased by the appre-
> hension that the powers of darkness were in league with his magical enemy.
> So her house was broken open, and under her bed were found certain
> uncouth images stuck full of pins, meant to represent and also to torment
> the poor provost, which she at length confessed to be intended for his
> destruction: she was therefore burnt in all the usual forms. Now there was
> little room for incredulity or compassion here; for she certainly wished
> and attempted to summon the powers of darkness in aid of her own
> malevolence.
>   I was amused at Sir Walter's caution in keeping so entirely clear of the
> second-sight: like myself, I am pretty confident he has a glimmering
> belief of, though not the same courage to own it.[26]

[24] Beers, *A History of English Romanticism in the Nineteenth Century*, New York 1901, p. 41.
[25] *Letters*, XI. 405–06, Oct.–Nov. 1830. Mrs Hughes's circumstantial reply of 15 Nov. may
be found in Wilfred Partington, *The Private Letter-Books of Sir Walter Scott*, [=Partington,
Letter-Books], London 1930, pp. 339–44. Her similar account of Mrs Ricketts, prepared for
the Rev. Richard Barham of Ingoldsby legend fame, was revised by him and made the last
entry in his notebook for 1836. R. H. D. Barham, *The Life and Letters of the Rev. Richard
Harris Barham*, London 1870, I. 305–15; J. H. Ingram, *The Haunted Homes and Family
Traditions of Great Britain*, London 1929, pp. 481–502.
[26] *Memoir and Correspondence of Mrs. Grant of Laggan*, ed. J. P. Grant, London 1844, III.
186–7. To [Scott] Mrs Grant writes, [30?] Apr. 1827, about "another authentic instance of

Correspondents continue to seesaw between belief and doubt or are noncommittally interested. Sir A. Edmondstone may soon gather material on a Lerwick wraith; meanwhile, he is disgruntled at the rationalistic pinning down of apparitions: "A mens sana in corpore sano cannot give into such sceptical garrulity." Not many months after delighting in Scott's stories at Abbotsford, J. L. Adolphus read his host's *Demonology*:

> I was (like many other people) a little scandalized at finding you protecting what Glanville would call the Sadducee side of the question—Too many of us, I am afraid, in reading a philosophical work on such a subject (at least when written by a man of imagination) will 'leave the pie, to gnaw‧ the streamer.' For my own part, I can muster credulity enough for a modest ghost-story; but the explanations do sometimes savour of the marvellous.[27]

The reviews of Scott's literary bone of contention express as great a range of opinion on the supernatural, from willing acceptance to intolerant scepticism, as the articles, books, and letters already quoted. Of these the first, coming before book publication, is probably based on an advance copy sent to the editor of *The Athenaeum*, whose critic displays considerable knowledge of Scottish words, lore, and places and refers to himself as "an old acquaintance" of Sir Walter's.

> It is the fashion of the present age to doubt everything, and believe nothing. That Sir Walter Scott is one of this latter generation, we have not the means of knowing; but certainly his mode of discussing this subject will carry alarm into the bosom of many a worthy family. Spectral illusion!— there is no illusion in it. . . . We are not to be cajoled out of our beliefs by a few well-chosen words. . . . Yet, though fallen from its high estate . . . witchcraft still flourishes; and old sagacious dames—some of whom we know—lift a tax equal to their support from the faith or the credulity of mankind. Even men lived within our own memory who were not only deemed *uncannie*, but who reckoned themselves such. Captain R—— was so sensible of the ill luck which followed whenever he looked on a churn or on a cow, that he avoided meeting his own dairy-maid driving the cows to pasture. . . . There is not a matron of sixty years or so in all the lowlands of Scotland, who could not, in one winter night, relate as many

the second sight . . . as lively at least as mine." And on a Friday night in Mar. 1828, she confides to him that the extent of her supernatural creed was not revealed in *Essays on the Superstitions of the Highlanders of Scotland*, London 1811, through fear of wounding her children by the ridicule brought on herself. After admitting that "I always believd well authenticated accounts of such appearrances," she relates how the apparition of two friends passed her gate "in broad daylight." "You see I take it for granted that you are Must be indeed from the habit of your mind in a limited sense a believer." Walpole.

[27] [Edmonstone], 26 Feb. 1831; [Adolphus], 11 Mar. 1831, in Walpole. For Adolphus' interest in Sir Walter's oral tales of "ghosts and wizards," see Lochhart, VII. 222.

legends of witches, fairies, and spirits, of good and evil, as would fill a goodly volume.[28]

In a similar vein, the reviewer of *The Atlas* humoursomely bemoans the "recantation of the orthodox faith avowed and boasted of by the author of *Waverley*. He is a heretic. . . . Ah, die when thou wilt, old Jack, all belief in ghosts will die with thee!"[29] The whimsical mood of *Atlas* and *Athenaeum* is hardly reflected in *The Court Journal*. The writer suggests that the subject is peculiarly adapted to Scott's "habits of study and thought," being one about which "he has, probably, read ten times more than any other person living." Then he appraises the *Demonology* as a philosophical attempt to sweep away that belief in the visible appearance of incorporeal spirits and in their intercourse with mortals which the Great Unknown's fiction has encouraged. His inference is that Sir Walter will write no more novels "founded on or very intimately connected with the superstitious beliefs of his own or any other country."[30]

In contrast to the dogmatic statement in *The Monthly Review* that tales of demons have been out of date for over forty years and that "not a man in a million . . . believes in ghosts,"[31] *The Gentleman's Magazine* has another opinion on the prevalence of superstition:

> The belief in ghosts, notwithstanding the intellectual advances of the present century, is still very general among those who have never contemplated the subject philosophically; and the doctrine of witchcraft is not yet eradicated from society; it still partially lingers amongst the vulgar and uncultured herd. To dispel these monstrous illusions appears to be the object of the Author of Waverley, in the present work.[32]

The article in *The Eclectic Review* is chiefly an attack on W. Newnham's *Essay on Superstition; Being an Inquiry into the Effects of Physical Influence on the Mind, in the Production of Dreams, Visions, Ghosts, and other Supernatural Appearances* (London 1830). But Scott is also found guilty of explaining too realistically the very phenomena on which belief in a supernal being rests. The reviewer cites Sir Walter's story of the man haunted by a skeleton (pp. 30–3) as haply an example of God's "severer punishment . . . commencing in this life the infliction of that horror on the soul which may perhaps form the chief part of future retribution"—hardly a fit subject for metaphysical investigation![33]

---

[28] *Op. cit.*, 18 Sep. 1830, pp. 577–82. See *Spectator* of the same date, pp. 733–7, for the story of a Wexford tailor's accusing an Irish schoolmaster of witchcraft (1830).

[29] *Op. cit.*, 3 Oct. 1830.   [30] *Op. cit.*, 25 Sep. 1830, p. 653.

[31] *Op. cit.*, Oct. 1830, pp. 286–302.   [32] *Op. cit.*, Oct. 1830, pp. 346–8.

[33] *Op. cit.*, Dec. 1830, pp. 501–16. The series of ten essays on demonology in *The Tatler*, 23 Sep.–7 Oct. 1830, though suggested by and containing criticism of Scott's volume, is of little interest. The last reviews show a distinct swing of the journalistic pendulum towards

Such critical diversity is not alone due to the liberal, orthodox, or literary bias of the particular reader. Scott himself is hard to pin down. In his discussion of ghosts and witches, he maintains "a middle course," refuses to combat the systems of previous demonologists or to set up one of his own, and yet indulges in a few loop-holed generalisations. Thus he is both entertaining in his narratives and bewildering in his philosophy. The orthodox should be satisfied with the statement that "the abstract possibility of apparitions must be admitted by every one who believes in a Deity, and his superintending omnipotence" and that "supernatural communication" cannot be denied in theory,[34] were it not that, having gone thus far, Scott disproves every modern case which he takes up. Logic demanded that, having ruled out unearthly doings, the author should reject the tenets which manifestations are supposed to validate. Sceptical readers, of course, objected to the book because it left intact the fundamental theories of demonology. But the majority thought it distinctly heterodox, if not heretical, especially when contrasted with the author's previous delight in and use of tales of wonder.[35]

Scott's cautious and compromising treatment of the uncanny in 1830, his Addisonian mixture of practical scepticism and theoretical belief, and his lawyerlike fondness for investigation are a culminating phase of a complex growth. His projects for a *Demonology* underwent considerable change, the emphasis shifting from antiquarian lore (with Surtees as collaborator) to a fine lark among absurd stories of apparitions (with the clever satiric Sharpe as collaborator), and finally to a general survey whose purpose was to advance his son Walter in the army (1823) or to pay off business debts (1830). In his youth, Scott was highly susceptible to the marvellous; in his middle age, imaginatively so; and in his last years, logically critical of given instances. The first period ended about 1801, and the second was in full vigour until about 1814 and in diminishing force until 1826, when loss of friends through death, financial catastrophe, strain, and waning health took away life's glamour.

adverse comment. See *Fraser's Magazine* (Dec. 1830) and "Noctes Ambrosianae" in *B.E.M.* (Nov. 1830, Jan. 1831). Scott's reaction to the last "abuse" may be found in *The Journal of Sir Walter Scott*, ed. J. G. Tait [=*Journal*], Edinburgh 1950 (18 Mar. 1831). Also see C. O. Parsons, "Manuscript of Scott's 'Letters on Demonology and Witchcraft,' " "Scott's 'Letters on Demonology and Witchcraft': Outside Contributors," and "The Interest of Scott's Public in the Supernatural," *N. & Q.*, CLXIV (1933) 276–7; CLXXXII (1942), 156–8, 173–4; CLXXXV (1943), 92–100.

[34] *Demonology*, pp. 47–8. Cp. *The Journal of the Rev. John Wesley*, ed. Nehemiah Curnock, London 1909, v. 265, May 1768.

[35] John Richardson writes Scott on 9 Nov. 1830: "Your views are to me quite rational & convincing—but it is amusing to witness the disappointment which people express at not finding you a thorough & implicit believer." Walpole.

During the major part of his creative life, Scott cherished superstition as a reminder of the past and as a poet's fanciful birthright. With his Aunt Margaret he could justly say, "It soothes my imagination, without influencing my reason or conduct."[36] As long as reason could be suspended, deflected, disciplined to function separately from the imagination, ghosts and gooseflesh could have their temporary way. These two domains are recognised in Scott's note on second sight in *The Lady of the Lake*: "If force of evidence could authorize us to believe facts inconsistent with the general laws of nature, enough might be produced in favour of the existence of the Second-sight." "Now universally abandoned to the use of poetry," second sight has passed from one province of belief into another.

The balance which Scott tried to maintain between conflicting faculties was destroyed at times in youth by the tyranny of imagination and in old age by that of reason. With increase of years and training in the sifting of evidence, Scott came ever nearer to eighteenth-century rationalism. Scepticism about the supernatural in its less purely religious forms dominates his discussion of witchcraft in the Second Series (1828) of *Tales of a Grandfather*, Chapter XIV. The Almighty no longer miraculously suspends natural laws; "the number of supposed witches seemed to increase in proportion to the increase of punishment," and they were practically forgotten when laws against them were abolished.[37] So David Hume reasons, "Witchcraft and heresy are two crimes which commonly increase by punishment, and never are so effectually suppressed as by being totally neglected."[38] Scott also reveals affinity to eighteenth-century thought in his comment on the Covenanters' successes and escapes, which "were imputed, not to the operation of those natural causes by means of which the Deity is pleased to govern the world, and which are the engines of his power, but to the direct interposition of a miraculous agency, overruling and suspending the laws of nature, as in the period of Scriptural history."

It was in keeping with his own growing rationalism that Scott came to feel that the new age, mechanical in its standards, had little taste for supernaturalism or for old-world studies. Alderson, Ferriar, and Hibbert had placed in a foolish light the old-fashioned ghost story told for a thrill and

[36] "My Aunt Margaret's Mirror," the original of the fictional relative being Scott's maternal great-aunt, Mrs Margaret Swinton. On Scott's duality, see *The Works and Life of Walter Bagehot*, ed. Mrs Russell Barrington, London 1915, III. 68–9.

[37] For belief in witches during Scott's own lifetime, see *Demonology*, pp. 340–2, and *Letters from and to Charles Kirkpatrick Sharpe*, ed. Alexander Allardyce [= Allardyce], Edinburgh and London 1888, I. 139, 346; II. 262.

[38] Hume, *The History of England*, new edn, New York 1879, III. 463.

not probed deeply. Such authors imposed on Sir Walter a sometimes irksome objectivity. Thus he regretfully ends his *Letters on Demonology and Witchcraft*:

> Tales of ghosts and demonology are out of date at forty years and upwards ... it is only in the morning of life that this feeling of superstition 'comes o'er us like a summer cloud,' affecting us with fear, which is solemn and awful rather than painful; and I am tempted to think, that if I were to write on the subject at all, it should have been during a period of life when I could have treated it with more interesting vivacity, and might have been at least amusing, if I could not be instructive.[39]

Scott, the public, and the supernatural as well are full of these tensions and contradictions. Religion may seem to warrant in theory what mature reason rejects in fact. The conflict of sense and sensation may turn an experience or a literary episode into an inartistic jumble. The impressionable Laird of Abbotsford who strikes a credulous visitor as believing the wonders he narrates may seem to an incredulous listener to be amused and objective. But on the whole Scott's wavering allegiance to imaginative and rationalistic values is a fair reflexion of the man and of his contemporaries. In both, receptivity was crossed by doubt and scepticism by glimmering conviction.

[39] *Op. cit.*, p. 401.

CHAPTER II

THE SCOTTISH LITERARY BACKGROUND

ALTHOUGH Scott's roots reach out toward many cultures, his taproot is fed by Scottish literature, tradition, and thought. There the spirit, the precedent, of his approach to the supernatural may be found. This chapter will concentrate on literary antecedents. The non-literary background will be considered in separate sections on witchcraft and other phenomena.

Scottish writers worked for the most part in an appropriate setting of nature and of events. The sudden changes of light, the lonely stretches of moor and hill, the deep glens, the threatening waters—all made the land-scape variously alive and, as it were, in league with powers beyond the natural. So with human happenings, which tended to peril, violence, betrayal, pride, greed, heroism, and sacrifice—to swift alternations of fortune. One dark and stormy night at the close of a presageful winter of thunder, lightning, and meteoric fire, Alexander III lost his way, fell from his horse, and broke his neck. Neglecting the warning of a Highland woman, James I crossed the Firth of Forth and was assassinated. James IV heeded neither the words of an apparition in St Michael's Church, Linlith-gow, nor the nocturnal voice at the Market Cross in Edinburgh crying the names of those to die. Like a *fey* man, he went against the English at Flodden and was slain with his nobles. Such omens and prophecies abounded and were not visited alone on the great. Deeds, scenes, and passions lent credit to the supernatural.

EARLY WRITERS

The unearthly is kept within bounds in ancient Scottish chronicles and historical verse romances. The muse of John Barbour is too realistic to explore every darkling byway. In *The Bruce*, completed in 1376, the Bishop of St Andrews exclaims on hearing that Robert Bruce has slain the Red Comyn,

I hop [that] Thomas prophecy
Off Hersildoune sall [verray] be
In him; for, swa our lord help me!
I haiff gret hop he sall be king.[1]

Although many prophecies, rightly interpreted, can be made to reveal that mysterious forces kindly shape Scotland's fortunes, Barbour does not develop the parallel between prophecy and fulfilment.

According to the poet, Edward I felt that he would die in the burgh of Jerusalem. Death came to him at Burgh-in-the-Sand. So much for English presentiment! Before telling another such story, Barbour becomes didactic on the subject of evil spirits and their words:

> The quhethir men said, enclosit he had
> Ane spirit, that hym ansuer mad
> Of thingis that he vald inqueir.
> Bot he wes fule, *forouten weir,   *a* without doubt
> That gaf treuth to that creature.
> For fendis ar of sic nature,
> That thai to mankynd has invy. . . .
> Quharfor oftymis will betyde,
> That quhen fendis *distrenȝit ar   *b* forced
> For till apper and mak ansuar,
> Throu force of coniuracioune,
> That thai sa fals ar and sa *fellouñe,   *c* wicked
> That thai mak ay thair ansuering
> In-till dowbill vndirstanding,
> Till dissaf thame that will thame *trow.   *d* trust

Thus reasons the Hermit of Engaddi in *The Talisman* when he misinterprets the stars. Nor is astrology beyond the pale of Barbour's interest. The poet's comment on vain astral lore corresponds to Guy Mannering's doubts about his genethliac insight into the three critical periods of Harry Bertram's life. Because it is possible to annul the apparent influence of the stars by changing the line of character development, man's fate is "na certane thing." In truth—

> . . . thouch a man his liff haly
> Studeit [swa] in astrology,
> That on the *sternis his hed he brak,   *a* stars
> Wiss men sais he suld nocht mak,
> His liftyme, certane *domys thre;   *b* predictions
> And *ȝeit suld he ay dout *quhill he   *c* yet
>   *d* until

[1] Barbour, *The Bruce*, ed. Walter W. Skeat, S.T.S., 2 vols., Edinburgh and London 1894, BK II, lines 86–9. The following quotations are from IV. 219–25, 230–7, 709–16, 746, 767–74.

> Saw how that it com till ending:
> Than is that na certane ᵉdemyng.   ᵉ foreknowledge

When Bruce's hostess foretells victory and kingship, Barbour considers astrological and necromantic attempts to penetrate the future.

> Me think, quha sais he knawis thingis
> To cum, he makis gret ᵃgabbingis.   ᵃ lies
> But quhethir scho [that] tald the king
> How his purpos suld tak ending.
> Wenit, or vist it ᵇvitterly,   ᵇ certainly
> It fell eftir all halely
> As scho said: for syne king wes he,
> And of full mekill [renomme].

Similarly, Scott tells of the Highland prophetess who tried to warn James I against going to Perth, where he was murdered. "It often happens, that when a remarkable deed is in agitation, rumours of it get abroad, and are repeated under pretence of prophecies; but which are, in truth, only conjectures of that which seems likely to happen."[2] After enjoying a mysterious event, it is wholesome for the reader to be braced by a rational explanation.

Altogether, Barbour was a man after Scott's own heart. Sir Walter's belief in the golden mean and his shunning of excess in all things (except land hunger and over-confidence in business) are paralleled in the medieval poet's praise of Bruce:

> ᵃVorschip extremyteis has twa;   ᵃ Valour
> ᵇFule-hardyment the formast is,   ᵇ Fool-hardiness
> And the tothir is cowardiss,
> And thai ar bath for to forsak. . . .
> For-thi has vorschip sic renouñe,
> That it is [mene] betuix thai twa.[3]

In like manner, one should not be too sceptical or too credulous about superstitions, which may best be represented—with reservations—as the beliefs of fallible men.

There is no rationalisation in *The Awntyrs of Arthure at the Terne Wathelyn*, a fourteenth-century alliterative romance which has been attributed to Huchown. Its rude and forceful didacticism requires that the "fowle

---

² *Grandfather*, First Series, p. 187.
³ Barbour, *The Bruce*, BK VI, lines 336–9, 346–7. See BK VIII for the central plot of Scott's *Castle Dangerous*. The passages cited may be found in *The Bruce*, ed. W. M. Mackenzie, London 1909, II. 85–90; IV. 189–311, 632–774; VI. 336–9, 346–7, and in George Eyre-Todd's translation, London and Glasgow 1907, pp. 19, 58–61, 69–73, 99–100.

fegouris" and "vgsum horribiliteis," as they were later called,[4] should be accepted as real, and that the transition from the mundane to the monstrous should be convincing. When Gawan and Queen Gaynour separate from the other hunters, it grows suddenly dark and stormy. Then a spectre appears, bare, "blake to the bane," and ringed with serpents. It is Gaynour's mother come to warn against the lust of paramours, against pride, lack of charity, and neglect of religion. "And nowe I am a gresely gaste, and grymly granes."[5] Weeping fearfully, the apparition begs for masses, reveals the brevity of Gaynour's life and the doom of the Arthurian order, and glides through the green groves. Agnes Mure Mackenzie conceives "Wandering Willie's Tale" as going back ultimately "to the grotesque ghost of the Tarne Watheling, as sure as Claverhouse or Fergus Macivor are in line of descent from Barbour's Good Lord James."[6] The Gothic punishments which Scott metes out to paramours in the Waverley Novels are closer to the ethical tone of the *Awntyrs*.

An old favourite of Scott's was Andrew of Wyntoun, who wrote his chronicle in the early years of the fifteenth century. Although Macbeth was rumoured to have been begotten on a willing woman by the devil in handsome mortal form and ' "his dedis were fell," ' Wyntoun will not say whether his conception was diabolical or human. As a grown man, Macbeth "herd . . . in his dremyng" talk of thane and king among three women whom he took to be weird sisters. When Macduff and Malcolm returned to Scotland, they astutely played on the king's superstitiousness:

> For thai wist weill þat Makbeth ay
> In [a]fayntsum fretis had gud fay,   [a] imaginary omens
> And [b]trowit ay in sic fantasy,   [b] believed
> As forouth this to ȝow tald I.

Macbeth's slayer did not share the crafty scepticism of his generals. In the heat of combat he cried out:

> For to þi fader I sall [a]þe send,   [a] thee
> That is þe deuill, for he þe gat.[7]

[4] "Sir John Rowll's *Cursing*," c. 1500, in David Laing, *Select Remains of the Ancient Popular and Romance Poetry of Scotland*, ed. John Small [= *Select Remains*], Edinburgh and London 1885, p. 217.

[5] *Select Remains*, p. 92; *Scottish Alliterative Poems*, ed. F. J. Amours, Edinburgh and London 1897, pp. 115–71 (the first of two adventures). For the source, a legend of Saint Gregory, see George Neilson, '*Huchown of the Awle Ryale': the Alliterative Poet*, Glasgow 1902, pp. 111–13.

[6] Blind Harry is also described as "a forerunner of Scott." Mackenzie, *An Historical Survey of Scottish Literature to 1714*, London 1933, pp. 60, 223–4.

[7] *The Original Chronicle of Andrew of Wyntoun*, ed. F. J. Amours, S.T.S., Edinburgh and London 1903–14, LIV. 198 (274, 278–80, 300). See Scott, *The History of Scotland*, Philadelphia 1830, I. 28.

Scott, too, keeps rumour alive without committing himself too positively, and he offers alternate interpretations of the marvellous. In passionate outbursts, a man may hurl *fiend* at the head of his enemy, but the evil of human nature, as the novelist hints, explains as much as infernal connivance. Then, too, cunning villains like Tomkins in *Woodstock* or Leicester's Varney may selfishly manipulate the credulity of others.

At the age of seven, Walter Scott feared that he might see the headless Fawdon at a window. With interest undiminished, he has the prince in *The Fair Maid of Perth* speak of Fawdon's ghost and adds a footnote, "The passage referred to is perhaps the most poetical one in Blind Harry's Wallace." If a Scottish prince is courteous enough to cite a bard as yet unborn, feeling perhaps that the resources of a national literature should be available to all, we need not boggle at chronology nor insist that Henry the Minstrel's *Sir William Wallace*, a rather pedestrian narrative, is enlivened by few purple patches.

After joining Wallace, Fawdon, "a man of dreadful size . . . threatening aspect, and iniquitous eyes . . . gruesome to the sight," seemed to lag behind treacherously in a retreat from the English. Wallace lopped off his head, and a pursuing hound was stopped by the smell of his blood. Hearing the blast of a horn at Gaskhall, Wallace encountered a frightful apparition at the gate and drew a cross. Unchecked, the "hellish spright" flung its gory head at the champion, who returned the pass, fled up the stairs, and threw himself out of a window. Wallace then thought that he saw the tower on fire and Fawdon, like another Ulrica at Torquilstone in *Ivanhoe*, on top of it. In closing this episode, the popular old bard wisely leaves the question to those deep in "dark philosophy"—

> . . . whether vested with compacted air,
> In Faudon's shape some demon did appear,
> Or, if the ling'ring soul, expell'd with pain,
> Strove to reanimate the corpse again.[8]

Although Blind Harry, unlike Barbour, does not provide a natural explanation (it is not always easy to rationalise a headless phantom), he does offer the reader a choice somewhat in the fashion of Scott's later summaries of possibilities.

In his "Remonstrance with Scotsmen for Having Soured the Disposition of their Ghosts and Faeries," William Butler Yeats commends the supernaturals of Hibernia as gay, graceful, and equable, and condemns those of

[8] The quotations are from William Hamilton of Gilbertfield's modernisation (1722) of Henry the Minstrel's fifteenth-century *Sir William Wallace*, Edinburgh 1812, pp. 50, 57-8. It may have been more read than the original.

Caledonia as gloomy, loutish, and malevolent. Although the ghosts of Fawdon and of Gaynour's mother would certainly not pass muster with Yeats, it is doubtful whether he would have considered the grotesque and terrible sufficiently leavened with humour, fantasy, and beauty in such conscious artists as Robert Henryson and William Dunbar.[9]

Henryson's "The Testament of Cresseid" shows the abandoned wanton rebuking Cupid for "hir greit Infelicitie." With a silver bell which can be heard "fra hevin unto hell," Cupid summons the seven planetary gods to advise him on punishment. Astrology reinforces the concept of character as doom and, with sacrilege and divine wrath, foreshadows narrative inevitabilities. Cresseid awakes from "this doolie dreame, this uglye visioun" of being condemned to exchange joy and comeliness for pain, disease, and melancholy. Her face, held in a mirror, is that of a leper. When Cresseid dies, the abomination of lovers, she leaves her spirit to Diana, "To walk with hir in waist Woddis and Wellis."[10]

Dunbar uses the dream less for moral than for humorous and satiric effects. "The Feigned Friar of Tungland" is a Satanic Turk who has a mad career of crime, disguise, and mishap in Europe. From his dream the poet is wakened by the jargoning of ducks frightened by the unholy aeronaut's fall into the mire. Dunbar's friar represents John Damian, King James IV's leach and alchemist. Three years after being made Abbot of Tungland in Galloway, the Frenchman cracked his thigh-bone trying to fly from Stirling Castle on birds' wings. Another of Dunbar's burlesque visions ("Lucina schynnyng in silence of the nicht") transforms Damian into a gryphon begetting Antichrist in aerial copulation with a she-dragon. His flight brings him to the abode of magicians, devils, and witches.

Dunbar descends into a nightmare world for the substance of three other poems. In one, on not persuading the stubborn poet to become a friar, "ane fieind" personating Saint Francis "vaneist away with stynk and fyrie smowk." In another, a cowardly cobbler and tailor, under the patronage of Mahoun and the Devil, clash in a farcical tournament. "Now trow this gif ye list," says Dunbar, not minding who sees the tongue in his cheek.[11] And in "The Dance of the Seven Deadly Sins," the last day of Carnival,

---

[9] Of course, not all Irish ghosts and fairies are good-natured. In fact, the contrast might be reversed by comparing Yeats's "Teig O'Kane and the Corpse" (*Irish Fairy and Folk Tales*) and Hogg's "Kilmeny."

[10] *The Poems and Fables of Robert Henryson*, 2nd edn, ed. H. Harvey Wood, Edinburgh and London 1958, pp. 103–26.

[11] Cp. the sophisticated ending of the anonymous poem, "Lichtoun Dreme," in which "Me thocht the king of farie had me tane": "That gentill aill is all the caus of dremis." *The Maitland Folio Manuscript*, 2 vols., S.T.S., ed. W. A. Craigie, Edinburgh and London 1919–1927, I. 173–5.

c. 1507, the tranced poet sees "baith heaven and hell." Heaven does not linger in memory. During the infernal revels, Mahoun is not amused by a dance of unshriven shrews and of the mortal sins, whose vigour is a measure of sinners' torment. The mood changes from the frightful to the farcical when Mahoun calls for a Highland pageant; the clatter of spoken Erse is so deafening—

> That in the deepest pot of hell
> He ªsmoorit them with smoke.[12]   ª smothered

Abbots, friars, cheating tradesmen, sinners, and Highlanders are given a rest in "Ane Littill Interlud of the Droichis [dwarf's] Part of the Play," which has been attributed to Dunbar. In thick-flowing rhodomontade which confounds his ancestry and consequence with folk heroes, witches, fairies, giants, and Arthurian chivalry, a dwarf cries the people to a play. Dunbar's energy and satiric thrust are closer to the genius of Burns than of Scott. It is noteworthy, however, that Nectabanus, or King Arthur, and his mate, Guenevra, or a Mohammedan houri, the dwarfish grotesques in *The Talisman*, arouse supernatural fear and give a crazed account of themselves which suggests a half-hearted borrowing from William Dunbar.[13]

The reader's wit must be nimble to follow Dunbar's pendulum as it swings between "real life and romance, everyday fact and the supernatural, things holy and things profane," the contradictions and possible harmonies of Scotsmen and their literature.[14] Less nimbleness is required by Gavin Douglas. Among the episodes of "The Palice of Honour" is the poet's dream of seeing in Venus's mirror Ossianic heroes, Friar Bacon and Friar Bungay, and such necromantic feats as turning a chicken-bone into a pack saddle, a penny pie into a parish church, and a nutmeg into a monk.

No less remarkable is the necromancy of Douglas's translation of the *Aeneid*. After calling on Pluto (Satan) and the Cumaean Sibyl (the Virgin

---

[12] *Scottish Poetry from Barbour to James VI*, ed. M. M. Gray, London 1935, pp. 143–6. John Speirs objects to any interpretation of the "Dance" as "a conscious blending of the comic with the horrible, the ghastly, the macabre"; its "savage folk-humour" is less sophisticated and more real than critics have supposed. *The Scots Literary Tradition*, 2nd edn, London 1962, p. 61.

[13] William Dunbar, *Poems*, ed. James Kinsley, Oxford 1958, pp. 43–58, 102–07. Also see the riotous *fabliau*, "The Freiris of Berwik," sometimes attributed to Dunbar, in *The Bannatyne Manuscript*, ed. W. Tod Ritchie, S.T.S., 4 vols., Edinburgh and London 1928–34, IV. 261–77: by pretending that Alesone's concealed lover, a black friar, is his familiar devil ("I hafe ane pege"), a white friar gets him cudgeled by the cuckold. The anonymous poem, "Lord Fergus Ghaist," *Bannatyne*, II. 303–05, wrings humour out of the acts and materials of conjuration; the wee spirit marries a fly and begets Queen Elpha and King Orpheus. The poem is reprinted in *Minstrelsy of the Scottish Border*, ed. T. F. Henderson [=*Minstrelsy*], 4 ls. Edinburgh 1902.

[14] G. Gregory Smith, *Scottish Literature*, London 1919, p. 10.

Mary) for inspiration in the Prologue to Book VI, the Bishop of Dunkeld defends Virgil's conception of the soul after death, the punishment of sin, and the reward of virtue against any charge of pagan, "vane superstitionis." Like Burns, the bishop has stirrings of pity for Satan-Pluto:

> Prince in that dolorus den of wo and pane,
> Nocht God tharof, bot gretast wreche of all.

The best known passage in the *Eneados* is a facile and inadequate summary of what Aeneas will see during his descent into hell:

> All is bot gaistis and elriche fantasies,
> Of browneis and of bogillis full this buke.[15]

The lines are important because they reveal that Douglas, through his transforming imagination, will people the Roman Hades with Scottish supernatural creatures. And hell itself will be "Scotland in its wilder aspects," as John Speirs so thoroughly demonstrates, the mists and storms, the caverns, "the mountainous and craggy wastes, the gloomy waters, and the wild and lawless inhabitants of these regions, as they might be viewed and feared at the oncoming of night."[16] Scott, too, has a sense of the fitness of deed and setting. Muschat's Cairn (*The Heart of Midlothian*) and Burley's cave in the Black Linn (*Old Mortality*) exude a potent spirit of place.

Early in the sixteenth century, Sir David Lindsay entertained his pupil with imitations of frightful beings, with prophecies, and with popular stories.

> And, sumtyme, lyke ane feing, transfigurate;
> And, sumtyme, lyke the greislie gaist of gye;
> In diuers formis, oft tymes, disfigurate. . . .

> The Prophiseis of Rymour, Beid, & Marlyng,
> And of mony vther plesand storye,
> Off the reid Etin, and the gyir carlyng,
> Confortand the, quhen that I sawe the sorye.[17]

---

[15] *The Poetical Works of Gavin Douglas*, ed. John Small, 4 vols., Edinburgh and London 1874, I. 65; III. 2, 6.

[16] Speirs, "The Scots 'Aeneid' of Gavin Douglas," *Scots Literary Tradition*, pp. 165–97.

[17] *The Works of Sir David Lindsay*, ed. Douglas Hamer, S.T.S., 4 vols., Edinburgh and London 1931–6, I. 4–5. Guy was a wife-haunting ghost. Lindsay's own use of the "aboundant-lie bledyng," didactic ghost of the murdered Cardinal Beaton is conventional ("The Tragedie"). The Red Etin is a three-headed giant whose story is lost. And the Gyre Carline is a giant mother witch whom Lindsay mentions in "Ane Satyre of the Thrie Estaitis" as the grandmother who taught Folly "the Prophesie of Marling" about a friars' war (*Works*, II. 401, 403). Her wounding of amorous Blasour, her escape as a sow from a castle besieged by the King of Fairie, and her marriage to Mahoun are told in "The Gyre-Carling," a poem which Scott quotes in the *Minstrelsy* (*Select Remains*, pp. 271–5).

Apparently confident in his pedagogy, Lindsay goes on to tell of "ane maruellous visioun" of Dame Remembrance, who takes him on an instructive tour from "the lawest hell" to heaven. "The Dreme" ends with an exhortation to James V. But seven years later, Lindsay represents the king's debauchery as such a reflexion on his education that court ladies shun his tutor as a devil ("The Answer to the Kingis Flyting").

Sir David's most successful foray into the supernatural is in "Squyer William Meldrum." After the young Scot has accepted Talbart's challenge, intended for the cowardly French, the English champion dreams that a cruel, black otter comes from the sea to attack him. In his bewilderment, he is rebuked by a companion for going against his faith in giving "credence till ane dreame." But when Talbart is unhorsed and wounded by the squire, whose shield displays an otter, he says ruefully, "I see weill my dreame wes trew."[18] Narrative tension is increased by a foreshadowing dream on which doubt is cast before it is impressively fulfilled. One of Scott's methods is to allow a dream to be realised after it has undergone the wholesome ordeal of logic or ridicule.

George Buchanan, the tutor of James V's grandson, James VI, has some interesting tales to tell of royalty in his Latin history of Scotland. When troubled by murder and other crimes, Kenneth III was visited at night by "terrible Apparitions. . . . At last, a voice was heard from Heaven, either a true one, as some think; or else, such an one, as his disquieted Mind suggested, (as it commonly happens to Guilty Consciences) speaking to him, in his Sleep, to this Sense"—Thou canst not escape punishment! And, indeed, Fenella did revenge on Kenneth the death of a son and a relative.[19] The historian offers a supernatural and a psychological explanation of the tenth-century king's experience, just as Scott lets the reader decide whether Sir John Ramorny, when sick, frightened, and remorseful, dreamed that "the shade of Queen Annabella stood by his bedside" to arraign him for corrupting her son, or was subject to a "species of phantasmagoria" which sketched "the countenance of the apparition" and dissolved it into nightmarish faces.

[18] Lindsay's Works, I. 152–61; The Book of Scottish Poetry, ed. Sir George Douglas, London 1911, pp. 146–56.

[19] Buchanan, The History of Scotland, a translation of his Rerum Scoticarum Historia, London 1690, p. 195. (The Fenella in Scott's Peveril of the Peak [= Peveril], is set as a spy on the Countess of Derby to avenge the execution of her uncle, William Christian.) Buchanan is even more critical of omens, weather magic, and astrology. Although the astrologers in Kenilworth and Quentin Durward are more complex than those attacked by Buchanan in the fifth book of De Sphaera, they have a common manipulative cynicism: "In order to provide greater license for planning every sort of crime and for giving the reins to it, the astrologer ascribes heaven to the misdeed, and encourages the follies of kings by excusing them, and imputes all to the innocent stars." James R. Naiden, The Sphera of George Buchanan, 1506–82 (repr. [1952]), p. 139.

THE REFORMATION AND THE SEVENTEENTH CENTURY

The Reformation found ammunition in demonology and witchcraft for its word battles. About 1583, Robert Sempill let forth his satiric rage in "The Legend of the Bischop of St Androis Lyfe, callit Mr Patrick Adamsone, *alias* Cousteane." Diabolically appointed to confound God's word, the Bishop served Satan for his tithes. When sick, this elf, this incubus, engaged a witch in—

> Reising the devill with invocationes,
> With herbis, stanis, buikis, and bellis,
> Menis members, and south runing wellis,
> Palme croces, and knottis of *a*strease,   *a* straws
> The paring of a preistis auld *b*tees. . . .   *b* toes

After Phetanissa, he employed another "vglie hund of hell." Accused of such alliances, he confessed but loosed the hags from jail and laid the blame on Pluto. Involved a third time, with "ane carling [hag] of the Quene of Phareis," the Bishop fled to Edinburgh and London, his penchant for evil undiminished.[20] A century later, this kind of scandal-mongering began to weave legends about the Stair family which Scott later used in *The Bride of Lammermoor*.

Seventeenth-century historians and theologians are prone to supernatural proofs that God is with the chosen and Satan with their enemies. The controversial temper of an Episcopalian stalwart like John Spottiswood (*The History of the Church and State of Scotland*) and of a Presbyterian champion like David Calderwood (*The True History of the Church of Scotland*) comes out in the latter's reference to John Lauder, a Cockburnspath minister who in 1619 reached the communion bread to one kneeling in "the popishe forme": "a black dogge start up, to snatche it out of his hand."[21] Devils and witches abound in James Kirkton's *The Secret and True History of the Church of Scotland . . . to the year 1678* and in Robert Law's *Memorialls* of happenings "from 1638 to 1684." These manuscript hoards

---

[20] *The Sempill Ballates*, ed. T. G. Stevenson, Edinburgh 1872, pp. 196–229. Patrick Adamson was cured by a wisewoman, Alison Pearson, who was accused by his enemies of witchcraft. A few years after her escape from the castle of St. Andrews, she was retaken, tried, and burned.

[21] Calderwood, *The History of the Kirk of Scotland*, ed. Thomas Thomson, 8 vols., Edinburgh 1842–9, VII. 360. Calderwood died in 1650 and Spottiswood in 1639. The Wodrow Society which brought out the best edition of his *History* is named after Robert Wodrow (died 1734), whose *History of the Sufferings of the Church of Scotland* and *Analecta: or, Materials for a History of Remarkable Providences, mostly relating to Scotch Ministers and Christians* are even richer mines of the supernatural.

were made accessible to the public in 1817 and 1818 by Scott's friend, Charles Kirkpatrick Sharpe.

Of more literary importance is the renewal of the short story out of witch and ghost tracts. *Newes from Scotland* (1591) is an exciting report on the attempt of sorcerer and witches on James VI's life. A century later, in 1696, a West of Scotland apparition figured in "A True Relation. . . ." (Edinburgh) and *New Confutation of Sadducism* (London), and in 1698, West of Scotland witches made a stir in *Narrative of the Sufferings and Relief of a Young Girl* (Edinburgh) and *Sadducismus Debellatus* (London). The shift from sensationalism or news to religious propaganda against scepticism and infidelity began in England at least as early as 1652. Regretfully admitting in *An Antidote against Atheism* that "the more weak and sunk minds of sensual mortals" cannot follow abstract argument, Henry More offers "strange . . . and undeniable Stories of Apparitions," racketing devils, and witches as evidence of immortality, God's oversight, and the reality of hell. More's disciple, Joseph Glanvil, supplies both logic and supernatural instances in *Saducismus Triumphatus* (1681). Up to 1726, the editions increasingly emphasised the exciting and entertaining proofs. Richard Baxter, Meric Casaubon, and the American, Cotton Mather, have More's and Glanvil's point of view, but John Aubrey is antiquarian, rather than tendentious, in his *Miscellanies* (1696). Richard Bovet, Nathaniel Crouch, and Edward Stephens are journalistic in approach, being sales- rather than soul-conscious, as is Defoe in "A True Relation of the Appari- tion of one Mrs. Veal" (1706).[22]

This advance towards narrative mastery was not without Scottish repercussions. A professor of natural philosophy at Glasgow University, George Sinclair (or Sinclar), introduced a Scottish story, "The Devil of Glenluce," in an appendix of *The Hydrostaticks*. But his impressive entry in the field was *Satans Invisible World Discovered; or, A Choice Collection of Modern Relations, proving evidently against the Saducees and Atheists of this present Age, that there are Devils, Spirits, Witches, and Apparitions* (Edin- burgh, 1685). Sinclair's stories have in common with the better English relations a movement from threat of danger to apprehensiveness to investigation and proof or discovery. Verisimilitude is usually achieved through detail about time, place, and persons, the apparent reliability of the source, and motivation. His superiority to other propagandic narrators depends on a more careful collection, selection, arrangement, rearrange-

---

[22] With the inclusion of "Mrs. Veal" in the fourth and later English editions of Charles Drelincourt, *The Christian's Defence Against the Fears of Death*, Defoe joins the controversial writers, although he only superficially belongs among them.

ment, and development of his materials. Thus he remained in print four times longer than Glanvil. He became household reading for generations of Scots and influenced Scott's *Guy Mannering* and "Wandering Willie's Tale," as well as Stevenson's "Thrawn Janet." His success may also have influenced Robert Kirk, the minister of Aberfoyle, to try a new weapon in the warfare "to suppress the impudent and growing Atheisme of this Age." This was *Secret Commonwealth* (1691), a treatise on elves, fauns, and fairies which Scott encouraged Robert Jamieson to edit for a wider public in 1815.[23]

EIGHTEENTH-CENTURY VERNACULAR POETRY

With the absorption of her Parliament into the English by the Treaty of Union of 1707, Scotland lost her political identity. The need for a compensatory sense of cultural identity began to be poignant. Perhaps the most effective agent in this reaction was Allan Ramsay (1684 or 1685 to 1758), whose anthologies, *The Ever Green, Being A Collection of Scots Poems, Wrote by the Ingenious before 1660*, in two volumes (1724), and *The Tea-Table Miscellany*, in four volumes (1724–37), performed a labour of revival, revision, imitation, and addition.

Ramsay's most important original work is a pastoral comedy, *The Gentle Shepherd* (1725), in Scots-English. For his setting the poet used the Newhall and Carlops estates in the parish of West Linton, Peeblesshire. In popular etymology, Carlops is derived from "carline's lowps [hag's or witch's leaps]" from one sheer rock to another.[24] Ramsay's host at Newhall was a distinguished lawyer, Sir David Forbes, whose judiciousness is represented in the character of Sir William Worthy. To these ingredients, popular superstition and upper-class responsibility, Ramsay added love interest from his earlier pastoral dialogue, "Patie and Roger."

Love and troth-plight are not affected by the discovery that Patie and his Peggy are cousins and gently born at that, being Sir William Worthy's son and niece. Even as peasants, they have been true to their birth and not

---

[23] For a fuller discussion, see C. O. Parsons, "Ghost-Stories before Defoe," *N. & Q.* CCI (1956), 293–8. The use of stories and argument to disprove spiritual intervention may be studied in John Webster, *The Displaying of Supposed Witchcraft* (1677), written by a Practitioner of Physick.

[24] William J. Watson, *The History of the Celtic Place-Names of Scotland*, Edinburgh and London 1926, p. 140; James B. Johnston, *Place-Names of Scotland*, London 1934, p. 126; *A History of Peeblesshire*, ed. James W. Buchan, 3 vols., Glasgow 1925–7, III. 109 (also see I. 186, 315; III. 124, 126–7). The modern version is that the larger rock was used by witches to mount their broomsticks.

superstitious. Bauldy, a genuinely lowborn shepherd, has the instincts of his kind and is credulous. When frustrated in love, he goes to buy Mause's help. Before approaching the witch and her cat, he reviews her powers:

> She can o'ercast the Night, and cloud the Moon,
> And mak the Deils obedient to her Crune.
> At Midnight Hours, o'er the Kirk-yards she raves,
> And howks unchristen'd *We'ans out of their Graves;   ^a children
> Boils up their Livers in a Warlock's ^bPow,   ^b skull
> Rins withershins about the Hemlock ^cLow;   ^c flame
> And seven Times does her Prayers backward pray,
> Till Platcock comes with Lumps of *Lapland* Clay,
> Mixt with the Venom of black ^dTaids and Snakes;   ^d toads
> Of this ^eunsonsy Pictures aft she makes   ^e unhealthy
> Of ony ane she hates—and gars expire
> With slaw and racking Pains afore a Fire;
> Stuck fu' of ^fPrins, the devilish Pictures melt,   ^f pins
> The Pain, by Fowk they represent, is felt.

In nervous conference, he repeats what folk say Mause has done: brought a changeling and a bad churning, frightened a mare, harmed barn and gear, caused a woman to lose her snood, and a man his way. Left to herself, Mause reflects on the hard luck of poverty, age, old-fashioned clothes, a lonely shelter, and a better education, "with a sma' Cast of Wiles," making her seem a witch to "this Fool" and "mony sic." But soon they will know what has brought her among them.

When Bauldy comes back after dark, the incensed Mause and Madge, as witch and ghaist, "fleg him." The clown hurries to Sir William Worthy with his tale of rough handling. He can't relax "Till in a fat Tar-barrel *Mause* be burnt."[25] No longer the practical joker who has excited oldsters by spaeing [foretelling] the sceptical Patie's fortune, Sir William comments to Patie's foster-father, Symon:

> What silly Notions crowd the clouded Mind,
> That is thro' want of Education blind!

Then he makes fun of the devil's dancing before "craz'd and poor" old women, appearing in the form of different beasts, leading aerial flights as well as flotillas in eggshells, and tumbling houseware about.

[25] In a note on his continuation of James I's "Christ's Kirk on the Green," Ramsay says that "the main Design of Comedy" is "to represent the Follies and Mistakes of low Life in a just Light, making them appear as ridiculous as they really are, that each who is a Spectator, may evite his being the Object of Laughter." Bauldy succeeds in obliterating the line between comedy and farce.

Whate'er's in Spells, or if there Witches be,
Such Whimsies seem the most absurd to me.[26]

The technique of using ridicule to make a belief humanly, rather than logically, untenable works with Symon, who, some decades before the repeal of the Witchcraft Act, agrees that suspicion doesn't fit the facts.

Matters are readily cleared up when Mause discloses that she is the former nurse of Peggy, whom she rescued from evilly-disposed relatives and laid at the shepherd Glaud's door. Thus she is the kind of sibyl whom Scott later found so useful, the Meg Merrilies or Magdalen Graeme who moves in a supernatural mist, takes pride in secret knowledge, and holds the key to identity. A correlation of social class with degree of credulity also serves Scott's purposes, as does antiquarian thoroughness in folklore coverage.[27]

Although *The Fortunate Shepherdess* is modelled on *The Gentle Shepherd*, the Buchan dialect of the narrative poem is more rugged and faithful than the modified Scots of the pastoral comedy. Alexander Ross's purpose is humbly Wordsworthian, "to set before the reader's eyes, in their plain and native colours, a variety of incidents in low life," based on observation of "the natural effects of the human passions on the conduct and manners of plain country people." In the first edition of 1768, the author uses folklore, night fears, and dreams, as well as allusions to the weird, in telling the story of a cattle-lifting, Lindy's separation from Nory while following the caterans, his release by the caterans' sister Bydby, Squire Olimund's love for Nory, the discovery that Nory's mother belongs to the gentry, Nory's marriage within her class to the squire, and Lindy's peasant marriage to Bydby.

After being "carefully corrected," the poem went into a second edition a decade later as *Helenore, or The Fortunate Shepherdess*. Nory and Bydby,

---

[26] Sir William reflects the more enlightened thought of Ramsay's day, not that of the time of action, which is shortly after Cromwell's death in 1658. More characteristic would be the attitude of Sir George Mackenzie, who insists in *The Laws and Customes of Scotland in Matters Criminal* (1678) on "the closest Relevancy and most convincing Probation" in investigating the very real crime of witchcraft.

[27] "The Gentle Shepherd," *The Works of Allan Ramsay*, ed. Martin and Oliver, S.T.S., 2 vols., Edinburgh and London 1951–3, II. 205–77. Goblins, brownies, ghaists, witches, elves and fairies, dreams, and devils appear in "Christ's Kirk on the Green," "Patie and Roger," "Up in the Air," "The Miser and Minos," "The Last Speech of a Wretched Miser," and "The Monk and the Miller's Wife" (based on "The Freiris of Berwik"): I. 67, 72, 76, 142–4, 174; II. 39, 66, 68, 150–3. In "Christ's Kirk," I. 76, the stanza on Nanny's grandmother, shrunken and "odd like" "auld Bessie," who was not let alone "Till she was burnt... Like mony mae," has the poignant lightness of touch of Burns's reversed pair, the young witch Nannie and her "reverend grannie," in "Tam o' Shanter." See I. 72, 142, 144 (also I. 82) for antiquarian notes on the "strange" and "whimsical Stories," the "odd Tales" of "old Women" and "Country" and "ignorant People" about brownies, the elf-shot, and shelly-coat. Burns is equally condescending in his notes to "Halloween."

in their separate searches for Lindy, had been frightened at night. In the revision, low-born Bydby also sees the fairies playing on pipes and whirling "in many a reel." Detecting the mortal spy, they swarm on her like bees "with unco fike and din." She must either be punished or put into service as cowherd or wet nurse. But first she is admitted to their banquet, at which the fairies again "danc'd and flang" before reporting their malefices—like witches—on Tam the steward and others. Then, roaring with fright, Bydby wakens from her nightmare.[28]

Burns treasured the poem and called its author "our true brother . . . a wild warlock." In "Tam o' Shanter," he seems to recall the episode of a voyeur descried by supernatural revellers and its phrasing, as well as the wedding festivities when "they lap they flang they ran" in reels and country dances, and the squire praised most the man "that highest leapt."[29]

"The Merry Wives of Musselburgh's Welcome to Meg Dickson," possibly anonymous, appeared in *A Collection of Scots Poems on Several Occasions* (1756), by Alexander Pennecuik *and others*. It is important because of its emphatic and original treatment of witchcraft. When Meg is about to be hanged in Edinburgh, "three clav'ring carlings" meet in Musselburgh. Lucky, "the auldest cummer of the three," born in 1651, bemoans the dispersal of their "gay large crew" since Halloween last. Now that "drunken Maggie" is in peril, there is no help from "auld Nick": "Pox tak' such de'ils." No passive complainer, Bessie plans that, so soon as Hangie cuts Meg down, she and Grissie will bring the body back in a Shetland cockle-shell "Gi'en by the auld good-man in hell, He's kind to me." Though Meg in her winding sheet looks like a "milk-white ghaist," the hags recover from their fright and devour the story of her capture, torment, and probation by the godly:

> I took them a' for worry-cows. . . .
> It was an unco' kind of session,
>   Sib to auld nick:
> I never met wi' sic oppression,
>   Since I was quick.

The hangman "girnt like a hell-feind"; "the de'il confound the fellow." Those "perfect diels," the surgeon lads, longed to rip up her wame. The persecutors' chaplain turned out to be the witches' "ain Mess John." And at one point, Lucky rounds on Meg, "The meikle De'il take her with His

---

[28] The editions of Ross's poem used are the first and second, 1768 and 1778, both published at Aberdeen.

[29] In "Tam o' Shanter," seeing "how Nannie lap and flang," Tam roars with delight and is pursued by the witches, "As bees bizz out wi' angry fyke."

cloven feet." So the world is nimbly turned topsy-turvy, and the pot calls the kettle black. All the cummers grow merry with drink and many a good crack.

This witch dialogue has elements in common with the talks of the octogenarian Ailsie Gourlay, "the auldest o' us three," Annie Winnie, and the paralytic in *The Bride of Lammermoor*: bitter jests about death, allusions to corpses and a winding sheet, the transport of cummers (by hemlock), "the very deil . . . turned . . . hard-hearted" so that no help comes from him, the persecuting "grit folk" with "breasts like win-stane" ("these hellicat quality, that lord it ower us like brute beasts"), the sudden accusatory turn ("mair o' utter deevilry" in Lady Ashton than in flights of witches), malice and grossness, and the making "a merry night o't" with tobacco, bread, ale, and "a drap brandy."

The bold irony and verve, the sudden twists and turns, of "The Merry Wives of Musselburgh's Welcome to Meg Dickson" place it in a tradition that may at times have gone underground from Dunbar to Burns but that never died out. It would seem to have helped renew the literary currency of folk belief, in its humour and terror, and thus to have prepared the way for Fergusson, Burns, and Scott.[30]

Robert Fergusson's range in the supernatural is from humour to macabre satire. In 1773 the Mortmain Bill proposed that charity assets be absorbed into an English-centred public fund which would pay a niggardly three per cent. The Edinburgh poet's counterblast, published in *Ruddiman's Magazine* a fortnight after the text of the bill was made known, was "The Ghaists: A Kirk-yard Eclogue." George Heriot and George Watson, two benefactors soon to be depersonalised, issue "Frae the dern mansions of the midnight tomb" as wan and grizly ghosts. Their "douff discourse" on the plunder of their hospitals is in rugged decasyllabic couplets which have the mournful cadence of the elder Hamlet's speech:

> Cauld blaws the nippin north wi' angry sough,
> And showers his hailstanes frae the Castle Cleugh . . .
>
> While owlets round the craigs at noon-tide flee,
> And bludey ^abawks sit singand on the tree . . .   ^a bats

---

[30] The burly anthology of Pennecuik and others went through a goodly number of editions. I have quoted from that of Edinburgh, 1769, pp. 37–46, a copy of which is in the Abbotsford Library. Alexander Pennecuik, who died in 1730, was the nephew of another poet, Dr Alexander Pennecuik (1652–1722). What William Brown calls "the spurious Edinburgh issue" [1750?], *A Compleat Collection of all the Poems . . . by . . . Alexander Pennecuik*, with "some Curious *Poems* by other worthy Hands," adds "A Warning to the Wicked, or, *Margaret Dickson*'s Welcome to the Gibbet": After the sins of ignorance, adultery, infanticide, lying, drunkenness, theft, "a false Repentance" and a fearful relapse, Meg ends "ten Times greater Devil than before."

> If ever aught frae sense cou'd be believ'd
> (And *b*seenil hae my senses been deceiv'd) ...   *b* seldom
> Tweed shall rin rowtin' down his banks out o'er,
> Till Scotland's out o' reach o' England's pow'r. ....

So monstrous is the Bill that the poet's feeling, as it bursts forth, disturbs nature and calls goldsmith and banker from their honoured rest. But more characteristic of Fergusson is his amused and casual way with wraiths, de'ils, and such folk in "To the Tron-kirk Bell," "Hame Content," and verse dialogues. Without leaving the fireside, country children learn "that fiends and fairies be | Sent frae the de'il to fleetch us to our ill":

> Frae *gudame*'s mouth auld warld tale they hear,
> O' *Warlocks* louping round the *Wirrikow*,
> O' gaists that win in glen and kirk-yard drear,
> Whilk touzles a' their *a*tap, and gars them shak wi' fear.   *a* top

Though "idle fancies" are passed on to children by gaffers, they do not disturb "life's brawest spring wi' reason clear."[31] In his bravest spring, Robert Burns recalls early guidance in ghaist-lore by an ignorant and superstitious "old Maid of my Mother's," Betty Davidson, who—

> had, I suppose, the largest collection in the county of tales and songs concerning devils, ghosts, fairies, brownies, witches, warlocks, spunkies, kelpies, elf-candles, dead-lights, wraiths, apparitions, cantraips, giants, inchanted towers, dragons and other trumpery.—This cultivated the latent seeds of Poesy; but had so strong an effect on my imagination, that to this hour, in my nocturnal rambles, I sometimes keep a sharp look-out in suspicious places; and though nobody can be more sceptical in these matters than I, yet it often takes an effort of Philosophy to shake off these idle terrors.[32]

[31] "The Farmer's Ingle," *The Poems of Robert Fergusson*, ed. Matthew P. McDiarmid, S.T.S., 2 vols., Edinburgh and London, 1954–6, II. 136–40; "The Ghaists," II. 141–5. Cp. Mark Akenside, *The Pleasures of Imagination*, 1744, BK I, 255–70. Scott's upbringing was similar:

> And ever, by the winter hearth,
> Old tales I heard of woe or mirth,
> Of lovers' slights, of ladies' charms,
> Of witches' spells, of warriors' arms.

(*Marmion*, Introduction to Canto III).
This pedagogic convention had already been spoofed by Richard Gall (1776–1801) in "The Hazlewood Witch":

> For mony lang year I hae heard frae my grannie,
> Of brownies an' bogles by yon castle wa',
> Of auld withered hags, that were never thought cannie,
> An' fairies that danced till they heard the cock craw.
> I leugh at her tales. ....

(Gall, *Poems and Songs*, Edinburgh 1819, p. 143.)

[32] Autobiographical letter of 2 Aug. 1787, to [Dr John Moore], in *The Letters of Robert Burns*, ed. J. DeLancey Ferguson, 2 vols., Oxford 1931, I. 106.

Between boyhood and early decline, Burns is at his best when tension exists between sceptic and believer, and when that tension is mediated by humour. Then he shares with Fergusson, "elder brother in the Muses," a son of the Enlightenment's nonchalance toward superstition and a man of imagination's capacity to participate. Functioning as a rationalist, the poet-folklorist who, in top form, abetted Captain Francis Grose, the antiquary, can off-handedly survey prophetic "charms and spells" in "Halloween," briefing the "philosophic mind" in preface and notes on the rude "passion of prying into futurity" of "the more unenlightened."[33] He can even deteriorate into "our warlock Rhymer" evoking guardian spirits and "a fairy train" as his facile stock-in-trade:

> (That Bards are second-sighted is nae joke,
> And ken the lingo of the sp'ritual folk;
> Fays, Spunkies, Kelpies, a', they can explain them,
> And ev'n the very deils they brawly ken them.)[34]

Usually, the Deil calls out the best in Burns as a poet. Through kenning him well, Burns came to associate the Devil with reality and with the honesty and courage to face up to it. Whereas God is a misty ideal whose followers are too often mired in hypocrisy, the deity of the nethermost is a talented birkie reduced to peasant status by the stiff-necked aristocrat of the skies. The poet offers advice to his "brunstane devilship" to be careful of the company he keeps; thinks of him in relation to landlords, politicians, and the idly affluent; sees Auld Hornie lurking for narrow, squabbling churchmen; hopes that "the meikle devil" may give Death and the exciseman their due; imagines him daunted by beauty; and in the end, despite the inroads of "bright wines and bonnie lasses rare" on "our sinfu' saul," remains on a first-name basis with "Nick."[35] The poet may range from

---

[33] Burns's introduction of Halloween in "Tam Glen" is less self-conscious. Cp. John Main (or Mayne), *Two Scots Poems*, Glasgow 1783, pp. 23-7: his "Hallow-e'en," first published in *The Weekly Magazine, or Edinburgh Amusement*, Nov. 1780, has the family gathering "'round a bleezing ingle-side" for the farm-wife's stories of bogles, fairies, and witches. The youngsters then try three kinds of divination to see or hear their future spouses, which leads "Jockie Mein" to conclude:
> But, 'twere a langsome tale to tell
> The gaits o' ilka charm and spell.
Had Burns followed this selective principle, he would not have written a static catalogue of divination methods. Main rises superior to folk belief, is aware that "customs vary wi' the times," and has an antiquarian footnote, but he is neither pedantic nor supercilious.

[34] "The Brigs of Ayr" and the poet's note on "haunted Garpal," whose banks are pertinaciously inhabited by "those fancy-scaring beings, known by the name of Ghaists."

[35] "Epitaph on Holy Willie," "Captain Grose," and "Epigram on Captain Francis Grose"; "Address of Beelzebub," "The Heron Ballads," "The Author's Earnest Cry and Prayer," and "The Twa Dogs"; "The Ordination" and "The Kirk's Alarm"; "Elegy on Capt. Matthew Henderson," "Scotch Drink," and "The Deil's Awa' wi' the Exciseman"; "Bonnie Lesley"; "Epistle to Colonel de Peyster."

scepticism to tradition, originality, and possible belief.[36] He may be crony, adviser, observer, alter ego, or possible victim of the Devil, yet he humorously keeps in the driver's seat.

In his "Address to the Deil," it is still the poet who calls the tune as it constantly changes from jocose to mock heroic, moral, popular, Masonic, Biblical, autobiographical, and compassionate. "Warlocks grim an' wither'd hags . . . in kirk-yards renew their leagues | Owre howkit [exhumed] dead," and Satan, tempest-borne, strips off kirk roofs. The Satan of Burns's most complex marshalling of the supernatural, "Tam o' Shanter," is somewhat grimmer, but still up to the same old tricks.

But before entering the Devil's orbit with Tam, we should look at the man. He moves in a female, a sex-oriented, world. He is away from home at the start and returning to it, temporarily subdued, at the end of his adventure. The home-body is a "sulky sullen dame," the moral shrew Kate, who would like to tame her mate. A lawful wife, with whom sex is lawful, she is scarcely bewitching. Tam prefers drink, "sangs and clatter," the pleasures of sex and conviviality—elsewhere. On Sunday, instead of sitting beside his wife in kirk, he may be tippling with Kirkton Jean at the Lord's House (the original inn was less ironically named Leddies' House). The night of his ride, Tam enjoys his ale with a well-loved crony, Souter Johnny, beside a blazing fire and exchanges "favours secret, sweet, and precious" with the compliant landlady, while an equally compliant landlord overlooks adulterous fondling. The contrast between grim checks and gay cheating, between the lawful and the forbidden in the natural world, is clear.

At the midnight hour when "Tam maun ride," he enters—as in a drunken dream—a world where all things are abnormally enlarged. This is immediately palpable in the elemental violence of thunder, lightning, wind, rain, and the flooded Doon. "The Deil had business on his hand." Tam's last contact with reality is his mare, Meg, who bears him past scenes of human turbulence and disaster—death, murder, and suicide—to the apparently blazing kirk. "Alloway's auld haunted kirk" can hardly be a symbol, as has been suggested, of narrow religious restraint of pleasure. Frequented for two and a half centuries by Catholics and by Reformers and abandoned to decay and the Devil some three years before Burns was born, it is completely stripped of power. Within its shell, licence is uninhibited by reason or moral control of any kind. With nightmarish

---

[36] "An' if a Devil be at a' " in "To Gavin Hamilton"; "Kellyburn Braes" (a shrewish wife too much even for the Devil); "Tam o' Shanter"; and "The Lord preserve us frae the Devil! Amen! amen!" in "Epistle to Colonel de Peyster," written the last year of Burns's life.

extravagance, evil, the starkly physical, has taken over. Warlocks and witches dance to the shrieking bagpipes of auld Nick in shape of "a touzie tyke, black, grim, and large!" Corpse candelabra, "a murderer's banes," "unchristen'd bairns," a hanged thief, blood-crusted weapons, an infanticidal garter and a parricidal knife form once more the image of human violence and woe.

At this point, the sexual pace quickens. The landlady has aroused Tam. There have been reminders of his state during the ride. Meg the mare is evoked in terms that are less equine than human.[37] In "Holy Willie's Prayer," there is a wanton named Meg:

> O Lord! yestreen, thou kens, wi' Meg——— ...
> An' I'll ne'er lift a lawless leg
> > Again upon her.

And Tam is—
> Weel mounted on his gray mare, Meg,
> A better never lifted leg.

Standing stones frequently have "a phallic significance."[38] Meg bears Tam past the "meikle stane." And now, perhaps, he is in a proper condition to respond to Nannie's performance. As the mirth grows "fast and furious," with louder piping and quicker dancing, each old witch, sweating and steaming, flings off all but her shirt. This far from titillating vision makes the poet wonder why Tam's stomach is not turned by sapless hags wildly leaping, staff in shrunken hand. He himself would give his only pair of breeches, right off his haunches, for one look at "plump and strapping" teenage girls in such a caper. Whereupon the wish conjures up the "winsome wench," Nannie.

Nannie is that indispensable member of a Scottish witch coven known as the Maiden.[39] Her name, significantly, is associated elsewhere in Burns's poetry with a lass "charming, sweet, an' young ... as spotless as she's bonie."[40] On her first night as an "enlisted" witch, she is poised between

---

[37] In "The Auld Farmer's New-Year Morning Salutation to his Auld Mare, Maggie," the sentiment and phrasing approximate those of the wife in "John Anderson, my jo."

[38] F. Marion McNeill, The Silver Bough, 4 vols., Glasgow 1957–. . . . I. 87, 179 n. 8.

[39] Op. cit., I. 133. The Maiden and hags of a coven have nature-myth overtones of spring and winter, growth and decay, Bride (the Maiden) and the Cailleach (Auld Wife). For survivals of the myth, see op. cit., II. 20, 120, 123–4, 126, 128–9 (with dancing), 131; III. 22.

[40] "My Nanie, O," and in "My Nanie's Awa," written after "Tam," Nanie is like a snowdrop, a primrose, a violet. But note the North-of-England use in nanny-catch, a mischievous sprite, and in nanny-house or nanny-shop, a brothel. English Dialect Dictionary and Oxford English Dictionary. The association of witchcraft and sex in Burns's poetry is fairly conventional, "witching" love, grace, or smile and "witchcraft o' Beauty's alarms."

Less conventional is the paradox in "A Prayer in the Prospect of Death": the Almighty Cause has formed the poet—

what she has been, her grannie's "wee Nannie," and what she will become, a destroyer of cattle, crops, and boats, the Maiden turned hag, "Lang after kent on Carrick shore!" Poignant and pretty, evil and deadly to be, she enriches Tam's eyes, a supple ballerina pulsing in the air to the devil's rhythms in a shirt bought for her when she was little. "Even Satan glowr'd, and fidg'd fu' fain." Master and Maiden seem on the verge of that act of initiation and subjection, of diabolical penetration, which witches confess to have been cold and painful. The moment when the novice's disposition is finally changed from passive abandonment to active malevolence is not reached. That incautious voyeur, peeping Tam, is wrought by this strange slip-tease to such a climax of appreciation that he cries out, "Weel done, Cutty-sark!" The witches fly after Tam, intent perhaps on punishing him in kind. But it is the mare that, reaching the crest of the bridge above the swollen waters of the Doon, pays with her tail. The poet's use of the term in "threshin' still at hizzies' tails" ("To a Gentleman") and "by my hen, an' by her tail" (an affair with Elizabeth Paton, thinly masked in "Epistle to John Rankine") would suggest that the sequence in "Tam" is not fortuitous:

> There at them thou thy tail may toss. . . .
> The fient a tail she had to shake! . . .
> But left behind her ain gray tail. . . .

Thus Burns, undergoing a kind of tumescence of the imagination, sends Tam on a journey from covert to manifest sexuality, from the conscious to the near chaos of the sub-conscious, from the natural to the super-natural. Wonder and ravishment end in fear, in shocked flight back to a less anarchic world. Tam has twitched the seven veils of time. Anticipating Margaret Murray's *The Witch-Cult in Western Europe* (1921), Burns reaches back through its debased and fragmentary form to the memory of a cult of fertility in which a pre-Christian god, incarnate as human or animal, represented nature's generative principle to witch communicants. Fantasy and humour act as relief to the intensity, psychic depth, and actual horror of "Tam o' Shanter," whose naked power is not matched in Scott's reticent fiction or in Scottish witchcraft literature.[41]

> With passions wild and strong;
> And list'ning to their witching voice
> Has often led me wrong.

Also see William Bell Scott, "The Witch's Ballad," *An Anthology of Carrick*, ed. Malcolm J. Finlayson, Kilmarnock 1925, pp. 169–73.

[41] Cp. John Spiers, "Tradition and Robert Fergusson," *Robert Fergusson 1750–1774*, ed. S. G. Smith, Edinburgh 1952, p. 104; David Craig, *Scottish Literature and the Scottish People 1680–1830*, London 1961, p. 109. The best interpretation of "Tam" that I know is in Thomas

EIGHTEENTH-CENTURY POETRY IN ENGLISH

As the eighteenth century advances, Scots writing in English gain confidence in dealing with the supernatural. But for the most part they work evasively, shifting the responsibility for superstition to the remote in rank, the peasantry; in place, the Highlands; or in time, the Gaelic past. Vernacular writers also describe the picturesque credulity of the peasantry for a public whose rationality is flatteringly assumed, but they tend more often to lose themselves in their subject.

The rustics in James Thomson's *Winter* (1726) fear the warning "demon of the night" and are clutched by "superstitious horror" when "the goblin-story" is told beside the fire. In *Summer* (1727), "as village stories tell . . . the fairy people throng" at night. Milkmaid and shepherd avoid the suicide's grave and the lonely tower which houses, "So night-struck fancy dreams, the yelling ghost." And in *The Castle of Indolence* (1748), either beguiled by "lone fancy" or glimpsing embodied "aerial beings," the Hebridean shepherd sees "A vast assembly moving to and fro."[42]

Dr John Armstrong, too, describes "surly Winter" as driving hinds to the fireside, where they tell "musty legends and ear-pathing tales," both aristocratic and plebeian, of madcap knights, "black necromantic bards," walking statues, air-built castles, tower- and dungeon-haunting ghosts, "church-yard belching flames at dead of night," giants, elves,

> And all the toys that phantasy pranks up
> T'amuse her fools withal.[43]

In *The Excursion* (1728) David Mallet uses the chiaroscuro of day and night, the mundane and the awful, peaceful and convulsed nature. His is not so much a symmetry of logic as of contrasting moods evoked by description and reflexion. For the darker side of nature, he summons Night's "secret *Horrors*, the distressful *Dream*, | And causeless *Fear*," which mock Fancy when Reason sleeps; the Murderer's flight from "the bleeding *Shadow* of the *Slain*"; the "griesly *Spectres*," aerial, fluvial, and igneous, of

Crawford, *Burns: A Study of the Poems and Songs*, Edinburgh and London, 1960, pp. 217–36. Also see William Montgomerie, "Tam o' Shanter," *New Judgments: Robert Burns*, Glasgow 1947, pp. 70–84. The text used is that of *The Poetical Works of Robert Burns*, ed. J. Logie Robertson, London 1960.

[42] *The Complete Poetical Works of James Thomson*, ed. J. Logie Robertson, London 1908, pp. 115, 192, 208, 263.

[43] "Imitations of Shakespeare," Armstrong, *Miscellanies*, 2 vols., London 1770, I. 153–4. If one accepts Armstrong's story that the poem was written in 1725 (*D.N.B.*), Thomson was forestalled as winter's bard by a boy of sixteen. Some forty-five years later, the poem was published.

waste places; and, though relegated to the far North, the spells and revels of sorcerer and witch.[44]

By choosing *The Grave* (1743) as his subject, Robert Blair joins the "graveyard poets." This category tends to obscure the originality he achieves through irony, pathos, horror, satire, and thought. When he is conventional, a great bell invisibly tolled, shrieks from "hollow tombs," and ambulant dead men give rise to rumour, "Strange things, the neighbours say, have happen'd here":

> (Such tales their cheer at wake or gossiping,
> When it draws near the witching time of night.)

He also has his "black demon" train of tempters; his "light-heel'd ghosts, and visionary shades" in mystic motion, "as fame reports"; his "grisly spectres"; his "horrid apparition," by moonlight, to a fearful and imaginative schoolboy. But when Blair speaks in his own voice, somewhat like Donne's, he jocularly wishes "some courteous ghost" to go beyond the routine of fatal warnings in order to *blab out* the secret of death and life thereafter. As soon as our turn comes to be ghosts, however, we shall probably husband our new knowledge with the same "stinted charity."[45]

According to the "Advertisement," the design of James Beattie's *The Minstrel; or, The Progress of Genius* (1771–4) is "to trace the progress of a Poetical Genius, born in a rude and illiterate age, from the first dawnings of fancy and reason," to minstrel stature. Although Edwin's birth in Scotia is not attended by any "strange event," "the visionary boy" likes to "dream of graves, and corses pale," and wailing, chain-clanking ghosts. He goes to a "haunted stream. . . . Where Fays of yore their revels wont to keep," and where he presently has a vision of a green–clad "host of little warriors," venerable minstrels, and "a troop of dames." Driven indoors by winter, he delights in an old woman's knightly, pastoral, and supernatural legends and ditties. But even a gifted shepherd can be too exclusively educated on fairies that revel by moonlight and on hags "that suckle an infernal brood" and show malice in flood or storm.

> . . . when to horror his amazement rose,
> A gentler strain the Beldam would rehearse,
> A tale of rural life. . . .

Most of the time Edwin is "rous'd" and nourished by "Gothic tale, or song, or fable old." Graduating from the beldam's care, he is counselled by a hermit sage: "Visionary fiends, an endless train," often attack "where

[44] Mallet, *The Excursion*, London 1728, pp. 11, 18–19, 23, 29–31.
[45] *The Poetical Works of Robert Blair*, London 1794, pp. 24–7, 44, 51–3.

no real ills affright." Phantoms, hags, and spell-muttering wizards can only be banished by "the Philosophick Spirit."[46]

It was much easier to pluck Beattie's "Gothic lyre" than to sound his philosophic note. In "The Sorceress," William Julius Mickle indulges a Gothic exuberance of fancy which anticipates the Romantic period in its least subtle moments. His new departure is to make a quick-paced plot hinge on the supernatural, with a fearful question introducing revelation and death. Earlier Scottish Augustans had been content to relate the un-earthly to folk culture and winter entertainment, to scenery and the terrors of night. Their conventionally grisly ghosts attract attention through rustic hearsay. The pleasures of superstition are regulated ideally by the golden mean. When reason is overbalanced by imagination, Beattie changes Edwin's mentors. Less concerned with balance, Mickle lets him-self go in the Countess of Leicester's lament, the omens attending her murder, and the haunting of "Cumnor Hall," an unacknowledged ballad which found larger utterance in Scott's *Kenilworth*.

As A. M. Oliver states in a valuable essay, "Their treatment of the super-natural is the most fruitful and the most individual contribution made by these Scots to English literature. . . . Wild scenery and the associated supernatural were especially identified with Scotland."[47] William Collins drew appropriate inspiration from his meeting with John Home in the autumn of 1749. In "An Ode on the Popular Superstitions of the High-lands of Scotland," the English poet exhorts his Lowland friend to poetise "Fancy's land . . . Where still, 'tis said, the fairy people meet," brownies do chores, and elf arrows fly. "Such airy beings awe the untutor'd swain." And long may "homely swains" nourish the fancy, not the fact, of wizards, second sight, will o' the wisp, the kelpie, and other prodigies.[48] Although Smollett is too much of a Scot to jumble Highland and Lowland wonders, he represents the "natural superstition" of Humphry Clinker, an English swain on a northern journey, as "much injured by the histories of

---

[46] Beattie, *The Minstrel . . . Book the First*, London 1771, pp. v, 18–19, 23–4, 31–2; *The Minstrel . . . The Second Book*, London 1774, pp. 21, 23–4. Amynter in John Langhorne, *Genius and Valour: A Scotch Pastoral*, 2nd edn, London 1764, pp. 8–9, philosophically rebuffs the Chorus of Shepherds, "No more of Leader's faery-haunted Shore." Langhorne was not a Scot, but John Logan, who was, allows his unphilosophic milkmaid to see "the Fairies, with their Queen, Trip hand-in-hand the circled green" ("Ode Written in Spring"). Logan, *Poems*, London 1781, p. 25.

[47] "The Scottish Augustans," *Scottish Poetry: A Critical Survey*, ed. James Kinsley, London 1955, pp. 141–4.

[48] *The Poetical Works of James Beattie, LL.D. and William Collins*, London 1823, pp. 318–26. In 1788, twenty-nine years after Collins's death, the "Ode" was published in two rival edi-tions in Edinburgh and London. The Scottish version was altered by Alexander Carlyle and Henry Mackenzie.

witches, fairies, ghosts, and goblins, which he has heard in this country."[49]

Native poets from Barbour to Fergusson kept a truer record of the fabulous than the Scottish Augustans, but the latter, in arousing curiosity south of the Border, helped to develop a wider public for Macpherson, Burns, and Scott.

REVIVALS: THE BALLAD AND OSSIAN

While eighteenth-century poets were condescendingly turning to peasants for the ingenuously picturesque, there was a revival of medieval ballads in which the popular imagination yearned toward the picturesque halls, weapons, and array, the passions and exploits, of the upper classes. In their treatment of the supernatural, at least, the older, anonymous composers show the greater sureness, skill, and integrity.

Ballad witches constrict, harm, or metamorphose people. Far from diminutive fairies love, enchant, and hold mortals, offer fatal gifts, impose taboos, dance at midnight or troop abroad on Hallowe'en. Agitated by love, hate, jealousy, or the excessive grief of the living, neurotic corpses come back as very substantial ghosts to regain their troth-plight, to carry off their lovers, to warn or to punish.

Steeped in ballad lore, Scott learned the value of supernatural accusation, foreshadowing, and mood. In "Kinmont Willie," when "the bauld Buccleuch" escapes over swollen Eden Water, Lord Scroope exclaims, "He is either himsell a devil frae hell, | Or else his mother a witch maun be." The temper of Royalists and Covenanters in conflict is the same. The night before his death in "The Battle of Otterburn," Douglas "dream'd a dreary dream." The omen of "the new moon . . . Wi' the auld moon in her arm" precedes the drowning of Sir Patrick Spens and his men. In "Edom o' Gordon," the leader sees "ill dooms" in the killing of a girl, and a sceptical follower tries to hearten him:

> "Wha looks to freits, my master dear,
>   It's freits will follow them;[50]
> Let it ne'er be said that Edom o' Gordon
>   Was daunted by a dame."

[49] After defining "Boggles" as "all beings which create an *earieness* in man," John Mac-Taggart humourously boasts, "In Scotland, more boggles are seen and heard of than there are in all the rest of the world." What are Welsh and Swiss spirits "to *warlocks* without end, *worricows, kelpies, spunkies, wraiths, witchies,* and *carlines?* . . . Accounts of these supernatural beings will . . . show that the Scots are a nation not only famous for religion, war, learning and independence; but also for superstition." *The Scottish Gallovidian Encyclopedia,* p. 77.

[50] For Mungo Park's smiling paraphrase of this passage when Scott remarked on "a bad omen," see the chapter on "Curses, Omens, Dreams, and Prophecies."

But when the lord comes home to his burning castle, "... soon i' the Gordon's foul heart's blude | He's wroken his dear ladye." (Leicester and Varney, as well as Rothsay and Ramorny, have the same superstitious master-cynical man relationship.) The action and feeling of the most ballad-like of Scott's novels, *The Bride of Lammermoor*, elaborate and refine the old broken love theme. An unpolished Ravenswood, "The Daemon Lover" returns for his "former vows"—

> "O fause are the vows o' womankind
> But fair is their fause bodie."[51]

Sir James Fergusson has found the dramatic ballad attitude "a characteristic of a people which views its whole national history in the light of legend."[52] This attitude was to be shared by Scott and Stevenson and, in a strange way, by James Macpherson. After combining, changing, and adding to Gaelic remains according to his vision of the past, Macpherson presented his partly derivative, partly creative work to readers as translations from Ossian (1760–5). In this he paralleled, though on a more impressive scale, what purifiers and sentimentalisers, tinkers and fakers, scholars and recreators of genius were doing with the ballad from Ramsay's *The Tea-Table Miscellany* (1724–1737) to Scott's *Minstrelsy of the Scottish Border* (1802–1803).[53] Attacks on Macpherson were perhaps due less to moral indignation than to resentment at being taken in by the pseudo-primitive. Ballads were, of course, the touchstone of the true-primitive.

In his early poetry, Macpherson swings from interest in Miltonic demonology to attempts at Gothic horror and to the creation of his own amorphous afterworld of ghosts. Death, "the grisly fiend," Ambition, the "virtue-hated fiend," and Discord, the "rav'nous fiend," appear in a juvenile poem called "Death." After emphasising violence and the terror of death, Macpherson turns to peace, contemplation, melancholy, and resignation in the last quarter of his poem. These are the components of his later retrospect of heroic war and woe from a time of sterile inactivity. The dissolving of factitious emotion and sensation into mood and

---

[51] Though his Margaret is faithful, even "Clerk Saunders" cannot rest: "Give me my faith and troth again, And let me fare me on my way." This and other quotations are from *Border Ballads*, selected by D. P. Bliss, London 1925. Also see L. C. Wimberly, *Folklore in the English and Scottish Ballads*, New York 1959. Ballads are briefly discussed in relation to *Minstrelsy* in the next chapter, "Apprentice Years."

[52] "The Ballads," *Scottish Poetry*, ed. Kinsley, p. 118.

[53] See Douglas Young, "A Note on Scottish Gaelic Poetry," *Scottish Poetry*, ed. Kinsley, p. 281: "James Macpherson . . . is now understood to have had somewhat the same relation to his original sources as Sir Walter Scott had in editing Border ballads. . . ." Note, too, Scott's authorship hoaxes and his mottoes from old plays, etc.

impressionism goes on in "The Hunter," which was perhaps written at the age of twenty. The poet seems bewildered by the diversity of his supernatural material, which includes dreams, "dire portents," phantom kings and a phantom sire, and a fairy kingdom like that in *A Midsummer Night's Dream*. As if to increase confusion, "his father Malcolm's phantom" appears to sleeping Donald. And into this Shakespearian, Christian, fictive jumble intrudes the later, Ossianic quality which would soon be so congenial to Macpherson's spirit:

> And the pale form is wrapt in gloomy night;
> Amid the breeze the dying words are lost,
> And nought is heard but the shrill whistling blast.

In 1758, when Macpherson was twenty-two, he published a thoroughly reworked "Hunter" as "The Highlander." The earlier demonological allusions are diffused into Gothicism. Thus, when he stands above sleeping Danes, young Alpin is like a stalking figure of the dead seen by "the midnight traveller": "At length the giant phantom hovers o'er | Some grave unhallowed, stained with murdered gore." And, pointing to "the streaming flood-gates of his breast," the "ghastly vision" of "a mangled man"—

> ... weakly says, "Revenge me, O my son!"
> I to reply—he hissed his way along,
> As breezes sing through reeds their shrilly song.

Here, Macpherson is groping his way from Gothic gruesomeness to Gaelic mistiness. The Gothic and the Ossianic strains are also mingled in "A Night-Piece," in which "A spirit whispers on the gale, ... | And ghastly horror rides the air," and in the more complex evocation of night in "The Six Bards": "Dark, dusky, howling is the night, cloudy, windy, and full of ghosts! The dead are abroad!" But by 1760, in *Fregments of Ancient Poetry*, the Ossianic note is sounded alone. Ghosts like grey mist or moonbeams ride on a meteor and depart "like a dream of the night," mournful in themselves, creating fear and love in others.

The assembly of ghosts is more numerous in the impressionistic prose epic *Fingal* of 1762. Spirits may be angry, sad, monitory, and prophetic. In their caves they talk of mortal men; they visit the sleeping or the waking, make music, even engage in vain combat with men; and they bear the newly dead to their hills. Although their voices are faint, they may be heard as wind, storm, or mountain stream. They move at noon and at night, in sunbeams, on the hills, or among mystic stones, and use "the whistling blast" or the whirlwind for transport. They resemble natural phenomena or are identified with them—the darkened moon, moonbeams, clouds, mist, buzzing flies or humming bees, meteors, and even lightning. When made one with nature, they may be interpreted rationally. Thus, in reply to the susceptible Connal, Cuthullin says of Crugal's ghost, "It was the wind that murmured across thy ear." Appropriately enough, on suffering a fall of valour, Cuthullin returns to belief.

These are fairly conventional ghosts. There are also ghosts-to-be: the living telling what they will do when dead or Fingal wishing his "falling people" to return to their native land and delight his soul in "silent dreams."[54]

The longer Macpherson was acquainted with ghosts the more he knew about them. In his second epic, *Temora* (1763), the outlines of a mythology begin to be clear. The insignificant in life are insignificant in death, being "folded in the vapour of the fenny field" or reedy pool and not released like heroes "on hills, nor mossy vales of wind." Over the grave of a warrior "the spirits of old . . . roll the mist, a grey dwelling" to shroud his ghost until the funeral elegy is sung to free him from the limbo of Loch Lego and to secure his fame. Fallen friends or foes, if not mourned and memorialised by bards and by stones or tombs, cannot go to their caves or "their airy halls."[55] The sphere and the variety of ghostly activity are also expanded. Ghosts appear on "the foam-covered waves." They can be formed and dismembered by the elements. They may fear the living, like those that fled when Fingal "struck the deep-sounding shield . . . the dismal sign of war!"[56] And they can be invoked.

In the shorter Ossianic narratives, ghosts continue to be single or multiple: "Erin's clouds are hung round with ghosts" and "the ghosts of thousands were near." Ancestral spirits are summoned by augury to answer the questions of dreamers ("Cathlin of Clutha" and "Cath-loda"). Chiefly important, however, are the more skilful use of setting, the elaboration of the eclectic mythology, and the intensification of the Gotterdämmerung mood. The emotional tone is made responsive to scenery. In "Sulmalla of Lumon," a stream crosses "a blasted heath" among "high broken rocks" and "bending trees":

> Near were two circles of Loda, with the stone of power; where spirits descended, by night, in dark-red streams of fire. There, mixed with the

---

[54] In "Lathmon," "the ghosts of those who are to fall" by Fingal's sword "are on the beams of his steel."

[55] In "Conlath and Cuthona," Conlath successfully appeals to Ossian to lay his ghost by transmitting his fame to posterity.

[56] In "The War of Caros," "the trembling ghosts of the dead fled, shrieking on their clouds," at the sound of Oscar's "terrible voice."

murmur of waters, rose the voice of aged men; they called the forms of night to aid them in their war.

Loda is Odin, the most clearly defined member of Macpherson's spectral pantheon. In "Carric-Thura," the "spirit of dismal Loda" comes "in his terrors" on a blast from the mountain, his eyes "like flames in his dark face," his voice "like distant thunder." Then, in Homeric rhodomontade, Fingal and Loda, the firm- and hollow-voiced, threaten each other. When they go beyond words, Loda's "flaming wrath" and "the blast of death" from his nostrils do not harm Fingal. Against Loda's "shadowy spear" is opposed Fingal's sword Luno, which "winds through the gloomy ghost," making it break up "like a column of smoke" disturbed by a boy's staff. "The spirit of Loda shrieked, as, rolled into himself, he rose on the wind." Loda has aspects of a weather god. But his dwelling, an "airy hall . . . marked with nightly fires," is like that of dead Gaelic heroes, and the resort of Northmen to spirit oracles is also the same, except for "Loda's stone of power." As a god dear to Scandinavia, which threatens Caledonia, Loda is Macpherson's nearest approach to a devil in a mythology which is singularly free from demonology and from an evil principle.

Like Loda, Malvina does double service as ghost and god, being a watcher of night and "lonely beam" as well as the muse of poetry, subject to invocation. When among the living, she is consoled by Ossian, who has seen Oscar's spirit in a dream: "There is a joy in grief when peace dwells in the the breast of the sad" ("Croma"). Out of this aesthetic intuition of the interdependence of opposite emotions[57] Macpherson creates the bitter-sweet mood in which his Ossianic prose-poems are steeped. The mood is sustained by a central concept, that life is a dream, and by a central figure, Ossian, old, blind, and lonely.

In "The Songs of Selma," after his failure to invoke the "ghosts of the dead," Colma says, "My life flies away like a dream: why should I stay behind?" The attraction and repulsion of the ghost world and the indistinctness of its boundaries make the characteristic death-wish less morbid than weak. That wish is not for total extinction but for a metamorphosis in which an earthly voice becomes an aerial one that will be both loved and feared by those yet living. Full of the same sad defeatism, Ossian, the last of the bards, the last giant "of the chiefs of old," endures life among "the sons of feeble men" and communes with ghosts. "Ossian

[57] Cp. "Comala" (to "frighten and please my soul"), *Temora* ("like the haunt of ghosts, pleasant and dreadful to the soul"), "Carric-Thura" (Fingal tells his bards, "Pleasant is the joy of grief!").

shall not be long alone. He sees the mist that shall receive his ghost" ("Berrathon"). Though he sings of godlike heroes and the twilight into which they are fading, "no bard shall raise his fame!" ("The Songs of Selma").

The Jacobite cause collapsed in 1746. In the fifteenth century, Beauchamp was perhaps the last true knight. Both James Macpherson and Sir Thomas Malory express their nostalgia for a vanishing age in terms of past ages, those of Ossianic heroism and Arthurian chivalry. Malory has the advantage of more intact sources, closer touch with the old order which he idealises, and greater narrative sweep and energy. Like Malory's, Macpherson's theme is the transitoriness of human glory, a prophetic, sweetly melancholy theme which may explain Ossian's hold on Napoleon. Transcience, decay, and *lachrymae rerum* are the burden of Ossian, who joins the numerous ghosts in mediating between the past and the present.[58]

Instead of mediating, Macpherson may blend "the voice of past times" with the voice of the present and future. Time is strangely telescoped in "The Death of Cuthullin," with Bragela's spirit inspiring Ossian to write of her as wife and widow and to desire her ghost to return home to dream of her hero. So brief is life, so lasting is the after-state, and so faint is the line between, that earthly and ghostly existence are almost simultaneous. And the mobile ghost is the soul as well: "Peace to thy soul, in thy cave, chief of the isle of mist!" In his dislocation of time, Macpherson seems to foreshadow modern writers, and, in his nebulous and ubiquitous spirits, the phenomena of mediums like Daniel Home.

Macpherson is original as well in his simplifying of mythology. Relieved of theology and complexity, his Ossianic afterworld is run by recent ghosts and is little affected by the few survivors of the old theocracies of good and evil. All is sadly sweet and vaguely consolatory. On her death, Malvina rises "like the beam of the east, among the spirits" of her friends. Feeble voices and "half-viewless" harps are heard. "Malvina ... beholds the unknown faces of her fathers," but her father Toscar is apparently recognisable. "His locks of mist" flying in the wind, "a smile ... on his grey, watry face," he cheers her, "Thy friends had passed away. The sons of little men were in the hall" ("Berrathon"). In a similar manner, but with a clearer purpose, Margaret Oliphant's Victorian stories of the unseen reduce religion and the afterlife to their simplest terms. Their success— and that of E. S. Phelps's *Gates Ajar* fiction after the American Civil War— was due to the easy comfort which they brought to thousands of readers.

[58] Rough sketches for the reflective, maladjusted Ossian are Macpherson's vague traveller and "musing hunter."

Macpherson's attitude toward the supernatural is not readily suggested by his imaginative accomplishment. His ghosts seem to have been given such prominence because Homer's supernatural machinery was too wonderful to go down in an Age of Reason. In a note to "Carric-Thura," the author attributes "the most extravagant fiction" of Fingal and the spirit of Loda to Ossian, who "said nothing but what perfectly agreed with the notions of the times concerning ghosts" as bodies subject to pain. A note to "Conlath and Cuthona" indicates that the ancient notion of ghost-raised storms "is still entertained by the vulgar," who think that spirits cause sudden blasts for locomotion. And a note to "Carthon" informs the reader that "the vulgar" refer the sudden starting of beasts to their seeing ghosts.[59] The implication is that a belief natural to a primitive state of society is both poetic and heroic. With general enlightenment, it sinks to the vulgar level and becomes matter for antiquarian comment by a Martin Martin, a James Macpherson, or a Walter Scott.

When sympathetic embodiment and rational disbelief are not divided between text and notes, Macpherson makes a character like Cuthullin objective and sceptical, uses qualifying phrases like "perhaps" and "seemed," or suggests in figurative language that ghosts are phenomena of light and weather. Moina's ghost is "like the new moon"; "the sound of his woods" may be the murmur of Erragon's ghost; and a newly fallen chief may be given a mist robe, a cloud-formed spear, and a "half-extinguished meteor . . . sword." Cuthullin's ghost voice is "like hollow wind in a cave: his eye a light seen afar"; and the stars look "dim through his form." So indefinite, in fact, is the animistic line between ghost and nature that the spirit of the mountain turns out to be "that deep and melancholy sound which precedes a storm" ("Dar-Thula").

Despite his neo-classic checks and balances, a full decade before Henry Mackenzie made the man of feeling popular James Macpherson gave wide currency to the ghost of feeling. He cast over the latter half of an age of supposed reason a euphoric melancholy which stimulated and released emotion and imagination. His faculty was an absorptive and integrative one which brought together elements from Gaelic traditional folk-story, English poetry, Greek and Latin epic, and Hebrew Bible. The product is a loose-jointed opus whose style is unified by repetition, rhythm, and tonal effects produced by mournful vowels. Questions of authenticity to Gaelic originals are more interesting than important in judging Macpherson, who is a creator, however faulty, and not a translator. His achievement is the prose-poetry of mood.

[59] Dogs are usually psychic, but in "Carthon" deer avoid the haunt of "a dim ghost."

In his criticism of Malcolm Laing's edition of *The Poems of Ossian*, Scott says that ghosts cannot be traced in any Gaelic ballads. For his "plurality" of ghosts, Macpherson fell back on "vulgar superstition . . . common to the Highlanders with the ignorant in all nations."[60] Though most effective at times, "the frequent and useless appearance of these impotent phantoms, impresses us rather with contempt, than with fear or reverence."[61] In more informal mood some fourteen months later (September 1806), Scott writes to Anna Seward that as "a very young boy" he "devoured rather than perused" Spenser and Macpherson and could remorselessly recite "whole . . . Duans" of Ossian. Despite his "progress in taste,"[62] Scott never completely shook off Macpherson's influence. The MacIvors in *Waverley* and Ranald of the Mist in *A Legend of Montrose* are given "those flowers of sentiment which Macpherson had taught the public to consider as the genuine attribute of Ossianic strain."[63] In a humorous episode of *The Antiquary*, Hector M'Intyre lamely defends the authenticity of Macpherson's Ossian against the attack of his Lowland uncle, Jonathan Oldbuck. Eight years later, in *St. Ronan's Well*, 1824, the unpredictable novelist excuses his poorest imitation of Macpherson: the Highland *miles gloriosus*, Captain Hector MacTurk, conceived his oration in "the periphrastic language of Ossian" before translating it into English.[64] And in 1828, Scott's modification of Ossian in the speech of Torquil of the Oak is moving and convincing (*The Fair Maid of Perth*). Scott's creation of mood through setting (Muschat's Cairn in *The Heart of Midlothian*) is both Ossianic and effective. As for ghosts, Scott can be as nebulous, as automatic, and as pretty as Macpherson at his worst, but seldom for long; ghosts are not Scott's *forte*. What Scott chiefly carried away from Ossian was a sense of high-flown rhetoric, romantic devotion, and the sadness

---

[60] *The Edinburgh Review*, VI (1805), 447. Scott's composite review, pp. 429–62, is partly devoted to the Highland Society Committee's *Report* on "the Nature and Authenticity of the Poems of Ossian: Drawn up . . . by Henry Mackenzie," Edinburgh and London 1805.

[61] *Op. cit.* For Scott's comment on Fingal's encounter with the spirit of Loda, see pp. 443–4, and for Ossianic ghosts in general, see J. S. Smart, *James Macpherson*, London 1905, pp. 82–3, 119–25. My quotations are from Laing's edition, 2 vols., Edinburgh 1805.

[62] *Letters*, I. 319–25. In this letter, Scott mentions his desire to write "a Highland poem . . . giving as far as I can a real picture of what that enthusiastic race actually were before the destruction of their patriarchal government." From his youth he has delighted in Highland traditions picked up from old Jacobite frequenters of his father's house.

[63] *The Edinburgh Review*, VI. 450. See Donald Davie, *The Heyday of Sir Walter Scott*, London, 1961, pp. 27, 113, on Scott's "Ossianic indulgence" in "Highland Minstrelsy," *Waverley*, ch. 22, and on the influence of his fabricated Ossianic prose on James Fenimore Cooper.

[64] Cp. *Letters*, I. 323: "We know from constant experience, that most highlanders after they have become compleat masters of English, continue to *think* in their own language and it is to me demonstrable that Macpherson *thought* almost every word of Ossian in Gaelic although he wrote it down in English."

of lost causes, all of which contribute to his vision of the Highlands.

To Allan Ramsay's Lowland backward look, Macpherson adds the nostalgia of a Highland Gael. More subtly and pervasively, Scott elevates nostalgia to the grand scale in the Scottish, English, and European backward look of the historical novel. Up to a certain point retrospection has been a stimulus and a comfort to the Scot; beyond that point it has tended to retard development, as with Stevenson, Neil Munro, and the Kailyard sentimentalists.

CHAPTER III

APPRENTICE YEARS*

SCOTT was long an apprentice to the craft of fiction. From boyhood, he exercised his talent on friends. Revision depended on felt and seen response. Indeed, if more versions of his many yarns were available, it might be argued that Scott's oral were superior to his literary gifts.[1] He was more natural and concise, more confident of his audience and therefore less obviously compelled to explain in order not to mislead, and less self-consciously literary. The development of his critical sense, along with the maturing of his taste as a reader of German literature, Gothic romance, imported and domestic ballads, and anecdotal tomes, favourably affected his own output. The specific training under consideration in this chapter, however, is Scott's work as translator, adapter, editor, and author of ballads and long narrative poems.

During a transient subjection to foreign literary models, Scott made hurried translations from the German. Under Gottfried August Bürger's gross spell he "excited mingled emotions of terror & pity"[2] with his rendering of "Der wilde Jäger" and "Lenore" as *The Chase, and William and Helen* (Edinburgh, October 1796). Horror, delight, and excitement, with some release for pent-up sexual forces, are at the core of such shockers as "William and Helen." When William does not return from a crusade, Helen blasphemes. That night her lover, with very little ghostly caution, rides up to the moated castle with sound-effects that are heavy, crashing,

---

* A fuller discussion appears in C. O. Parsons, "The Supernatural in Scott's Poetry," *N. & Q.*, CLXXXVIII (1945), 2–8, 30–3, 76–7, 98–101. Also see Paul Kroeber, *Romantic Narrative Art*, Madison 1960, pp. 133–4, 168–87, 191–2.

[1] Cp. Frederick A. Pottle's comment on Scott's "vivid notes" and introductions: "In fact, to a mature reader the professed fictions often suffer by comparison with the unacknowledged ones." "The Power of Memory in Boswell and Scott," *Essays on the Eighteenth Century Presented to David Nichol Smith*, Oxford 1945, p. 187.

[2] John Ramsay, 30 Nov. 1796, Walpole. Lockhart slightly misquotes Ramsay and omits his praise of the morality: "When could supernatural power be better displayed than in punishing an impious oppressive Lord, & a love-lorn damsel that despised & quarrelled with the supreme disposer of events who giveth and taketh away." Cp. George Chalmers and William Taylor, 6 and 14 Dec., for opposite opinions on softening the original and giving "the English world the moral, without the fright." *Id.* and Lockhart, I. 253, 255.

clattering, ringing, and clanking. Then, remembering that a spectre is abroad, Scott tones things down to a tap, "a rustling stifled noise," tinkling staples, and a whispering voice. Once the "deadly cold" gallant has his betrothed mounted behind him, he dashes off at midnight on a hundred-mile gallop, compelling church-yard corpses and gallows tenants *en route* to be his wedding guests. Scott is chiefly interested in fabulous horseman-ship and in the gruesome.[3] The steed turns out to be an illusion, the await-ing guests "unhallowed ghosts," the bridegroom "a ghastly skeleton," the cheated bride a cadaver, and their chamber a gaping grave. Subtle and symbolic touches are wanting (the dancing ghosts *howl* the funeral song), and the pathos inherent in the contrast between "the bridal guests" expected and those actually confronted is not developed. The criterion is the taut nerve, and the justification, or sop to conscience after an emotional orgy, is the moral that a despairing heart should not protest against Heaven's decrees.[4]

In "The Chase," another moralising poem about a brutal horseman, the Wildgrave destroys crop, herd, and flock, violates the Sabbath, and defies sanctuary. When joined by a white and an infernally swarthy huntsman, the supernatural debaters of medieval art and drama, he harkens only to his "dark-brow'd friend." Then, much in the spirit of "The Ancient Mariner" (published two years later), the "oppressor of creation fair" is condemned:

> Be chased for ever through the wood;
> For ever roam the affrighted wild;
> And let thy fate instruct the proud,
> God's meanest creature is His child.

Hell-hounds and grisly hunters rise from the earth to join the eternal pursuit of the Wildgrave, who flees through caverns by day and athwart the sky at night.[5] And this explains the phenomenon of the wild huntsman

[3] Cp. William Harrison Ainsworth's account of Dick Turpin's ride to York on Black Bess (*Rookwood*, 1834) and James Grant, *The Captain of the Guard* (1862), ch. 50: Sir Patrick Gray's horse, fleeing from Thrave, "rushed on at a frightful pace, as if it was enchanted, or bestrode by an evil spirit, like that of Lenore in the ballad of Burger." In Washington Irving, "The Spectre Bridegroom," "The baron nearly frightened some of the ladies into hysterics with the history of the goblin horseman that carried away the fair Leonora; a dreadful story, which has since been put into excellent verse, and is read and believed by all the world."

[4] For the wide diffusion of the story, see Antti Aarne, "The Types of the Folk-Tale," tr. Stith Thompson, *Folklore Fellows Communications*, xxv. no. 74, Helsinki 1928, p. 61.

[5] Scott writes Joanna Baillie about his often repeating verses from the anonymous poem, *Albania*, "with some sensation of awe. . . . The remarkable superstition . . . consists in hearing the noise of a chace with the baying of the dogs the throttling sobs of the deer the hollo' of a numerous train of huntsmen and the 'hoofs thick beating on the hollow hill.' " *Letters*, II. 525 (4 Aug. 1811). Cp. the classic story of Actaeon, the sinful hunter hunted.

as reported by peasants, but ascribed by more prosaic souls to the flight of geese.

There is more realism in the original ballads than in Scott's paraphrases, which underscore the didacticism in transferring "the general effect" to the page. The translator is too impatient, too ill at ease with German, to render every phrase scrupulously.[6]

Although the young Scottish poet also achieved a version of Goethe's "Erlkönig," the cruder horrors of Bürger were still more within his range. "The Erl King" (1798)[7] has the naïve straightforwardness appropriate to a "goblin story . . . to be read by a candle particularly long in the snuff."[8] But it fails to imitate the orignal in suggestion through tone colour. The sinisterly sweet persuasion of the Black Forest apparition, which is so effectively reproduced by Schubert, becomes a mere jingle in the English rendering.

In *Anne of Geierstein,* Scott speaks of the "many spirit-stirring tales" which have followed the *Götz von Berlichingen* of "an author born to arouse the slumbering fame of his country." Among the tales influenced by Goethe's supercharged drama of a robber-knight with an iron hand are *Marmion, Ivanhoe,* and *Anne of Geierstein.*[9] In Scott's translation of 1799,[10] strong passion, perfidy, and courage build up an impression of demonic energy. The portrayal of male violence tends to supplant penetrating analysis, as it does in *Rob Roy, The Heart of Midlothian, Kenilworth,* and *The Fair Maid of Perth.* It is one of the ironies of literature that Scott generously admired Goethe's early work and was less responsive to his mature achievement.

"Frederick and Alice" is an imitation of Crugantino's song in Goethe's *Claudine von Villa Bella.* When Frederick leaves France and his dishonoured Alice, the lady curses, prays, and dies a week later on the stroke of four. At that very hour, the heartless soldier and his horse experience supernatural terror. Another week passes, and Frederick seeks shelter from

---

[6] C. O. Parsons, "Scott's Translation of Bürger's 'Das Lied von Treue' " ("The Triumph of Constancy"), *Journal of English and Germanic Philology,* XXXIII (1934), 242–3.

[7] Kelso *Mail,* 1 Mar. See William Ruff, "Walter Scott and The Erl-King," *Englische Studien,* LXIX (1934), 106–08.

[8] Advice to [Miss C. Rutherford], Oct. 1797. *Letters,* I. 76.

[9] Carlyle considered *Götz* "the prime cause" of *Marmion,* etc. *The Works of Thomas Carlyle,* London 1898–1901, XXIX. 58. Also see Lockhart, I. 297; William Macintosh, *Scott and Goethe,* Glasgow 1925. Cp. the secret tribunal in *Anne of Geierstein,* 3 vols., Edinburgh 1829, and *Götz* (v. xi); Paul M. Ochojski, *Walter Scott and Germany,* Ph.D. dissertation in TS. (1960), Columbia University, CH. III, "The Road to Berlichingen."

[10] Appearing during "the first volunteering enthusiasm in this country," the translation powerfully impressed many amateur militarists with "its fine warlike tone, and lofty character of sentiment throughout." P.K. in a review, *B.E.M.,* XVI (1824), 385.

a storm in ruins. Led by ghastly lights to an iron door, he is received among deceased friends and relatives at a funereal banquet. Alice, a demon lover in the vestments of the grave, joins the reception of the perjurer, who must now "bid the light farewell!"

Although "Frederick and Alice" is somewhat less lurid than "William and Helen," it heightens the sensationalism and the implied didacticism of Goethe's lines.[11] Its brevity, mistily graphic setting, cumulative horror through a pattern of numbers (four and seven), accelerating exchange of the unearthly for the earthly, reservation of the demon-lover *motif* for the climax, and abridgment of the moral combine to make this "extremely rude" ballad (with Mat Lewis improvements) highly effective in its *genre*. Like "Frederick and Alice," "Wandering Willie's Tale" in *Redgauntlet* makes use of a strayed human's intrusion on a hellish gathering among ruins. While curtailing conventional details and intensifying native raciness, the short story again combines realistic touches with a suggestive vagueness.

Scott is more definitely the adapter than the translator in *The House of Aspen*, a "*rifacimento*" of Veit Weber's (Leonhard Wächter's) *Die heilige Vehme*. Though written shortly after the version of *Götz*, this companion-piece to Mat Lewis's *The Castle Spectre* "and the other drum and trumpet exhibitions of the day" soon struck its author as no better than a "Germanized brat."[12] In the tragedy, Gertrude's dream of the burial of the screaming Baroness of Aspen approximates, rather than accurately prefigures, the catastrophe. It develops that the baroness poisoned her first husband, whose brother is vengeful. While being tried by the secret tribunal, the poisoner stabs herself. Throughout, the casualness with which the dream is taken destroys its ominousness. Another unachieved effect is that of the haunted hemlock marsh, scene of battle slaughter and source of the fatal poison. A trooper's avoidance of the marsh elicits a jest about "nursery bugbears." Suspense is disproportionately built up before an earthly squire's appearance by an apparition tale and the Radcliffian technique of fears and countervailing ridicule. And strangely enough, nothing is made of the potentially terrifying approach of two muffled

[11] Goethe's 42 lines are amplified in the first 81 of Scott's 88-line version. See *Claudine von Villa Bella: Goethes erste Lottedichtung*, ed. Willy Krogmann, Berlin 1937, p. 56.

[12] *Letters*, I. 123 (7 or 8 Dec. 1801). By 17 May 1811, it seems in retrospect "a sort of half-mad German tragedy," owing something perhaps to Schiller's *Der Geisterseher* and Naubert's *Hermann von Unna*. It was published in 1829. Other *Germanized brats*, translated from plays by Iffland, Steinsberg, and Maier, were stillborn in 1796–7. Of these, Jakob Maier, *Fust von Stromberg* contains a message from Fust's dying brother which may have influenced the Lady of Branksome's instructions to Sir William of Deloraine for the recovery of Michael Scott's wizard book from the tomb (*Lay of the Last Minstrel* [=*Lay*], I. xxii). Duncan M. Mennie, "Sir Walter Scott's Unpublished Translations of German Plays," *M.L.R.*, xxxiii (1938), 234–9. Though close, the translations are of poor quality.

members of the secret tribunal to a watchfire to seize their victim. Scott makes two beginnings, a prophetic dream and a mood-creating scene, manages his materials awkwardly, and fails to cap the expected climax. On the credit side, the operation of the secret tribunal is more believable in the play than in the later novel, *Anne of Geierstein*, and the resort to the supernatural is remarkably restrained for the time in which *The House of Aspen* was written. But Scott is still in German bondage.

"The Fire-King," published in *An Apology for Tales of Terror* (1799), is professedly a German-derived ballad on the elemental salamander. As in *Anne of Geierstein*, the fanciful belief in a creature of flame is unconvincingly coupled with eastern fire worship. Forgetting "fair Rosalie" while on a crusade, Count Albert watches by mystic, caverned fire in order to win the Soldan's daughter Zulema. An immeasurably tall, formless Fire-King gives the Count a sword which will be all-conquering as long as he renounces Catholic sway. "Unwittingly" the faithless knight, while fighting Christians, breaks the taboo and slays Rosalie, disguised as a page. The renegade's soul flies to the Fire-King. In an atmosphere of sombre violence, the inaccurately conceived externals of an eastern faith—chiefly of the Zoroastrian god of fire—are exploited for the trumpery appeal of strangeness and terror. To counteract the knight's Christian safeguards, Lebanese priests sing "many dark spells of their witchcraft." This eclectic approach to the supernaturalism of remote periods and places will reappear in such novels as *The Talisman*.

Scott's more creative work is inspired by immediate experience or by Scottish legend and history. Although the subject of one of his first original poems is his beloved Williamina Belsches, the supernatural obtrudes itself. Conjecturally the hill of Caterthun, on which the lines were written 5 May 1796, could have been the scene of Danish blood sacrifice on the altar of Odin:

> Or if we trust the Village tale
> A wayward maid in witching hour
> When stars were red and moon was pale
> Reard thy dread mound by magic power.[13]

For the moment emotion yields to curiosity about ancient ritual and to the evocation of spirit of place by means of local lore. While Williamina is sacrificing him to the will of her mother, the poet juxtaposes romantic feeling and the weird. In the like predicament of *The Bride of Lammermoor*, the novelist fuses love and the supernatural.

---

[13] First published in Grierson, *Scott*, p. 37.

In "The Gray Brother," the first of three fragmentary poems written between 1799 and 1802, Scott combines native materials with a lingering exoticism. While taking from Alexander Peden the episode of divine service being impeded until a devil in the congregation is expelled, he shifts the scene from Ayrshire to Rome and transforms the Cameronian divine into the Pope and the obnoxious witch into Lord Albert, a Scottish pilgrim. But the pilgrim returns to his homeland, where a Gray Friar who has come 5,000 miles to give absolution prepares to hear the wanderer's confession. The fragment ends as the assoiler lays his "ice-cold hand" on Lord Albert's neck. Whether the Gray Brother is a vengeful ghost or a devil is not revealed. The confession was to have been based on a tradition from near Lasswade, where Scott was living: Learning of the guilty commerce between his daughter and an abbot, a father destroys the lovers and their go-between by setting fire to the house of assignation. When Peden is next called on, to help in characterising morbidly superstitious Covenanters in *Old Mortality*, he will be allowed to do his work on his own heath and in the caves of the persecuted saints.

Another fragment, "The Shepherd's Tale," relates a legendary adventure in a cavern of the Eildon Hills. When a fugitive from Clavers' oppression ventures into a "spell formd den ... hewn by Daemons hand,"[14] an aged man, or brownie, who uses a dead man's hand as a candelabrum, promises him a way of revenge devised by Michael Scot. If he makes the right choice between a sword and a horn, he may rouse the knights-dormant and rule over all Scotland. The timorous refugee reaches for the horn and is hurled out of the cave to die on the mountain side.[15] The incorporation of an incident from "persecution's iron days" in a Border legend which usually makes Thomas of Ercildoune the master of ceremonies is none too successful. Although the hand of glory may be more defensible in "The Shepherd's Tale" than in *The Antiquary*, it is outlandish garnishing in either narrative. But the ballad itself is a firm step in the direction of harmonising Scottish history and real character.[16]

Still another fragment, "Cadyow Castle," written in 1802, is set in the *Lay* frame, with the modern minstrel tuning his Border harp at the request

[14] First printed in Lockhart, I. 307-13. For the "Correct Text of 'The Shepherd's Tale,'" see my note in *N. & Q.*, CLXIV (1933), 75-6. This "imperfect ballad," on paper watermarked 1798, was written between 1799 and 1801.

[15] For other accounts of warriors sleeping in a cavern until their deliverance by a brave man, see Patrick Kennedy, *Legendary Fictions of the Irish Celts*, London 1866, pp. 173-4, and *The Denham Tracts*, ed. James Hardy for the Folk-Lore Society, XXIX (1892), 121-8.

[16] Scott intended to use a purer form of the Eildon story in the prose romance, *Thomas the Rhymer*, which he left unfinished. Appendix I of the General Preface of the Waverley Novels. The adventure of Canobie, or Canonbie, Dick is also told in *Demonology*, Letter IV.

of Lady Anne Hamilton. The story harks back to 1569 and Hamilton of Bothwellhaugh's murder of the Regent Murray for the seizure of his house and the eviction of his wife, who went mad and died. Interest is centred on the absence of Bothwellhaugh from his chief's hunting party, the remembered raid, and the arrival of Bothwellhaugh with an account of Murray's death. The ballad has sufficient reality and scope to sustain both the allusion to a "sheeted phantom" wildly gliding with "a shadowy child" in her arms and Bothwellhaugh's report that his Margaret's ghost shrieked triumphantly over the bleeding regent. Neither the supernatural content of "Cadyow Castle" nor the phrasing rises much above the conventional. Its superiority depends on the unadulterated quality of its superstition,[17] which contributes to the main action without dominating it. Scott's characterisation of second-sighted Allan M'Aulay, in *A Legend of Montrose*, emphasises the hereditary influence on a child of its mother's expulsion and insanity.

Scott's intention is more fully evident in a brace of ballads completed in 1799, "Glenfinlas" and "The Eve of St. John." In the latter, the Baron of Smaylholme returns from a mysterious expedition to learn that his lady and her lover have met the last three nights on Beacon Hill. This news astonishes the husband, who remembers slaying Sir Richard under the Eildon Tree three nights ago. On the Eve of St John, the lover appears as a ghost in his lady's bower to announce that he is damned and must wander near the trysting place, because "lawless love is guilt above." As a sign enforcing this moral, the spectral sinner lays his hands on the lady and on an oaken beam, leaving an indelible burn on animate and inanimate matter alike. Thereafter, the adulteress and the murderer do conventual penance. Even while returning to "the scene of the Editor's infancy," Scott is bound to the demon lover, ethical warning, supernaturally intensified punishment for sexual sin, and eclecticism.[18]

As Scott reports to Anna Seward, "All Scotchmen prefer the Eve of St John to Glenfinlas, and most of my English friends entertain precisely an opposite opinion."[19] The Scots favourite has more artistic unity, and the English more energetic variety. Within the framework of a coronach for Lord Ronald, "Glenfinlas" reveals how the Highland chief met his death

[17] In the poet's day, tradition kept alive the woes of Lady Bothwellhaugh, who seems to have haunted both the ruins of Woodhouselee and the new Woodhouselee some four miles distant. See the note on Woodhouselee, "Cadyow Castle" ("She always appears in white, and with her child in her arms") and Scott to [Lady Anne Hamilton], 29 Jul. 1802 in *Letters*, I. 149.

[18] For instance, the tradition of spirits whose touch scorches is Irish. Scott discusses both fiery-handed and icy-handed (Gray Brother) contact in a note to "The Eve of St. John."

[19] 29 Jun. 1802 in *Letters*, I. 147.

while hunting with his Hebridean friend Moy. The action belongs to a time when the red deer were hunted with bows and arrows, and the scene is near the poet's favourite Loch Katrine and Ben Ledi. Sheltered in a hut on a moonlit night, Lord Ronald longs for the presence of Glengyle's daughter Mary. In spite of second-sighted Moy's reporting death-damps on his friend's brow, corpse-lights, and the cry of Ronald's Warning Spirit, the amorous chief descends a dell for a tryst with Mary. Later, Moy refuses to let a green-clad huntress wile him out in search of the lovers. The spirit then expands horribly,[20] a storm rips the hut apart, and fragments of Lord Ronald rain from the sky on his virtuous friend. The youth has been torn to bits by a succubus disguised as a wayward Lady of the Glen.

Scott manages to jumble Highland legend and second sight with Welsh corpse-lights,[21] Rosicrucian "Lady of the Flood" and "Monarch of the Mine," and conventional literary terror. On this he imposes the deadening effect of Ossianic and neo-classical poetic phrasing. Ossian speaks in "fast by Moneira's sullen brook," "since Enrick's fight, since Morna's death," "stern huntsman of the rigid brow," and "the rousers of the deer." The Highland hunter of Scott's prose introduction reappears as a knight, "pretty lasses" as "fairest of our mountain maids," and "Green Women" as "wayward Ladies."[22]

In an article devoted chiefly to E. T. W. Hoffmann,[23] Scott quotes from a letter of Lord Webb Seymour about the death of cruel, fey Captain John Macpherson on the night of 14 February 1799. According to the common people, the bothy of the deer-hunters was wrecked by some supernatural power. With the years, the story took on the outlines of "Glenfinlas," so that James Hogg[24] and others came to assume that Lord Ronald's catastrophe was modelled on the Black Captain's. Unfortunately for romantics and source-hunters, Macpherson was seventy-six at the time

[20] Of great antiquity is the story of a very tall witch (or deer-priestess) who, offended by a hunter's killing deer without seeking permission or paying a tribute of venison, attacks him in his bothy at night. J. G. McKay, "The Deer-Cult and the Deer-Goddess Cult of the Ancient Caledonians," *Folk-Lore*, XLIII (1932), 154–5.

[21] See "On some Popular Superstitions in Wales," *B.E.M.*, III (1818), 193–5.

[22] See Lockhart, I. 303, on the allegation of the poet's "German use of his Scottish materials" and of the superiority of the prose introduction to the elaborated ballad.

[23] "On the Supernatural in Fictitious Composition," *F.Q.R.*, I (Jul. 1827), 60–98. For a letter of Macpherson's daughter, Helen Macburnet, demanding that Scott issue "a public apology" for traducing "the good name of a person who lives not to defend himself," see Abbotsford Mss., 23 Jan. 1828. Also see *F.Q.R.*, II (Feb. 1828,) 352–4, and 1–2 Apr. 1828 in *Journal*, p. 513, for the unsatisfactory retraction of the "raw-head and bloody bones story"; Walpole (correct date probably Apr. 1828) for Anne Grant's defense of Scott's 1827 account.

[24] "On this calamitous event, Walter Scott's beautiful ballad of Glenfinllas [*sic*], is said to have been founded." *The Spy*, ed. James Hogg, Edinburgh 1811, p. 103.

of his death, which was on 2 January 1800. Scott probably contributed to the growth of the Macpherson legend.

Inasmuch as Scott is actually discussing prose fiction in the article, one comment is significant: "the feeling of superstitious awe annexed to the catastrophe . . . could not have been improved by any circumstances of additional horror which a poet could have invented . . . the incidents and the gloomy simplicity of the narrative are much more striking than they could have been rendered by the most glowing description." The reviewer would probably have admitted that in "Glenfinlas," which has just these additional horrors and glowing descriptions, his mature standards of simplicity and reality are violated.

This judiciousness appears as early as 30 July 1801, in a letter to Dr Currie. Their novelty having been exhausted in literature, ghosts are out of fashion. "I think the Marvellous in poetry is ill-timed & disgusting when not managed with moderation & ingrafted upon some circumstance of popular tradition or belief which sometimes can give even to the improbable an air of something like probability."[25] This is, as it were, Scott's declaration of independence from the Monk Lewis school of spectral licence. After the publication of Lewis's *Tales of Wonder* (1801), with contributions by Scott, the two men diverged in their use of the weird. Throughout his career, the "Monk" was an admirer and imitator of German sensationalism. Never conscious that fear is short-lived in its intensity, he numbs his readers with sheer excess. His is not the art of relieving tension.

Scott's emancipation from Lewis and the German variety of horror (never to be taken as absolute) was due to developing taste, to good example, as of Joanna Baillie's plays, and to the collecting of folk ballads for *Minstrelsy of the Scottish Border* (published 1802–3). As editor, reviser, and imitator of ballads, he could learn much about consistency of tone and easy transition from the land of men to that of elves from "The Young Tamlane" and its story of a lover *borrowed* from the Queen of Fairies by fair Janet. In "The Twa Corbies," with simple inevitability the reader enters a realm where crows talk with unearthly knowledge of a slain knight and his "white banes, when they are bare." The corbies' cynical insight is not wanting in the three witches of *The Bride of Lammermoor*. "Clerk Saunders" offers a critical measuring-stick for Scott's own demon-lover ballads. There is pathos in the lover's death and his return for release from troth-plight, for the love which a living man has felt goes with him to his earthy bed. The moral is not hammered in. There is a remarkable

[25] *Letters*, I. 121. The unfinished ballad "of the kind" mentioned by Scott may be "The Shepherd's Tale."

underpinning of the supernatural with realistic detail in "The Wife of Usher's Well." At the crowing of the cock, when three ghosts must leave their mother's house, they sadly part from familiar things, barn and cow-house and "the bonny lass, | That kindles my mother's fire." The con-centrated malignity of witchcraft is released in "Willie's Ladye" when the mother-in-law magically binds the child in the young wife's womb, "But she sall die, and turn to clay, | And you sall wed another may." These native examples of artful supernaturalism could hardly be ignored.

And they were not ignored in the long narrative poems to which Ernest A. Baker refers, "Scott was writing Waverley novels in verse for ten years before he began writing them in prose."[26] The first of these rhymed tales, The Lay of the Last Minstrel (1805), is an accretive work which grew beyond the limits of a literary ballad for Minstrelsy of the Scottish Border. Starting as "a wild rude legend of Border diablerie"[27] about a brownie, it soon encompassed "the customs and manners which anciently prevailed on the Borders of England and Scotland" in the middle of the sixteenth century. For this purpose, Scott used a plot later basic to many a Waverley novel: love difficulties arising from hero and heroine's being in different camps; final happiness against a background of strife.

The supernatural constantly exudes from events. The representative of each rival house has magical powers, the Lady of Branksome Hall through arts learned from her Padua-educated, shadowless father, and Lord Crans-toun through his goblin page. The lady uses charms for cures, longs for a magic book from Michael Scot's tomb in Melrose Abbey, and has secret knowledge of events. No less determined than Lady Ashton in The Bride of Lammermoor to direct her daughter's love, she ignores the prophecy of elemental river and mountain spirits.[28] Yet the prophecy is fulfilled, not because of the probabilities of circumstance and human nature, but because of the happy ending. Like the White Lady of The Monastery, that supernatural hybrid, Gilpin Horner,[29] creates obstacles only to brush them

[26] Baker, The History of the English Novel, London 1924–39, VI. 130. The opening chapters of Waverley were laid aside about the time the Lay was written.

[27] Lockhart, II. 22. In a way, the Lay contains the legendary overflow of the Minstrelsy. Letters, I. 237.

[28] In The Ruminator, 1 Apr. 1807 (London 1813), I. 42–3, Sir Samuel Egerton Brydges objects to the sprites' dialogue as needless and unpoetical, forming "no part of the local superstition of the Lowlands."

[29] The original Gilpin Horner was a farmhouse sprite. So many critics have attacked the page that one defender may be quoted. In a letter to [Scott] of 4 Jun. 1805, Ellis concentrates on moral, rather than folklore, versatility. "It cannot fairly be required that, because the goblin is mischievous, all his tricks should be directed to the production of general evil. The old idea of goblins seems to have been that they were essentially active, & careless about the mischief they produced, rather than providently malicious." Ms. Letters from George Ellis Esq., N.L.S., 73 f.

aside. The goblin—or brownie—page has no soul, can not be slain, is able to transform himself and others, and is malevolent to mortal men. When his narrative task is done, he vanishes amid storm effects.

The *Lay* itself is as much of a supernatural tangle as Gilpin Horner. Allusions to wraiths and fairies, as well as Harold's song of the ominous shroud, the kelpie, the warning illusion of Roslin chapel in flames, and the drowning of Rosabelle, are of the Border, with a Highland overtone or two. A reference to the soldier "who spoke the spectre-hound in Man" (roused again in *Peveril of the Peak*) takes the reader somewhat afield. So does the survey of Norse lore in Harold's native Orkneys, which is like a prospectus of Scandinavian materials in *The Pirate*: "And much of wild and wonderful | In these rude isles might fancy cull." And with Fitztraver's song of Cornelius Agrippa's showing Geraldine to Surrey in a magic mirror (a theme resumed in "My Aunt Margaret's Mirror"), the reader finds himself on the other side of the North Sea.

No character in the *Lay* acts the part of sceptic, as Scott's Waverley heroes do. The chasm between past and present is shakily bridged by the seventeenth-century narrator, who cautions his aristocratic audience, "I cannot tell how the truth may be; | I say the tale as 'twas said to me." In later work, Scott seldom equals the vagueness of the old minstrel's reservations, which leave the house of magic as firm as it was built.

In his first long poem, Scott falters in lessons partially mastered in shorter pieces. He casually and unconvincingly relates strange beings to the basic action, thereby falling short of the unity of superstition and *locale* which is sketchily achieved in "Cadyow Castle." The translation of a Border brownie into a grotesque all-purpose agent shows the kind of taste which lapsed in "Glenfinlas."[30] The assembling of native—and imported—superstitions in a poem of scope was generally valuable practice. The narrative problems encountered in the *Lay* were later solved, although the solutions were not consistently borne in mind.

In *Marmion* (1808), Scott partially unfolds the mystery of his own reaction to the supernatural. He imagines that, after sitting on a necromancer's grave, he muses over a "mystic lay" until he comes under its wild sway, hears unearthly voices "in the bittern's distant shriek," and recreates the unhallowed wizard-priest "Till from the task my brow I clear'd | And smiled to think that I had fear'd." The time, the place, the

---

[30] For lingering echoes of Lewis, *The Monk*, see Paul Staake, *A Critical Introduction to Sir Walter Scott's Lay of the Last Minstrel*, Meerane 1888, pp. 21–3.

mood, and the poet's thoughts effect a very willing suspension of disbelief, which is pleasurably indulged before being revoked.

In addition to pleasure, the romancer is justified by culture history in going back to tales "of witches' spells, of warriors' arms," of men jostling "conjuror and ghost, | Goblin and witch!" Beginning with the wraiths, ghosts, and portents of the classics, the universality of such beliefs sanctions their narrative use:

> All nations have their omens drear,
> Their legends wild of woe and fear. . . .
>
> Such general superstition may
> Excuse for old Pitscottie say.

Robert Lindsay of Pitscottie, Gervase of Tilbury, and John Fordun supply Scott with supernatural incidents which he follows more closely than he does the sources of his later works. There are tales of Alexander III's consulting a wizard about the future of his kingdom and unhorsing an elfin knight; of James IV's being warned by "a ghostly wight" not to war against the English; and of a spectral summoner's naming those who must appear before an infernal tribunal (all these men fell with James IV at Flodden in 1513).

Two kinds of doubters react to these marvels, the rational and the self-willed. De Wilton appeals to Heaven against the summoner and later suggests that the spectacle was a peace-maker's "juggle." Marmion, on the other hand, having no fixed principles, professes a "sceptic creed" and holds that natural law never is contravened by "superhuman cause." Said to be almost as sceptical about religion as about superstition, he is ashamed to believe; yet he wearies of doubt and becomes paradoxically open to credulity. He takes his vanquisher in single combat—actually De Wilton—to be a "mortal enemy" dead long ago.

The attitude toward constructive and destructive modes of doubt in *Marmion* will be familiar to readers of the Waverley Novels, as will the characterisation of Marmion, the treatment of the supernatural, and the eclectic use of source-material. A man of strong and contending passions like Robertson in *The Heart of Midlothian*, Lord Marmion is not his own man or God's, but the Devil's. The supernatural is brought in, time is allowed to intervene, then an explanation is offered. At one point the emotions are stirred; at another the mind is satisfied. And the urge to combine various lores, as well as such consciously literary garniture as Lord Gifford's magical accoutrements, "a quaint and fearful sight," does not prevent Scott from integrating the weird episodes in his plot and achieving unity of tone.[31]

The characters in *The Lady of the Lake* (1810) breathe the rarefied air of fairy-land: "So wondrous wild, the whole might seem | The scenery of a fairy dream." The heroine is "a fay in fairy land," ladies call themselves "weird women" who sing "charmed rhymes" and cast spells on wandering knights, the Knight of Snowdoun hears "fairy strains of music," a boat is a "fairy frigate," and a sword is fairy-forged. The minstrel's ballad of "Alice Brand" is about a human captive in Elfland. The fairy allusions are responsive to the spirit of the action. When Coir-nan-Uriskin (Goblin Hollow) becomes part of the setting, the supernatural mood begins to darken, for the fays and satyrs that visit it by moonlight will "blast the rash beholder's gaze." The entire narrative is encased within "Harp of the North" lyrics in which an enchantress wakes and stills the strain.

Except for an intrusive "River Demon" and a "fatal Ben-Shie," when superstitions are introduced, as George Brandes points out, it is "because they belong to the period and the people, not because they are mysterious."[32] The frightening dream of the Knight of Snowdoun, the "prophecy of fear" and of hope of gray-haired, second-sighted Allan-bane and the *taghairm*, or divination, of Brian the Hermit—all come true. Of these piercings of the future, Brian's is the most impressive and unusual. Wrapped in the still warm hide of a milk-white bull, the seer lies on a cliff ledge beside a thunderous cataract awaiting his revelation:[33]

> Which spills the foremost foeman's life,
> That party conquers in the strife.

No word of obtrusive reason breaks the descriptive spell except bluff Malise's permissible boast that Clan Alpine's omen and assistance are the sword and not augury. If he wishes, the reader may refer the two-edged prediction to the seer's knowledge of the clan and to the half-mad state induced by Brian's strained vigil, his morbidly secluded life, and belief in "his mysterious lineage." It is said of Brian the Hermit, as it might be of Burley in *Old Mortality* or of the Hermit of Engaddi in *The Talisman*,

[31] The contrast between the *Lay* and *Marmion* in this and other respects is great, as Lewis rather one-sidedly indicates in a letter of 2 Oct. 1807: "I am afraid though, that however great may be its merits, I shall still prefer 'The Last Minstrel,' for Erskine tells me, that there is nothing of the wonderful employed in it, and Ghosts, Fairies, and Sorcerers (as you well know) are with me a *sine qua non*." Walpole.

[32] Brandes, *Main Currents in Nineteenth Century Literature*, New York 1923, IV. 114.

[33] *Taigheirm* is defined in Spence's *Encyclopaedia of Occultism* as "a magical sacrifice of cats to the infernal spirits, formerly practised in the Highlands and Islands of Scotland." Sleeping on or in the hides of newly-sacrificed animals was the ritual at several Greek and Roman oracles preliminary to prophetic dreams. The latter is certainly the more poetic ceremony.

"The desert gave him visions wild." He traces his paternity like Merlin[34] to a "Phantom Sire." "Bred between the living and the dead" like Allan M'Aulay in *A Legend of Montrose*, he is "gifted beyond nature's law."

In defence of Brian's marvellous genealogy, Scott refers to the studious and godly Black Child, Son to the Bones, whose mother while warming herself at a fire of dead men's bones was impregnated by the ashes.[35] The poet generalises in the same note:

> He may differ from modern critics, in supposing that the records of human superstition, if peculiar to, and characteristic of, the country in which the scene is laid, are a legitimate subject of poetry. He gives, however, a ready assent to the narrower proposition which condemns all attempts of an irregular and disordered fancy to excite terror, by accumulating a train of fantastic and incoherent horrors, whether borrowed from all countries, and patched upon a narrative belonging to one which knew them not, or derived from the author's own imagination.

In both *The Lady of the Lake* and *Marmion*, Scott does—despite temptations to stray—effect an artistic union among superstitious observances, locales, and period. When he is most sure of his craft, the poet is his own best guide.

In writing *The Vision of Don Roderick* (1811), the *Ivanhoe* of his poetic romances, Scott follows the advice of the Mountain Spirit in the Introduction:

> Decay'd our old traditionary lore, ...
>
> No! search romantic lands. ...
> ... themes for minstrelsy more high than thine.

Suspecting that he has exhausted his readers' interest in Scottish subjects, of which little remains except the vulgar "belief in the existence and nocturnal revels of the fairies" (Scott's note), the modern minstrel hopefully looks to Spain. His supernatural exotic is a tradition of King Roderick's defiance of a prophecy that only the last ruler of his line will seek to know the future in an enchanted vault near Toledo. Fatally daring, Roderick sees a representation of his own defeat by the Moors in 714. Emboldened by his evocation of the entombed Michael Scot in the *Lay*, and by the example of Calderon's *La Virgin del Sagrario* and Rowley's *All's Lost by Lust*, the poet plunges into the eighth century and emerges with wondrous creatures of

---

[34] Cp. "the fiend-born Merlin" in the pageant of *Kenilworth*, ch. xxxvii.

[35] Scott's acknowledged source is Walter Macfarlane, *Geographical Collections relating to Scotland*, a manuscript in the Advocates' Library since edited by Sir Arthur Mitchell for the Scottish History Society, VOLS. LI–LIII, Edinburgh 1906–8. See LII. 162.

the deep which are unsuited to our atmospheric pressure.[36] In his search for novelty, Scott wanders too far from familiar terrain.

Unfortunately, in his next long poem, *Rokeby* (1813), Scott's psychological realism turns into melodrama.[37] Motivation is rather carefully worked out, but the springs of feeling, more closely approached, prove to be geysers. The author remarks that tales of native terror beside a Christmas fire, the "universal sway" of "this vain ague of the mind," can be delightful. But "fierce Bertram" Risingham, early "train'd in the mystic and the wild," learns on distant seas of the phantom ship, the sale of Lapland winds, ghastly meteorology, and bloody pirates' fear of haunted keys. No wonder that, haunted by the frightfulness of his own crimes, he looks like "a murderer's ghost," is a ghost-seer in his own right, and half insanely infers that Mortham has buried his Indian treasure in a tomb to be watched by ghosts. Demonology supplements the characterisation. Fiends stir in the ruffian when his anger breaks forth; he calls on Hell and is heard; in short, he is like one sold to the Devil.

When with his diabolical followers, Bertram seems like Milton's "Master-Fiend." One of the subordinate imps, Guy Denzil, believes neither in "the visionary tales of eld" nor in religion. As complete a sceptic as Henbane Dwining in *The Fair Maid of Perth*, he is "vow'd to every evil, | [and] Might read a lesson to the devil." The mind of Bertram's quondam friend, Mortham, caught in "Superstition's nets," is "by anguish forced astray," but Matilda, like Annot Lyle in *A Legend of Montrose*, can "charm his evil fiend away." Even the hero, Redmond, has been "nurtured while a child | In many a bard's traditions wild."[38]

Counterpoises to this general credulity may be found in the poet's qualifications: the time of his story is "that simple day," and remorse is really more to be feared than haunting ("What spectre can the charnel send, | So dreadful as an injured friend?"). Denzil's cynicism and Wilfrid's startled scorn of Bertram's wild creed also help the reader to keep his balance. However, Wilfrid, who is as moodily introspective as Scott's friend, R. P. Gillies, is not an entirely convincing doubter.

Rokeby may be thought of as an unintentional testing ground for narrative

[36] Although Scott's "last Gothic King of Spain" may have influenced Landor, Southey, and Washington Irving, these authors of drama, poem, and sketch stress the Spanish King Arthur's violation of Florinda, treasonable revenge, and the mystery of his death.

[37] For Scott and melodrama, see Henry A. White, *Sir Walter Scott's Novels on the Stage*, New Haven 1927, pp. 210–26, and Allardyce Nicoll, *A History of Early Nineteenth Century Drama*, Cambridge 1930, I. 91–6, 100.

[38] The harper's catalogue of his musical repertory (v. ix) includes:

> Fairy tale to lull the heir,
> Goblin grim the maids to scare.

methods soon to be used in the novels. As in *The Heart of Midlothian*, there are haunted scenes: places which retain the names of Norse deities, although they are lovely enough for fairies' feet, and a brook visited by a murdered Borderer. But these scenes create general atmosphere and are not carefully linked to the action. The Buccaneer terrors and the sale of winds tried once and found acceptable will be used more fully and appropriately in *The Pirate*. The early conditioning which creates human susceptibility is clearly shown. Lucy Ashton will soon bend before a gale of eerie legends in *The Bride of Lammermoor*. A mind which remorse and horror have unhinged sees a real presence as spectral. General Harrison will make the same mistake in *Woodstock*. Although the historical background of the poem is the Civil War, not much is made of the interplay of public and private events. The state of belief in 1644 is sketched with the simple purpose of contrasting individuals. Ghosts and devils make no contribution to the study of party, class, or religious differences, but they will later in *Old Mortality*.

Altogether, the analysis of human evil, often in demonological terms, is attempted too often, and the differentiation, in spite of Bertram's brutality, Denzil's heartless doubt, and Mortham's domestic tragedy, is not sufficiently clear-cut. A band of human fiends is introduced, but the Iago mentality is subordinated in interest to the savagely forceful one. When similar bands appear in *Kenilworth* and *The Fair Maid of Perth*, there will be more contrast among the members and more complexity in the master mind.

Scott makes *The Bridal of Triermain* (1813) an Arthurian tale to "charm romantic ear." Long ago, Gyneth, daughter of King Arthur and the fay Guendolen, was trained to avenge her deserted mother on mankind. When she allowed a tourney for her hand to turn into slaughter, she was doomed by Merlin to remain inanimate until freed by a knight. At the time that Sir Roland de Vaux of Triermain wakes and weds his sleeping beauty, she is 501 years old. The narrative is flexible enough to include references to Druids, goblins, genii, demons, mountain spirits, and nymphs. Scott's romance is partly reminiscent of *Sir Gawain and the Green Knight*, Boiardo, Spenser, and fairy tales, and partly anticipatory of *Locksley Hall, Maud*, and *Great Expectations*.[39] As a novelist Scott seldom has his feet so completely off the ground, except in Agelastes' somewhat similar tale of the enchanted Princess of Zulichium in *Count Robert of Paris* and the quest for

[39] The attempt to hoax the public into believing that William Erskine wrote the *Bridal* probably accounts for the pre-Tennysonian note. (Both *Locksley Hall* and *Maud* may have been influenced in plot and mood by *The Bride of Lammermoor*, a favourite of Tennyson.)

Thomas the Rhymer's manuscripts in *Castle Dangerous*. As creative energy wanes in verse or prose, Scott gains artificial assurance through wizardry.

Two verse narratives, *The Lord of the Isles* (1815) and *Harold the Dauntless* (1817), appear too late to be considered apprentice pieces of the Author of Waverley, but they do come before such novels as *Castle Dangerous* and *The Pirate*. The dramatic vigour of the Bruce's career is muted in *The Lord of the Isles*, as is that of the Douglas in *Castle Dangerous*. In both stories, the heroine dresses as a boy and provides confused and conventional love-interest which stultifies the Zeitgeist. The strange beacon light which draws Bruce to the mainland is explained by "superstitious credence." But, whether tricky, magical, celestial, infernal, or meteoric, "I know not —and it ne'er was known." This broaching of possibilities, without a definite resolution, is in the manner of the fifteenth-century Scottish minstrel, Blind Harry. The antiquarian note quoting Joseph Train on the supposedly weird origin of Bruce's Bogles' Brae fire is typically Scott's, as is the partial nurture of young Allan on supernatural tales.

Harold the Dauntless opens with a confession that reading in the supernatural cures *ennui*. If so, the tale itself contains enough antidotal demonology, magic, and witchcraft to banish the *ennui* of a normal lifespan. To begin with, Danish Count Witikind, his son Harold, and Jutta the Sorceress worship devils, each one "a God of heathen days." Harold is variously shown as believing in, serving, or opposing devils. He has the look, the laugh, and the speech of "the arch-fiend incarnate in flesh and in bone," and when he is possessed by demons, fond Eivir, disguised as Gunnar the page, has musical skill to charm them away. He is also aided by a Christian palmer, a "phantom gray" monitor before whom yelling imps disperse. And in a final "wild scene of fiendish strife," Harold vanquishes Odin before turning Christian.[40] A fiend's earlier declaration that Harold's powers, strength, and dauntlessness are of hell defines abundant and ungoverned berserk vitality as demonic. With different emphasis the concept is basic to the characterisation of Cleveland the pirate, Robertson the seducer of Effie Deans, and other Waverley villain-heroes.

Jutta, a witch of the true *Malleus Maleficarum* breed, is also to be reckoned with. Though menaced by "penal fires," this supernatural anachronism engages in the "mean mischief" (Harold's phrase) of travelling with preternatural speed, commanding storms to destroy grain, slaying cattle with

---

[40] This ethical characterisation, in which Christianity represents the imposition of controls on boundless energy, is supplemented by the ballad legend of the Castle of the Seven Shields in which the wishes of the seven daughters of a Druid are carried out by "the Outcast of heaven."

spells, cursing with her eyes, and hag-riding sleepers. Norna of *The Pirate* is in part foreshadowed by Jutta, who summons "mighty Zernebock" as the later sibyl does Trolld, and—"one woman . . . alone"—is "the last, the feeblest of thy flock." Like Ailsie Gourlay in *The Bride of Lammermoor,* she dies unrepentant.

The apposite and the inapposite are joined in *Harold.* The storm spirit, the mermaid, the ghost-seer, the ghoul, goblin, and night-hag (nightmare), a mortal mistaken for a phantom warrior, ominous birds, Druid-Norse-Christian mythology—all find their place. In this romance of the Scandinavian past, as in *The Pirate,* the antiquary-poet heaps up detail. But the very profusion conceals poverty, as it does in Landor's *Gebir* and Southey's *Madoc.* So much of the Norse world as can be captured externally is there —and little more. The sagas have greater simplicity and truth.[41]

*   *   *

With experience, Scott became convinced of the superiority of native to factitious and imported lore. Agreeing with his correspondent, Dr Currie, that tales of wonder flag in interest because "the wonders put each other out of countenance,"[42] he relegated German *diablerie* and Gothic terrors more and more to the background until he could speak with objectivity of "the faults attachd to that slovenly composition, the German ballad."[43] How different, one wonders, would his art have been if he had turned for his first inspiration to the demon-lover theme in popular ballads and in William Julius Mickle's "The Sorceress; or, Wolfwold and Ulla"[44] rather than in Bürger's "Lenore." The gloomy aegis of the startling, rather than the great, works of German literature[45] was virtually inimical to his genius, except as an initial stimulus. Whenever he returned to that influence in episodes of *The Antiquary, The Monastery,* and other fiction of his mature years, grotesqueness is inevitable. Just as Scott's literary career began none too auspiciously with foreign models, so it ended—in an artistic second childhood. As the sources of creativity ran dry, he searched his memory for German founts to use in *The Surgeon's Daughter* and *Anne of Geierstein,* and later read "stupid German novels in

[41] For the poet's background materials in the verse romances, see Rose Marie Grady, *The Sources of Scott's Eight Long Poems,* a thesis abstract, Urbana 1934; Georg Hofmann, *Entstehungsgeschichte von Sir Walter Scott's "Marmion",* Königsberg 1913, pp. 51–5.

[42] *Letters,* I. 118, n. 1 (1801).

[43] 4 Aug. 1811 in *Letters,* II. 526.

[44] Mickle, *Poems, and a Tragedy,* London 1794, pp. 141–55. Mickle's "Cumnor Hall," not included in this posthumous collection, did influence *Kenilworth.*

[45] In his "Essay on the Drama" (1814), Scott regrets that the best German writings have not been made known to the English. Kotzebue is more accessible in translation than Goethe, Schiller, or Lessing. *The Miscellaneous Prose Works of Sir Walter Scott,* Boston 1829, VI. 287.

hopes a thought will strike me when I am half occupied with other things."[46]

The poet-novelist's exposition of critical principles may mislead the reader into expecting a continuous realisation of theory in creative practice.[47] It would be logically gratifying to trace in Scott a consistent advance from exotic imitation to mastery of native traditions, scenes, and superstitions. There is instead a zigzag improvement with occasional relapses into borrowed and whole-cloth wonders. Creative in cycles like Thomas Hardy, Scott apparently forgets the lessons learned in previous works when an inferior poem or novel is on the anvil. This unevenness of achievement in the verse romances blinded some contemporaries to the merits of "the Old Ballad style of poetry," so that they exclaimed with the anonymous author of *The Caledonian Comet*:

> Oh! hear the drooping Muse's call,
> Release her from this Gothic thrall,
> Disperse the cobwebs, rubbish, dust,
> The magic spells, and ancient rust.[48]

Though wholesome, the protest ignores the vivifying sense of the past which at times transforms the pageant and its trappings into reality. It also ignores the tentative achievements of Scott's apprentice years and the growth in understanding of the problems involved. The unchecked profusion of supernatural creeds and creatures yields in his best work to greater restraint, coherence, and appropriateness. Haunted places create an atmosphere which is congenial to the action. Witchcraft and demonology help to characterise rebels as well as the romantic protest against social, traditional, and religious restraints. But when Scott fails to make popular beliefs reinforce character and action, he can lose himself in Arthurian, Norse, and Gothic realms. Much yet remains to be done before verse trials become prose accomplishments.

[46] *Journal*, p. 718 (27 Feb. 1831). See also F. W. Stokoe, *German Influence in the English Romantic Period 1788–1818*, Cambridge 1926, pp. 63–4, 87; *Sir Walter Scott To-day*, ed. Grierson, London 1932, pp. xi–xii.

[47] Thus Mody C. Boatright is tempted into unconvincing schematisation in his excellently documented article, "Scott's Theory and Practice concerning the Use of the Supernatural in Prose Fiction in relation to the Chronology of the Waverley Novels," *P.M.L.A.*, L (1935), 235–61.

[48] [John Taylor], *The Caledonian Comet*, London 1810, p. 17. Cp. Walter Freye, *The Influence of "Gothic" Literature on Sir Walter Scott*, Rostock 1902, pp. 1–53, in which parallels are persistently misrepresented as sources.

Chapter IV

THE WAVERLEY NOVELS

1. Influences and Critical Theory

BEHIND the crowded pageant of the Waverley Novels extends the long and at times indistinct perspective of the author's experience, his contact with men of varied knowledge, his reading, his retentive and transforming memory, and his constantly active imagination. One of the novelist's most characteristic literary habits is the eclectic use of materials, which undergo so thorough a reworking that they seem, when pointed out, no more than hints or suggestions. Source-hunting often oversimplifies Scott's curious interweaving of details from traditionary lore, desultory antiquarian reading, and personal observation. Differences between the source and the fictional incident may be the result of creativity, of caprice, or of deliberate avoidance of apparent plagiarism. On reading Horace Smith's *Brambletye House*, Scott observes that whole pages have been lifted from Defoe's *A Journal of the Plague Year*: "When *I convey* an incident or so, I am [at] as much pains to avoid detection as if the offence could be indicted in literal fact at the Old Bailey."[1] The chances of Sir Walter's being indicted for literal borrowing are rather small, for most of his conveying is from a bounteous, though none too accurate, memory of "old and odd books, and a considerable collection of family legends."

The concentration of this study on the novelist's use, rather than on the provenience, of supernatural materials permits a brief consideration of the sources of his inspiration. The detailing of borrowings and adaptations is for the most part outside its scope. The Waverley Novels contain unearthly episodes with the realistic grip of ballads like "The Wife of Usher's Well" or the violent horror of chapbooks. *The Talisman* has the quality of such medieval romances as *Guy of Warwick* and *Richard Cœur de Lion*. Scott's villains and witches owe much to Shakespeare. The self-assurance of many a ghost in popular drama is not lacking in the Waverley breed.

---

[1] *Journal*, p. 249 (18 Oct. 1826).

Spenser hovers over passages in which glens and woods call for rather harmless spirits to people them, and over the Archimago-like treachery of Agelastes in *Count Robert of Paris*. The Biblical and Miltonic imminence of mysterious power, brief and indistinct, is sometimes achieved by Scott.[2] And above all, he is sustained by the example of his own national literature from Barbour to Burns.

Extensive reading in the solemnly sensational classics of witch and devil literature and in anecdotal histories of many nations afforded Scott an abundance of non-Scottish lore which he more frequently mastered in its outlines than in its essence. Scandinavian sagas are stocked with sooth-saying runes, stone, treasure, and tomb legends, magic and the elements, and pre-Christian Norse gods, references to which are heavily concentrated in *The Pirate*.[3] Although Scott is usually too rational, even heavy-handed, to rise to the high fantasy of Celtic wonder, he approximates it occasionally. In a grosser sphere, the appearance in a Waverley novel of conspiratorial protagonists with an outlaw complex, of the secret tribunal, of heroines resembling elemental spirits, of Rosicrucian mysteries, of Harz demons and spectral huntsmen, quite properly suggests the influence of the early, romantic Goethe and of second-rate German literature.

Gothic romance is often mentioned as yielding ore to Scott, who was partly bred on such fare. Ranging from pleasurable melancholy to grotesque sensationalism, the Gothic novel exploits the mystery and terror of strange settings, deeds, and times. Its primary end is to startle the reader rather than to illuminate the past. Whenever Scott intends the supernatural to be interesting in itself rather than to create atmosphere or to advance the plot, and whenever he traces the horrors to mechanical devices, trickery, or secret passages, the influence of the Gothic novel may be suspected.

Although Scott never completely freed himself from the impression made by specious Gothic historical fiction, he was critical of its practitioners. And it is in his lives of those pioneers of weird romance, Horace Walpole and Ann Radcliffe, that his own use of the supernatural, whether in prose fiction or narrative poetry, finds its critical rationale. Even as late as 1820, when Scott set about writing the lives of the novelists, the

---

[2] Cp. Woodstock, ch. xv: "So much is the influence of imaginary or superstitious terror dependent (so far as respects strong judgments at least) upon what is vague or ambiguous."

[3] "Is it too much to suggest that the novelist may have been helped to find himself by the saga-writer?" Both the Waverley Novels and the sagas combine "the heroic with comedy and plain downright realism." Edith C. Batho, "Sir Walter Scott and the Sagas," *M.L.R.*, XXIV (1929), 411. Also see P. R. Lieder, "Scott and Scandinavian Literature," *Smith College Studies in Modern Languages*, II. 1 (1920), 8–57.

incognito of the Great Unknown still permitted him to formulate theories of the craft without being judged by his own standards. After the frayed mask of anonymity had been dropped, the comparison of the novelist's expressed theory with his actual practice was not made by his contemporaries; yet it is one which may be entered into profitably.

Although it later appeared in Ballantyne's Novelists' Library, the life of Walpole was first published some three years before *Waverley*.[4] It is important as containing views on which practical difficulties have little effect. In his analysis of *The Castle of Otranto*, Scott states that Walpole intended more than the evocation of surprise and horror. His object was the depiction of domestic life and manners in feudal times, together with the supernaturalism to which devout credence was then given. And he successfully reconciled natural and marvellous happenings. "Romantic narrative," Scott proceeds to explain, "is of two kinds,—that which, being in itself possible, may be matter of belief at any period; and that which, though held impossible by more enlightened ages, was yet consonant with the faith of earlier times."[5] *Otranto* belongs to the latter class, but Walpole is at fault in making his marvels recur too frequently. The supernatural is allowed to appear *en plein jour*, being presented so accurately and distinctly as to dispel that mysterious obscurity which alone agrees with our conception of disembodied spirits.

On the score of simplicity and impressiveness, Walpole's unexplained wonders (such as gained credence in Gothic times) are preferable to the marvels of Mrs Radcliffe, who compromises between the two kinds of romantic narrative by proposing natural causes. There are several objections to Mrs Radcliffe's method: (1) it performs a needless task in an avowed work of fiction by relieving the reader's spirits of supernatural terror; (2) not only does it cheat the indignant reader into sympathy with horrors which are later explained away, but it also destroys the eager interest of a second reading; and (3) its realistic solutions are frequently as improbable as the prodigious events themselves.[6] When called upon to do

[4] *The Castle of Otranto: a Gothic Story*, Edinburgh 1811. The copy in the N.L.S. has an autograph note: "The introduction to this book was written by W Scott and the frontispiece was drawn by Daniel Terry of Covent Garden Theatre

W. Scott
29th December 1813"

[5] Scott, *Lives of Eminent Novelists and Dramatists* [=*Lives*], new edn, London and New York 1887, p. 541.

[6] Cp. *Letters*, v. 398 (15 Jun. 1819), in which Abel Moysey is commended for not referring the supernatural to natural causes in his anonymous novel, *Forman*: "Witchcraft . . . is a species of machinery of which the author of a work of fiction is entitled by all the rules of composition to avail himself. But these lame explanations are more improbable than the existence of the black art itself and always disgust the reader."

so, a reader will admit the belief in unearthly agency, but once his author has agreed to account for all occurrences, he has a right to expect a natural, ingenious, and complete explanation. Still, it must be remembered that our ancestors were more responsive to the eerie than we are. "A transient, though vivid impression, is all that can be excited by a tale of wonder, even in the most fanciful mind of the present day."[7]

After writing his short life of Horace Walpole, Scott saw reason to modify his rather dogmatic statements. Guided by his own taste as a reader, he had awarded the narrative palm to Walpole for introducing into *The Castle of Otranto* the superstitions that would have been acceptable to the characters in their day and for refusing to stultify the cumulative effect by natural explanations. But in his comments on *The Mysteries of Udolpho* in the life of Mrs Radcliffe, he wavers between his own point of view and that of the novel-reading public, whose reactions he had come to know. The critical result is more practical, though less logical and conclusive.

Mrs Radcliffe awakens fear by means of obscurity and suspense,[8] but her devices for creating expectancy are somewhat too obvious and her ultimate solutions are often paltry and inadequate. Then Scott generalises: "Ghosts and witches, and the whole tenets of superstition, having once, and at no late period, been matter of universal belief, warranted by legal authority, it would seem no great stretch upon the reader's credulity to require him, while reading of what his ancestors did, to credit for the time what those ancestors devoutly believed in."[9] The phrase "it would seem" is significant. That some readers of the Waverley Novels had failed to accept instances of ancestral belief is evident from Scott's earlier and anonymous explanation of their frequent introduction:

> The traditions and manners of the Scotch were so blended with super-stitious practices and fears, that the author of these novels seems to have deemed it incumbent on him, to transfer many more such incidents to his novels, than seem either probable or natural to an English reader. It may be some apology that his story would have lost the national cast, which it was chiefly his object to preserve, had this been otherwise. There are few

[7] *Lives*, p. 542. Coleridge expresses a contrary opinion in his criticism of *Udolpho* for *The Monthly Review*, Nov. 1794: "The reader experiences in perfection the strange luxury of artificial terror without being obliged for a moment to hoodwink his reason, or to yield to the weakness of superstitious credulity." Quoted by Montague Summers in *The Gothic Quest: a History of the Gothic Novel*, London 1938, p. 136.

[8] Elsewhere, Scott distinguishes between Mrs Radcliffe's sensational and his own psycho-logical use of the marvellous: "My object is not to excite fear of supernatural things in my reader, but to show the effect of such fear upon the agents in the story [*Woodstock*]." *Journal* pp. 87–8 (3 Feb. 1826).

[9] *Lives*, p. 568.

F

families of antiquity in Scotland, which do not possess some strange legends, told only under promise of secrecy, and with an air of mystery; in developing which, the influence of the powers of darkness is referred to.[10]

This then is the novelist's difficulty: readers expect amazing events, yet some of them balk at uncanny instrumentality, the hags, devils, and apparitions once dear to our forebears; they also object to wonders being devitalised by the tardy discovery of a prosaic origin. Some writers try to avoid the dilemma by remaining in the no man's land between ancient faith and modern incredulity. Phantoms are brought forward and prophecies are fulfilled without any commitment on the author's part as to their supernatural, imaginary, or coincidental source. "This is, however, an evasion of the difficulty, not a solution; and besides, it would be leading us too far from the present subject, to consider to what point the author of a fictitious narrative is bound by his charter to gratify the curiosity of the public, and whether, as a painter of actual life, he is not entitled to leave something in shade, when the natural course of events conceals so many incidents in total darkness. Perhaps, upon the whole, this is the most artful mode of terminating such a tale of wonder, as it forms the means of compounding with the taste of two different classes of readers"[11]—those who desire a complete unravelling and those who resent such sceptical pedantry.

The hesitancy is characteristic both of Scott's criticism and of his use of the weird in fiction. Walpole's method is an excellent one and should be acceptable to readers; so too is Mrs Radcliffe's, when ingeniously employed. As for the expedient of leaving the manner of solution to the individual reader, that has much to recommend it and perhaps suits contemporary attitudes best.

John Buchan suggests that "what was needed was a writer who could unite both strains, for in the mediaeval world the two had been inseparable, the mystery and the fact, credulity and incredulity, the love of the marvellous and the descent into jovial common sense."[12] But it is a mistake to suppose that the nineteenth-century mind could approximate the medieval tolerance of violent contrasts and mutual contradictions. More complex than the blending of the faith and unfaith of some bygone age,

[10] Q.R., XVI (1817), 435. Although this criticism of Old Mortality and The Black Dwarf is ostensibly by William Erskine, the manuscript is in Scott's handwriting. It is not known how much the novelist's friend actually contributed.

[11] Lives, p. 568. The outlines of Scott's discussion of the supernatural in fiction, with exclusive reference to Charles Maturin and Mrs Radcliffe, appear in his criticism of Dennis Jasper Murphy's (Maturin's) Fatal Revenge, London 1807, in Q.R., III (1810), 344-7. The subject is taken up again in Scott's review of E.T.W. Hoffmann in F.Q.R., I (1827), 60-98.

[12] Buchan, Sir Walter Scott, London 1932, p. 129.

the task is primarily one of reconciliation between the credulity of the past and the comparative scepticism of the present—the artistic adjustment of one period to the comprehension of another. To achieve this Walpole's method is inadequate because it offers no adjustment at all. Seeing an age through its manners, customs, and superstitions may be a literary *tour de force*, but it can be naïve and even boring when the eyes are apparently those of a contemporary of the action.[13] Mrs Radcliffe's procedure is even worse, being a mere congeries of tricks; and the third system is one of shifty noncommitment. Actually, however, by leaving the problem of a narrative desideratum unsolved, Scott achieves greater variety, as well as more unevenness, than Horace Walpole or Mrs Radcliffe.

That variety may best be surveyed in a topical arrangement of Waverley lore. As far as possible, the sequence in which the topics are discussed will be that of Scott's arriving at his fullest or most significant use of each superstition (*i.e.*, the warning spirit in *Waverley*, the sibyl and astrology in *Guy Mannering*, German *diablerie* in *The Antiquary*, and so on).

2. THE WARNING SPIRIT

The warning spirit hovers in time half-way between ghosts and sibyls. Ghosts are reminders of the past, its violence and unappeased desires. Devils, witches, magicians, poltergeists, elemental spirits, and fairies, belonging more to the belief of the past than of the present, are also reminiscential. Soothsayers, astrologers, second-sighted persons, and sibyls utter predictions which make men turn their eyes to the future. When he is a dead seer whose remembered words indicate the shape of things to come, the prophet may bind past, present, and future. But this service to the imagination should be better performed by the warning spirit, which has an emotional connexion—whether yearning or vindictive—with the mortal whose fate it knows. Unfortunately, that spirit can be like history, apter to confuse than to forewarn.

Futile and inconclusive as it was, Scott had some experience of warning spirits. In his anecdotal vein, R. P. Gillies tells of Scott's encounter with a figure in dusky brown drapery during his residence at Ashestiel (1804–12). Returning home one evening shortly after sunset, the poet be-

[13] As an example, Allan Cunningham, *Sir Michael Scott*, London 1828, is an attempt "to gather from history, tale, and tradition, the torn and scattered members of popular superstition, and . . . to unite them into one consistent narrative" (Preface). The story rambles endlessly without selection or climactic development. See David Hogg, *Life of Allan Cunningham*, pp. 275–7.

held the form in a green open space some quarter of a mile distant. When he rode to within a few yards, his "friend all in an instant vanished." Fifty yards farther on, he looked back, saw the apparition, and spurred toward it. "I must candidly confess," Scott reports to Gillies, "I had now got enough of the phantasmagoria; and whether it were from a love of home, or a participation in my dislike of this very stupid ghost, no matter, Finella did her best to run away, and would by no means agree to any further process of investigation.[1] I will not deny that I felt somewhat uncomfortable, and half inclined to think that this apparition was a warning of evil to come, or indication, however obscure, of misfortune that had already occurred."[2]

Even more disappointing was the mermaid of Scott's crest which "never boded me either good or evil," unlike the heraldic mermaid which played "the Banshee a prophetess of woe" in the *Narrative* of Lord Byron's grandfather, the Hon. John Byron.[3] Some five years after writing to Byron, Scott enlightens the credulous Mrs Hughes about the emblazoned lady who bears the sun in her right hand and the crescent moon in her left. She is "supposed to represent the spirit Threshie-wat who used to appear to light him [Wat Scott of Harden] through the Cheviot hills—with a lanthorn in each hand which for dignitys sake has been since converted into the Sun & Moon by the heralds."[4] But this guiding spirit only benefited ancestors.

After Lady Charlotte's death, Scott sustained visitations and warnings. On 12 September 1826, he thought he heard his wife call him by a familiar name of endearment. On waking, however, he reminded himself that such impressions are echoes of the past, not forebodings of the future.[5] Before setting out for London to gather material for his nine-volume *Life of Napoleon*, Sir Walter records this incident in his Journal for 11 October

---

[1] In the animal's nervousness, the adventure verges on second sight, a vision which is usually indicative of death or disaster: "That Horses see it is likewise plain, from their violent and sudden starting, when the Rider or Seer in Company with him sees a Vision of any kind, Night, or Day." Martin Martin, *A Description of the Western Islands of Scotland*, London 1703, p. 306.

[2] Gillies, *Recollections of Sir Walter Scott*, pp. 170–2. Cp. opening of "Relation XXIX" in George Sinclair, *Satan's Invisible World Discovered*, ed. T. G. Stevenson [= Sinclair], Edinburgh, 1871, p. 187.

[3] To (Byron) 28 Mar. 1822, in *Letters*, VII. 121.

[4] 25 Dec. 1827 in *Letters*, X. 347 (305). See Charles Rogers, *Genealogical Memoirs of the Family of Sir Walter Scott*, London 1877, pp. lxxi–lxxii. The motto, "Reparabit cornua Phoebe," is susceptible of amusing cattle-lifting mistranslation. Cp. Captain Walter Scot, *A True History . . . of the Right Honourable Name of Scot*, 3rd edn, Hawick 1786, PT I, p. 48:

> Nights-men at first they did appear,
> Because moon and stars to their arms they bear.

[5] *Journal*, p. 229.

1826: "My wife's figure seems to stand before me, and her voice is in my ears—'S——, do not go.' It half frightens me."[6]

* * *

Had Scott been more than gently born, his warning spirits might have been less amateurish. During his tour of Scotland, Thomas Pennant learned that "every great family had in former times its Daemon, or Genius, with its peculiar attributes."[7] Thus the *Bodach an dun*, ghost of the hill, the *Bodach Gartin*, and other spirits haunted ancestral houses which, unlike Abbotsford, had an atmosphere of age and tradition. "The *Boddach* of the Highlanders," as Scott describes them in a review of the *Culloden Papers*, " 'walked the heath at midnight and at noon.' "[8] In a Gaelic folk tale, a gray old man known as the Bodach Glas gains power over a king's son by winning a game of shinty.[9] The Montgomeries, Earls of Eglinton, were visited by a Bodach Glas on the eve of family disasters. If this warning spirit identified itself with the Cunninghams, hereditary enemies of the Montgomeries, it must have been exultant and hateful.[10]

Such, at least, is the animus of the fictional Bodach Glas or Gray Spectre which makes itself visible to Fergus MacIvor in *Waverley* as "a tall figure in a gray plaid," and again, the night before the proud chief's execution at Carlisle, takes shape in a slip of moonlight, smilingly beckoning to the last descendant of its ancient enemy. Tradition identifies this Bodach Glas as the spirit of Halbert Hall, a Lowlander whose life was taken by Fergus's ancestor, Ian nan Chaistel, some three centuries before, in a quarrel over the division of booty.[11] After announcing catastrophe and death to successive chiefs of the MacIvor clan, this should certainly be its farewell earthly appearance.

The warning spirit could perform two valid functions in *Waverley*, by inducing a mood of fatalistic resignation in the Highland chief and by

---

[6] *Op. cit.*, p. 243. A certain grimness settles on these visions of the night because of the earlier precautions against body-snatchers' opening the Dryburgh Abbey grave of Lady Scott. *Letters*, x. 44; cp. xi. 125.

[7] Pennant, *A Tour in Scotland:* MDCCLXIX, 4th edn, London 1776, pp. 156–7.

[8] Q.R., xiv (1815–16), 289–90.

[9] "The Tale of the 'Bodach Glas,' " tr. Mrs Mary Mackellar, *The Celtic Magazine*, xii (1887), 12 ff. Cp. Alfred Nutt, "Notes on the 'Bodach Glas,' " xii. 106. For another gray spectre, see the spiteful Duine-glase-beg, i.e., the Little Gray Man, in Walter Gregor, "Guardian Spirits of Wells and Lochs," *Folk-Lore*, iii (1892), 68.

[10] For a full discussion of possible sources, see C. O. Parsons, "The Bodach Glas in *Waverley*," *N. & Q.*, clxxxiv (1943), 95–7.

[11] Cp. Scott's Shetland Diary for 23 Aug. 1814: "Gruagach, a sort of tutelary divinity, often mentioned by Martin in his History of the Western Islands, has still his place and credit, but is modernized into a tall man, always a Lowlander, with a long coat and white waistcoat." Lockhart, iii. 228.

operating on readers' sympathies so as to increase the poignancy of his death. Scott's handling of the Bodach Glas, however, falls somewhat short. The apparition is introduced rather perfunctorily, and it does not take a significant part in the emotional and narrative crises leading up to the self-willed tragedy. Then, too, attention is needlessly distracted from the spectral warning and its elaboration by Edward Waverley's ill-timed scepticism.

While evoking the Bodach Glas, Scott combines three techniques for the narrative use of the supernatural. As author, he offers no forthright comment on the vision, thus leaving the explanation, if one is required, to the reader. But he does insinuate an explanation in the unbelief of the ardently romantic hero (Scott considers him a figure of straw): "Edward had little doubt that this phantom was the operation of an exhausted frame and depressed spirits working on the belief common to all Highlanders in such superstitions." And at the same time he reveals the susceptible temperament of the Highlander through Fergus's acceptance of the apparition and the import of its message.[11a]

When he introduces the warning spirit incidentally, Scott may resort to a summary of the thoughts and emotions aroused through apprehension. Thus when Julian, in *Peveril of the Peak*, follows mute Fenella to the Countess of Derby's apartment, her mournful step, inarticulate moaning, and afflicted wringing of the hands make the young man shudder:

> As a Peaksman, and a long resident in the Isle of Man, he was well acquainted with many a superstitious legend, and particularly with a belief, which attached to the powerful family of the Stanleys, for their peculiar demon, a Banshie, or female spirit, who was wont to shriek, 'foreboding evil times;' and who was generally seen weeping and bemoaning herself before the death of any person of distinction belonging to the family. For an instant, Julian could scarce divest himself of the belief, that the wailing, gibbering form, which glided before him, with a lamp in her hand, was the genius of his mother's race come to announce to him his predestined doom.

Since Fenella is elsewhere likened to a sylphid, a familiar, and a changeling, there is not much opportunity to develop any of the supernatural parallels except the last. But her attachment to Julian, "like that of the prophetic spirit to his family," can only portend ill. In this passage on the

[11a] In a marginal note on the episode, Coleridge calls "Sir Walter, an orthodox cosmolater," whose "half and half" method jumbles "the simplest principles of pathology," "the full effect of superstition for the *reader*" through marvellous coincidence, and "the credit of unbelief for the writer." *Coleridge's Miscellaneous Criticism*, ed. T. M. Raysor, Cambridge, Mass., 1936, p. 322. In *The Pirate* as well, Scott "relates as *truth*" what he "as an enlightened man" disclaims believing (p. 332).

family banshie, Scott is less the novelist than the antiquary or folklorist seeking an illustration of a widespread belief.

Indeed, so great is his imaginative appreciation of the Irish banshie that he persistently associates odd-jobs, and even male, attendant spirits of Scotland with her.[12] Perhaps, he felt that Scottish lore would be richer if it possessed a counterpart of Maturin's "tale of the Banshi; it is, like her own music, pleasant and mournful to the soul."[13]

More sadistic than pleasant is the story of the Bahr-geist, Vanda of the Red-Finger, in *The Betrothed*. After two years of marriage, a Briton wife was deprived of a finger and strangled by order of her Saxon mate, Baldrick. In penance, each female descendant of the House of Baldringham must spend one night in the murdered lady's chamber, there to receive a sign from the ghost's whole or mutilated hand of her happy or hapless future. It is the lot of the heroine, Eveline Berenger, "the last branch of her house," to see "a fierce expression of vengeful exultation" on the face of the apparition, which holds up "the bloody hand as witness of the injuries with which she had been treated while in life" and menaces the frightened girl. Eveline herself, like Fergus MacIvor in *Waverley*, does not hesitate in her belief, while Rose Flammock, a rather unconvincing twelfth-century sceptic, speaks of trickery and "an obsolete family superstition." Like Edward Waverley and Scott's contemporary, Dr Samuel Hibbert, Rose seeks a physical source: Surely, Eveline has been afflicted by the nightmare, which "is by leeches considered as no real phantom, but solely the creation of our own imagination, disordered by causes which arise from bodily indisposition." Scott offers no explanation in his own right, although he does hint at a less fanciful interpretation in his reference to Eveline's "boding vision or dream."

Unlike the Bodach Glas of Scott's first novel, Vanda is at times friendly —in fact, strangely alternates between malevolence and beneficence.[14] "The Bahr-geist is, therefore," Eveline tells Rose, "sometimes regarded as the good genius, sometimes as the avenging fiend, attached to particular families and classes of men." After making Eveline shudder at the

[12] See *The Lady of the Lake*, III. viii, nn.; *Demonology*, pp. 351–2.

[13] Charles R. Maturin, *The Milesian Chief*, London 1812, I. 177.

[14] Scott's source, Lady Fanshawe's *Memoirs* in manuscript (published 1829), also suggests that this contradictory mixture of affection and hate. The spirit, appearing on the night of a death in an Irish family, was "in white, with red hair and pale ghastly complexion: she spoke loud, and in a tone I had never heard, thrice, 'a horse;' and then, with a sigh more like the wind than breath, she vanished. . . . This woman was many ages ago got with child by the owner of this place, who murdered her in his garden, and flung her into the river under the window." Scott allows Eveline to narrate her own adventure, as does Lady Fanshawe in the seventeenth century. Cp. the haunting of Pausanias by murdered Cleonicé in "Cimon," *Plutarch's Lives*, tr. Bernadotte Perrin, Loeb Classical Library, II. 420–3.

devastating prophecy, "Widowed wife, and wedded maid, | Betrothed, betrayer, and betrayed!" the vision returns in a dream and "seemed to repeat or chant":

> All is done that has been said!
> Vanda's wrong has been y-wroken—
> Take her pardon by this token.

As the plot glides toward a happy ending, clouds lift and menace dissipates in a dream.

In *The Highland Widow*, the visitant is not the intermediary of an ancestor or of someone injured by an ancestor. It is the sadly knowing spirit of a father, a mountain robber shot down by the soldiers, trying to save his son. His widow and antagonist, Elspat MacTavish, is the pronouncer, instrument, and fellow victim of a curse. Some of her neighbours look on her as a witch who joins the Devil at the time of her death. Destiny-driven, she is represented by Scott as much in terms of Greek tragedy as of Highland superstition. The impression of deeds and influences beyond the reasoned control of man or ghost is enhanced by the setting, which is unlucky and haunted.

Three points of view create tension, Hamish's automatic duty to his regiment (the new Hanoverian order), the mother's blind honour and loyalty (the outmoded Highland order), and the spectre's sense of inevitable change (mediating a transfer of loyalty). Hamish is passive, Elspat is active and tragically effective, and the dead father is active and ineffective. When Elspat wants to urge Hamish to desert his regiment and become a cateran like his father, "it seemed to her heated imagination as if the ghost of her husband arose between them in his bloody tartans, and, laying his finger on his lips, appeared to prohibit the topic." Later, the embodiment of the warning spirit becomes more definite. A tall, shadowy, gliding High-lander appears to young Hamish in the twilight when he comes home just before rejoining his regiment. The figure "first pointed to Elspat's hut, and made, with arm and head, a gesture prohibiting Hamish to approach it, then stretched his hand to the road which led to the southward, with a motion which seemed to enjoin his instant departure in that direction." Through temporising in his obedience, Hamish drinks whisky drugged by his mother, overstays his time, slays a friend sent to put him under military arrest, and dies before a firing-squad.

The irony of a reiver's ghost warning his son back to a regiment which serves a Hanoverian king is somewhat lessened by the author's hint that the soldier thus interprets some natural happening, for "his heated imagination" probably "exaggerated into superstitious importance some very ordinary and accidental circumstance." After the wordless encounter, a similar hint is repeated to the too credulous reader: "The plaided form was gone—Hamish did not exactly say vanished, because there were rocks and stunted trees enough to have concealed him." There is, however, no sceptical friend to argue against "the universal turn of *Hamish's* countrymen for the marvellous," and the warning paternal spirit, whether a subjective or objective phenomenon, is effectively and consistently introduced.

As warning spirits, Vanda and Fenella are either unnecessary or trumpery garnishing; the Bodach Glas is only supplementary to the self-dooming fanaticism of Fergus MacIvor; and the freebooter's ghost intensifies a reality which is profound and moving in its own psychological right. Scott was out of his time and place in *The Betrothed* and *Peveril of the Peak*. *Waverley* and *The Highland Widow* have Highland lore in common, but the later and shorter work reveals greater sensitivity, power, and maturity in the use of the warning spirit.

3. THE SIBYL

If a potential warning spirit lingered on instead of dying in the prime of life, it might well become a sibyl. In an ageing or aged person, past suffering and present misery, even insanity, may be twisted into confidence in supernatural power or knowledge of the future. The balanced Scott found unbalanced, obscure, melodramatically vehement misanthropes, hermits, and sibyls fascinating.

On his voyage to the Shetland Islands in 1814, Scott fills his diary with rich lore which is employed imaginatively in *The Lord of the Isles* and *The Pirate*. One of his experiences, recorded on 17 August is that of meeting Bessy Millie:

> An old hag lives in a wretched cabin on this height, and subsists by selling winds. Each captain of a merchantman, between jest and earnest, gives the old woman sixpence, and she boils her kettle to procure a favourable gale. She was a miserable figure; upwards of ninety, she told us, and dried up like a mummy. A sort of clay-coloured cloak, folded over her head, corresponded in colour to her corpselike complexion. Fine light-blue eyes, and nose and chin that almost met, and a ghastly expression of cunning, gave her quite the effect of Hecate. . . . We left our Pythoness, who assured us there was nothing evil in the intercession she was to make for us, but that we were only to have a fair wind through the benefit of

her prayers. She repeated a sort of rigmarole which I suppose she had ready for such occasions.... So much for buying a wind. Bessy Millie's habitation is airy enough for Æolus himself, but if she is a special favourite with that divinity, he has a strange choice.[1]

Here a reader finds many of the essentials of Scott's fictional sibyls: a lonely, eerie dwelling; age and a startling appearance; mysterious words; cunning and credulity mixed; contrasting attitudes toward the old woman's pretensions; a final note of scepticism.

* * *

In Scott's first sibyl, Meg Merrilies, the characteristics of the sisterhood combine more fitly than in any of her successors. Feeling at home in gypsy lore, a subject to which he had devoted a good deal of study,[2] Scott has in Jean Gordon the gift of a compelling human prototype for the prophetess of Derncleugh. His debt to her is paid in the Introduction (1829) to *Guy Mannering*.

The gypsy's uncanniness is made all the more probable by her belonging to a race which the common people suspected of devilish pact. That the wandering bands were feared is evident in the Fifeshire country-folk's practice of throwing salt in the fire "to set at defiance the *witchcraft*, of which they believed these gypsies were possessed."[3] Fortunes were usually spaed by old women who made use of a network of informants to gather startling data. Supernatural dread might even be inspired in order to intimidate and fleece country lasses. These often became so excited when fortunes were told with corn-riddle and scissors that, after the gypsy had

[1] Lockhart, III. 203–04. Scott's classical allusions recall the prototype of Shetland and Waverley pythonesses, the "maddened" Sibyl of Cumae in Virgil, *Aeneid*, BK. VI, chanting "her perplexing terrors . . . truth wrapped in obscurity," and, shrunken and old in Petronius, *Satyricon*, complaining, "I want to die." For a prescient parody, see the sale of winds by Lapland witches in James K. Paulding, *The Lay of the Scottish Fiddle*, London 1814, Canto I, xiii and Note 4 (1st edn. 1813).

[2] See Lockhart, IV. 64: Scott "*dictated* to Pringle a collection of anecdotes concerning Scottish gypsies, which attracted a good deal of notice." These anecdotes appeared in "Notices concerning the Scottish Gypsies," *B.E.M.*, I (1817), 43–58, 154–61, 615–20. Scott's written contribution was a review of Weissenbruch, *Ausführliche Relation*, Frankfurt 1727, "On the Gypsies of Hesse-Darmstadt in Germany," *B.E.M.*, II (1817–18), 409–14; see Walter Simson, *A History of the Gipsies*, ed. James Simson, London 1865, p. 79, and G. F. Black, *A Gypsy Bibliography*, London 1914, p. 155. Scott speaks of having found Weissen-bruch "amidst heaps of treatises on diablérie, astrology, chiromancy, rhabdomancy, alchemy, &c . . . while the philosophers, poets, and amateurs of the City, rivalled each other in the wish to appropriate manuals of the black art" at John Ballantyne's sale of foreign books in Dec. 1817. See also John Hoyland, *A Historical Survey of the Customs . . . of the Gypsies*, York 1816, pp. 93–4.

[3] W.S. [Walter Simson], "Anecdotes of the Fife Gypsies," *B.E.M.*, II. 526; William Chambers, *Exploits . . . of the most remarkable Scottish Gypsies*, 3rd edn, Edinburgh 1823, pp. 32–3.

muttered incantations in Romany and cried out, "Turn riddle—turn—sheers and all," they fled lest the Devil himself should appear to them on the spot.[4] Stories were frequently circulated about the miraculous fulfilment of gypsy prophecies[5] as well as about *glamour*, or hypnotic power, the latter an area which Scott does not explore in *Guy Mannering*.[6]

Possessing the secrets of her race and utterly convincing in the exercise of very keen faculties, Meg Merrilies evokes from her acquaintances and even from her creator a variety of reactions, which in themselves contribute to a rounded, rather than a one-sided, characterisation. She is called "*malefica*," "no canny," an "ancient sibyl," an "intractable sorceress," a "witch," and a "hag of Satan"—the last, fitly enough, by Hatteraick. To Colonel Mannering she appears in a less fantastic light than to Hatteraick, whose brain is conventionally stocked with kobolds and fiends; to Dominie Sampson, who splutters a tangle of book and countryside witch lore; or to Dandie Dinmont, in whom personal courage finally masters superstitious fright.

Mannering's astrology is finely contrasted with Meg's power of divination, a display of which he chances to see in the ruins of Ellangowan Castle. The gypsy is spinning a tri-coloured woollen thread, singing a charm the while, "Twist ye, twine ye! even so | Mingle shades of joy and woe." When her supply of yarn runs out, Meg measures it: "A hank, but not a haill ane,—the full years o' threescore and ten, but thrice broken, and thrice to oop [unite]; he'll be a lucky lad and he win through wi't." This prognostic is at once more vivid, native and credible than the mathematically exact fifth, tenth, and twenty-first years of the astromancer.

Some five years later, the prediction is followed by the famous "prophecy, or anathema, of Meg Merrilies," which is launched on Ellangowan's head in anger over the ejection of the gypsies from the laird's estate. Antithetical and rhetorical, with the authentic ring of prophecies immemorially circulated on the Border, it opens: "This day have ye quenced seven smoking hearths,—see if the fire in your ain parlour burn

---

[4] Simson, *History of the Gipsies*, pp. 231-2.

[5] After the appearance of *Guy Mannering*, poetic forecasts, some of them presented as real, became popular in magazines. In "The Gipsy's Prophecy," a sibyl vaguely warns a lady with raven hair, "I can give thee but dark revealings," and speaks of the stars and of doom, "a broken heart, and an early grave!" *The Edinburgh Magazine*, XVII (1825), 551. Cp. "The Gipsie's Prophecye," *G.M.*, XCV. PT I (1825), 224; "The Gipsy's Malison," *The Complete Works of Charles Lamb*, ed. R. H. Shepherd, London 1892, p. 721; C. G. Leland, *Gypsy Sorcery and Fortune Telling*, London 1891, pp. 188-93.

[6] But see Scott's note on "the gypsies' glamour'd gang" in "Christie's Will," *Minstrelsy*, and on "All was delusion" in *Lay*, III. ix.

the blyther for that. Ye have riven the thack off seven cottar-houses,—look if your ain roof-tree stand the faster. Ye may stable your stirks in the shealings at Derncleugh,—see that the hare does not couch on the hearth-stane at Ellangowan." The laird soon has cause to remember his doom, the last clause of which is a distinct echo of a rhyme current in Teviotdale in Scott's day and thought to have come from Thomas of Erceldoune's lips:

> The hare sall *kittle on my hearth stane,   *a* litter
> And there will never be a Laird Learmont again.[7]

Scott's treatment of the parallel birth prophecies includes a hint that the almost meticulous confirmation of sibylline and astrological forecasts may be explained by coincidence, a narrative evasion which falls under the novelist's own criticism of Mrs Anne Radcliffe for her paltry and insufficient adjustment of natural causes to preternatural effects. The prophetic machinery, however, is diversified by robust scenes, and the astrologer and the sibyl are in themselves such authentic characters that they almost persuade us to overlook this inconsistency. They lend as much interest to the unearthly as they gain from it. Through their efforts to restore Harry Bertram to his rights after predicting evil crosses in his life, they provide a certain artistic cohesion between the chief supernatural elements in *Guy Mannering*.

Colonel Mannering says of Meg: "Many of her class set out by being impostors, and end by becoming enthusiasts, or hold a kind of darkling conduct between both lines, unconscious almost when they are cheating themselves, or when imposing on others." This psychological formula is less applicable to the most original of the Waverley line of sibyls than to the wise women who follow after her. Without being close copies of their fictional prototype, Norna of Fitful Head and Mother Nicneven are conceived in the spirit, rather than in the letter, of the gypsy.[8]

---

[7] *Minstrelsy*, IV. 101–02. Cp. Gideon Kemp's fulfilled prophecy in John Galt, *Ringan Gilhaize* (1823): "The foul toad and the cauld snail [may yet] be the only visitors around the unblest hearth o' Carswell."

[8] "For Norna, who will be pronounced a new hash of Meg Merrilies, I think those peculiar superstitions, the shocking death of her father, and her own insanity, make a very clear distinction, and people would allow it if she were but made a *little* old woman instead of a tall one." *Letters of Lady Louisa Stuart to Miss Louisa Clinton*, ed. J. A. Home, Edinburgh 1901, p. 212 (undated letter written shortly after 4 Jan. 1822). If Scott could not get Meg out of his mind, neither could his imitators. On 9 May 1823, the Rev. Thomas Streatfeild, author of *The Bridal of Armagnac*, London 1823, writes Sir Walter that his tragedy "originated in a conversation relative to the Sibyl of Derncleugh, and that Adelaide was an attempt to 'graft the self devotion of Meg Merrilies upon a character of feminine softness. Little Meg was long her nom de guerre, and Mr. S. would be well satisfied should Sir Walter Scott admit that she retained any resemblance to her mighty mother.' " Walpole.

Although the suspicion of witchcraft is cast on Magdalen Graeme, as when the Lady of Avenel's waiting-maid Lilias and Doctor Luke Lundin suggest a ducking in the loch, her chief characteristics are those of a sibyl. She moves through the plot of *The Abbot* as though in a fateful trance, alluding to "my weird" and "the sphere of the Vision." Some external agency, vow, or spell seems to compel her, but so nebulous is the compulsion "that it was not easy to decide whether she made any actual pretensions to a direct and supernatural call." Later she reappears as Mother Nicneven, bearing the name of the Scottish Hecate[9] and the character of a "weel friended . . . auld popish witch-wife," a sorceress, a reader of the heavens, a folk mediciner with herbs and spells, a prophetess, a poisoner, a possessed demoniac, and a saint. She perversely wraps her service to Catholicism, Queen Mary, and her grandson Roland Graeme in obscurity. In her last important scene, Mother Nicneven is given the characterisation which Scott wishes us to bear in mind. "Assuming the mien and attitude of a Sibyl in frenzy," with "an enthusiasm approaching to insanity," she utters the metaphorical and inspired "oracle of a Pythoness."

The chief function of Mother Nicneven is that of an eerie, yet human, guardian angel to her grandson Roland. As such, she travels hither and thither "like a ghost," makes arrangements behind the scenes, overreaches herself in obstinate interference, and imparts a general air of mysterious destiny to certain episodes. Without her assistance, the action could advance with ease, and she impresses the reader as an intrusive rather than an essential agent. She resembles Meg Merrilies, who is the guardian angel on earth of Harry Bertram, but she differs from her in not carrying conviction wherever she goes.

Another of Scott's wild, awesome, and even repellent guardian angels is Norna of Fitful Head,[10] whose charge—or lonely woman's fixation—is Mordaunt Mertoun. The author touches her, like Mother Nicneven, with insanity, imposture, and self-deception, in order to set her off from such a famous prototype as Meg Merrilies. When novelty fades, effects must be heightened.

Norna's whole history is perhaps best traced in the change in her dress. She is first introduced as wearing, among other garments, a velvet jacket stamped with figures, a girdle "plated with silver ornaments, cut into the

[9] See Donald A. Mackenzie, *Scottish Folk-Lore and Folk Life*, London and Glasgow 1935, pp. viii, 149–51; Thomas Davidson, *Rowan Tree and Red Thread*, Edinburgh and London 1949, pp. 8–9 ("Nicniven, the . . . Mother witch of the Scottish peasantry . . . a mysterious divinity").
[10] Fitful Head is a place name whose applicability unfortunately extends beyond geography. *Norna* comes from the Norns, the three giant fatal sisters of Norse mythology.

shape of planetary signs," and an astrologically embroidered apron.[11] Her staff, which somewhat resembles a divining rod, is "engraved with Runic characters and figures." A skilled make-up artist and costumer, tall, rugged Norna also knows what words and gestures are appropriate to her character. But when the action draws to a close and "this unfortunate victim of mental delusion" must regain some measure of reason in order not to mislead credulous readers any further, she takes to the Bible, denies her powers, dismisses her dwarf familiar, and changes to clothes "of a more simple and less imposing appearance."

The range of Norna's supernatural repertory is suggested by numerous epithets. To forthright Mistress Baby Yellowley, Norna can be none other than a witch. To some she is an insane woman and a cheat; a randy quean, a spaewife, a prophetess of evil, and a warlock thief; a priestess, a pythoness, a sorceress, a sybil, a divining woman, a mistress of the elements, a fatal sister, and a reim-kennar. To others she is the bondswoman of the Christian Devil and of the pre-Christian dwarf Trolld.

In contrast to the disparate characterisation of Norna by different acquaintances is the consistent attempt of the novelist to make her case clear. Although Norna is the cousin of solid Magnus Troil, she is descended from a family of pretenders to magical power. Her own father, Erland, taught her "whatever of legendary lore Scald and Bard had left behind them." Maddened by remorse over her father's death, Norna, or Ulla Troil as she was christened, gains some release from suffering by aiding Mordaunt Mertoun and by arousing awe in superstitious breasts. Possessed of "a considerable income," as well as an extensive knowledge of "secret passes and recesses," Norna is able to receive news, give orders, impose secrecy, take short-cuts and appear or disappear bafflingly. These Radcliffian explanations, however, are reserved for the last third of the novel.[12] Their intrusion makes Norna doubt her own occult gifts and, like the Hermit of Engaddi, regain comparative sanity.

[11] Scott writes [Miss Smith] about her costume as the Witch Dame of Branksome in *The Lady of Buccleuch*: "The Lady when engaged in her magical intercourse with the Spirits should I think have a sort of stole or loose upper scarf with astrological hieroglyphics of the planets." 5 Apr. 1811 in *Letters*, II. 471. In *The Abbot*, Mother Nicneven "was dressed in a long dark-coloured robe of unusual fashion, bordered at the skirts, and on the stomacher, with a sort of white trimming resembling the Jewish phylacteries, on which were wrought the characters of some unknown language." Cp. Lord Gifford's "wizard habit strange" in *Marmion*, III. xx. Meg Merrilies does not wear the highly conventionalised dress which Scott usually thinks proper to a sibyl.

[12] In the light of Scott's own practice, it is ironical to find the Introduction (1 May 1831) to *The Pirate* ending in this fashion: "The professed explanation of a tale, where appearances or incidents of a supernatural character are referred to natural causes, has often, in the winding up of the story, a degree of improbability almost equal to an absolute goblin narrative. Even the genius of Mrs. Radcliffe could not always surmount this difficulty."

Besides her plot service as universal fixer, Norna of Fitful Head has a subtle, almost atmospheric function. As an antiquarian storyteller, Scott could hardly set a tale in Zetland without harking back to the distant past, as when Norna challenges effete Zetland males: "The women have not forgotten the arts that lifted them of yore into queens and prophetesses." Although survivals from pre-Christian times are freely sprinkled throughout *The Pirate*, ancient ways and beliefs are symbolised by, and concentrated in, the figure of Norna. Just as Ulrica brings elder Germanic lore into the pageantry of *Ivanhoe*, so Norna keeps the Norse past alive. In making irony and frustration the chief results of her fanatical conservatism, Scott is faithful to the nature of cultural lag.

* * *

Scott's self-deluded female enthusiasts, though cunningly differentiated in other respects, have certain things in common: their dress is strange; their features are wildly expressive; they inspire awe by spacing fortunes and penetrating the future, a skill made substantial by a garnering of facts which seems no less than miraculous to the ill-informed; and they chant or sing their prophecies in an exalted manner. These sibylline verses become more and more opaque with Meg Merrilies' successors, in keeping with conscious deception.[13]

Whatever the degree of their real or factitious vitality, the sibyls fit into the same basic narrative pattern. As ubiquitous and almost omniscient agents, capable of advancing the action at awkward points by helping other characters out of tangles, these *deae ex machina* render the service of such *dei ex machina* as Flibbertigibbet and Edie Ochiltree. With their help, the hurried plot-maker slips out of many a tight place.

They are also useful to the novelist in his role as culture historian. In *The Pirate*, Scott analyses the attitudes toward witchcraft in different stages of civilisation,—veneration in early society, detestation with the increase of religion and knowledge, and eventual suspicion of imposture. These three stages may also be traced in reactions to the sybils, Norse Norna, Catholic Mother Nicneven, and gypsy Meg.

[13] Or, perhaps, they imitate great Merlin's practice, which Fordun describes, "plura quasi prophetice cecinit ad intelligendum obscura; quae, quousque contingant, nullatenus aut vix a quoquam discerni valeant, sed contingentia saepius, vel postquam acciderint citius elucidari putantur." John Fordun, *Scotichronicon*, ed. Goodall, I. 121 (BK III. ch. xvii).

4. Astrology

Scott's concern with the stars was imaginative and antiquarian, not dogmatic. Its quality can be suggested by an unpublished letter of Christmas Day, 1829, in which G. R. Ainslie adds to the novelist's curious library:

> I read somewhere, that you have a collection of book[s] on judicial astrology, I met with the subject of this note in Paris, at a stall, I thought it might hold its place on your shelves, as a link in the chain, from the period of that celebrated science holding its sway over the minds of most men, to the present, when its empire is somewhat reduced as to limits.[1]

Lockhart discriminatingly remarks on the caution underlying his father-in-law's enthusiasm:

> He delighted in letting his fancy run wild about ghosts and witches and horoscopes—but I venture to say, had he sat on the judicial bench a hundred years before he was born, no man would have been more certain to give juries sound direction in estimating the pretended evidence of supernatural occurences of any sort.[2]

In his youth and during the intermittent suspension of disbelief which served him as a popular writer, Scott could participate in Lady Hester Stanhope's conviction: "A clever man will, from his knowledge of the stars, look even at a child and say, 'That child will have such and such diseases, such and such virtues, such and such vices;' and this I can do."[3] Lady Hester's power over the Druses rested largely on her divination and prophecy.

*   *   *

Walter Scott was early introduced to the narrative value of astrology by a servant of his father's, the old Highlander, John MacKinlay, who believed in his story as firmly "as in any part of his creed." Once, a benighted traveller found his way to a country seat in a remote part of Galloway. In courteous exchange for hospitality, he cast the horoscope of an infant whose birth had broken the spell of ten childless years. When it was known that the heir of the house must face a cruel temptation on or about his twenty-first birthday, the sage arranged that the crisis be met in his house in the south of England. There, the youth was assailed by an evil influence with the memory of his sins ("like a swarm of demons") and was inveigled to despair by Satan himself. The victim leaned for support

---

[1] Walpole.   [2] Lockhart, VII. 413.
[3] *Memoirs of the Lady Hester Stanhope*, London 1845, II. 253.

on his faith and on the Holy Bible; whereupon, the fatal hour having passed, "the demon retired, yelling and discomfited."[4]

The admittedly derivative plot of *Guy Mannering* may be said to have passed through two refining processes, the first of which operated directly on John MacKinlay's wondrous narrative. Scott was inspired to project a tale about a doomed person whose virtuous efforts were "forever disappointed by the intervention, as it were, of some malevolent being," but whose victory over destiny was won in the end. In the second refining process, this plan was modified into its present form. Thus the astrological element is important in Chapters III–VI, an experimental beginning after which it is abandoned as no longer retaining "influence over the general mind sufficient even to constitute the mainspring of a romance."

Guy Mannering is represented as sharing in his early youth an old clergyman's enthusiasm for the stars and as acquiring great knowledge of the art before he comes to a full realisation of its absurdity. Thus on learning of the birth of an heir to Ellangowan, he falls into the humour of casting the nativity, a suggestion jokingly made by the laird when he rejects Meg Merrilies' offer to spae the fortune. On erecting his scheme, the Englishman multiplies the single peril of the old legend into three crises falling in the child's fifth, tenth, and twenty-first years. Worse still, the danger threatened in the twenty-first year coincides exactly in time with the disaster which Mannering has earlier made out in the horoscope of his sweetheart, Sophia Wellwood (later his wife).

No wonder Mannering wavers momentarily in his scepticism before returning to his common-sense attitude. After advising Ellangowan that no "sensible man can put faith in the predictions of astrology," he makes a point of giving him a sealed paper, with instructions not to open it until five years have passed. Ellangowan's superstitious wife makes a small velvet bag for the paper and hangs it as a charm round her son's neck. Strange to say, two of the intimations come true: young Harry Bertram is kidnapped by smugglers and gypsies at the age of five, and some sixteen years later, he is bested in a duel with Colonel Mannering, who wrongly suspects him of intimacy with his wife, Sophia.

---

[4] Still another version of the story, set in "fair Yorkshire," is preserved in *The Durham Garland*, which Lockhart believes Scott must have read in his boyhood. Lockhart, III. 405–14. MacKinlay's oral narrative need not be a corrupted Scottish version of *The Durham Garland*, as Lockhart supposes; it may be a cognate legend. Some time before 7 Nov. 1814, Joseph Train, Gallovidian folklorist and excise-officer, sent Scott a third version of the tale, which is described as "a local story of an astrologer, who calling at a farm-house at the moment when the goodwife was in travail, had, it was said, predicted the future fortune of the child, almost in the words placed in the mouth of John M'Kinlay, in the Introduction to Guy Mannering." Lockhart, III. 308–09, 316.

Feeling his authorial responsibility, Scott pauses to warn readers against taking the three forebodements too seriously: "It will be readily believed that in mentioning this circumstance, we lay no weight whatever upon the pretended information thus conveyed. But it often happens—such is our natural love for the marvellous—that we willingly contribute our own efforts to beguile our better judgments." Scott next suggests explanations of the coincidence. But the prophetic fulfilment is so remarkable that the reader is likely to forget the author's cautionary remark in Chapter IV about "singular chances which sometimes happen against all ordinary calculations."

Such, at least, is the interpretation of one reader, J. A. McWhirter of Edinburgh, who writes to Scott on 18 December 1828, that astrology has been his "amusement" since the appearance of *Guy Mannering*. Indeed, "the 'Nativity' of Sir Walter Scott would be invaluable; as it would tend to prove either the truth, or the falsehood of the General Principles of that Science in which our forefathers reposed such implicit faith."[5] Critics, too, have been puzzled by the disparity between theory and narrative practice. C. D. Yonge, for one, surmises that "we may also, perhaps, see in the tale traces of a lurking fancy that there was somewhat more foundation for the claims of astrology to be reckoned among the sciences, than was generally admitted."[6]

The jargon of the art or science, with which the novelist became acquainted in such works as William Lilly's *Christian Astrology* (London 1647), lends a certain quaint raciness to the opening chapters, in which Mannering's point of view approximates Scott's. Both men involve themselves in difficulties by playfully attempting to revive the interest of previous studies. Both enjoy running over "all the hard terms of art which a tenacious memory supplied, and which . . . had been familiar to *them* in early youth." Deceptively warmed by a reminiscent afterglow, Scott unhesitatingly projects his tale of wonder, but—as the words flow—

[5] Walpole. In the Introduction (Jan. 1829) to *Guy Mannering*, Scott mentions this offer to cast his horoscope as an instance of modern belief in the stars and their influence. Another instance would be *The Spirit of Partridge: or, the Astrologer's Pocket Companion, and General Magazine*, published for the London Astrological Society in 1825. As did the Napoleonic era and its troubled aftermath, the Second World War stimulated soothsaying, so much so that Bishop Frank R. Barry warned Englishmen against the undermining of character and national morale by superstition. The United States had 30,000 practicing astrologers at the time. *Newsweek*, 3 May 1943, pp. 74, 76, 78.

[6] Yonge, *Life of Sir Walter Scott*, London 1888, p. 84. Also see J. W. Lake's "Memoir of Sir Walter Scott": "It [*Guy Mannering*] treats the supernatural agency not as a superstition, but as a truth; and the result is brought about, not by the imaginations of men deluded by a fiction, but by the actual operation of a miracle, contrary to the opinion and belief of all the parties concerned." *The Poetical Works of Sir Walter Scott*, Philadelphia 1836, p. xiii. For contrasting protests against Scott's use of astrology, see Andrew Lang's Introduction to *Guy Mannering*.

rationality warns him that he is misguiding himself and his public. He then becomes circumspect and faint-hearted. In this, one of his character- istic procedures with the supernatural, he shies away from the unearthly, recurring to it spasmodically, as in *Woodstock*, or else changes to a diffident, compromising attitude, inartistically juxtaposing the real and the unreal, as in *The Black Dwarf*. In the present novel, however, Mannering's departure from Ellangowan offers a plausible excuse for playing down the astrological *motif*.

Convinced that the action of *Guy Mannering* was of too recent a date (1765) for the introduction of astrology, Scott removes the planetary art further and further from the present in *Kenilworth, Quentin Durward*, and *The Talisman*. Although belief was almost universal in 1575, 1468, and 1191, Scott adopts the additional precaution of presenting it as the tool of crafty charlatans or madmen.

In the sixteenth century, the tragi-comic symbiosis of astrologers or alchemists and patrons, deteriorating into parasitism, was not rare. Just such a "great league and confederacy" resulted from the Earl of Leicester's introduction of Albert Laski (Albertus Alasco) to Dr John Dee. The Polish prince "did aspire much higher" and was promised kingship by a spirit through the intermediacy of Dee's treacherous scryer, Edward Kelly.[7] In *Kenilworth*, Leicester is partly modelled on Laski, Alasco (indebted in name only to Laski) on Dee, and Varney on Kelly.

The ambitious Earl of Leicester's conference with his astrologer Alasco is prefaced by a clear statement about "this pretended science": "It is well known that the age reposed a deep confidence in the vain predictions of judicial astrology...." The astrologer bears many a warning label. In his earlier guise as Dr Demetrius Doboobie, he is vulgarly reported to be a white witch, a conjurer, and "the devil's crony." Superstitiously learned Master Erasmus Holiday calls him Rosicrucian, palmist, discoverer of stolen goods, weapon salver, gatherer of herbs to make men invisible, searcher after the universal elixir and the philosopher's stone. To his former assistant, Wayland Smith, he is a basilisk with "as much of the demon about him ... as ever polluted humanity." And to Richard Varney, who is far more subtle in the ways of evil, Alasco's mixture of stars, alchemy, physic, poison, and intrigue is no more than "philosophical charlatanry" and "the mystery of cheating."

[7] *A True & Faithful Relation of What passed for many Years Between Dr. John Dee ... and Some Spirits*, London 1659, Meric Casaubon's Preface and p. 139. This book is in the Abbots- ford library. Cp. John Aubrey, *Brief Lives*, ed. Andrew Clark, Oxford 1898, I. 213–14: Dee "used to distill egge-shells, and 'twas from hence that Ben Johnson had his hint of the alki- mist, whom he meant."

This partially self-blinded impostor has come into Varney's power and must serve him. Using Varney's information, the small, aged, long-bearded adept holds out to Leicester, the bait of royalty, "a prouder title ... an higher rank." Although the Earl is "superior to his time" in all but one superstition, Alasco unexpectedly admits that the stars, which are subject to God, can only "show the natural and probable course of events." In these words the complexity of his nature is revealed: trickery, intellectual energy, and unbalanced idealism coexist in his talk and actions. His eyes are ratlike, his bearing noble. He dies poisoned by the sulphurous fumes of his own laboratory. Long suspect of "intercourse with the invisible world," he has much of the aspiration and more of the degradation of Marlowe's Doctor Faustus. In his portrayal of Alasco, Scott rises above the stereotypes of astrology to mingle pathos, grandeur, and horror.

In *Quentin Durward*, Louis XI has need of the pensioned astrologer, Martius Galeotti, to judge the courage and future good fortune of the young Scottish archer in conducting the Countess of Croye to the Bishop of Liége. Unlike Alasco, the versatile Galeotti is nobody's tool. When disgusted with the King's donative, he considers serving Cardinal Balue, "and it shall be his Eminence's own fault if the stars speak not as he would have them." The last references to Galeotti discourage credulity. The King's sight pierces momentarily through the mists of superstition when he exclaims: "Confess that I am a dupe, thou an impostor, thy pretended science a dream, and the planets which shine above us as little influential of our destiny, as their shadows, when reflected in the river, are capable of altering its course." To Petit-André he is a legerdemain fellow. And the novelist regrets that the imprisoned Galeotti put his great learning and talents "to the mean purposes of a cheat and an impostor."

Neither a man of the world nor a court sage resorts to astrology in *The Talisman*, but a hermit who—as Alberick of Mortemar—was confessor to a sisterhood, seduced a nun, and drove her to self-murder. Distracted by guilt, the hermit "gibbers, moans, and roars" over her grave in the vaults of Engaddi, all of which has the ring of Monk Lewis without that Gothic novelist's morbid elaboration. Although the hermit is "a mad priest" to King Richard and an "insane fanatic star-gazer" to Saladin, both princes listen to his predictions. Altogether, he is a wayward spirit "fluctuating between madness and misery," a cross between Scott's astrologer and sybil, sharing with the latter an egomaniac's urge to chart the destiny of others through prophecy. Thus he sees in the stars bloody peril for the Lion Hearted—humiliation, captivity, and early death without offspring. Later, the realisation that he has mistaken the astral message about the marriage of Edith Plantagenet to a prince sleeping in his grotto (Kenneth of Scotland rather than Saladin) chastens the relentless anchorite: "God will not have us break into His council-house, or spy out His hidden mysteries." It should be added for our comfort that, after renouncing astrology, the Hermit of Engaddi seldom has "frenzy fits." Saladin's own rejection of astrology as a science which "misleads those whom it seems to guide"[8] underscores the novelist's criticism of a system which has for centuries betrayed over-credulous men.

The omission of astrology from *Count Robert of Paris* is rather curious. Scott's partial source, Anna Comnena's brilliantly objective history of the reign of her father, Alexius I, contains a brief digression on astrology. The princess explains the recentness of the discovery and gives the names of famous Egyptian practitioners in Constantinople. Although the Emperors opposed instruction in the art as making "people of a guileless nature reject their faith in God and gape at the stars . . . there was no dearth of astrologers at that time." Anna herself studied astrology in order to pass fair judgment on it.[9] Scott sprinkles the marvellous over several episodes of the novel but withholds command of the stars from the intriguing sage, Agelastes. He may consciously have avoided repeating the character of Alasco or Martius Galeotti.

★   ★   ★

Scott's chief use of astrology is not to suggest the intellectual texture of a period, because it is introduced rather inappropriately in *Guy Mannering*, which is set in the reigns of George II and III, and it is omitted from *Count Robert of Paris*, in which the belief would have characterised the times accurately. When Scott has Colonel Mannering, an honest amateur who has little faith in his own hobby, make two valid predictions, he does so for a narrative end, to create suspense through a horoscopic forecast of plot-development. Elsewhere, he treats astrology as a grandiose, chiefly aristocratic illusion which reveals men's natures. Although much attention is paid to the splendid dupe—Leicester, Louis XI, or Saladin—the interest is mainly centred on the starry adept. This magnificent scamp may be part cheat and part devotee, complete impostor, or sincere victim of his own pretensions, but, whatever his motivation, he is complex, startling, theatrically satisfying.

[8] Saladin's inconsistency should be noted. His talisman, "composed under certain aspects of the heavens, when the Divine Intelligences are most propitious," cures only when water in which it is dipped is given to the patient at "the fitting hour."

[9] Anna Comnena, *The Alexiad*, tr. Elizabeth A. S. Dawes, London 1928, pp. 148–50 (VI. vii).

5. German Diablerie

Scott gains confidence on removing astrology from Scotland and from modern times. With German *diablerie* the case is different. He feels over-confident on Scottish soil and in the fairly recent past.

When demonology, magic, impudence, and imposture are mixed in different proportions in a Waverley novel and superadded to the character of an expatriate German, the result is German *diablerie*. Melodramatic jargon is part of the formula. The concoction is tried out in *Guy Mannering*, with Captain Dirk Hatteraick[1] bellowing such phrases as "Es spuckt da!" and "Strafe mich helle!" In a brief scene, the skipper slurs Meg Merrilies' connexions, calling the gypsy "tousand deyvils" and "Mother Deyvilson." Although "it shall never be said that Dirk Hatteraick feared either dog or devil," the kidnapper of Harry Bertram is himself associated with the Devil by other characters. Thus the Laird of Ellangowan splits his personality into "half Manx, half Dutchman, half devil!" The effect of all this bluster is to give a diabolical colouring to the naturally evil character of a piratical smuggler who is hard-favoured, gross, and superstitious. The pigment may be heavy, but the canvas can hold it.

Many years before writing *The Antiquary*, Scott undoubtedly became acquainted with the legend-encrusted career of Rudolf Eric Raspe, a "starving German literatus, whose name I have forgot."[2] By birth a Hanoverian, Raspe stole precious coins from the cabinets of his employer, the Landgrave of Hesse, was arrested, and escaped to England, where he worked in a German coffee-house, translated, became assay-master and store-keeper of Cornish mines, and compiled his celebrated Munchausen chapbook. In Scotland, he was employed to make a mineralogical survey of the Highlands. His eagerness to discover hidden wealth and bestow illusory prosperity is reminiscent of Sir Robert Sibbald's determination "to find out ye Bed or Vein of Gold in Scotland. And this opinion I hold to be good: for I ever will be of ye same mind, that there is both a Bed & Vein of Gold in Scotland."[3]

Among the many proprietors who listened greedily to Raspe's Midas words was pompous, bustling, benevolent, project-crammed Sir John

---

[1] The skipper bears the homonym of "an old wizard, whose real name was Alexander Hunter [Hamilton], though he was more generally known by the nickname of Hatteraick, which it had pleased the devil to confer upon him," whom Scott knew through Sinclair. See *Demonology*, pp. 300–03; Robert Chambers, *Domestic Annals of Scotland*, Edinburgh 1858, II. 32–3; and Lang's note on Hatteraick. The nickname seems to combine *hatter*, bruise with blows, with *ache*, make to ache.

[2] 26 Nov. 1812 in *Letters*, III. 198.   [3] Sibbald's Ms. Collections, N.L.S., p. 37.

Sinclair. In the latter part of 1789, the "ingenious traveller" located lead on Sir John's Hill of Skinnet in Caithness. At this point tradition begins to take over. It makes Sinclair the German adventurer's chief dupe, exposes the trick as the planting of Cornish ores in Caledonian earth, and climaxes the whole with the unmasking of the cheat.[4] It is to this incident that Scott probably refers in the Advertisement to the first edition of *The Antiquary*: "The knavery of the Adept . . . is founded on a fact of actual occurrence."

The bare outline of Dousterswivel's activity will suggest how close his Scottish career is to Raspe's—that is, when it is stripped of the excrescence of German *diablerie*. A native of Westphalia, this "tall, beetle-browed, awkward-built man" dangles prospects of caverned wealth before the eyes of Sir Arthur Wardour, who guarantees the money advanced by an English company for mining copper at the Glen-Withershins works.[5] For two years Dousterswivel alternately tricks and bleeds Sir Arthur, even going so far as to bury a small horn of "Scotch, English, and foreign coins, of the fifteenth and sixteenth centuries," in order to excavate it, after magical preliminaries, for his patron's encouragement. When the inevitable exposure comes, Dousterswivel leaves the country.

The transformation of the clever, shifty, scientific adventurer, Rudolf Eric Raspe, into the stupid swindler and devotee of magic, Herman Dousterswivel, is not unaccountable. Scott's stereotypic association of the Teuton with ill-assorted *diablerie* goes back to his early absorption in Gothic tales and Bürger ballads. He stuffs his mongrel with gobbets cut from demonological treatises, the jargon of charlatanry being supplied by Reginald Scot's *Discoverie of Witchcraft*, from ghost-books, astrology, and unnatural natural history. This curious balderdash crosses cultural and temporal lines to include sympathies and antipathies, *magia naturalis*, the cabala, the *magisterium*, Rosicrucian mysteries, the divining rod, the glory hand, the *arcanum*, the Mighty Hunter of the North, sigils, and planetary influence.

Within this range of outlandish superstition, the most striking incident is the midnight treasure-hunt of Dousterswivel and Sir Arthur Wardour.

---

[4] *The Book of Days*, ed. Robert Chambers, II. 85–6. See C. O. Parsons, "Sir John Sinclair's Raspe and Scott's Dousterswivel," *N. & Q.*, CLXXXIV (1943), 63–6; John Carswell, *The Prospector*, London 1950, pp. 227–9, 260.

[5] Here as elsewhere, Scott's names are often self-interpreting. *Withershins*, direction contrary to the course of the sun, suggests bad luck. In *Guy Mannering*, Vanbeest Brown and Dandie Dinmont cautiously make their way across a treacherous swamp called Withershins' Latch. A *douster* is a user of the divining rod. See C. O. Parsons, "Character names in the Waverley Novels," *P.M.L.A.*, XLIX (1934), 284. Llwyvein remarks that "Dousterswivel sounds very much like deuced swindler." "The Subtleties of Scott's Names," *The Knickerbocker*, XLVIII (1856), 114.

In the ruins of St Ruth's priory, the digging is advanced by a "simple suffumigation" and "the suitable planetary hour"—all by the light of the last full moon. Lovel and Edie Ochiltree are a concealed audience whose coughing and sneezing break up the unusual performance.

The details of a search interrupted by some elemental, animal, or human disturbance and usually accompanied by magical incantations were already familiar to Scott. Perhaps his favourite passage in William Lilly's *Life* was the one in which James I's clockmaker, Davy Ramsey, John Scott, and the astrologer sought wealth in the cloisters of Westminster Abbey, using the hazel rod for detection. At a depth of six feet their labourers struck a heavy coffin which they neglected to open. A tremendous wind sprang up, extinguished their torches, and made the rods ineffectual. Then, despite Lilly's dismissal of the blustering demons, his party was forced to abandon its project about midnight, having been laughed at and derided by thirty spectators.[6]

Another such hunt figures among the earliest hoaxes in the dazzling career of Count Cagliostro, occultist and adventurer, who is characterised by Jonathan Oldbuck as a modern pretender "to the mystery of raising spirits, discovering hidden treasure, and so forth." Young Cagliostro is reported to have cullied Marano, a Sicilian goldsmith, into believing that he had an immense hoard concealed in a grotto and thus to have won more than sixty pieces of gold for use in magical preliminaries. When the time came to dig, Marano set to with a will, only to be rewarded with a merciless beating by Cagliostro's confederates in the guise of infernal spirits. On Marano's discovering the fraud, Cagliostro fled.[7]

Still another search for treasure-trove is that described by Charles Kerr in a letter to Scott of 21 May 1790, which Wilfred Partington considers direct source material for *The Antiquary*: "Peel Castle [Isle of Man] has the greatest remains of antiquity of any place here: 'twas the ancient Cathedral. A story had circulated here that the church plate was concealed

---

[6] The anecdote occurs in *The Lives of those eminent Antiquaries Elias Ashmole, Esquire, and Mr. William Lilly*, London 1774, pp. 47–8, and it is quoted by Scott in "Some Traditionall Memorialls on the Raigne of King James the First," *Secret History of the Court of James the First*, Edinburgh 1811, I. 264–6, and in the note on David Ramsay in *The Fortunes of Nigel*. In his copy of William Ramesey, *Vox Stellarum. Or, The Voice of the Starres*, London 1652, Scott wrote a summary of the story, adding, "Poor D. Ramsey who had brought a huge sack to carry off the treasure was obliged to return *re infecta*." See *Funk & Wagnalls Standard Dictionary of Folklore, s.v.* fairy wind: "People seeking to dig up fairy treasure are often stopped by a terrific gale of wind." Scott also knew of John Napier's agreement to hunt for hidden riches in Fast Castle. See his letter to [James Skene], Easter Monday, 1830, in the latter's *Memories*, p. 170, and Andrew Lang, n. 34 on *The Antiquary*.

[7] *The Life of Joseph Balsamo, commonly called Count Cagliostro*, London 1791, p. 5. See also "Count Cagliostro," *The Works of Thomas Carlyle*, XXVIII, 268–9.

in a vault of the castle. The Bishop gave liberty to a friend of mine to inspect it. He employed two men to dig into the vault; and they had got about 21 feet deep when a gentleman here, knowing what they were about, who had hidden himself under ground, bellowed in a most fearful tone at a time they were surrounded with skulls, etc; and frightened the poor devils to such a degree that nobody in the Island will attempt to disturb these secret repositories again."[8] Dousterswivel, too, has searched for "de great huge pieces of de plate so massive . . . and de silver cross," in Westphalia. His Scottish performance seems to be taken from William Lilly and Charles Kerr, with a possible hint or two from Cagliostro's escapade.[9]

When he resorts to German *diablerie*, Scott is unconvincingly eclectic. Given his conception of Dousterswivel, the problem is basically one of reconciling oral lore about a mining cheat with bookish lore about a parasitical magician. Scott fails to restrict his character to such superstitions as are peculiar to miners or native to Germany. His practice in the Waverley Novels is to supply his characters with action invented out of whole cloth or pieced together from antiquarian gleanings, wide-ranging reading, imagination, and observation or experience. Dousterswivel is furnished a hotch-potch of acts and information from oral tradition about Raspe and Sinclair, esoteric books, and imagination, but there is no real involvement of author to keep the balance true. On the whole, if the engrafting of German *diablerie* on the distinctly Scottish tale of *The Antiquary* seems awkward and inappropriate, it is representative of the discordant and infelicitous, though spasmodic, influence of German literature on Scott's art.

6. Local Legends

Abbotsford is a tribute to Sir Walter's skill in unifying local lore and supplying its deficiencies. The land itself, known as "Clarty [dirty] Hole"

[8] Partington, *Post-Bag*, p. 321. Cp. throughout "the easily authenticated history of Benedict Mol, the treasure-digger of Saint James," in Borrow, *The Bible in Spain* (1843), chs. 13, 27, 33, 41–2; Herbert Jenkins, *The Life of George Borrow*, New York 1924, p. 353.

[9] John Robert Moore suggests the influence of Daniel Defoe's story of a peddler's digging for silver under apparition guidance. "Scott's *Antiquary* and Defoe's *History of Apparitions*," *Modern Language Notes*, LIX (1944), 550–1. See also *Narratives of the Days of the Reformation*, ed. J. G. Nichols, Camden Society, LXXVII (1859), 333: William Wicherley confessed on 23 Aug. 1549, that he and a confederate "digged for treasure and found none. But as they were working in the feat, ther came by them alongst the highway a black blynde horse, and made this deponent and other with hym to ronne their wayes, for it was in the nighte." Cp. G. L. Kittredge, *Witchcraft in Old and New England*, Harvard Univ. Pr. 1929, pp. 158, 212.

in franker days, could offer scant inducement to buy, for it was undrained, infertile, and expensive; in fact, it had lost "almost all natural pith, and was reduced to what in Scripture is termed a field of stones."[1] Scott himself speaks of it as altogether unpromising before his improvements began to take effect and admits that people abused him "for buying the ugliest place on Tweedside."[2] But the Eildon Hills were the focal point of Border tradition, and it was inevitable that Scott, the enthusiastic student of local history and antiquities, should take root between the Eildons and the storied Tweed.

Almost every guest at Abbotsford was shown Huntly Bank and the Rhymer's Glen, where True Thomas met the Fairy Queen, as well as the Bogle Burn, beside which she rode. In 1817, Washington Irving was given a tour of these haunts and was regaled with verses on the marvellous visit to fairyland.[3] Scott also took his American visitor for a row on Cauldshiels Loch, the land adjacent to which had been purchased in July 1813. The loch was notable for "a bogle in the shape of a water bull, which lived in the deep parts, and now and then came forth upon dry land and made a tremendous roaring, that shook the very hills." The Laird of Abbotsford did not choose to contradict the tale that a man still living had seen the bull; such fables were a part of the soil and, besides, he fancied amphibious hobgoblins.[4] Irving is rather vague about being taken to the top of hills which afforded a spacious prospect. These were undoubtedly the Eildons, from which Scott later told Tom Moore he could point out thirty places famous in Scottish song.[5] Among the thirty was Smailholme Tower, known to Scott as a boy, which reportedly housed a human skull that would, if carried away, return straight to its repository.[6] In descending the Eildons, Scott may have reminded tourists of the famous witch-meetings at the neighbouring windmill of Kippilaw.

Captain Basil Hall records in his Journal of 30 December 1824 an

[1] "October 6, 1832. Supplement. Life of Sir Walter Scott," *Chambers' Edinburgh Journal*, 1 (1833), 8 n. The name "Cartley Hold" (*hold*, either a fort or a holding) is used in W. C. Fraser, "Oral Traditions about Sir Walter Scott," *Transactions* of the Hawick Archaeological Society (1932), p. 30.

[2] *Letters*, III. 158–9, 400.

[3] Irving, *Abbotsford and Newstead Abbey* [=Irving, *Abbotsford*], Philadelphia 1835, pp. 54–5; see also pp. 69, 77. Irving was at Abbotsford from 30 Aug. to 3 Sep. 1817.

[4] *Op. cit.*, pp. 80–1; see also Lockhart, III. 63–4, 402–03. The King's-Moorloch in Selkirkshire, source of the Ale, was the abode of a better known water cow. Alexander Jeffrey, *The History and Antiquities of Roxburghshire and Adjacent Districts*, 2nd edn, Edinburgh 1855–64. I. 58. Cp. *Letters*, II. 318; *Journal*, pp. 435–6; James Hogg, *The Mountain Bard*, Edinburgh 1807, pp. 94–5; John Leyden, *Journal of a Tour in the Highlands and Western Islands of Scotland in 1800*, ed. James Sinton, Edinburgh and London 1903, p. 13.

[5] Moore, *Memoirs*, IV. 336–7.

[6] Scott, *The Border Antiquities of England and Scotland*, London 1814–17, II. 151.

excursion to the Rhymer's Glen, into which Scott would not let his holiday party descend until he had related the full romantic story, "so that . . . our imaginations were so worked upon by the wild nature of the fiction, and still more by the animation of the narrator, that we felt ourselves treading upon classical ground; and though the day was cold . . . I do not remember ever to have seen any place so interesting as the skill of this mighty magician had rendered this narrow ravine, which in any other company would have seemed quite insignificant."[7] That evening Scott read his guests the poem on Thomas of Ercildoune's fairy adventure. It was probably with the object of delighting such parties that he saw to the construction of steps to the Rhymer's Waterfall, a dam, and a footpath in 1818.[8]

The identification of Dick's Cleugh—or Rhymer's Glen, as Scott preferred to call it—with the scene of True Thomas's encounter with the Queen of Elfland is entirely factitious. The Eildon Tree, or rather Eildon Stone, traditionally supposed to mark its site, is on the declivity of the easternmost Eildon Hill near the Bogle Burn, between two and three miles from the literary laird's ravine, which lies at the base of the western Eildon. The location of the real Huntly Bank differs from that proposed by Scott in being within sight of the Eildon Tree and in having an extended view.[9] That Scott consciously effected this transfer of a legendary site to his own property need not be doubted.[10] No task could be simpler for the recorder, adapter, and creator of Border lore. In the absence of the colourful legends which give personality to place, Scott invented or transplanted traditions so that an interesting scene might not lack storied significance. J. B. S. Morritt's Memorandum of Scott's visit to Rokeby in 1812 suggests this eagerness to capture or to manufacture the folk *genius loci*:

> From his boyish habits, he was but half satisfied with the most beautiful scenery when he could not connect with it some local legend, and when I

[7] Lockhart, v. 376. Scott writes Daniel Terry on 25 Dec. 1816, that he has acquired "a quiet invisible sort of a dell where a witch might boil her kettle in happy seclusion among old thorn trees & scathed oaks in a deep ravine." *Letters*, IV. 328. Visits to the dell are recorded in J. G. Lockhart, *Peter's Letters to his Kinsfolk* (1819), LII: Mrs Mary Ann Hughes, *Letters and Recollections of Sir Walter Scott*, ed. H. G. Hutchinson [=Mrs Hughes], London 1904, pp. 69, 209, 270; Moore, *Memoirs*, IV. 340; Charles R. Leslie, *Autobiographical Recollections*, ed. Tom Taylor, Boston 1860, pp. 60, 256; R. F. Butler, "Maria Edgeworth and Sir Walter Scott," *Review of English Studies*, New Series, IX (1958), 25, 39.

[8] Lockhart, IV. 184. The cascade had to be repaired nine years later. *Journal*, pp. 381, 418.

[9] Robert Chambers, *Popular Rhymes of Scotland*, new edn, London and Edinburgh, 1870, p. 213; *The Romance and Prophecies of Thomas of Erceldoune*, ed. J. A. H. Murray, London 1875, E.E.T.S., LXI. li–lii.

[10] *Letters*, VII. 275, contains frank comment by the Laird on the two sites. Cp. John Smith, "The Geology and Romance of the Rhymer's Glen," *Transactions* of the Hawick Archaeological Society (1931), pp. 36–9.

was forced sometimes to confess, with the Knife-grinder, 'Story! God
bless you! I have none to tell, sir'—he would laugh, and say, 'then let us
make one—nothing so easy as to make a tradition.'[11]

In his combination of fervour and sly humour, Scott reflects the
imagination and native common sense of his fellow Borderers. The rich
legends which made every feature of their beloved hills and valleys glow
with meaning, the supernatural tales which set their nerves tingling with
sympathetic horror—these were too dear to their hearts to be torn out by
destructive reason.

★　　★　　★

Unlike German *diablerie*, that unassimilated refugee in the Waverley
Novels, local legendry is perfectly at home. Although many of the folk
beliefs of the Border appear in *The Black Dwarf*, their charm has been
veiled by the unpopularity of the narrative. The action itself, projected
against a background of countryside lore, is happily introduced by just
such a legend as the common people preserved for generations to explain
peculiar rock formations or otherwise unaccountable groupings of
druidical stones. Hobbie Elliot fearfully approaches a knoll near the
centre of Mucklestane-Moor, where a huge column of unhewn granite is
encircled by lumps. According to tradition, the main shaft was once a
witch whose deadly malice caused "the ewes to *keb*, and the kine to cast
their calves," and it was on this very heath that she revelled with "sister
hags" and "diabolical partners." Crossing the moor one day with a flock
of geese which she intended to sell at a neighbouring fair, the witch,
enraged at the birds for scattering, blurted out, "Deevil, that neither I nor
they ever stir from this spot more!" An attendant fiend promptly
metamorphosed the hag and her refractory poultry into the Grey Geese
of Mucklestane-Moor. And thereafter the moor was haunted by kelpies,
spunkies, and demons, the former fellowship of the witch's orgies.

In a letter of 31 July 1829, Scott assures James Skene that the setting of

---

[11] Lockhart, III. 16. Morritt quotes George Canning's *Anti-Jacobin* parody of Southey, "The
Friend of Humanity and the Knife-Grinder" (1797). Scott, *Rokeby*, I. xx; II. x; IV. ii, contains examples of the adjustment of legend to *locale*. For remarks on Scott as a legend-maker,
see R. L. Stevenson, *Edinburgh Picturesque Notes*, new edn, London 1889, pp. 59–60, and
Life, Letters, and Journals of George Ticknor, Boston and New York 1909, I. 283. There is a
thoroughly retouched portrait of the Laird of Abbotsford in "Bracebridge Hall," *The Works
of Washington Irving*, new edn, New York 1854, VI. 357: "I have mentioned the Squire's
fondness for the marvellous, and his predilection for legends and romances. . . . In his love
for all that is antiquated, he cherishes popular superstitions, and listens, with very grave
attention, to every tale, however strange; so that, through his countenance, the household,
and, indeed, the whole neighborhood, is well stocked with wonderful stories."

the legend is his own creation: "Of the places in the *Black Dwarf*, Meikle-stane Moor, Ellisla[w], Earnscliff are all and each *vox et praeterea nihil.*"[12] (Skene was the artist of a *Series of Sketches of the existing Localities alluded to in the Waverley Novels*, issued in twenty numbers during 1828-9.) But the legend itself owes much to a humorous ballad called "The Grey Geese of Addlestrop Hill." Setting out one ominous Friday morning with her twenty grey geese, Dame Alice tripped, tore her kirtle, and heard a raven croak. "And thrice by the way went the gander astray | Ere she reach'd the foot of the hill." A wild, tattered, pale-eyed hag wanted a goose but was denied; whereupon, she cursed amid storm effects. When Alice awoke from a trance, she found that her geese had been transformed into grey stones. In fulfilment of an old prophecy, these Gloucestershire stones were later used by Warren Hastings, "a sage . . . from the East country," in improvements on his estate.[13] Scott's Elshender the Recluse also breaks up a petrified flock.

In borrowing an English ballad story, the novelist strips it of minimising humour, sets it in Scotland, and is sensitively responsive to popular beliefs. Thus he restores to it the naïve folk character of many a stone legend, both of Scotland and England.[14]

Scenes brooded over by deeds or haunted by mortals who have sinned, blasphemed, or suffered in the past invite more turmoil and strange beings. The weird repute of Mucklestane-Moor serves the narrative purpose of preparing for the *bogilly* introduction of Cannie Elshie, with whose original Scott early became acquainted. About 16 October 1796, he visited Dr Adam Ferguson, whose eldest son conducted the imaginative guest to the cottage of David Ritchie, a local eccentric:

> The dwarf passed to the door, double-locked it, and then, coming up to the stranger, seized him by the wrist with one of his iron hands, and said, "Man, ha'e ye ony poo'er?" By this he meant magical power, to which he had himself some vague pretensions, or which, at least, he had studied and

[12] *Letters*, XI. 223.

[13] *G.M.*, LXXVIII (1808), 341-3. The ballad was pointed out as a source in *The Book of Days*, ed. Robert Chambers, II. 245-7.

[14] J. B. S. Morritt writes Scott about the three Devil's Arrows and the Yorkshire witch who supplied the bowstring. Walpole (5 Jun. 1809). Other legends explain stone groups as the awful memorials of human wickedness, Sabbath-breaking, or too close contact with the Prince of Darkness: four clusters of druidical stones being a Somersetshire bridal party which danced to the devil's piping; the Eleven Shearers, Roxburghshire reapers of corn on Sunday; and three grey stones, an Aberdeenshire girl (for a time betrothed to the Devil), her baking *girdle* and *spartle*. *Choice Notes from "Notes and Queries." Folk Lore*, London 1859, pp. 182-3; Jeffrey, *History of Roxburghshire*, I. 177-8; III. 315; *Ancient Scottish Ballads*, ed. George R. Kinloch, London 1827, pp. 150-2. Cp. W. Fordyce Clark, *The Shetland Sketch Book*, Edinburgh 1930, pp. 64-5; Lowry C. Wimberly, *Folklore in the English and Scottish Ballads*, New York 1959, pp. 35-7.

reflected upon till it had become with him a kind of monomania. Mr Scott disavowed the possession of any gifts of that kind, evidently to the great disappointment of the inquirer, who then turned round and gave a signal to a huge black cat, hitherto unobserved, which immediately jumped up to a shelf, where it perched itself, and seemed to the excited senses of the visitors as if it had really been the familiar spirit of the mansion. "*He has poo'er,*" said the dwarf, in a voice which made the flesh of the hearers thrill within them, and Mr Scott, in particular, looked as if he conceived himself to have actually got into the den of one of those magicians with whom his studies had rendered him familiar.... When they had got out, Mr Ferguson observed, that his friend was as pale as ashes, while his person was agitated in every limb.[15]

This incident rests on the authority of Sir Adam Ferguson, Scott's lifelong friend and a famous anecdotist. The appearance of *The Black Dwarf* (1816) and of the Introduction (1830) in the Magnum Opus inspired a flood of inquirers who added so many true and fictitious details about the life of David Ritchie that Scott himself may have faltered in distinguishing nicely between knowledge of Bowed Davie gained before and after writing his novel. Scott seems not to have been acquainted with *An Elegy on David Ritchie* (1812) or the privately-printed *Short Account of David Ritchie* (July 1816), either of which would have nipped Scott and Erskine's curious reference to Bowed Davie as "perhaps still living."[16]

Among the antiquarian investigations of the Peeblesshired warf with which the novelist and his readers were regaled are John Anderson's identification of the original in *Blackwood's Edinburgh Magazine* for June 1817, the account in the *Edinburgh Magazine* for October 1817, William Chambers' *Life and Anecdotes of the Black Dwarf* (1820), and the second edition of Robert Chambers' *Illustrations of the Author of Waverley* (1825). After such a spate of biographical material, it is amusing to find Joseph J. Archibald writing to Scott from Greenock on 10 March 1831: "I have lately become acquainted with a very intelligent old man who informs me that he has often aided the Black Dwarf.... But ... he is possessed of such a degree of effrontery as to declare that all the publications connected with honest David are very incorrect. Have you ever seen our prodigy's life written by an old shepherd of the name of Tweedie?"[17] Scott's reply of 16 March reduces his source material to a simple, yet sufficient,

---

[15] William Chambers, *Chambers' Edinburgh Journal*, II (1834), 99. Cp. Scott's remark to Washington Irving: "These cats are a very mysterious kind of folk. There is always more passing in their minds than we are aware of. It comes no doubt from their being so familiar with witches and worlocks." Irving, *Abbotsford*, pp. 37-8.

[16] Anonymous critical article in Q.R., XVI (Jan. 1817), 443.   [17] Walpole.

minimum: Professor Ferguson and his family supplied information about the three-and-a-half-foot misanthrope, and "I saw him myself."[18]

All accounts of Bowed Davie agree in making him a humanity-hater who was easy to take offence, superstitious (he used charms against witchcraft), and proud of his uncanny reputation among the common folk. These are the ingredients which Scott uses in the person of the Black Dwarf, spiteful moroseness and the creation of fear as a protection against the curious and as a source of prestige.

In a somewhat cruder form, the elements of this characterisation are to be found in the Northumbrian Brown Man of the Muirs, about whose ugly, stumpy, supernatural, and malevolent self Robert Surtees has much to record (or to invent) in a letter of 9 November 1809. Scott's enthusiasm is strong, "Your 'Brown Man of the Muirs' is a noble fellow."[19] While Scott's Elshender is still living on Mucklestane-Moor, Hobbie Elliot's grandam thinks him none other than the Brown Man. After the dwarf's disappearance, most of the countryfolk are convinced of his renewal as the malignant Man of the Moors, who makes their ewes *keb* and loosens wreaths of snow on poor wayfarers. With few exceptions, however, Scott does not achieve a composite of Elshender's two originals; the folklore alloy tends to break up into its component parts.

In the characterisation of Elshender the Recluse, Scott works on two planes: (1) folk response to a spitefully brooding dwarf with mysterious antecedents and apparently supernatural power, and (2) psychological probing into the physical and social causes of misanthropy. These approaches parallel different attitudes toward the original, David Ritchie—those of the dwarf's working-class neighbours and of the Fergusons, to whom motivation would be more interesting than superficial appearances. In the novel, the folk response varies. Hobbie Elliot mistakes the homunculus for a witch, a ghost, a Pict, a bogle, and the Devil. As the rustics become more used to the prodigious labours on the solitary hut, they cease to regard Elshender as a phantom but still cling to the idea that, through diabolical contacts, he has a familiar as an assistant. Nor does Canny Elshie discredit these rumours, which rise like incense to his ego; in fact, he strengthens them by his strange habits, sullenness, worldly knowledge, and medical skill. Popular apprehension is quickened when the Wise Wight of Mucklestane-Moor disappears. Some say that he has been carried off by the Evil One for entering a consecrated building.

In the elaboration of his plot, Scott leaves the figure of David Ritchie

[18] *Letters*, XI. 487.

[19] Surtees, *The History and Antiquities of the County Palatine of Durham*, London, 1816-40, I. 41; *Letters*, II. 299. Cp. *The Black Dwarf*, ch. i, n.

more and more in the background as he leads up to the revelation that
Elshender the Recluse is actually Sir Edward Mauley, who has been
driven into seclusion by deformity and an unfaithful betrothed. Scott's
analysis of Sir Edward's misanthropy is sound enough in its general outlines, but it is at times external, melodramatic, and artificial.

The failure of *The Black Dwarf* is due to the unachieved transformation
of plebeian David Ritchie into an aristocratic dwarf and from the lack of
variety in the morose subject. A few chiaroscuro effects are added to the
sombre portrait by the introduction of Border scenes and folk beliefs.
Fairy lore, legends, and superstitions yield a certain artistic symmetry
through being grouped round the figure of Canny Elshie, whose appearance and disappearance are accompanied by eerie tales. But even
though folklore and legendry serve as vivid, yet partial and unevenly
distributed, relief, the Black Dwarf remains—like Nectabanus and his
diminutive mate in *The Talisman* and Sir Geoffrey Hudson in *Peveril of the
Peak*—a grotesque.[20]

Scott creates a foreboding gloom in *The Bride of Lammermoor* by
introducing witches, prophecies, omens, and a fountain legend. The last
traces back to a Lord of Ravenswood who, every Friday at sunset, met and
wooed an enchanting damsel near the Mermaiden's Well. Father Zachary
urged that the strange being departed at the sound of the vesper bell in
order to return to her proper hellish abode and that, if the ringing of the
bell were delayed half an hour, the false naiad would turn into a fiend and
vanish amid sulphurous fumes. When the lady knew that she had been
tricked, she despairingly bade her lover farewell and sank into the fountain,
leaving its waters troubled and bloody.[21]

"From this period the house of Ravenswood was supposed to have
dated its decay. . . . All . . . agreed, that the spot was fatal to the Ravenswood family; and that to drink of the waters of the well, or even approach
its brink, was . . . ominous to a descendant of that house." It is to this
fountain that Edgar carries Lucy after rescuing her from the wild bull,
and with its water he recalls her to consciousness. After the ill-starred pair
break a piece of gold and plight their troth by the Mermaiden's Well,
they are startled by the whizz of an arrow. A raven transfixed falls to the

[20] A fuller discussion may be found in C. O. Parsons, "The Orginal of the Black Dwarf,"
Studies in Philology, XL (1943), 567-75.
[21] This legend somewhat resembles stories told of the German nixies. See "Popular
Mythology of the Middle Ages," *Q.R.* XXII (1820), 361 n., and the brothers Grimm,
Deutsche Sagen, Berlin 1911, I. 57-72. Scott enlightens Washington Irving on the subject:
"Our streams and lochs are like the rivers and pools in Germany, that have all their Wasser
Nixe, or water witches." Irving, *Abbotsford*, pp. 80-1.

ground at Lucy's feet, staining her dress with blood.[22] Whatever land it visits, the raven presages anguish and death.[23] At the moment of her death, old Alice appears to Edgar at the Mermaiden's Well.

Although it belongs to the large body of tales in many countries about the destructive malice of sea and fountain women,[24] the legend of the Mermaiden's Well is genuinely Scottish. In atmosphere it is similar to the story of the Maiden Well near the Ochil Hills, supposed haunt of fairies and of a treacherous water sprite. "When invoked a thin mist arose over the well disclosing a lady of most ravishing beauty. The result, however, was always fatal to the would-be wooer, for he was invariably found dead next day by the well side."[25] Scott does not keep such interesting and dangerous company without suggesting a realistic explanation: Raymond Ravenswood had jealously slain a beautiful, but lowly, maiden, whose blood dropped into the water of the well.[26] Whether it is the fateful *locale* of guilt or heedlessness, the Mermaiden's Well ties the doomed and decaying line of Ravenswood to a tragic moment in a past from which it cannot break free.

Reversing his treatment of place lore, Scott does not in *Kenilworth* present a tale long current in the countryside. Instead, he adapts and invents circumstances which give rise to a local legend. Deserted by his master, Dr Demetrius Doboobie, a servant avoids those people who "confound learned skill with unlawful magic," assumes the name of Wayland Smith, and reappears as a mysterious farrier who lurks underground, at the sign of the stone ring, on "a bare moor." A traveller must tie his horse to an upright stone, whistle thrice, place a silver groat on a flat stone, and retire until the unseen workman's hammer stops clinking. Even after Flibbertigibbet has blown up the forge, fables spring up so eagerly that "the wild legend of Wayland Smith" persists in the Vale of Whitehorse to this day and the farrier himself predicts that his fame will haunt the site "long after *his* body is rotten."

Taking "the liberty to pillage the stores of oral tradition," as well as Camden's *Britannia*, Scott goes back beyond Elizabethan times to a

[22] Cp. the far less effective use of colour symbolism in William Meinhold, *Sidonia the Sorceress*, tr. Lady Wilde, London 1894, II. 47: Bishop Francis "broke a bottle filled with red ink which stood thereon, and the said ink (alas! what an evil omen) poured down upon Duke Philip's white silk stockings, and stained them red like blood."

[23] See Dalyell, *Darker Superstitions of Scotland*, pp. 414–16.

[24] See, for instance, *P. Gasparis Schotti . . . Physica Curiosa, sive Mirabilia Naturae et Artis*, Würzburg 1667, I. 362.

[25] Alexander Fraser, *Northern Folk-Lore on Wells and Water*, Inverness 1878, p. 31.

[26] Cp. *Memoirs of Lady Fanshawe*, London 1829, pp. 85–6; Elliot O'Donnell, *The Banshee*, London and Edinburgh, [1920], pp. 36–7.

H

vestigial belief in a Teutonic Vulcan, Wayland Smith, who was supposed to live invisible in a stone barrow on the chalk hills north of Lambourn, Berkshire. If horsemen withdrew from sight, this Wayland would shoe their mounts for money.[27] By postdating the origin of "an idle tradition," the novelist shows how it might arise.

In the opening chapter of *Anne of Geierstein,* the guide Antonio relates the legend of Mount Pilatus. Pontius Pilate lived for many years on the wild mountain before plunging into the lake at its summit. Ever since that day the undrowned body or the spirit of the proconsul has haunted the Infernal Lake washing its hands and portending tempest by means of dark clouds. Although the Philipsons are "too good Catholics to . . . doubt . . . the story," young Arthur is audacious enough to cry out a challenge, "*Vade retro*! Be thou defied, sinner!"[28] With fearful howling and groaning, the inevitable storm descends on the noble merchants, separating them and almost killing the younger. An ominous legend has helped to represent the peril in elemental forces.

Scott's attitude toward Catholicism is brought out more clearly in another episode, in which the treacherous Brother Bartholomew is allowed to pad the narrative with a Virgin Mary legend. In the likeness of a sacred image which he had refused to ferry across the Rhine one stormy day, Our Lady appeared to repentant Hans and said that, her chapel in Kirch-hoff having been destroyed, she would stay with him. Then Hans converted his hut into a chapel and himself into a chaplain. "The figure was supposed to work miracles." Since these words are a paraphrase of Brother Bartholomew's, the Protestant author's refusal to concede too much may be amusing, but it is not realistic. Scott respects the antiquity of Catholicism but not its fables, which are hesitantly used as incidental ornaments.

Supernatural local legends in the Waverley Novels range from indigenous effectiveness in *The Black Dwarf* to anachronism and superficiality when Scott departs from the land and lore he knows intimately. In *The Bride of Lammermoor,* the traditional tale is melodramatic but its

[27] John Timbs, *Ancestral Stories and Traditions of Great Families,* London 1869, pp. 320–1. Mrs Hughes writes [Scott] on 19 Feb. 1821, "The village children religiously believe the old legend of the visionary Smith; and often visit the spot to hear the clink of his hammer." Partington, *Post-Bag,* p. 151. And on 15 Mar., Mrs Hughes has "a little sketch of Wayland Smiths forge," very correctly drawn by her son, for the Great Unknown. Walpole. Scott associates Wayland, as he does other strange beings, with the northern duergar.

[28] For Scott's source, see Louis Simond, *Switzerland,* Boston 1822, 1. 133–4. *Pileatus,* cloud covered as with a felt-cap, may have been corrupted into *Pilatus.* A less ornamented version, taken from Felix Hemmerlin of Zurich, is given in G. G. Coulton, *The Medieval Village,* Cambridge Univ. Pr. 1925, pp. 271–2. Cp. *The Poetical Works of Dr. John Leydon,* London and Edinburgh, 1875, pp. 11–12, 283–4.

ominous application is powerful. Such stories represent a variety of haunting in which the interest is focused on the event as much as, or even more
than, on a lingering ghost or an impression of place. The difficulty of
combining legend, *locale*, and attached human or divine spirit seems to
have been too great for Scott's hasty methods of composition. The
narrative stands out at first, although it may fade from memory as other
qualities of place are emphasised. This is true of the Scottish novels. In
the brief use of the Wayland Smith legend by tricksters or in *Anne of
Geierstein*, local tales are connected with scenes transiently visited. They
have a guide-book brilliance, the tone of an official conferring of romantic
interest on chosen places.

7. Ghosts*

Through the riches of folk and family lore, local legends supply a link to
a past which haunts and impinges on the present in many ways. Much
more comprehensively, the genealogist, the historian, the antiquary, the
historical novelist, and the ghost-seer quicken the feeling of oneness with
the lineal and national past. In these capacities Scott displays that "attitude
towards the past unthinkable to Englishmen" which Robert Louis
Stevenson attributes to the Scotsman, who cherishes the memory of good
and bad ancestors and has a burning "sense of identity with the dead even
to the twentieth generation."[1] As somewhat of a lifetime authority on
ghosts, Scott gathered stories, had some experiences of his own, and was
reputed a congenially hair-raising raconteur.

As a collector, he listened sympathetically, became involved through
knowing ghost-seers, then turned rationalist and investigator. As late as
1817, Scott distinctly remembered the commencement of "a most dismal
ghost story" which one servant girl related to another over the embers of
the little master's nursery fire. Walter, then about six, was curious, but he
covered up his head rather than be frightened out of his wits for the rest
of the night.[2] An arresting comment on such early experience is offered
by Robert Jamieson's query in an undated letter [?1807]: "Do you let
him [Scott's elder son Walter, age about six] hear ghost stories? A *boy* of
genius cannot hear too many of them, after a certain age, if they are told

---

* Although R. Th. Christiansen is very persuasive on the "connection" between fairies and
the dead, I shall follow Scott in keeping ghosts and fairies separate. "Scotsmen and Norsemen: Cultural Relations in the North Sea Area," *Scottish Studies*, I (1957), 30–7.

[1] Stevenson, *Weir of Hermiston*, ch. v.   [2] *Letters*, IV. 381–2.

him at first in a proper manner & by a proper person.—But he is much too young for them yet."[3] At the age of seven, the future poet feared that Blind Harry's Spectre of Fawdon would show his headless trunk at one of the windows.[4] And five years later, he gained the Earl of Buchan's praise by reciting poetry with great spirit—"it was the apparition of Hector's ghost in the Æneid."[5]

In his manhood, Scott was deeply impressed by three ghost-stories because of the seers' mad eccentricity or suicide. Tragically central was Viscount Castlereagh (later Marquis of Londonderry), whom Scott associates with another seer, at times unnamed, at others identified as Stanhope and as Lord Erskine.[6] The shadowy Stanhope may be the "late nobleman" about whom Scott has this tale to tell in 1830:

> He had fallen asleep, with some uneasy feelings arising from indigestion. They operated in their usual course of visionary terrors. At length they were all summed up in the apprehension, that the phantom of a dead man held the sleeper by the wrist, and endeavoured to drag him out of bed. He awaked in horror, and still felt the cold dead grasp of a corpse's hand on his right wrist. It was a minute before he discovered that his own left hand was in a state of numbness, and with it he had accidentally encircled his right arm.[7]

[3] Abbotsford Mss., N.L.S. For the harmful effects of tales of horror on children, see *The Edinburgh Review*, XLVII (1828), 129, and the chapbook, *An Account of Some Imaginary Apparitions, the Effects of Fear or Fraud*, Stirling 1801:

> Would you your tender offspring rear,
> With minds well form'd, devoid of fear,
> Ne'er let the nurse with idle tale,
> Of Ghost their infant ears assail;
> Of Bug-a-boo! or Chimney Sweep!
> To terrify them into Sleep.

[4] Lockhart, VII. 214; Henry the Minstrel, *The History of . . . Sir William Wallace*, modernised by William Hamilton, Edinburgh 1812, pp. 50, 57–8. For a somewhat similar Galloway legend, see Partington, *Post-Bag*, pp. 107–09. Also see "The Ghost of Fadon" by Scott's friend, Joanna Baillie.

[5] Lockhart, VII. 190; 25 Apr. 1829 in *Journal*, p. 629. In the Prefatory Letter to *Peveril*, Scott refers to "the effect of the apparition of Hector's phantom on the hero of the Æneid—

> Obstupui, steteruntque comae."

Aeneas is not appalled, nor does his hair stand up nor his voice stick in his throat, when Hector appears to him in sleep blood-soiled and gashed (Virgil, *Aeneid*, II. 268–97). But see II. 774, and III. 48, in which the spectral form and voice are those of Creusa and Polydorus.

[6] Cp. Thomas Moore's diary entry of 24 May 1828: "Told Lady Holland I had inquired of Scott, according to her wish, who was the *second person* he meant when he said he had been assured by two people of their having themselves seen ghosts, and that both of these people afterwards put an end to themselves. This introduced ghost stories." *Memoirs, Journal, and Correspondence of Thomas Moore*, ed. Lord John Russell, 8 vols., London 1853–6, V. 283 (Stanhope).

[7] *Demonology*, p. 45.

In this anecdote, however, the apparition is subordinated to the illusion of touch, which a less reticent Scott could have explained by his own dream that, after her death, "poor Charlotte" lay asleep beside him.[8]

Unlike the suicide, kind, credible, sensible Stanhope, "Tom Erskine was positively mad. I have heard him tell a cock and a bull story of having seen the ghost of his father's servant, John Burnet, with as much sincerity as if he believed every word he was saying."[9] Lady Sydney Owenson Morgan has preserved Lord Erskine's story, as he told it to the Duchess of Gordon on 9 February 1811. On his return to Edinburgh (?1768) after having been away from Scotland for a considerable time, Erskine was approached by the family's old butler, who was "greatly changed, pale, wan, and shadowy, as a ghost." After desiring Master Tom to intercede with his father, the Earl of Buchan, for a sum owed by the steward, he mysteriously disappeared. Upon enquiry, Erskine found that the butler had been dead several months. Deeply affected, he recovered the money and turned it over to the butler's widow.[10] Although in after years Erskine grew "flighty," his death on 17 November 1823, was a perfectly natural one.

Far different was the death, on 12 August 1822, of Lord Castlereagh, who ended his life by severing the carotid artery. While admitting that he never saw the Lord Chancellor in his best days, Scott gropes toward an understanding of his character. Probably "subject to aberrations of mind which often create ... phantoms" (1822), he was a man of "sense and credibility" (1826) who was also "moody and maddish" (1829).[11] Seven years after he heard the story of the Radiant Boy from Castlereagh's lips "at one of his wife's supper parties in Paris in 1815," Sir Walter writes to Lady Abercorn:

> I remember his once telling seriously and with great minuteness the particulars of an apparition which he thought he had seen. It was a naked child, which he saw slip out of the grate of a bedroom while he looked at the decaying fire. It increased at every step it advanced towards him, and again diminished in size till it went into the fireplace and disappeared. I could not tell what to make of so wild a story told by a man whose habits were equally remote from quizzing or from inventing a mere tale of

---

[8] "I believe the phenomena of dreaming are in a great measure occasiond by the *double touch*, which takes place when one hand is crossd in sleep upon another. Each gives and receives the impression of touch to and from the other, and this complicated sensation our sleeping fancy ascribes to the agency of another being, when it is in fact produced by our own limbs acting on each other." 11 Jun. 1826 in *Journal*, p. 184.

[9] 20 Apr. 1829 in *Journal*, p. 627.

[10] Lady Morgan, *The Book of the Boudoir*, New York 1829, I. 87–9. Lord Erskine is described as delightful, paradoxical, frequently incoherent, and even affectedly mad.

[11] 28 Aug. 1822 in *Letters*, VII. 227; 1 Nov. 1826 in *Journal*, p. 263, and 20 Apr. 1829, p. 627.

wonder. The truth is now plain that the vision had been the creation of a temporary access of his constitutional infirmity.[12]

Lockhart, who was often present when his father-in-law repeated the story, recalls some of the "great minuteness": With its frightful increase in stature, the naked child "assumed the appearance of a ghastly giant, pale as death, with a bleeding wound on the brow, and eyes glaring with rage and despair."[13] No wonder that Scott admits to his journal on 1 November 1826, "He is gone. . . . I shall always tremble when any friend of mine becomes visionary."[14] Castlereagh and the fatal sequence of melancholy, ghost-seeing, and suicide had been brought vividly to mind by a visit to Paris.

The sequence was reversed some twenty-seven days later when Scott's nerves were shaken by news of the suicide of Colonel Thomas Huxley, his niece's husband. The man had been quiet, inoffensive, seemingly "free from all those sinkings of the imagination which render those who are liable to them the victims of occasional low spirits." That night Scott was visited: "Awaked from horrid dreams to reconsideration of the sad reality; he was such a kind, obliging, assiduous creature. I thought he came to my bedside to expostulate with me how I could believe such a scandal, and I thought I detected that it was but a spirit who spoke, by the paleness of his look and the blood flowing from his cravat. I had the nightmare in short, and no wonder."[15] Not even Sir Walter's Stoicism, "the only philosophy I know or can practice," could save him from despondency after that.

[12] 13 Sep. 1822 in *Letters*, VII. 240–1. Lady Abercorn replies from Florence, 15 Oct. 1822: "I never heard of his having named it to any one else, which I think proves it was the imagination of a disordered brain at the moment, did you ever hear of it from any other person?" Walpole. For the lord's mental condition see *Memoirs and Correspondence of Viscount Castlereagh*, ed. Charles Vane, Marquess of Londonderry, London 1848–53, I. 83; Sir Archibald Alison, *Lives of Lord Castlereagh and Sir Charles Stewart*, Edinburgh and London 1861, III. 175–8. And for fuller accounts of the Radiant Boy, see Mrs Catherine Crowe, *Ghosts and Family Legends*, London 1859, pp. 93–7; R. H. Barham, *The Ingoldsby Legends*, ed. R. H. D. Barham, London 1870, II. 381–2; Ingram, *The Haunted Homes and Family Traditions of Great Britain*, London 1929, pp. 43–51; "The Purgatory of Suicides," *The Poetical Works of Thomas Cooper*, London 1877, pp. 89–94, 107–08. "Cut-throat Castlereagh" reportedly appeared on the island of Stromboli concurrently with his death many miles away. Edward John Trelawny, *Recollections of . . . Shelley and Byron*, London 1906, p. 123.

[13] Lockhart, v. 214. Both Tom Moore and Mrs Hughes were similarly regaled, but they differ from Lockhart in saying that Scott first heard the story by his own request at the Duke of Wellington's house and not at 30 Rue du Faubourg St. Honoré. Moore, *Memoirs, Journal, and Correspondence of Thomas Moore*, IV. 337–8, and Mrs Hughes, pp. 71–2.

[14] *Journal*, p. 263. Cp. *Demonology*, pp. 356–7.

[15] *Journal*, pp. 284–5. Where Scott's acres met Buccleuch's and Kippilaw's, there was a self-murderer's grave. "The spirit of Wattie Waeman wanders sadly over the adjacent moor to the great terror of all wandering wights who have occasion to pass from Melrose to Bowden." 14 Apr. 1824 in *Letters*, VIII. 255. Waeman seems to have kept out of the Laird of Abbotsford's way.

Interest in ghost stories and acquaintance with seers may have set the stage for the nightmare appearance of Colonel Huxley. But years before, Scott had been a would-be, involuntary, or deceived seer steadied by a retroactive scepticism. Each of the three incidents has survived in more than one version. An anonymous reviewer of the *Letters on Demonology and Witchcraft* tells of having seen the spectre of Catherine Lindsay in the ruins of Falkland Palace one autumn evening. Pale of face, with disordered locks, misty, glaring eyes, and an unearthly voice, the *revenante* described the court of James V (1528–42). Sharing the seer's reverential awe, young "Watty" Scott championed the tale, "returned evening after evening to the lonely hall, and waited in breathless expectation for the heavenly visitant, for such she was." Later, Sir Walter referred to "an unhappy maniac . . . at Falkland Palace, the disorder of whose mind . . . appears to have infected many persons who conversed with her."[16] This yarn reveals Scott's reaction-pattern to the marvellous—an enthusiastic curiosity followed by an urge to discover the natural cause. Thus, when Tom Moore repeated Rogers' story of a phantom appearing between two lovers at the Berlin opera, Scott "evidently did not like the circumstances being left unexplained."[17]

Once Sir Adam Ferguson and Scott saw "a very hideous looking fellow. . . . Scott did not deny it, but said they were both 'fu' [drunk],' and not very capable of judging whether it was a ghost or not."[18] This anecdote of Sir Adam's helps to identify the "modern poet" mentioned in a review of Dr John Ferriar's *An Essay towards a Theory of Apparitions*. The poet accompanied a friend to an oyster tavern, perhaps after a Friday meeting of the Club.

> They were shown into an inner room, and sat down to table. Here they were joined, as they believed, by an unknown person, whom neither of them knew; but it is to be remarked, that his appearance was unaccompanied by any circumstances of terror. He neither swallowed his oysters, shell and all, or did any thing which could subject him to suspicion. They lost sight of him they knew not how; and on going into the next room and inquiring about their uninvited guest, were assured by those who had remained there during the whole time they were within, that no one had passed through that apartment, which afforded the only means of access to their own. It may, perhaps, be objected to any inference drawn

[16] *The Atlas*, 3 Oct. 1830. See also C. O. Parsons, "Journalistic Anecdotage about Scott," *N. & Q.*, CLXXXIII (1942), 339–40.

[17] Moore, *Memoirs*, v. 286.

[18] Abbotsford Mss., N.L.S.; Moore, *Memoirs, Journal, and Correspondence of Thomas Moore*, IV. 337.

from this anecdote, that the imagination of the two gentlemen in question had probably been warmed with wine.[19]

A third ghost adventure can be referred neither to possible journalistic fabrication nor to drink, but to optical illusion. Not long after the death of Byron at Missolonghi on 19 April 1824, Scott saw the *eidolon* of his friend in the Abbotsford armoury. According to James Skene,

> The account of Byron's death had reached Sir Walter in the morning, and had of course been the subject of conversation throughout the day. Towards dusk Sir Walter had parted from me in the library, and as he came round by the entrance hall, which was ornamented by armour and curiosities hung around the walls, and dimly lighted by the stained-glass windows, a cloak carelessly thrown over a suit of armour in the corner, and surmounted by a head-piece upon which a gleam of party-coloured light fell, took to his eye so exactly the form, attitude, and even features of his departed friend, that he was for a moment staggered with the resemblance, which his imagination assisted in completing. The deception was so perfect that it was only upon a close approach that it yielded to the reality. Upon rejoining me in the library he mentioned the circumstance, and observed that it was the most perfect illusion he had ever met with, but the light had shifted by the time we returned to look at it again, and in no position could we recall the spectre.[20]

First the tingling nervous shock, then the investigation. In his own version of this *deceptio visus*, Scott describes his companion as a "young friend" (certainly no just epithet for Skene in 1824) and says that the figure resolved itself into "a screen, occupied by great-coats, shawls, plaids, and such other articles as usually are found in a country entrance-hall."[21] As Tom Moore remembered the story told by Scott in London on 25 May 1828, Anne Scott was the other party and the delusion was "the effect of either the moonlight or twilight upon some drapery that was hanging up."[22]

During certain crises in his life, Scott's early love, Williamina Belsches, or his wife Charlotte appeared to him, but these ladies belong to the realm of dreams and warning spirits. With the passage of years, Scott's

[19] *Q.R.*, IX (1813), 310–11.
[20] Skene, *Memories of Sir Walter Scott*, ed. Basil Thomson, London 1909, pp. 62–3. Less interesting spectres at Abbotsford were the factitious one sponsored by a merry party, but not countenanced by Scott, and the ghostly appearance of the bust of Shakespeare. Lockhart, VII. 58; Mrs. Hughes, p. 257.
[21] *Demonology*, pp. 38–9.
[22] Moore, *Memoirs, Journal, and Correspondence of Thomas Moore*, v. 286. For the roaming abroad of Byron's spirit from 1810 to 1821, see *op. cit.*, VI. 14; Moore, *The Life, Letters and Journals of Lord Byron*, new edn, London 1920, p. 456: Mrs Catherine Crowe, *The Night Side of Nature*, London 1848, I. 291; Lord David Cecil, *Melbourne*, London 1955, p. 130.

interest in ghosts changed without greatly diminishing. On 26 January 1832, Sir William Gell accompanied the dying novelist to the sea-girt and ruined villa of Pollio near Naples. "It was by no means the recollection of Pollio that induced Sir Walter to make this excursion. A story existed, that out of an opening in the floor of one of the rooms in this villa a spectre robed in white occasionally appeared, whence the place had acquired the name of *La Casa degli Spiriti*, and none had presumed to inhabit it."[23] Scott's last word on ghosts seems to have been addressed to Sir William: A spook painted white on tin can at dusk "be instantly made to vanish by turning the edge almost without thickness toward the spectator."[24]

Scott's reputation for telling delightfully gruesome tales was early established, and additions to his large collection of ghost-stories poured in from books, anecdotal friends, and even correspondents. Demonia's poetical epistle of 26 November 1805, has high praise for "Gilpin Horner":

> And each Member amongst us this Motto has got
> That for Tales of Hobgoblins of Ghosts & *what not*
> No Mortal in Britain is like Walter Scott.[25]

In a letter of 17 August 1809, Lady Abercorn mentions the poet's recent trip to London, "The Princess of Wales wrote me word she had seen a great deal of you and that you told a great many ghost stories."[26] Whenever Scott found an ear as sympathetic as that royal lady's, he poured into it a whimsical farrago of traditions, anecdotes, and spectre narratives. Thus he promises Lady Charlotte Rawdon, if she visits him, much entertainment from old ballads, family legends, "and tales of Ghosts and fairies without measure or limit."[27]

Scott's attitude toward his tales of wonder may have fluctuated according to his mood and audience, but three of his auditors agree on the general impression. Washington Irving, visiting Abbotsford in 1817, notices that the laird treats superstitions with "a sly and quiet humour"

---

[23] Gell, *Reminiscences of Sir Walter Scott's Residence in Italy, 1832*, ed. James C. Corson, London 1957, p. 7 (pp. 26, 32); Lockhart, VII. 348. See W. R. Hamilton, "Notes on a Roman Villa on the Coast of Naples, near the Hill of Pausilippo," *Transactions* of the Royal Society of Literature, III. PT I (1839), 113.

[24] Gell, *op. cit.*, p. 35.

[25] Walpole. Scott's reply, playfully refusing the invitation to Admiral Elliot's Christmas party, promises amends:
> Fear not. I'll bring sweet horrors soon,
> Shall make delighted list'ners swoon.

See C. O. Parsons, "Walter Scott in Pandemonium," *M.L.R.*, xxxviii (1943), 244–9.

[26] Walpole; Partington, *Post-Bag*, pp. 47–8. See *The Diary of the Right Hon. William Windham 1784–1810*, ed. Mrs Henry Baring, London 1866, *s.d.* 23 Apr. 1809.

[27] *Letters*, II. 233.

which does not conceal his strong enthusiasm.[28] Some ten years later, J. L. Adolphus describes his host as unwilling to put the supernatural to the test of belief or disbelief: "In no instance, however, was his colloquial eloquence more striking than when he was well launched in some 'tale of wonder.' The story came from him with an equally good grace, whether it was to receive a natural solution, to be smiled at as merely fantastical, or to take its chance of a serious reception."[29] The painter Haydon had Scott to breakfast on 5 May 1828: "I started ghosts. . . . He told us some curious things, affecting to consider them natural; but I am convinced he half thought them supernatural. Sir Walter Scott has certainly the most penetrating look I ever saw, except in Shakespeare's portraits."[30]

The wink, the twinkling eye, the whimsically curling lip, the bended brow, and the knowing look of oral telling suggest an infinite variety of interpretations. On the printed page, however, Scott can be less effective, stultifying his effects with awkward and disillusioning substitutes for conversational techniques. As a writer, perhaps through distrust of an audience not personally known to him, he sometimes forgets his own dictum on unrationalised marvels:

> A supernatural tale is, in most cases, received as an agreeable mode of amusing society, and he would be rather accounted a sturdy moralist than an entertaining companion, who should employ himself in assailing its credibility.[31]

*   *   *

Many ghosts flit through the pages of the Waverley Novels. At the head of this spectral line are Henry Morton, a live man taken for a *revenant*, and old Alice, a spirit appearing at the moment of its body's decay. After discussing Scott's treatment of illusion and possible reality, I shall review the diversity and function of his other ghosts.

The mistaken belief that a person is dead may lead to supernatural complications. Believing Henry Morton drowned, Edith Bellenden feels her lover's appearance at the window to be the visitation of a ghost. The apparition in *Old Mortality* follows an ominous echo of Edith's sigh, and the head is seen just as the lady is resolving that "no vain illusions [shall]

[28] Irving, *Abbotsford*, pp. 74–5.   [29] Lockhart, VII. 59.
[30] *The Autobiography and Memoirs of Benjamin Robert Haydon (1786–1846)*, ed. Tom Taylor, London 1926, II. 441.
[31] *Demonology*, p. 356. To see how much is lost in printed versions of ghost and wonder stories told by Scott or to him, glance at the *Demonology*, pp. 383–6; *Journal*, pp. 667, 740; *Letters*, VII. 240–1; Partington, *Letter Books*, pp. 339–44; Lockhart, II. 187–8, 344; 213–14, 296–7, 347–8, 384–5; VII. 284–5; Mrs Hughes, pp. 71–2, 76, 137.

recall the memory of other days." The immediate effect is to convince the heroine that "Heaven and earth, the living and the dead, have leagued themselves against this ill-omened union" with Lord Evandale against the counsels of her heart.

The very substantial ghost is seen by Lady Emily as a shadow and by Halliday. The conviction grows in Lord Evandale that Edith's agitated and overstrained imagination has conjured up the phantom. The chaplain offers three explanations: the appearance was a true ghost, a striking and deceptive similitude, or Morton himself. But the reader is not left long in doubt, the author almost immediately providing a circumstantial account of Morton's actual visit to Fairy Knowe.

The narrative service rendered is that Edith breaks off her engagement ("*she* cannot marry whose union disturbs the repose of the dead") and that eventually the course of true love does run smooth. The episode is rich in incidental spirit lore, such as the belief that those who have met a violent death should only haunt the place where they have been hanged or shot and that excessive lamentation distresses the dead. The latter is found in folksongs and ballads (e.g., "The Unquiet Grave") of many countries from India to Ireland. In ballads the dead lover may return to take his "faith and troth again," to summon his lady, or to protest against her fickleness. The sweetheart is, of course, the seer, as in "Clerk Saunders":

> And Clerk Saunders stood at may Margaret's window,
> I wot, an hour before the day.[32]

Since the events in *Old Mortality* take place in the latter half of the seventeenth century, Edith Bellenden's belief that her lover's spirit has returned to rebuke her is not surprising. Yet Scott traces the incident to the eighth chapter of Defoe's *The History and Reality of Apparitions*, in which Alexander's psychic double appears twice to his scheming stepmother, crying "Here!" and "Hold!" The bewildered young man himself arrives from the East Indies several months later to protect his rights *in propria persona* and to hearten his tormented father.[33] An investigator of Scott's literary background who ignored more romantic parallels of a dead or supposedly dead lover in order to favour Defoe's almost disinherited youth would hardly gain a hearing—without the confirmation of

---

[32] *Minstrelsy*, III, 226. See Scott's "Advertisement" to *The Pirate* for the ceremony by which a woman guarded against a ghostly visit by resuming her troth. And for excessive mourning, see Nathaniel Hawthorne, "Graves and Goblins" (1835); Lowry C. Wimberly, *Folklore in the English and Scottish Ballads*, pp. 103–04, 109–10, 230–3, 256–60, 306.

[33] *The Novels and Miscellaneous Works of Daniel DeFoe*, Oxford, 1840, XIII. 152–66; "Defoe on Apparitions," *B.E.M.*, VI (1819), 206–7.

the author's own note. This is, however, a fairly typical illustration of the thorough reworking to which Scott subjected borrowed material.

In *Ivanhoe* Scott once more confounds the living and the dead. When the hero is about to sue for Rowena's hand, Cedric reminds him that Athelstane's grave is not yet closed: "The ghost of Athelstane himself would burst his bloody cerements, and stand before us to forbid such dishonour to his memory." Whereupon Athelstane, in mortuary garb and "like something arisen from the dead," startles their nerves. The warrior is no departed mortal whose spirit must be set at rest, but a living man who has broken from a dungeon after being stunned by a blow at Torquilstone. Such is the melodramatic casuistry which Scott's change of plot, at Ballantyne's request, forces on him. However, some passing insight into the effect of fear on veracity is afforded by Friar Tuck's report to Allan-a-Dale on his encounter with the shrouded Saxon: "My quarter-staff . . . glided through his body as it might through a pillar of smoke!"

Yet again, this time in *Woodstock*, the apparently dead refuse to be actually dead. Nehemiah Holdenough tells Everard that the ghost of his college friend, Joseph Albany, has appeared, although he saw the being, when in mortal mould, hurled from the battlements of Clidesthrough Castle into a deep lake. "This strange vision," with "its pale, ghastly countenance," is twice seen reflected in a mirror and once in direct line of sight. Nineteen chapters later, Holdenough is frightened by Dr Anthony Rochecliffe, who makes it clear that as Joseph Albany he swam to the shore of the lake. Everard's scepticism about Holdenough's relation is Addisonian some sixty years before the master of the golden mean in controversy: "I do not deny the existence of such preternatural visitations. . . . Though I grant the possibility of such things, I have scarce yet heard of an instance in my days . . . well fortified by evidence."[34] As for the ghost, it is factitious and, in the overcrowded, super-haunted lodge of Woodstock, superfluous.

Conscious trickery is used in the same narrative to pass off a human being as a ghost. Like another raving, grimacing Burley, guilt-stricken General Harrison fights incarnate and infernal devils single-handed. One devil presses a handkerchief against its left side and resembles the actor-soldier, Dick Robison, who was murdered by Harrison after surrendering on Naseby Field. The spirit, with the distinctive jewel in its ear, comes to summon Harrison, who wants to put the conflict off till the great battle of Armageddon. Harrison follows his apparitor, only to fence against

[34] Ch. xvii. Cp. Everard's objection to Holdenough's universal receptivity in ch. x.

unresponsive air. When he receives the story from Tomkins, Everard marvels at this confirmation of the belief "that the spirits of the slaughtered have strange power over the slayer." The conception of a ghost staunching its accusatory wound as it returns to earth to persecute its half-mad slayer is effectively worked out some fifteen chapters before the heavy-handed Radcliffian explanation is given. Joceline Joliffe admits that, following Tomkins' advice, he dressed like the player to frighten the Roundhead commissioner.

The assortment of ghosts in *Woodstock* is certainly generous, ranging from the crude racketing devil (discussed in the section on poltergeists) to a ghost-in-the-making. Having killed Tomkins in order to protect Phoebe, Joceline Joliffe immediately begins to fear spectral reprisals—"I wish no ghost may haunt me!"—despite the dying man's forgiveness. The tension is increased by the forester's vow, on catching the rascal (then Philip Hazeldine) deer-stealing, that the hide should be Tomkins' winding-sheet or his own. Before he has lapped Tomkins in the stiff hide, the dog Bevis, or some devil in his shape, brings him the murdered man's glove. Tomkins' eye, fixed in hatred, terror, and reproach, pursues him. But the burial, with Dr Rochecliffe's aid, apparently lays the body and the potential ghost at one and the same time. Scott's portrayal of Joceline's rising fear is brief, varied and yet centred in its emphasis, perfectly adjusted to the man and the morbid state of his emotions after homicide. Incipient haunting at Woodstock is more pulse-quickening than palpable haunting.

Ghostly claptrap of a different kind may be found in *Castle Dangerous*. The medieval Byronic hero, Sir James Douglas, shows versatility. A spectral knight, he fades from Sir Aymer's view. On another occasion, "the ghastly cavalier" tells uncomfortable Lady Augusta de Berkely that he may "melt from *her* side like a phantom which dreads the approach of day." He dons armour painted to represent a skeleton, with ominous owls on shield and helmet. Exceeding height and leanness make the fantastic Knight of the Tomb appear like an apparition rising from the grave, a madman, a supernatural being, and even the King of Terrors. Obviously, it is not plot necessity but Scott's interest in the macabre moods and devices of chivalry which fits the quixotic warrior with skeleton armour.[35]

Scott's closest approximation of a real ghost is in *The Bride of Lammermoor*. The seer, Edgar Master of Ravenswood, is a moody, fortuneless

[35] The interest appears earlier in Scott, *Essay on Chivalry* (1814), in which the use of Lancelot's skeleton to confer knighthood on a bachelor is mentioned. *The Miscellaneous Prose Works of Sir Walter Scott*, Edinburgh 1827, VI. 80.

seventeenth-century gentleman who despises "most of the ordinary prejudices about witchcraft, omens, and vatication" and, on one occasion, resolves that his imagination will not again "beguile *his* senses." Later, protesting against Lucy Ashton's broken troth, Edgar revises Scott's analysis of his Byronic character. Family honour, friendly advice, reason, and superstitious portents have not shaken his fidelity. "The very dead have arisen to warn me, and their warning has been despised." When in the grip of strong emotions, Ravenswood is as it were destiny-driven and doomed by his own nature. He rises above rational and supernatural considerations, without denying either.[36]

The apparition of old Alice to the Master of Ravenswood is hesitantly introduced with a hint about the self-created illusion of an excited mind. At the Mermaiden's Fountain, the Master associates its fatal reputation with the *old sibyl's* warnings against any connexion with the usurping Ashton family. Then Scott temporises: an author must tell a tale as he has received it; oral transmission tends to colour a tale; "this could not be called a Scottish story, unless it manifested a tinge of Scottish superstition." The incident *is said* to be that his horse rears in terror as Ravenswood sees a woman in a greyish mantle. When he approaches the figure on foot, the Master recognises blind Alice, shrouded. The apparition rises, holds up a shrivelled hand, noiselessly moves its withered lips, and glides away. Alternate explanations are suggested by the author's phrasing, "whether it was real, or . . . the creation of a heated and agitated imagination."

Wondering whether Alice can actually have leagued with the Devil, Ravenswood takes time off to investigate. Thus he discovers that Alice's death and the appearance coincide in time, that the deceased sent a peasant to fetch him, and that she yearned passionately to renew her warning. While he sits by thwarted Alice's corpse in her cottage, Ravenswood returns to his questions: Was it an ocular deception? a visitation through the force of deathbed desires? a breach in nature's laws without a purpose being made known?

Altogether, the ghost's *raison d'être* is none too clear. If some warning were conveyed to the lover, the episode would add to the prophecies, omens, and strange monitions which he thrusts aside in his march to destruction. As a case of earthly frustration seeking ghostly fulfilment, it is incomplete and tends to focus interest on Alice rather than on the

---

[36] The master-and-man contrast in *The Bride of Lammermoor*, roughly parallels that in *Rob Roy*. When Ravenswood returns unexpectedly at night to Wolf's Crag, the comic-relief servant, Caleb Balderstone, calls out, "Aroint ye!" As he "would sooner face fifty deevils" than his master's ghost or wraith, he will not unbolt the door until he is sure that Ravenswood and Bucklaw are men of flesh.

Master. The incident, weighed down as it is with verification and—the coincidence established—with Edgar's dubious soliloquies, does not build toward the catastrophe.[37]

Waverley ghosts not yet mentioned serve as figures of speech, adjuncts of humour and local colour, and revelations of psychological states as well as of repressed and obsessional lives. Figurative ghosts contribute little to atmosphere, dread, or suspense. The description of the heroine in *The Abbot* is literary trimming, nothing more: "Catherine Seyton, on her part, sate still like a lingering ghost, which, conscious of the awe which its presence imposes, is charitably disposed to give the poor confused mortal whom it visits, time to recover his senses, and comply with the grand rule of demonology by speaking first." In *The Betrothed*, however, a figure of speech is combined with an instance of mistaken ghost fright. When Eveline and Rose make themselves known at night to Rose's father, Wilkin Flammock, and Father Aldrovand, the lady explains her appearing on the walls of the Garde Douloureuse "like a wandering spirit that cannot take slumber or repose." Just before this, harrowed by the "two white forms," the Fleming has exclaimed, "Es spuckt—there are hobgoblins here!" and the priest, his teeth chattering, has tried a Latin exorcism.

Never truly superstitious, Frank Osbaldistone is at least susceptible, in moments of despair or high excitement, to the chimerical. When Frank keeps a mysterious tryst with a stranger, he resolves that "he should not have the apology for silence proper to apparitions, who, it is vulgarly supposed, cannot speak until they are spoken to." He and Rob Roy glide along "like mute spectres." As the hero's superstitiousness is merely fanciful and transient, it is best conveyed in figurative language.

Whimsy entices spirits into the "Introductory Epistle" of *The Fortunes of Nigel*. As usual in a crowded and ancient house, the author is sentenced "to the *haunted apartment*. I have, as a great modern said,[38] seen too many ghosts to believe in them, so betook myself seriously to my repose." Then appears the ghost of Betty Barnes (Betsy Baker), John Warburton's cook-maid, who, when among the living, ignorantly burned or *put under pye bottoms* some fifty-five Elizabethan and Jacobean dramatic manuscripts.

[37] An anonymous critic slashes out at old Alice's ghost as "one of the most idle and gratuitous apparitions that ever was conjured up to frighten the king's liege subjects." *The Edinburgh Monthly Review*, II (1819), 168.

[38] "A lady once asked me if I believed in ghosts and apparitions. I answered with truth and simplicity: No, madam! I have seen far too many myself." S. T. Coleridge, *The Friend*, ed. H. N. Coleridge, 4th edn, London 1844, p. 195. Mr Flosky, a literary take-off on Coleridge, has a similar idea: "I can safely say I have seen too many ghosts myself to believe in their external existence." T. L. Peacock, *Nightmare Abbey*, London 1818, p. 179. Cp. *Demonology*, p. 35.

Her shade reveals to the Author of Waverley that certain greasy and unconsumed fragments may still be found in the coal-hole.

The humorous anecdote may enter the narrative itself, as in *The Bride of Lammermoor*. The simultaneous approach of two carriages to Sir William Ashton's gateway reminds Scott somewhat inconsequently of the hypochondriac profligate who, on his deathbed, saw a spectre at a certain hour. A friend, wishing to effect a cure, had someone dress up to imitate the phantasm. "Mon Dieu!" exclaimed the patient, "il y en a deux!" The conjuring of apparitions by diseased senses appealed to Scott. It supplied drolly effective anecdotes for social or literary use and yielded readily to natural explanation.

Dousterswivel and Sir Arthur Wardour's hocus-pocus search for treasure in *The Antiquary* is broadly comic. While waiting for the fun, Edie Ochiltree mentions Sanders Aikwood's stories of "worricows and gyre-carlins" haunting the walls of St Ruth's, only to hint at the conventional explanation of nocturnal poaching and smuggling. "Nae believer in auld wives' stories about ghaists," Edie yet realises that he is in a fit place for spirits and calls the approaching treasure-hunters "mortal or of the other world." The show breaks up after the spies, Edie and Lovel, fall to coughing and sneezing.

Local colour is provided by ghosts that flit within fixed spatial limits and have no urge to be free-lances.[39] These neighbourhood ghosts abound in *The Antiquary*. Edie easily frightens "Dousterdeevil" with "reports that auld Misticot walks." Edie and Steenie Mucklebackit flee from a white-clad rider at the Countess of Glenallan's funeral, thinking him "a spirit, or something little better." Oldbuck pokes fun at old Caxon the hairdresser for insisting that he has seen a ghost at the Humlock-Knowe. Against this widespread popular dread of spooks, which generally distinguishes the lower classes from the upper, is set Oldbuck's intolerance of any nonsense about contemporary "ghaist or fairies, or spirits walking the earth, or the like o' that." Yet the antiquary proses to Lovel about a unique broadside in his collection, *Strange and Wonderful News... of certain dreadful Apparitions... seen in ... 1610*. True to his class and hobby, Jonathan Oldbuck has numismatic, archaeological, and historico-legendary credulity.

Psychologically, the shock of a sudden, unusual, or unexpected human encounter may be represented in ghostly terms. When reason and the

---

[39] Meg Merrilies intends to become a fixed spirit: "for if ever the dead came back amang the living, I'll be seen in this glen mony a night after these crazed banes are in the mould." The White Woman of Woodstock also belongs to this class.

observant faculties regain control, the ghostliness fades away. Thus in *The Antiquary* Elspeth tells the Earl of Glenallan that when her cottage was visited by his mother "pale and ghastly as if she had risen from the grave," she at first seemed not of this earth. After the visitant was recognised as a mortal, the startling effect of the meeting still lingered: "I durstna speak first, mair than if I had seen a phantom." In *The Heart of Midlothian*, Jeanie Deans, terrified by remembered "stories of apparitions and wraiths," takes some time to realise that the figure emerging from the copsewood is her exiled sister's "ain living sell." Effie impishly proves her materiality with a pinch. Once freed from strangeness, the meeting and the dialogue subside to a more commonplace level.

The previous state of mind of two characters may lead to double deception involving superstitious fear. Emotion is intensified by being rechannelled. In *The Pirate*, Minna Troil, hearing sounds of strife between her sister's lover and her own serenader, goes out to see who is wounded. She hears Claud Halcro singing an ominous song about crime, vengeance, and burial. Then old Halcro, who—despite travel—has not "rid himself of his native superstitions," sees the mute, white-clad figure and tries to conjure it away. His "wild and unearthly" rhyme calls on the saints for aid against every possible weird opponent—good or evil, airy, earthy; ghost once human; pixie strayed from its ring, or nixie from its spring. Halcro's spell being spoken, "the conjured phantom" confesses herself and becomes even more like a pale spectre on learning that corpse-lights have been seen in the harbour.

A monomania such as avarice may drain a living man of vitality until he seems no more than a phantom. In *The Fortunes of Nigel*, the hero gets into quite a state while reading *God's Revenge against Murther*. The candles falter; the tapestry writhes. Then old Trapbois, for whose convenience "a private passage long disused" is remembered, creeps from behind the arras, his withered hand stretched towards a gold piece. His "bloodless countenance, meagre form, and ghastly aspect" impress the less than daring hero as spectral.

Through sin or error, a life may dwindle into reclusiveness, broken by stealthy, mostly nocturnal appearances. Though virtually dead in the flesh for many years after Lord Dalgarno has pretended to marry her in Spain, Lady Hermione attaches herself to the Heriots like an anaemic Scottish brownie, occupies a torchlit suite, and sleeps in her coffin. Food is left for her in a "whirling-box," and she silently attends the family devotions. Glimpsing her own face in a mirror, Lady Hermione thinks it "the visage of a ghost" and is aware that she seems "a bloodless phantom" to the few who see her. Richie Moniplies suspects George Heriot of keeping a spirit besides having a cloven cloot and prowling after Nigel's soul. This turns out to be Richie's drunken garnishing of Jenkin Vincent's bamboozling account.

Against the Gothic background of the lady's morbid, elusive, fairy godmother existence, the author's confidence in the "Introductory Epistle" to *The Fortunes of Nigel* is amusing: "all is clear and above board"; the White Lady of Avenel and her kind are banished. However, in giving Margaret Ramsay the money with which to free Nigel Olifaunt, Lady Hermione seems more like Lady Bountiful than "Master Heriot's ghost." As an agent in the plot, she decreases in spectral interest as her human involvement increases.

Fate-driven characters may be like tormented spirits. In *St Ronan's Well*, Clara Mowbray, the victim of her own weakness and of consequent doom, is "like the wretched creatures who, it is said, lie under a potent charm, that prevents them alike from shedding tears and from confessing their crimes" (her own comparison). Haunted by "wandering visions" with which she confuses the real presence of Francis Tyrrel and his scheming half-brother, Valentine Bulmer, she is a "delusion of Satan" (an old hag's idea) who looks "like something from another world . . . Mat Lewis's Spectre Lady" (Lady Penelope's words) and who appears here and there before her death in the manner of apparition, phantom, or vision. There are scattered references to the ill-starred heroine's "mental malady." Scott intended Clara to be another Effie Deans or Zilia de Monçada in frailty. The prudish Ballantyne argued against this conception without removing the attendant atmosphere of guilt and punishment.

A person may withdraw from the world because of his crimes, psychic wounds, or fixations, or he may lurk in secret chambers under religious or political proscription. Of the many stories of these ghostly refugees, one told to Scott by his great-aunt, Mrs Margaret Swinton, has to do with the "singular vision" of the murderess, Mrs MacFarlane, in Sir John Swinton's house. This narrative suggested an incident in *Peveril of the Peak*, in which the Catholic Countess of Derby slides back a secret panel and appears before Julian Peveril and Alice Bridgenorth. Having been enlightened by nursery tales about "the terrors of the invisible world," little Julian is at first frightened, then thinks the apparition a delusion, and at last converses with the strange lady. Such ghostly sensations, Scott realises, cannot be protracted without weakening their effect.

In *Rob Roy*, the sudden appearance of Diana with her attainted, Jacobite father, Sir Frederick Vernon, makes Frank Osbaldistone think himself distracted or in the presence of "spirits of the dead." Frank's servant, Andrew Fairservice, falls into an excellent, though conventional, man and master contrast in his instant responsiveness to the supernatural. After seeing a ghost, he tremulously reads the fifth chapter of Nehemiah to keep other frightful apparitions at a distance. Much later, he notes a resemblance between his moonlight bogle and a portrait of Diana's grandfather. When the unearthly phenomenon is finally explained away, Andrew stubbornly persists in considering Sir Frederick a "ghaist," as in a sense he is. If an existence sinks far below normal vitality through clinging to the dead past, its furtive, solitary, hunted quality is appropriately expressed as bloodless and ghostly.

★　　★　　★

There is a purely literary and incidental quality about many of the Waverley ghosts. As for the others, when they are not cases of mistaken human identity, doubts are cast on their spectral nature, so that they wander in a limbo between illusion and unearthly reality. The effective ones may appear to unbalanced persons, but they are chiefly seen by common folk, whose reason has not been sophisticated by education. Much more interested in response to the ghostly than in the ghostly *per se*, Scott is for the most part satisfied with the trappings of spirit return. In the least characteristic of the ghost passages, the resurrection of Athelstane, fright is a narrative end, but here, as in the study of Joliffe's fear of being haunted, the object is not the Gothic one of startling the reader but the realistic one of observing the effect of a given emotion on fictional characters.[40] Ghostly experiences, except when they contribute to the feeling of time and place, are intended to disclose states of conscience and of consciousness, states which would otherwise require subtle and painstaking analysis. Whether ghosts are merely ornamental, play havoc for a short time with the hero's imagination, or perform other tasks, Scott concentrates on metaphor, humour, local colour, tradition, folk character, repressed and doomed lives, distortion of reality, and psychological revelation.

8. Haunted Places

Spirit-possessed rooms, castles, and *locales* appealed tremendously to Scott, who could feel in them what Henry James calls "the sense of the past" suffusing the present. His experiences in haunted settings, both outdoor

[40] An exception, "The Tapestried Chamber," is discussed in the section on haunted places.

and indoor, were varied. In the summer of 1793, he passed a night at Glamis Castle, hereditary seat of the Earls of Strathmore. Protected by the third person singular, he describes his sensations frankly in his "Biographical Notice of Horace Walpole" (1811):

> He who, in early youth, has happened to pass a solitary night in one of the few ancient mansions which the fashion of more modern times has left undespoiled of their original furniture, has probably experienced, that the gigantic and preposterous figures dimly visible in the defaced tapestry,— the remote clang of the distant doors which divide him from living society,—the deep darkness which involves the high and fretted roof of the apartment,—the dimly-seen pictures of ancient knights, renowned for their valour, and perhaps for their crimes, the varied and indistinct sounds which disturb the silent desolation of a half-deserted mansion,—and, to crown all, the feeling that carries us back to ages of feudal power and papal superstition, join together to excite a corresponding sensation of supernatural awe, if not of terror.[1]

Using the first person some nineteen years later, Scott is more confident of his self-control. After mentioning a murder committed within the castle walls and referring to the famous secret chamber,[2] he becomes reminiscential:

> I was conducted to my apartment in a distant corner of the building. I must own, that as I heard door after door shut, after my conductor had retired, I began to consider myself too far from the living, and somewhat too near the dead. . . . In a word, I experienced sensations, which, though not remarkable either for timidity or superstition, did not fail to affect me to the point of being disagreeable, while they were mingled at the same time with a strange and indescribable kind of pleasure, the recollection of which affords me gratification at this moment.[3]

During his cruise with the light-house commissioners in 1814, Scott was almost uniformly responsive to the atmosphere of the scenes he visited. Here is his comment on "a horrible ugly gulf" in the cave of Smowe,

---

[1] *Lives*, p. 539. In Perceval Landon's "Thurnley Abbey," Colvin sleeps in a chamber with Queen of Sheba tapestry which is not fastened at the bottom: "I have always held very practical views about spooks, and it has often seemed to me that the slow waving in firelight of loose tapestry upon a wall would account for ninety-nine per cent of the stories one hears." *The Supernatural Omnibus*, ed. Mantague Summers, London 1931, p. 102.

[2] Scott's silence about the Ogilvies' being starved to death in the chamber leads Andrew Lang to suggest that the legend may have come into being after the visit of 1793, but failing memory and hasty composition may account for the lapse. The legend is given in Ingram, *The Haunted Homes and Family Traditions of Great Britain*, pp. 98–100. For spectral gambling in the hidden room, see William Howitt, "Visits to Remarkable Places. Glammis Castle," *Howitt's Journal*, II. (1847), 122, and for some melodramatic nineteenth-century adventures in Glamis, see Elliot O'Donnell, *Scottish Ghost Stories*, London 1911, pp. 265–93.

[3] *Demonology*, p. 398; Lockhart, I. 210–13.

Sutherlandshire: "A water kelpy, or an evil spirit of any aquatic propensities, could not choose a fitter abode; and, to say the truth, I believe at
our first entrance, and when all our feelings were afloat at the novelty of
the scene, the unexpected plashing of a seal would have routed the whole
dozen of us."[4] Of Scott's susceptibility to "that dread lake," Coruisk on
the Isle of Skye, William Erskine says: "I remember, that at Loch Corriskin,
in particular, he seemed quite overwhelmed with his feelings; and we all
saw it, and retiring unnoticed, left him to roam and gaze about by himself."[5]

It was on this voyage that Scott visited Dunvegan Castle, Skye, 23–4
August, when John Norman MacLeod of MacLeod, twenty-fourth chief,
was in the midst of alterations costing £4,000 and including mock turrets
and battlements in the romantic style.[6] During the first day, Scott's host
showed him a famous Fairy Flag that, when fitly used, drew herring into
the loch, stimulated fertility, and increased the number of the clan in
battle. The silken banner, said to have been the gift of the Queen of
Fairies, had brought victory twice and was reserved for a third fight, after
whose bloody close the fairy mistress would come to carry it and the
standard-bearer away. The conversation, appropriately enough, turned on
supernatural themes: "We learn that most of the Highland superstitions,
even that of the second-sight, are still in force."[7]

The very surroundings of Dunvegan had the eerie gloom and grandeur
of a Radcliffian romance. Thus environed, Scott seems to have expected a
grisly titillation from sleeping in the haunted apartment, to which he was
introduced about midnight. But, wonder as he might at his callousness, he
was chiefly excited by a comfortable bed in which he fell asleep "without
thinking of ghost or goblin."[8] In after years, Scott came to look on this
experience as a turning-point in his reaction to uncanny places. Replying
to the confession of Miss Anne Wagner of Liverpool, "I believe in the
identity of both" devil and ghost,[9] Scott takes time on 7 February 1828,
to recall his night at Dunvegan Castle:

> I cannot say that I am a believer in the return of departed spirits but I
> heartily regret the days when I did entertain that very interesting opinion

[4] 19 Aug. 1814 in Lockhart, III. 213.
[5] W. Forbes Gray, *Scott in Sunshine & Shadow*, London 1931, p. 12. See Lockhart, III.
234–5 (August 25); *The Lord of the Isles*, III. xiii–xvi.
[6] See *The Book of Dunvegan*, ed. R. C. MacLeod, Aberdeen 1938–9, I. xxxvi, xxxviii, xlv;
II. 49.
[7] Lockhart, III. 228.   [8] *Demonology*, p. 401.
[9] Walpole, letter stamped 6 Feb. 1828. Miss Wagner was the aunt of Felicia Hemans,
author of *The Sceptic* and other poems. See R. S. Cleaver, "Sir Walter Scott and Mrs. Veal's
Ghost," *Nineteenth Century*, XXXVII (1895), 271.

... ghosts are only seen where they are believed. But whether recon-
cileable to the understanding or not they are most interesting to the
imagination and I shall always remember with pain the loss of the
sensation. . . . The Lady [of Dunvegan] asked me in courtesy whether I
would chose to sleep in the Haunted Chamber which of course I preferd
and was told many stories of its terrors. It certainly was [the] finest scene
I ever saw for a ghost. . . . All this I saw the quarter of which would have
been sufficient at a more imaginative time of life to suggest strange matters
either for waking hours or dreams

> But woe is me
> The wild romance of life was done
> The real history was begun

I felt nothing but that I had had a busy day had eaten a good dinner had
drunk a bottle of excellent claret and was much disposed to sleep—And
so to my eternal shame without troubling myself about the ghost of
Rorie More or anyone of his long line I went to bed and slept quietly till
my servant calld me in the morning.[10]

Although Scott lingers wistfully over the sudden loss of early susceptibility, his progress from credence through sympathy to controlled
imagination was actually gradual, beginning before 1814 and continuing
many years after that date. Confidence in his growing scepticism frequently led Scott to assume in later years that his incredulity was always
uppermost, but it had once been bottommost.

*　　*　　*

Within the sweep of the Waverley Novels, in which the past lays hold
of the historic consciousness, the imminence of that past, immediate or
remote, may be experienced through warning spirits, local legends, or
ghosts. Eerie places may represent ancient but obscure wrongs, woes, and
frustrations channelled by the popular imagination into the present.
Scott's haunted scenes are visited by bands of weird beings or by individual
spirits, which may seek domestic shelter or take to the open country.
Whether tricksters, creations of the heated fancy, or unrationalised pre-
sences, the haunters help to create atmosphere of place through sharpening
the significance of present acts in an unchancy setting.

[10] C. O. Parsons, "Scott's Experiences in Haunted Chambers," *Modern Philology*, xxx
(1932), 103–05; *Letters*, x. 371–3; xii. 128–9. Cp. Mrs Hughes, pp. 329–30. Scott's bedroom
was the one occupied by Samuel Johnson in 1773. In his Journal for 31 Dec. 1824, Captain
Basil Hall records an instance of equal insensibility on Scott's part: "in the course of a conversation about ghosts, fears in the dark, and such matters," Scott mentioned his being forced
to occupy the same room, but not bed, with a corpse in a crowded country inn. "I laid me
down, and never had a better night's sleep in my life." Lockhart, v. 384–5.

The outdoor haunting in the Waverley Novels is of narrow valleys, stone groups, moors, and crags—confined, desolate, and dangerous spots. Scott makes the dark possession of forbidden places in *The Heart of Midlothian* and the deeds perpetrated in them horrifying in proportion to the guilt which he wishes to externalise. Spirits hovering over crags, valley, and cairn both commemorate and personify bygone hate. Muschat's Cairn, like Egdon Heath, menaces the actors. Effie's lover, Robertson, commands Butler to have her sister Jeanie meet him at the Cairn, which had been erected to the memory of a man who cruelly murdered his wife.[11] "It was in such places, according to the belief of that period ... that evil spirits had power to make themselves visible to human eyes." There wild Madge has her moonlight chats with Ailie Muschat of the slit throat, and the tie between the wickedness of days gone by and of the present is strengthened by Madge's message from Nicol himself to Ratcliffe, "Blithe will Nicol Muschat be to see ye, for he says ... he wad be ravished to hae a crack wi' you—like to like, ye ken." To "this ominous and unhallowed spot" comes Jeanie Deans in such an overwrought state of mind that the sudden appearance of Robertson from behind the heap of stones seems that of the fierce fiend.

Indeed, the whole region is fearfully possessed. Butler meets that "ruined archangel," Robertson, in a dell which was once the resort of bloody duellists and suicides. A boy of Leith has sported with the fairies in caves under the cliffs, and witches have met on Saint Leonard's Crags and the Chase. The acts and agonies of characters in *The Heart of Midlothian* are connected with gory, evil-frequented scenes which provide a ghastly background for human passions.[12]

The spectral atmosphere of Mucklestane-Moor in *The Black Dwarf* chiefly expresses the native grotesqueness of folk beliefs. Attentive to supernatural tales from childhood, Hobbie Elliot finds the heath "an unco bogilly bit." And well it may be, for after sunset it is still "the ordinary resort of kelpies, spunkies, and other demons, once the companions of the witch's diabolical revels, and now continuing to rendezvous upon the same spot." Scott's unwillingness to let this landscape mood become

[11] See *The Last Speech and Confession of Nicol Muschet*, Edinburgh [1721]; the expanded version, *A True and Genuine Copy* ... [Edinburgh? 1725?] and its reprint, *The Confession* ..., Edinburgh, Glasgow, London, 1818. The stones may have been thrown on the pile by wayfarers in order to give the murdered woman rest. See Ignazio Silone, *Bread and Wine*, tr. David and Mosbacher, New York and London 1937, p. 51.

[12] Scott may well have influenced Stevenson in *Weir of Hermiston*: Deil's Hags, or Francie's Cairn, where the Praying Weaver of Balweary was shot by Claverhouse, is the ominous site of Archie's meetings with Christina and his murder of Frank Innes, her seducer (the killing was in the plan of the unfinished novel).

oppressive is evident in the encounter between Earnscliff and Elliot. The latter, whistling to quell his superstitious fears, hears a friendly shout *behind* him. Instead of trembling in the deceptive presence of the Enemy, Hobbie immediately welcomes human companionship. Thus reinforced, Hobbie turns bold regarding "worricows and lang nebbit things about the land" and "the auld carline hersell." But like a Scottish Bob Acres, his courage oozes when, by the shifting light of a clouded moon, he thinks he sees Auld Ailie. Protectively, he considers firing on the apparition, repeating a short prayer, and taking to the bog. The strange being, actually the Black Dwarf, next reminds the young farmer of a ghaist, a bogle, and Humphrey Ettercap, who died in the bog five years ago. When he gets home, mercurial Hobbie talks about being "mistrysted wi' bogles in the hame-coming," with the Devil or the "auld Peghts [Picts]," and perhaps—the next morning's reflexion— with the ghost of a stone-mason. Throughout this experience, Hobbie's better educated companion, Earnscliff, dashes ineffectual cold water on his warm imaginings, climaxing his scepticism with a rather self-conscious statement, "I am of opinion that preternatural visitations are either ceased altogether, or become very rare in our days." Despite Earnscliff, the spooky character of Mucklestane-Moor, substantiated by the Black Dwarf, is almost consistently maintained.

A lighter atmosphere pervades *The Monastery*, whose scenes are frequented by airy beings much in the spirit of the *genius loci* in *The Lady of the Lake*. As Scott says in his Introduction of 1830, the Melrose and Tweedside *locales* lay "almost under the immediate eye of the author," a neighbourhood that could easily yield traditions, ruins, and such narrative ornaments as fays and water-bulls. But the enchanted setting is taken freely, not slavishly, from the purlieus of Abottsford—the Allen rolling along its bed, through the Fairy, or Nameless, Dean [Glen], the strangely hollowed stones known as fairy cups, saucers, and basins; Boldside and its decaying, fairy-visited churchyard; the moonlit bank of the Tweed, "a scene that Oberon and Queen Mab might love to revel in."

Scott's comment to Lockhart on the contrast between *The Monastery* and *Ivanhoe* holds true for the reader: "It was a relief to interlay the scenery most familiar to me with the strange world for which I had to draw so much on imagination."[13] And yet the setting, like the White Lady of Avenel, is not free from eclecticism. Glendearg is described in the romance as the habitat of the Brown Man of the Moors, a creature which had been transplanted four years earlier in *The Black Dwarf* from Northumberland. One of the recesses of Glendearg is called *Corrie nan Shian*,

---

[13] Lockhart, IV. 350.

which is corrupted Gaelic for the Hollow of the Fairies.[14] Now, there is no particular reason for a Tweeddale hollow to bear a corrupted Celtic name except that Scott's mind was working on the analogy of a cavern near Loch Katrine, *Coir-nan-Uriskin*.[15] The author's allusion to "the elementary spirits by which the valley was supposed to be haunted" introduces another folklore importation whose only excuse may be to keep that supernatural refugee, the White Lady, from dying of homesickness. To the eerie infestation of Glendearg, Scott adds the more truly local agency of Lowland fairies, spectres, and devils. Despite the visiting spirits, the impression left by the setting, as distinct from the story of *The Monastery*, is refreshingly native. The soil is tradition-soaked, and the lore as a whole is indigenous. Much of this success is due to Scott's long practice in blending Scottish legend with local sights for the benefit of Abbotsford guests.

The charmed scenery of Glendearg fades from view during a discussion in *The Abbot* between Roland Graeme, secretly a Catholic, and Adam Woodcock, openly a Protestant. Fearing saint and devil, Roland thinks the goblins may punish his companion for profane song and talk. Adam considers the "wandering spirits" but "bubbles in the water, or shadows in the air," used by priests to gull laymen. The Reformed faith has disenchanted the vale of Glendearg:

> From haunted spring and grassy ring,
>   Troop goblin, elf, and fairy;
> And the kelpie must flit from the black bog-pit,
> And the brownie must not tarry.

Notable landmarks may evoke mysterious antiquity while revealing the state of mind of the beholder. Thus, when Cleveland wakes repentant on board his sloop in *The Pirate*, the Standing Stones of Stennis seem in the grey dawn "like the phantom forms of antediluvian giants, who, shrouded in the habiliments of the dead, came to revisit, by this pale light,

---

[14] The Prelude of Scott's play, *MacDuff's Cross* (1823), opens:

> Nay, smile not, Lady, when I speak of witchcraft,
> And say, that still there lurks amongst our glens
> Some touch of strange enchantment. . . .

Cp. T. Crofton Croker, *Researches in the South of Ireland*, London 1824, p. 82: Fairies are supposed to frequent the most romantic Irish dells, called "gentle places."

[15] See *The Lady of the Lake*, III. xxv:

> By many a bard, in Celtic tongue,
> Has Coir-nan-Uriskin been sung,
> A softer name the Saxons gave,
> And call'd the grot the Goblin-cave.

Cp. Patrick Graham, *Sketches of Perthshire*, 2nd edn, Edinburgh 1812, p. 121; *Demonology*, p. 113.

the earth which they had plagued by their oppression and polluted by their sins, till they brought down upon it the vengeance of long-suffering Heaven." One of these stones lingers as a memorial of ancient ritual, straying from other lands and other faiths into the present. Through a hole in its shaft, lovers clasp hands and take the Promise of Odin.

Ill-fated deeds and sites, to the folk imagination, are in the keeping of irritable powers. In "The Highland Widow," the desolate glen where Michael Tyrie tells Elspat that her son has been killed by a firing-squad and where he is cursed by her is haunted by the *Cloght-dearg* or Redmantle. While tracing such superstition to days of Popery or even paganism, the minister surrenders to the gloomy setting. Just as he is blaming the accidents in the steep glen on the overflowing of a torrential stream, his name is called by Elspat. Momentarily he fears that "the Evil Being, whose existence he had disowned, was about to appear for the punishment of his incredulity." Then Elspat appears from behind the rocks like Robertson at Muschat's Cairn or the Hermit of Engaddi in the desert. With her reddish tartan mantle, her distorted features and wild eyes, she is "no inadequate representative" of the *Cloght-dearg*.

It is not lucky to speak of certain things where they have chanced, even though no gyre-carlin, witch, fairy, bodach, brownie, or bogle is known to be concerned. Mischance comes to him who intrudes on Elspat's solitude. Donald MacLeish does not want to linger near Elspat's oak-tree, for "the place is not canny," and after her death Highlanders avoid the tree because her ghost then frequents it. During life and after death, natural and traditional eeriness serve as background to Elspat's ungoverned grief and despair. Scott makes actions, scenes, and Elspat's words sustain each other.

When Scott turns from haunted terrain to haunted chambers, he has among his many resources the gleanings of his friends. Among the Abbotsford MSS. in the National Library of Scotland is a group of tales written on paper watermarked 1800 and bearing this note by Scott: "The following Manuscript Legends were communicated to me by Lord Webb Seymour who wrote them down at my request. The first has appeard in print in different shapes & languages and is I believe the foundation of a modern Tragedy in which all the people are killd except-ing one who was supposed to have been dead at the beginning of the play."

The first is a parlour tale of terror in which a horseman who has lost his way in a lonely countryside is offered shelter by the owner of a goodly mansion. Because the house-guests are numerous, the only free room, long unoccupied, is one that is dreary with "age & decay,—the tapestry & the furniture of the bed were moth-eaten." After sleeping about two hours, the traveller awakes to find a shape "hovering over the dying embers." When prevented from escaping, the intruder, "a withered old man in a squalid dress," confesses that he was the master of the house some twenty years ago before his only son shut him up in a turret and tricked the neighbourhood with a mock funeral. Long deprived of a fire, he has crept toward the warmth through a door which his keepers failed to lock. On the traveller's urging restoration of rights, his guest exclaims, "No, no, no, no,—say not a word about it,—'Tis the hand of heaven!—I murdered my father!" and rushes back to his penitentiary.

By shifting the emphasis from creepiness of setting to the afterlife, momentarily, and then to the strangeness of this life, Lord Webb Seymour keeps up the melodramatic interest. In Scott's narratives, an incident belongs in the discussion of ghosts if the apparition is dominant and in the present section if atmosphere of place is stressed. "The Tapestried Chamber or The Lady in the Sacque" combines the two emphases in a short story which is intended to arouse fear, is free from any hint of Radcliffian explanation, and is not attacked by any sceptical character.[16]

In May 1807, Scott was told the story by Miss Anna Seward of Lichfield, who had "an authentic source," and he became acquainted with at least one other version. Perhaps after subjecting it to oral tryouts, Scott published "Story of an Apparition" anonymously in *Blackwood's Edinburgh Magazine* for April 1818 and, expanding its length four-and-a-half times, "The Tapestried Chamber" by the "Author of Waverley" in *The Keepsake for 1829* (printed in 1828).[17] Both published versions recall the *silky*, a species of ghost chiefly known in Northumberland. The Silky of Denton Hall, near Newcastle, for one, is described as a "somewhat hard and severe"-faced old woman who appeared to visitors at the manor-house in an old-fashioned gown, "the distinct rustle of *whose* silk" was audible.

> There is some obscure and dark rumour of secrets strangely obtained and enviously betrayed by a rival sister, ending in deprivation of reason and death; and that the betrayer still walks by times in the deserted hall which she rendered tenantless, always prophetic of disaster to those she encounters. . . . Visitors . . . had actually given way to these terrors so far as to quit the house in consequence.[18]

[16] Although "a complete skeptic on the subject of supernatural appearances" the day before, Lord Woodville does not try to explain his guest's experience as a dream, a vagary of the imagination, or an optical illusion, Instead, he believes and immediately sets about closing up the tapestried chamber.

[17] For a fuller discussion, see C. O. Parsons, "Scott's Prior Version of 'The Tapestried Chamber,'" *N. & Q.*, CCVII (1962), 417–20.

[18] M. A. Richardson, *The Borderer's Table Book*, Newcastle-upon-Tyne 1846, VIII. 310–16 (cp. VII. 181–5). See C. O. Parsons, "Scott's Use of the 'Silky,'" *N. & Q.*, CLXIV (1933), 76–7.

Scott's plot and setting, as well as the silky, are conventional enough. The association of that movable piece of ancestral furniture, a ghost, with a tapestried chamber is *de rigueur*.[19] Both versions relate that an officer, staying at the country seat of an old friend whom he has not seen for years, is conducted to the only apartment left vacant by guests—a bedroom newly opened up and warmed by a wood fire. At midnight a woman penetrates this room and, at a sound from the bed, turns on the soldier a face grisly with evil passions and the sunken pallor of death. Next morning he is anxious to leave his friend's residence, protesting urgent business— elsewhere. Before his departure, however, he is taken through the family portrait gallery, where he recognises his sunless visitant in the painting of a lady who had dishonoured the line by committing incest and murder in the very chamber which he has quitted.

The versions differ in such details as the time of action, 1737 or after 1781; the century in which the phantom lived and sinned, the sixteenth or seventeenth; the location, northern or western England; and the possible or actual presence of tapestry. The important differences are those of arrangement. *Blackwood's* prepares for the adventure with a family legend half narrated and broken off with significant glances at Colonel D. and describes the apparition at the time of its visit. The *Keepsake* has General Richard Browne tell of his experience when pressed by his host, Lord Frank Woodville. Ghostly etiquette is more closely observed in *Blackwood's*, with the figure, dressed in an ancient silk robe, gliding into the room noiselessly. In the *Keepsake*, the general is "suddenly aroused by a sound like that of the rustling of a silken gown, and the tapping of a pair of high-heeled shoes." Of course, ghosts are too immaterial for any sound except speech, which is permitted them after they have first been spoken to.[20]

Scott's first use of Anna Seward's story is direct, vigorous, and effective, though sometimes too condensed; his second use, while superior in the

[19] On 31 May 1819, John Ballantyne "slept in a singular old chamber hung with Tapestry" at Brahan Castle: "There only wanted a Ghost to have completed my apartment, & I was told next morning there was one in the passage." *Private Diary 1819–1821*, Morgan Library, New York City. See W. W. Fenn, "In the Room with the Arras," *Woven in Darkness. A Medley of Stories, Essays, and Dreamwork*, 2 vols., London 1885, I. 20–46. There is a parodic description of a "gloomy chamber . . . its walls hung with tapestry exhibiting figures as large as life," in Jane Austen's *Northanger Abbey*.

[20] The ghost of Mrs Heber, confined to "no definite ghost room" in Sacheverell Sitwell's Northamptonshire manor house, was not properly brought up. Whether in tapestried room or along the passages at Weston, she disturbed sleepers in 1873 by " 'a most extraordinary noise of rustling silk . . . the sound of a file, filing away very near' " and " 'of little high-heeled boots walking to and fro.' " Sacheverell Sitwell, *Poltergeists*, New York 1959, pp. 25–8.

description of the "horrible spectre," is awkward in construction and longwinded. Without referring to *Blackwood's* or consciously differentiating among oral and printed versions, he seems in "The Tapestried Chamber" to have aimed at the hasty strength, the dramatic presentation, the conversational, yarning mood of "Story of an Apparition": "I will not add to, or diminish, the narrative by any circumstance, whether more or less material, but simply rehearse, as I heard it, a story of supernatural terror." But he falls short. The reduction of his debt by marketing more words and the tired search for old subjects to be reworked tend to diffuse the ghostly effects in the version admittedly by the "Author of Waverley."[21]

In a playful vein, unlike that of his short story, Scott may represent a haunted room as an architectural heirloom which lends spice to anecdotes and affords an interesting adventure to hardy guests. At Monkbarns, Lovel's entry into nocturnal possession of the "charmed apartment" is preluded by the Antiquary's jocose remarks about phantasms going out of fashion and by Grizel Oldbuck's rather confused account of the Fairport town clerk, Rab Tull. Rab was visited in the Green Room by ancestral Aldobrand Oldenbuck's bewhiskered ghost, which conducted the punch-fortified functionary to a cabinet where a deed lay forgotten that made Grizel's grandfather triumph in a lawsuit.[22]

With such a preparation, Lovel can hardly be indifferent to his sleeping quarters. His first sensation is borrowed from Scott's experience at Glamis Castle:

> Step after step Lovel could trace his host's retreat along the various passages, and each door which he closed behind him fell with a sound more distant and dead. The guest, thus separated from the living world, took up the candle and surveyed the apartment.

The sixteenth-century tapestry with its forest green and its "grim figures," as well as the faded green bed, should keep up the ghostly illusion, but at this point susceptible young Scott of Glamis becomes middle-aged Scott of Dunvegan, and Lovel obligingly reflects his creator. The hero cannot fix his mind on ghost yarns, for hopeless love distracts him.

> He almost regretted the absence of those agitated feelings, half fear, half curiosity, which sympathise with the old legends of awe and wonder. . . . He endeavoured to conjure up something like the feelings which would, at another time, have been congenial to his situation, but his heart had no room for these vagaries of imagination.

[21] The manuscript of "The Tapestried Chamber" in the British Museum has a number of words crossed out or added but no revision of the strictly supernatural parts.

[22] See the chapter, "Curses, Omens, Dreams, and Prophecies," n. 28.

Old rumours of haunting may be renewed in order to protect and conceal living men. Smugglers in *The Antiquary* and Royalists assisting the fleeing prince at Woodstock Lodge make superstition serve their ends. Arnheim, the successive abode of elemental Hermione, Sybilla, and mysterious Anne of Geierstein, whose father Albert has a magical prestige, is described as well defended by frightful reports spread through the countryside. In *Rob Roy*, Sir Frederick Vernon chiefly restricts his movements to the library and turret of Osbaldistone Hall, which the servants say lie "on the haunted side of the house." The library, a "chamber of evil fame," yields access through Rashleigh's apartments to the turret stair, which none of the servants will ascend "for fear of bogles and brownies and lang-nebbit things frae the neist warld." Sounds, words, and the sight of an unidentified person—all arousing fears of the unknown —confer nightly sanctuary on this quarter. In a similar manner, Janet Gellatley's reputation as a witch makes it easy for her to maintain a hideout for the proscribed Baron of Bradwardine in *Waverley*.

Reports of haunting may condition the reader to strange events and to manifestations of present evil. Ruinous Graffs-lust, possessing "no good name" because it is "liable to be haunted by beings from another world," is the scene of Anne of Geierstein's double-ganging. In Rashleigh Osbaldistone's frequenting of the shunned library, there is a suggestion that bad passions may hover in the air like a malignant spirit. And in *Kenilworth*, both the helplessness of Amy Robsart and the relentless machinations against her are supernaturally intimated. When she comes to Kenilworth with the futile hope of putting her life in order, Amy is lodged in Mervyn's Tower, which is irregularly visited by a murdered Welsh prisoner. Although a somewhat humorous glimpse of the phenomena is later given in jailer Staples' allegation that the groans, howls, and clashings in the tower are really dreadful when the wind rattles and the thunder growls, the atmosphere created does serve a purpose. In her lonely room, Amy, who has grown pale and thin through suffering, is herself mistaken by Tressilian for an apparition. Finally, when fate, mischance, evil, and human weakness have brought Amy to her death, Cumnor Hall is deserted through fear of "supernatural noises," which are promptly explained by Scott as the groans and screams of Anthony Foster starving and suffocating in his treasure cell.[23] These obvious, elucidation-weighted instances of

[23] Cp. the unrationalised treatment in William Julius Mickle's "Cumnor Hall," quoted in Scott's Introduction (1831) to *Kenilworth*:

And in that Manor now no more
Is cheerful feast and sprightly ball

haunted room and hall are slight and incomplete in themselves, but in the larger interplay of irrational and inhuman forces expressed in terms of demonology, witchcraft, and astrology, they sharpen the pathos of Amy's vain struggling.

Whenever Scott enumerates weird denizens, he substitutes a method of haste for the careful evocation of the spirit of place. In *Peveril of the Peak*, Holm Peel on the Isle of Man is traditionally peopled by "goblins, ghosts, and spectres ... saints and demons ... fairies and ... familiar spirits." For practical purposes, this universal haunting of the fortress must be reduced to the antics of the banished Duchess Eleanor of Gloucester's "discontented spectre," which is sufficiently versed in ghost-lore to dissolve at the crowing of a cock or the tolling of a church bell; of the elfin Fenella, who is the object of confused superstitious regard and dread; and of the Mauthe Dog, whom we shall encounter later.

Again in *Woodstock*, and with more skill than in *Peveril of the Peak*, Scott combines popular lore about a venerable and therefore visited structure with the recent pranks of marvellous tenants. Woodstock Lodge has a general reputation for eerie concourse which makes "men afeard to harbour there after nightfall." And its vicinity, according to the Reverend Nehemiah Holdenough, local Presbyterian minister, has always been haunted by "a demon of one or the other species"—the "Demon Meridianum," a spectral huntsman or a whole band of clamorous hunters chasing the stag (as in Scott's early translation of Bürger's "Der wilde Jäger"), and the "Demon Nocturnum." To this theory of round-the-clock haunting, the sceptical Markham Everard perforce objects, but not without being warned against siding with atheists and witch-advocates in combating supernatural evidence. Later the clergyman explains that there are gradations in spirit possession of "this ancient and haunted mansion." The Devil, drawn to scenes of lust and murder, sits in Rosamond's Tower in the likeness of the poisoned mistress of Henry II; next in fearsomeness is that "haunt of evil spirits," Victor Lee's room.

In his childhood, Everard heard stories of Lee's ghost roaming through the lodge. And as a man he sleeps in the bedchamber and is unstrung when his fears are justified by the sight of a figure like Victor Lee holding a veiled lady by the hand. Even a pistol-shot at six-foot range does not dis-

> For ever since that dreary hour
> Have spirits haunted Cumnor Hall.

Amy's ghost walks in Alfred D. Bartlett, *An Historical and Descriptive Account of Cumnor Place, Berks*, Oxford and London 1850, pp. 10–11. See Sister M. Eustace Taylor, *William Julius Mickle*, Washington 1937, pp. 73–7.

compose the forms. Hesitating for a moment between two identifications, "supernatural beings" or "designing men," the Colonel settles on "dexterous combination," the master key to the goings-on of Woodstock ghosts, devils, and poltergeists. (Perhaps the servants are frightened away from Woodstock less by mysterious footfalls and voices than by lapses in pay.) No wonder that, faced with unfair competition, the older, more sedate generation of ghosts provides atmosphere but keeps out of sight. In *Woodstock* as well as in *Peveril of the Peak*, overemphasis on tricky and unconvincing present animation entangles the lineage of superstition in many a bar sinister.

The services which Scott requires of haunted places range all the way from grotesquerie, humour, and delight to terror, tragic suggestion, and symbolic evil. A haunted scene may be used by the author to reveal states of mind, foreshadow events, or link past and present through continuity of belief, or by his characters to conceal themselves, cloak their activity, or frighten their enemies away. Of course, achievement is not invariable. For instance, in establishing contact with the present, the past may deepen the sense of guilt, as in *The Heart of Midlothian*, or it may meaninglessly project its evil on the guiltless, as in "The Tapestried Chamber."[24] When Scott requests the partnership of the reader's imagination, as in much of the outdoor haunting, he creates and preserves his mood. When he is explicit and explanatory, as in many of the indoor scenes, he is heavy-handed. The sense of obscure, yet potent, mystery which Scott admired in the supernaturalism of *Job* and *Paradise Lost* must be pervasively, not pointedly, evoked.

9. WITCHCRAFT[*]

Scott's interest in witchcraft was virtually conterminous with his lifetime. The fear that witches—and later fairies—could substitute manikins or changelings for humans, especially infants, had descended from classical times. After a formal system of witchcraft beliefs spread over Europe, the sorceress acting as midwife was said to baptise babies "in name of the devill privately," and injunctions were finally issued against the exercise of diabolical arts by midwives.[1] Scott possessed three counter-charms

[24] Note the very meaningful intrusion of the vile dead on the living in Henry James's *The Turn of the Screw*.

[*] Another treatment may be found in Mody C. Boatright's admirable "Witchcraft in the Novels of Sir Walter Scott," *University of Texas Studies in English*, XIII (1933), 95–112.

[1] Robert Law, *Memorialls*, ed. C. K. Sharpe, Edinburgh 1819, pp. 125–6; *Visitation Articles and Injunctions of the Period of the Reformation*, ed. W. H. Frere, London 1910, II. 372.

against such evils or, what is very likely, one charm which was so enthusiastically and variously named and lauded that it seemed like three.

The flat, heart-shaped, chocolate-coloured stone amulet, mounted in silver filigree, which was his mother's, had a small ring set in the top, so that it could be hung around the necks of lying-in women and babies to preserve them from sorcery and witchcraft.[2] One of Scott's servants, George Walkinshaw (born about 1786), may have had this in imperfect memory when he told of his master's purchase of some "lammer beads" (amber beads) which were later reset and given to Margaret Charlotte Carpenter soon after Scott married her:

> They were the pride of the good lady's heart, and held in high esteem by the old people of the country side for their sanatory virtues. Besides possessing many other occult qualities, they were known to be a sure charm against the malign influences of witchcraft, and an infallible remedy for sore eyes.[3]

The "good lady" was probably the former owner of the *beads*, not Charlotte Scott. Still another charm—or account of the same charm— was the toadstone which Scott describes as shielding "pregnant women from the power of demons, and other dangers incidental to their situation."[4] The mysterious stone, actually the petrified tooth of a fossil fish, "might be procured entire by burying the toad in an ant-hill to consume its flesh, and its genuineness was supposed to be ascertained by a toad raising itself and snatching at it when put within reach!"[5] Less sensational is Scott's description of the toadstone in a letter to Miss Joanna Baillie, who made the purse in which it was kept:

> III. A toadstone, a celebrated amulet which was never lent to any one unless upon a bond for a thousand merks for its being safely restored. It was sovereign for protecting new born children and their mothers from the power of the fairies and has been repeatedly borrowed from my mother on account of this virtue.[6]

The Lee Penny, later used in *The Talisman*, and Scottish curing stones may have suggested to Scott the heavy bond exacted for safe return.

[2] M. M. Maxwell Scott, *Abbotsford: the Personal Relics and Antiquarian Treasures of Sir Walter Scott Described*, London 1893, p. 56, and exhibit card at Abbotsford.

[3] George Allan, *Life of Sir Walter Scott*, Philadelphia 1835, p. 118.

[4] *Minstrelsy*, II. 363, n. I. Mrs Hughes adds that the toadstone was supposed to "ensure a safe delivery." Mrs Hughes, p. 70.

[5] Dalyell, *Darker Superstitions of Scotland*, p. 408 (also see pp. 130-2, 135-6); John Brand, *Popular Antiquities of Great Britain*, ed. W. C. Hazlitt, London 1870, III. 97-9; G. F. Black, "Scottish Charms and Amulets," *Proceedings* of the Society of Antiquaries of Scotland, XXVII (1893), 506-09; Radford, *Encyclopaedia of Superstitions, s.v.* gems, toad.

[6] 4 Apr. 1815 in *Letters*, III. 102; XII. 487.

What the humble toadstone borrows from better-known amulets, it repays in Scott's understanding of the concern Meg Merrilies feels for the heir of Ellangowan in *Guy Mannering*, "Wha was to hae keepit awa the worriecows ... and the elves and gyre-carlings frae the bonny bairn?"[7]

As a collector, Scott was interested in oral lore and books as well as superstitious objects. When travelling through Perthshire and Forfarshire in the spring of 1796, he spent a night at Montrose with his old tutor, James Mitchell, who sadly relates that the young advocate's chief purpose was apparently not attendance at the Court of Justiciary in its northern circuit, but the collection of "ancient ballads and traditional stories about fairies, witches, and ghosts."[8] A friendly competitor, R. P. Gillies, has this comment on Scott's persistent search for books on witchcraft:

> It soon became an agreement betwixt Mr. Ballantyne and myself, that whenever there occurred a fresh arrival of old treasures, I should be present at the unpacking of the boxes, and make my own selection, only with this caveat, that if any "witch-books" came in the way, these were to be put aside for Sir Walter Scott. Under this generic title he ranked all books and tracts, not only relating to witches, but to daemonology, ghosts, apparitions, warnings, prophecies, &c., having for a long time been sedulous to form a large collection in this department, with a view to compose, one day, an original work on the subject.[9]

Abbotsford became cluttered like an antiquarian museum. So great was its store that gifts went out to societies and fellow collectors. On 31 January 1827, Mr James Bowd presented Scott with a heart which he had found fifteen years ago in the floor rubbish of a Dalkeith house occupied some half-century previously by cattle-tenders. The same day, Scott transferred this relic to less occupied hands: "Called on Skene to give him for the Antiquarian Society a heart, human apparently, stuck full of pins ... it is in perfect preservation."[10] James Skene did not fall into the error of supposing the heart to be human. In fact, he learned from Mr Bowd that a woman past eighty—

> recollected, in her youth, a bad disease having got amongst the cattle in that quarter, and particularly among those kept in the house in question;

---

[7] Cp. R. H. Cromek, *Remains of Nithsdale and Galloway Song*, London 1810, p. 292: "Mothers frequently frighten their children by threatening to give them to *M'Neven*, or the *Gyre Carline* [mother witch]."

[8] Lockhart, I. 112–13 (see also I. 239). Confused by the misdating of some of Scott's letters, Lockhart refers the trip to the autumn of 1796.

[9] Gillies, *Memoirs of a Literary Veteran*, London 1851, II. 10–11. The omitted criticism of *Demonology*, Scott's "original work," is more detailed in Gillies, *Recollections of Sir Walter Scott, Bart.*, London 1837, pp. 132–3.

[10] *Journal*, p. 313.

and that she knew that it was then the practice, when such calamities befell their cattle, for the country people to take the heart of a calf, as a representative for the heart of the witch by whose malice their cattle were visited, and to place it on a spit before the fire, sticking in a pin at every turn, until it was completely roasted, by which the witch was subjected to a simultaneous operation of proportional severity in her own bosom. . . . The heart thus prepared was secretly deposited near the cattle; and no doubt the one in question had been of that description.[11]

Scott later saw the counter-charm as "the withered heart of some animal stuck full of many scores of pins."[12] Three decades ago, a small jar was found at Abbotsford containing a lump like dried clay, held together by what seemed to be human hair. A note in Scott's hand attests it to be a "witch's charm."[13] This is probably the *instance*, used elsewhere, "that the belief in witchcraft is only asleep":

> In a remote part of the Highlands, an ignorant and malignant woman seems really to have meditated the destruction of her neighbour's property, by placing in a cowhouse, or byre, as we call it, a pot of baked clay, containing locks of hair, parings of nails, and other trumpery. This precious spell was discovered, the design conjectured, and the witch would have been torn to pieces, had not a high-spirited and excellent lady in the neighbourhood gathered some of her people, (though these were not very fond of the service,) and by main force taken the unfortunate creature out of the hands of the populace. The formidable spell is now in my possession.[14]

The jar was delivered to Scott by a young laird, the friend of Mrs Maclean Clephane of Torloisk, who writes on 27 June 1813:

> I . . . have given him a small gallipot directed to you in which you will find a witch's spell which once was breathed full of bad wishes and looked into by evil eyes. This ammunition, it seems, hits point blank, for the spell—with three others—made away with no less than six cows. So the one I have sent may be said to have killed a cow and a half to its own

---

[11] *Archaeologia Scotica: or Transactions of the Society of Antiquaries of Scotland*, III (1831), 300–01. The heart is now in the Scottish National Museum of Antiquities, Edinburgh. An illustration appears in E. D. Longman and S. Loch, *Pins and Pincushions*, London 1911, p. 37. Cp. *N. & Q.*, Second Series, I (1856), 415.

[12] *Demonology*, p. 340.

[13] *The Scotsman*, 7 Oct. 1931. See Longman and Loch, *Pins and Pincushions*, p. 38, and for the magical use of an earthen pot William Drage, *Daimonomageia*, London 1665: "One was so bound [incapacitated in generation] by an earthen Pot, threw by a Witch into his Well, with some ceremonies."

[14] *Demonology*, pp. 339–40. For the vulgar persuasion of witchcraft in Scott's day, see James Paterson, *A Belief in Witchcraft Unsupported by Scripture*, Aberdeen 1815, p. i: "One necessitated, by official duties, frequently to converse with men in the ordinary ranks of life, and to gain an acquaintance with their sentiments, must observe how generally a belief in Witchcraft prevails among them, and the strong conviction they feel of its truth." Cp. *op. cit.*, p. 21.

share. They were placed above the byre door of the farmer who lost his *beasts* (as he called them); and he believes so religiously in their bad consequences that he sent for a famous Tobermory wizard to set matters to rights. He called them "Wicked machines"; and vowed with many oaths needless to mention that if he could discover who did it "he would let them see a bonfire." I suppose you understand the meaning of that without a glass.[15]

Scott needed no glass to understand a threat to burn. Some help in understanding what was far more difficult, the heart of a witch, came to him as Sheriff of Selkirkshire, an office which he held from 16 December 1799, almost to the time of his death. He circumspectly tells the story of an old woman who supported herself in a lonely part of Scotland by raising chickens, a work at which she was so handy that she was said to prosper by unlawful means. Finding it hard to get feed in the lean years (about 1800), she applied to a farmer for a peck of oats, but he refused: he had already measured out his grain for the Dalkeith market. Soon after her uttered wish that evil might befall his produce, a wheel dropped off one of the carts ejecting sacks into the river—*damnum minatum, et malum secutum*.[16] The farmer consulted the county Sheriff—Scott avoids naming himself— who pointed out that the laws against witchcraft had been repealed and that the whole thing was merely an accident. But when the Sheriff, expressing scepticism, advised the old woman to be cautious, she was piqued: "I kenna how it is, but something aye comes after my words when I am ill-guided, and speak ower fast."[17]

*   *   *

The kindly rationalism of Sheriff Scott and of his friend, the Highland lady, is parted between Reuben Butler and Duncan of Knockdunder, a

---

[15] Partington, *Post-Bag*, pp. 99–100.

[16] This legal formula, by which many a witch was condemned to the stake, is illustrated by the following passage: "The main thing proven, was her threatening such as refused to give her money, and some evil accidents befalling them shortlie thereafter." *Chronological Notes of Scottish Affairs, from 1680 till 1701: being chiefly taken from the Diary of Lord Fountainhall*, ed. Sir Walter Scott, Edinburgh 1822, p. 261. Also see R. H. Robbins, *The Encyclopedia of Witchcraft and Demonology*, New York 1959, *s.v.* Maleficia. In *The Bride of Lammermoor*, when Ailsie Gourlay menaces Johnie Mortsheugh with "Let's see if the pins haud," the musical sexton retorts, "I take ye a' to witness, gude people, that she threatens me wi' mischief, and forespeaks me. If ony thing but gude happens to me or my fiddle this night, I'll make it the blackest night's job she ever stirred in."

[17] *Demonology*, pp. 340–2: "The story . . . contains materials resembling those out of which many tragic incidents have arisen." Scott twice says that he is well acquainted with the circumstances. The deduction that he was the Sheriff is made in *Spectator* for 18 Sep. 1830, p. 736. Selkirkshire, with fewer than 25,000 inhabitants, may still be described as a lonely part of Scotland. Donald Carswell, *Sir Walter*, London 1930, p. 167.

Highland captain, in *The Heart of Midlothian*. David Deans maintains that Ailie MacClure "practises her abominations, spaeing folks' fortunes wi' egg-shells, and mutton-banes, and dreams and divinations, whilk is a scandal to ony Christian land to suffer sic a wretch to live; and I'll uphaud that, in a' judicatures, civil or ecclesiastical." To the Captain, Ailie is a white witch who "only spaes fortunes, and does not lame, or plind, or pedevil any persons, or coup cadgers' carts, or ony sort of mischief; put only tells people good fortunes, as anent our poats killing so many seals and doug-fishes, whilk is very pleasant to hear." And to Butler, she is "no witch, but a cheat . . . practising her impostures upon ignorant persons"— for profit. Not wanting the rabble to duck Ailie, the Captain persuades Butler to admonish her privately and not to bring her before the kirk session.

Whether she is supernatural help, harm, or hoax, Ailie MacClure is paltry beside the antipathetic pair of witches, Madge Wildfire and her "deevil's buckie" of a mother, Meg Murdockson. Among characters living under Providence or under Fate, Meg and her mad daughter represent the extreme of lawlessness in the godless natural dispensation.[18] Violent in her graspingness, Meg Murdockson may have encouraged the love-affair between Madge and George Staunton as a means of rising in the world. She does away with the bastard child and hates Staunton and his sweetheart, Effie Deans, with a ferocity which is intensified by her delusion of diabolical confederacy. The *idée fixe* of this "vindictive fiend" is revenge, "the best reward the devil gives us." But, having been Staunton's wet-nurse, she has a curdled drop of human kindness in her breast: "Though he has made me company for the devil, if there be a devil, and food for hell, if there be such a place, yet I cannot take his life."[19]

Madge openly calls her rancour-hardened mother a witch who has sailed through the air and over the waves with her gudeman, Satan. Beside a charcoal fire, Meg seems a "Hecate at her infernal rites," and when repeatedly called "Mother Blood," she "brayed and howled like a demoniac." As Frank Levitt tells Madge, "You have not such a touch of the devil's blood as the hag your mother, who may be his dam for what I know." When the witch and her dark kinsman do not agree, poor Madge's back pays. Mother and daughter are not alike in evil. Meg is

---

[18] See P. F. Fisher, "Providence, Fate, and the Historical Imagination in Scott's *The Heart of Midlothian*." *Nineteenth-Century Fiction*, x (1955), 99–114.

[19] Meg's scepticism at this point is in keeping with Scott's belief that delusion is not unbroken and that supreme evil may raise the villainous above superstition. The latter interpretation, however, usually applies to better educated scoundrels who sneer at ignorant credulity.

naturally evil, but Madge errs through lack of guidance, a yielding nature, giddy vanity, and final insanity.

In flickers of sanity, Madge longs for her mother's blessing of "lang syne" and for her "puir wean," whose death brought on her infirmity.[20] But she understands lunacy in demonological terms, "my auld acquaintance the deil" having brushed her lips with his wing and laid his broad black palm on her mouth, so that good thoughts and words have become foolish songs and sayings. The moon shines for her pleasure and is the tutelary planet in whose light she dances, "and whiles dead folk came and danced wi' me . . . ony body I had kend when I was living." Muschat's Cairn is made more fearful by her conceit of talking to the murderer Nicol Muschat and his wife Ailie between bat-flying and cock-crowing time, and of calling Ailie out by moonlight to wash her bloody corpse-sheet. In Madge Wildfire's words, the note of pathos characteristic of Elizabethan and Jacobean mad scenes sounds once more. She is a figure of pathetic, as her mother is of melodramatic, power.

But Scott is hardly sentimental about his witches, who have taken a blameworthy road and must suffer. When Meg Murdockson is hanged near Carlisle, Dame Hinchup calls her "nae witch, but a bluidy-fingered thief and murderess." At this, the bystanders malign the realist as an English witch defending a Scotch sister. Meg is preserved to startled memory in a broadsheet. The "hellicat devil" Madge is ducked by butchers and graziers whose cattle are plagued by a witch-induced distemper and is belatedly rescued, insensible and dying, by a magistrate.

In both hanging and ducking, Scott is less interested in relating the victims' last moments than in revealing the passions and superstitious fears of the mob. Such phrases as "the gallows-tree," "the tall aërial ladder," "the executioner," and "the present victim of the law" indicate that the people are not taking justice directly into their own hands against Meg. The last English execution was in 1682, the last Scottish one in 1722, and both English and Scottish statutes against witchcraft persecution and prosecution were repealed in 1736.[21] The hanging of Meg Murdockson in 1737 is therefore anachronistic, but the non-judicial drowning of Madge Wildfire is probably not.[22] Indeed, as late as 1743, Presbyterians convened

[20] The original of Madge Wildfire, as Scott points out, was Feckless Fanny, whose low-born shepherd lover was shot by her father. Apparently, the only superstitious garnishing of Fanny's story is that several people who crossed the crazed wanderer were mysteriously punished.

[21] Wallace Notestein, *A History of Witchcraft in England*, Washington 1911, p. 369; *Demonology*, pp. 338–9. The law (9 George II, ch. 5) went into effect on 24 Jun. 1736. *The Statutes: Revised Edition*, London 1871, II. 401.

[22] For mob violence similar to that practised on Madge Wildfire, see *The Tryal of Thomas Colley*, 2nd edn, London 1751?; *Demonology*, pp. 272–3.

at Edinburgh declared any withdrawal of penal inflictions sinful and "contrary to the express Law of God!"[23]

Scott goes back to a period of much greater supernatural activity and more widespread belief for his most compelling evocation of witches. The realistic kernel of the Gallovidian family legend on which *The Bride of Lammermoor* is based is that, on 12 August 1669, Janet Dalrymple married Baldoon; on 24 August, she was taken from her parents' house of Carscreugh to her bridal home, where on 12 September she died suddenly and was buried some eighteen days later. This tragic series of events inspired legend-makers to pierce the mystery in their fashion and political opportunists to defame the powerful Dalrymples.

The fablers evolved four different combinations of deeds and motives: (1) the bride, marrying against her mother's will, received a parental curse and was stabbed by her husband, who went mad; (2) forced to marry Baldoon despite her engagement to Lord Rutherford, the bride stabbed her husband and went mad; (3) on the wedding night, Rutherford slipped in through the bedroom window and wounded his rival; and (4) after calling on her diabolical master to claim her if she broke troth with Rutherford, the girl married Baldoon, who received a mauling and lost his bride as well. Thus there are four vengeful characters: the mother working through the husband, the wife, the lover, and the fiend punishing a vow-breaker. The prime mover in the first three versions is the inhumanly strong-willed mother, and, in the fourth, the fatally treacherous daughter.

Softening the bride's treachery into weakness, Scott uses both these strands of motivation. He seems to have rejected the first version as making the bridegroom the mere automaton of the mother's strange power and to have become acquainted with the third only after the publication of his novel. The fourth he recalls incidentally, as in this passage: " 'And is it true then,' mumbled the paralytic wretch, 'that the bride was trailed out of her bed and up the chimley by evil spirits, and that the bridegroom's face was wrung round ahint him?' " The second version was the best for Scott's purposes.

Although the political fable-makers slurred the character of Janet Dalrymple, their hatred of her father, James Dalrymple, who had risen rapidly from Lord of Session in 1657 to Knight, Baronet, Lord President, Privy Councillor of Scotland, and Viscount Stair, induced more direct attacks on Lady Stair. In lampoons and memoirs, she was represented as a witch who gained preferment for her family through hellish compacts,

[23] Law, *Memorialls*, p. cvii.

a sorceress who promised affluence so long as her coffin stood upright above ground, a daughter of Beelzebub—

> Whose malice oft wes wreckit at home,
> On the curst cubs of her owne womb.[24]

In his vituperative "Satyre on the Familie of Stairs," Sir William Hamilton of Whitelaw consistently pictures Viscount Stair as vacillating and two-faced, and his wife as heartlessly domineering. In fact, the family line is devil-tainted:

> It's not Stair's bairnes alone Nick doth infest,
> His children's children lykewise are possest.[25]

Scott roughly parallels these contemporary portraits in *The Bride of Lammermoor*. Realising, however, the absurdity of burdening his plot with maternal witchcraft and diabolical retribution, yet unwilling to abandon the theme altogether, Scott makes the mother more credible and relates the daughter's madness to witchcraft outside the family. Thus he allows the tragedy to develop on two levels, one of romantic realism and another of superstitious lore. Despite Ailsie Gourlay's ascription of witchcraft to Lady Ashton and Lucy's responsiveness to the weird, the central figures move on the first level, sometimes descending to the second, where they meet old Alice Gray's apparition, sexton Johnie Mortsheugh, and three crones who act as chorus to the catastrophe of the main action.

Scott carefully differentiates among lesser characters who are reputed to be witches. Alice Gray, for one, a dependent of the Ashton family and former servant of the Ravenswoods, is maliciously described by young Henry Ashton as "a witch, that should have been burned with them that suffered at Haddington." Mortsheugh knows that she must be buried six feet deep in a warlock's grave "or her ain witch cummers [cronies] would soon whirl her out of her shroud for a' their auld acquaintance." Alice belongs to that class of suspected women for whom Mause pleads in Allan Ramsay's pastoral play, *The Gentle Shepherd* (1725), II. iii:

> This fool imagines, as do mony sic,
> That I'm a witch in compact with Auld Nick,
> Because by education I was taught
> To speak and act *aboon their common thought.   *above

---

[24] "Inscriptione for Lord Stair's [the son's] Tomb," *A Second Book of Scottish Pasquils &c.*, Edinburgh 1828, p. 70.
[25] *A Book of Scottish Pasquils &c.*, Edinburgh 1827, p. 54; *A Book of Scotish Pasquils. 1568–1715*, Edinburgh 1868, pp. 189, 370.

The old hags who take "a singular and gloomy delight" in preparing Alice Gray's body for its narrow house remind Ravenswood of the witches in *Macbeth*, whose literary descendants they are.[26] Inasmuch as crones are wont to gather in mystical triads, Scott's group is made up of Ailsie Gourlay, an octogenarian, Annie Winnie, a lame woman,[27] and a nameless paralytic wretch. While this third prong of evil is ironically left to guard the corpse against witches and fiends, her more active companions hirple forth to cull rosemary in Alice's garden, where their cankered desire for power and revenge on real or imaginary foes is laid bare:

"They prick us and they pine us, and they pit us on the pinnywinkles for witches; and, if I say my prayers backwards ten times ower, Satan will never gie me amends o' them."

"Did ye ever see the foul thief?" asked her neighbour [Ailsie].

"Na!" replied the other spokeswoman; "but I trow I hae dreamed of him mony a time, and I think the day will come they will burn me for't."

Believing in the possibility of a pact with the Devil, resenting his denial of aid and bounty, verging on auto-suggestion, they relish rousing terror in the credulous and gleefully hobble along the pitmirkie paths of misanthropy. These misery-demented women foresee a short and painful life for both Edgar Ravenswood and Lucy Ashton. When Annie Winnie gloats over the Master of Ravenswood's handsome body, "He wad mak a bonnie corpse—I wad like to hae the streaking and winding o' him,"[28] Ailsie Gourlay is not reassuring. It is written on his brow that "dead-deal will never be laid on his back." Again, at the bridal, second-sighted Ailsie asserts that Lucy's "winding sheet is up as high as her throat already,

[26] See Wilmon Brewer, *Shakespeare's Influence on Sir Walter Scott*, Boston 1925, pp. 281–4. Joanna Baillie's tragedy, *Ethwald*, PT I (1802) changes Macbeth into an ambitious thane who penetrates the Druid's Cave, where three post-Druidic Mystic Sisters, three Mystics, an Arch Sister, and their invisible Master grant him visions of a crown and sceptre and of "a crowned phantom, covered with wounds," as well as sounds of "Mercia's woes."

[27] Her name probably came from an Edinburgh trial of 20 Dec. 1644, in which Agnes Finnie was charged with causing the death of William Ffairlie, because the boy called her "by nick-name 'Annie Winnie.'" *Some Unpublished Scottish Witchcraft Trials*, ed. George F. Black, New York 1941, p. 20. In Walter C. Smith, "The Confession of Annaple Gowdie, Witch," Annie Winnie rides a broom to join her coven of thirteen in a kirk. *Poetical Works*, London 1906, pp. 33–4. Ailsie Gourlay also comes from appropriate stock: "In a witch trial recorded in Humble Kirk Session Register (23 Sep. 1649) one Agnes Gourlay is accused of having made offerings of milk" to the fairies underground. Spence, *Encyclopaedia of Occultism, s.v.* Scotland (Highlands).

[28] " 'He's a bonny corpse,' she [Meg Merrilies] muttered to herself, 'and weel worth the streaking.'" Cp. Scott's fireside anecdote in Mrs Hughes, p. 292: "Two old women whose office it was to lay out the dead were in the Churchyard when their Laird's son passed: he heard them say: 'Hech, lass look to winsome Mr. Peter—he'll be a bonny corpse to streck': it so affected him, that he fell ill and died soon after." The senile necrophilia of these women is less latent than manifest.

believe it wha list." Appearing at the bride's funeral to gloat with her cummers over the discomfiture of the mighty, Ailsie pursues Ravenswood like an embodied fury, "If auld freets [omens] say true, there's ane o' that company that'll no be lang for this warld."

Ailsie Gourlay is famous for cures of mysterious diseases by herbs selected with due regard to planetary hours, words, signs, and charms. "She 'spaed fortunes,' read dreams, composed philtres, discovered stolen goods, and made and dissolved matches as successfully as if, according to the belief of the whole neighbourhood, she had been aided in those arts by Beelzebub himself." More carefully individualised than her sister hags, the Wise Woman of Bowden surpasses them in keen malice and warped intelligence. Such is the agent employed by Lady Ashton to tend her daughter and soften her will with superstitious legends. To this unnatural conspiracy Lucy, whose taste runs to stories trimmed with "supernatural horrors," is an easy victim. Ailsie's tales cunningly grow in sombre terror as they centre more sharply on the doomed house of Ravenswood. With the virtual unhinging of the girl's mind, submission to her mother's more ambitious marital schemes is assured.

Sensing that a prolonged acquaintance with his hags would both pall on the reader and destroy the artistic balance between light and shadow, Scott restricts their activity to the last third of *The Bride of Lammermoor*. Their literary labours are three: they advance plot (through Ailsie), intensify mood by their running commentary on the puniness of doomed characters, and inspire interest in themselves as self-deluded witches. Enthusiasm about the last achievement leads Joanna Baillie to suggest to the Great Unknown that Mr Cleishbotham or Pattieson write a novel on *The Witch*:[29]

> I can imagine a malevolent mind in those days by degrees actually believing that it acted by power from the devil, and to trace those steps would be very curious and subtle, and give much insight into human nature.[30]

On Miss Baillie's following her own advice in a tragedy, *Witchcraft*, Scott unconsciously commends his earlier fictional interpretation in his comment:

[29] In its early planning stage, *The Witch*—renamed *Redgauntlet*—was perhaps intended to contain the contrast between witchcraft and Quakerism which Archibald Constable had suggested for *Peveril*. *Constable and his Literary Correspondents*, III. 212, 287, 290.

[30] 28 Jun. 1819 in *Familiar Letters of Sir Walter Scott*, Boston 1894, II. 46–7. For a discussion of fatal self-accusation coming from hags' blind infatuation and of the influence of *The Bride of Lammermoor* in shaping this motivation, see the Appendix to *Witchcraft*. Joanna Baillie, *Dramas*, London 1836, III. 483–4. Miss Baillie writes Sir Walter about her tragedy: "I am inclined [to] think favourably of it. Renfrew Witches upon a polite stage! Will such a thing ever be endured!" Undated fragment in Walpole.

I shall be curious to see it. Will it be real witchcraft—the *Ipsissimus Diabolus*—or an impostor, or the half-crazed being who believes herself an ally of condemnd spirits, and desires to be so? That last is a sublime subject.[31]

In developing his sublime subject, Scott uses as the groundwork of his plot a family legend with which he has been familiar from youth through the oral versions of his mother, Mrs Margaret Swinton, Mrs Anne Murray Keith, and William Clerk. To the crude and hackneyed plot of heartless parent, compliant child, and certain tragedy he perhaps adds something from William Sampson's play, *The Vow Breaker* (1636).[32] When Lucy tries not to be a vow-breaker by writing to the Master of Ravenswood for her release, Lady Ashton lays hold of the letter. Here and elsewhere in *The Bride of Lammermoor*, Scott's problem is not so much one of invention as of modification. Refining the primitive violence of his sources, Scott maintains a duality of mood and action by allowing his chief persons to work out their destinies against the dark background of witch-lore—the flower of much reading in early trials—and of country-side superstitions. Omens, presages, and spoken doom impart the narrative tightness of folk literature.

Whether restrained by attacks of pain from wasting time on digressions, clumsy rationalism, and stultifying literariness or by the power, movement, and economy of the Dalrymple legend, Scott works with a sure hand. He narrates directly and swiftly, paring his fictional materials to the quick. Although Scott came out of his trance of concentration to be shocked by the unmasked force of his narrative, he never surpassed his objectification in warped characters of the evil and irrationality inherent in life.[33]

*   *   *

Witchcraft, somewhat varied, reappears in several of the Scottish novels. Brief passages in *Waverley* are like a preview of the accusation and defence of Ailie MacClure in *The Heart of Midlothian* and the self-delusion of crones in *The Bride of Lammermoor*. The popular dread of witches, the meagre grounds, the prejudice and rare enlightenment of the upper class, and the urge to confess under punishment, the sorry materials of many a Scottish witch case, are sketched in humorously yet with an eye to the

[31] 22 Jul. 1827 in *Journal*, p. 376. For Scott's most thoughtful and humane treatment of witchcraft outside fiction, see *Grandfather*, Second Series, (1828), ch. xiv.

[32] *The Vow Breaker* is in the Abbotsford Library. There are sensational chapbook versions of the play.

[33] See C. O. Parsons, "The Dalrymple Legend in *The Bride of Lammermoor*," *The Review of English Studies*, XIX (1943), 51–8.

darker shadings. When Edward Waverley is a guest in the house of Tully-Veolan, he learns from Rose Bradwardine that her father, moved to "a strange defiance of the marvellous," once triumphantly stood up for Janet Gellatley—"born on his estate"—against Whig gentry and ministers who arraigned her as a witch. "The infallible grounds [were] that she was very old, very ugly, very poor, and had two sons, one of whom was a poet, and the other a fool." When imprisoned, partially starved, and deprived of sleep, she became convinced that she had been accosted by the Devil and had performed wonders as a channel of his power. The lairds' and divines' shame at fleeing when the witch shrilled, "I see the Evil One sitting in the midst of ye," as well as the Baron's defence, led to Janet's release.[34] But the general fear, shared even by Bailie Duncan Macwheeble, of the hut and haunted glen in which she lives lingers on, so that the attainted Jacobite Baron of Bradwardine later hides in the unsonsy place. Only once after she is freed from the charge of witchcraft does Janet sink into self-deception: "And for that Inch-Grabbit [rapacious heir-male of the Bradwardine estate], I could whiles wish mysell a witch for his sake, if I werena feared the Enemy wad tak me at my word."

In *The Antiquary*, the way is prepared for the emotional tensions and revelations of Elspeth o' the Craigburnfoot's deathbed confession to the Earl of Glenallan by such clues as Jenny Rintherout's hint, "D'ye think yoursell that she's no uncanny?" Maggie Mucklebackit's defence of her mother-in-law hardly dispels the suspicion: "Canny, ye silly tawpie! think ye ae auld wife's less canny than anither?—unless it be Ailison Breck; I really couldna in conscience swear for her." A witch allusion may contribute to atmosphere of place, as in *Rob Roy*. The landlady in the wild and inhospitable Clachan of Aberfoil is "the Hecate," Jeanie MacAlpine. "Her black hair, which escaped in uncombed elf-locks from under her coif, as well as the strange and embarrassed look with which she regarded us, gave me the idea of a witch disturbed in the midst of her unlawful rites."

The grosser aspects of witchcraft are for the most part avoided or, at least, played down in the Waverley Novels. Lady Lochleven's cruel treatment of captive Mary in *The Abbot* draws from the Queen a re-

---

[34] In a note, Scott locates the original episode in "the south of Scotland," where "an old clergyman" shielded "a poor insane creature" from his zealous brethren. In his introduction to Thomas Potts's "A Wonderfull Discoverie of Witches in the Countie of Lancaster" (1613), Scott quotes the description of that "dangerous witch" Chattox: "She was a 'very old, withered, spent, and decrepid creature; her sight almost gone, her lips ever chattering and walking, but no man knew what.' " *Somers Tracts*, 2nd edn, ed. Walter Scott, London 1810, III. 95.

flexion on early frailty. "That stain is the very reverse of what is said of the witch's mark—I can make her feel there, though she is otherwise insensible all over." The revolting detail which Scott figuratively veils is probably not the true witch's mark, a teat from which a familiar sucked milk or blood, but the devil's mark, *signum pacti*, which neither bled nor felt pain.[35]

Although witch-finders flourished in the seventeenth century, Scott makes his sole "trier of witches," Gaffer Pinniewinks,[36] active in Elizabethan *Kenilworth*. After being ordered to put Wayland Smith to the probation, Pinniewinks sharpens his pincers and his probing awl, and Dame Crank, the Catholic laundress, opines that the Devil will make Wayland's flesh insensitive. But the fortunate farrier has left the Vale of Whitehorse with Tressilian, "to whom I owe it, that Gaffer Pinniewinks is not even now rending my flesh and sinews with his accursed pincers, and probing every mole in my body with his sharpened awl (a murrain on the hands which forged it!) in order to find out the witch's mark." Thus Scott adds the witch-finder to his narrative illustration of culture history without having to describe the actual search for Devil's or witch's mark.

Scott does not gaze on the revels of Kirk Alloway with Burns or hasten to the Brockenberg with Goethe. Perhaps because the witches' Sabbath was more variously reported on the Continent than in England or Scotland, he permits Annette Veilchen to characterise Anne of Geierstein's father, Count Albert, as one who has "sailed to the mountains of the Brockenberg, where witches hold their sabbath." More interested in the picturesque, typical, and humanly revealing aspects of the supernatural than in its sensationalism, Scott makes no use of that eclectic, pagan-heretico-parodic carnival. The Sabbath swept anointed witches through space to the presence of the goat demon, to the kiss of shame, sacrilegious rites, infant sacrifice, obscene feasting and dancing, and unnatural copulation. Its climax was sexual. As a narrator, Scott refrains,[37] nor does he picture lone witches stirring up love and lust or inflicting sterility and

[35] See Montague Summers, *The History of Witchcraft and Demonology*, 2nd edn, New York 1956, pp. 70–7; Robbins, *Encyclopedia of Witchcraft and Demonology*, *s.v.* devil's mark, pricking, shaving, and witch's mark; and James Fraser, *Chronicles of the Frasers*, ed. William Mackay, Edinburgh 1905, pp. 446–7 ("the spell spot").

[36] *Pinniewinks* is an instrument of torture with holes for the accused's fingers, which are squeezed by means of pegs. His name suggests that the gaffer is more a torturer extracting confession than a witch finder or pricker discovering potential victims at so much a head.

[37] In "Ancient Sorceries," Algernon Blackwood strikes the balance between past and present stages of belief in an indirect evocation of the witches' Sabbath which is chastened without being weakened. *Prince of Darkness*, ed. Gerald Verner, London 1946, pp. 79–145.

impotence. His utmost limit is the suggestion of necrophilia in senile hags.

After drawing uncomfortably close to the sick imaginings, the sadism and the cruelty, of witchcraft in his novels from 1818 to 1821, Scott returns to the more conventional manifestations. When female thoughts, deeds, or emotions go far beyond the norm, he tends to express human extremes in supernatural terms. In *The Fortunes of Nigel*, Mrs Ursula Suddlechop tries to worm out of Margaret Ramsay the secret of her god-father's ghost in order to uphold her character as "Mother Midnight," in competition with Mother Redcap. Fertile in suspicion, she slurs the Ramsays' laundry-maid under her breath, "I hope she will go to the devil in the flame of a tar-barrel, like many a Scots witch before her!" Pro-curess, hidden agent, and wisewoman, as well as milliner, Mrs Suddlechop adds the spice of witchery to her unlawful occupations.

The animus against the prosperous of Scott's triad reappears in the "grumbling crone" of *St Ronan's Well* who harbours the dying Hannah Irwin. When Lord Etherington and Lady Penelope Penfeather leave the cottage of this pauper, not without a farewell gratuity, she bursts out, " 'The Almighty guide your course through the troubles of this wicked warld—and the muckle deevil blaw wind in your sails,' she added, in her natural tone." Her keeping Clara Mowbray out, through fear of a delusion of Satan, gives Scott a chance to explain her witch-like attitude. "The old hag was one of those whose hearts adversity turns to very stone, and obstinately kept her door shut, impelled more probably by general hatred to the human race than by the superstitious fears which seized her."[38]

⋆　　⋆　　⋆

Scott is on shaky supernatural ground whenever he leaves the country and the historical periods best known to him. A sense of the theatrically effective replaces dramatic feeling and an intimate knowledge of the tex-ture of beliefs. This is evident in *Ivanhoe* (1820), his most extensive excursion into witchcraft outside Scotland. Ulrica, the daughter of mur-dered Torquil Wolfganger, is a farrago of witch, fury, demon, evil angel, heathen goddess, sibyl, and revenge-maddened mortal, constant in no single aspect. In Cedric's presence she speaks of "the demon who has governed my life" and thinks it would be well to turn to the fiends of

[38] In a note on the muttered curse, Scott comments: "The author has made an attempt in this character to draw a picture of what is too often seen, a wretched being whose heart becomes hardened and spited at the world, in which she is doomed to experience much misery and little sympathy."

Christianity, "to Woden, Hertha, and Zernebock—to Mista, and to Skogula, the Gods of our yet unbaptized ancestors." "The Saxon witch Ulrica" cruelly haunts the death-bed of Reginald Front-de-Boeuf, whom she goaded into killing his father. He yearns to live until this "incarnate fiend" goes to hell fires through a flesh-devouring bonfire. When Ulrica sets fire to Torquilstone Castle, the antics on a turret of this anachronistic "fiend of a Saxon witch"[39] lay bare her mystery: she is maniacal.

After melodramatically disposing of the Saxon, "Urfried," who has been twisted like a witch by suffering, hate, and madness, Scott brings on his stage an entirely different sorceress, the young and beautiful Jewess, Rebecca. "The pupil of the foul witch Miriam," who was burned at the stake, is accused of using talismans and spells, working cures by means of cabalistic charms, and infatuating Brian de Bois-Guilbert through sorcery. This last charge is chiefly pressed at the trial, and in "those ignorant and superstitious times" she is found guilty on three immaterial counts, her race, her medical skill, and her sexual attractiveness. After being sentenced, Rebecca is stripped of Satanic amulets. Although the stake is ready for its victim, the timely appearance of Ivanhoe as her champion in trial-by-combat and the miraculous collapse of Sir Brian before striking a blow release the Jewess from the charge of witchcraft and sorcery.

Rebecca's trial, condemnation, and rescue serve the fictional purposes of arousing sympathy for the accused innocent and of creating suspense. The narrative is reminiscent of Le Morte Darthur, in which Sir Mador accuses Guenevere of poisoning his cousin with an apple, courtiers are reluctant to defend the queen, a great fire is built around an iron stake, and Lancelot, arriving at the last minute, victoriously takes up the challenge. Like Sir Thomas Malory, Scott is eclectic in his portrait of antique manners. Malory offers the simple explanation, "Suche custommme was vsed in tho dayes."[40]

But Scott is also interested in concise characterisation through opposed responses to the same situation. Thus Lucas de Beaumanoir, Grand Master

[39] See H. C. Lea, A History of the Inquisition of the Middle Ages, New York, III. 534: "It is quite likely, indeed, that the gradual development of witchcraft from ordinary sorcery commenced about the middle of the fourteenth century." Note Scott's frank admission in the "Dedicatory Epistle": "It is extremely probable that I may have . . . introduced, during the reign of Richard the First [1189–99], circumstances appropriated to a period either considerably earlier, or a good deal later than that era." His defence for the introduction of Negro slaves is that a romancer need only "restrain himself to such [manners] as are plausible and natural, and contain no obvious anachronism" (n. ii).

[40] Malory, Le Morte Darthur, ed. H. Oskar Sommer, London 1889–91, I. 734 (BK XVIII, ch. 6). See also R. S. Forsythe, "Two Debts of Scott to Le Morte d'Arthur," Modern Language Notes, XXVII (1912), 52; The Chronicle of Froissart (1387), tr. Lord Berners, London 1901–03, IV. 369.

of the Temple, in his stern conviction of Rebecca's guilt and his prejudiced conduct of the trial, is "the hoary bigot" (Bois-Guilbert's phrase) and as such not unlike some of Scott's own Covenanters. Both Albert Malvoisin, Preceptor of Templestowe, and Conrade Mont-Fitchet are willing to manufacture evidence against Rebecca. Cynically realistic Malvoisin would condemn the fair witch in order to clear Bois-Guilbert, who is revolted by the policy of "this calm hypocrite." Of course, Bois-Guilbert does not consider Rebecca a sorceress. Reluctantly accepting his comrades' strategy, he still protests against the "folly and fanaticism" of the proceedings, "Will future ages believe that such stupid bigotry ever existed!" The younger knights ascribe Bois-Guilbert's bewitchment to "the power of her real charms, rather than of her imaginary witchcraft." And before the formal accusation is uttered, Prior Aymer lightly and jokingly characterises Rebecca as a seductive second Witch of Endor. Having felt the advantage of Rebecca's mystic unguents, Higg the Saxon peasant persists in his bewildered devotion to the accused. Without being able to disbelieve the solemn charges of the court, the crowd at the trial feels sympathy for Rebecca. And her father, Isaac of York, ominously remembers that charges of necromancy are too often excuses for evil measures against his race. Thus a cross-section of twelfth century psychology is exposed by the reactions of various persons to Rebecca's plight.[41]

* * *

Between 1814 and 1824 Scott thought of witchcraft as characteristic of periods and places he was bodying forth in fiction. His witches, Jewish, pre-Christian, and Christian, range from the exotics of *Ivanhoe* to the embittered hags of the Scottish novels. The imputation may be tangential or direct; romantic, atmospheric, even humorous, or grotesque and sinister; figurative and fleeting or revelatory of the profoundest human maladjustment. When the suspicion is unfounded, Scott uses it as a test of the accusers, but when the woman is actually witchlike in her hatred of humanity, she becomes the subject of analysis. In one case it may represent local feeling as it is brought to the surface by an object of prejudice; in the other it may suggest the causes and consequences of solitariness, frustration, poverty, oddity, criminality, and insanity in all their pathos, sordidness, or horror.

Scott's narrative review of witchcraft is convincing and almost complete. When, as in *The Heart of Midlothian*, Scott moves in the eighteenth

---

[41] For the anomaly of a Jewish witch, see Robbins, *Encyclopedia of Witchcraft and Demonology, s.v.* Jewish witchcraft.

century, his omissions are historically sound because belief was then weaker and less ritualistic. In stories of earlier centuries what is neither presented nor implied is for the most part too gross, morally and aesthetically, for imaginative use. The novelist has in mind a distinction later generally formulated in *The Pirate*: "Superstition, when not arrayed in her full horrors, but laying a gentle hand only on her suppliant's head, had charms which we fail not to regret," even in days of "reason and general education." Because there is no question of real compact with the devil, Scott does not rationalise obtrusively. Considered as a moral state, not as a system of perverse power, witchcraft can hardly be said not to exist.

10. Second Sight

For aid in defining second sight, Scott turns not to Highlanders but to Dr Johnson: "an impression, either by the mind upon the eye, or by the eye upon the mind, by which things distant and future are perceived and seen as if they were present." Scott adds that "the spectral appearances thus presented, usually presage misfortune ... the faculty is painful to those who suppose they possess it; and ... they usually acquire it while themselves under the pressure of melancholy."[1] Second sight comes in most instances as a premonitory vision to the eyes, a cry to the ears, or an odour to the nostrils, and it sometimes affects animal, as well as human, seers.

Possessing great imaginative appeal and susceptible at times to demonstration through coincidence, second sight long retained its hold on the Scottish—and particularly on the Highland—mind. That many contemporaries believed in second sight is indicated by several anecdotal letters addressed to Scott. Nor was the novelist's antiquarian correspondent, Joseph Train, remiss in forwarding instances which had been communicated to him. There is the "curious & what might seem well authenticated instance of the Second Sight" related to J. Stewart Hepburne in Rannoch by his cousin, Colonel Macdonald of Dalchosnie (*i.e.*, the

---

[1] Note to "Glenfinlas," *Minstrelsy*, IV. 155. Cp. [Archibald MacDonald of Inverlocky], *The Second-Sighted Highlander*, London 1715, p. 5; Dalyell, *The Darker Superstitions of Scotland*, p. 475, "In the strictest acceptation, the second sight is the discovery of subsisting incidents"; Alexander Macgregor, *Highland Superstitions*, 5th edn, Stirling 1937, p. 40, "the faculty of seeing otherwise invisible objects" and events; Lewis Spence, *Second Sight: Its History and Origins*, London 1951, pp. 15–25. Definitions known to Scott are in Martin Martin, *A Description of the Western Islands of Scotland*, p. 300, and Robert Kirk, *The Secret Commonwealth of Elves, Fauns, & Fairies*, ed. Andrew Lang, London 1893, p. 40 (earlier editions, 1691 and 1815).

L   P.W.D.

plain of victory), who "solemnly believed it true." The Colonel's grandfather, John of Dalchosnie, was once told by an alarmed neighbour that
he had clearly seen a well-convoyed funeral without being able to distinguish the face of a mourner on a white horse or to learn the name of the
dead. When Allan More heard that he had not been seen in the numerous
company, he was needlessly distressed. An old gentleman soon died and
at his funeral everything fell out as in the vision. Allan More accompanied
the mourners on a white horse, borrowed for the occasion when his own
horse met with an accident.[2]

Another case is mentioned in an undated and unsigned manuscript
collection of clan lore which was probably set down by a MacKay.[3] In
the Braes of Lochaber, Dòmhnull Bàn a'Bhòchdain (Donald Bain of the
Goblin, who "was for many a long year, harassed and *harried* by a goblin
that infested his house") made a second-sighted prediction that a Laird of
Glengarry would be lost by sailing close to a white house. More than
thirty years afterwards, a Glengarry who feared the spoken doom was
drowned near the white house of Inverscaddel. Circumstantiality is
characteristic of this and other such tales, which were often repeated as
proof of the reality of second sight.

As a Lowlander, cut off from mountain mists and Gaelic inspiration,
Scott could hardly expect to have a complete experience of the second
sight. Once in the gloaming he did see a phantom cart drawn by a horse
which was led by a man. "At once, the whole tumbled down the bank"
and vanished. When a belated servant returned from Melrose some two
hours after the vision, his provision cart slipped down the brae. But there
was no loss or injury. So much for the imaginative Laird's supernatural
portent![4]

It is possible that, by a suspension of disbelief, Scott artificially prolonged his fanciful attachment to second sight. Byron is very positive
about the matter: "Who can help being superstitious? Scott believes in
second-sight."[5] But in 1830, when he brings out *Letters on Demonology
and Witchcraft*, Scott fails to discuss the subject. All he does is mention
the trick of turning one's cloak, "recommended, in visions of the second-
sight, or similar illusions, as a means of obtaining a certainty concerning

[2] Unaddressed letter of 9 Aug. 1828, in Train Ms., N.L.S., volume, 296v–7v ff. Several
folklore communications have been bound together for convenience of reference; the
present letter may possibly have no connexion with Joseph Train as collector or transmitter.
[3] *Op. cit.*, 353v f. See also Partington, *Post-Bag*, pp. 278–9; Allardyce, II. 452.
[4] John Morrison, "Random Reminiscences of . . . Scott," *Tait's Edinburgh Magazine*, x
(1843), 577, and Mrs Hughes, pp. 79–80. Such phenomena are discussed by J. G. Campbell in
Witchcraft & Second Sight, Glasgow 1902, pp. 120–81.
[5] Thomas Medwin, *Journal of the Conversations of Lord Byron*, New York 1824, p. 67.

the being which is before imperfectly seen."[6] One should hesitate before attributing this partial silence, as does Mrs Grant of Laggan, to "a glimmering belief" which Scott is afraid to confess.[7] Oversight or hesitancy about logically assailing a superstitious dogma which was cherished by many a friend and acquaintance may account for the omission.

Although the novelist does not express himself as fully or as clearly as one might wish, his attitude toward second sight seems to have been that of eighteenth-century rationalism. He would probably agree with Professor James Beattie, who argues in a letter to Mrs Montague (probably written in 1772) that instances of second sight are ambiguous and the revelations themselves frivolous. One never hears of learned, sensible, observant men endowed with second sight; only the ignorant, superstitious, and young are favoured.[8] In his "Essay on Poetry and Music," Beattie credits the "trifling and ridiculous visions of seers" to "a distempered fancy," coincidence, or the combination of credulity and imposture.[9]

★　　★　　★

Whenever Scott sets his action in the Highlands or takes a Lowland hero there, he values second sight as illustrative of regional life and beliefs. The culture phenomenon is free from the grosser tenets of demonology and witchcraft. The only restraint on the author's imaginative sympathy, therefore, is rationalism, which is destructive only when it is not tempered by humour.

The most extended treatment is in A Legend of Montrose, into whose plot-fabric second sight is firmly woven. The novel "was written chiefly with a view to place before the reader the melancholy fate of John Lord Kilpont, eldest son of William Earl of Airth and Menteith, and the singular circumstances attending the birth and history of James Stewart of Ardvoirlich, by whose hand the unfortunate nobleman fell" (Scott's Introduction, 1830). The bare contemporary account of George Wishart is that, after mortally wounding Lord Kilpont, by whom he had ever been "treated with the greatest familiarity and friendship, insomuch, that that very night they had slept together in the same bed," James Stewart fled from Montrose's to Argyle's camp, where he soon rose in favour.

[6] *Op. cit.*, p. 178.

[7] *Memoir and Correspondence of Mrs. Grant of Laggan*, ed. J. P. Grant, III. 187.

[8] Sir William Forbes, *An Account of the Life and Writings of James Beattie*, 2nd edn, Edinburgh 1807, I. 285–9. Beattie's scepticism was scarcely all-inclusive: "Not that I mean to deny the existence of ghosts, or to call in question the accounts of extraordinary revelations, granted to individuals, with which both history and tradition abound."

[9] James Beattie, *Essays*, 3rd edn, London 1779, pp. 169–74.

It was said that, won over by bribes or hoped for rewards from the Covenanters, he meditated treachery but failed to enlist Kilpont in the assassination of their leader. On being repulsed, he silenced his confidant.[10]

Dissatisfied with this motivation, Scott falls back on the resources of love, legend, and the supernatural. He makes Allan M'Aulay (Ardvoirlich) jealous of Annot Lyle's evident preference of Lord Menteith (Lord Kilpont). Then he incorporates a story of the Ardvoirlichs long treasured in his memory. The Children of the Mist slew Drummond-ernoch in the forest of Glenartney and placed his severed head on a table in the house of Ardvoirlich, where his sister came upon it. She fled shrieking and demented into the woods, from which at last she was led back home. Not long after, a son was born to the unhappy woman—James Stewart of Ardvoirlich, who displayed in his young manhood great strength coupled with a temper "moody, fierce, and irascible." He it was who stabbed Lord Kilpont in "a fit of sudden fury or deep malice long entertained."[11] In the novel, Lord Menteith is made to say that Allan M'Aulay's mother has undoubtedly impressed upon his mind many superstitious ideas and that his imagination, "which, probably from the circumstances preceding his birth, was constitutionally deranged," has been fed with the wild and terrible notions of the mountaineers. The ground being laid, Scott endows Allan with second sight.

The seer encourages the popular report of his communion with beings of another world, and his own recklessness in battle sustains the rumour that he bears a charmed life. In his gloomy seizures, a cloud comes over his mind, present reality grows dim, and the veil of futurity is rent asunder. Out of these attacks, like Saul at the sound of David's harp,[12] he is often drawn by the strains of Annot Lyle's "clairshach." The most persistent of his visions is that of a Highlander dirking his friend. With unconscious irony, he warns Menteith: " 'I repeat to you, that this weapon—that is,

---

[10] Wishart, *Memoirs of the most renowned James Graham, Marquis of Montrose*, Edinburgh 1819, pp. 83-4. (The Latin original came out in 1647 and translations in 1648-52, 1720, and 1756.) The same explanation is given in *Grandfather*, Second Series, London and Glasgow 1923, pp. 123-4, ch. 9. See John Buchan, *Montrose*, London 1949, p. 165.

[11] This is the story as told in the author's Introduction. Cp. *Q.R.*, XIV (1815-16), 308; Robert Chambers, *Illustrations*, p. 172: "She [Lady Ardvoirlich] regained her senses after the birth of her child; but it was remarkable that the son whom she bore seemed affected by the consequence of her terror. He was of great strength, but of violent passions, under the influence of which he killed his friend and commander, Lord Kilpont." On 15 Jan. 1830, Robert Stewart of Ardvoirlich sent Scott the family tradition about the murder. The two men had quarrelled in their cups over Kilpont's prevention of a duel between his friend and Alexander Macdonald. In neither version does the motivation have a supernatural tinge.

[12] Scott may have had 1 Sam. 16: 23 in mind: "And it came to pass, when the evil spirit from God was upon Saul, that David took the harp, and played with his hand: so Saul was refreshed, and was well, and the evil spirit departed from him." See *Letters*, VIII. 414.

such a weapon as this,' touching the hilt of the dirk which he wore, 'carries your fate.' " Later, in converse with another seer, Ranald MacEagh, Allan confides his worst fears:

> "Repeatedly," he said, "have I had the sight of a Gael, who seemed to plunge his weapon into the body of Menteith,—of that young noble- man in the scarlet laced cloak, who has just now left the bothy. But by no effort, though I have gazed till my eyes were almost fixed in the sockets, can I discover the face of this Highlander, or even conjecture who he may be, although his person and air seem familiar to me."
>
> "Have you reversed your own plaid," said Ranald, "according to the rule of the experienced Seers in such case?"

This Allan has done, and the phantom has appeared with its plaid reversed in dreadful token that the seer will hold the knife. The omen, however, is but partially realised, since Lord Menteith recovers from the wound inflicted by his comrade.

Before the stabbing, the voice of incredulity is heard. Lord Menteith declares his doubts to Montrose of the supernatural origin of Allan's second sight: "I think that he persuades himself that the predictions which are, in reality, the result of judgment and reflection, are supernatural impressions on his mind, just as fanatics conceive the workings of their own imagination to be divine inspiration." And after the stabbing, unbelief insists that "Allan's supposed vision was but a consequence of the private suggestions of his own passion, which, having long seen in Menteith a rival more beloved than himself, struggled with his better nature, and impressed upon him, as it were involuntarily, the idea of killing his competitor."

Although so much Scots rationalism in the reign of Charles I is ex- travagant, it is not forced on the reader in such a way as to destroy his interest in M'Aulay's central insight. Nor is the dramatically inevitable fulfilment impaired by questions of primacy among preternatural power, highly developed human faculty, and the urging of passion. In Scott's hands, second sight foreshadows events, heightens their poignancy, and reflects Highland character.

★   ★   ★

Because of its Highland setting, *Waverley* is appropriately garnished with allusions to second sight. When Donald Bean regrets the death of that gifted seer, Donnacha an Amrigh (Duncan with the Cap), he is reminded of the son Malcolm. But Donald questions the skill of the modern *taishatr*:

He told us the other day we were to see a great gentleman riding on a horse, and there came nobody that whole day but Shemus Beg, the blind harper, with his dog. Another time he advertised us of a wedding, and behold it proved a funeral; and on the *creagh* [foray], when he foretold to us we should bring home a hundred head of horned cattle, we gripped nothing but a fat bailie of Perth.

Naturally, such a bungling man of vision is not allowed to foresee the death of Colonel Gardiner. Instead, as Callum Beg levels his fusee at the reconnoitring Englishman, an unnamed old Highland seer stays his arm: "Spare your shot; his hour is not yet come. But let him beware of to-morrow,—I see his winding-sheet high upon his breast."[13] Callum turns pale and obeys. There is no attempt to explain away this true penetration of futurity.

In the Waverley Novels, belief in second sight depends more on a person's place of birth than on his general credulity. Convinced that the appearance of the Black Dwarf always presages troublous times, Hobbie Elliot's Border grandmother recalls that "they said the second-sighted Laird of Benarbuck had a communing wi' him some time afore Argyle's landing, but that I cannot speak to sae preceesely—it was far in the west." In *The Highland Widow*, "General ——," half-Lowlander, half-Englishman, says of mountain enthusiasm and loyalty, "These are Highland visions . . . as unsatisfactory and vain as those of the second sight."

The geographical line is equally clear in *The Two Drovers*. When that sibyl and witch, Janet of Tomahourich, is walking the lucky sunwise "*deasil*" three times round her nephew, Robin Oig, she stops with the exclamation, "There is blood on your hand, and it is English blood." His dirk, too, which gleams brightly to other eyes, shows Saxon blood to her. The women join in urging Robin to give up his luckless weapon, "saying few of his aunt's words fell to the ground."[14] Robin complies so far as to surrender the dirk to Hugh Morrison ("you Lowlanders care nothing for these freats"), who agrees to keep it "if you are feared for the auld spaewife's tale." Later, when Robin's English friend, Harry Wake-

[13] At an ill-fated wedding, Ailsie Gourlay is sure that the Bride of Lammermoor's "winding sheet is up as high as her throat already." And the MacGregors were heartened to attack a superior force by a second-sighted clansman's assurance "that he saw the shrouds of the dead wrapt around their principal opponents" (Introduction to *Rob Roy*). In her ballad, "The Moody Seer," Joanna Baillie follows the belief through all its stages. Macvorely sees what looks like a kerchief "round *Malcolm's* brogues," than "a shroud, Raised mid-way to thy breast," and before shipwreck and drowning "the white shroud gather'd high." *Dramatic and Poetical Works*, 2nd edn, pp. 801–03.

[14] For a statement that Scott's story is based on fact, see *The Caledonian Mercury* (Edinburgh), 6 Mar. 1828. "Almost uniformly some member of the families connected with Robin Oig, has been distinguished for . . . the second sight."

field, knocks him down in a quarrel over the pasturing of cattle, memory of his *"Muhme's"* [*sc.*, his aunt's] utterance "confirmed *his* deadly intention." What Robin Oig will do is through Janet's vision of blood made known to the reader, who is held by the power of the inevitable and by the inherent interest of words and deeds leading up to the killing.

When Scott takes his readers to fifteenth-century France in *Quentin Durward*, his action is so remote from seventeenth and eighteenth century Scotland that he can indulgently ridicule second sight. Robust old Ludovic Lesly thinks more highly of the pretensions of "second-sighted Saunders Souplejaw, the town-souter of Glenhoulakin," than of Galeotti's prophecies. "He foretold that all my sister's children would die some day; and he . . . foretold to myself one day, that I should be made by marriage." Fortunately, Isabelle of Croye's hand is promised to whoever brings the Wild Boar of Ardennes' head to the Duke of Burgundy. Lesly expands Souplejaw's foresight to include "the fortune of our house," calls on the seer back home to hold his own, and achieves the exploit. By transferring the reward to his nephew Quentin, he manages to fulfil a very elastic prophecy.

*　　*　　*

In the Waverley Novels the gift of second sight chiefly belongs to minor characters, who are nameless or named only in passing. The treatment of the phenomenon ranges from simple and incidental to complex and significant. It is humorous or serious and, if serious, rationalised or unrationalised. The Callum Beg, Robin Oig, and Allan M'Aulay passages in *Waverley*, *The Two Drovers*, and *A Legend of Montrose* proceed from simple to complex; as the length of presentation increases, the author's willingness to leave second sight unexplained decreases. In the last two narratives, the stubborn yet passive agent, dimly foreknowing, moves in tranced resignation, like the Master of Ravenswood, through his bitter role. As present and future happenings are strangely knit together, the gloom of fatality descends on human events. Curiosity is not deadened by second-sighted foreshadowing, or by omens, prophecies, or warning spirits, because narrative suspense depends more on the manner in which action unfolds than on the unexpectedness of the acts themselves.

A Legend of Montrose contains hints of a return to the rational heavy-handedness which crumples the fabric that imagination spreads before the reader. But it is preserved intact by Scott's shifting interest from culture, race, and *locale* to psychology. The same man is seer and stabber. Nurture and a fearful knowledge of self contribute more to the growth of the illusion than native soil or strain, although these background factors help to create the doomed set of mind. Like Brian of "mysterious lineage" in *The Lady of the Lake*, Allan M'Aulay is the subject of an enquiry into the hereditary, prenatal, and environmental influences that predispose a man to melancholy, which is conducive to second-sighted visions. A principal character has the power; therefore, as seer, he is individualised rather than typified. Attention is directed to his psychic wound more than to his victim's physical wound. Thus a study of the conditioning of the psychic personality is achieved.

11. ELEMENTAL SPIRITS

In confecting *The Monastery*, Scott goes far afield in search of novelty. Retrospectively, in the Introduction of 1830, he admits that the expediency of obtruding the marvellous in fiction has been disputed and "wellnigh exploded" by contemporary critics[1] and that the revels of fairies and the saturnalia of witches, as figments of an out-at-elbows creed, are no longer acceptable to the popular imagination. Abandoning, at least temporarily, the more vulgar forms of Scottish superstition, Sir Walter turns to the almost forgotten Paracelsian and Rosicrucian doctrine of elemental spirits which flourished in the seventeenth and early eighteenth century.

In his treatise, *Liber de nymphis, sylphis, pygmaeis et salamandris et de caeteris spiritibus* (1566), published a quarter-century after his death, Paracelsus explains that the nymphs or undines of the water element, the sylphs of the air and forest, the pygmies of earth, and the salamanders of fire are coarse and large if their *chaos* or abode is subtle, fine and small if their life medium is heavy and dense. Among these bodily gradations, the nymphs most resemble men, whom they wish to marry in order to gain immortal souls; sylphs are larger and stronger than men. Not to be confused with mere beasts, ghosts, and demons, these elementals magnify God's glory. Pygmies and salamanders are sufficiently spiritual to warn and protect mankind by seeing into the past and the future. The salamanders or vulcans serve men by forging mineral treasures, and other elemental beings guard these treasures until the time comes for their use. All these creatures can pass through walls, yet they have blood, flesh, and bones; they also talk, eat, sleep and reproduce.[2]

[1] Satiety may have been induced by the revival of old ballads and the importation of German books, with their ineludible "apparitions and the mysteries of haunted castles." But the poet is still privileged to introduce the return of the dead and "the struggle of evil beings for an ascendancy over human nature." "Indeed some of Scott's works excite the feelings of superstitious fear and traditional awe in a degree that has never been surpassed." "Some remarks on the Use of the Preternatural in Works of Fiction," *B.E.M.*, III.(1818), 648–50.

[2] *Four Treatises of ... Paracelsus*, trs. Temkin, Rosen, Zilboorg, and Sigerist, Baltimore 1941, pp. 215–53.

In somewhat altered form these beliefs crossed the Channel. Thomas Heywood draws his materials from such writers as the eleventh-century Byzantine philosopher, Michael Psellus, rather than from contemporary Rosicrucians recently under attack by Gabriel Naudé. In *The Hierarchie of the blessed Angells* (1635), he cautiously points out the influence of spirits on human beings: "Some haue affirmed . . . That those Æthereall or Fierie, stirre vp men to contemplation: the Airy, to the businesse and common affaires of this life: the Waterie, to pleasure: the Earthy, to base and gripple auarice."³ But the translations of *Le Comte de Gabalis* in 1680 and 1714 take the curious beyond mere speculation to the technique of making spirits serve adepts. By means of the grand cabala, initiates of the Rose Cross can get in touch with a variety of elementals that surpass mankind in longevity, having a life span of several centuries. Expose a glass of "conglobated Air, Water, or Earth" to the sun for a month; then rarefy it.

> 'Tis wonderous what a magnetick Quality each of these purify'd Elements has to attract *Nymphs, Sylphs,* and *Gnomes.* Take but ever so small a Dose thereof every Day for some Months, and you'll see the Republick of *Sylphs* fluttering in the Air, and *Nymphs* making to the Banks in Shoals, and the Guardians of Wealth spreading forth their Treasures.⁴

Inasmuch as these spirits know and love God and wish to attain immortality through union with man, most of the stories about them concentrate on attempted intermarriage and its failure because of a taboo imposed by the occult mate and broken by the husband.⁵ Baron de la Motte Fouqué's *Undine* is a water-spirit that secures a soul by marrying a mortal man, only to lose it when Sir Huldebrand of Ringstetten falls in love with Bertalda.⁶ The German novelist's *Undine* is the direct inspiration of Scott's White Lady of Avenel.

³ *Op. cit.,* London 1635, p. 229 (also pp. 503–10, 543–53); on p. 507, the White Nymph is referred to as a watery sprite. Also see Robert H. West, *The Invisible World: A Study of Pneumatology in Elizabethan Drama,* Athens, Georgia 1939, pp. 23–4.

⁴ Nicolas de Montfaucon de Villars, *The Count of Gabalis,* London 1714, p. 23; the abbe's "entretiens sur les sciences secrètes" first appeared in Paris in 1670. This "questioning and cautiously satirical" "comic romance" has not been in high favour with the initiate. See Hargrave Jennings, *The Rosicrucians,* 7th edn, London n.d., pp. 427–8; A. E. Waite, *The Brotherhood of the Rosy Cross,* London 1924, p. 14 n. 2, 573. The airy elemental has a satirical role in Alexander Pope's "The Rape of the Lock" (1714) and a moral one in *The Sylph* (1779), an epistolary novel attributed to Georgiana Duchess of Devonshire (see I. 195–6, *passim*).

⁵ There are interesting parallels and contrasts in Apuleius' story of Cupid and Psyche, in which the mortal breaks a taboo by looking at her immortal and divine husband. After magical labours performed, Psyche is made immortal and reunited to Cupid.

⁶ Paracelsus contends that a soul once gained by a nymph cannot even be lost by separation from the human mate. Scott makes the mistake of supposing that La Motte Fouqué's Undine loses immortality by wedding a mortal.

Like an over-confident gardener, Scott has hardly transplanted the naiad from German to Scottish soil, to a period too early for Rosicrucian fancies or euphuism, before he grafts the white lady onto the water nymph. Only Collin de Plancy's conception of *femmes blanches* can match this hybrid: "Quelques-uns donnent le nom de femmes blanches aux sylphides, aux nymphes, ou à certaines fées qui se montraient en Allemagne."[7] Among these sheeted ghosts, the most famous, the German "weisse Frau," is a castle spectre that materialised in Prussian royal palaces as a warning of approaching death.[8] The Irish white ladies double as banshees, but those of England, Wales, and the Isle of Man are no more than white-garmented spooks which revisit the spots where treasure has been concealed or crimes have been committed.[9] Although Scotland has not been particularly congenial to white ladies, its few examples conform to the Southron type. Neither the banshee nor the *revenant* has any connexion with water, except superficially when a fountain or a river is the *locale* it revisits.

Lost in a maze of clarification, Scott compares the banshee activity of his undine-white-lady to that of Highland and Milesian attendant spirits, thereby adding a third personality to his eerie anomaly. He refers to May Mollach, who "condescended to mingle in ordinary sports, and even to direct the Chief how to play at draughts."[10] Perhaps, the supremely farcical character of May Mollach, whose sex is not fixed, is best illustrated by the services rendered to Grant of Tullochgorm:

> In old there frequented this Family a Spirit called Meg Mulloch. It appeared like a little Boy, and in dark nights would hold a candle before the Goodman, & shew him the way home, and if the Goodwife would not come to bed, it would cast her in beyond him, and if she refused to bring what he desired, it would cast it before him.[11]

[7] Collin de Plancy, *Dictionnaire Infernal*, 2nd edn, Paris 1825–6, III. 33. (1st edn, Paris 1818).

[8] E. Cobham Brewer, *Reader's Handbook* and *Dictionary of Phrase and Fable; Chambers's Enclyclopaedia, s.v.* White Lady; John Aubrey, *Miscellanies upon Various Subjects*, 5th edn, London 1890, p. 118. Cp. Karoline von Woltmann, "Die weisse Frau," *Neue Volkssager der Böhmen*, Halberstadt 1821, pp. 1–118, which also permits the wholesale interference of a white lady in human affairs. In *The Gothic Quest*, London n.d., pp. 223–4, Montague Summers mentions Christiane Naubert, "Die weisse Frau," *Die neuen Volksmärchen der Deutschen*, (1789–92).

[9] C. O. Parsons, "Association of the White Lady with Wells," *Folk-Lore*, XLIV (1933), 295–305.

[10] Also see *The Lady of the Lake*, III. vii, note on "the fatal Ben-Shie's boding scream;" *Minstrelsy*, I. 152.

[11] Sir Robert Sibbald's Ms. Collections, N.L.S., p. 288. Cp. Aubrey, *Miscellanies upon Various Subjects*, p. 192.

Now, the Maid of the Hairy Arms is certainly more akin to the goblin or the grotesque all-purpose brownie than to the banshee, as the following anecdote will suggest:

> Sir Normand MackLeod's opponent in the game of tables was advised of a successful move by the butler. "The Fellow own'd that he never play'd in his life, but that he saw the *Spirit Browny* reaching his arm over the Players head, and touched the Part with his finger, on the Point where the Table-man was to be plac'd."[12]

Scott's White Lady of Avenel, then, is a mixture of elemental sprite, castle spectre and attendant spirit, goblin and brownie—poetry, terror, and burlesque exemplified in a being whose actions are guided, not by "feeling or reasoning," but by "temporary benevolence or caprice."[13] True to her nature, these actions are a patchwork of native and outlandish elements.

In a note Scott states that the use of the bodkin as a reminder of humble ancestry "is borrowed from a German romance, by the celebrated Tieck, called Das Peter Manchen, *i.e.* The Dwarf Peter." R. P. Gillies' memory is more reliable at this point: his friend knew the tales of Christian Heinrich Spiess (1755–99). Among these he spoke "with peculiar interest of the 'Petermänchen,' a production of *diablerie*, which his own genius had probably invested with interest, such as no other reader could have discovered in it."[14] Scott was probably impressed by the scornful use of a horseshoe to recall a blacksmith ancestor in Spiess' *Das Petermänchen* (Prague and Leipzig, 1793) during his early burst of enthusiasm for German literature. Otherwise, he could have taken the hint from Pope's "The Rape of the Lock," in which high-bred Belinda's weapon, "a deadly bodkin," is described as "The same . . . | Her great-great-grandsire wore about his neck, | In three seal rings." More native is the provenance of Father Philip's ducking, which is a Tweedside legend of a horseman's obligingly taking a mermaiden up behind him. In the middle of the river, she tries to pull him into the water—and fails because, glimpsing

---

[12] Martin Martin, *A Description of the Western Islands of Scotland*, London 1703, p. 320.

[13] The White Lady's half sisters of the fountain and the sea are consistently malicious. See P. *Gasparis Schotti . . . Physica Curiosa, sive Mirabilia Naturae et Artis*, Würzburg, 1667, I. 362.

[14] Gillies, *Recollections of Scott*, p. 72. See also Bertel Kothen, *Quellenuntersuchung zu Walter Scotts Romanen "The Monastery" und "The Abbot"*, Weimar 1931, pp. 58–9; for Fouqué's influence, pp. 57–8, and Stokoe, *German Influence*, pp. 80–1; and throughout Richard Warner, *Illustrations, Critical, Historical, Biographical, and Miscellaneous, of Novels by the Author of Waverley*, London 1824, II. 115–20, 169–225. Scott seems not to have known the two volume translation of Spiess, *The Dwarf of Westerbourg*, London 1827, which was published three years before the annotation of *The Monastery*.

her character, he has loosened the buff belt to which she clings.[15]

This is but a part of the White Lady's total activity, which can be briefly summarised. She first appears to guide Mary Avenel and her companions through a bog. Then, when Father Philip, sacristan of St Mary's Monastery, takes Alice Avenel's vernacular Bible from her, the White Lady mounts behind him on his mule, ducks him in the ford, seizes the Holy Book, and returns it to the Avenels. After it is taken by Father Eustace, she again recovers it and protects the sub-prior from murderous Christie of the Clinthill as well. On being invoked by Halbert Glendinning in a manner reminiscent of the conjuration of a demon, she obeys the summons and conducts him through the earth to a cavern, where he secures the Bible.[16] And she indicates to Mary Avenel the place where Halbert has hidden the fugitive volume. More conventionally, she performs the duty of a sympathetic spirit whose visitation is foreboding when she appears wringing her hands to the sub-prior and to Mary, Edward, and Halbert just before the death of Lady Avenel.

When Halbert calls up the versatile attendant spirit a second time to ask what it is that takes his mind off manly sports, she rhymes of love and gives him a silver bodkin to remind his rival, Sir Piercie Shafton, of his tailor origin. She appears to him unbidden before he engages with Sir Piercie but capriciously keeps her distance when the knight seems mortally wounded. Then she closes up a grave which has been miraculously dug for the duellist, though not occupied, and strangely heals his wound. It is by her advice that Edward Glendinning enters the monastery, and she is seen by him bidding farewell to her holly and fountain.

The unconvincing episodes in which the White Lady takes part, as well as her uncongenial folklore elements, are awkwardly placed in the Tweed-side setting. For a time that pleasant setting seemed to call for different action. "The Monastery was designed, at first, to have contained some supernatural agency, arising out of the fact, that Melrose had been the place of deposit of the great Robert Bruce's heart."[17] On its way to or from the Holy Sepulchre as a surrogate for King Robert I, who could not keep his vow of pilgrimage, the royal heart was held up in Spain, where its protector, the Good Sir James Douglas, died fighting the Moors.

[15] See Thomas Wilkie, Old Scots Songs A.D. 1814, Ms. 122, pp. 117–19, N.L.S.; Leitch Ritchie, Scott and Scotland, London 1835, pp. 63–4; and my "Association of the White Lady with Wells." (In an earlier variation of the trick, Scott has Ewan of Brigglands loosen a horse-belt in order to let Rob Roy escape while crossing the River Forth.)

[16] See Hibernicus, "Scott and Homer," N. & Q. CLXXIII (1937), 171: The relation of the White Lady to Halbert is "modelled on that of Minerva to Telemachus."

[17] Scott's Introduction (1831) to The Abbot.

Recovered by Sir William Keith, it was brought to Melrose Abbey, where it apparently refused to lie still. Had Scott followed his original plan, the White Lady would probably not have been without fantastic employment. The energy she consumed keeping track of the Avenel Bible could just as well have been expended guarding Robert Bruce's wayward heart.

* * *

As Paracelsus explains the generation of elementals, the offspring of an abnormal birth is monstrous, giant, siren, dwarf, or will-o'-the-wisp. The White Lady is a suspicious combination of giant in strength and will-o'-the-wisp in caprice. Fenella, in *Peveril of the Peak*, seems also to have been an obstetrical problem. This nimble, diminutive young lady, with her conspiratorial pretence of deafness and dumbness,[18] has something of the nature of a near-dwarf, a *bona fide* will-o'-the-wisp, and a siren *manquée*. Her elemental category is fixed by an actual dwarf, Sir Geoffrey Hudson, in his defence of "this sylph" or "sylphid"[19] against the cynicism of King Charles II. For Fenella's life, though free, is sexually blameless.

On various occasions, Fenella is likened to a fairy changeling, a banshee, and a familiar. More mundane ingredients in her life and character came from Goethe's Mignon,[20] a lawsuit over the rescue of a "tumbling lassie" from a mountebank, and the pretended dumbness of a servant in the household of Scott's grandfather. Perhaps, the fictional waif also derives a trait from the slayer of King Kenneth II in A.D. 995—that "ffenela, quhome nature had formet to deceiue."[21]

As the illegitimate daughter of the vengeful, intriguing Edward Christian and a Moorish woman, Scott's Fenella comes by her restlessness

[18] Scott would have known of Jennet Douglas, who was dumb for a time, "whether really or counterfeitly, its hard to determine": Sinclair, pp. 1–18.

[19] Although Scott interchanges the words *sylph* and *sylphid*, the latter is a young or small sylph. Denizen of air and forest, the sylph may have taken her generic name from *sylvestris* and *nympha*. After the time of Paracelsus, the sylph decreased in size and coarseness until she took on the quality of her chaos, the air. In his *Description of the Isle of Man*, George Waldron says that Manxmen would not hesitate to credit any of the absurdities in *The Count of Gabalis* (quoted in n. viii, *Peveril*).

[20] For Goethe's unfavourable comment on Scott's borrowing, see 18 Jan. 1825 and 31 Jan. 1827 in *Conversations With Eckermann*, New York 1901. Coleridge identifies Scott's grossest literary sin as the degradation of Goethe's exquisite creation into the "repulsive nondescript grotesque . . . Fenella." *Coleridge's Miscellaneous Criticism*, ed. Raysor, p. 335. Meg Merrilies, Norna, and the White Lady are also products of fancy, not of imagination (pp. 329–30).

[21] John Leslie, *The Historie of Scotland*, ed. E. G. Cody for the S.T.S., Edinburgh and London 1888–95, I. 296. See *Chronicles of the Picts, Chronicles of the Scots . . .*, ed. William F. Skene, Edinburgh 1867, index *s.v.* Finuele, the lady of *perfidia*; Skene, *Celtic Scotland*, 2nd edn, Edinburgh 1886–90, I. 380. When the trickery of her dumbness is disclosed by Charles II, Fenella speaks of herself as one "whose life has been spent in practising treason on others." Also see Lockhart, I, 240, 361.

and guile naturally. She resembles the White Lady in serving her creator as a trouble-shooter. Whenever the narrative skein is too complicated, she untangles it, and whenever the skein hangs limp and straight, she is there to tangle it. Unlike the conventional *deus ex machina*, whose function is terminal, this remarkable goddess-and-devil-from-the-machine is on hand throughout the plot.

Scott verges on anachronism in *Peveril of the Peak*. He incorporates late Rosicrucian elaborations of the elemental schema in *The Monastery*, whose action is earlier than the publication of Paracelsus' treatise, and in *Anne of Geierstein*, whose action concludes before the birth of the occult physician. In observing the social status of the belief, he is less careless. Rosicrucian tenets were never popular. Distinguished at different times by learning, quackery, and polite acceptance, elemental spirits like the stars moved in aristocratic circles. For that reason, if for no other, the nymphean component of the White Lady must shudder at some of the country company she has to keep, but Fenella does not become a sylph until she is discussed in the presence of royalty. In *Anne*, Lady Hermione of Arnheim is dead when Donnerhugel tells her story, and an appropriate mist of the fabulous past descends on her aristocratic person.

"Donnerhugel's Narrative" is about Anne's grandfather, Baron Herman of Arnheim, a student of the mystic sciences, his guest Dannischemend, a Persian brother of the Sacred Fire pursued by avengers of the Secret Tribunal, and the Zoroastrian's beautiful daughter Hermione. Baron Herman first saw slight, agile, perfectly formed Hermione on a pedestal whose lamp had been removed in order to give the newcomer an appropriate perch. The maiden was an *ignis fatuus* in the dance, supernaturally alert in games, deep-read in forbidden lore, and possessed of a strange affinity for her decorative opal. When Dannischemend left Arnheim at the end of a year and a day, he warned his noble pupil not to ally himself with Hermione, for—as his own example too well proved—happiness could not come of such a union. Of course, the infatuated baron married Hermione. They named their first-born Sybilla (fortune-teller, prophetess) and at the christening, when challenged by a malicious guest, Baron Herman broke the unexpressed taboo by flicking holy water on his wife's forehead. A drop, falling on the opal, extinguished its light. Within two hours the baroness was reduced to "a handful of light-grey ashes," and the heedless husband followed her quintessential remains to the grave exactly three years later.[22]

---

[22] See *Funk & Wagnalls Standard Dictionary of Folklore, s.v.* opal: "It was highly thought of as a gem until the 19th century when it came to be regarded as a gem of ill omen. This is

That Rudolph Donnerhugel may be too straightforward and un-imaginative to preserve the lady's history is implied by Scott in Arthur Philipson's expressed surprise at the soldier's hidden talents. In his narrative, Scott allows his fancy to wander to salamanders and their sister elementals, sylphs and nymphs, via sun and fire worship in a Near Eastern creed. This association of the beliefs of different ages, lands, and religions is anticipated by the motto of Chapter XI, which at the same time directs the reader's attention away from Persia to Europe:

> These be the adept's doctrines—every element
> Is peopled with its separate race of spirits.
> The airy Sylphs on the blue ether float;
> Deep in the earthy cavern skulks the Gnome;
> The sea-green Naiad skims the ocean-billow,
> And the fierce fire is yet a friendly home
> To its peculiar sprite—the Salamander.

The elemental characteristics of Hermione are diverse. "An aerial being" almost "formed of gossamer" and a linnet "dropped from the sky on the tendril of a rosebud," she resembles those post-Paracelsian sylphs which are "compos'd of the purest Atoms of the Air."[23] She is one with La Motte Fouqué's nymph, Undine, in her mortal union and its tragic dissolution. And after her fading away, she is called a will-o'-the-wisp, "Maiden of the Fiery Mantle," "Lady of the spark,"[24] and—strange jumble of Rosicrucian terms!—"the Nymph of the Fire, the Salamander." These and other specific Rosicrucian terms are for the most part excluded from the narrative itself, cropping up instead in the telltale chapter motto and in subsequent reference to the incidents. After writing in the fanciful spirit of Rosicrucian belief, Scott becomes objectively conscious of what he has done and puts up his markers outside the domain itself.

Other markers, or vestiges, are much fainter. On one side of her house, Scott's sylph is a very refined descendant of supernaturals, sometimes succubi or demons in female form, that shun the consecration of the Mass—until caught. Her rude forebears appear in *Richard Coer de Lion*, the *Gesta Romanorum*, Giraldus Cambrensis, Gervase of Tilbury's *Otia*

---

probably due to Sir Walter Scott's novel, *Anne of Geierstein*." Queen Victoria's patronage helped to bring the opal back into favour. In 1878–85, however, an opal spread death in the household of King Alfonso XII of Spain. See Radford, *Encyclopaedia of Superstitions, s.v.* gems.

[23] *The Count of Gabalis*, p. 21.

[24] This addition in Scott's handwriting is in *Anne of Geierstein*, Edinburgh 1829, VOL. I, interleaf facing p. 317 (Treasury Room of the Harvard College Library). It has not been incorporated in any text I have used.

Imperialia, and John Fordun's *Scotichronicon*.[25] On the other side of the house, his lady of the opal derives from the fairies of folk literature that dread holy water and from beings whose souls reside in jewels. Her last phase is transformation into a human being. As Sybilla's daughter, Anne of Geierstein, informs Arthur Philipson, "All these things were confused in popular tradition, and the real facts turned into a fairy tale."

But the fairy-tale is more than a pleasant interpolation. It sanctions some of the interpretations of Anne of Geierstein, who is descended, as Donnerhugel says, "more or less directly from one of those elementary spirits which have been talked of both in ancient and modern times." Wavering Arthur Philipson does not know whether to regard her as "the daughter of . . . an elementary spirit," a "wandering spirit of the elements," "an elementary spirit" attended by a demon, an ocular illusion, an apparition, an angel, or a mortal maiden.[26] To her kindly old uncle, Arnold Biederman, she is a propitious domestic fairy, and to his dull-pated son Sigismund, a very mysterious damsel, if not worse, a goblin, a ghost, a double-ganger, or a devil in vestal form. But this hocus-pocus as to her real nature is dropped when, two-thirds of the way through the novel, the Baroness Anne of Arnheim chooses to explain her baffling feats to Arthur.

These marvels and their Radcliffian elucidation include the rescue of Arthur Philipson from prison (her father's expedient to obtain a messenger to the Swiss); her warning to Philipson on the road (a disguising dress from her father and information from Sigismund); her spectral passing of sentries at night on the Graffs-lust bridge (the use of a secret passage, with the deliberate cozening of poor Sigismund, in order to meet her father); and her apparent double existence inside and outside the walls of Brisach (the presence of her maid, dressed for the part, among the Swiss). Even with "these mysteries explained," the reader may feel cheated. Anne of Geierstein's excursion into the supernatural is clumsier than her grandmother Hermione's.

★   ★   ★

[25] C. O. Parsons, "Demonological Background of 'Donnerhugel's Narrative,' " *Studies in Philology*, xxx (1933), 604–10. Other significant influences or parallels may be found in Godwin, *St. Leon* (1799), the sheltering of an adept; Jean d'Arras, *Melusine* (c. 1387), return of a supernatural mother to her children; Lockhart, v. 384, Scott's story of a French lady who dwindled to "a small heap of grey ashes" when a dancing partner unlooped her mysterious black velvet girdle.

[26] Cp. John William Polidori, *Ernestus Berchtold*, London 1819, p. 69, in which the hero wonders whether a beautiful young woman met in the Swiss Alps was "a vision" or "my guardian angel, who invested that form?" The heroine's father, like Anne's grandfather, has studied strange lore with a man of the East, and like Anne's father, he is under the suspicion of wizardry.

Although Scott often proves to be his own best critic, he is singularly blind to the artistic defects of his elemental spirits. When the public all too obviously disapproves of the White Lady of Avenel, he inserts an *apologia pro arte sua* in the Introductory Epistle to *The Fortunes of Nigel*:

> I think she is a failure myself; but rather in execution than conception. Could I have evoked an *esprit follet*, at the same time fantastic and interesting, capricious and kind; a sort of wildfire of the elements, bound by no fixed laws, or motives of action; faithful and fond, yet teazing and uncertain. . . . I must invest my elementary spirits with a little human flesh and blood—they are too fine-drawn for the present taste of the public, [which] . . . ought to allow for the capriccios of what is, after all, but a better sort of goblin.

In describing herself as formed of the ether blue, with blood of the unfallen dew, the White Lady reveals that she is under the same illusion as her creator. Instead of being too ethereal, the spirit is so palpable, so freakishly energetic, that her numerous interventions lead to a familiarity that breeds indifference, if not boredom. As for Scott's distinction, the weakness is not of execution alone but of conception too. But Scott learns from experience. Under an increasingly human interpretation, his elementals change from the consistently supernatural, the White Lady, to the intermittently so, Fenella and Anne.

As a character, Anne, despite the awkwardness of retrospective explanations, is the most convincing of the lot. And as a fictional embodiment of Rosicrucian tenets, "Donnerhugel's Narrative" is the most successful. Despite a fairy-tale prettiness of phrase, it has the atmosphere of the demon-wife experience modified by the more pathetic and moving fancy of the union of an elemental spirit with a human being. Against the background of flight from the secret tribunal, forbidden arts, and Persian mysteries, the actual difference between Hermione and the Baron Herman in racial culture, religion, and temperament explains their attraction under the shadow of taboo. Because it is a family legend, fact transformed by the popular imagination, the short tale has a *raison d'être*.

But the reason for Scott's creation of female elementals is much less clear. His nymphs and sylphs are fascinating, unpredictable, even lawless, and at the same time kind, faithful, and loving. Their morals and temperament may be read in their bodies, which are delicate, shapely, and boyishly slender. Tomboys with budding breasts, they are undeveloped, unawakened, and pure, though pubescently skittish. As long as the elemental fiction is kept up, they are free from sexual taint not only in their present life but in their remote origin. Apparently loose-laced, Fenella is innocent:

M   P.W.D.

Indeed, she seems rather a sylphid of the Rosicrucian system, than aught more carnal; being slighter, lighter, and less than the females of common life, who have something of that coarseness of make which is doubtless derived from the sinful and gigantic race of the antediluvians.

Scott is thinking of the "giants in the earth in those days . . . when the sons of God came in unto the daughters of men" (Genesis VI. 4). The account in the Book of Enoch (IX. 8–9; X. 9) is more detailed:

And they have gone to the daughters of men upon the earth, and have slept with the women, and have defiled themselves, and revealed to them all kinds of sins. And the women have borne giants, and the whole earth has thereby been filled with blood and unrighteousness. . . . "Proceed against the bastards and the reprobates, and against the children of fornication: and destroy [them]."[27]

In this awful miscegenation of fleshly and spiritual all sexual sin began. But from this burden all elementals, creatures of another descent, are free. This freedom Scott gladly confers on his heroines, among whom Diana Vernon has been most generally admired. For greater objectivity, I shall borrow a description of eighteen-year-old Diana from Edgar Johnson, who finds her the "proudest masterpiece" among the character portraits of *Rob Roy*, "gay and lively," at times discouraged, fine of spirit, gallant, brave, intelligent, full of "fire and charm," vivacious, fresh, and "uninhibited." "Neither coarse in conversation nor unchaste in conduct," she is—as much as a lady may be—a hoyden.[28] Die Vernon is an appealingly humanised elemental who is unencumbered by Rosicrucian jargon. Nor does she lack the sexual ambiguity of her kind.

Lucy Ashton's "sylph-like form . . . mantled in azure silk," her grace and sweetness, so impress the Master of Ravenswood that "she seemed to be an angel descended on earth, unallied to the coarser mortals among whom she deigned to dwell for a season." But when her latent sexuality is conjured up by submission to a mortal misalliance, Lucy stabs her husband and goes mad.

Although this undoubtedly is not the way Scott thinks of himself as regarding women, the image persistently breaks through. So persistently that it cannot be dismissed as the pretty verbiage with which a robust, extraverted writer disposes of love and sex, so that he may get on to more

---

[27] *The Apocrypha and Pseudepigrapha of the Old Testament in English*, ed. R. H. Charles, Oxford 1913, II. 193–4 (also 233). See Flavius Josephus, *Jewish Antiquities* (I. iii, 1), tr. for Loeb Classical Library by H. St. J. Thackeray, London and New York, 1926–43, IV. 35.

[28] *Rob Roy*, ed. Edgar Johnson, Boston 1956, p. xv. For the masculine element in Diana's nature, see Alexander Welsh, *The Hero of the Waverley Novels*, New Haven 1963, pp. 187–9.

important narrative matters. Of course, there is Williamina Belsches, who rejected her cousin, Walter Scott, married William Forbes, and died thirteen years later. It is not unlikely that she is the one who must linger in a pre-nubile, delightfully uncommitted state, novel after novel. A heroine's slow physical maturation may or may not express psychic retardation in her creator. But the sexual image projected in Scott's heroines—and most clearly in his elemental spirits—is one of a boyishly supple girl who stops short of womanhood.[29]

12. FAIRIES

As a boy Walter Scott looked wistfully at the green hillocks frequented by fairies and wished that he might sleep by them and be carried off to Fairyland, except for the cantrips played on several human guests.[1] His state of mind seems to have been that of William Butler Yeats, who says in *Reveries over Childhood and Youth* (1914):

> I wandered about raths and fairy hills and questioned old women and old men and, when I was tired out or unhappy, began to long for some such end as True Thomas found. I did not believe with my intellect that you could be carried away body and soul, but I believed with my emotions and the belief of the country people made that easy.

During Scott's lifetime, fairies were still articles of a living Border faith. The story of a souter's being transported by the fairies from the Peat Law to Glasgow was readily credited by the common people. And did not an old woman see them dancing in the Chicken-Acre with "antic capers, often on one leg, and altogether too fantastic for clumsy human limbs"?[2] Abbotsford itself had "more than one place celebrated for the resort of the fairies."[3]

John Hugh Lockhart, Sir Walter's infant grandson, was watched over with peculiar anxiety by a maid. Scott whimsically reassures his son-in-law: "I have a capital amulet against Catherines alarms but alas the spell which fairies fear is safe lockd up in the old cabinet at Abbotsford." And to his son Walter he writes four days later: "No fears exist saving those of little Catherine for the baby lest the fairies take it away before the

[29] This is true as well of John Buchan's women. Janet Raden in *John Macnab* is "like an adorable boy." Scott's heroines are discussed more fully in the chapter on "Methods."

[1] Irving, *Abbotsford*, p. 83.
[2] T. Craig-Brown, *The History of Selkirkshire*, II. 154–5. See *Demonology*, p. 126.
[3] *Letters*, X. 242–3.

Christening."[4] What Catherine dreaded was the substitution of a change-ling, a puny and morose fairy suckling which could be got rid of by making it laugh. She probably had her own interpretation of John Hugh's ill health and of his death when ten years old.

Numerous were the fairy-tales of actual credence or admitted illusion which were directly transmitted to Scott. Of these one may be repeated. A lady told the man of letters that, when a girl, living with Lord Lovat's family at Castle Downie, she had seen Prince Charles and his fleeing attendants appear unexpectedly after the Battle of Culloden (1746). "Impressed with the belief that they were fairies, who according to high-land traditions, are visible to men only from one twinkle of the eye-lid to another, she strove to refrain from the vibration, which she believed would occasion the strange and magnificent apparition to become invisible."[5]

When some boys paid Tom Purdie back for calling "fairy-stones . . . common chucky-stanes," the Laird entered into the fun and warned his shepherd, "Those green hill-folk have strange ways with them, Tom, and sometimes make a lodgment in the shape of a pinch of snuff, and dance a reel upon a man's midriff—the devils that rushed into the herd of swine are angels compared to these fairies when they are angered."[6]

As a sheriff, Scott dipped into fairy lore. While conducting Tom Moore over the Abbotsford estate in 1825, Scott called his attention to the opposite bank of the Tweed as a favourite resort of dancing fairies. A shepherd, Alexander Laidlaw, "declared before him, in his judicial capacity, that having gone to pen his sheep about sunrise in a field two or three miles further down the river, he had seen little men and women under a hedge, beautifully dressed in green and gold; 'the Duke of Buccleugh in full dress was nothing to them.' 'Did you, by the virtue of your oath, believe them to be fairies?' 'I dinna ken; they looked very like the gude people' (evidently believing them to be fairies). The fact was, however, that these fairies were puppets belonging to an itinerant show-man, which some weavers, in a drunken frolic, had taken a fancy to and robbed him of, but, fearing the consequences when sober, had thrown them under a hedge, where this fellow saw them."[7] When Mrs Hughes appeared at Abbotsford in 1828 for her second bustling, chatty visit, she

---

[4] *Letters*, VI. 387, 390. James Curle's note on the amulet is: "The Luckenbooth brooches were pinned to a child's garments between birth and baptism." See Ian Finlay, "The Luckenbooth Brooch," *The Scottish Companion*, ed. Rhoda Spence, Edinburgh 1955, p. 12, for their potency against witches. Cp. *Demonology*, p. 125; Petronius, *Satyricon*, 63.

[5] Scott's article on the Culloden Papers, *Q.R.*, XIV (1815–16), 328.

[6] George K. Matthews, *Abbotsford and Sir Walter Scott*, 2nd edn, London 1854, pp. 51–3, (also 147–50).

[7] Moore, *Memoirs*, IV. 331 (29 Oct. 1825). The incident was in April, *Letters*, IX. 95–7.

also heard the story of the Galashiels lads who stole the puppets exhibited at Selkirk.[8]

*   *   *

Scott remarks that "fairies . . . are certainly among the most pleasing legacies of fancy" in folklore and literature.[9] Three aspects of this legacy impinged on his own life: the changeling, fairy abduction, and name-euphemism as a safeguard against fairy malignancy. All three reappear in his fiction.

Fenella is a person about whose supernatural attributes few can agree in *Peveril of the Peak*. She is more frequently referred to as a changeling than as a familiar, a banshee, or even a sylphid. Manxmen readily assume that the diminutive, apparently deaf-mute maiden has been exchanged for some mortal infant before baptism. Such changelings are usually defective in some organ. Though she has the "attributes of the irritable, fickle, and dangerous race," she dislikes to be called the Elfin Queen. Yet she wins power over the superstitious by wearing green, the fairy colour, and by imitating "the pigmy folk." The general belief is that the Countess of Derby's *Elf* laughs and sings "with the invisibles of her own race" and dances with "the fairies in the haunted valley of Glenmoy" or joins the mermaids while her double attends the Countess.[10] A ship's captain discusses with Julian Peveril the foolish islanders' belief that "she is a wechsel-balg—what you call a fairy-elf changeling." He has seen a real one at Cologne, a large eater very unlike Fenella, but the girl was once a rope-dancer's apprentice. Julian smiles inwardly at the notion "that the little mute agent was aided in her machinations by the kindred imps, to whom, according to Manx superstition, her genealogy was to be traced."

In thus differentiating between upper and lower class credulity, Scott is not following his authority, George Waldron, whose *Description of the Isle of Man* (1726 and 1731) he quotes in a long note on "Manx Superstitions." Waldron's tales illustrative of those "first inhabitants" and present residents of the Isle of Man, the fairies, are drawn from the experiences of gentle and country folk, of learned and illiterate alike. Not being island-born, Peveril is hardly typical, and his creator does make the belief in Fenella's fairy extraction more widespread than similar Scottish

[8] Mrs Hughes, p. 293. Instances of puppets mistaken for magical devices and *diablotins* are given in Antoine Gachet d'Artigny, *Nouveaux Mémoires d'Histoire, de Critique et de Littérature*, Paris 1749–56, v. 123–4, and Scott's note on Mrs Anne Turner in *The Fortunes of Nigel*.

[9] *Demonology*, p. 120.

[10] Scott may be borrowing from witchcraft. When a witch flies to a Sabbath to dance and dissipate with her cronies, she may leave behind a demon or a bundle of straw to personate her.

and English superstitions in his other narratives. For "the Isle of Man, beyond other places in Britain, was a peculiar depository of the fairy traditions," which were strengthened and variegated by the Norse conquest.[11]

Even if the newly-born are not supplanted by fairy infants before baptism, as children and as adults they will still be in peril. In *Guy Mannering* the precentor reports the deceased minister of Kippletringan's "opinion that the bairn [Harry] was only conveyed to Fairy-land for a season" after his disappearance from Ellangowan.[12] Adults fare badly, being snatched away without any proxies left to fill their shoes and perhaps intended as a part of the dreadful tribute to hell:

> And pleasant is the fairy land,
> But doleful 'tis to tell,
> That once in every seven years,
> We pay a tiend to hell.[13]

When Conachar runs from the clan battle at Perth in cowardly fear and kills himself, a legend arises that, "snatched from death by the *Daoine Shie*, or fairy-folk," he wanders a mournful phantom through waste and wood (*The Fair Maid of Perth*). About Thomas the Rhymer, whose love passages with the Queen of Elfland were scarcely clandestine, "the general belief was, that he was not severed from the land of the living, but removed to the land of Faëry, from whence he sometimes made excursions" in order to prophesy (*Castle Dangerous*). Ignorance of the time and manner of True Thomas's death makes this interpretation of his departure from middle-earth seem plausible enough. But with Thomas we have advanced in supernatural-mortal relations from the unwilling to the willing abduction—to the theme of the fairy mistress.[14]

Few are likely to be ostracised from mundane life by a changeling or, later on, to be dragged or lured to Fairyland. More may see the vindictive little people, and all should refer to them courteously in order to escape their wrath. Indeed, a fairy's codification of etiquette, reward, and punishment has long made human ignorance of the law no excuse.

---

[11] *Demonology*, p. 129.

[12] See Andrew Lang's note on this passage in the Border Edition of the Waverley Novels and the essay, "On the Fairies of Popular Superstition," in *Minstrelsy*.

[13] "Tam Lin" in M. G. Lewis, *Tales of Wonder*, 2nd edn, London 1801, p. 232; "The Young Tamlane" in *Minstrelsy*.

[14] This theme in "Donnerhugel's Narrative," *Anne of Geierstein* does not include the mortal lover's ageing rapidly and becoming a pile of dust after the taboo is broken; instead, the offended supernatural mistress turns to dust.

Gin ye ca' me imp or elf,
I ^arede ye look weel to yourself;   ^a advise
Gin ye ca' me fairy,
I'll work ye muckle ^btarrie;   ^b vexation
Gin guid neibour ye ca' me,
Then guid neibour I will be;
But gin ye ca' me ^cseelie wicht,   ^c seelie wicht,
I'll be your freend baith day and nicht.[15]   polite name
                                   for fairy

In Hobbie Elliot's remarks to the sceptical Earnscliff, Scott humorously suggests the correct way to speak of fairies and hints at the decline of belief: "And it's for certain the very fairies—I mean the very good neighbours themsells (for they say folk suldna ca' them fairies) that used to be seen on every green knowe at e'en, are no half sae often visible in our days." Hobbie has never seen a *good neighbour*—only heard one; but his father, homing partly sober from fairs, saw many in his time (*The Black Dwarf*).

As a fellow student of popular antiquities, Scott was well acquainted with the work of two Aberfoil clergymen, Robert Kirk's *An Essay . . . of the Subterranean . . . Invisible People . . . Elves, Faunes, and Fairies . . . among the Low-Country Scots*, and Patrick Grahame's *Sketches of Perthshire*.[16] The introduction of fairies in *Rob Roy* almost inevitably results. As Bailie Nicol Jarvie accompanies Frank Osbaldistone to the Clachan of Aberfoil, he points out a beautiful hill which contains the caverned "palaces of the fairies." Prompted by the Bailie's ill-disguised timorousness, the novelist explains these "airy beings, who formed an intermediate class between men and demons, and who, if not positively malignant to humanity, were yet to be avoided and feared, on account of their capricious, vindictive, and irritable disposition." In a whisper Nicol Jarvie reveals, "They ca'

[15] Robert Chambers, *Popular Rhymes of Scotland*, p. 324. The taboo on speaking the names —among others—of gods, demons, witches, and totem animals results in such flattering or harmless euphemisms as Jehovah, Auld Hornie, Mother Midnight, and Grandfather (the bear). Use of the stark name may be sacrilegious, insolent, or defiant, as in the attempt to gain power over a being. It may also disastrously suggest that the named one act according to its nature.

[16] *Demonology*, pp. 163–7. Scott is responsible for the 1815 edition of Kirk's small book, retitled *A Secret Commonwealth*: W. T. Lowndes; Seymour de Ricci; P. M. Barnard, *Catalogue*, Tunbridge Wells 1916, p. 7; *Letters*, IV. 38. In a new edition of *Rob Roy*, perhaps with "Sabbath" Grahame in mind, Scott speaks of Dr Patrick Grahame as dead, whereupon the clerical antiquary writes the fictionist: "The unearthly being who now addresses you may be no more than a Fairy Changeling," etc. Partington, *Letter-Books*, p. 338 (31 Dec. 1829). Scott restores Grahame to life in a note to the Introduction (1830) of *A Legend of Montrose*. Scott's only long note in *Rob Roy* deals with "the most peculiar, but most pleasing, of . . . Celtic superstitions," the fairies that are still supposed to haunt the source of the Forth river.

them *Daoine Schie*, whilk signifies . . . men of peace,—meaning thereby to make their gude-will." Although it is well to follow this cautious procedure, the lights of the hamlet and the proximity of the manse inspirit the Bailie, who then declares all such matters but "deceits o' Satan, after a'."

In *The Monastery* Scott reverts to the character of fairies and the shunning of their name through fear of retaliation. The part of Glendearg called *Corrie nan Shian*, or Hollow of the Fairies, is visited by that "whimsical, irritable, and mischievous tribe" which is sometimes "capriciously benevolent" to men but more often inimical. Human neighbours neither repeat the dread place-name nor speak good or ill of the "imaginary beings," which also exact secrecy about their revels. When Martin and Tibb Tacket are setting out across "wild land," the wife rebukes her mate for mentioning the good neighbours when about to pass their haunts.[17] Because the White Lady of Avenel seems to be a part-time fairy, as well as ghost and angel, Dame Glendinning tries the combined strength of red string, rowan tree, and witch-elm against her before consulting Father Eustace. "Be here! that I should have named their unlucky names twice ower!"

Fairies occasionally show a genial side. Ailie Dinmont pleasantly evokes a haunted well when she recommends her sheets to Vanbeest Brown as having been "washed wi' the fairy-well water." But their kindness is often illusory. Like the contract money of the Devil, their gifts may turn worthless on the morrow. When young Osbaldistone's flattery gives way to confused silence, Diana Vernon is reminded of the fairy-tale character who "finds all the money which he had carried to market suddenly changed into pieces of slate" (*Rob Roy*).[18] If not illusory, their kindness is extended on very strict conditions. In *The Pirate*, thinking he is to leave the islands, Mordaunt Mertoun tries to return to Norna her "fairy gift [a chain wrought by the drows], that it may bring more lasting luck to some other than it has done to me." But Norna seriously warns him neither to despise nor to court "the gift of the nameless race." The reader further learns, from Minna Troil, what every local child knows, "that fairy treasures, if they are not wisely employed for the good

---

[17] In the note on this passage, Scott gives his tale of the shepherd's mistaking puppets for fairies a thorough literary grooming.

[18] On receiving money from the Black Dwarf, Hobbie Elliot protests, "I dinna like to use siller unless I kend it was decently come by; and maybe it might turn into sclate-stanes, and cheat some poor man." And in *The Pirate*, Baby Yellowley fears that Norna's payment for hospitality "will be a sclate-stane the morn, if not something worse." Cp. *Nicolai Remigii Daemonolatreiae Libri Tres*, Lyons 1595, BK I. ch. 4; William Godwin, *St. Leon*, London 1799, III. 234.

of others, as well as of those to whom they are imparted, do not dwell long with their possessors."[19] Triptolemus Yellowley also owns a treasure, which he has not used, abused, or spoken of, "whilk they say muckle offends them whom we in Scotland call Good Neighbours, and you call Drows."[20]

The Shetland drows or trows, "the legitimate successors of the northern *duergar*, and somewhat allied to the fairies," are unfriendly hill and sea folk descended from Scandinavian trolls. As local colour of the northern islands they are somewhat faded, because Scott keeps thinking of them in terms of their more polished southern cousins, the fascinatingly mercurial Lowland fairies.[21]

Scott generally prefers popular to literary lore. His fairies come from woods, fields, and hill caverns rather than from Spenser, Shakespeare, and Drayton. But when Scott leaves home base, the folk note grows faint. The literary fairies in *Ivanhoe* rudely jostle their country kin without sending them away. When Wamba the Jester hears horsemen approaching, he flippantly ventures that "they are come from Fairy-land with a message from King Oberon."[22] Gurth rebukes him for talking of such matters while a frightful storm is brewing. When Ivanhoe disappears from the tourney field at Ashby, it is "as if the fairies had conveyed him from the spot."

At times, wishing to convey the charm of a heroine, Scott lapses into the imagery of Fairyland, as he does elsewhere into that of elemental spirits. His fairies are then no longer the dangerously capricious native variety but the anaemic hybrids of children's stories. Annot Lyle in *A Legend of Montrose* is "the most beautiful little fairy certainly that ever danced upon a heath by moonlight." This "fairy queen of song and minstrelsy" tames moody Allan M'Aulay and seems to Lord Menteith "the lightest and most fairy figure that ever trode the turf by moonlight . . . so that Titania herself could scarce have found a more fitting representative."

[19] These exigent fairies seem to model their behaviour on Matt. xxv: 24–30, in which a servant, proving to be wicked, slothful, and unprofitable with one talent, is deprived of what he has and cast "into outer darkness."

[20] Cp. Shakespeare, *The Winter's Tale*, III. iii: "This is fairy gold, boy, and 'twill prove so: up with 't, keep it close. . . . We are lucky, boy; and to be so still, requires nothing but secrecy." Ben Jonson, Fletcher, and Massinger also refer to the need of keeping "fairy favours" or "fairies' treasure" secret.

[21] For Shetland trows, see *The Fairy Mythology*, London 1833, I. 260–72, by Thomas Keightley, who depends on Samuel Hibbert, *A Description of the Shetland Islands*, Edinburgh 1822, pp. 444–52.

[22] Twelfth-century Wamba refers to the king of the fairies in thirteenth-century *Huon de Bordeaux*, introduced to the English in Lord Berners's translation of 1534 and popularised in *A Midsummer Night's Dream*.

In the pretty triteness and repetition of these descriptions, Scott is trying to express something that is for him inexpressible, or else he is revealing a middle-aged novelist's lack of interest, ignorance, or hesitancy in portraying young womanhood.

In order to emphasise the strangeness of human traits, Scott may fall back on fairy-tale types. So it is with the Baroness of Steinfeldt in *Anne of Geierstein*, an old lady of "insatiable curiosity and overweening pride." Put down in a contest over precedence, this "malicious fairy in a minstrel's tale" calls her host a sorcerer and her hostess a demon and quits the christening party. Like one under a curse, Lady Hermione dies that very day and, exactly three years after her funeral, the baron is entombed.

★   ★   ★

Scott faithfully retains the darker shadings along with the streaks of benevolence in fairyism. But while revealing the caution of the common people against malice, he also suggests the fading vitality of the whole tissue of beliefs. When his own imaginative sympathy weakens, he may try to characterise a heroine by means of fairy metaphor, but the effect is that of a changeling temporarily ousting an engaging mortal. Any loss of grip on narrative reality may encourage the stereotyped elves of fairy tales to appear. Throughout the Waverley Novels, the incidental references to fairy haunts and habits outnumber the episodes, as they do in Scott's anecdotes and letters. These scattered allusions are often more ornamental than functional, but many of them contribute to local colour and are delightful or dramatic according to the temper of the folk. If fairies linger for a time, it is because they are drawn by credence among common men who cling to a native faith.

Fairy lore in *The Monastery* inspired a shepherd to write expressing his sentiments and asking the Author of Waverley "whether ye really believe in the existence of such Beings."[23] Scott was not a believer but a connoisseur. As such he was fascinated by the ever-changing pattern of overlapping superstitions. Despite the pretty fancies of men of letters, the fairy nature strangely harboured aborigines, ghosts, elementals, demons, and witches. The family tree sent down its roots to early people subdued into lurchers, the dead or their essences, personified nature spirits, fallen angels and their accomplices. They haunted places like ghosts, and they contracted mortal unions like elementals. Like demons, they raised gales to frighten diggers from treasure. And, like witches, they stole milk, cows, unbaptised children, sacrificed infants and grown people to the Devil, and

[23] 24 Jun. 1820 in Partington, *Letter-Books*, pp. 321–2.

rode to mass revels on sticks, stalks, and beasts.[24] Yet fairy lore refined much grossness out of the practices it shared with demonology and witchcraft.

13. DEMONOLOGY

As a child Walter Scott almost fell into the clutches of Auld Hornie. He was cared for by a maid who grew to hate him because he kept her from a sweetheart in Edinburgh. "She confessed to old Alison Wilson, the house-keeper, that she had carried me up to the Craigs, meaning, under a strong temptation of the Devil, to cut my throat with her scissors, and bury me in the moss." After her discharge from Sandy-Knowe, she is believed to have gone mad.[1] Adults sometimes called in the Fiend as an agent to enforce obedience. "When I was a boy," Scott informs the attentive Mrs Hughes, "I used to be told that there was risque in presenting guns or pistols at people even though I knew they were unloaded for that the Devil might load them for the purpose of putting me to shame."[2]

Not only a tempter but an entertainer, the versatile enemy of mankind could enliven stories by his presence. Among young Walter's many rela-tives and acquaintances who were spirited fireside narrators was his brother Robert, whose tales are still fresh in memory when the novelist describes Coffin-key in *The Pirate*. On this low island the crew abandons Cleveland to the pitiless demons and spectres of the Equinoctial Line, with whom he is supposed to be in league. Finally the hardy pirate is but "little alarmed by visionary terrors" which come into focus as bushes, driftwood, or wreaths of mist. A footnote fixes the source of all but Scott's rational explanation:

An elder brother . . . used to astonish the author's boyhood with tales of those haunted islets [in the West Indies]. On one of them, called, I believe,

[24] In ballads "witches and fairies, especially in the matter of their supernatural powers, are often indistinguishable," and ghosts and fairies show "striking resemblances." Lowry C. Wimberly, *Folklore in the English and Scottish Ballads*, p. 165.

[1] Lockhart, I. 15–16, and Mrs Hughes, p. 215. "Upon this marvellous story Mr. Lockhart makes no comment, and its incredible character and want of confirmation makes me believe it had no existence beyond some gossip's tale which the author of Waverley may have heard in after life." Sir Walter Scott and his Contemporaries, I. 10–11, anonymous Ms., life, Forster Collection, Victoria and Albert Museum, London. (The Mortons' housekeeper in *Old Mortality* is named Alison Wilson, and Muschat's Cairn in *The Heart of Midlothian* is haunted by Ailie, whose husband cut her throat.)

[2] *Letters*, XI. 230; Mrs Hughes, p. 323. Cp. Law, *Memorialls*, pp. 229–30: "Certainly it is Sathan that prompts the hearts of men and children to such presumptuous actings to adven-ture to shoot guns, whereof they are ignorant whether charged or not, and to present them to others in a frolick way." For the fourth Duke of Buccleuch's account of his youthful dread of devils, see Partington, *Letter-Books*, pp. 308–09, and *Huntingdon Library Quarterly*, II (1939), 341–2.

Coffin-key, the seamen positively refused to pass the night, and came off every evening while they were engaged in completing the watering of the vessel, returning the following sunrise.[3]

These are late eighteenth-century echoes of a devil-lore which grows darker and more complex the further Scott as story-writer penetrates the past. In his late twenties and early thirties, Scott was a highly imaginative, often susceptible amateur demonologist. He was not alone. While pursuing such life interests as languages, literature, the theatre, divinity, antiquarian research, county history, and even tortured self-knowledge, seven of his friends likewise made a hobby of demonology. Of these men, "Monk" Lewis, C. K. Sharpe, Robert Surtees, R. P. Gillies, and Charles R. Maturin shared various degrees of advantage of birth; parental indulgence; frail, ill, or uncertain health; fits of moody melancholy; spare time; bookishness and an active fancy; and early stimulus by story-tellers steeped in local balladry and traditions. Of vigorous common stock, John Leyden and James Hogg were homespun geniuses who stood alone in their eccentric self-assurance.

Scott himself exhibits traits of both decadent and sturdy demonologists,[4] and thus his enthusiasm has many facets. Between 1802 and about 1805, he was a highly valued Hobgoblinite, or fashionable demonolater, in the Pandemonium of the Elliots of Minto. On Christmas Day 1805, he writes to the secretary-poet of the club:

> Of ghosts & kelpies I've a store.
> And some shall squeak & some shall roar,
> At Teviot's mount, by pale blue light,
> When Devilish tales e'en Devils fright....
>
> I'll sing ye many a merry ploy,
> Shall make Deils wag their tails with joy.[5]

[3] There flock the damned—there Satan reigns and revels,
And hence yon Isle is called "The Isle of Devils"!

Matthew Gregory ("Monk") Lewis, *The Isle of Devils*, London 1912, p. 12 (1st edn, 1827). Writing to Scott, Mrs Maclean Clephane encloses her poem, dated 11 Jan. 1814, on three men who, sleeping on the Isle of Lunga in Nov. 1813, were harassed and pursued by Devils. The poetess advises adventurers to say a prayer before landing on Lunga:

And let your skiff be moor'd to land,
But let her not stranded be
Nor be caught by the fangs of the Island Fiends
When before you lies the sea!

Abbotsford Mss. (letter of Sep. [1814]), N.L.S. Also see Lockhart, I. 149.

[4] C. O. Parsons, "Scott's Fellow Demonologists," *M.L.Q.*, IV (1943), 473-93.

[5] This versified epistle is in reply to Demonia's invitation to a party, at which Scott is to instruct Hobgoblinites "in mystical lore ... to teach them to conjure ... to make their Teeth chatter at Goblin or Ghost." Walpole; C. O. Parsons, "Walter Scott in Pandemonium," *M.L.R.*, XXXVIII (1943), 244-9.

In his early forties Scott was consulted by morbid acquaintances who often described their despondency and ill health in demonic terms. James Ballantyne, William Stewart Rose, and Sir James Stuart were possessed by blue devils and demons of melancholy. Gillies was afflicted by "most formidable fiends": "*From my own experience* I can affirm that there is a certain state of mind & Body in which Apparitions such as those which appear in the Highlands . . . actually do present themselves to the Eye with all the horrible reality of Supernatural Visitation."[6] Scott's advice to defy the foul fiend by having some set routine of work appealed less to Gillies than his own negative remedy of avoiding "preternatural excitement." As a patient, with his moods of exultation and depression, his conviction that dreams are truer than reality, and his "*diabolical resources*," Maturin also proved difficult.[7]

In the latter part of his life, Scott sometimes found that distraction, melancholy, or strong emotion could be expressed vividly in the imagery of demonism. The Devil slipped into toasts and proverbs as well. When Abbotsford was finished, the Laird let the servants have a ball at which he drank their health: "All your good helthes and cheep meal, and may the Divell rock them in a creel that does not wish us all weel." During his financial setbacks, Scott went into conference with James Ballantyne at Abbotsford and, on being interrupted by his butler, sent him packing: "The divell is with me, and harrowing the verrey soul out of me." Half an hour later he rang the bell and added, "Now he has left me with breath, but that is all."[8]

★   ★   ★

Demonology serves many purposes in the Waverley Novels, from slight allusions to the embodiment of folklore, the passions of history, character contrasts, and moral values. Before attempting to survey demonry in the Scottish and in the non-Scottish novels of Sir Walter, I shall discuss "Wandering Willie's Tale" (*Redgauntlet*) as illustrative of the narrator's method of fusing details from a large body of tradition.

Among the many seventeenth-century personages who were accused of diabolical intimacies, not the least notable bondsmen of Satan were Sir Robert Grierson of Lag, John Graham of Claverhouse, and Major Thomas Weir. The animosity stirred by Lag, "Clavers," and Weir, though definitely

---

[6] 29 Jan. 1812 in Walpole.

[7] *The Correspondence of Sir Walter Scott and Charles Robert Maturin*, Austin, Texas 1937, p. 14.

[8] "Memoirs of William Dalgleish," ed. G. E. Mitton, *The Cornhill Magazine*, Third Series, LXX (1931), 744; LXXI (1931), 221.

crossed with political feeling, was religious. Covenanters traced the brutal persistence of Lag and Claverhouse in hunting down conventiclers to a league with Satan, in which they exchanged their immortal souls for success in exterminating God's chosen vessels. This is Robert Wodrow's conclusion to an anecdote of Sir Robert Grierson's inhumanity:

> Dreadful were the acts of wickedness done by the soldiers at this time, and Lagg was as deep as any. They used to take to themselves in their cabals the names of devils, and persons they supposed to be in hell, and with whips to lash one another, as a jest upon hell.[9]

Since the demonic interpretation of Grierson's activity and connexions prevailed among Covenanters during his own lifetime, a tradition in which his more human features may be made out is of particular interest. One of "Bluidy" Lag's tenants died owing "considerable arrears of rent." When the factor approached the widow with a choice of full payment or eviction, the poor woman went to Lag and silently walked round him several times. She had heard that "his honour had a right side and a wrang ane, and as she had a favour to ask of him she wanted to try gin she could fin out his right side." Upon learning the details of the widow's story, Lag sent her to his house, where he later joined her with two papers, one a discharge of the arrears, and the other a nineteen-year lease of the farm at a moderate rent.[10]

Still another legend about payment of arrears and the just action of the Laird of Lag was current in Galloway. It is probably the widow's story accommodated to Lag's death of apoplexy, an event which made the substitution of the creditor's death for the debtor's almost inevitable. The fuller legend appears in a note to Joseph Train's *Strains of the Mountain Muse* (Edinburgh 1814): The unexpected passing of the Laird of Lag prevented one of his lessees from obtaining a receipt for a tardy payment of rent. The young Laird, for his part, refused to accept the farmer's word in lieu of a voucher. On his way home that night, the disconsolate man was joined by a stranger who conducted him to a castle in the wood whose gate was opened by Lag's deceased porter. On entering the hall, the living man recognised Pate Birnie tuning his fiddle and several persecutors mingling in the company. The Laird himself wrote out a receipt, whereupon the

---

[9] Wodrow, *The History of the Sufferings of the Church of Scotland*, ed. Robert Burns, Glasgow 1830–5, IV. 242. Also see John Howie, *The Judgment and Justice of God Exemplified*, Glasgow 1782, p. 61. Macaulay transfers this anecdote to Claverhouse, of whom Wodrow had previously been writing. For Black Beard's (Captain Teach's) similar love of *diablerie*, see Daniel Defoe, *A General History of the Pyrates*, 2nd edn, London 1724, *passim*.

[10] Abbotsford Mss., N.L.S. "Lag's Right Side" is in a group of songs and tales watermarked 1812 but written down as late as 28 Nov. 1819, the recitation date of one of the songs. Scott's informant was probably Joseph Train or one of that antiquary's assistants.

stranger led his bewildered companion back to the road.[11] This second legend contains a highly conventionalised episode, that of a trip to Hell or to a mysterious castle in a wood or of the intervention of wizard or ghost.[12] Its articulation with the Lag saga, of course, requires the actual settling of the arrears in order to motivate the tenant's infernal visit.

The castle incident may be found in yet another short story, "The Bewitched Fiddler." Matthew Wilmart lost his way in the forest of Hesdin. Guided to "a magnificent chateau" by the gleam of a light, he came upon a multitude of people eating, playing games of chance, and dancing. Matthew's fiddle was hung on a golden nail by a page whose fingers charred the part they touched. When the newcomer stared at the features of any guest, "a sort of thin mist shrouded his face," but he did recognise his violin teacher in the fiddlers' gallery—old Barnabas Matassart, dead some thirty years. At that sight he cried out shakily, "Holy Virgin, have pity on me!" Instantly, fiddlers, dancers, and chateau vanished, leaving not a rack behind. Next morning, old Matthew was found lying at the foot of a gibbet.[13]

In "Wandering Willie's Tale," when told to return after a twelvemonth to pay homage for the protection received, Steenie Steenson protests, "I refer myself to God's pleasure, and not to yours." All goes dark around him and he sinks to the earth like one dead, only to regain consciousness next morning in the old churchyard of Redgauntlet parish. Scott's narrative divergences from Train's version of the second legend are often matched not by such stories as "The Bewitched Fiddler" but by demonological lore attached to leading persecutors and Covenanters. In its transit from one man to another, this lore acquired unity, so that its application to Sir Robert Redgauntlet is artistically effective.

[11] *Op. cit.*, summary of pp. 191–5.

[12] Tenant pays rent, but "harsh and cruel squire" dies; "even more wicked wife" demands second payment; poor man goes to wizard, who conjures squire "all wrapped up in flames" and obtains receipt. A. H. Krappe, *The Science of Folk-Lore*, New York 1930, pp. 97–8. Debtor dies but appears to son in dream to tell where receipt is, thus discomfiting grasping creditor in court. St. Augustine, *De Cura pro Mortuis Gerenda*, summarised by Noel Taillepied in *A Treatise of Spirits*, tr. Montague Summers, London n.d., p. 68. Also see "The Bewitched Fiddler."

[13] *Storys of the Bewitched Fiddler, Perilous Situation, and John Hetherington's Dream*, Glasgow n.d., pp. 3–12. The chapbook also follows Matthew Wilmart's unhappy adventures after the fearful night. A similar story is told of a benighted farmer by George Waldron in *A Description of the Isle of Man* (Scott used the 2nd edn of 1731 in *Peveril*) and is repeated by Joseph Train in *An Historical . . . Account of the Isle of Man*, Douglas 1845, II. 154–5. Cp. chapbook, *Satan's Warehouse Door: Or Water Willie's New Mode of Purifying his Hands*, Glasgow 1808; *Demonology*, pp. 126–8. Also see Count Jan Potocki (1761–1815), *The Saragossa Manuscript*, tr. Elisabeth Abbot, New York 1960, p. 23: After supernatural experience, "I awoke . . . under the gallows of Los Hermanos, and beside me—the corpses of Zoto's two brothers!"

In *An Elegy in Memory of that valiant Champion, Sir Robert Grierson of Lag*, the fifth and earliest known edition of which came out twenty years after Lag's death, the Prince of Darkness says of his favourite, "He bore my image on his brow, | My service he did still avow."[14] Although the image is metaphorical rather than physical, Scott's Sir Robert Redgauntlet is distinguished by "the visible mark of a horse-shoe in his forehead, deep-dinted, as if it had been stamped there." At this point, a curious shift may be noted; life and legend, instead of influencing fiction, begin to be influenced by it. The steps are these: (1) in a note to "Wandering Willie's Tale" the author explains, "I have heard in my youth some such wild tale as that placed in the mouth of the blind fiddler, of which, I think, the hero was Sir Robert Grierson of Lagg, the famous persecutor"; (2) the popular mind identifies fictitious character with original; and (3) it is reported that Lag's descendant and Scott's acquaintance, old Robert Grierson, in accessions of wrath, displayed a clearly defined horseshoe on his forehead.[15]

Among the Abbotsford MSS. in the National Library of Scotland is a collection of transcripts including an extract from George Sinclair's *Satan's Invisible World Discovered* (1685) made on paper watermarked 1825 and docketed by Scott, "Red Gauntlet Major Weir." Although the copy itself is not in Scott's hand and is of a later date than the novel, which was published in June 1824, it is interesting as containing the actual source of Redgauntlet's infernal stigma:

> She [Jean Weir] put back her head-dress, and seeming to frown, there was seen an exact Horse-shoe shaped for nails in her wrinckles. Terrible enough I assure you to the stoutest beholder.[16]

Scott borrows still another particular from Sinclair's account of the Weirs, notorious Major and fanatical sister. Being dated from the place of torment, Steenie's receipt is thrown into the fire by Sir John Redgauntlet. Resisting combustion, "away it flew up the lum, wi' a lang train of sparks at its tail, and a hissing noise like a squib." The professor of philosophy and mathematics at the University of Glasgow is equally quaint:

[14] *An Elegy ...*, 5th edn, corrected and enlarged (1753), p. 4. The 10th edn of 1773 is quoted in Crockett, *Scott Originals*, p. 353, and in Alexander Fergusson, *The Laird of Lag*, Edinburgh 1886, p. 166.

[15] "The Laird of Redgauntlet," *Macmillan's Magazine*, LIV (1886), 116.

[16] Sinclair, Postscript. C. K. Sharpe first identified the horseshoe: "the frown of the family of right belongs to Mrs. Jean Weir, the celebrated Major's sister, who was hanged for a witch, &c., in the year 1679 [1670]." Allardyce, I. 4. See Robert Chambers, *Illustrations*, pp. 224–7, for information probably drawn from Sharpe. Jean's sorceress mother also bore this inappropriate brand of Satan (the horseshoe was a widespread countercharm against witches, his chosen agents on earth).

There was another clout found [in the Weirs' house] with some hard thing in it, which they threw into the fire likewise; it being a certain root, which circled and sparkled like Gunpowder, and passing from the Tunnel of the Chimney, it gave a crack like a little Cannon, to the amazement of all that were present.

When she [Helen Stewart, whose desertion by the devil duplicates Major Weir's plight] had hung some little time on the Gibbet, a black Pitchy-like ball foamed out of her mouth: and after the fire was kindled, it grew to the bigness of a Walnut, and then flew up like Squibs into the air, which the Judge yet living attests.[17]

John Graham of Claverhouse, Viscount Dundee, also contributes to Scott's account of Sir Robert Redgauntlet. According to tradition, Claverhouse received from the Devil a black horse on which he "out-stripped and *coted*, or turned, a hare upon the Bran-Law, near the head of Moffat Water, where the descent is so precipitous that no merely ... mortal rider could keep the saddle."[18] He was likewise proof against lead shot: "The superstitious fanatics ... averred that they saw the bullets recoil from his jack-boots and buff-coat like hailstones from a rock of granite."[19] Redgauntlet, too, is vulgarly reported to have "a direct compact with Satan" which renders him "proof against steel" and re-pellent to bullets; they "happed aff his buff-coat like hailstanes from a hearth." And he rides "a mear that would turn a hare on the side of Carrifra-gawns [a steep mountainside in Moffatdale, Dumfriesshire]."

Learned in demonology and country tradition, Scott chooses no detail from kindred materials which does not harmonise with his conception of Sir Robert Redgauntlet or of his original, the Laird of Lag. Fitting con-tributions are also exacted from Claverhouse and Major Weir. Thus, without weakening its simple effectiveness, he infinitely enriches a source legend which he has long known and which his friend, Joseph Train, has revived in 1814. "Wandering Willie's Tale" also recreates the superstitious

[17] Sinclair, Postscript.
[18] *Old Mortality*, n. xi on "Claverhouse's Charger." Cp. the spectre horsemen who rode along the sheer side of Souterfell. John Timbs, *Abbeys, Castles, and Ancient Halls of England and Wales*, 2nd edn, ed. Alexander Gunn, London 1872, III. 314–16. Also see Wordsworth, "An Evening Walk," 1793, ll. 175–90 (in revised version, ll. 192–211).
[19] *Old Mortality*, ch. 16. See n. xv on "General Dalzell"; Allardyce, II. 190–1; *Edinburgh and the Lothians*, ed. Theo Lang, London 1952, p. 159, for bullets glancing off General Tom Dalzell's buff coat and boots. Also see John Howie, *Judgment and Justice of God Exemplified*, pp. 50–1, and Sharpe's Ms. jottings on Claverhouse, Jul. 1808, in Mark Napier, *Memorials and Letters illustrative of the Life and Times of John Graham of Claverhouse, Viscount Dundee*, Edinburgh 1859–62, I. 283. The heaviness of Dalzell's riding-boots still preserved at his former home, The Binns, and the thickness of Claverhouse's dented, but not pierced, coat of pressed deerskin, kept at Glamis Castle, offer a natural explanation of their wearers' in-vulnerability.

milieu in which seventeenth century Covenanters and Cavaliers fought over their irremediable differences. Variety within the bounds of artistic congruity, realism of manners and incident, gruesomeness free from cautionary disquisition, rapid narration, vigorous, earthy dialect—all combine in the masterful execution of Scott's most popular short story.[20]

★   ★   ★

In the Waverley Novels, incidental references to the Devil, as well as proverbs, may characterise the speaker, advance the plot, or indicate the superstitious temper of an historic period. Folk wisdom is imbedded in the proverbs, even when they are repeated by fairly sophisticated persons:

> "Blow for blow, as Conan said to the Devil." [Fergus MacIvor, to his sister Flora, in *Waverley*; cp. Note XIII.]

> "The devil is ever most to be feared when he preacheth." [Father Eustace, to Christie of the Clinthill, in *The Monastery*.]

> It is better to "fleech the de'il than fight him." ["The Highland Widow."]

> "The devil has factors enough to utter his wares." [Catharine Glover, to Henry Smith, in *The Fair Maid of Perth*.]

Other passages combine the qualities of proverb and epigram:

> "The deil flay the hide o' it to sole his brogues wi'!" Meg Murdockson exclaims to her daughter Madge, to whom Frank Levitt then says, "We shall have the devil to pay here, and nothing to pay him with." [*The Heart of Midlothian*.]

> "You look on me as the devil looks over Lincoln," says Dame Ursula. "It is ill talking of the devil, mother Midnight," Jenkin replies. ". . . I am at that pass, when they say he will appear to wretched ruined creatures, and proffer them gold for the fee-simple of their salvation.". . . "Thou knowest every place by the river's side as well as the devil knows an usurer." [Dame Ursula, to Jenkin, in *The Fortunes of Nigel*.][21]

---

[20] A more detailed analysis of Scott's sources may be found in "Demonological Background of . . . 'Wandering Willie's Tale,' " *Studies in Philology*, xxx (1933), 611–17. Since writing the article, I have read "a problematical claim" for a Fifeshire source of Steenie's recovery of the receipt: James Wilkie, *Bygone Fife*, Edinburgh and London 1931, pp. 295–8. The Grierson legend, which is not mentioned by Mr Wilkie, is much closer to Scott's narrative. For an interpretation of the short story as "closely linked with the main theme of the novel" through its study of "master-servant relations in old Scotland," see David Daiches, "Scott's *Redgauntlet*," *From Jane Austin to Joseph Conrad*, edd. Rathburn and Steinmann, Minneapolis 1958, pp. 56–7. For my discussion of the father/son theme, see ch. v.

[21] For standard Devil proverbs, see Andrew Henderson, *Scottish Proverbs*, ed. James Donald, new edn, Glasgow 1881, pp. 11–12, 106.

Still other allusions give vigour to oaths or relate to tenets of demonism:

> "The fiend go down my weasand with a bare blade at his belt if we part
> before my dirk and his best bluid are weel acquainted thegither." [Rob
> Roy, concerning Rashleigh Osbaldistone.]

> "Such gifts from such hands [those of Charles II disguised as an old
> fortune-teller] are a kind of press-money which the devil uses for enlisting
> his regiment of witches; and if they take so much as a bean from him, they
> become his bond slaves for life—Ay, you look at the gewgaw [a ruby
> ring], but tomorrow you will find a lead ring and a common pebble in its
> stead." [Joceline Joliffe, to Alice Lee, in *Woodstock*.]

The humour, the joy of exaggeration, in some of the Scots sayings is
lacking in Joceline's English warning. Although it has been said that the
Devil can hardly be a native of Scotland, because he has never gone around
in a kilt,[22] he has been seen in trews. There is a camaraderie in Burns's
"Address to the Deil." The best way to get along with the Earl of Hell is
to treat him democratically. At times, Scott pokes fun at those who take
the Enemy too seriously. Minister Bide-the-Bent pompously reproves
Girder the cooper for his cursing, "The taking in our mouths the name of
the great enemy of our souls is an exposing ourselves to his temptations"
(*The Bride of Lammermoor*).

The very presence of the royal author of *Daemonologie* (1597) in *The
Fortunes of Nigel* requires the delivery of dogmatic opinions on forbidden
lore. The brains of Scotsmen left in their native land seem to James I
"hirdie-girdie, like sae mony warlocks and witches on the Devil's
Sabbath-e'en," and George Heriot "stares as if he took his native prince
for a warlock! us that are the very *malleus maleficarum*, the contunding and
contriturating hammer of all witches, sorcerers, magicians, and the like;[23]
he thinks we are taking a touch of the black art oursells!" A shadow of
the Satanic falls on Lord Dalgarno, who speaks of his gypsy page, Lutin
or Goblin, as "a very devil" for discovery of persons "as if by art magic."
Ever obedient to his master's conjuring-rod, this "imp of Satan" can teach
any but "real fiends" more mischief than he can learn. Another character,
Jenkin Vincent, despairingly tells Sir Richie Moniplies of his drift Devil-
ward, which inspires the Scotsman to pun on the Devil Tavern. Underworld allusions in *Nigel* parallel Scott's use of demonology to characterise

---

[22] Ronald MacDonald Douglas, *The Scots Book*, New York 1935, p. 107.

[23] The reference is to the central treatise of demonography, the *Malleus Maleficarum* or
Hexenhammer of Jacob Sprenger and Henry Kramer (1486), a manual of doctrine and practice culminating in witch tracking, torture, and trial. It went through five English editions
during James I's lifetime.

the credulous, the villainous, or the weak, but in each case a humorous turn is given to the device.

Scott's suppressed *Private Letters* is an antiquarian hoax written a year earlier than *Nigel,* of whose royal portrait it contains a sketch. James worries about a shrewd and subtle priest of Baal who "copieth his master the Devil in seekinge whose sowle he may devowre." But his pedantry is most nagging in enquiry about a Jesuit sorcerer's "strange forayne owle." Because "unlawful and devilishe artes" are more abhorrent "than treasone itselfe," "prudent men, well travelled in discoverie of witchcrafte," must privily "marke whether the owle carrie itselfe at all poyntes like unto an ordinarie owle" or like an imp or familiar.[24] The King actually advanced from fearful belief in 1590-2, when the North Berwick witches confessed plotting his marine destruction, to very hardheaded scepticism.[25] But to Scott he remained "the witch-persecuting James I," author of "a deep work upon Demonology, embracing . . . the most absurd and gross of the popular errors," a Dominie Sampson with power and a printer.[26]

Some of the "popular errors" may be found in *The Abbot.* Like fairies, Old Scratch does not enjoy being painted as black as he really is. A waiting-woman rebukes Wingate for his soft words about the Papists:

> "If one were to speak to you about the devil himself, you would say there were worse people than Satan."
> "Assuredly I might say so," replied the steward, "supposing that I saw Satan standing at my elbow."
> The waiting-woman started.[27]

Magdalen Graeme thinks Roland's being twice drawn into the Avenel house is like the inability of destructive spirits to enter "unless they are invited, nay, dragged over the threshold." To illustrate the belief, Scott quotes from James Ridley's *Tales of the Genii* of 1764 and Coleridge's "Christabel."

[24] Scott, *Private Letters of the Seventeenth Century*, ed. Douglas Grant, Oxford 1947, pp. 83–90. Andrew Lang's "An Unpublished Work of Scott," *Scribner's Magazine*, XIV (1893), 733–48, is a shortened version. The courtier writing Letter VIII does not know whether Jesuit magic is trickery or the cooperation of Beelzebub. Cp. Scott, *The History of Scotland*, Philadelphia 1830, II. 306–07.

[25] *Newes from Scotland*, London [1591], reprinted by the Roxburghe Club in 1816. The king is defended by George Lyman Kittredge, "English Witchcraft and James the First," *Studies . . . Presented to Crawford Howell Toy*, New York 1912, pp. 1–65, reprinted in Kittredge, *Witchcraft in Old and New England*, Cambridge, Mass. 1929, pp. 276–328.

[26] Lord Somers, *A Collection of Scarce and Valuable Tracts*, 2nd edn, ed. Walter Scott, London 1810, III. 161 (also 95); *Demonology*, p. 246.

[27] So it is with the Devil worshipers of Iraq: "The Yezedis, curious folk, are convinced that there is a good deal of evil in the world, and that it is more sensible to propitiate Satan, who is in charge of it, than the nicer deities." John Gunther, *Inside Asia*, New York and London 1939, p. 537 n. 3.

Embarrassing reversals can best be explained as diabolical. Discomfited in a duel, vain Sir Piercie Shafton pretends that Halbert Glendinning may have dealings with Satan or, at least, be instigated by him (*The Monastery*). Warming up, the knight suggests to the Sub-Prior that the Devil may have fought him in the likeness of Halbert and then transported his body from the scene. Or sorcery and bewitchment may have been involved. Psychologically, the modern equivalent is, "Luck was against me."

Although the suspicion of diabolical pact may be cast on Halbert, Elspat of the Tree, and other characters, not much use is made of a grosser aspect of demonolatry, the confederate's receiving a familiar—usually an animal—as the Devil's liaison. The being that works with the Black Dwarf on the moor always disappears when anyone approaches the newly built cottage. Against Earnscliff's suggestion that it may be the recluse's shadow, Hobbie Elliot protests that Elshie is "ower far in wi' the Auld Ane to have a shadow." Besides, the shadow gets between Elshie and the sun. On another occasion, Hobbie is sure that he has come on "a wizard holding intercourse with his familiar spirit," mistaking a money-filled fur pouch near the spot where the familiar vanishes for a badger or a terrier. Although the companion later turns out to be human, he contributes much to Elshie's reputation of having leagued himself "with other powers, deformed to the eye and malevolent to the human race as *him*self."

When a devil's or a familiar's materialisation is not due to mistaken identity, his real presence may be suspected in a friend, relative, or faithless retainer. Hannah Irwin's confession in *St Ronan's Well* makes her more variously sinister than Ailsie Gourlay in her influence on Lucy Ashton. If she reveals her guilt to any but a clergyman, she will be carried away body and soul by "the Evil Spirit, whose servant I have been." She has directed her cousin, Clara Mowbray, in a course of corrupting, romantically perverse reading. Then, seduced by "another yet blacker, if blacker could be," Valentine Bulmer, a "demon" whose agent she becomes in further evil, she enviously and clearsightedly sets out to destroy Clara's virtue. In a passage which Scott excised at James Ballantyne's request, "the devil and Hannah Irwin" triumph when Clara and Bulmer's half-brother, Francis Tyrrel, sin together. Hating both persons, she helps Bulmer impersonate Tyrrel in a midnight marriage to Clara. "Oh! if fiends laugh, as I have heard they can, what a jubilee of scorn will there be, when Bulmer and I enter their place of torture!"

Nor is this the limit of Satan's aid to evil, fractious, and passionate mankind. Like the Devil at the heels of a sinner "who nursed diabolical purposes," Captain Hector MacTurk is eager to ignite the touchwood of any quarrel. And when John Mowbray, a man of "ungovernably strong" passions, loses control through wine, hot riding, and shame over Clara's disgrace, he is tempted by "an evil spirit" to stab his sister with a hunting-knife. "Yonder I could almost fancy I see him fly, the wood, and the rock, and the water gleaming back the dark-red furnace-light that is shed on them by his dragon wings!" In these passages, the author's shocked revulsion from the crimes he invents and divulges finds expression in the melodramatic intensity of his Devil imagery.[28]

When he develops the wages-of-sin theme in *The Heart of Midlothian* and *The Surgeon's Daughter*, Scott does not make the mistake of removing the sin. His loathing of extra-marital relations, whether his brother Daniel's or a fictional character's, is again voiced in demonic terms. The good characters in the earlier novel believe in the Devil's existence and resist his influence; the bad scoff, waver, or believe and submit. Robertson, the seducer of Effie Deans, commands the preacher, Reuben Butler, to have Jeanie Deans meet him at Muschat's Cairn by moonlight. Butler questions whether he has not encountered "the Roaring Lion," a fiend whose manly beauty cannot conceal his designs or cloak his passionate, suspicious, melancholy, mocking nature. In a similar mood, David Deans speaks of his runaway daughter as in "the bonds of Satan . . . wi' that son of Belial." When her father suggests a way of saving Effie through deceit, Jeanie suspects that she has been tempted by Satan's assuming Deans' "voice and features." Going to meet Robertson at night, Jeanie fears that her grief and despair may subject her to the Devil's temptations. Alone at a murder-cursed landmark, she at first mistakes the distracted Robertson for a fiend and later wonders whether he is "a maniac, or an apostate spirit incarnate."

Robertson (George Staunton) is a melodramatic, guilt-seared, Byronic sinner whose references to himself as mad, frantic, fearless, merciless, forsaken by the good and abandoned to "an evil being" do little to lessen Reuben's, David's, or Jeanie's dread. Together with Levitt, Captain John Porteous, who before his lynching seems "agitated by some evil demon," and Ratcliffe, a regular *deevil's peat* and the worst villain "out o' hell," he breathes the sulphurous air of demoniac violence and abandon. To Jeanie he impatiently declares himself free from cloven feet, taloned hands, or horned head, only to admit in his autobiographical confession that he has "turned out a fiend." And to Reuben, with "a contortion of

---

[28] Meg Dods has a lighter touch in her comment on the curative water of the Well: "Folk had a jest that St. Ronan dookit the Deevil in the Waal, which garr'd it taste aye since of brimstane."

visage absolutely demoniacal," "I am the devil!" And so he is morally.

Effie, his leman before she is his lady, is the victim of an ungoverned passion which—in its grossest form—sweeps Meg Murdockson to malignity and Madge Wildfire to madness. Ruled by selfhood, she breaks the moral code and, unhappily like Scott's villains, is sucked into a vacuum of disbelief. When she is distracted, Effie thinks that the Devil may be putting bad thoughts into her mind. But later, as Lady Staunton, she is "inaccessible to supernatural terrors." Of course, the culprits must suffer. Consequently, Effie's bastard, the Whistler, "a born imp of Satan" without a Christian name, is a *reductio ad horrendum* of moral anarchy who finds his element at last among "wild Indians," but not before he has become an outlaw, shot his father, set a house on fire, and driven his mother into a convent.[28a]

Bad as the Whistler may seem, Richard Middlemas, the illegitimate son of Zilia de Monçada and Richard Tresham in *The Surgeon's Daughter*, is even worse. By suddenly appearing to his mother in India, after many years of separation, he kills her through shock. That "apostate spirit," General Witherington (Tresham that was), exclaims stagily: "Behold me—see you not my hair streaming with sulphur, my brow scathed with lightning?—I am the Arch-Fiend—I am the father whom you seek." Then he drives Middlemas from his sight with a curse, "My son!—thou art the fiend who hast occasioned my wretchedness in this world, and who will share my eternal misery in the next." The young man shoots his colonel in a duel, plots to sell his sweetheart to Tippoo Saib, betrays English and Indian leaders alike, and is at last trampled to death by a retributive elephant. Thus a pre-Victorian lesson on the consequences of unchastity is underscored by demonology.

The use of demonology to bring out religious, as well as moral, differences has been suggested by Covenanters' legends about their persecutors ("Wandering Willie's Tale") and by the attitudes of three Presbyterians, Reuben Butler and Jeanie and David Deans, the last narrowly and rigidly sectarian. When Scottish Presbyterians refused the imposition of Episcopalianism and took to open-air conventicles and rural hideouts, they developed the manias of persecuted folk. Prophecy descended on enthusiastic preachers, angels hovered over worshippers, and miracles were performed to aid escape. Opposed to the chosen ones of God were Royalists whom Satan mounted on supernaturally surefooted black

---

[28a] For an informed analysis of the novel in Calvinistic terms, see Winifred Lynskey, "The Drama of the Elect and the Reprobate in Scott's *Heart of Midlothian*," *Boston University Studies in English*, IV (1960), 39–48.

steeds, shielded from bullets,[29] and equipped with familiars. Sometimes bypassing their human agents, hellish spirits intervened directly to lame the Covenanters' horses, to betray their footsteps to the pursuers, or to terrify their saints "by ghastly apparitions in the dreary caverns and recesses where they were compelled to hide themselves."[30]

For his short sketch of Ellangowan's ancestor in *Guy Mannering*, Scott extracts the quintessence of superstitions about the aristocratic anti-Covenanters. Fiery-tempered Donohue Bertram got drunk every day, "held orgies with the Laird of Lagg," joined Claverhouse at Killiecrankie, and at Dunkeld "was shot dead by a Cameronian with a silver bullet (being supposed to have proof from the Evil One against lead and steel) . . . his grave is still called the 'Wicked Laird's Lair.' "

One year later, Scott expands this sketch in *Old Mortality*. Not only does the reader catch dramatic glimpses of Claverhouse through the blood-shot eyes of his enemies, but he has the soldier's words and actions to consider, as well as Scott's mature, though idealised, portrait. According to "superstitious fanatics," Claverhouse—like General Tam Dalzell—wears bulletproof garments; his coal-black horse is a gift from the arch-fiend; and his life is charmed—"it's lang or the deil dies." Like Grierson of Lag, he is reported to drink a cup of warm blood every morning before breakfast. To this the movingly ironic contrast is Claverhouse's declaration that, as a youthful campaigner, he felt that each drop of blood shed on the battlefield came from his own heart. Forced to put down conventicles in order to preserve Episcopacy, he sets about his task with sad fatalism. Death is nothing, military and personal honour everything. But because the harsher and crueller sides of his character are noted, a tense balance is maintained throughout the narrative. On the one hand is the agent of divine vengeance and political expedience against ignorant, mistaken religionists, and, on the other, the brilliant tool of the Devil against the godly.

What Scott has achieved is a double analysis of Bonny-Dundee-Bloody-Clavers,[31] which he reinforces by contrasting John Graham of

[29] In *A Legend of Montrose*, it is not the Royalist-Covenanter struggle but a clan feud which evokes this superstition. To Ranald Son of the Mist, Allan M'Aulay, ruthless enemy of his clan, is "the fiend incarnate" against whose charmed life bullets, dirks, and arrows are unavailing.

[30] *Grandfather*, Second Series, p. 266. Cp. James Hogg, *The Mountain Bard*, Edinburgh 1807, pp. 92–4, n. on "Mess John."

[31] Scott's painting of the Great Dundee led his "Whig and Cameronian" friend, John Morrison, to tell how Bloody Clavers—"his look altogether diabolical"—rode and wheeled his horse on the coping of a parapet in Dumfries. Morrison, "Random Reminiscences of Sir Walter Scott," *Tait's Edinburgh Magazine*, x (1843) 628.

Claverhouse and John Balfour of Burley. Claverhouse is as awesome to the Covenanters as an invulnerable "supernatural being," and the Cameronian extremist, Burley, is "the devil incarnate" to the Royalists. Any resemblance is deceptive. Like Archbishop Sharpe, Claverhouse is proof against imputations; Burley is not, and his delusion comes to be shared by comrades.[32] When Morton finds Burley in a solitary cave, he is at the peak of a seizure, his firelit face "that of a fiend in the lurid atmosphere of Pandemonium." His reason unhinged by the gloom of hiding places, danger, and a melancholy and remorseful imagination, Burley struggles against the Evil One with sword and Bible.[33] The virulence of hate and fear in embattled partisans, expressed symbolically, becomes diabolical help, hindrance, or possession.[34] The devilry of clashing religious, political, and social ways of life generally reveals supposititious rather than real villainy.

Scott's real villains, Iago-like artists in evil, require some focus of their malevolence.[35] In *Rob Roy*, the Osbaldistone household considers Rashleigh a master of spirits because of his knowledge of ancient languages, current events, and science. As his brother Wilfred declares, Rashleigh need not dread "ghaist or barghaist, devil or dobbie." He converses with unseen beings and watches for bogles at night. While quieting ghost-startled Andrew Fairservice, Frank Osbaldistone indirectly offers the key, "Fear nothing from the next world; the earth contains living fiends, who can act for themselves without assistance." The diabolical overtones are heard again in Rashleigh's death-scene, when he curses the patrimony which descends to Frank and, after his last breath, retains "the grin and glare of mortal hatred."

Scott assembles a carefully differentiated band of villains in *The Fair*

---

[32] Bothwell, a Royalist, is exceptional in that he is to his slayer, Burley, a "well-beloved and chosen agent" of Satan and to his commander, Claverhouse, a newly won servant of the Devil. This is not his view of himself.

[33] Cp. the words of a gifted seer who hides in a haunted Galloway cavern, *The Heart of Midlothian*, ch. 15: "It is hard living in this world—incarnate devils above the earth, and devils under the earth! Satan has been here since ye went away, but I have dismissed him by resistance; we will be no more troubled with him this night." See n. ix; Patrick Walker, *Biographia Presbyteriana*, Edinburgh 1827, 1. 68, 169 (drowning Devil), 288–9 (Grierson of Lag).

[34] This is true of Catholic-Protestant prejudice as represented in early Waverley Novels. In *The Monastery* when she learns that she must lodge Henry Warden for several days, Dame Glendinning protests that this heretic "may bring the great horned devil himself down upon us all," breaking through the very walls. Scott's position is clear in his comment on Robertson's (Sir George Staunton's) beads, crucifix, and hair shirt: "His sense of guilt had induced him to receive the dogmata of a religion, which pretends, by the maceration of the body, to expiate the crimes of the soul." (*The Heart of Midlothian*.)

[35] Cp. Thackeray's Chevalier de la Motte in *Denis Duval* (1864) and Richard Blackmore's Caryl Carne in *Springhaven* (1887), two villains unsupported by demonology.

Maid of Perth. The climax of their machinations, after the thwarted abduction of Catharine Glover and the attempt on Henry Smith's life, is
the starving of Prince David. Behind this crime lurks the Duke of Albany,
like the Earl of Leicester in *Kenilworth.* Sir John Ramorny, the Prince's
master of the horse, is the leader of the triad of evil-doers. Henbane
Dwining, a dwarfish, spiteful, medical Iago who denies alliance with or
belief in the Devil, is the subtle one. And Bonthron is the brutish tool.
In each characterisation demonological references occur, and Dwining's
demonism is associated with magic as is Rashleigh Osbaldistone's. When
Dwining promises to rescue Bonthron from the gallows "into the land of
faëry, like King Arthur," credulous Sir John suspects him of charms and
witchcraft. His "willing fiend . . . must have the aid of Satan," with whom
the unconsciously ironic knight refuses to traffic. Bonthron's evasion from
the gallows is credited by some Perthmen "to the foul fiend himself."
Later, when Bonthron appears at Falkland, the dungeoned Prince believes
that he has been "judged and condemned; and the most abhorred fiend
in the infernal regions is sent to torment me!" While Dwining and
Ramorny gleefully commiserate over the Prince's ebbing health, Catharine
marvels that these can be "earthly men, and not incarnate devils."

In "his diabolical musing," Dwining turns against Ramorny and against
the Royal Burgh of Perth, whose incubus he means to be. "Like the nightmare, I will hag-ride ye, yet remain invisible myself." When the "poor
dwindled dwarf" circumvents formal justice by taking poison, Lord
Balveny, mistrusting glamour, sorcery, and spells, has the corpse hanged
as a safeguard against "his foul spirit" returning to a ready home. Altogether, with his "native malignity of disposition," Dwining is a more
persistent, less well motivated misanthrope than the Black Dwarf. By
not being obtruded on the reader too much, he gains in effectiveness. All
three confederates, stupid Bonthron, vindictive Ramorny, and intensely
crafty Dwining,[36] move through the plot with infernal auras over their
heads. Only when they are forcibly withdrawn from the action by rope
or poison is the way clear for man, maid, and happiness ever after.[37]

Not only does the Devil stand behind active Iagos, but he whispers
advice to passive Hamlets. Minds of a gloomy and despairing cast are
represented in Scott as inviting melancholic, even demonic, occupants.

---

[36] In *Victory* (1915), Conrad distributes comparable roles to brutal Pedro, rapacious Martin
Ricardo, and sinister Mr Jones, "the insolent spectre on leave from Hades."

[37] There is incidental Devil lore in *The Fair Maid of Perth*: To Simon Glover and Henry
Smith, both Lowlanders, it seems that "the devil will have the tartan." Smith thinks that
priests may raise Devils. The armourer's housekeeper, Luckie Shoolbred, dreads the minstrel
lass, Louise, as a witch under the power of Satan.

This is suggested in the portrayal of the Master of Ravenswood, last representative of a ruined line. A peasant view is that Ravenswood "evoked some evil fiend" who tampered with events. Toward the end of *The Bride of Lammermoor*, this hint of a fiend-driven or fiend-like nature is renewed in Bucklaw's demand that his rival receive fair play "were he the devil come to fly away with the whole house and generation," as well as in Scott's description of his riding off "with the speed of a demon dismissed by the exorcist."[38] A kind of encouragement flows from the words and acts of a pretty assortment of witches and from remarks about the Devil's temptations. Ravenswood denies giving in to the temptation of secretly pursuing revenge, but the energy of his asseveration reveals the inner conflict, as when he rebukes blind Alice, "Be silent, woman! is it the devil that prompts your voice?"

Admitting that the Devil has been at his elbow, the wastrel Bucklaw finds that the Old One is dealing just as cunningly with Ravenswood, who perforce agrees:

> It is too true, our vices steal upon us in forms outwardly as fair as those of the demons whom the superstitious represent as intriguing with the human race, and are not discovered in their native hideousness until we have clasped them in our arms.

The novelist, too, puts in a word for a more realistic understanding of tragic causation: "Alas! what fiend can suggest more desperate counsels, than those adopted under the guidance of our own violent and unrestrained passions?" The fiend has at least helped characterise a darkly moody hero.

It is fitting that a Devil who faithfully attends mankind throughout life should enter prisons and lurk in the halls of death. Although a dimly seen visitor can be mistaken for an apparition, frightened imagination may insinuate that the Devil is abroad. Thus it is in *A Legend of Montrose* when M'Callum More mysteriously appears in the dungeon of Dugald Dalgetty and Ranald MacEagh. "All Highlanders are superstitious. 'The Enemy of Mankind is among us!' " cries Ranald. Dalgetty, with his polyglot lore, tries exorcisms in Latin, Spanish, and German, looks for the Scottish cloven foot or the German horse's hoof assigned to the Devil, at last falls into the lighter mood of quibbling about the intruder's passing through the keyhole. The dramatic, then humorous, heightening of the effect of an unexpected encounter is part of Scott's narrative stock-in-trade.

Far less conventional are the prison experiences of Gilbert Glossin

---

[38] See G.G.L., "Shelley and Scott," *N. & Q.*, CLXXI (1936), 60.

and that "half devil," Captain Dirk Hatteraick. The Dutch smuggler chokes the lawyer until his face blackens and "the head was turned backward over the shoulder, as if the neck had been wrung round with desperate violence." Then he drives a bone into a crevice, fastens a cord to it, bends his knees, and hangs himself.

> The worthy Mr. Skriegh and other lovers of the marvellous ... still hold that the Enemy of Mankind brought these two wretches together upon that night by supernatural interference, that they might fill up the cup of their guilt and receive its meed by murder and suicide. [*Guy Mannering*.]

Here Scott works in the spirit rather than the letter of demonology, digesting much material about Auld Hangie and his earthly associates and bringing together tensely, yet humorously, both natural and supernatural explanations. The background may be sketched briefly. As Lambert Daneau reminds readers of *A Dialogue of Witches*, "Satan himselfe hath strangled many sorcerers in prison, or beaten them to death with his fistes."[39] When involved in Renfrewshire witch activity of 1696–7, John Reid, a smith, escaped being hanged and incinerated on the Gallow Green of Paisley in this fashion: "Another Man also confes'd, But the *Devil* Strangled him in Prison, for he was found sitting in a Chair with a Cord about his Neck but slack and ty'd to no thing."[40] And in *The History of the Shire of Renfrew*, George Crawfurd explains the Devil's eagerness to forestall justice: "A report prevailed, and gained full credit, that one of the condemned, *viz.* a wizart, was strangled in his chair by the devil, least he should make a confession to the detriment of the service."[41]

The chief victim of wizards and witches, Christian Shaw, was *thrawn* like Glossin—and like Stevenson's Thrawn Janet. "Her forehead [was] drawn forcibly about toward her shoulders. ... All the parts of her body becoming rigid and extended like a corpse, her head was twisted round."[42] Out of these crude but potent sources Scott draws the substance of an

---

[39] *Les Sorciers* (1564), translated into Latin as *De Veneficis* (1575) and then into English, London 1575, ch. 4. There is a copy of the *Dialogue* in the Abbotsford library.

[40] *A Relation of the Diabolical Practices of above Twenty Wizards and Witches ... of Renfrew ... 1697*, London [1697], p. 4. Scott owned four later and fuller accounts: Sir Francis Grant, *A True Narrative of the Sufferings and Relief of a Young Girle*, Edinburgh 1698, and his *Sadducismus Debellatus*, London 1698; Richard Boulton, *A Compleat History of Magick ...*, London 1715–16, II. 51–165; *From Authentic Documents. A History of the Witches of Renfrewshire*, ed. John Millar, Paisley 1809. See J. G. Cochrane, *Catalogue of the Library at Abbotsford*, Edinburgh 1838, pp. 145–7, 150, 272.

[41] *Op. cit.*, Paisley 1782, p. 319. Scott owned this edition and one of 1818. See his paraphrase of the passage in *Demonology*, p. 334 (cp. 322–3).

[42] *A History of the Witches of Renfrewshire*, new edn, Paisley 1877, pp. 81, 92. This is a reprint of the 1809 account (see n. 40), with additional extracts, etc.

episode of murder and suicide in prison which combines horror, realism, and humour.[43]

Prison is not, of course, the only place where the wicked may meet their Destroyer face to face. Intense folk dread of the Black Dwarf generates the rumour that the fatal trickster has borne him away for entering a consecrated building and thus breaking an article of his compact. As for the Highland widow, Elspat MacTavish, "the credulous thought that the evil spirit under whose influence she seemed to have acted had carried her away in the body."

If the body remains within mortal reach, its preparation for burial may be touched with demonology. The incident in *The Bride of Lammermoor* has been mentioned. In *The Highland Widow* the body of Allan Breack Camcron, deprived of life by Elspat's son Hamish, is laid out. Insight into the widow's character is highlighted by the gruesomeness of the dialogue.

> "I would as soon dress a corpse when the great fiend himself—God sain us—stood visibly before us, as when Elspat of the Tree is amongst us.—Ay—ay, even overmuch intercourse hath she had with the Enemy in her day."
>
> "Silly woman [answers a female mourner who has called Elspat a "bloody sorceress" to her face,] thinkest thou that there is a worse fiend on earth, or beneath it, than the pride and fury of an offended woman, like yonder bloody-minded hag?"

*   *   *

As far as the Scottish novels are concerned, Scott's review of the Devil's intrusion into human affairs may appropriately end with this repeated hint that diabolism is passional, not supernatural. Inasmuch as Old Nick does not fully renew his bag of tricks at every frontier, there will be some duplication in the non-Scottish narratives. Scott will tend to depend more on bookish lore than on a fine synthesis of reflexion on folkways, observation of survivals, and reading. And he will try to particularise an age or a country through its demonology.

The eighteenth chapter of *The Antiquary* may be discussed here, because the short story, "The Fortunes of Martin Waldeck," read to picnickers in the version of Isabella Wardour, "a lover of fairy-land," comes from the German, Dousterswivel. How the charlatan came on the tale Scott cannot remember—perhaps in the Abbotsford library, where "Die goldenen Kohlen" appears in a copy of Friedrich Gottschalk's *Die Sagen*

---

[43] For a fuller discussion of sources, see C. O. Parsons, "The Deaths of Glossin and Hatteraick in *Guy Mannering*," *Philological Quarterly*, xxiv (1945), 169–74.

und Volksmärchen der Deutschen (Halle 1814).[44] A summary of the original plot will show what Scott and Miss Wardour choose to make of the action. Deceived by the clear moonlight into thinking it is morning, a poor miller's maidservant finds that she has no tinder. Seeing a charcoal-burner's fire on a mountainside, she encounters strange men and thrice fills a vessel with glowing coals which go out on the hearth. On her third trip, a voice warns, "Nun komm nicht wieder!" At midnight, both fire and mysterious figures vanish. The maid creeps back to her bed frightened, and in the morning the miller finds virgin gold on his hearth. A rich man, he builds a large and beautiful house.

Scott's thorough revision extends the action to three years in the reign of Emperor Charles V (1519–56) and localises it in the hamlet of Morgenbrodt among the Harz mountains. After introductory padding about the superstitiousness of miners and foresters, the Brocken spectre as a projection of the seer's refracted shadow,[45] the temerarious preaching of an ambulant friar against local demons, and the unlucky consequences of accepting the wayward Harz demon's gifts, Scott begins. Martin Waldeck, the youngest of three charcoal-burners, thrice dares to approach the night fire of the hairy and gigantic Harz demon for wood to rekindle his fire. Each time the fire goes out, but next morning three large lumps of gold are found in the dead ashes.

The Harz demon can now gloat, "How like you the fire MY coals have kindled!" To the day of death and retribution, wealth conjures up in Martin's nature the fiends of pride, avarice, cruelty, and oppression. The combination of supernatural tale and ethical instruction is a development of the baleful gift *motif* in folk literature, in which moral values may inhere. Scott's legend begins and ends rather heavily and suffers from the too explicit pointing of "a sound and valuable moral." Though well told, it has lost much of its folk quality. But it has gained an ironic new dimension. Seeing her father swindled by Dousterswivel's promises of mineral wealth and hidden treasure, Isabella turns "a very trumpery and ridiculous legend" into a lesson which is read aloud in St Ruth's Priory. Not heeding the filial warning of "miseries attendant upon wealth, hastily attained and ill-employed," Sir Arthur Wardour returns to the ruins at night with Dousterswivel, who makes a fool of him.

In *Ivanhoe*, earlier creeds linger in an ostensibly Christian age. The

[44] F. Holthausen, "Die Geschichte von Martin Waldeck in W. Scotts 'The Antiquary,'" *Beiblatt zur Anglia*, XXIX (1918), 280–3; M. F. Mann, *op. cit.*, 375–6. These notes were called to my attention by Professor Hans Hecht of Göttingen, in a letter of 20 Dec. 1932.

[45] See Preface by "W." to "Treatises on the Second Sight," *Miscellanea Scotica*, III (1818–19), 5–8.

speech of that "old housefiend" Urfried, or Ulrica, frenzied by violation and loss of father and brothers, is peppered with pre-Christian gods and Christian devils, "May the evil demon Zernebock tear me limb from limb." Athelstane jokes about Zernebock's having taken over the castle during his absence, and Cedric impatiently cries out, "May the fiend fly away with me, and leave me in Ifrin with the souls of Odin and of Thor!"[46] Allusions to Christian demonology can be almost as literary and factitious. Bois-Guilbert thinks that "a legion of fiends" has given Rebecca her pride and resolution. And De Bracy remarks that "the fiend laughs, they say, when one thief robs another; and we know, that were he to spit fire and brimstone instead, it would never prevent a Templar from following his bent."

Other passages have a truer ring, as when Prince John adapts a proverb, "Threadbare cloaks of penniless dogs have not a single cross in their pouches to keep the devil from dancing there."[47] Or when Friar Tuck, the jolly hermit of Copmanhurst, fears "the devil and his imps" no more than man but cautiously avoids the subject before morning devotions. The master of all evil is held responsible whenever great skill, strength, or grimness disturbs the medieval imagination. As the Black Knight of Fetterlock storming Torquilstone, Richard Coeur-de-Lion terrifies a veteran soldier, who exclaims, "He is the devil!" And Locksley's bowmanship so far transcends human ability that the astonished yeomen proclaim him "no man of flesh and blood" but a devil.

Demonology in *Kenilworth* chiefly centres on the relations of Flibbertigibbet and Wayland Smith and of Sir Richard Varney and his associates. As he spreads Wayland's diabolical fame and tyrannises over the credulous folk mind, Flibbertigibbet acts like an irresponsible familiar. An erratic elf, loutish and undersized, he is wildly derisive in quip, gesture, and grimace. Nicknamed Hobgoblin by his playfellows, he is appropriately mischievous without being completely ill-natured. Before blowing up Wayland's underground smithy, he cockily asserts, "I have more of the hobgoblin about me than you credit." But the wreckage and the report that "the devil hath flown away" with the farrier in fire and smoke are

---

[46] For Zernebock, the Devil of the Prussian Slavs, see Q.R., XXII (1820), 360; P. R. Lieder, "Scott and Scandinavian Literature," *Smith College Studies in Modern Literature*, II. No. 1 (Oct. 1920). Chernobog was the Western Slavonic black god of night and evil. Cedric may have in mind the Teutonic underworld, Niflhel or Niflheim ("Mist-world"), but Odin is fonder of Valhalla. *Larousse Encyclopedia of Mythology*, New York 1960, pp. 255, 259, 294.

[47] In *Woodstock*, Joceline Joliffe speaks of the Devil's dancing in moneyless pockets. Both silver and the cross on a coin are demonifuges.

kindly services. On his reappearance as a masquerader bound for Kenilworth, he drops the hobgoblin and becomes a diablotin, a "most hopeful
imp of darkness," "a limb of the devil in good earnest," and a "prince
of cacodemons." Altogether, he is the best of Scott's contradictory
grotesques, compelling belief by the puckish verve which he inherits
from his versatile progenitor, Fliberdigibbet.[48]

According to their several capacities, countryfolk, the comic pedagogue
Holiday, and others regard Wayland Smith as a sorcerer, an adept, "the
Devil's foot-post," and "the evil un." Gammer Sludge sews "a sprig of
witch's elm" in Flibbertigibbet's doublet to protect him from the farrier,
who fears that he will one day be "taken up for a wizard." Before he is
rescued from such peril by his familiar, Wayland talks of having "Talpack
with his fiery lance" at command and generally invites trouble. The only
persons to doubt Wayland's supernatural character are Flibbertigibbet,
who finds him "something queer" though no devil, a landlord who considers him a cheat and a scoundrel, and the sceptical Edmund Tressilian.
Once he has become Tressilian's servant and left the Berkshire moor,
Wayland sloughs his devil nature. In the Elizabethan pageantry of
Kenilworth, it is time for him to yield place to less extrinsic devils.

In a soliloquy, Varney energetically boasts of being driven by the lust
for pleasure, power, and retaliation. "On, good horse, on—the devil
urges us both forward." But when the astrological "vassal of hell itself,"
Alasco, declares that Sir Richard is "a worse devil" than his own enmeshed
self, the ruthlessly clearsighted nobleman says that he is a mortal man
seeking gratification and advancement by mortal means. Apparently a
tool, this eloquent and "malicious fiend" actually nose-leads the Earl of
Leicester, who admits that his servant has mastery. When the Earl is about
to avow his marriage in the presence of Queen Elizabeth, Varney—"born,
as it appeared, to be his master's evil genius"—defeats his "better angel."
"With a mixture of fiendish feelings," Varney schemes to win the Countess Amy in order to revenge himself on her for previous scorn. On the
culmination of his utter wickedness in the imitation of Leicester's signal
and the trap-door murder of the countess, Anthony Foster exclaims,
"Varney, thou art an incarnate fiend!"

Always shaping the weakness, credulity, greed, and ambition of other
men to his own ends, Varney becomes the chief of a sinister band.

---

[48] "Frateretto, Fliberdigibbet, Hoberdidance, Tocobatto were foure deuils of the round, or
Morrice, whom Sara [Williams] in her fits, tuned together, in measure and sweet cadence."
Samuel Harsnet, A Declaration of egregious Popish Impostures, London 1603, p. 49. Cp. Edgar's
description of "the foul fiend Flibbertigibbet" in King Lear (1605), III. iv.

Cynically reviewing the variety of retainers a man like the Earl of
Leicester must have, Varney mentions cabalists "for conjuring up the
devil," swordsmen to "fight the devil when he is raised and at the wildest,"
and Puritans like Foster to "defy Satan, and do his work at the same time."
Some folk believe that the secretive Foster has "sold himself to the devil
for treasure." Michael Lambourne thinks of Foster as an "undermining
fiend," and Varney wakes the sleeping hypocrite to further mischief with
the exclamation, "The devil has not discharged you from service yet."
Doctor Alasco, studying "devil's divinity" in his "pandemonium" or
laboratory, is recalled "to the affairs of hell" by Varney. He is, to Foster's
way of thinking, the Devil who brews poison. Of Lambourne, Varney
says, "If the devil were to choose a gossip, I know no one more fit for the
office." Although Lambourne has no faith in the aristocratic pursuits of
astrology and alchemy or even in plebeian ghosts and goblins, he does not
imitate Varney in believing "nothing in earth, heaven, or hell." He
accepts the Devil in order that some such being may carry Varney off
when death looms.

In demonic atmosphere, Sir Richard Varney's fictional career reflects
Leicester's Commonwealth (1584) and Elias Ashmole's *Antiquities of Berkshire* (1719), both of which represent the wretch as blaspheming God and
saying that "all the devils of hell did teare him in pieces." Freed from the
hampering beliefs of his fellow men, Scott's character often revels in evil
for its own sake. In this his mentor is Iago, whose influence is apparent at
the end of Chapter XXI and elsewhere in the novel. Feeling that such a life
transcends the expressiveness of strictly realistic methods of portrayal,
Scott leans on Shakespeare and the Devil.[49]

In *Peveril of the Peak*, Chiffinch speaks of Edward Christian as having
"the cunning of the devil for a pilot." This prompts the Duke of Buckingham to enquire about "Christian's familiar ... that little Numidian witch,"
Fenella (actually Christian's half-Moorish daughter). Here, the allusion to
a strangely efficient helper, coming from a lord, is sophisticated rather than
superstitious. It is different with Sir Geoffrey Peveril's son Julian, usually
"no ready believer in the supernatural," when he is cast into prison like
an active partisan. His mood is operated on by dreams of "gliding spirits,
gibbering phantoms, bloody hands, which, dimly seen by twilight, seemed
to beckon him forward." Faced with a "nocturnal demon" that makes his
hair bristle, he wakes his prison mate, Sir Geoffrey Hudson, to tell him
that a devil may be in their room. Instantly, the dwarfish knight lights a

[49] Cp. David Freeman's interpretation in "Sir Walter Scott's Villains," *The Dublin Review*,
CXCV (1934), 305–16.

O   P.W.D.

candle, which equals *fuga daemonum* in its power to drive off "goblins, and evil or dubious spirits."

During a second visit, the soft-voiced intruder teases poor Julian with figurative and vague replies to his questions. His fears, however, do not keep him from reasoning on his adviser's earthly or unearthly status, mistrusting his imagination, and testing grates. We learn later that, with a knowledge of prisons surpassing that of turnkeys, the ubiquitous Fenella has made her way to the hero's strong room. Apparently, the daintier the damsel acting *pro tempore* as a supernatural agent the tougher the assignment given her. In this instance, human identification is longer deferred than usual.

The Iago touch reappears in *Quentin Durward*. Louis XI rather resents the religious and astrological scepticism of his barber-counsellor, Oliver Le Diable. After all, his namesake, the devil, "believes and trembles." But the supreme villain must go beyond good and evil—beyond faith and fantasy. To be fair, although his nickname is "expressive of his evil propensities," Oliver is "scarcely so completely identified with Satan" as to lack all human feeling. By making the willing servant diabolic, Scott tangentially characterises the royal master whose behests are base.

Having encouraged a supposed devil to visit a despairing prisoner in Scotland and England, Scott shifts the scene to Wales in *The Betrothed*, borrows a bit from Jacob's wrestling match with the angel, and changes the motivation. Disguised as a palmer, Sir Hugo de Lacy comes to his dungeoned nephew to test him. But Damian has heard of beings that tempt men to give up their salvation. "Such are the fiend's dearest agents, and in such a guise hath the fiend himself been known to appear." Once rid of his shackles, Damian wrestles with the palmer in order to discover whether he is "man or fiend." His doubts are soon dispelled by a reassuring proof of human prowess.

The experiment with exotic contrasts in demonology, begun in *Ivanhoe*, is continued more successfully in *The Talisman*. When Saladin guides Sir Kenneth through the wilderness of the forty-day fast to the hermit of Engaddi's cavern, the Scottish knight dwells on Christ's temptation and "the foul spirits" which, when expelled from mortal bodies, haunted waste places. Holy men having driven demons into the desert, travellers must advance warily.[50] The Saracen's conversation is too much like that of "some gay licentious fiend" eager to seduce a Christian on storied

[50] For the Tempter's "wonted impudence in desert places," see the interpolated tale of Duke Henry the Lion's Lybian adventures in J. K. A. Musäus, "Melechsala," tr. Thomas Carlyle in VOL. I of *German Romance*, Edinburgh 1827.

ground. His tale of the demon origin of the Kurdish tribes, his own declared descent "from the Dark Spirit," Eblis, and his chanted hymn to Ahriman, "the Evil Principle" of the Persians, make the Christian fear that he is consorting with an omnifarious demonolater. And the apparition of the lean hermit convinces him for a time that the Prince of Darkness has been conjured up. This adventure, climaxed by the knight's meeting the "flail of all . . . devil-worshippers," the demented holy man, skilfully opposes religious cultures through two men's responses to the desert *genius loci*—the Saracen's daring and exultant, the Christian's cautious and reverent.

Intestine contrasts are ironic, for among the Crusaders there is "a worse Pagan" than "the heathen Saladin." King Richard's objection to Giles Amaury, Grand Master of the Templars, as leader of the Christian host is that he is "an idolater—a devil-worshipper—a necromancer—who practises crimes the most dark and unnatural, in the vaults and secret places of abomination and darkness." Thus, about 1191, with admirable prescience, Richard makes Amaury guilty of corruption which may have entered the Temple some sixty-five to a hundred years later. Secrecy, pride, and wealth aroused fear, envy, and greed, which were rationalised in 1307–14 as charges of worship of the idol Daphomet (Mahomet) or else the Devil in the shape of a cat, collaboration with the Moslems, heresy, sorcery, and sodomy.[51]

In the case of Oliver Cromwell, the charges were more specialised and more suited to extended fictional use. Roundheads and Royalists set their tongues wagging during the two phases of the Civil War: Prince Rupert, "the Mad Cavalier," was "a magician; a notion increased by his austere manner, sallow complexion, and a large favourite dog, alias familiar [also taken for the devil], his constant companion,"[52] and the ruthless commoner made a diabolic pact before his victory at Worcester.[53] The Lord Protector's death during a tempest, on the anniversary of his triumphs at Dunbar and Worcester (3 September 1650, 1651, and 1658), was recognised by anti-Commonwealth men as a bonded victim's being whisked off by the Devil. Although this lurid synchronology, mentioned in Scott's *Life of Napoleon Buonaparte* and *Tales of a Grandfather*, Second Series, falls

[51] Edith Simon, *The Piebald Standard: A Biography of the Knights Templars*, Boston and Toronto 1959, pp. 279–337. The last Grand Master of the Temple, Jacques de Molay, was burned at the stake on 19 Mar. 1314.

[52] *Letters from Archibald, Earl of Argyll* [ed. C. K. Sharpe], Edinburgh 1829, p. 26, n. 1.

[53] T.M., PT 4 (1660), pp. 31–2, of Clem. Walker, *The Compleat History of Independency*, London 1661; Laurence Echard, *The History of England*, London 1707–18, II. 712–13, 825; and *True and Faithful Narrative of Oliver Cromwell's compact with the Devil for seven years*, 2nd edn, London 1720.

outside the scope of *Woodstock*, it helps to set the tone of "A Tale of the Year Sixteen Hundred and Fifty-One."

The distribution of demonological suspicion in *Old Mortality* between Royalists and Covenanters is partial in *Woodstock*, with the burden resting heavily on one character. The Cavalier, Roger Wildrake, calls Cromwell "the devil's darling," "the devil" with whom he tussles, and food for a voracious devil. "Noll hath certainly sold himself to the devil, and his lease will have an end one day." Old Sir Henry Lee holds similar views: Although the Devil can raise up a favourite, he cannot give him long tenure; the Devil has slackened pressure on his agents lately; the Devil (Cromwell) may sometimes be honoured "for his burning throne." Not only do the King's men consider Cromwell Devil-propped, but his own followers say that "there are times when the evil spirit cometh upon him as it did upon Saul." Aware of this propaganda, Cromwell protests to that "busy fiend," Pearson: "Think'st thou, like other fools, that I have made a paction with the devil for success, and am bound to do my work within an appointed hour, lest the spell should lose its force?" In an age of witches, witch-finders, and hellish compacts, the great are not unscathed.

Besides shifting credit for human superiority, demonology may explain an otherwise incredible degree of evil in man's nature. In *Anne of Geierstein*, the ruthless and grasping governor, De Hagenbach, yields justice as reluctantly as the denizens of Hell. On one occasion, however, he protests that "the devil is not quite so horrible as he is painted." By 1829, this method of characterisation has become all too familiar in the Waverley Novels, as has the device of the perplexed prisoner. Therefore, Scott merely suggests the former and tries for variety in the latter by introducing two visitants, one of whom is suspect. The Black Priest of St Paul's and Anne release Arthur Philipson from a dungeon in the town of Brisach. The hero wonders, "Has she conjured up this earthlike and dark demon to concur with her in my deliverance?"

In *Count Robert of Paris*, set in Constantinople in the eleventh century, Scott achieves novelty by factitious means. Agelastes, a crafty sage, tries to induce Hereward, of the Emperor Alexius Comnenus' Varangian bodyguard, to join a plot against the throne. The old man asserts that he can command the oracular spirit of the broken statue of Anubis and that he knew Hereward's grandfather Kenelm—"in the body or in the spirit." Fearful of being seduced from Heaven by such words, the simple Anglo-Saxon defies seduction of men, necromancers, and fiends. Agelastes later talks of the baseness and absurdity of human embodiments of the Evil

Principle. But both Hereward and Frankish Countess Brenhilda are deaf
to the enticements of his tongue. The noble lady has the satisfaction of
seeing the daring thinker interrupted in the midst of blasphemy against
"the Christian Satan" and strangled by Sylvan, an ape resembling "the
fiend himself" come to punish infidelity.

When the man of "signs, names, periapts, and spells" fails to win
Hereward over, the head of the Varangian Guard, Achilles Tatius, tries
other tactics. Men like the philosopher, he tells the soldier, "will pretend
to possess the most unbounded power over elements and elemental spirits
. . . to cause the absent to appear . . . and the dead themselves to burst the
cerements of the grave," while using more natural means of gathering
information. The channel of this information, command of which apparently verges on the supernatural, is later made known to the reader.
As for Agelastes himself, he is one of Scott's Iagos, lifting himself above
the creeds of men and selfishly manipulating the beliefs of others. A
melodramatic end is what he asks for—and gets.

* * *

The remoter a Waverley novel is from Scotland or the eighteenth
century, the more likely its demonology is to be grotesque and bookish.
After passing his literary prime, Scott leans more and more on stereotypes.
Thus appearances in forlorn places, especially dungeons, and in desolate
periods of a man's life become for the Devil a conditioned reflex. Resisting
the inertia of habit, Scott seeks to vary the pattern, but the variety
achieved is less often essential than self-conscious and superficial.

When Scott is using demonology more effectively, it may be incidental,
proverbial and allusive, as it is in the author's conversation, lending the
colour and intensity of the credulous past to the matter of more enlightened times. Or it may be pawky and humorous, gruesome and thril-
ling, dramatic and unexpected, historic and popular, moral and revealing.
At his peak, Scott is complex and controlled, using humour as a fixative
of horror and, in "Wandering Willie's Tale," making natural and supernatural explanations reinforce each other. In the portrayal of religious
persecution and the embodiment of political and class conflicts, in the
transfiguration of partisan prejudice in the racy tale that is sifted through
Willie's consciousness, Scott achieves an unflawed native quality and
reaches his high water mark in demonology.

As a novelist, however, Scott considers demonology a method of
characterisation as well as an index of cultural differences. In extreme
variations from the norm, fictional Iagos, Hamlets, and Byronic heroes,

there is a Satanic base. If a man wilfully cuts his anchor rope, he drifts deeper and deeper into a Sargasso Sea of selfhood, moody, perverse, fanatical, violent, ultimately evil. Indeed, certain people can be imaginatively conceived as unleashed on the world by a god of evil.[54]

Thus Scott develops a melodramatic ethical concept involving bold character contrasts and retribution for wicked deeds, with remorse, distraction, and cruel death descending on the sinner and inevitable depravity on the illegitimate offspring (if the sins-of-the-fathers theme is included). There is certainly no profundity—and only occasional subtlety—in this narrative schema of values. The continued influence of the moralised supernatural terrors of Bürger's ballads is traceable in Scott's rewards and punishments, which are perhaps transitional to the more human and convincing ethics of Elizabeth Gaskell and George Eliot.[55]

14. THE POLTERGEIST*

The racketing devil, later known as *poltergeist*, enjoyed its greatest vogue in the seventeenth century. With moronic malice, it tore sheets from beds, slammed doors, dropped bags of stones on the floor, and whirled furniture about the room. Thomas Heywood refers indifferently to pugs, hobgoblins, fairies, and Robin Goodfellows as the impish source of this kind of persecution, which he jinglingly particularises:

> In solitarie roomes These vprores keeps,
> And beat at dores to wake men from their sleepes
> Seeming to force locks, be they ne're so strong,
> And keeping Christmasse gambols all night long.
> Pots, glasses, trenchers, dishes, pannes, and kettles
> They will make dance about the shelues and settles,
> As if about the Kitchen tost and cast,
> Yet in the morning nothing found misplac't.[1]

In 1661–3, a kinetic and telekinetic spirit called the Drummer of Tedworth disturbed John Mompesson by knocking, beating, rattling, jingling, and rustling, lifting, plucking, scratching, shaking, throwing, filling, emptying, and hiding or stealing anything on which it could lay

---

[54] This is suggested in Scott's poem, *The Vision of Don Roderick* (1811), Conclusion, vi. Compare the note on stanza 48 and the Royalist attitude towards Cromwell in *Woodstock*.
[55] Cp. throughout Mody C. Boatright, "Demonology in the Novels of Sir Walter Scott: A Study in Regionalism," *University of Texas Studies in English*, xiv (1934), 75–88.

* Scott does not use the convenient term *poltergeist*, which seems not to have entered the language earlier than Catherine Crowe, *The Night Side of Nature* (1848).
[1] Heywood, *The Hierarchie of the blessed Angells*, London 1635, p. 574.

its hands or commands.[2] Before the rattling ghost slipped into folklore as pranksome and vengeful, it had a minor place in Thomist doctrine. Men are subject to three kinds of physical attack by devils: internal *possession*, external *obsession*, and environmental *infestation*. The last is manifest in "noise-making, throwing things about, breaking articles of furniture, mysterious knocks on doors and walls, and so on."[3] The religious context was restored when the rector of Epworth, John Wesley's father Samuel, was annoyed in 1716–7 by knocking, jarring of metal objects, rattling of pewterware, clapping of doors, lifting of latches, and clattering of windows.[4]

The scratching of the Cock Lane Ghost in 1762[5] and the affliction of Mary Golding of Stockwell and her niece in 1772 by the uncanny levitation and aerial projection of glass and china,[6] when discovered to be frauds, brought the poltergeist into some disrepute. So much so that Scott was hopeful "that the grosser faults of our ancestors are out of date,"[7] including the poltergeist. But, with its medium (frequently an adolescent) and its mobile material phenomena, poltergeisterie is perhaps a crude forerunner of modern spiritualism. The Society for Psychical Research has no lack of cases for serious investigation.

Scott himself became an investigator in 1818. The ghostly clatter was of a highly specialised type described by Noel Taillepied in 1588: "It is known that when new houses are being built the neighbours have heard the sawing of wood, the rattling and soughing of cords, bricks being placed in order, and mortar pounded, as if carpenters, stonemasons, plasterers and other workmen were all busy at their several employments."[8] On Thursday, 30 April, Scott writes to Daniel Terry about the unfinished and exposed state of Abbotsford, resulting in a strange commotion at two a.m. on 29 April. At the same hour the following morning

[2] Sinclair, pp. 55–75; Joseph Glanvill, *Saducismus Triumphatus*, London 1681, PT I, pp. 89–118, (for similar relations, pp. 254–92); Joseph Addison, *The Drummer: or, the Haunted House* (acted in 1715); Sitwell, *Poltergeists*, pp. 112–24, 214–29.

[3] Walter Farrell, *A Companion to the Summa*, New York 1941, I. 425.

[4] Adam Clarke, *Memoirs of the Wesley Family*, New York 1824, pp. 136–67; T. M. Jarvis, *Accredited Ghost Stories*, London 1823, pp. 142–54; Sitwell, *Poltergeists*, pp. 80–90, 157–88. Cp. the biographer's own experience in his *Account of the Religious and Literary Life of Adam Clarke*, New York 1837, pp. 86–7.

[5] *The Beauties of all the Magazines selected, for the Year 1762*, I. 81; Charles Churchill, *The Ghost*, London 1762; Andrew Lang, *Cock Lane and Common-sense*, new edn, London 1894, pp. 161–70. References to the hoax occur in the lives, letters, and works of Johnson, Walpole, Hogarth, and other contemporaries.

[6] *Demonology*, pp. 376–9, which none too accurately follows William Hone, *The Every-Day Book*, London 1826–7. See Sitwell, *Poltergeists*, pp. 132–3, 289–98.

[7] *Demonology*, p. 402.

[8] Taillepied, *A Treatise of Ghosts*, tr. Montague Summers, London [1933], p. 79.

the racket was heard again, as of heavy boards dragged through the new part of the house, and the Laird, his lady being "rather *timbersome*," vainly investigated "with Beardie's broadsword under *his* arm." Scott grumbles at George Bullock's delay in not sending the needed doors and windows from London and continues: "If there was no entrance but the key-hole, I should warrant myself against the ghosts. We have a set of idle fellows called workmen about us, which is a better way of accounting for nocturnal noises than any that is to be found in Baxter or Glanville."

A letter of 2 May from Terry conveys the news of the furnisher's "sudden & unexpected" death "on Wednesday evening between 9 & 10 oclock—leaving the whole house in utter confusion."[9] And long after, Lockhart reports that the temporal "coincidence [of the second pother at Abbotsford and Bullock's death], when Scott received [William] Erskine's minute detail of what had happened in Tenterden street, made a much stronger impression on his mind than might be gathered from the tone of an ensuing communication" of 4 May about the "melancholy summons." Twelve days later, in a letter to Terry, Scott resumes the subject:

> Were you not struck with the fantastical coincidence of our nocturnal disturbances at Abbotsford with the melancholy event that followed? I protest to you the noise resembled half-a-dozen men hard at work putting up boards and furniture, and nothing can be more certain than that there was nobody on the premises at the time. With a few additional touches, the story would figure in Glanville or Aubrey's Collection. In the mean time, you may set it down with poor Dubisson's warnings, as a remarkable coincidence coming under your own observation.[10]

Despite perplexity and then shock, Scott immediately measures his experience against those recorded by Joseph Glanvill, Richard Baxter, and John Aubrey.[11] The "few additional touches" are not difficult to supply. In the oral version heard by Mrs Hughes, Skene, and Lockhart,[12] the

---

[9] Abbotsford Mss. N.L.S.

[10] *Letters*, v. 133–4, 136–9, 147–8, 157, 170; Lockhart, II. 344; IV. 138–43. The warnings of the Edinburgh dentist, John Du Bisson, and his death are related in a letter to [Morritt] of 1 Jul. 1811. *Letters*, II. 507. For carpenter-haunting, see the chapbook, *A most Strange and Dreadful Apparition . . . at the House of Mr. John Thomas . . .* (1680), pp. 4–5; John Bernard, *Retrospections of the Stage*, London 1830, II. 237–42.

[11] *Saducismus Triumphatus* (1681); *The Certainty of the World of Spirits* (1691), ch. ii, 7, etc.; Aubrey, *Miscellanies upon Various Subjects* (1696 and, "with large Additions," 1721), IX. "Knockings," etc.

[12] The episode is retold, with variations, in Mrs Hughes, pp. 257–8. James Skene adds a parallel from a letter to Scott: "What is still more curious, it appears that a family in the neighbourhood of London, whose house also Mr. Bullock was employed to furnish, was disturbed on the same night by extraordinary noises of a similar description, which they also had mentioned in a jocular manner by letter addressed to Mr. Bullock the day after his death." Skene, *Memories of Sir Walter Scott*, p. 62.

four-to-five-hour gap between event and supernatural notice is closed up. And in its finished form, as recited to John Morrison at Scott's breakfast table, noisy workmen are forgotten in order to make Bullock wholly responsible for the waking of his employer's wife:

> My wife awakened me at midnight, and declared that "Mr. Bullock must be returned from London, for I hear him knocking in the dining-room." I prevailed with her to fall asleep, for it must be all nonsense; but she again awakened, and assured me that she not only heard his hammer knocking in the usual way, but heard him speak also. In order to satisfy her, I arose and examined the premises, but nothing was either to be seen or heard. On the second day after, a letter, sealed with black, arrived, stating that poor Bullock was dead,—mentioning the hour, which exactly agreed with the time he was heard in the dining-room by my wife.[13]

Of course, houses usually have to age before they become congenial to ghosts. Abbotsford did not have to wait. It began naturally enough in 1817 with Scott's remark about the library, "The west wind would blow the devil through the walls horns & all."[14] Thirteen months later, the poltergeist arrived. And according to Mr Hope Scott, even after Sir Walter's death "unusual voices, and supernatural footsteps" continued to be heard in a certain part of the house.[15]

*　　*　　*

Although *Woodstock*, the novel in which Scott makes capital of the noisy ghost, was completed on 26 March 1826, its narrative content may have been milling round in the author's mind as early as October 1822, when he contracted to produce "another unnamed 'work of fiction.' "[16] Eager to freshen, as well as to augment, his knowledge of the frightful invasion of Woodstock in October and November 1649, Scott may have discussed the incidents with Mrs Mary Ann Hughes on her visit to Abbotsford in May 1824. That antiquarian lady reverts to the subject in a letter of October 3: "I send you the extract from Dr Plotts history of Oxfordshire containing the devilries acted at Woodstock which you told me you wished to have & which I could not get at till I came to the great Babylon."[17] The passage from Robert Plot's *Natural History of Oxfordshire*, 2nd ed.

---

[13] Morrison, "Random Reminiscences of Sir Walter Scott," *Tait's Edinburgh Magazine*, x (1843), 626; Morrison heard other versions from other sources.

[14] Letter of [?] Mar. 1817 to [Daniel Terry]. *Letters*, IV. 399; V. 117.

[15] Frederick G. Lee, *The Other World*, London 1875, II. 98–9.

[16] Lockhart, v. 237–8. Lockhart erroneously refers to the contract with Constable as having been fulfilled *three* years after it was drawn up.

[17] Walpole, in which may be found Mrs Hughes's letter of 31 Oct. 1824.

(Oxford 1705), pp. 210–214, is a sober rehearsal of diurnal wonders, to which Mrs Hughes adds:

> This contrivance was the invention of Joseph Collins of Oxford otherwise called Funny Joe, who having hired himself for Secretary, under the name of Giles Sharp, by knowing the private traps belonging to the house, & the help of Pulvis fulminans & other chemical preparations, & letting his fellow servants into the scheme carried on the deceit without discovery to the very last—insomuch that Dr Plott relates the whole as fact.

Although he recalls the narrative in Dr Plot, Scott wants to know the authority for "the explanation—a very natural and probable one and a sign that old Noll's saints were not quite so confident in their superiority to Satan as their gifted pretensions would have made one suppose."[18] His informant's source for both Dr Plot and "the explanation of the Wood-stock *devilries*" turns out to be secondary and none too easy to come by, *The Beauties of all the Magazines selected. For the Year 1762.*[19] "What authority they have for divesting the story of the supernatural I know not, but I recollect I always felt sorry to think it was not the Devils own work, & that he left it unfinished" (October 31). With this shaky warrant for Funny Joe's duping of the Commissioners Scott has to be content. As he indicates in the Preface to *Woodstock*, he possesses no copy of Plot and only "ancient and imperfect recollections" of some disclosure of the trickery in "a book or a pamphlet" read may years before.[20]

In the novel, strange tales of manifold revenants and spectre huntsmen in and about Woodstock Lodge create a *gemütlich* atmosphere for a pol-tergeist that torments and ejects the Commissioners from royal Wood-stock, which they are bent on disparking. Roger Wildrake ushers in the reign of supernatural terror by spying on the Commissioners' servants and treating them to a diabolical roar and grimace. The real eruption follows: the violent shutting of a door, driving of nails, sawing, a loud clap of thunder, the rustle of silk, the mewing of a cat, growling of a dog, squeaking of a pig, puzzlingly familiar voices, music, sudden gleams of light, forms, a tussle in which a head is broken, the overturning of Colonel Desborough's bed and a tub of ditch-water to drench him with, the clash of fetters, "visions of men in armour, horses without heads, asses with horns, and cows with six legs, not to mention black figures, whose cloven hoofs gave plain information what realm they belonged to,"

---

[18] 6 Oct. 1824 in *Letters*, VIII. 391–2.

[19] I. 77–80. Mrs Hughes misdates the volume 1761. Her note appears on p. 79, col. 2. See also Joseph Taylor, *Apparitions*, 2nd edn, London 1815, pp. 102–3.

[20] Scott forgets Mrs Hughes's refresher course and Relation VI in Sinclair, in which George Sinclair refers all the prodigies to unearthly agencies.

bituminous odours, and hellish bobbery generally. While some of these afflictions are Scott's facile inventions, others may be traced to George Sinclair's collection, no recondite volume to the novelist:

> October 17, 1649 [the action is shifted to 1651 in *Woodstock*]: Something . . . hoyested up their Beds-feet so much higher than their heads, that they thought they should have been turned over and over: and then let them fall down with such a force, that their bodies rebounded from the bed a good distance, and then shook the Bed-steads so violently, that themselves confest their Bodies wer sore with it.
>
> November 2: And upon the Servants in the Truckle-Bed, who lay all the time sweating for fear; there was first a little, which made them begin to stir, but before they could get out, there came a whole Tub full, as it were of stinking Ditch-water down upon them, so green, that it made their Shirts of that colour too.[21]

Scott clearly differentiates those chiefly aimed at by the mummery at Woodstock. The Hon. Colonel Desborough, victim of bed-tilting and dousing, is described as an indolent blockhead who drinks heavily when terrified by the poltergeist and seeks safety in prayer and Bible. Another aspect of supernatural fear appears in Master Joshua Bletson, M.P. for the borough of Littlefaith, a blaspheming coward who trembles visibly and covertly uses the Bible as counter-spell while pretending incredulity. In his reactions, Major-General Harrison (discussed in the section on Ghosts) is more complex than his fellow Commissioners, Bletson and Desborough. Another character, the Presbyterian divine, Master Nehemiah Hold-enough, believing implicitly in bodily presence at Woodstock, sets forth dogmatically and consequentially to wage war on the Fiend.

As for the hero, although Scott does admit that he "had the usual credulity of the times," Markham Everard manages to return to the solid rock of scepticism after a period of wavering. Refusing to believe that the laws of nature have been temporarily suspended, he is generally rational and unflurried. The phenomena, after all, are referable to confederacy—though perhaps with the aid of conjuration and witchcraft. Hardly a full-time doubting Thomas, Everard does not too insistently take the supernatural machinery apart.[22]

---

[21] Sinclair, pp. 33, 37. The incident of one Commissioner's mistaking another, who has just risen from bed in his shirt, for the noisy Devil and attacking him may have suggested Markham Everard's grapple with "a tall figure in white" which turns out to be Wildrake, newly waked from sleep.

[22] Cp. Horatio (Horace) Smith, *Brambletye House; or, Cavaliers and Roundheads* (1826), admittedly written in Scott's vein. The hero, Jocelyn Compton, being "more free from superstition and credulity than most of his contemporaries," is "little disposed at any time to superstitious fears." 3rd edn, 1826, II. 84, 320.

But Scott does. When criticised by James Ballantyne for imitating Mrs Radcliffe, Scott succinctly notes, in the Journal for 3 February 1826, what he considers the difference in his aim: "Many will think with him—yet I am of opinion he is quite wrong. . . . My object is not to excite fear of supernatural things in my reader, but to show the effect of such fear upon the agents in the story—one a man of sense and firmness [Everard]—one a man unhinged by remorse [Harrison]—one a stupid uninquiring clown [Desborough]—one a learned and worthy but superstitious divine [Holdenough]. . . . The book turns on this hinge and cannot want it."[23] But the *longueurs* inescapable in wonders strung out without climactic effect on a dead narrative level cannot be so easily rationalised. Although the analysis of fear in *Woodstock* is skilful, it is based on complications which are disproportionate to the plot-service rendered.

Scott adds, "I will try to insinuate the refutation of Aldiboronti's exception into the prefatory matter." The insinuation turns out to be less a refutation of Ballantyne's argument than a belated truncation of the poltergeisterie. "I might have gone much more fully into this part of my subject, for the materials are ample;—but, to tell the reader a secret, some friendly critics were of opinion they made the story hang on hand; and thus I was prevailed on to be more concise on the subject than I might otherwise have been" (Preface).

When taken to task by his printer, Scott had nearly finished the second of his three volumes. A little less than two-thirds of the way through *Woodstock* he shifts his emphasis from supernatural works to natural deeds, eschewing demon pranks from the end of Chapter XXII to the middle of Chapter XXIX. Although the King's visit to the lodge properly ends the fantastic horse-play, the dearth of later allusions to Trusty Tomkins' successful sleights and the cursory explanation of devices used are probably the not unwholesome fruits of Ballantyne's criticism. In fact, after the first flush of annoyance at being schooled, Scott apparently enjoyed leaving his supernatural maze. An entry in the Journal for 10 February suggests as much: "This morning I had some good ideas respecting *Woodstock* which will make the story better. The devil of a difficulty is, that one puzzles the skein in order to excite curiosity, and then cannot disentangle it for [the] satisfaction of the prying fiend they have raised."[24]

An untangling of the twisted skein is implicit in Everard's general comment on Royalist responsibility for the commotion. Toward the end of *Woodstock* Scott must make good. But his only solution is the Radcliffian one to which he objects—at least in *gothic* fiction:

[23] *Journal*, pp. 87–8.   [24] *Op. cit.*, p. 97.

The bold assertion of the actual existence of phantoms and apparitions seems to us to harmonize much more naturally with the manners of ancient times, and to produce a more powerful effect upon the reader's mind, than any attempt to reconcile the superstitious credulity of feudal ages with the philosophic scepticism of our own, by referring these prodigies to the operation of fulminating powder, combined mirrors, magic lanterns, trap-doors, speaking trumpets, and such-like apparatus of German phantasmagoria.[25]

To escape the charge of paltriness or implausibility earlier levelled at the Radcliffian method, Scott offers a master key with simple notching rather than a special key for each enigma. If the reader fails to open the lock, the fault is his, not the author's. The secret is that Trusty Tomkins, Dr Rochecliffe, Phoebe Mayflower, and Joceline Joliffe are hobgoblin impersonators. The hoax is kept up by means of the network of rooms and hidden passages accessible through Victor Lee's apartment. Disguises, concealed springs, and enough cordage and machinery to overturn Desborough's bed are the appliances. Serving both Royalists and Roundheads, Tomkins takes part in the eerie masquerade to frighten the Commissioners away and to gain information about King Charles for Oliver Cromwell.

Scott's actual management of the poltergeist is not compressed and emphatic but diffuse. Most of the old relations which could have served as models were daily records of inexplicable annoyance, often singularly lacking in continuity and exhibiting a keen *penchant* for bathos. In like manner, though in refined form, Scott heaps up his wonders with little regard for the conventional time of reckoning, which he largely replaces with a blanket explanation.[26]

★   ★   ★

[25] Criticism of Horace Walpole in *Lives*, p. 542.

[26] The same supernatural clutter, high purpose and fumbling execution may be found in Scott's play, *The Doom of Devorgoil* (published 1830, not acted). See Scott to [Daniel Terry], 12 Mar. 1817–2 Mar. 1818, in *Letters*, IV. 402–06, 438; V. 43, 61, 100. Through distrust of the audience, Scott omits a projected "ghosts' banquet" and proceeds with a cruel ancestral spectre whom he considers materialising as a returning kinsman with a thorough knowledge of "all the secret holes & hiding places of the castle." Having evolved a "wholly fantastic" plot, he brings in "our old Castle spectre the German Barber" and Owlspiegle's assistant, Cockledemoy, to shave conceited Gullcrammer. To such ingredients are added a few pinches of general haunting, accursed household, knowing palmer, prophecy, scepticism, exorcism, witchcraft, and magical conditions. Like Ballantyne, Terry may have banished other eerie beings by his letter of 11 Feb. 1818, objecting to the sudden and repeated introduction of goblins that are "very liable to weaken if not destroy the admission and effect of the serious & potent spirits subsequently & shortly to appear." Abbotsford Ms., N.L.S. (Cp. Scott to [Morritt], 14 Jan. 1818 in *Letters*, v. 50–1.)

In Scott's reaction to the Abbotsford poltergeist, excitement, emotional involvement, search for a material cause, and creative reshaping jostle each other. No trickery coming to light, the investigator is untempted to mar what develops into an effective anecdote. Because there is suspected fraud in the celebrated Woodstock case, his interest follows a different course, recreation of the deception and unintentionally anticlimactic exposure. The Abbotsford specimen offers better material; Scott works more freely and is, in his earlier attempt, the better artist.

In electing to use the Woodstock poltergeist as fictional apparatus, Scott does not observe the statute of limitations on superstitions that are ludicrous and outmoded. For the most part, historical fiction is restricted to such deeds and beliefs as quicken the imagination when bygone scenes are re-enacted. Lifeless happenings and superstitions properly attract the shortsighted antiquary but not the living novelist. At best the reader can only feel a transient sympathy for characters who tremble at gross, transparent antics.[27] Thus the very real merit of *Woodstock* is not due to supernatural confusion worse confounded, but to vigorous scenes and arresting contrasts between Roundheads and Royalists.[28]

15. MAGIC

Whether magic was white, black, or mechanical—healing, harmful, or theatrical—it appealed to Scott. In fact, the Northern Magician lived in the *locus classicus* of Scottish wizards whose traditionary exploits he almost equalled in the evocation of lays, prose tales, and the petrous romance of

[27] Note William Hazlitt's comment in his *Conversations of James Northcote, R.A.*, ed. Edmund Gosse, London 1894, pp. 157–8: "The plot turned chiefly on . . . a very mechanical sort of phantoms who dealt in practical jokes and personal annoyances . . . instead of supernatural and visionary horrors. It was very bad indeed, but might be intended to contrast the literal, matter-of-fact imagination of the Southron with the loftier impulses of Highland superstition."

[28] I have not discussed Scott's Introduction (1 Aug. 1832) to *Woodstock*, for it is largely based on reading done for annotation purposes. The Introduction liberally quotes William Hone, *The Every-Day Book*, II. 291–5, which identifies the source Scott remembers having read "more than forty years since" (cp. *Demonology*, p. 375): "The Authentic Memoirs of the memorable Joseph Collins of Oxford" in *The British Magazine; Or, the London and Edinburgh Intelligencer* for Apr. 1747 or a printed extract from the periodical. It is rather curious that the explanation which Scott completely trusts was given with journalistic glibness some hundred years after the event. See also Aubrey, *Miscellanies upon Various Subjects*, p. 84; J. N. Brewer, "Oxfordshire," *The Beauties of England and Wales*, VOL. XII, PT. II, London 1813, pp. 392–3; Edward Marshall, *The Early History of Woodstock Manor*, Oxford and London 1873, pp. 204–05, with the author's Supplement (1874), pp. 14–18. In the Appendix, Scott reprints "The Woodstock Scuffle" (1649) and Thomas Widdowes, "The Just Devil of Woodstock" (1660), neither of which was known to him before Oct. 1831. Both are mentioned by Anthony à Wood in *Athenae Oxonienses*, ed. Philip Bliss, London 1813–20, III. 398–9.

Abbotsford. There was Michael Scot, whose magical powers were the subject of what Thomas Dempster calls "innumerabiles aniles fabulae." According to tradition, the Eildon Hills, which dominate Tweeddale, formed one large peak until this potent magus imposed on one of his fiendish labourers the task of splitting the mountain into three separate masses.[1] And it was rumoured of another wizard, Merlin, that he slept with Arthur and the knights of the Table Round in an enchanted vault beneath the Eildon Hills, awaiting the bugle note which would arouse him to the service of the living.

While preparing "Thomas the Rhymer" for the *Minstrelsy* and editing *Sir Tristrem* with a long disquisition on the prophet-poet, Scott probably began a fragmentary prose romance which was to have commemorated that hero as *The Lay of the Last Minstrel* later revived the fame of Michael Scot. In the General Preface to his Magnum Opus, Sir Walter discusses this early project of a chivalrous tale in the style of *The Castle of Otranto*. It was to have been stocked with "Border characters and supernatural incident" and to have turned "upon a fine legend of superstition which is current in the part of the Borders where he had his residence": Many years ago a horse-dealer, Canobie Dick, encountered a venerable man on Bowden Moor, just west of the Eildons. They fell to chaffering and the trader sold the stranger two horses for gold of an antique coinage. One night, after having disposed of several more mounts advantageously, Dick hinted that a dry bargain was unlucky; whereupon the buyer led him by a concealed passage into the Lucken Hare, a witch-haunted eminence between the southern and central peaks of the Eildons. Passing stalls in which were coal-black chargers and recumbent knights, weapon in hand, they came to the upper end of the immense, torch-lit hall, where a sword and a horn lay on a table of olden time. Making himself known as Thomas of Ercildoune, the prophet, bard, and magician declared that the horse-dealer would be King of Britain if only he chose wisely between sword and horn. When Dick fixed upon the latter, thunder rent the cavern, man and beast came to life:

> Woe to the coward, that ever he was born,
> Who did not draw the sword before he blew the horn!

After being whirled out of the hall and down the precipitous bank, Dick lived just long enough to tell some shepherds of his uncanny

[1] James Hogg, *The Three Perils of Man*, London 1822, II. 151; *Lay*, II. xiii, n. Science and tradition are not entirely at variance, for "Eildon with its remarkable three peaks is but one hill; and the whole is essentially of the same geological character." George Tate, "Notes on the Geology of the Eildon Hills," *History of the Berwickshire Naturalists' Club*, v (1868), 4.

adventure.[2] Thus, besides being organiser and supply-agent of renascent Arthurian chivalry, Thomas of Ercildoune acts as guide to the Eildon vaults whenever he meets a man who may break the charmed sleep of the knights for good.

In writing of his land investments to John Richardson, Scott crows, "My wings... will probably soon flap the Eildon Hills."[3] He was approaching the storied slopes and vast caverns of which Michael Scot may be called the deviser, Merlin the tenant, and Thomas of Ercildoune the guide.

But when one turns from the magic of the legendary past to the Border present, there is a sad falling-off. Grand geological changes give place to petty cures. Folk remedies may be magical in their use of charms or in the transmission of animal vitality to the sick. A popular cure was early tried on lame Watty. "Some one had recommended that so often as a sheep was killed for the use of the family, I should be stripped, and swathed up in the skin warm as it was flayed from the carcass of the animal."[4] This occurred in the home of the boy's grandfather, who could have cited John Moncrief's *The Poor Man's Physician* as an authority for wrapping paralysed members in lambs' skins, applying "the hot lungs of a sheep" in cases of convulsion, or warming the parts affected in a fresh-killed "Ox or Sheep's Belly."[5]

Long after being involved in the sheepskin, Scott writes to the Duke of Buccleuch about the superstitious leechcraft suggested for an attack of cramp and jaundice: "The most extraordinary recipe was that of my highland piper John Bruce who spent a whole sunday in selecting twelve stones from twelve south running streams with the purpose that I should sleep upon them and be whole."[6] Innocent as this survival of white magic

---

[2] The tale also appears in *Demonology*, pp. 136–40. For variants and parallels, see Mrs Hnghes, pp. 112–13, 115; M. A. Richardson, *The Borderer's Table Book*, VII. 37–46; J. F. Campbell, *Popular tales of the West Highlands*, Edinburgh 1862, IV. 36–7; *The Denham Tracts*, ed. James Hardy, XXIX. 121–8. In his *Scenes of Infancy*, PT II, John Leyden makes Thomas undergo the test which is usually applied to another adventurer:

> In iron sleep the minstrel lies forlorn,
> Who breathed a sound before he blew the horn.

[3] 22 Sep. 1817 in *Letters*, IV. 531; also 508 ("a sort of fairy land marching with Abbotsford"), 529, 539. For the Eildons in portraits of Scott by Lawrence and Wilkie, see X. 129–30, 168.

[4] Lockhart, I. 16. See also *Letters*, X. 27; Mrs Hughes, p. 215; Andrew Lang, *The Life and Letters of John Gibson Lockhart*, London 1897, I. 405.

[5] Moncrief, *op. cit.*, 3rd edn, Edinburgh 1731, p. 2. Cp. *C. Plini Secundi Naturalis Historiae Libri XXXVII*, ed. Carolus Mayhoff, Leipzig 1897, V. 66–7; Samuel Pepys's *Diary* for 19 Oct. 1663; Law, *Memorialls*, p. lxx; J. S. Forsyth, *Demonologia*, London 1831, pp. 58, 61 (1827 edn reissued).

[6] 15 Apr. 1819 in *Letters*, V. 348. The Duke died in Lisbon five days after this letter was written.

may seem, on 21 July 1603, James Reid was convicted of sorcery and burned, one of the charges being that the Devil had taught him to use "south-running water as a healing charm, and enchanted flints, to the prejudice of many," and in 1623 Thomas Greave, a wizard, was burned "for curing diseases, by making sick persons pass several times through hanks of yarn, washing their shirts in south-running water, and the like."[7]

It is rather a descent from south-running streams to parlour magic, but such is the progress won by the march of intellect and education. When the comedian and ventriloquist, Charles Mathews, visited Abbotsford in January 1826, bringing "his black art tricks," Scott's butler was perturbed:

> I said to Sir Walter that I had heard of witches and warlocks, but if he had not sumething of that kind about him, there was worse; for no man could go through such devilish tricks without sumething uncommon about them.
> "He will laff hearty when I tell him you think he is a warlock—"[8]

Sir Walter was interested in the melancholy temperament, as well as the accomplishments, of Charles Mathews. There was something almost ominous about the man. In 1822, Scott dined with Sir Alexander Boswell and the comedian in Castle Street, Edinburgh. Boswell died on a duelling field two or three days later: "I never saw Sir Alexander more." And in 1815, he lunched with Mathews, John Scott of Gala, Daniel Terry, and Lord Byron, whose "beautiful pale face [was] like a spirit's—good or evil." "I never saw Byron so full of fun, frolic, wit, and whim: he was as playful as a kitten. Well, I never saw him again. So this man of mirth, with his merry meetings, has brought me no luck."[9] Boswell and Byron, though exceptionally lively table companions, had the traits of "fey [doomed]" men.

"A strange story about town of ghost-seeing" is recorded in Scott's *Journal* of 16 October 1831. Lord Prudhoe and Colonel Felix had seen a magician in Grand Cairo draw a black pentacle in a boy's palm and—after certain rites, perfuming, and suffumigation—evoke figures as through an

---

[7] Law, *Memorialls*, pp. l–li. See also Craig-Brown, *History of Selkirkshire*, I. 449; Dalyell, *Darker Superstitions of Scotland*, pp. 84–7.

[8] "Memoirs of William Dalgleish," ed. G. E. Mitton, *The Cornhill Magazine*, pp. 88–9. Among Scott's retainers, George [Walkinshaw?] matched the butler in superstitiousness: "He was a firm believer in ghosts, and warlocks, and all kinds of old wives' fable." Irving, *Abbotsford*, pp. 73–4. Nothing magical seems to have attended the visit of that "arch-deceiver," M. Alexandre Vattemaire, to Abbotsford in 1824. See Scott's "Lines addressed to Monsieur Alexandre, the Celebrated Ventriloquist"; a nameless "ventriloquist and partial juggler," 25 Apr. 1829 in *Journal*, p. 629.

[9] Lockhart, III. 337–8, 373; V. 153–4; VI. 10, 168, 189. Mathews himself seems not to have been superstitious. Note the incident of his renting a haunted room in York. Mrs Anne (Jackson) Mathews, *Memoirs of Charles Mathews, Comedian*, London 1838–9, I. 247–56.

aperture in the hand. Seven flags appeared, then a Sultan's splendid tent amid hosts. The person to be summoned was named. Shakespeare, for one, was invested with flesh once more. For a modest sum, as Scott also learned, two gentlemen had received instruction in the art of spirit-raising. "The truth of a story irreconcilable with the common course of nature must depend on cross examination. If one should find, while at Malta, that they had an opportunity of expiscating this matter, though at the expence of a voyage to Alexandria, it would hardly deter me." About 23 November, Scott writes to Lockhart from Malta that the letters of an excellent Arabic scholar would seem to show confederacy of one kind or other.[10]

The more disillusioning life became, the more interest Scott felt in the mechanics of illusion. Sir William Gell gives an instance of May 1832:

> Some of the party went out to walk round the battlements of the Castle [of Bracciano] by moonlight, and I think a ghost was seen among the usual accompaniments of such situations. A ghost, said Sir Walter, is best made by painting it with white on tin, "for in the dusk after it had produced its effect it could be instantly made to vanish by turning the edge almost without thickness toward the spectator."[11]

The death of Scott a few months after his explanation of optical trickery revived all the old imagery about the Magician of the North. "Thy wand, O magician! is broken." "The minstrel sleeps!—the charm is o'er."[12] But the magic, like the legendary feats of Michael Scot, lived on.[13]

*   *   *

[10] Journal, pp. 750–2, 771; The Journal of Sir Walter Scott, ed. David Douglas, Edinburgh 1890, II. 421, n. 1. Scott does not mention that ink was poured into the boy's palm to form a magic mirror in which a sweeper, seven flags, troops, tents, and a sultan appeared. See Leon Delaborde, "Magie Orientale," Revue des deux Mondes, Second Series, III (1833), 332–43; Q.R., LIX (1837), 195–208; E. W. Lane, An Account of the Manners and Customs of the Modern Egyptians, 5th edn, ed. E. S. Poole, London 1871, I. 332, 337–47.

[11] Gell, Reminiscences of Sir Walter Scott's Residence in Italy, 1832, ed. James C. Corson, London 1957, p. 35; Lockhart, VII. 367.

[12] James C. Corson, "Verses on the Death of Scott," N. & Q., CLXXVII (1939), 417–19. In the Dedicatory Epistle of Ivanhoe, Scott uses similar figures of speech in discussing the historical "resuscitation by . . . sorceries" of "the Scottish magician" or "the Northern Warlock."

[13] The obvious comparison between Michael and Walter Scott, suggested by the Lay, has been repeated, one must admit, almost ad nauseam:

> Long since the enchanter's gone, the dreams no more
> Of superstition's day, enthrall the soul;
> But lo! Dun Edin owns fresh magic lore,
> Another Scott renown'd whilst ages roll.

This quatrain is from "The Scotch Magician," a poem sent to [Scott] on 15 Dec. 1824, by an admirer, J. M. Longmire. Walpole. See also B. S. Nayler, A Memoir of the Life and Writings of Walter Scott, Amsterdam 1833, p. 4; Charles Mackay, Forty Years' Recollections . . . from 1830 to 1870, London 1877, I. 202–5; Harold Nicolson, Sainte-Beuve, Garden City [1956], p. 179.

The only narrative of Scott's which fully depends on magic is "My Aunt Margaret's Mirror." In its oral form this *Keepsake* offering of 1828 was related to the boy Walter by his great-aunt, Mrs Margaret Swinton, who also supplied the plot of *Halidon Hill* and a version of *The Bride of Lammermoor*.[14] A spinster who used a human skull as a candle-holder, "she entertained largely that belief in supernaturals which in those times was not considered as sitting ungracefully on the grave and aged of her condition ... one of her own family had been an eyewitness of the incidents" in the Magic Mirror.[15] Hearing this tale from Scott's lips, Mrs Hughes reports that it happened to his grandmother and her sister, who was married to Sir Archibald Primrose, "a most wicked and abandoned man."[16] The two ladies went to a conjurer in the Canongate to learn of the doings and intentions of the missing husband. Using a glass, the man of skill revealed Sir Archibald leading a Flemish girl to the altar and being prevented by Lady Primrose's brother, sword in hand. Mrs Hughes pauses to comment on the narrator:

> It is not possible to describe the effect with which he tells anything supernatural: the deep, impressive tones of his voice, the overhanging brow, the intense expression of his eye which seems fixed beyond the sphere in which he sits as if he were looking into the world of spirits, altogether produce a sort of creeping sensation which tho' it does not last, is very powerful while the great magician is uttering the spell.[17]

Besides making early use of the mirror story in conversation, Scott introduces it in *The Bride of Lammermoor* as an exploit of Ailsie Gourlay's:

> I find, I say, it was charged against her, among other offences, that she had, by the aid and delusions of Satan, shewn to a young person of quality, in a mirror glass, a gentleman then abroad, to whom the said young person was betrothed, and who appeared in the vision to be in the act of bestowing his hand upon another lady. But this and some other parts of the record appear to have been studiously left imperfect in names and dates, probably out of regard to the honour of the families concerned.[18]

[14] Lockhart, v. 159; *Peveril*, n. ii, "Concealment of the Countess of Derby."

[15] Scott's Introduction of Aug. 1831.

[16] This is obviously a lapse of memory. The actual hero—and villain—was James Viscount Primrose, who died in 1706. Chambers, *Traditions of Edinburgh*, I. 250; *Major Fraser's Manuscript*, ed. Alexander Fergusson, Edinburgh 1889, II. 104, n. There was a Sir Archibald Foulis Primrose of Dunipace, Bart., whose wife Mary, unlike the long-suffering Lady Primrose of tradition, died two days after her husband's execution on 15 Nov. 1746. Sir Robert Douglas, *The Scots Peerage*, ed. Sir J. B. Paul, Edinburgh 1904–14, VII. 220, 222.

[17] Mrs Hughes, pp. 148–9. In this version, Scott is represented as having received the story from his mother, who in turn got it from her mother.

[18] Scott elsewhere foreshadows plots which are more fully developed in time. Cp. the crusading Wilibert in *Waverley*, ch. iv; "The Noble Moringer"; and *The Betrothed*—1814, 1819, 1825.

In its expanded form, the narrative was twice written. "Tale of the Mysterious Mirror," a first draft completed on 3 December 1827, failed to meet the critical approval of Cadell and Ballantyne.[19] On 13 April 1828, Sir Walter records in his Journal: "Amused myself by converting the *Tale of the Misterious Mirror* into *Aunt Margaret's Mirror*, designed for Heath's what-dye-call-it. Cadell will not like this, but I cannot afford to have my goods thrown back upon my hands. The tale is a good one, and is said actually to have happend to Lady Primrose, my great-grandmother having attended her sister on the occasion."[20] With this judgment Tennyson was later to agree: "Scott's short tale, *My Aunt Margaret's Mirror* (how little known!), he once spoke of as the finest of all ghost or magical stories."[21]

The final version tells of Jemmie Falconer's visit to a Paduan doctor in Edinburgh to gain knowledge of her vanished husband, apparently on a military campaign abroad. After she has accepted the condition of strict silence during seven permitted minutes—"as he pretended"—of mirror vision, there is sweet and solemn music and Damiotti returns with pale, rigid features and in a different garb. The sable chamber has five torches and a large mirror which reflects two crossed swords, a human skull, and a foreign Bible resting on an altar. The peccant spouse is imaged on the point of marrying a teen-age foreigner when he is prevented by an officer (Jemmie's half-brother, who is killed in the inevitable duel). The Scottish wife disturbs the mystic revelation with an exclamation and, at the end of seven tense minutes, the scene fades away. Damiotti announces that the mirrored events are strictly, or almost strictly, contemporary. But when news does arrive of the enactment of the scene at Rotterdam, the time interval is loosely extended to "some days."

Despite Scott's assertion that he is giving "a mere transcript . . . with very little embellishment" of what he heard at the fireside, he manages somewhere in the series of oral and literary revisions to change the conjurer from a Scottish Wise Man, or Wise Woman, into a Paduan doctor. Neither the reader nor the author knows quite what to make of Baptista Damiotti. At times he seems little more than a Jacobite agent or a quack using a reputation for magic to attract patients; at others he is apparently an adept with real powers, a man wracked and tortured by his own gift. As with his other esoteric characters, Scott indulges in a wide range of roughly synonymous epithets, some of them not too felicitous. The Italian is labelled a villain-rascal-rogue, a conjurer, sorcerer, and necromancer, a user of "charms and unlawful arts," "an expounder of futurity,"

---

[19] Lockhart, VII. 88.   [20] *Journal*, p. 521.
[21] Andrew Lang, *Alfred Tennyson*, New York 1901, p. 219.

a fortune-teller, a soothsayer, a sage, a man of art, the master, and this Italian warlock.

Having relaxed into a trite and artificial conception of supernatural paraphernalia, from which he never entirely frees himself, Scott must introduce cabalistic instruments and exoticism and substitute outlandish superstition for native lore. But mirror-conjuring, the mainspring of the plot, is recurrent in the annals of British, as well as Italian, superstition. Thomas Nash's *The Unfortunate Traveller* (1594) associates the mirror theme with Italy, as does William Turner's story of Sir Marmaduke Langdale and the Italian magus.²² But English Anne Bodenham was accused of showing Sarah Goddard's chamber in a glass, "the Bed turned up the wrong way, and under that part of the Bed where the Bolster lay . . . the poyson in a white paper."²³ And Hodge, a white witch, displayed the face of a thief in a mirror.²⁴

Artistically compensating for crediting the mirror ceremony to a visiting Paduan doctor's skill, Scott sensitively adjusts the narrative to the temperament of Aunt Margaret. An unforced chat with her nephew leads the old lady into the shadowy recesses of the past. Before coming to her story, the narrator describes the state of mind which makes her afraid to look into the dimly-lit depths of the mirror at the figures that may take shape there. Her superstition ("which I do not wish to part with") comfortably separates her from the living and prepares her for the dead. She is joined to the present by "the steady light of reason" and to the past by "the twilight of illusion." Aunt Margaret is the inspiration of Scott's most appealing analysis of the superstitious mind.

While sailing between the Scylla of rational explanation and the Charybdis of unchecked credulity, Scott keeps a fairly even keel. Resorting to a sister contrast that is somewhat reminiscent of the Deans and the Troils, he presents the passive, fitfully obstinate, unintelligent wife as a believer and bold, high-principled, intelligent Lady Bothwell as a sceptic. To the author's suggestion that Damiotti may have profited by secret news, Aunt Margaret replies that Lady Bothwell found so many difficulties

²² Turner, *A Compleat History of the Most Remarkable Providences . . . in this Present Age*, London 1697, p. 59. Cp. the "brood mirour of glas" in Chaucer's "Squire's Tale," ll. 81–2, 132–41.

²³ Edmund Bower, *Doctor Lamb Revived*, London 1653, p. 6.

²⁴ W.P., *The History of Witches and Wizards*, London 1700[?], pp. 125–7. Cp. *The Famous History of Fryar Bacon*, London 1766, p. 96, and E. T. W. Hoffmann, "The Golden Pot" in Thomas Carlyle, *German Romance*, II. 246: "It is not, as with others of her tribe, by cards, or melted lead, or grounds of coffee, that she divines to you; but after certain preparations, in which you yourself bear a part, she takes a polished metallic mirror, and there rises in it the strangest mixture of figures and forms, all intermingled; these she interprets, and so answers your question."

after canvassing such possibilities that even she inclined to a supernatural explanation. Thus Scott' wisely follows his informant's theory of the proper way to tell a weird story. Only "fools and children" will accept certain prodigies as true, but everyone can enjoy the sensations of a blanching cheek, a tingling ear, and a "slight shuddering." An effective renewer of a tale of terror, after expressing "his general disbelief of all such legendary lore," will present his narrative as still having something inexplicable in it.[25]

*   *   *

The variety of magic in the Waverley Novels will be somewhat less bewildering if it is considered in two ways—as literary when it appears in figures of speech or fairy-tale and as more functional when it emphasises the difficulty of man's progress from birth to death. The literary use, however, is not unrelated to character, as will be seen in *The Abbot* and *Count Robert of Paris*.

In their obedience to mysterious inner and outer compulsions, Waverley heroes and heroines seem at times like Spenser's knights and ladies moving in a domain of glamour. A hero is often like a shuttlecock kept in the air by the battledores of a coy damsel, an enigmatic protectress, and the Northern Magician. Puzzled by superior intelligence, rapid human transit, or his own hidden identity, he may feel himself to be in the grip of fate or, at least, of spells. When Roland Graeme follows the nimble-footed Catherine Seyton into a miserable Kinross cottage, instead of his inamorata he finds the stagily fatidical Mother Nicneven, or Magdalen Graeme. When she moralises volubly and reproachfully, for once the hero rebels:

> I have been treated amongst you . . . as one who lacked the common attributes of free-will and human reason, or was at least deemed unfit to exercise them. A land of enchantment have I been led into, and spells have been cast around me—every one has met me in disguise—every one has spoken to me in parables—I have been like one who walks in a weary and bewildering dream. . . . If one must walk with masks and spectres, who waft themselves from place to place as it were in vision rather than reality, it might shake the soundest faith and turn the wisest head.

Perhaps, only a trumpet summoning Roland to action in the cause of Queen Mary can "dispel the chimerical visions by which I am surrounded." Here the terms of enchantment, though figurative, vividly

[25] For G. P. R. James's apology and assertion of innocence of plagiarism in a similar fictional incident, see James, *Darnley; or, the Field of the Cloth of Gold*, London 1910, 159, n. (1st edn, 1830), and Partington, *Letter-Books*, p. 236.

present the dilemma of the passive hero who wearies of being acted upon. Roland is crying out against the author of *The Abbot* as much as against his grandmother Magdalen.

In *Count Robert of Paris*, Agelastes tells the Frank a tale of enchantment. Arriving at the court of the island Princess of Zulichium, a Zoroastrian Magus was soon enslaved by her charms. Sensitive to mockery, the old magician cast a spell on castle and occupants, so that for many years a fast sleep held the gay and the young in thrall. When Artavan de Hautlieu tried to free the "nymph of fifteen" by kissing her, she was transformed into a dragon and flew out of a window "uttering loud wails of disappointment" (three kisses would have been sovereign). In his oversubtle attempt to persuade Count Robert to change his course of travel, Agelastes fails as he almost invariably does in his designs on stolid Northerners. Although Scott's pretty fairy-tale is suspended in a narrative vacuum, it does illustrate racial differences.[26]

Scott's more functional use of magic, in the life-cycle of man, begins with birth. Though uninformed of the infant's birth minute, Meg Merrilies wishes to protect Harry Bertram from worriecows, elves, and gyre-carlings. She sings Saint Colme's charm, with its jumble of magical herbs, animal lore, and saints. Mr Skreigh, the superstitious precentor, has his own version of Harry's birth and disappearance. The father has been too tolerant of those familiar-attended witches, the Egyptians, and particularly of Meg, "maist powerfu' with the Enemy of Mankind," who "as gude as said she would have him [Harry], body and soul, before three days were over his head." Five years later, Meg—"or her master in her similitude"— wrests the bairn from Kennedy's arms. The precentor also makes Guy Mannering, caster of the boy's horoscope, a gray-bearded ancient who vanishes after warning of the Evil One's power over poor Harry. Most effective is the gypsy's magic, which picturesquely suggests the actual mystery of birth (as later of death), together with the folk dread of foul spirits which await an unguarded moment to take possession of soul or body.

When maidens long "to ken wha suld wed me," they may use the charm tried by Elspeth in *The Monastery*. But "I ken there is little luck in Hallowe'en sights." As she recalls the adventure, "I had not winnowed the last weight clean out, and the moon was shining bright upon the floor,

---

[26] Cp. the dictum in "An Essay on Romance" that there is a stronger "tendency to the marvellous" in oriental than in northern romance. *The Miscellaneous Prose Works of Sir Walter Scott*, Edinburgh 1834, VI. 147. In *The Talisman*, Sir Kenneth has no tale of wonder to match Saladin's account of demon ancestry.

when in stalked the presence of my dear Simon Glendinning, that is now happy. . . . He held up an arrow as he passed me, and I swarf'd awa wi' fright." It was no use trying to persuade her afterwards that it was all a trick of Father Nicolas the cellarer and Simon holding "Cupid's shaft." The "Cantrip" was surely ominous, for after the marriage "the grey-goose wing was the death o' him after a'!" In this compressed episode, humour, superstition, realism, and *lacrimae rerum* mingle.[27]

Troth-plighting is a serious matter. In *The Pirate*, Minna Troil is willing to bind herself to Cleveland until he releases her. But "the promise of Odin, the most sacred of our [surviving] northern rites," must be witnessed by the Norse spirit which guards the Standing Stones of Stennis. Their hands will be joined through the hole in a pillar and their faith pledged. The revelation that Cleveland is a pirate releases Minna from the arrangement and from a gruesome ordeal, for the story of the original pirate involved the execution of Gow and the sweetheart's withdrawal of troth by touching the dead man's hand.[28] Neglect would result in visitation by ghost or demon lover. Here, Scott is less interested in the historical appropriateness of the ritual than in the contrast between old and new, in the romance of survival. Undoubtedly, Thomas Hardy would have gone through with the vestigial promise of Odin, placing the solitary lovers in the ageless and unresponsive stone circle and allowing Minna's high romantic fervour to sweep her to her doom.

The action of *Count Robert of Paris* is six centuries earlier than that of *The Pirate*. Yet it is during a revival of "old superstitions" that Hereward and Bertha plight their troth at a stone circle over which Odin, "who was, while alive, a bloody and cruel magician," presides.[29] When they meet in Constantinople, their constancy seems still well assured by pre-Christian magic, but they want to propitiate the newer, more powerful Christian deity by renewing their vow according to non-heathen rites. To the bookish and none too harmoniously blended beliefs of the novel the lovers add an experiment in pantheism.

[27] See Burns's note on "Halloween," l. 182, "To winn three wechts o' naething": " . . . and the third time an apparition will pass through the barn, in at the windy door, and out at the other, having both the figure in question, and the appearance or retinue, marking the employment or station in life"; McNeill, *The Silver Bough*, III. 36–7, 148 n. 8; and Radford, *Encyclopaedia of Superstitions*, s.v. Hallowe'en and, for bad luck in charms, Sweethearts (Calling).

[28] Advertisement to *The Pirate*; F. J. Child, *The English and Scottish Popular Ballads*, Boston 1882–98, II. 227, n; McNeill, *The Silver Bough*, II. 73, 87, 95–6, 145, n. 2; Allan Fea, *The Real Captain Cleveland*, London 1912, pp. 18–19. When the course of married love does not run smooth, magic may also be resorted to, as in "My Aunt Margaret's Mirror."

[29] For Odin as magician, see *Demonology*, p. 99; H. C. Lea, *A History of the Inquisition of the Middle Ages*, New York 1911, III. 404; *Larousse Encyclopedia of Mythology*, pp. 258–62.

Health is an important object of magic. When Magnus Troil brings his
daughter Minna to Norna with an affection of the heart, the sibyl readies
a charcoal-filled chafing-dish, a crucible, and some sheet lead. Having long
expected her visitors, she soon lights the fuel ("probably by some chemical
combination of which the spectators were not aware"). With her usual
facility in improvisation, Norna chants verses of gratitude to the elemental
fire spirit before melting lead and pouring it into water. But, just as a
reader of tea-leaves may not be inspired by the foliation in a cup, Norna
finds no meaningful design. While the lead is melting a second time,[30] she
propitiates the Spirit of the Winds with verse and a handful of gray hair.
Returning to "the dubious twilight, which best suited her character
and occupation," she pours again and finds that a bit of lead now forms a
human heart.

> She who sits by haunted well,
> Is subject to the Nixie's spell;
> She who walks on lonely beach,
> To the Mermaid's charmed speech;
> She who walks round ring of green,
> Offends the peevish Fairy Queen;
> And she who takes rest in the Dwarfie's cave,
> A weary weird of woe shall have.

Having dared do these things, Minna is in "a demon's hold." "That the
cause of your sickness and sorrow may cease" Norna attaches the heart to
a gold chain in a necklace. The spell ends with the hiding of the "fairy
gift" in the girl's bosom, where it is to lie secret until the vague and
mysterious prophecy is fulfilled. No hint of the gift must pass Minna's
lips or its efficacy will be lost.

Having performed his task as poet-novelist, Scott as antiquary remarks
that Zetlanders of "the lower orders" have recently worked the lead spell
in order to replace a human heart stolen by a demon. "As this simple and
original remedy is peculiar to the isles of Thule, it were unpardonable
not to preserve it at length, in a narrative connected with Scottish
antiquities." The twenty-eighth chapter serves, therefore, as a folklorist's
act of piety.

When Edward Waverley is hurt during a Highland stag-hunt, a gray-
bearded leech-conjurer thrice walks the lucky, sunwise "*deasil*"[31] round

---

[30] Perhaps, the lead should have been poured through the wards of a key or the teeth of a
comb. Each pouring weakens the power of the spell. W. Fordyce Clark, *The Shetland Sketch
Book*, pp. 39–40. Also see McNeill, *The Silver Bough*, III. 35.

[31] The "deasil" is also performed around a corpse, *e.g.* that of Gilchrist MacIan, chief of the
Clan Quhele, in *The Fair Maid of Perth*.

him before muttering spells—"Gasper-Melchior-Balthazar-max-prax-fax"—and boiling herbs gathered under a full moon.[32] Waverley, of course, admits the healing properties of the herbs, moon or no moon, but rejects the spells. Curious about his host's attitude, he finds Fergus un-critical. The episode is rich in local colour and in Highland-Lowland contrasts.

The curative Lee Penny, Scott's *Talisman*, has for centuries been the subject of superstitious, romantic and antiquarian interest. The roughly heart-shaped stone, set in an Edward IV groat,[33] was involved in a trial of 1629, in which the husband of the witch Isobel Young was found to have used water in which the charm was dipped to cure his diseased cattle.[34] Although ailing bestial were chiefly advantaged by the stone, it was also a specific for human fevers, infections, and hydrophobia. Like the Stone of Ardvoirloch, which also hailed from the East, and the Lockerby and Black Pennies, the Lee Penny was only lent out if a large sum were deposited for its return.[35]

The talisman legend is that Sir Simon Lockhart of Lee was entrusted with the heart of the Bruce after Sir James Douglas was slain by Spanish Moors. Instead of depositing the heart in the Holy Land, he brought it back to the high altar of Melrose Abbey. Meanwhile, Sir Simon had fought in Palestine and captured a Saracen prince from whose wife he obtained, besides the ransom already agreed on, a talisman which fell from her purse.[36] In Thomas Gaspey's *The Witch-Finder*, the first fictional work to make use of the Lee Penny, the "wife of the prisoner" owns the charm,[37] but in Scott's Introduction (1832) to *The Talisman*, it belongs to "the aged mother of the captive" Emir.

Freely supplementing the simple legend, Scott returns the Lee Penny to

[32] The Catholic charm used during the gathering is adapted from Reginald Scot, *Discoverie of Witchcraft*. Cp. Ailsie Gourlay in *The Bride of Lammermoor*: "Her Pharmacopeia consisted partly of herbs selected in planetary hours, partly of words, signs, and charms."

[33] J. Y. Simpson, "Notes on Some Scottish Magical Charm-Stones," *Proceedings* of the Society of Antiquaries of Scotland, IV (1863), 222–4. The belief in Scott's day that the coin was of Edward I's reign clashes with the tradition of Eastern origin after the death of Robert the Bruce. See Dalyell, *Darker Superstitions of Scotland*, pp. 157, 680; Joan Evans, *Magical Jewels of the Middle Ages*, Oxford 1922, pp. 178–9; McNeill, *The Silver Bough*, I. 93–4.

[34] Hugo Arnot, *Collections and Abridgement of Celebrated Criminal Trials in Scotland*, Glasgow 1812, p. 396, n.; Law, *Memorialls*, p. liii.

[35] See William Henderson, *Notes on the Folk-Lore of the Northern Counties of England and the Borders*, p. 164, for the offer of Yorkshire farmers "not very long ago" to forfeit their large deposit in order to keep the stone.

[36] *G.M.*, LVII. PT II (1787), 1045–6; William Andrews, "The Lee Penny," *The Reliquary*, XVI (1875–6), 87–9.

[37] Gaspey, *The Witch-Finder; or, The Wisdom of Our Ancestors*, London 1824, II. 81–5. The talisman has no plot significance in this historical romance of the times of Matthew Hopkins (active 1645–6).

the East and shifts attention from a cure-all for cattle to a medicine for man. Before being permitted to tend King Richard, Adonbec the Hakim must demonstrate his healing skill on a lesser person. This he does on an apparently dying sergeant, who breathes the fumes of a mysterious liquid before drinking a cup of water in which "a small silken bag" of unrevealed contents has been steeped for five minutes. The virtue of "this most holy elixir" is, of course, so miraculous that the physician may then administer a similar draft to the King, followed by an infusion of "the small red purse." As the Hakim later explains to his royal patient, his talisman, "composed under certain aspects of the heavens, when the Divine Intelligences are most propitious," must be used by a self-controlled sage who has fasted and done penance.[38] It must cure twelve sick persons every month or its power will depart and the adept and his last patient will die within the year.

When Sir Kenneth defeats Conrade, Marquis of Montserrat, in judicial combat, Richard the Lion-Hearted persuades Saladin, whom the reader now recognises as El Hakim, to use the talisman on the traitorous knight. Hesitating between the rival claims of magic and romantic justice, Scott lets the stone benefit Conrade but sees to it that the Grand Master of the Templars wakes him from his charmed sleep to poniard him. In a final paragraph, Scott has Saladin send the talisman to Sir Kenneth, Prince Royal of Scotland, as a wedding present. And the prince in turn bequeaths it to Sir Simon of the Lee,[39] "in whose ancient and highly honoured family it is still preserved."

Although the importance of the Lee Penny to the action is slight, its presence is characteristic. While Scott is wandering in distant lands and centuries, touched with nostalgia for his native heath, he takes with him a Scottish hero, a belief or magical object and—like Antaeus when his feet touched mother earth—renews his strength through the contact. As in a fairy tale, the talisman, validated by the physician's purity and a favourable planetary hour, functions benignly and—its work done—vanishes with the other conjured figures, *locales*, and airy impedimenta of romance.

---

[38] Cp. William Lilly, *History of his Life and Times*, London 1822, p. 232: "Neatness and cleanliness in apparel, a strict diet, and upright life, fervent prayers unto God, conduce much to the assistance" of astrologers or their aids, the speculators. The Hakim speaks of the disadvantages of "indulgence of sensual appetite" in a sage, as also does [Lilly], *op. cit.*, pp. 222, 227. See Francis Grose, *A Provincial Glossary*, London 1811, p. 271; *Demonology*, p. 350.

[39] Scott's chronology at this point is off in the realm of faëry, where a century is but as a day. In Scott's own lifetime, Sir Simon's representative as custodian of the Lee Penny "was not altogether without some" faith in it. Lady Louisa Stuart's letter of 2 Jul. 1825, to Scott in W. Forbes Gray, "Friends of Sir Walter," *The Cornhill Magazine*, Third Series, LXXIII (1932), 263–4; Abbotsford Mss., N.L.S.

Whereas the action of talismans is usually positive, that of amulets and certain charms is negative, protective, and preventive.[40] Like many a Scotsman, David Ritchie, original of the Black Dwarf, was a great believer in the power of rowan tree. On 6 May 1818 Scott's folklore field man, Joseph Train, writes to him about a rowan twig bound in a cow's tail:

> Of the Cow's tail I can only say that the skin to which it belonged was brought from Scrobbermore in the Parish of Minnigaff about a month ago to one of the Tanyards in Newton-Stewart. What they call the Charm is rather different from any that I have seen before. The Rowan-tree I think appears to have been burnt at each end and by the small stubbles that still remain I am of opinion there has been some kind of herb rolled up in the red cloth. The circumstance of finding this Charm caused me to inquire if there was any reputed witch in the neighbourhood of Scrobbermore I soon found that a thousand anecdotes could be easily gathered to prove the wife of the Rowan tree Toll [?] (which is nearly adjoining Scrobbermore) to be a witch of the most malignant description which in some measure accounts for the precaution used by the gude wife of Scrobbermore although it did not preserve the life of her cow.[41]

Highland cattle, being very susceptible to spells, are protected by St Mungo's knot. The power of the guardian saint, with the knotting of the hair at the end of the tails, is too much for the crooked skill even of a witch. Thus, in *The Two Drovers*, Robin Oig shields his cattle from witches' cantrips; he has no such counter-agent against his own ticklish sense of Highland honour. Although witches are more feared than wizards, in *Kenilworth* Gammer Sludge guards her Flibbertigibbet against Wayland Smith with witch's elm.

Torquil is convinced in *The Fair Maid of Perth* that the weak spirit of his foster son, the cowardly Conachar, is due to magic and the evil eye. The hour that Conachar was born a bat put out the torch, and the infant was fed doe's milk. On the sacred isle of Iona, Saint Columba will remove his white doe's heart; the stolen human heart will return to his breast. Meanwhile, Torquil will see that Conachar's sword is steeped in holy

---

[40] Scott uses amulet and talisman interchangeably. But see E. W. Smith and A. M. Dale, *The Ila-speaking Peoples of Northern Rhodesia*, London 1920, I. 250: "Talismans are used to bring good luck or to transmit qualities, while amulets are preventive in their action." Also *Funk & Wagnalls Dictionary of Folklore*, *s.v.* amulet and talisman.

[41] Train Ms., N.L.S., folio 70v. For "an occult mixture of rowan-tree twigs with scraps of red cloth bound with texts of Scripture in a cow's hide" which was presented to Scott by the excise officer in the early part of 1815, see John Patterson, *Memoir of Joseph Train*, Glasgow 1857, p. 43. Mrs Grant of Laggan seems to have made a similar gift to Scott's collection. Magical protection of cattle is discussed in Dalyell, *Darker Superstitions of Scotland*, pp. 5, 9; Thomas Davidson, *Rowan Tree and Red Thread*, pp. 59, 77–8.

water and that vervain, rowan tree, and St John's wort are placed in his crest for clan battle. And when Conachar has a temporary accession of courage, Torquil rejoices that "the foul spell" and "the tardy spirit" are vanquished.

Conachar points to Henry Smith, his rival for the love of Catharine, as —figuratively—"the fell enchanter." Horrified that his fosterling has engaged in battle with "accursed mail" from the armourer's hands,[42] Torquil encourages him to "resist the witchcraft." Desperately he tries to loosen the grip of "the foul wizard" by unclasping Conachar's coat of mail. When Torquil is slain by Smith before Conachar can put on a dead foster-brother's war-gear, the old Highlander's clumsy shift ironically helps to motivate the young chief's flight. Charms and counter-charms, as well as second-sighted visions, so intensify the impact of temperament on action that the blazoning of character in crisis seems like a supernatural revelation.

Besides raising an illusory barricade between men and inimical beings, witchcraft, disease, spells, and inconstancy, magic confers command over weather. The whipping up of storms to wreck ships and drown men is not a specialty of Scott's sibyls.[43] Instead, they tame storms and bid favourable winds to blow for smugglers and other clients. When Captain Dirk Hatteraick is introduced in *Guy Mannering*, impatient at his crew's being delayed half an hour, he exclaims to Meg Merrilies, "Come, bless the good ship and the voyage, and be cursed to ye for a hag of Satan!" The technique of the gypsy is vaguely described as "reciting or singing, and gesticulating with great vehemence." After Meg has helped release the soul of a dead seaman, a live sailor comments on the squally weather which it will encounter, and another says, "Now old Meg may pray for his last fair wind, as she's often done before."

Weather-control is after all a side-line with Meg, but a chief stock-in-trade of Norna of Fitful Head. When Norna comes at night to reveal her past history to the frightened Troil sisters, she tells how, to the accompaniment of storm effects at the Dwarfie Stone, she evoked "the unshapely and indistinct form of Trolld the dwarf." Her desire was "the power of the Voluspae and divining women of our ancient race; to wield, like them, command over the elements; and to summon the ghosts of deceased heroes from their caverns,[44] that they might recite their daring deeds, and

---

[42] A realist, Smith holds that "spells may be broken by true men" and that strength of arm is sufficient against charmed armour.

[43] For the attempt of Satan and the North Berwick witches to strand or to overwhelm the vessel of James VI of Scotland, see *Newes from Scotland*, London 1591; *Demonology*, pp. 309–15; Charles Mackay, *Extraordinary Popular Delusions*, New York 1960, pp. 494–501 (a reprint of 2nd edn, 1852).

[44] Cp. P. H. Mallet, *Northern Antiquities*, London 1770, I. 147: "Others dragged the ghosts of the departed from their tombs, and forced the dead to tell them what would happen."

impart to me their hidden treasures."[45] In veiled words, the dwarf intimated that the aspirant was the first woman in a thousand years to acknowledge his sway. For this and for her courage, after she had deprived her father of life, he would reward her with "power . . . o'er tempest and wave." (Spectral heroes and treasures were out of the question.) Then, much like his European cousins, the stunted demon disappeared "in a thick and sulphureous vapour." Later, Norna guiltily feels that she has become "Sovereign of the Seas and Winds" by causing her father's death.

Long before the reader is startled by this case history, Norna demonstrates her gift by subduing a storm with a chanted incantation. But we need hardly follow her meteoric career to be convinced of her obsession. In a lonely, remorse-ridden, passionate nature, weather supremacy becomes an expression of megalomania.[46] Divested of some of its trumpery aspects, the characterisation of Norna is impressive. At times masterfully presented, she appears too often as "Queen of the Elements" speaking with "the voice of the Reim-kennar."

Power, learning, or skill surpassing that of less ruthless or accomplished men readily draw on a unique character the imputation of magic. In the first chapter of *Waverley*, Scott humorously reviews the different types of fiction promised by Radcliffian, German, sentimental, and modern sub-titles. If he calls his story *"Waverley: a Romance from the German,"* readers may expect "a profligate abbot, an oppressive duke, a secret and mysterious association of Rosicrucians and Illuminati, with all their properties of black cowls, caverns, daggers, electrical machines, trap-doors, and dark-lanterns." Little did Scott realise at the time (professedly November 1, 1805) that he would return in weary seriousness to his own satirical recipe. *Anne of Geierstein* has its profligate Black Priest of St Paul's, its oppressive Duke of Burgundy, its Rosicrucian tenets, and its "Initiated, answering to the modern phrase of Illuminati," with the accompaniment of a subterranean vault, trap-door, and descending bed, black-cowled men, symbolic sword and rope, daggers, black torches, solemn ritual and set phrases. The examination of John Philipson by the Secret Tribunal has no plot function and is introduced merely for the horror factor of the ceremonial

---

[45] Here Norna may be confusing sorceresses with kemps, or champions, who wrested weapons and treasures from the ghost- and fiend-protected tombs of the dead. See *Demonology*, p. 103.

[46] The sibyl's former lover, himself considered "uncanny," sarcastically refers to "the mistress of the potent spell" as changing the wind by a twitch of her cap and getting rich by the sale of winds to the port-bound. By these words he reduces Norna to the pathetic level of her original, Bessie Millie. (See n. iii, "Sale of Winds," in *The Pirate*.)

underground proceedings conducted by Anne's father, Count Albert.[47]

The Count is one of Sir Walter's violent characters whose lack of self-command is evident in his vengefulness toward opponents, his diabolical autocracy and love of subterranean conspiracy. Whether he is at the moment the Black Priest of St Paul's or a Carmelite monk, he fancies himself defended by a spell. Although Count Albert is a judge of the Secret Tribunal, Annette Veilchen is bold enough to describe her mistress's father as one who has gone to the witches' Sabbath or, at least, "on a hunting-party with the Wild Huntsman." In her eyes the nobleman is a wizard and his agent, Ital Schreckenwald, an incarnate devil. Albert's nephew, Sigismund, more than half suspects him of using conjuring books to command supernatural speed[48] and helpers and, having "gambled away his soul," of being subject to seizure by the Devil after death. Duke Charles of Burgundy loads the absent Count with such epithets as wearer of the "conjurer's cap" and "accomplice of sorcerers." Fear of approaching death somewhat slackens the stern fibre of Count Albert, who foresees happiness and fame for his daughter and Arthur Philipson. Throughout, the imputation of magic is less a tribute to Albert's knowledge than an expression of fear of his turbulent, vindictive nature.[49]

The grandfather of Anne of Geierstein is variously suspected of being an alchemist, a sorcerer, and a companion of supernatural beings. According to Anne and her cousin, Rudolph Donnerhugel, Count Herman's laboratory research, his study of astrology and mystic lore, his power as a judge of the Secret Tribunal made him inscrutable to the common mind, which superstitiously aspersed his learning. When envious and jealous, Donnerhugel is less objective. When Arthur Philipson strikes a pole, severs a string, and kills a bird with three arrows from the mighty bow of

[47] Scott's translation (1799) of Goethe, *Goetz von Berlichingen* includes a scene in the Secret Tribunal (v. xi) and a Preface referring to "excellent romances" which have made the Tribunal known to the English: C. B. E. Naubert, *Herman of Unna*, tr. anon., London 1794, 1796) and his *Alf von Deulmen*, tr. A. E. Booth, London 1790, 1794. In *Herman of Unna*, comments *The Monthly Review*, New Series, xv (1794), 21, "the perpetual recurrence of its [the tribunal's] incomprehensible interference has all the *marvellousness*, without the *incredibility*, of supernatural agency." See also James Boaden's adaptation, *The Secret Tribunal*, London 1795, Act II, in which Ida—like Anne of Geierstein—visits the hero in a castle dungeon; James Skene, "A Subterraneous Structure in Swabia . . . connected with . . . the Secret Tribunal" (dated 1824), *Archaeologia Scotica*, III (1831), 17–39; Carl Bröker, *Scotts "Anne of Geierstein*," Kiel 1927, pp. 73–82.

[48] Cp. Robert Chambers, *Traditions of Edinburgh*, I. 281. William Duke of Queensberry (d. 1695) was believed by the Covenanters to have the art of transporting anywhere by mere volition.

[49] In *Rob Roy*, the dread of Rashleigh Osbaldistone's magical power is the response of "ignorance and bigotry" to his scientific, historic, and linguistic acquirements and to his volcanic and evil passions. And in *Ivanhoe* the illiterate De Bracy considers the Saxon letter of defiance to Front-de-Boeuf and his allies as "magic spells for aught I know."

Buttisholz, he ascribes the triumph to chance, illusion, magic, or witchery.[50]

Magic, too, is associated with the close of life's hazards. When Meg Merrilies tends a dying ruffian, she has an appropriate rhymed spell, partly Catholic in tone, which helps the soul struggle free from the body. But, the words not being prepotent, she turns to the magico-symbolic action of drawing bolt, lifting latch, and opening door to afford suggestive passage to the spirit. At death she sets lighted candles at head and feet and places a trencher of salt[51] on the breast of the corpse. Through opening the door rather than setting it ajar, Meg adds to the excitement of Harry Bertram's entrance. The folk belief is that an open door may let the soul out and some frightful being in.

In sympathetic magic, as distinguished by Sir James Frazer, Meg's manipulation of bolt, latch, and door would be *homeopathic*, like producing like. And the testimony of blood against a murderer would to some extent be *contagious* magic, the part being identical with the whole.[52] Scott's interest in the magical justice of the bier-right, evident as early as 1797, finds full expression in *The Fair Maid of Perth* in 1828. After the slaying of Oliver Proudfute, the authorities of Perth order that the body be laid out in the Church of St John, that masses be said for the revelation of the murderer, and that each suspect member of Ramorny's household pass before the bier and call on God to witness his innocence. As Sir Louis Lundin explains the ordeal, making the corpse the prime detector rather than the blood, "The antipathy which subsists between the dead body and the hand which dealt the fatal blow . . . will awaken some imperfect life," and blood will flow from the wounds. The women who prepare the body for the ceremony chant verses which translate Lundin's medieval science into terms of the "mystic force" by which the "viewless Essence," aroused by "strange sympathies," will send forth avenging blood.[53]

[50] In *Ivanhoe*, superlative archery is credited to diabolical agency. Cp. Chambers, *Traditions of Edinburgh*, I. 224 n: William Sinclair (d. 1778), an expert with bow and golf club, was believed to have *the black art*.

[51] Salt was considered a symbol of eternity. See McNeill, *The Silver Bough*, I. 60.

[52] Frazer, *The Golden Bough: A Study in Magic and Religion*, abridged edn, New York 1958, pp. 12 ff., 267 ("the belief that the soul is in the blood"), and 283 (locks and doors at time of death).

[53] The belief in cruentation flickers up in Scott, *The Two Drovers*, in which the drinkers at Haskett's Inn, sobered by the fatal dirking of Harry Wakefield, expect the wound to "send forth fresh streams" when Robin Oig looks on his victim; and again in his tragedy, *Auchindrane*, III. iii, in which Quentin's corpse bleeds when touched by the six-year-old daughter of his murderer. Cp. Lady Dunce's warning to Sir Davy in Otway, *The Soldier's Fortune* (1681), Act IV: "Oh come not near him, there's such horrid Antipathy follows all murders, his wounds would stream afresh should you but touch him." Also see Taillepied, *Treatise of Ghosts*, pp. 86–7; Dalyell, *Darker Superstitions of Scotland*, pp. 36–42, 179–80; James Fraser, *Chronicles of the Frasers*, ed. William Mackay, Edinburgh 1905, p. 517.

When Henbane Dwining, an accessory to the murder, reluctantly enters the house of the bonnet-maker to bleed his sick orphan, the ignorantly grateful mother thrusts her husband's chaplet into the apotheca ry-surgeon's hands. Although Dwining usually rises above all superstition, he returns "the ill-omened gift" with the impatient excuse, "I know no legerdemain—can do no conjuring tricks." One of the gossips at work on Proudfute's mortal part observes "a large gout of blood." Whether it is blood or liquid balm is then disputed.

The actual ceremony of the bier-right is solemnly performed. Ramorny's page fears that his knowledge of the assassin will implicate himself, but no blood flows. Others pass through the trial unimpeached by the corpse. While awaiting his turn, Bonthron suffers horribly and then refuses to confront Proudfute. "What do I know what juggling tricks may be practised to take a poor man's life?" Instead he faces Henry Smith in trial by combat, is defeated, sentenced to be hanged, and miraculously rescued through a contrivance of Dwining's. Thus Scott avoids the alternatives of making the corpse bleed or allowing the murderer to undergo the bier-right like a guiltless man. The solution is at least more convincing than Bois-Guilbert's death of guilty internal tension before he actually meets Ivanhoe's lance.[54]

*   *   *

Whereas religion is lawful entreaty and submission to powers of good, magic is unlawful invocation of and control over powers of good or evil. Magic may be black or white, negative or positive, antipathetic or sympathetic. Within these generous limits, the magic in the Waverley Novels is connected with persons, acts, and objects—with conjurers, spells, and talismans. It is involved in the search for security from storms and inimical agents; for skill, power, health, and justice; for knowledge of hidden things. It affects infants and dying men, as well as adults in crucial moments of love sickness, engagement, and desertion, at secret trials, sports rivalry, and bloody struggles. Some magicians engage in what is to them a true art; others are conscious tricksters, encouraging superstitious reports in order to protect their unsanctioned activities; and still others are men of learning or of unfathomable pursuits who are vulgarly suspect. When

[54] There is a slight use of magic in *The Fair Maid of Perth* for humorous contrast. When the riotous Duke of Rothsay visits Sir John Ramorny, he jokingly suggests a magical transfer of afflictions. Let someone drink wine for his handless henchman, and "he shall be cured vicariously." The elevation of Bacchus will be Ramorny's and the dreg-like after effects the actual drinker's. But the comic note declines into the pathetic as Ramorny continues to "look something ghastly."

Scott plays up the magician or the potent relic, he tends to be artificial, conventional, and literary. With charms, spells, and rites he achieves his greatest success in expressing the mystery and terror of incalculable forces and the pathos of man's safeguards and struggle against his destiny.

16. Curses, Omens, Dreams, and Prophecies

The past may be joined to the present by legends and beliefs, by ghosts and haunted places. The link between present and future may be some form of prediction. Scott was interested in the foreshadowing as well as in the supernatural and psychological conditioning of the future by curses, prophecies, dreams, and evil omens. He delighted, for instance, in frequently repeating the story of a witch who distressed James Hogg's maternal forebears, the Laidlaws, in the sixteenth century.

> In some evil hour, her husband, the head of his blood, reproached her with her addiction to the black art, and she, in her anger, cursed the name and lineage of Laidlaw. Her only son, who stood by, implored her to revoke the malediction; but in vain. Next day, however, on the renewal of his entreaties, she carried him with her into the woods, made him slay a heifer, sacrificed it to the power of evil in his presence, and then, collecting the ashes in her apron, invited the youth to see her commit them to the river. "Follow them," said she, "from stream to pool, as long as they float visible, and as many streams as you shall then have passed, for so many generations shall your descendants prosper. After that they shall like the rest of the name be poor, and take their part in my curse." The streams he counted, were nine.[1]

In telling the tale, Scott and his friend, William Laidlaw, pointed out that all the Laidlaws were landless men except Laird Nippy of the Peel, who—"think whatever we choose of it"—obligingly went bankrupt and removed the one flaw in a supernatural yarn which Scott always spun "with an air that seemed to me [Lockhart], in spite of his endeavours to the contrary . . . grave."

In his "Farewell to Mackenzie, High Chief of Kintail," Scott laments over one whose talents shone forth though "Fate deaden'd *his* ear and imprison'd *his* tongue." On 11 January 1815, death had come to Francis Humberston Mackenzie, Lord Seaforth, the last of his line. The event apparently tallied with a prophecy uttered about 1670. The story was that, while the third Earl of Seaforth was in Paris, his lonely Countess summoned Kenneth Odhar, the Brahan Seer, to question him about her lord.

[1] Lockhart, II. 187–8.

After putting his eye to the hole of a magic white stone, Kenneth admitted, with great reluctance, that he had seen the nobleman kneeling, and kissing a fair woman's hand. In shame and rage, Lady Seaforth ordered the seer to be executed. Kenneth's valediction was doom on the house of Mackenzie, whose last member would be deaf and dumb and would outlive his sons. As a sign, when four great contemporary lairds— Mackenzie of Gairloch, Chisholm of Chisholm, Grant of Grant, and MacLeod of Raasay—were buck-toothed, hare-lipped, half-witted, and speech-impeded, these disasters would be imminent.[2] The prediction began to be fulfilled when, at the age of twelve, Francis Mackenzie lost his hearing and was for a time deprived of speech by an attack of scarlet fever. And in time his four sons predeceased him.

The death of Lord Seaforth moved Sir Humphry Davy to reflect that seemingly unrelated events, fragments of a universal plan about which we know nothing, may actually be connected.

> If the popular and antiphilosophical view of omens, prophecies, and prodigies be correct, this is the only philosophical solution that can be given. The apparent ravings of Thomas the Rhymer [Sir Humphry's substitute for the local seer, Kenneth Odhar], respecting the Mackenzie family, have no natural connection with the remarkable event of which I am an historical witness; no more than the rattling of the wheels of a carriage at an inn door with the death of poultry, which, however, we know is the remote cause.[3]

In a more emotional vein, Scott writes J. B. S. Morritt on 19 January 1815: "You will have heard of poor Caberfaes [Mackenzie's] death— what a pity it is he should have outlived his promising young representative. . . . I do fear the accomplishment of the prophecy that when there should be a dumb [deaf] Caberfae the house was to fall." Two days later, he tells Morritt that "Caberfae's" hearse has just gone by: "There is something very melancholy in seeing the body pass, poorly attended and in the midst of a snow storm whitening all the sable ornaments of the undertaker and all corresponding with the decadence and misfortune of the family." And on the same day he writes Elizabeth, Marchioness of Stafford, in a somewhat sceptical mood which is the rational aftermath of his uninhibited first impressions: "All the Highlands ring with a prophecy that when there should be a deaf Caberfae the clan and chief shall all go to

---

[2] Sir John Burke, *Vicissitudes of Families*, London 1869, I. 169–84; Alexander Mackenzie, *The Prophecies of the Brahan Seer*, Stirling 1899, pp. 71–6.

[3] John Davy, *Memoirs of the Life of Sir Humphry Davy, Bart.*, London 1836, II. 72. Lockhart gives the reference but not the quotation.

wreck, but these predictions are very apt to be framed after the event."[4] Morritt himself "heard the prophecy quoted in the Highlands at a time when Lord Seaforth had two sons both alive and in good health—so that it certainly was not made *après coup*." Both Sir Humphry and Sir Walter regarded the prophecy as having been wonderfully fulfilled.[5]

The Mackenzies and the Laidlaws were the victims of vengeful prophecies, which are both causative and prescient. Omens prefigure but do not generate good or ill. On being told of the Welsh *Mort Bird*, Scott readily instances the Scottish "warning bird":

> And the Raven had flapped at her window-board,
> To tell of her Warrior's doom.[6]

When Scott parted from his Selkirkshire friend, Mungo Park, in September 1804, the explorer's "horse stumbled & nearly fell. As he recoverd him I said 'thats a bad omen Mungo' to which he answerd laughing '*freits* follow those that look to them.' "[7] After all, Park was the seventh child in a family of thirteen. He returned to the Niger in 1805 and was drowned in the Bussa rapids early the following year. In 1827, postponements of the Duke of Buccleuch's coming-of-age dinner because of an accident and a death made Scott exclaim, "I am not superstitious, but . . . God avert bad omens!"[8]

Toward taboos which, when neglected, may be ominous, as toward omens, Scott's attitude varies from playful to serious. On 26 August 1814, Scott occasioned no little consternation among the sailors of the lighthouse yacht on which he was cruising the Scottish islands. He had broken a taboo of the sea by carrying on board ship a human skull from a cave on the Isle of Eigg. Later, when the weather turned bad, Captain Wilson found the cause to be the landsman's rash plunder.[9]

---

[4] *Letters*, IV. 14, 19, 22. A staghead, *caberfae*, is the bearing of the Mackenzie family.

[5] Lockhart, III. 319 n. Less portentous is the episode of Scott's ten year old niece Eliza's "threatening to prophesy evil" of American Indian women. She hit the mark on occasions, but Mrs Tom Scott "put a stop to her predictions." *Letters*, VIII. 263.

[6] John Morrison, "Random Reminiscences of Sir Walter Scott," p. 575 ("The Lady of Ellerslee").

[7] *Freits*, omens. 24 Apr. 1815 in *Letters*, IV. 54, to [John Wishaw], editor of Park, *Journal of a Mission to the Interior of Africa in the Year 1805*, 2nd edn, London 1815; "Addenda," pp. iv, vii–ix; Lockhart, II. 13–14; Stephen Gwynn, *Mungo Park*, London 1934, p. 156.

[8] 22–3 Nov. 1827 in *Journal*, p. 435.

[9] Lockhart, III. 240, 276. The captain had kept an eye on his own men to prevent any removal of bone relics to the yacht. R. L. Stevenson, "Scott's Voyage in the Lighthouse Yacht," *Scribner's Magazine*, XIV (1893), 499. Dead bodies and mummies aboard ship are also unlucky. John Aubrey, *Remaines of Gentilisme and Judaisme*, ed. James Britten, London 1881, p. 67. Scott's " 'awsome fancy for an auld girning skull' " puzzled and frightened his "superstitious housemaids." Irving, *Abbotsford*. p. 46; Lockhart, I. 236.

When he is serious about taboos, Scott places himself on the safe side by accepting usage which has venerable human sanction. Lockhart tells of the novelist's hurried departure from London after receiving the honour of a baronetcy in 1820, "for he had such respect for the ancient prejudice (a classical as well as a Scottish one) against marrying in May, that he was anxious to have the ceremony in which his daughter was concerned over before that unlucky month should commence."[10] Thus, like the less sophisticated couple in John Galt's *Annals of the Parish* (1821), Sophia Scott and John Gibson Lockhart were married on 29 April:

> Miss Lizy [Kibbock] and me were married on the 29th day of April, with some inconvenience to both sides, on account of the dread that we had of being married in May; for it is said—
> > 'Of the marriages in May,
> > The bairns die of a decay.'[11]

Poor John Hugh Lockhart, first offspring of the Great Unknown's daughter and his future biographer, did not escape the fate of children of May marriages. He *died of a decay* at the age of ten, having come within the baleful orbit, as it were, of that month which the Romans considered sacred to the dead.[12]

Somewhat in Roman fashion, Scott resorted to augury when worried by finances. On 3 April 1826, he planted two or three fatidic acorns in order to "judge by their success in growing whether I will succeed in clearing my way or not."[13] Where reason fails to give assurance, the imagination may find a way. Later in this troubled year, Scott's dead wife twice appeared to him in dreams. Earlier in his life, the *eidolon* of his

[10] Lockhart, IV. 366–7. On 28 Mar. Scott writes his wife that the wedding can be arranged for 28, 29, or 30 Apr. and he mentions to Archibald Constable "that ceremony which cannot with good luck be performed in May." *Letters*, VI. 156, 159. Cp. *Demonology*, pp. 95–6.

[11] *Op. cit.*, ch. 6. Cp. Joseph Train, *Strains of the Mountain Muse*, Edinburgh 1814, p. 9: "In the metropolis of Ayrshire, young persons are unwilling to be married in the month of May, lest such an untimely connection should be chastised by the production of an idiot."

[12] In May prowling ghosts were to be feared. *The Fasti of Ovid*, tr. Sir James Frazer, London 1929, IV. 52–7. On 10 Oct. 1820, Lady Abercorn sends Scott from Lausanne an explanation found in "an account of the pays de Vaud": "What amused me most was the marriages in May and I shall transcribe what it says—'Un Mariage ne serait pas présumé heureux s'il etait béni dans le mois de Mai, parceque ce mois est reputé de mauvais augure. Ce préjugé existait dejà longtems avant Jesus Christ: il vient d'une loi des anciens romains, par laquelle les femmes publiques ne pouvaient se marier que dans le mois de Mai. Les femmes honnêtes évitaient soigneusement ce mois là, crainte de passer pour privilégiées.' I was glad to find out the cause of this superstition." Walpole. Also see *Journal*, p. 771 (Malta, 22 Nov. 1831).

[13] *Journal*, p. 147. "A symbol of endurance, strength, and triumph," the oak and its leaves were considered prophetic by the Greeks and the ancient Aryans. *Funk & Wagnalls Dictionary of Folklore, s.v.* oak. In the thirteenth book of *Dichtung und Wahrheit*, Goethe tells of knife augury to discover whether he would become an artist.

disdainful sweetheart had been solicitous. "On the eve of unlucky events Williamina is said to have appeared to him in his sleep."[14]

One of Scott's last utterances on superstitious observances, however, is in a very different vein. Edward Cheney records in his Journal for 10 May 1832, that, wishing to keep Sir Walter in Rome, he reminded him that Friday was a most unlucky day for departure. "He answered, laughing, 'Superstition is very picturesque, and I make it at times stand me in great stead; but I never allow it to interfere with interest or convenience.' "[15] Here Scott makes the mistake of assuming that an attitude functional to a time when infirmity and loss of money and friends had taken the glamour out of life was characteristic of his entire life.

★   ★   ★

Prophecy in the Waverley Novels usually conveys the impression of fated events and the impotence of human will. Although the significant action, condition, or coincidence is often accompanied by disaster, it may bring happiness. Whatever the outcome, through its very nature as advance notice of crisis, prophecy contributes to narrative suspense.

Prophecy is a basic part of one of the three plots of *The Fair Maid of Perth*. The novel ends in happy union for the Lowland lovers, punishment for the Scottish Prince's murderers, clan defeat and suicide for the chief Highland character—in Lowland comedy, judicial melodrama, and Highland tragedy. Although these plots are interrelated, they are for the most part self-sustaining. Thus the Highland plot can be said to trace a prophecy, the attempts to avoid its fulfilment, and the blind rush of events—with ironic human assistance—to the appointed end. During a period of defeat for the Clan Quhele, chieftain Gilchrist MacIan's wife gives birth to a son who is nursed on doe's milk in the forest. Because of "an ancient prophecy ... that the power of the tribe should fall by means of a boy born under a bush of holly, and suckled by a white doe," the infant, on the restoration of the clan's prestige, is sent to Perth under the name of Conachar (Hector MacIan) to be secretly reared by Simon Glover.

Some eighteen years later, Conachar's foster-father, Torquil of the Oak, nullifies this safety measure. Being "Taishatar, or a Seer ... supposed to have communication with the invisible world," Torquil produces forced

---

[14] Edwin Muir, "Walter Scott," in *From Anne to Victoria*, ed. Bonamy Dobrée, New York 1937, p. 533. Also see my chapter on the Warning Spirit.
[15] Lockhart, VII. 378.

fire, "*Tine-egan*,"[16] evokes a fiend, and learns that Conachar will be the only combatant in the clan battle at Perth to emerge unwounded. Interpreting this to mean victory, Torquil threatens to withdraw with his eight sturdy sons from the list of thirty Clan Quhele champions unless Conachar is recalled from banishment to join the warriors. When they must choose between two superstitions, time-steeped "ominous presage" and "Tine-egan," the clansmen incline to the newer mode. In the end both the prophecy and the Fiend's words are true. Deception comes from human misinterpretation. As in *The Talisman*, where the stars prove reliable and the hermit gazer is fallible, Scott is satisfied to let the original prophecy stand and to embarrass the human seer. This compromise is highly effective, offending neither the sceptical nor the credulous.

The content of prophecy may be withheld in order to titillate interest. When the Philipsons become the guests of Arnold Biederman in *Anne of Geierstein*, their host refers vaguely to a prophecy about the bow of Buttisholz, which the hero not only bends but handles with surprising skill. Although the information is never vouchsafed, the prediction obviously has to do with success in love, and Arthur's marriage to Anne confirms the foresight of an anonymous seer.

Perhaps, Scott has most fondness for the prophets who allow him to relax with a jingle. In *The Antiquary*, while exhausting his estate, Sir Arthur Wardour futilely remembers "an old prophecy in our family":

> If Malcolm the Misticot's grave were fun',
> The lands of Knockwinnock are lost and won.

Sir Arthur does his best to get house, land, and fortune *lost*, and Edie Ochiltree, alternating as licensed beggar and *deus ex machina*, is fortunately more handy in seeing them *won* again. Old sayings and prophecies in *The Bride of Lammermoor* are like voices plaintively trying to penetrate consciousness. That "female Tiresias,"[17] Blind Alice, says, "If my mortal sight is closed to objects present with me, it may be I can look with more steadiness into future events." Despite this compensation, the truth she speaks is unheeded. Too impatient for consistency, the Master of Ravenswood calls her "more superstitious" and less fearful of "old superstitious saws" than Caleb Balderstone, who repeats the words of True Thomas:

[16] See *A Gaelic Dictionary*, Herne Bay 1902, III. 943, for use of *teinéigin* as an antidote against cattle diseases, bewitching, and the evil eye. *Fire of necessity*, or *neidfyre*, was a magical flame kindled by the friction of wood in a house in which all other fires had been extinguished. Two men officiated. It was not a method of conjuration.

[17] Robert C. Gordon, "*The Bride of Lammermoor*: A Novel of Tory Pessimism," *Nineteenth-Century Fiction*, XII (1957), 119–20.

When the last Laird of Ravenswood to Ravenswood shall ride,
And woo a dead maiden to be his bride,
He shall stable his steed in the Kelpie's flow,
And his name shall be lost for evermoe!

Thomas the Rhymer's reputation as a prophet is too great for his words to be contradicted, so that he is not compelled, like the fickle Vanda of *The Betrothed*, to modify or expand his verse in the light of events. But in Scott's last novel, *Castle Dangerous*, Thomas the Rhymer's initial prophetic stress on re-edification of the castle is changed to military retaliation. A story is told of the minstrel's appearing as a long, lean, wild, and hairy phantom, attended by hart and hind,[18] to announce "the doom of Heaven, that as often as the walls of Douglas Castle shall be burnt to the ground, they shall be again rebuilt still more stately and more magnificent than before." Interest is then spread thin over the prophet, his prediction, and his manuscript lays. Bertram the minstrel tells how Hugo Hugonet found the lay of *Sir Tristrem*,[19] only to see it removed as if by an invisible hand. This starts an exhibition of book jugglery reminiscent of the restless Bible in *The Monastery*. In this region of fairy tale quest and magic, Hugonet is not "destined" to remove the book and dauntless Bertram is.

After reciting some of True Thomas's mystifying verses, replete with animal imagery and vague prediction, Bertram imaginatively interprets them. Then Greenleaf, a curiously rationalistic archer, offers counter-explanations. But the debunking process, whimsical, satirical, and anachronistic at the same time, hardly compensates for a huddled climax which prophecy has inadequately foreshadowed.[20] Thomas and his literary remains have lured the author down the paths of antiquarian digression.

Usually, Scott's prophets are heard from the grave; his soothsayers, palmists, and oracles are contemporary to action. In *The Abbot*, Mary Queen of Scots is despondent on the eve of her escape from Loch Leven because "it was foretold me by a soothsayer in France, that I should die in prison, and by a violent death." The accomplished facts of history and those not yet accomplished in fiction menace her.

[18] By their appearance in Ercildoune, these gentle animals had warned Thomas that he must quit this world for the land of faëry. *Minstrelsy*, IV. 83; *Demonology*, p. 136.
[19] In his edition of the lay, Scott attributes it to Thomas of Ercildoune. *Sir Tristrem*, 3rd edn, Edinburgh 1811, p. xlviii; Lockhart, I. 413,416. It would follow from this captivating theory that the first classical English romance was written in Scotland. Although George P. McNeill, editor of *Sir Tristrem* for the S.T.S. in 1886, also argues for the *Rhymer's* authorship, the majority of scholars have doubted this or have at most allowed Thomas the credit of a translation.
[20] Scott also fails to catch up dangling plot threads in the search of archer and minstrel for "the dingle bearing the ominous name of Bloody Sykes." While tracking down portentous place-names, they are baffled and interrupted, and nothing comes of the matter.

Although they contribute to gypsy atmosphere, the soothsaying references in *Quentin Durward* do not blend into the action as easily as do the astrological efforts of Martius Galeotti. Burgundy's envoy, Count de Crèvecoeur, retorts to Louis XI, "The noble Duke uses not to enquire of witches, wandering Egyptians, or others, upon the destiny and fate of his neighbours and allies." But the superstitious monarch, on Oliver the Devil's advice, has consulted a treacherous Bohemian, Zamet Maugrabin. Louis believes in the powers of the heathen descendants of the star-gazing Chaldeans; yet he overreaches himself in testing the gypsy's skill and in letting out secrets which are valuable to the Duke of Burgundy. Zamet's powerlessness to foresee his own execution is typical of soothsayers, whose understanding is darkened when self-applied.

When Zamet's brother Hayraddin is his party's guide, Quentin suspects him of planning betrayal. In a scene of ironical banter and cross-purposes, the hero asks the gypsy to read his palm.[21] In keeping with a literary convention of card and chess games, palmistry allows characters to act and speak on two planes of possible meaning. In addition, Hayraddin's routine prediction of a "large fortune by marriage . . . and . . . successful love" is truer to the mark than second-sighted Saunders Souplejaw's referring the same prophecy to Quentin's freedom-loving uncle.

Varying his explanation with the company he keeps, Hayraddin comments on foreknowledge. When Quentin puts sceptical questions about the pretended insight of his race, the Zingaro describes the gift as instinctive. To lanzknecht Heinrick's objection about his not foreseeing his brother's hanging, he cynically replies that, had he known that Zamet would betray Louis to the Duke of Burgundy, he could have foretold the execution. He also rebuts the Countess Hameline's accusation of lying about the stars and her success with Quentin. "And so they *had* decreed your union, had both parties been willing—but think you the blessed constellations can make any one wed against his will?" Admittedly, all Hayraddin's craft is based on human and fallible guesses.

Thus, through Hayraddin's frankness with mentally sluggish characters like the German mercenary and the foolish Countess, Galeotti's revelation

[21] Scott's distinction at this point that palmistry was as much a matter of faith in the fifteenth century as phrenology in the nineteenth is too clear-cut. For modern chiromancy, or *hand-divination*, see J. S. Forsyth, *Demonologia*, London 1831, p. 147, and Jane Anne Cranstoun's letter to [Scott] of 18 Apr. 1796: "Far be it from me to affirm that there are no diviners in the land. The voice of the people and the voice of God are loud in their testimony. Two years ago, when I was in the neighbourhood of Montrose, we had recourse for amusement one evening to chiromancy . . . either my letters must have been inspected, or the devil was by in his own proper person. . . . Now that you are on the spot . . . you are not standing on holy ground." Lockhart, I. 240; Walpole.

in soliloquy, and Souplejaw's humorously obvious or inaccurate pro-
nouncements, Scott deflates all gypsy, astrological, and second-sighted
pretensions to knowledge of the future. Credibility aside, the novelist
finds the superstitions intrinsically interesting and useful.

Divination is an equally hoary practice. A sheep's blade-bone is consulted in *Waverley* (scapulomancy) and "mutton-banes" help Aily Mac-
Clure spae fortunes in *The Heart of Midlothian*. In *Anne of Geierstein* the
self-consciously tragic queen admits to Arthur Philipson that she has
spent six hours on the brink of the caverned and abysmal Lou Garagoule,
performing strange heathen-Christian rites in order to wrest future
knowledge from subterranean spirits, from the oracles of Roman days.
"Misfortunes have rendered her superstitious." But "the demons of
Garagoule" are silent about Lancastrian Margaret's chances of returning
to the English throne. Before her death, the Queen does Christian penance
for having tried to consult pagan oracles. Lacking plot-significance, the
episode still contributes to the reader's understanding of Margaret, and of
the author's absorption in the survival of ancient ceremonies.

Unlike these non-malicious methods of learning what is to happen,
curses are malicious attempts to control the future. Scott ventures nothing
as lurid or single-minded as John Paslew's curse in Ainsworth's *The
Lancashire Witches* (1848): his enemy's descendants shall be "a brood of
adders, that the world shall flee from and crush." Eighty years later,
Lancashire suffers from nests of witches whose careers of hellish pacts,
attendant familiars, aerial rides, and Sabbaths end in death. John Mure, in
Scott's play, *Auchindrane*, impotently longs for the power to wither with
vengeful words:

> 'Tis vain to wish for it—Each curse of mine
> Falls to the ground as harmless as the arrows
> Which children shoot at stars! (II, i)

In the Waverley Novels, curses stamp an ominous pattern of action on
men's minds and throw as much light on the utterer as on events. Meg
Merrilies' "keen-edged malediction" (discussed in the chapter on sibyls)
is a revelation of the gypsy and a rhetorical projection of the Laird of
Ellangowan's feckless way of life as well as a curse. In *The Highland Widow*,
failing to turn her son into a mountain freebooter like his father, witchlike
Elspat exclaims, "Stay! or may the gun you carry be the means of your
ruin—may the road you are going be the track of your funeral!" Then, to
protect Hamish, the uncontrollably violent mother directs her evil words
against herself. Ironically, it is Elspat who implements her curse by

drugging the youth so that he will not rejoin his Lowland regiment. Raising his gun against the search-party, Hamish, the involuntary deserter, must in turn face a firing-squad. When Elspat learns of her son's death from the minister, she launches a malison against his eyes, ears, and tongue. May the Evil One speak in his prayers, may his congregation turn against him, may heaven's thunder still his voice for ever! The Biblical vehemence and completeness of this curse call for no fulfilment. The supernatural overtones of the earlier curse heighten the effect of fatally wilful human passions.

A sense of the future may be conscious in those who have presentiments or a feeling of personal fatality and unconscious in those who are *fey*. External phenomena have less influence at the moment of presentiment than the individual's own fears and convictions, which foreshadow events. Philipson's apprehension in *Anne of Geierstein* is far from idle. As night—"dark as a wolf's throat"—is yielding to dawn, the Swiss and the traitorous Italians sweep irresistibly through the Burgundian camp. A discussion of premonitions in *Count Robert of Paris* introduces no individual experience but a general state of distrust, alarm, and conspiracy in Constantinople. Just as birds and beasts have an "ominous sense of a coming tempest," so may uncultivated human nature undergo "prescient foreboding."[22] Education leads us to "disregard those natural feelings, which were originally designed as sentinels by which nature warned us of impending danger. Something of the kind, however, still remains, and that species of feeling which announces to us sorrowful or alarming tidings, may be said, like the prophecies of the weird sisters, to come over us like a sudden cloud."[23] The whole episode is a rationalisation of Plutarch's and Shakespeare's prodigies in the street before a revolution in human affairs.

When a Byronic hero wanders into a Waverley novel, he usually makes it known that his presence is blighting. Robertson tells Jeanie Deans, "I ... have been the destruction of the mother that bore me—of the friend that loved me—of the woman that trusted me—of the innocent child that was born to me." The span is three generations. Such Byronism is demonic Calvinism: Robertson is "predestined to evil here and hereafter." Scott's Byronic women are more pathetic, therefore less melodramatic, in their confessions. Both dethroned Mary in *The Abbot* and

[22] Also *Castle Dangerous*, ch. xix. Scott's willingness to believe in *prescient foreboding* is fairly evident.
[23] *Macbeth*, III. iv, 110–12, one of Scott's favourite quotations:

Can such things be,
And overcome us like a summer's cloud,
Without our special wonder?

exiled Margaret of Anjou in *Anne of Geierstein* pathetically feel that "all must perish" who love them or are loved by them. Each has "an ill-omened hand."

Other persons may show signs of being doomed without recognising their fate or being concerned about their impingement on the lives of friends. Before the defeat and death of Charles of Burgundy, John Philipson notices that the "once fiery Duke" has become more like "a shrouded phantom." An unusual gentleness reminds the Englishman that his superstitious nurse, Martha Nixon, "a northern woman," used to say "that any sudden and causeless change of a man's nature . . . indicates an immediate change of his fortunes . . . for evil most likely . . . is impending over him whose disposition is so much altered." The same novelist who insensibly transforms the Shetland drow into a Scottish fairy (*The Pirate*), wishing to be accompanied in distant lands by familiar lore, gives his southron noble a northern nurse.

Philipson is, of course, harking back to the superstition of the fey person. Of Scott's several definitions of the word, perhaps the best is in *The Pirate*. When Basil Mertoun is headstrong, a comment is, "Fey folk run fast; and the thing that we are born to, we cannot win by [escape]." And on careful Baby Yellowley's becoming warmly hospitable, her brother thinks that the poor woman "must be *fey*," having but a short time to live. "When a person changes his condition suddenly, as when a miser becomes liberal . . . he is said, in Scotch, to be *fey*, that is, predestined to speedy death, of which such mutations of humour are received as a sure indication."

Before he is slain by smugglers, Frank Kennedy, the excise officer in *Guy Mannering*, acts "fie," exhibiting "those violent spirits" which "the common people . . . think a presage of death." He is rash enough to get into trouble. And before Captain Porteous is lynched in *The Heart of Midlothian*, he becomes diabolically agitated, his step falters, his eyes grow wild, and his speech is confused: "Many remarked he seemed to be *fey*." The belief is given an ironical turn in *The Fair Maid of Perth* when Simon Glover, hearing that Oliver Proudfute has been talking of death and burial all day, asks the blustering bonnet-maker whether he is fey. "No, not a whit—it is not my own death which these gloomy fancies foretell—I have a strong horoscope, and shall live for fifty years to come." After borrowing Henry Smith's coat-of-mail, Proudfute is mistaken for a better man and assassinated in the streets of Perth.

If the fey person, instead of being blind, consciously and courageously expects the imminent, there is no frantic temperamental change. The narrator of "My Aunt Margaret's Mirror," knowing that dissolution is near, becomes only mildly fey. The first stone turned up in digging the old chapel ground is just two centuries old, bearing the date 1585 and the name of a former Margaret Bothwell. "I think it betokens death," and the lady is "abstracted and disposed to silence." Whether the effect is to be nostalgic, as with Aunt Margaret, tragic, ironic, or humorous, Scott deftly brings out the fey quality in character. The exception is the Duke of Burgundy, to whom the exported superstition is too self-consciously applied.

Omens are portentous signs vouchsafed to ready and unready participants in action—and to those bystanders known as readers. Their frequency tends to be greatest in novels like *The Bride of Lammermoor* (or *Wuthering Heights*) which increase their sensuous and emotional thrust by evading the mind. Ravenswood stoops to recover a gold coin which Blind Alice rejects, as he rejects her warning. He breaks it and gives half to Lucy as a sign of troth-plight, which is broken soon. It evokes the scene of love declared, the Mermaiden's Well, whose legend is ominous. By a witch's trick, the threatening portrait of Sir Malise of Ravenswood, the Revenger, glowers once more from the wall at the Ashtons. After Lucy Ashton's death, Ravenswood rides to a duel with her brother in a hat with "a large sable feather." He spurs too near the Kelpie's Flow, and only the feather is left in sight by the quicksand.[24]

Although there are several birds of ill omen, the raven easily carries away the honours. Scottish witches were thought capable of raven-transformation, the blackness of the plumage matching their Satanic master's complexion. The village hags croak like ravens anticipating plague over Lucy's death and Ravenswood's doom—"if auld freets say true"—as the thirteenth among the funeral company. In *The Highland Widow*, the raven is invoked by the narrator or by frenzied women to screech, scream, and line its nest with human hair. The legend of Mount Pilatus, whose apostate haunter discharges tempests at men's heads, prepares travellers for the terrors of a Swiss storm in *Anne of Geierstein*. Then, as Arthur Philipson clings to a tree after a landslide, "flights of owls, bats, and other birds of darkness" and an "ill-omened and ill-favoured" vulture perturb him. "The foul bird, was she the demon of the place to which her name referred [*Geierstein* or Vulturestone]?" Could she, "like a raven or hooded crow by a dying sheep," foresee a feast? But in

[24] In *Anne of Geierstein*, Margaret of Anjou throws the mocking emblems of royal power, the rose and black feather, to the tempestuous wind. When the red rose of Lancaster is blown away from her, the exiled queen "accepts the omen"; she will go "to waste and desolation" with the feather.

The Talisman, the royal crusader brushes aside such fancies: "When you bid Richard Plantagenet fear that a danger will fall upon *him* from some idle omen, or omitted ceremonial, you speak to no ignorant Saxon, or doting old woman, who foregoes her purpose because a hare crosses the path, a raven croaks, or a cat sneezes."

In *Ivanhoe*, Scott makes a similar distinction between races, which replaces his more usual master-man and mistress-maid contrasts in scepticism and credulity. Whereas the Saxons were "of all people of Europe ... most addicted to a superstitious observance of omens," the Normans "had lost most of the superstitious prejudices which their ancestors had brought from Scandinavia." When Saxons leave the Convent of St Withold's, the clamour of "a large lean black dog" makes Athelstane recommend turning back, because a man must eat again to cancel the omen of a monk's, a hare's, or a vocal dog's crossing his path. Cedric's recognising the dog as Gurth's keeps up the humour. Poor Fangs' howl of greeting proves ominous only to himself when he is wounded by a javelin. The brief incident runs the gamut from learned comment to transient fear, humour, and pathos too rapidly to create a definite impression.

Perhaps, Scott was too fond of dogs to sense their ominousness. The Mauthe Dog in *Peveril of the Peak* is a taxidermic spectre, and the canine "presage" in *Woodstock* turns to nothing except in the fearful soul of Joceline Joliffe. When Bevis brings the glove of Tomkins to his murderer, Joliffe, it howls and scratches at the hall door. Sir Henry Lee remarks that "long howls are said to be ominous," recalling that, on the death of his father, Bevis's grandsire bayed the night through.

Weapons may be foreboding. The dirk with which Robin Oig kills his friend in *The Two Drovers* appears bloody to a second-sighted aunt, who places a taboo on its use. In the end the "wanchancy" and "fatal" dagger is a symbol of its owner's obdurate Highland honour. In *Anne of Geierstein*, Steinernherz, Sir Archibald de Hagenbach's executioner, has a sword whose fall "infallibly announces the presence of him who shall feel its edge." Like an ambiguous Greek oracle, this omen has variant readings. It is not John Philipson, the disguised Earl of Oxford, who parts with his head but Steinernherz's master.

Claud Halcro in *The Pirate* is fascinated by the natural wonder of phosphorescence or dancing corpse-lights, which can "bode no good." To Minna Troil, he repeats an old poem which ends, "There shall corpse lie stiff and stark." Human events seem to concur, for Mordaunt is seriously wounded in a struggle with the pirate. Until the hero begins to mend, the omen serves a narrative purpose. Triptolemus Yellowley contributes humour in his huffish catalogue of lazy-man omens: getting out of bed "wrong foot foremost," stepping over the tongs, turning "about the boat against the sun," seeing an owl, meeting "an uncanny body," having a rabbit cross one's path, and dreaming of a roasted horse.

Triptolemus is not clever enough to turn superstitiousness to his own advantage, as is Roland Graeme in *The Abbot*. "The fate of her sons made her [the Lady of Lochleven] alive to omens, and a corpse-light, as it was called, in the family burial-place, boded death." Roland cries out that he sees corpse-candles[25] in the churchyard vault and, while the lady-jailer's attention is distracted, substitutes false keys for the ones which will free Mary Queen of Scots from her island prison. Irony complicates the scene with the lady's decision that the light, actually a signal, comes from the gardener's hut and is not supernatural. On the eve of her brief evasions, Mary's hand is "damp and cold as marble." The Queen watches the defeat of her army from the castle in which she first held court after marrying Darnley. "What but evil can Mary's eyes witness from this spot!"

While fairy gifts are often unlucky, human gifts are occasionally so. When Allan M'Aulay in *A Legend of Montrose* offers Annot Lyle a casket of jewelry, she chooses a ring without noticing at first that it bears "a death's head above two crossed daggers." "This ill-omened gift," Allan reveals, "was the mourning ring worn by my mother in memorial of her murdered brother." In this light, Annot's "I fear no omens" and Allan's conjecture that sceptical Lord Menteith "may not live to see the event of the omen" are not reassuring. When Menteith, after being dirked by M'Aulay, recovers in defiance of physical and artistic probabilities, the novelist reports a revision of popular opinion: the portentous ring "related to the death of the bride's father" some months after Annot's marriage to Menteith.

Most of these omens are sufficiently explicit. But Scott's omens are most powerful and most true when they are implicit. When a Waverley novel has maximal narrative density and tension and minimal surplusage and artifice, words, acts, and objects take on a double meaning, the immediate or partial and the ultimate or contextual. The ominous, ironic, and tragic are richly intertwined in *The Highland Widow*. Each omen is complex because it glances in more than one direction. Thus in an essential episode whose

[25] "What in *Wales* are called *corps candles*, are often imagined to appear, and foretell mortality." Thomas Pennant, *A Tour of Scotland, 1769*, Chester 1771, p. 160. In Scott's tragedy, *Auchindrane* (1830), III. i, corpse-lights dance on the water before the murder of Quentin Blane.

verbal markers are redundant, Hamish drains "his parting cup" of drugged
liquor, "of which he would have held it ominous to have left a drop"; he
is drinking to his mother's health, "and may we meet again in happiness,
in spite of your ominous words." He wakes to find himself a deserter and to
see his mother as his destroyer.[26] Given Elspat's mad dream of a "Highland paradise," her hatred of "the churl Saxons," her ignorance of change,
her archetypal momism, and "her ain wicked will," and every move she
makes in relation to her son, the New Highland man, is bound to be
tragic. If tragedy is in the nature of things and therefore inevitable, every
step toward the catastrophe must be ominous, because it contains every
subsequent step.

In fine, Waverley omens are a ready and concise way of tightening
interest by foreshadowing events. Whenever they throw no light on the
future, they do on the character of the believer. They may be words,
actions, or illusions, birds, beasts, or objects, places or times (the reference
in *The Abbot* to the "fatal union" of Mary and Bothwell "in the fated
month of May"). They are mostly seen but some are heard or felt. They
are humorous, ironic, or tragic. They may be understood prospectively
or retrospectively, and several with tragic irony are aimed over obtuse
fictional heads at the reader.

In a way, dreams are omens that come to sleepers. They are also nocturnal presentiments, the piecing-together of subconscious knowledge, and
the expression of desire. Images of slumberous reverie are immediately
adjusted to external reality in *Guy Mannering* when Glossin's voice rouses
his imprisoned confederate, Hatteraick, who exclaims: "I dreamt this
moment that Meg Merrilies dragged you here by the hair, and gave me
the long clasped knife she used to wear,—you don't know what she said."
The heedless lawyer remains—and is strangled.

Scott's fullest treatment of dreams is in *The Antiquary*, which combines
narrative interest, humour, and realism. In unconscious preparation for
Lovel's experience in the tapestried Green Room, credulous Grizel Oldbuck tells a tale of Rab Tull's being visited there by the spectre of Aldobrand, an ancestral Oldbuck, who indicated where a forgotten deed might
be found. Her brother attacks the story as an olio of superstition, exaggeration, and oneiro-energised memory. Even its originality is suspect, Saint
Augustine having long before told of an apparition's informing its son

---

[26] V. S. Pritchett cites Hamish's discovery that he has overslept his furlough as a "real
omen." The minister tells him what day it is, "Had you been where you should have been
yesterday, young man, you would have known that it was God's Sabbath." Hamish knows
that the place he should have been was not the local church but the camp at Dumbarton.
Pritchett, *The Living Novel*, New York 1947, pp. 59-60.

where a debt-acquittal could be found.[27] Scott was actually more deeply interested in Grizel's anecdote than the delightful whimsy of the scene might indicate. This is clear in the long note on "Mr. R——d's Dream," which explains his partial source as an instance of "the fortuitous coincidence of actual events with our sleeping thoughts" or, on second thought, of the recapture in sleep of details lost to waking memory.[28]

After Lovel joins the dreamers by seeing a huntsman emerge from the tapestry in the Green Room, change into Aldobrand Oldenbuck, and open a foreign tome, he discusses the significance of dreams with his host. Several of the customary interpretations are canvassed: "deceptions of imagination," "juggling tricks" to excuse inclination, "motives which originate in our own wilful will," and occasional consonance "to future events." As for the German motto which Lovel remembers from his dream and which, when translated, encourages him to persevere, he must have heard it before he dreamed it. Thus the dream evaporates like a mist under the powerful sun of the antiquary's reason. Elsewhere, Oldbuck's account of a nurse's military dream and Dousterswivel's "dream dat you dream tree times" are humorous and grotesque.

When devising dreams to create atmosphere for a mysterious visit, Scott writes to a stereotype. Before Fenella's disembodied voice is heard by Julian Peveril in prison, he has preparatory dreams of "gliding spirits, gibbering phantoms, bloody hands, which, dimly seen by twilight, seemed to beckon him forward." In *The Pirate*, Minna and Brenda Troil sleep together in the same bed and have dreams which are "varied by the moods and habits of the sleepers." Minna beholds a mermaid beckon to her from a seaside cavern, "while her wild notes ... denounced, in prophetic sounds, calamity and woe." Brenda sees herself with family and friends, attempting a sprightly song, yet changing to "the deep tones ... and melancholy notes of Norna ... chanting some wild Runic rhyme." Both highly imaginative Minna and satirical, though responsive, Brenda

---

[27] Although Oldbuck does not mention his authority, it may have been Aubrey, *Miscellanies upon Various Subjects*, rather than the church father. See pp. 56–7. Dante is said to have appeared to his son Jacopo in a dream to reveal that thirteen lost cantos of the *Paradiso* were in a recess behind a wall mat. Francis MacManus, *Boccaccio*, London 1947, pp. 203–04.

[28] Citing the case again in his anonymous review of John Galt, *The Omen*, for *B.E.M.* of Jul. 1824, Scott rejects both supposed coincidence and supernatural visitation and adds, "We may one day return to" this subject. *The Prose Works of Sir Walter Scott*, Edinburgh 1834–6, XVIII. 351–3. For a study of the Rutherford story, see C. O. Parsons, "Anecdotal Background of Rab Tull's Dream," *Scottish Notes and Queries*, Third Series, XI (1933), 162–3. Scott gives a natural explanation of a dream of James V in his *Grandfather*, First Series, p. 307. A favourite story of his was that Miss Hepburn dreamed that her youngest brother was shot and lay dead on the floor. The actual tragedy was enacted on the morning of 8 Oct. 1715. *Op. cit.*, Third Series, pp. 124–5.

wake in terror at the same moment to find that "the sounds, which had suggested their dreams, were real, and sung within their apartment." Norna has come at the fated hour to unveil her past. For this factitious scene dreams appropriately set the stage. Thereafter, in keeping with her dream, Minna, on the death of her pirate, leads a subdued and charitable life. Minna, through circumstance and tragic predisposition, clarifies her vague prefigurement, and Brenda, despite sad strains, hears wedding music at last. In *The Betrothed*, the reference of visions of sleep to external happenings is combined with preparation for a pleasant visit. Eveline Berenger dreams of her father's consoling ghost and of blonde Vanda of the Red Finger's shift from resentment to benevolence. The warning spirit's kiss and pressure of the hand merge into the reality of fairhaired Rose's bending to touch and wake her mistress with a budget of happy news.

Scott does not rise again to the starkness of Hatteraick's dream or to the various light thrown on Lovel's dream. Instead, he falls for a time into a formula of dream as anticipation or corroboration of a human visit. Then he achieves pathos and irony in dreams dictated by fear and ambition. In *St Ronan's Well*, Clara Mowbray warns her brother against broils; she cannot sleep now without dreaming that he is the victim of a fight. Later, in a duel, John kills his sister's perfidious husband, Lord Etherington. The dream is not spelled out, and it receives emotional, more than factual, substantiation. In *Anne of Geierstein*, Steinernherz has a dream that Sir Archibald de Hagenbach will ennoble him. The ruffian's obsession is fed by a law that a headsman may win a title by nine single-stroke executions of nobles. His patron is the ninth. But at this point, perhaps, we should break off, remembering John Mowbray's advice to Clara, "If you begin to tell your dreams, we shall never have done. . . . I entreat you . . . to keep your visions to yourself."

*   *   *

Knowledge of the future may be thrust upon a character or it may be actively sought. Whether it is a heritage from the past or a phenomenon of the present, prophecy is usually imposed upon consciousness. The consulting of palmists and soothsayers and the use of augury, on the other hand, involve effort on the part of the curious. Without human intermediacy, the sense of the future may come to the receptive as presentiment and to the unreceptive (unadaptable) as fey behaviour, understood only by others. Signs may be revealed to both the impressionable and the unimpressionable as omens, if they are awake, and as warnings or foreshadowings, if they are asleep. Most of these manifestations are potentially helpful but only hazily informative. Usually no ill will is felt, but curses, uttered in the present or descending from the past, come from premeditated or impulsive malice shaping the future to the purposes of revenge.

An unhappy protagonist may be menaced from within by a tragic flaw like that of Oedipus or Orestes and from without by avenging conventions. If he is active, he will invite doom by challenging it, and if he is passive, he will know the futility of struggle. The function of dreams and prophecies is to emphasise man's lot. The end of wisdom, perhaps, is a character's accepting the mature stoicism voiced in the novelist's Journal. But most characters do not push things to a conclusion. Despite forebodings, they survive through compromise.

The great variety of prefiguring devices in *Anne of Geierstein*, which has a happy ending, suggests that omens do not always provide symbolic intensification. Instead, they may inadequately mask superficiality and haste. Many effects shakily supported by prognostics could have been achieved by more incisive characterisation and actual acquaintance with the scenes described. There is no substitute for insight and knowledge. At their best, however, presages in the Waverley Novels unite at least the overtones of profound characterisation with a philosophy of overruling forces that are psychological, natural, and supernatural. The fact that the characterisation is seldom profound and the philosophy is uncertain weakens, without nullifying, the impact of the portents.

17. ASSORTED SPIRITS AND SUPERSTITIONS

Although miscellaneous beings and beliefs in the Waverley Novels have been discussed elsewhere,[1] the subject may be briefly renewed. Scott's multifarious activity as a garnerer of out-of-the-way tomes, relics, and supernatural lore was in full swing by his twenty-first year, when he made notebooks the depositories, among other items, of "extracts about witches and fairies . . . notes on the Second Sight, with extracts from Aubry [*sic*] and Glanville."[2] Years later, guests at Abbotsford were shown the curiosities which covered walls, crammed chests, and stood ready for inspection in halls. Nor were the treasures of "numerous old carved oak cabinets, filled with the strangest things—adder-stones of magical power —fairies' rings . . ."[3] and the rarities of book presses left unsung.

---

[1] C. O. Parsons, "Minor Spirits and Superstitions in the Waverley Novels," *N. & Q.*, CLXXXIV (1943), 358–63; CLXXXV (1943), 4–9.
[2] Lockhart, I. 201.
[3] *Op. Cit.*, v. 383 (Captain Basil Hall's Journal for 31 Dec. 1824).

From the purchase of chapbooks in boyhood to the gift of the first edition of George Sinclair's *Satan's Invisible World Discovered* (1685) at the end of his life,[4] Scott was a joyous bibliomaniac. Gifts, trades, and above all purchases, resulting from his own searches or those of booksellers and bustling acquaintances,[5] built up a collection which cried out to be better known. As Amédée Pichot remarks after an inspection, "Ce serait déjà un curieux livre que le catalogue de cette bibliothèque, où j'ai remarqué entre autres plus de cinq cents ouvrages sur la magie et les sorciers."[6] In partial response to this need, Scott began dictating to William Laidlaw on 5 September 1830, "a sort of *catalogue raisonnée* of the most curious articles in his library and museum," entitled "Reliquiae Trottcosienses, or the Gabions of Jonathan Oldbuck."[7]

Years of dabbling in almost every department of the supernatural supplied Scott's memory and his pen not only with the more usual information on ghosts, witches, elemental spirits, devils, and fairies, but also with odd practices and beliefs, with foreign apparitions and beasts from another world which might resent being ignored in this study.

SUPERSTITIONS

That Scott was a sincerely, though non-institutionally, religious man, with a tincture of the heathen Stoic, can hardly be doubted. The mystery of man's relation with his Maker was too solemn for him to make it the subject of fiction. Something could be ventured, however, when pageantry, violence, ignorance, or enthusiasm made religion picturesque, melodramatic, or superstitious. Scott both disapproves of and delights in

[4] After Scott's refusal to pay John Stevenson's price, four guineas, the copy was bought by Charles Kirkpatrick Sharpe, traded to David Laing, and given to Sir Walter (probably in April 1831, although Scott's date is April 1832). See Ms. letter and notes in first edition, Abbotsford Library; the Prefatory Notice of T. G. Stevenson's reprint (1871), pp. l–li; Allardyce, II. 450–1.

[5] The most enthusiastic and successful scouts for witch books were Ballantyne, Constable, Henry Weber, and Daniel Terry. For methods of acquisition, see Thomas Constable, *Archibald Constable and his Literary Correspondents*, Edinburgh 1873, III. 301; T. C. Croker, 28 Aug. 1827, in Walpole; Scott's note in Berthelemy Cocles, *Le Compendion . . .* , Paris 1546, Abbotsford Library.

[6] Pichot, "Trois Jours chez Sir Walter Scott," *Revue de Paris*, XXX (1831), 130. Cp. "Abbotsford," *The Anniversary*, ed. Allan Cunningham, London 1829, p. 97. It was Pichot who gave his friend Nodier the Scottish goblin story of *Trilby ou Le Lutin d'Argail*. "Préface Nouvelle," VOL. III, *Œuvres de Charles Nodier*, Paris 1832–7.

[7] Lockhart, VII. 218. See "Gabions of Abbotsford," *Harper's New Monthly Magazine*, LXXVIII (1889), 782; M. M. Maxwell Scott, "Sir Walter Scott on his 'Gabions,' " *The Nineteenth Century and After*, LVIII (1905), 630; Nathaniel Hawthorne, *The English Notebooks*, ed. Randall Stewart, New York 1941, p. 342.

religious extremes, whether evident in Catholic fetish and fanfare or in Cameronian fanaticism. Startling contrasts appeal to him. In *Woodstock*, Tomkins is killed while trying to assault Phoebe: "The soul, dismissed from its earthly tenement in a moment so unhallowed, was gone before the judgment-seat." In the first edition of *Waverley*, he omits the name of Colonel James Gardiner. Later, he identifies the profligate doubter whose conversion by blazing light and a vision of Christ crucified makes him an object of almost superstitious regard to young soldiers. The narrative is general, detail and tactful scepticism being reserved for a note.[8]

When the religious substance of one age merges into the superstition of a later day, it becomes more properly matter of fiction. In *The Monastery*, Catholic All-Hallow Eve becomes folk Hallowe'en and is more expressive of the people than of the Church. Because "they that are born on Hallowe'en whiles see mair than ither folk," Mary Avenel sees the effigy of her dead father in breastplate, hawk on hand, and penetrates the meaning of "signs, words, and actions." As the Spirit of Avenel grows up, her birth on a day of unloosed spectral power, as well as her fragility, pallor, and shyness, inspires "mysterious awe." When he realises that the White Lady's mystic activity makes human competition supererogatory, Scott interprets the gifts of the last representative of a family in decay as insights of a sensitive, introspective, anaemic girl.[9] "This pale hectic phantom" (Sir Piercie's words) fitfully appears in the light of decadence and mental pathology, with laughter-loving, healthy Mysie Happer, the miller's daughter, acting as foil.[10]

Scott observes in *The Pirate*, "The auguries of Hallowe'en in Scotland [are] considered partly as matter of merriment, partly as sad and prophetic earnest." Sympathising with both attitudes, he could follow certain common Scottish practices as ties to his culture and people without too insistently raising the question of acceptance or doubt. Presentiments and birthmarks were different. To follow Scott's reasoning, although many presentiments are partly traceable to unconsciously gathered or retained information and to the unobtrusive operation of almost dormant primitive

[8] *Waverley*, n. iii. See Philip Doddridge, *The Most Remarkable Passages in the Life of the Honourable Colonel James Gardiner*, Falkirk 1805, pp. 14–16, and *The Life of the Honourable Col. James Gardiner*, Greenock 1812, pp. 9–10. Scott owned the first edition of Doddridge, Edinburgh 1747. Cp. the version in *Autobiography of the Rev. Dr. Alexander Carlyle*, ed. J. H. Burton, Edinburgh 1860, pp. 16–19: Gardiner read Gurnall's *Christian Armour* until past the hour of assignation with a surgeon's wife and became a better man.

[9] Cp. Scott's psychological use of Hallowe'en and M. W. Hartstonge's schematic and sensational use in *The Eve of All-Hallows*, London 1825, whose heroine, Adelaide of Tyrconnel, is born, marries, and dies on Hallowe'en (see particularly I. 192–3, influence of her nurse, 201–27, and III. 69–85, 152). The three-volume novel is dedicated to Scott.

[10] For Dame Glendinning's Hallowe'en "cantrip," see the chapter on magic.

faculties resembling those of animals, they are still not entirely explicable. And birthmarks are even less so. The family of Redgauntlet has the mark of a horseshoe traced on the forehead "by the mysterious law of nature," and Lilias Redgauntlet has five blood-specks on her arm as "a mark by which mysterious Nature has impressed, on an unborn infant, a record of its [Jacobite] father's violent death and its mother's miseries."[11] Scott does not follow the Greek dramatists in using the birthmark as an identification tag. Instead, he transforms it into a symbol of individual character and family woe.

When one culture cuts across another, the prejudice aroused often turns into superstitious fear and hate. In *Ivanhoe*, four Negro slaves tending the faggots at the stake seem like "demons . . . the familiar spirits with whom the witch [Rebecca] had communed, and who, her time being out, stood ready to assist in her dreadful punishment." A Jewess, Rebecca belongs to a people whose necromancy and spells Gurth and Higg, the Saxon serfs, dread. The Norman aristocrat, Lucas de Beaumanoir, has the power to bait Jews, whose medicines are little more than "devices of Satan." Ironically, the Grand Master's own Knights Templars "are charged with studying the accursed cabalistical secrets of the Jews, and the magic of the Paynim Saracens." Suspicion is like a Chinese puzzle.

Thus groups and races may be characterised by their own beliefs or by the fears they inspire in others. The less Scott knows about a race, the more likely he is to catalogue creeds and observances and let the matter go at that. In *Count Robert of Paris*, such oddments as Egyptian superstitions, diabolic religious rites, and the haunted, ruinous temple of Cybele suggest the interplay of cultures against the flat and unconvincing back-drop of polytypic Constantinople.

More familiar terrain was that of the Shetland Islands, which Scott visited in 1814. His gleanings, rich in trows, witches, fairies, and change- lings, included a wind-vending Hecate and tales about mermaids, a sea- snake, second sight, lead charms, and the Dwarfie Stone.[12] Supplemented by much reading in saga and antiquarian tome, these findings went into *The Pirate*, most copious among the Waverley novels in racial super- stitions. Standing stones and curious metalcraft are credited by "the uni- versal superstition of the Zetlanders" to supernatural artisans and builders. Despite Protestant ministers, safety at sea is purchased by stealthily

[11] Also see *Redgauntlet*, ch. xviii, n.; *Grandfather*, Third Series, p. 464: the mark of a broad axe on the neck of the Countess of Cromarty's son is "a striking instance of one of those mysteries of nature which are beyond the knowledge of philosophy."

[12] Lockhart, III. 155–6, 199–201, 203, 228; *Letters*, III. 535 [1814]. The following year, some of the material was used in *The Lord of the Isles*.

visiting the abandoned church of Saint Ringan barefoot, by walking around the ruins three times sun-wise ("*deasil*"), offering a coin, and withdrawing head-averted to avoid seeing the saintly skeleton. Ancient stone axes are preserved as "thunderbolts" which will keep lightning away. And in "a land of omens and superstitions," the evil eye is of course feared. Scandinavian drows, dwarfs and giants, sorcerers, mermaiden chanting "prophecies of future events," sea kraken, other-world kings, shoupeltins or tritons, nereids, rhyming voluspae, Norse gods transformed into "powerful spirits for good or evil" under an imperfectly assimilated Christianity, phantoms, corpse-lights, pixies, spirits of air, earth, and water, the Devil, witches, wraiths, warlocks, familiars, fairies, and precipice demons shoulder each other across the pages of the novel.

The most important single belief in *The Pirate* is that the rescuer of a drowning man will meet disaster. Whatever the basis—physical risk, desire for undisputed possession of flotsam, or vengefulness of water-monsters deprived of their prey[13]—Cleveland develops "an instinctive aversion" for his rescuer, Mordaunt Mertoun, and stabs him in a fray. The temperamental dissimilarity of the two men and their mistaken rivalry in love give human substance to an old superstition.

Altogether, Scott makes his narrative a cultural crossroad. Everything gains definition through contrast. Nominally Protestant fisherfolk slip back to the sites of ancient worship. Despite the lapse of centuries, sooth-saying survives—or is made to survive. Scott revels in one of his favourite conceptions, the overlapping and intermixture of cultures. But so many vestigial folkways are introduced that the effect is kaleidoscopic rather than steadily focused.

STRANGE BEINGS

The less run-of-the-mill supernatural beings in the Waverley Novels are uncanny beasts, creatures of cavern, water, or earth's crust, mortals immortally punished, and deformed and double persons.

Animals

If there is an imaginative fitness in ravens being ominous, unfamiliar apes and black dogs can well be diabolical and spectral. One of Scott's additions to the plot groundwork of "Wandering Willie's Tale" is the

---

[13] *The Pirate*, n. IV, "Reluctance to Save Drowning Men"; James M. Mackinlay, *Folklore of Scottish Lochs and Springs*, Glasgow, 1893, p. 7.

"ill-favoured jackanape," Major Weir, whose name is taken from a wizard executed in 1670 at Edinburgh. This "foul fiend in his ain shape" is turned into a scapegoat by the dead Laird's son, who gives out that Sir Robert Redgauntlet's pet stole Steenie's receipt, blew its master's whistle, and capered on the coffin.[14] At several points, the ape—or monkey—is like a grotesque symbol of the ruthlessness of persecuting cavaliers and the violent superstitiousness of their foes.

Another simian character is the seven-foot ourang-outang, Sylvan, which is as huge as a gorilla and as talented as a chimpanzee.[15] Count Robert of Paris takes this fantastic turnkey to be "the Devil himself, or some of his imps," a double-portion jackanapes, or, perhaps, a meta-morphosed human being. Whether appearing through a trapdoor or from behind a curtain, Sylvan shows a predilection for the theatrical. And in strangling Agelastes after the philosopher has sneered at the crude Christian concept of Satan, the ourang-outang opts for melodrama. Falling short of the exotic impact which he thinks his subject warrants, Scott turns to the imperial menagerie for an assistant.

An ordinary black dog may be ominous when it howls (*Ivanhoe*) or expressive of melancholy when it keeps quiet (Scott's *Journal*, 11 May 1826). But in *Peveril of the Peak*, the extraordinary Mauthe Dog haunts the secret way from garrison guard room to castle keep. As he is led down the passage by Fenella, Julian nervously recalls the legend of a soldier who followed the "dog or devil" with drawn sword and died of terror.[16] In his version of George Waldron's "very impressive story," Scott condenses his original, changes the spaniel to a mastiff, makes the drunken guard follow the dog instead of wishing that it would follow him, and has the passage abandoned, rather than closed up, after the soldier's death. He pushes the date of the episode back from 1671 to the reign of James I and needlessly omits the "great noise" heard by the less daring guards.[17] The advantages are greater compression, a more frightful dog, a bolder

[14] Major Weir is actually imitating a corbie crow which perched on the coffin of Sir Robert's historical original, Sir Robert Grierson of Lag, and accompanied it to the grave-yard. Alexander Fergusson, *The Laird of Lag*, Edinburgh 1886, pp. 145 ff.

[15] Cp. the fluting ourang-outang of Lord Monboddo (1714–99) and the parliamentarian, Sir Oran Haut-ton, in Thomas Love Peacock's *Melincourt* (1817).

[16] See "De'il Dogs" in John MacTaggart, *The Scottish Gallovidian Encyclopedia*, London 1824, p. 166.

[17] George Waldron, *A Description of the Isle of Man*, ed. William Harrison, Douglas 1865, pp. 12–13. Scott used the second edition of 1731. Reversing the Manx words, Scott mistook Doog or Dhoo (cp. Gaelic *dhu*, black) for dog. In "The Spectre Dog of Peel Castle. The 'Manthe Dhoo' of 'Peveril of the Peak' ", *Borderland*, 1 (1894), 472–5, an anonymous writer suggests that the Manthe Dhoo reappeared as the Black Dog of Santon in the eighteenth and nineteenth centuries.

challenge to the supernatural, and a temporal softening of crudity. The passage must be left open for Fenella's and Julian's use, but no narrative purpose is served by the remembered legend. It has value as giving colour of time and place.

Dobbies

A purebred dobby, or household sprite, might be puzzled by the Dobby's Walk in *Peveril of the Peak*. The first Squire of Moultrassie Hall, a melancholic and perhaps suicidal brewer, "was supposed to walk in this sequestered avenue, accompanied by a large headless mastiff, which, when he was alive, was a particular favourite." Moonlight, sad thoughts, gloomy elms, and the ghost-story combine to make Lady Peveril pay a momentary "debt to the superstitious belief of the times" when she sees Major Bridgenorth, who has been away. Throughout this incident, the setting, contrasted folk and aristocratic credence, and actual events blend admirably.

Brownies

Much truer to type is the brownie, defined by Scott as a familiar spirit "believed in ancient times to supply the deficiencies of the ordinary labourer." A moron compared with sprightlier beings like the fairies, the brownie is good-natured in nocturnal chores, ill-natured in occasional rough treatment of women. It is easily pleased and just as easily offended. Both Sir Walter and his friend, James Hogg, display an almost sentimental attachment to the last of the south Scottish lubber spirits, the Brownie of Bodsbeck. In the second volume of his novel, however, Hogg confesses, "This celebrated Brownie was no other than the noted Mr John Brown, the goodman of Caldwell."[18] And Scott, always more cautious than the Ettrick Shepherd, admits that such superstitions "are too limited, and too much obliterated from recollection, to call for special discussion."[19] Appropriately, his use of the brownie for local colour is as fragmentary as the vestiges of the belief in the nineteenth century.

Sobered by the adventure of a gudewife with the Brownie of Ben-ye-gask, the landlady of the inn at Aberfoil will not set foot in her stable after dark. "It was aye judged there was a Brownie in our stable, which was just what garr'd me gie ower keeping an hostler."[20] The brownie-like

---

[18] Hogg, *The Brownie of Bodsbeck*, Edinburgh 1818, II. 76.
[19] *Demonology*, pp. 353–4. Also see *Minstrelsy*, I. 148, n.
[20] Cp. "the wylie auld wife" who hires Aiken-drum in "The Brownie of Blednoch," *The Poetical Works of William Nicholson*, 3rd edn, Castle-Douglas 1878, pp. 77–82.

sound from within comes from Andrew Fairservice, who fears to venture farther in the Rob Roy country. In *The Heart of Midlothian*, when Jeanie Deans goes one morning to the mansion house of her rejected suitor, Dumbiedikes, and finds no one stirring, she shakes down fodder for a neglected cow. A sleepy servant screams, "Eh, sirs! the Brownie! the Brownie!" and flees. By means of the brownie, the management of this "castle of the sluggard" is humorously revealed, and a reason is given for the red-faced old housekeeper's ungracious reception of industrious Jeanie.

Bogles

Sir Walter had in his possession a letter from John Scott to William Scott of Maxpopple, dated 6 January 1823, which mentions a neighbourhood bogle resembling the racketing devil of Woodstock. "The Village of Cauldshiels was on the East side of Rhymers Glen—The ruins of the houses are still visible—I have heard that a ghost, or Bogle so *pelted* the door of the last inhabitant of that place that he was obliged to abandon his dwelling."[21]

The Scottish bogle may become familiar with mortals, but it is still to be feared. The Black Dwarf is "mair like a bogle than a living thing." In *The Bride of Lammermoor*, Mysie the cook is reluctant to lay hands on the old broodhen for a makeshift meal. "Ou, she's sitting some gate aneath the dais in the hall, and I am feared to gae in in the dark for the bogle; and if I didna see the bogle, I could as ill see the hen, for it's pit-mirk." And in *St Ronan's Well*, John Mowbray reminds his sister Clara that, as a boy, he went forth to meet the bogle in the upper orchard and found the cow-boy wrapped in a shirt stealing pears. Nor is he now frightened by "the raw-head and bloody-bones."[22] The boast is ironic. Instead of drubbing a cow-boy, headstrong Mowbray kills the Earl of Etherington and contributes to Clara's death.

Goblins

Scott's infrequent goblins appear figuratively in the shape or nature of man or as bugbears with which the crafty seek to tyrannise over the weak.

[21] Endorsed by Scott, "Names of places in Thos. the Rhymer": Abbotsford Ms. N.L.S.
[22] The servants' hall in *Waverley* is astonished with "raw-head and bloody-bones stories." In a Ms. play of Feb. 1805, *The British Soldier; or, Life's Campaign*, III. iii, a servant brings Miss Lucretia some books: "Every one ha' got some frightful name (opens one of the books) 'Raw-head & Bloody bones: a Romance in three Volumes.' " Henry E. Huntington Library, Larpent 82. M. 4. The bugbear was also used to keep children in subjection: "This boggart... I was seriously informed, preferred to breakfast on the bodies of naughty children, nicely roasted!" Charles Hardwick, *Traditions, Superstitions, and Folk-Lore*, Manchester 1872, p. 131.

Although goblins are the mischievous and even malignant English cousins of bogles, they sometimes migrate. The deep-voiced, square-built, long-armed Rob Roy seems to Frank Osbaldistone ferocious, cunning, and unearthly like "the old Picts who ravaged Northumberland...a sort of half-goblin half-human beings." When told in *Kenilworth* to make "the out-of-doors frightful to her [Amy Robsart], with tales of goblins," superstitious Anthony Foster replies to Varney, "I trifle not nor toy with my dead neighbours of the churchyard" and such like.

Kelpies

Water perils are imaginatively concentrated in the kelpie, a spirit which lurks near lakes, fords, and treacherous currents to warn or to lure those who are to be drowned. Assuming horselike shape, the kelpie may offer the unwary a fatal means of crossing water. The motto of the fourth chapter of *The Heart of Midlothian* is taken from "Kelpie": "The hour's come, but not the man." A footnote explains that a water spirit was thus complaining when the fey horseman rode up and, despite warning human voices, plunged into the flooded stream.[23] The fictional character similarly driven is Captain John Porteous. At a salmon-spearing in *Guy Mannering*, "the light diminished to a distant star that seemed to twinkle on the waters, like those which, according to the legends of the country, the water-kelpy sends for the purpose of indicating the watery grave of his victims." The Tweedside legend which inspired the White Lady's ducking of Father Philip in *The Monastery* concerns a mermaid, probable substitute for an earlier kelpie. In *The Abbot*, the monk has had time to recognise his abandonment "to the misguiding of a water fiend,[24] whereby he had been under a spell," as a punishment for his deception about a marriage ceremony. Altogether, the kelpie is too rudimentary to play other than a burlesque or allusive role.

Drows

Drows or trows, according to Scott, are "somewhat allied to the fairies, residing, like them, in the interior of green hills and caverns." More frequently hostile than friendly to man, these subterranean people, as they are called in the Faeroes,[25] are particularly dangerous at midnight. They

---

[23] A better verse and a better version are quoted from Hugh Miller in Isabel Cameron, *A Highland Chapbook*, Stirling 1928, pp. 121–2: "The hour, but not the man, has come."

[24] Although De Bracy in *Ivanhoe* asserts that "a water-fiend hath possessed" the weeping Rowena, no kelpie ever functions as a lachrymose genius.

[25] Lucas Jacobson Debes, *A Description of the Islands and Inhabitants of Foeroe*, Anglicised by J[ohn] S[terpin], London 1676, pp. 365–6, etc.

are also skilled metal-workers. In *The Pirate*, Norna's present of a "gifted chain, which all in our isles know was wrought by no earthly artist, but by the Drows, in the secret recesses of their caverns," is undervalued by Mordaunt as an ineffectual "fairy gift." Triptolemus, the outlander, and Norna, who should know better, also prettily confuse Norse drows with Scottish fairies, "the nameless race." And Brenda says that her sister Minna "would like much to have a little trow, or fairy, as the Scotch call them, with a green coat, and a pair of wings as brilliant as the hues of the starling's neck, specially to attend on her."[26]

The Duergar

Elsewhere, Scott relates the drow to the English fairy (or Gothic elf), whose "prototype . . . is to be sought chiefly in the *bergelfen*, or *duergar*, of the Scandinavians."[27] The duergar may go back in turn to the diminutive Lapps, Finns, and Letts who fled from the more powerful Asae.[28] Being excellent metallurgists and meteorologists, these dwarfish refugees worked in underground hideouts and, gaining a supernatural reputation, were associated, or confounded, with German kobolds, English goblins, and Scottish bogles, as also with the vivacious fairy kind.

It is in terms of "the genuine duergar" who figures in Robert Surtees' hoaxing legend of his last appearance in Northumberland and in Leyden's ballad, "The Cout of Keeldar," that Scott conceives the traditionary side of the Black Dwarf's nature. The misanthropic-benevolent protagonist slowly emerges from the mists of folk superstition into humanity and, at the close of the action, takes on again the characteristics of the duergar.

Dwarfs

The common or separate origin of superstitions, rites, and beings,[29] Norse influence, modification and intermixture, island and mainland variations fascinated Scott. Possible combinations and relationships seemed to have no ending. Sir Walter is confident that the *drows* "may . . . be

[26] Of course, fairies formed part of the mixed supernatural population of the Shetlands. Robert Stevenson, the lighthouse engineer, lost a box-measuring line with which he intended to show Scott the dimensions of the Stones of Stennis. A boy who found the line threw it away, fearing that "it had belonged to the Fairies." *Scribner's Magazine*, xiv (1893), 498. The quotation is from Stevenson's "Reminiscences of Sir Walter Scott," written the year of the engineer's death (1850) and edited by his grandson, R.L.S.

[27] In his essay "On the Fairies of Popular Superstition," *Minstrelsy*, Scott credits this identification to Dr John Leyden.

[28] See *Joannis Schefferi von Strassburg Lappland*, Frankfurt 1675, p. 46; Thormodus Torffaeus, *Universi Septentrionis Antiquitates*, Copenhagen 1705, p. 100.

[29] See the discussion of disjunct origin or "one common source" in *Peveril*, n. viii, "Manx Superstitions."

identified with the Caledonian fairies" in most respects except their name, which is "a corruption of Duergar or *dwarfs*."[30] Mindful of the intertwining family trees of short, stumpy, malicious earth spirits and of undersized aborigines, whether Lapps or Picts, Scott gives his human dwarfs strange and forbidding traits. Superstitious shrinking from the abnormal suggests a terminology for mental and physical aberration.

The Black Dwarf, Scott's first portrait in the small, was followed by Norna's square-built errand boy, Nick Strumpfer or Pacolet, in *The Pirate*. With his disproportionately large, ugly head and his dumbness, the manikin disturbingly reminds people of "the very demon Trolld," Old Nick, and a goblin that Latin will conjure away. When "the said dwarf, devil, or other apparition" disappears, it is conceivably on a dragon's back. On another occasion, this ambulant gargoyle emerges from a subterranean passage "like some overgrown reptile." Scott does penance for this monster of nature and of art in *Peveril of the Peak*, in which he consistently presents Sir Geoffrey Hudson as a physical oddity whose human company the noble and the well-formed desire.

Scott's last venture was his boldest, a dwarfish couple in *The Talisman*. Rising through a trapdoor in a Gothic chapel, Nectabanus bears a lamp which gleams on his hideous, lump-headed, strangely garbed figure. Spellbound, Sir Kenneth is reminded of "gnomes, or earthly spirits, which make their abode in the caverns of the earth." This impression is intensified when a whistle conjures up a shaggy browed, flashing-eyed female, "Guenevra, his lady and his love," who glibly identifies her mate as "King Arthur of Britain, whom the fairies stole away from the field of Avalon." Summoned by a voice, Queen Berengaria's dwarfs blow out their lights and leave the Scottish knight in the dark. Such dwarfs belong, of course, to the trappings of medieval romance, although their usual function is not to sweep out chapels but to accompany damsels on missions, as in *The Faerie Queene*.[31]

Without agreeing completely with Ruskin that Scott's dwarfs evidence a diseased mental tendency in their creator,[32] one can regard them as lapses in artistic taste. Although dwarfs fit into the diverse and none too symmetrical pattern of life, they can hardly be made the subject of morbid fictional study. (Misanthropy, it may be noted, is not stressed in Walter de

---

[30] *Demonology*, pp. 122–3.

[31] In Spenser's poem, Una's dwarf has this conventional, as well as an allegorical, task to perform. Also see *Le Morte Arthur*, ed. J. Douglas Bruce, London 1903, p. 61.

[32] "Fiction, Fair and Foul," *The Works of John Ruskin*, ed. Cook and Wedderburn, London 1903–12, XXXIV. 263 ff. Besides the dwarfs discussed above, Ruskin has in mind the goblin page in the *Lay*, Cockledemoy in *The Doom of Devorgoil*, Flibbertigibbet, and Fenella.

la Mare's *Memoirs of a Midget*.) They bring with them into the pages of the Waverley Novels the decadent appeal of the malformed and the repellent.

Wild Huntsmen

The wild huntsman is introduced in one of Scott's earliest pieces, "The Chase," a translation of Bürger's "Der Wilde Jäger," and at the end of his literary career. The first presentment is for an immediate sensational and moral effect, and the last helps the reader understand a culture background. In *Woodstock*, Holdenough declares that the forest near the lodge is the scene of a spectral hunt in which a lone, green-clad rider of the twelfth century asks at noon the direction of the stag's flight. Although the action of *Count Robert of Paris* is in the eleventh century, the heyday of the belief is referred to the indefinite past. A distant trumpet-note in the streets of Constantinople reminds Hereward of Hampshire tribal fathers' story "of invisible huntsmen, who were heard to follow with viewless horses and hounds the unseen chase through the depths of the forests of Germany." But Hereward shakes "such childish fancies" off. Scott's youthful absorption has turned into caution.

Double-Gangers

Wraiths, "a species of apparition, similar to what the Germans call a Double-Ganger,"[33] receive incidental attention in *A Legend of Montrose* and *The Pirate*. The "dismissed spirit" of old Alice in *The Bride of Lammermoor* is seen just after death, whereas a conventional wraith is a likeness which usually appears just before the mortal double's death. The Scottish co-walker has a longer span of activity.

Among the multiple explanations of the heroine's physical duplicity in *Anne of Geierstein*, Sir Walter suggests a preternatural double. Sigismund Biederman warns against Anne's sending "any of your double-gangers to me . . . come in what shape they list." Sigismund forgets that double-walkers, "those aërial duplicates of humanity," must retain the shape of their prototypes. Until Anne's explanation of her ubiquity is forthcoming, the reader is likely to share Arthur Philipson's bewilderment, "While strictly alike in shape and lineament, was the one a tenant of the earth, the other only a phantom?"

---

[33] *A Legend of Montrose*, n. ii. "Wraiths." Cp. an anonymous review of E. T. A. Hoffmann, *The Devil's Elixir* (translated by Scott's friend, R. P. Gillies) in *B.E.M.*, XVI (1824), 57. Although Scottish wraiths are similar to the "*doppelganger*; that is to say . . . a man's being haunted by the visitations of *another self—a double* of his own personal appearance," German authors seem to have richer materials or to make better use of "their country-people's old tales."

As a double-ganger, Anne of Geierstein, who is ordinarily "gentle, candid, pure, and simple," becomes independent, resourceful, adventurous, mysteriously fascinating. Her personality is probably not split by this device but expanded to reveal a side of woman's nature which is often stultified by social restraints.

*　　*　　*

The plentifulness of miscellaneous superstitions and otherworld creatures which accompany the more conventional stock-in-trade of Waverley supernaturalism suggests why Scott has at times been accused of encouraging credulity. To the undiscriminating, interest in and acceptance of certain phenomena may be synonymous. But the quality of Sir Walter's interest is generally clear. He likes the colour and quaintness of bygone beliefs; his more serious preoccupation, however, is with men in relation to their times. To the understanding of past cultures, the creatures with which men have peopled their imagined world and the folk-creeds to which they have adhered have much to contribute.

CHAPTER V

SCOTT'S METHODS AND ACHIEVEMENTS

SCOTT'S methods and achievement must be sought out in the temporal and spatial range; the multiplicity of actions, motives, and people; the variety of appeal in largely accretional plots; the strange welter of truth and falsity, insight and melodrama, the universal and the antiquarian particular of the Waverley Novels. In them the supernatural is introduced subtly and mechanically, functionally and ornamentally, sympathetically and analytically. For Scott was convinced that the uncanny added light and shadow to a story.

The reading public was on the whole appreciative of the supernatural in literature. In an age of transition from the gloomier to the more fanciful tenets of superstition, that public ranged from ready credulity to stubborn rationality. As a man of imagination, Scott himself enjoyed the unexplained sensation, but as an advocate, a sheriff, and a man of reason, he delighted in probing the mechanics of supernatural fraud. Thus he was in a position to be all things to almost all readers and to please those who shared his changing and contradictory attitudes. Readers had several choices: they could concentrate on the experience and ignore any explanation; they could reverse the process; or they could with Scott combine the advantages of temporary belief and objective scrutiny.

Whatever the drawbacks of this eclecticism, it seems to have been widespread in the early part of the nineteenth century. Artistically, perhaps what was needed was an indulgent presentment of former times in which the illusion of older superstitions would be preserved without the reader's being led into an emotional debauch. The response must be finely balanced between over-susceptibility and cold rationality. And this equipoise could be achieved, not by obvious statements, but by an expressive handling of characters and situations. The reader's reward would be twofold, a spirited, though imaginary, participation in bypast life and a not too obtrusive, ironic sense of superiority.

Through its reactions the public issued critical caveats to its most popular novelist. The English were generally less responsive to the supernatural than the Scots. Yet folk beliefs were too integral a part of Scott's fictional world to be removed because of the Southron. At best, they could be modified by dispersed sceptical hints and declarations. The public, English or Scottish, was not interested in the grotesque pure and simple or in long-outgrown marvels. A distinction must be made between wonders which, commanding almost universal credence among one's proximate forebears, could still give the nervous system at least a momentary shock and those which were but the fossil curiosities of a remote past.

Scott could be blind to this line of demarcation, nor did he thoroughly understand why readers objected to such hybrids as the White Lady of Avenel. His nervous changing of subject and *locale*, as well as the attribution of his own work to fabricated authors, all to satisfy the public's craving for novelty, did not improve his vision. Thus many of Scott's clumsy attempts to warn readers against participating in the beliefs of his characters result from a puzzled distrust of a heterogeneous public which it was his responsibility not to mislead.[1] Influenced by the demands of that public and by his own varying attitudes and choice of method, Scott is sometimes objective and sometimes subjective in his uncritical delight in the marvellous. Striking the right note seems to be with him more a matter of intuition and feeling than of conscious effort.

Setting

When a landscape seems to be called for, Scott often provides one in the manner of Poussin, Salvator Rosa, or a gentleman on the grand tour. He may even shorten his labours by referring to the painter or traveller whose style he is approximating, as he does to Hogarthian scenes and faces. But when the setting seems to call for appropriate action,[2] he is usually less self-conscious. The Fairy Dean is sensitively evoked in *The Monastery*, but the capers of the White Lady are hardly appropriate. Like James Macpherson and Mrs Radcliffe, Scott is better at creating eeriness than calling up eerie beings. When the dimension of time is added, past events, held in suspension by atmosphere of place, haunt the present.

[1] Cp. *Four Discourses on Subjects relating to the Amusement of the Stage*, Cambridge 1809, pp. 27–9, in which James Plumptre objects to theatrical representation of secrets of the invisible world. "May not these exhibitions tend, and have they not tended to keep up such a belief amongst an ignorant populace, and afforded an opportunity for the success of impious imposture?"

[2] Note the conclusion of Scott's enthusiastic description of Perth and Perthshire in the first chapter of *The Fair Maid of Perth*: "It is therefore natural, that, whilst deliberating on what might be brought forward for the amusement of the public, I should pitch upon some narrative connected with the splendid scenery which made so much impression on my youthful imagination, and which may perhaps" set off "the imperfections of the composition. . . ."

Scott is at his best in conveying awe, suspense, mystery, and personal feeling through nature. When an Edward Waverley or a Frank Osbaldistone penetrates the Highlands, interest quickens. Entering Highland passes, caves, glens, and recesses is like slipping from the conscious into the unconscious, womblike, enfolding, dream-freighted, or from the illusion of free will into the substance of fate. A border is also being crossed between what is and what might be, reality and romance, between selfish causes and lost causes, the calculating present and the impulsive past. This excitement and tension may be due to a symbolic re-enactment by Scott of his own crossing of the border between youth and manhood, fancy and sober control. Because renewed choice is renewal of possibility, to go back in order to re-emerge is a way of briefly recapturing what is lost.

Plot

The three basic Waverley plots reveal the narrative function of the supernatural. The plots concern civil strife, the hero's identity and rights, and honour. With these actional focuses may be combined sister or brother contrasts and the wages-of-sin theme. The first two plots are typically used in *Waverley* and *Guy Mannering*, and the third is chiefly developed in the short stories.

In the *strife* plot, the problem of worth and status is complicated by war rather than by parentage, as in the *identity* plot. Hesitating between two opposed causes, the hero, a moderate himself, may be precipitated into rebel ranks by some act of severity on the part of authority. Conflicts are also set up by reason and imagination, policy and romance, with love increasing the tensions. With its larger issues, civil strife gives rise to, intermingles with, sets off, or opposes individual desires. While Highlanders and Lowlanders, Hanoverians and Jacobites, Royalists and Covenanters, Reformers and Catholics, English and Scots, Normans and Saxons, French and Burgundians, Crusaders and Saracens (or Greeks) clash, individuals are thrown together or thrust apart, and the hero chalks up for himself human debits and credits in both camps. The *dénouement* brings peace after hostilities, the reward of pardon and marriage for the good man, and the punishment of death or disgrace for the bad.

In civil or national strife, the degree of credulity of leaders, factions, religions, and races emphasises conflict in which a mediator moves in the no man's land between opposites. A young man who neither goes to the Hanoverian extreme of practicality nor shares the Highland Jacobites' faith in second sight, medical thaumaturgy, or the warning spirit, Edward Waverley is alternately attracted toward the rational and the imaginative way of life. Henry Morton, a moderate Presbyterian in *Old Mortality*, who loves a Royalist maid and shelters a fleeing Covenanter, is a man of equilibrium among contestants who vigorously wield both the word, in accusation of Devil-compact, and the sword. The strife in *A Legend of Montrose* is again between Royalists and Covenanters, with Annot Lyle broaching the problem of *identity* and transcending marshalled antagonism in her love. The larger issues are neither linked with superstition nor brought out fully by other means. In the central clash between rivals in love, second sight, which is almost always associated with personal rather than group misfortunes, helps to differentiate individuals and to heighten effects. In *Woodstock*, Royalists are distinguished in part by their astutely playing on the supernatural fear of their enemies and Roundheads, by their being almost uniformly taken in. The cheat, Joseph Tomkins, crosses the boundary between contending forces, as does the reasonable, though not completely intrepid, hero.

The more distant the place and the time in which Sir Walter unfolds his *strife* plot, the more likely he is to distinguish individuals effectively, rather than groups, by popular culture beliefs. This is true of the conflict of Louis XI and Charles the Bold in *Quentin Durward*, which is carefully worked out in relation to their degree of faith in soothsaying. The French King's dependence on astrology and the superstitious externals of religion and his confidence in Oliver the Devil add to a complex portrait. It is also true of the accusation of witchcraft against Rebecca in *Ivanhoe* and the double-ganging activity of the Swiss maiden in *Anne of Geierstein*. There is a superficial return to the difference of racial beliefs in *Count Robert of Paris*, with the Franks giving in temporarily to exotic fears.

In *The Bride of Lammermoor*, civil strife narrows to family rivalry between a decadent Tory-Episcopalian and a rising Whig-Presbyterian family. Torn by the conflicting loyalties of honour (revenge) and of love, the Master of Ravenswood looks toward the protagonists of the Highland short stories. Incalculable forces, expressed in terms of fate, prophecy, omens, and witchcraft, menace him and his beloved. Like the *identity* heroes, Ravenswood has an "old sibyl" in the person of Alice, but he will not let her become his picturesque guardian spirit and suffers accordingly. Her apparition is like a symbol of the futility of resisting man's doom.

The *identity* plot hinges on proof of the hero's (or heroine's) status—political, religious, social, romantic, or hereditary—and of his marital eligibility. Ignorance of or uncertainty about parentage and legitimacy creates obstacles and suspense. If the discovery of a Waverley hero's identity and the full assertion of his rights depended on the young man alone, he would probably go through life bearing a chance name and lose both his inheritance and his lady because he could not justify his claim to either. But devils are leagued against him and a sibyl, or a guardian angel with a *penchant* for hero-worship, counterplots on his side. Thus the diabolical skipper, Dirk Hatteraick, and the more astute, legal devil, Glossin, are arrayed against Harry Bertram in *Guy Mannering*. Despite fictional pretence, Bertram's coming into his own has little to do with the Colonel's astrology or Meg Merrilies' predictions. What is essential is the wise-woman's entirely natural recognition of Vanbeest Brown as the kidnapped heir, as well as her opportune and constant help thereafter.

When the manufacture of narrative difficulties out of *identity* problems has gone on long enough, Sir Walter may neglect the makeshift in order to concentrate on the young person's rights. This changeover emphasises the conflict between good and evil, as in *Kenilworth*. The recognition of Amy Robsart as the Countess of Leicester, with the rights attached to her station, is hopelessly striven for by Tressilian and by Wayland Smith, who has shed his supernatural cloak on giving up farriery. The opposition, made up of a subtle Devil with astrological, canting, and cynical aides who are half-human and half-fiendish, is too much for her weak innocence. And in *The Fortunes of Nigel*, the hero is almost kept from preserving his ancestral fortunes by Lord Dalgarno, whose wickedness has much complexity and whose diabolism is symbolised by his page Lutin. The guardian angel is a cloistered phantom absorbed in her own wrongs (Dalgarno is her evil genius, too) and therefore deficient in energy, ingenuity, and ubiquity. Nigel is freed when the ghostly Lady Hermione prosaically supplies the enterprising heroine, Margaret, with money. In his plot of rights and identity, Scott makes hellish evil central, but the supernatural aspects of the forces of good are mostly superficial.

Honour in conflict with some other loyalty is usually the theme of Scott's short stories. The incompatible allegiances of "The Two Drovers" are Highland honour and friendship with an Englishman; of "The Highland Widow," honour, upheld by the older generation, and friendship and acceptance of the new English order, upheld by the younger; of "Death of the Laird's Jock," Scottish honour and English honour mortally asserted by two champions; and of "My Aunt Margaret's Mirror," family honour and its betrayal by a husband who is punished. In so far as it conforms to the dominant short-story theme, "The Tapestried Chamber" shows the lurid dishonour of the past spectrally disturbing the blameless present.[3] In the Highland tales, the honour compulsions are too strong to be expressed by realistic methods alone. When the hero himself becomes the battleground,[4] the clash of irreconcilable standards and cultures is so tragic that the disaster can best be prefigured by a second-sighted aunt in "The Two Drovers" and by a paternal warning spirit in "The Highland Widow."

Scott often combines different narrative patterns. The Deans, Reuben Butler, and other fixed dwellers in *The Heart of Midlothian* would probably have achieved equilibrium and happiness in their relations among themselves if an external force had not broken into their otherwise secure Eden.[5] The serpent is Robertson the fallen and the uprooted, who brings sin and turmoil with him. Demonology and witchcraft are freely associated with Robertson, his comrades, his early victim, Madge Wildfire, and her vengeful mother, Meg Murdockson. Effie's weakness and scorn of her strong sister's credulity seduce her from a safe, commonplace home into Robertson's fearful orbit. The plot strands of sister *contrast, wages of sin,* and Robertson's *identity* as Sir Edmund Staunton's son, with the fey Porteous briefly introducing civil *strife* when he challenges the people and is mobbed, are closely connected with supernatural lore. The moral is carefully pointed in the final address to the "Reader": "The evil consequences of our crimes long survive their commission, and, like the ghosts of the murdered, for ever haunt the steps of the malefactor."

The Pirate repeats the combination of *The Heart of Midlothian*, a splendid villain's *identity, wages of* (Norna's) *sin,* sister *contrast,* and *strife* (the government against piracy). Although a sibyl protects the hero, her real usefulness—as with the grandmother of Roland Graeme in *The Abbot*—is much less clear than that of Meg Merrilies. The villain, Clement Cleveland, despite the rumour of his forming a league with the demons of Coffin-key, is less melodramatically portrayed than Robertson. These Byronic anti-heroes tend to share illegitimacy and, before the action begins, the seduction of women around whom weird legendry gathers. And later, without deflowering Minna, Cleveland incapacitates her psychically for loving or marrying another man. Whether with these men or with

[3] For a discussion of these tales, see Lord David Cecil's Introduction to Scott, *Short Stories*, Oxford University Press 1934, and the same critic's *Sir Walter Scott*, London 1933, p. 60.
[4] Cp. Prosper Mérimée, *Colomba*, in which a happy ending is none too convincingly imposed on a similar conflict.
[5] The similarity to Milton, *Paradise Lost* is mostly figurative. Although Robertson joins a certain magnificence to his depravity, the fallen Eve cannot reassert human dignity. In Scott's novel, there is no ultimate human ennoblement through the discipline of sin, struggle, and accomplishment.

Richard Tresham in *The Surgeon's Daughter*, with Norna or with Clara Mowbray in *St Ronan's Well* as planned by Scott, carnality makes the difference. It thrusts the sinner from this world into a limbo of ghosts, demons, visionary powers, and remorse.

In *The Talisman*, despite his misreading of the true message of the stars, the Hermit of Engaddi prepares the way for revelation of the hero's *identity* and assertion of his *rights* (to high marriage). The hermit also contributes much to monarchic *contrast* by the unmatched responses he draws from Richard and Saladin. The *strife* which one might expect between crusaders and infidels yields in importance to dissension within the crusaders' camp and to a contest of courtesy between Saladin and Richard. Much of this friendly rivalry depends on the magical talisman. The *identity* and *rights* of Conachar as chief of his clan in *The Fair Maid of Perth* are opposed by prophecy and advanced by second sight and magic, and the outcome of clan *strife* is dependent in part on his recognition. The strife between courtiers and townsmen is emphasised by the bier-right which helps to reveal the bonnet-maker's murderer. And the machinations of Robert III's brother against the Prince are associated among the tools of his crime with demonology.

Whatever his narrative line or combination of lines may be, Scott is not entirely impersonal in his choice of subject. Parallels in the lives and personal conflicts of the fiction-writer and his relatives often lend an immediacy to the treatment. Sister contrasts, the temperamental diversity of brothers, and the two sides of a wavering hero's nature are to be found in Scott's daughters, in himself and his brothers, and in his own complex nature. As was right and proper in a world ruled by social forms, reason, expediency, and the heart, the parentage and identity of Lord Downshire's ward, Margaret Charlotte Charpentier, and the status of Walter Scott were established before their marriage.[6] The wages-of-sin theme may have been stamped on Scott's consciousness by his Sandy-Knowe nurse whose "wild fellow" of a sweetheart "had [probably] done and said more to her than he was like to make good." Some time after being tempted by the Devil to kill Watty, she apparently went insane like another Madge Wildfire.[7] Or the issue may have been realised for the novelist by his brother Daniel's failings (it is not likely that Scott knew of his mother-in-law's life after she left Charpentier). Scott may change the period and the characters in his novels, but the central situations remain real and meaningful to him.

[6] Grierson, *Scott*, pp. 46–66.
[7] Lockhart, I. 15–16.

Many weird manifestations in the Waverley Novels, however, are factitious and far from real or meaningful. Dousterswivel illustrates Sir Arthur Wardour's mineralogical gullibility and provides Lovell a means of winning the favour of the heroine's father by saving him from ruin. Despite such services, this fantastic is on the whole a narrative *persona non grata* in *The Antiquary*. Either Henry Morton's ghost or his real presence, accepted as such in *Old Mortality*, would prevent Edith from marrying Lord Evandale, so that the apparition-mistake adds little except momentary spirit-complication of the usual nick-of-time intervention. Whether as true or misapprehended supernatural agents, in their obtrusive and capricious activity the White Lady of Avenel and Fenella are plot excrescences. Although she undergoes a temperamental change because of plot necessity, Vanda has no significant function in *The Betrothed*. And the quest for prophecy in *Castle Dangerous*, when it serves inadequately in anticipating action, becomes a distracting fictional side venture.

Characterisation

Those two great components of fiction, doers and their deeds, characters and plots, are so interrelated that much of the discussion of plot has applied to characterisation as well. Enough has already been said about villains in the comment on villainy. But other characters may be more specifically considered in relation to the function of the *raisonneur*, contrasted sceptics and believers, class differences in credulousness, the hero's attitudes, and sex and the supernatural.

In speaking for the author, the *raisonneur* offers an escape from the difficulty of introducing the unearthly without losing balance. Ideally his scepticism serves many purposes, the most important being that it frees the author from the embarrassment of stepping forward in his own person to argue for natural cause and that it gives the reader a rational point of view from which to survey the action. The drawbacks are equally obvious. Too often the *raisonneur* is a makeshift adjustment to inconsistency in narrative theory and practice and to lack of subtlety in handling character and situation. While keeping alive the rational values, sceptical mouthpieces, whether old or young, male or female, act as irksome checks on the reader's imagination. Many of them seem to be moderns anachronistically let loose in ages past. But, no matter what Scott's method, lack of method, or combination of methods may be at the moment, the reader cannot go wrong intellectually if he clings to the coat-tails of the *raisonneurs*, after making sure that the doubter is not the villain as well.

Perhaps, Scott's most boldfaced *raisonneur* and guide to the perplexed reader is the remarkable archer of *Castle Dangerous*, Gilbert Greenleaf. He astutely defines prophecy as "some old forgotten rhyme, conjured out of dust and cobwebs, for the sake of giving courage to . . . rebels." By means of treasonable predictions and even worse offences, "men, pretending to have the assistance of the devil, do impose upon the common people." More than that, when publicised, forecasts "are very apt to cause the very mischances which they would be thought only to predict." Such penetration is scarcely explained by Gilbert's admission that he is "borrel" (unlearned) or by the author's revelation that the bluff soldier is prejudiced against fanciful minstrels and their craft.

The humbly-born archer's fellow *raisonneur* is Sir Aymer de Valence, who is just as impatient with the minstrel Bertram. For his story of a presageful and "ghastly spectre" at the wedding of Alexander III of Scotland and Lady Juletta de Dreux, Sir Aymer has an explanation, a skeleton figure was tactlessly included in the nuptial pageant.[8] Thomas the Rhymer or no Thomas, prophecy is not enforced by "the will of Heaven."[9] Ironically, in the light of what follows, Bertram's sense of harmony between prophecy and the trend of events is less than senile, and the well-born knight's insouciance shows the English invader's inability to estimate the strength of his Scottish foe.[10]

The opposition of scepticism and belief may have moral as well as intellectual significance. Utter imperviousness to the supernatural indicates frivolity or hardness of heart; too great susceptibility, weakness. The ideal young man or woman feels the influence of superstition but rises above it like eighteen year old Grizell Hume, who took food to her Presbyterian father, Sir Patrick, when he hid from arrest in the family vault:

> She had been bred up in the usual superstitions of the times, about ghosts and apparitions, but the duty which she was discharging to her father banished all such childish fears.[11]

If the moral issue of submission were not involved in *The Heart of Midlothian*, the superstitiousness of the God-fearing Jeanie Deans might

[8] See W. S. Crockett, *The Scott Country*, 6th edn, London 1930, pp. 41–2.

[9] See *Grandfather*, First Series, pp. 46–7; Scott, *History of Scotland*, London 1830, I. 48–9.

[10] Sir Aymer also exercises his scepticism on a vanishing horseman, a sibyl, and Lazarus Powheid, whose talk of "fleshless warriors" he impatiently labels "a fiction too gross to charm to sleep a schoolboy." An ancient, emaciated, half-crazed plotter, Lazarus moves among the entombed Douglases in an atmosphere of graveyard prescience. He is an effective study in the macabre and Scott's most carefully drawn sexton.

[11] *Grandfather*, Second Series, p. 301. Grizell Hume has points of resemblance to Jeanie Deans and to Ida Munster, heroine of "a very good little German romance." C. B. E. Naubert, *Herman of Unna*, 2nd edn, tr. anon., London 1794, III. 156–7; *Letters*, II. 495.

have been conferred, by psychological right, on the uncontrollably romantic Effie. Instead, Jeanie, who has heard ghost and devil stories "from her infancy,"[12] trembles before the unknown and is irreproachable. Except for being spoiled, Effie the sinner has the same early conditioning as her sister, yet she is "inaccessible to supernatural terrors." When marriages are contracted, Effie is bound to her seducer, whose lips form Satan's name more frequently than God's. Their illegitimate son is untamed and diabolical. Jeanie is united to Reuben Butler, who considers disbelief in witches or spectres "an undeniable proof of atheism." With low-born Effie and well-born Robertson, self-centred rejection of a part shakes the whole structure of belief. Paradoxically, therefore, minds which scorn superstition at the time of the belated repeal of the witchcraft law are represented as wayward and blasphemous, and temperaments which accept an outmoded creed are admirably compliant to the will of God and man. The values implied do not fit into a consistent ethical pattern; rather, they suggest a fragmentary and emotional appraisal of good and bad individuals.

What Scott was confusedly trying to articulate in *The Heart of Midlothian* through sceptic-believer contrasts comes out more clearly in *The Pirate*. The illicit lover, Basil Mertoun, is thrust beyond faith of any kind by his flaunting of moral law. A solitary, sneering, iconoclastic, even uncanny person, "he was totally without the superstitious fears of the country." The pirate Cleveland, his illegitimate son, has "no sympathy whatever" to waste on spirits or visionary terrors and comes to no happy end. But for Basil's legitimate son, the good Mordaunt, "who had much of romance in his disposition, these superstitions formed a pleasing and interesting exercise of the imagination . . . half doubting, half inclined to believe." In his curiosity about Norna's weather powers, "his incredulity went no farther than doubts." Although Mordaunt later joins others in suspecting madness, he temperamentally unites traits of the sisters, Minna and Brenda Troil, and thus remains consistently inconsistent—and convincing.

Norna's pretensions are a touchstone by which the "extremely different" sisters are tested. To talented, romantic Minna, who delights in "every tale of wonder," Norna is an instrument of fate; to gay, satirical Brenda, whose weak nerves subject her to fears which her reason ridicules, Norna is made terrible by partial insanity. Minna accepts the sibyl's confession, but Brenda seeks an explanation in "imaginary crime" dream-evoked at the Dwarfie Stone. When they see Norna performing the lead

[12] Note Scott's comment on the reading public of 1818: "The incredulity of the age has rendered us strangers to the nature and extent of her feelings."

heart charm, the patient, Minna, believes and is resolute; Brenda, with her "bounded comprehension" (Norna's words), disbelieves and is afraid.

> In our own more enlightened days, there are few whose undoubting mind and native courage have not felt Minna's high-wrought tone of enthusiasm; and perhaps still fewer, who have not, at one time or other, felt, like Brenda, their nerves confess the influence of terrors which their reason disowned and despised.

Throughout, Scott reveals a fondness for the lofty-minded Minna. But, like Norna, with whom she has much in common, she must give up the fictions of rhyme and saga. Thus "she learned to exchange the visions of wild enthusiasm which had exerted [exercised] and misled her imagination, for a truer and purer connexion with the world beyond us." Brenda, with more judgment, strikes her creator as somewhat tame. In the struggle between sense and sensibility, Scott is not as wholeheartedly on the side of sense as is that artist in cameo, Jane Austen.

Contrasted sisters are replaced in *The Betrothed* by mistress and free-spoken maid. Reversing Mrs Radcliffe's procedure,[13] Scott gives the benefit, or the burden, of rationality to the attendant and the luxury of imagination to the highborn damsel. When "with an overstrained eye, and an imagination heated with enthusiasm," Eveline Berenger vows at the shrine of Our Lady of the Garde Doloureuse that she will reward her rescuer even with her hand, the image overpowers her with "supernatural awe" by seeming to smile and nod assent. Of all this "her faith permitted her not to question the reality." Rose Flammock's advice to her mistress regarding the vigil in the chamber of the Red Finger is to "bid defiance to this antiquated and, I think, half-pagan superstition," which may be compounded "as much of trick as of supernatural agency." She discusses continued worship of pre-Christian elemental spirits, nightmare due to "bodily indisposition," and "the great and perhaps yet undecided question" (Scott's words) of final separation from the earth after death or of permitted communication. Although the "guilt of heresy" would cling to the denial of spirit return, the Flemish maid can at least doubt the frequency of such visitation. Thus Eveline's imagination is neutralised by Rose's logic, and her experience of the beyond loses force when discussed. But Rose's hardiness of mind, like Brenda Troil's, is not matched by that

---

[13] "The enlightened philosophy likewise! young ladies [in Radcliffian romance] arguing with their maids against their belief of ghosts and witches, when a judge durst not have expressed his doubts of either upon the bench." *Letters of Lady Louisa Stuart to Miss Louisa Clinton*, ed. J. A. Home, Edinburgh 1901, p. 55 (cp. p. 212), 10 Feb. 1820. Of course, in Restoration and eighteenth-century plays, as in Roman comedy, the servant lives by his wits and is often the greater realist. Scott's debt to drama has not been adequately explored.

of her body, which trembles at the slightest sound during her watch outside the ghostly chamber. When Eveline is ready to tell her confidante of the bahr-geist's appearance, Rose professes ignorance of such matters. Her father has discouraged her from listening to tales of terror, because she would see enough evil spirits "without *her* imagination being taught to form such as were fantastical." As so often in verse and prose, Scott makes the point that rationality or susceptibility chiefly reflects early upbringing. What Eveline's childhood training has been may easily be conjectured.

Despite Rose Flammock's analytical powers, superstitiousness usually increases as Scott's non-historical characters descend the social ladder. Sir Henry Lee's daughter Alice is apparently aware of this when she scornfully advises "a fortune-teller by Rosamond's Well," "You must carry your tricks of fortune-telling and palmistry to the women of the village—We of the gentry hold them to be either imposture or unlawful knowledge" (*Woodstock*).[14] Within the upper class, temperament and education make a wide difference. The whimsical scepticism of the antiquary, Jonathan Oldbuck, offers no real impediment to the gullible abandon of his sister Grizel in telling the story of Auld Rab Tull's dream.

Circumstances may drive a character outside the thought pattern of class and time. Thus the middle-class Fair Maid of Perth develops opinions that are "refined . . . beyond those of the age she lived in," a consequence of Father Clement's tuition. Because of the stark necessity to live by their wits, Scott's *gamins*, such as Dickie Sludge (Flibbertigibbet), and his desperate men, hardened and soured by life, know too much about taking people in to be readily taken in themselves.

The low-born, of course, have picturesquely low folk notions. As Scott remarks in *St Ronan's Well*, "Love of evil presage . . . is common in the lower ranks." Notwithstanding his tags of learning, Dominie Sampson in *Guy Mannering* comes from the people and accepts ghosts and evil hags "as an article indivisible from his religious faith." When he sees Meg Merrilies at the haunted Kaim of Derncleugh, countryside fears well up and he splutters Latin to drive the danger away. Even after giving in to Canidia's stew and smuggled brandy, the tremulous pedant can hardly free his spirit from that "harlot, thief, witch, and gypsy" or his tongue from exorcism. In his farrago of popular fears, scraps of learning, and eccentricity, the dominie is a humorous victim of witch fright. Nor is he out of character when he rejects the "altogether vain, frivolous, and

---

[14] Alice's sweetheart has already assured a clergyman, "Trust me, what you hear from the villagers is the growth of their idle folly and superstition."

unsatisfactory" science of astrology as "the resource of cheaters." Because it is a middle-class and aristocratic prepossession, astrology has had no early warping influence on his mind, which considers the phenomenon in maturity and dismisses it.

In general, then, Scott's unheroic commoners are governed in their attitudes by the locale, period, and class to which they belong. His heroes and heroines, on the other hand, find it much more difficult to be consistent because of contrary loyalties to plot, truth of character, and the need to be exemplary. Scott's own undirected reading and enthusiasm were brought within bounds by the discipline of the law, of a marriage perhaps more sensible than romantic, and of mature responsibility buoyantly faced. At times his heroes—and heroines to some extent—represent the days of unchecked youth; at others, the period of growing self-mastery. Or these aspects may be assigned to close friends, as to Darsie Latimer and Alan Fairford in *Redgauntlet*. With Scott's young people, as has been suggested, old wives' tales or a sound upbringing makes the difference between subjection to or mastery of superstition.

The wavering hero is, unfortunately for all despisers of puns, a familiar figure in the Waverley Novels.[15] Though rather ineffectively, the waverer bodies forth Scott's own combination of the pleasures of imagination with the security of reason. Edward Waverley, William Lovel, Patrick Earnscliff, Edgar Ravenswood, the Earl of Menteith, and Colonel Markham Everard, men of heart and hand, are far from distinguished in intellect or judgment. While playing a sceptical role which is foreign to their natures, they tend to reflect with Edward when he thinks of the Bodach Glas, "What, can the devil speak truth?" For the most part, in what concerns the unearthly, they are narrative wet blankets.

Although Tressilian plays second fiddle in *Kenilworth*, he has the conventional hero's qualities without his success in love. He hesitates momentarily before deciding that Amy Robsart is not an apparition or the illusion of "a heated imagination." But when he sees Wayland Smith and Flibbertigibbet in a flickering light, he immediately soars above "that age of superstition." The reason for his immunity is that "nature had endowed Tressilian with firm nerves, and his education, originally good, had been too sedulously improved by subsequent study to give way to any imaginary terrors."

---

[15] In *Waverley*, Scott describes young Waverley as having a "wavering and unsettled habit of mind," which "wavered" between two plans, and quotes a newspaper innuendo about "the *Waverin Honour*" of Waverley Honour, the family seat. The hero of Sir Walter's last novel, *Cast Dangerous*, is middle-aged "Walton the Unwavering." See Donald Davie, *The Heyday of Sir Walter Scott*, London 1961, pp. 46, 104.

In *Anne of Geierstein*, Arthur Philipson unpredictably pendulates from "ardent imagination" to sensible objectivity. As a man of fecund fancy, he inclines to belief in the heroine's elemental ancestry and in her ethereal vagaries. And as a man of critical outlook, though not "positively incredulous" about apparitions, he shakes off the impression that Anne's flitting form is spiritual and turns his mind to more solid reflexion. In his unwillingness to accept the uncanny as long as "ordinary rules" can be made to apply, Arthur follows the teachings of his brave, intelligent father. But the father has premonitions and toys with the Scottish idea of fey persons. By not always living up to his rational precepts, the elder Philipson, too, becomes a waverer.

Lacking an introspective gift, Scott clumsily fumbles toward a realisation of his own comfortably divided nature in his heroes. His approach to the other sex, to his heroines, is complicated and confused by reticence and inhibition. There is much surface truth in the common assumption that, with very few exceptions, Scott fashions straw-stuffed narrative dolls with sufficient blood to blush but not to pulsate; that, in avoiding scenes of passionate love, he dissolves feminine reality in an idealising solution of polite flattery and aloof regard. Of course, his heroines display little manifest sexuality, but few are lacking in latent sexuality. Indeed, Scott's tribute to the power of sex is that, while apparently playing it down, he unconsciously emphasises it. With him, suppression, transformation, and evasion become mutilated expression. Because of this difficulty, apparently disproportionate attention will be paid to innocent, weak, and sinful young women. As the most numerous, the innocents offer a good starting-point.

The exoticism of Scott's innocents is not unknown in real life. It appears in the no less fantastic, though certainly less moral, mistress of Lord Byron. Caroline Lamb galloped bareback at fourteen, assumed boyish disguises, exulted in trousers, scorned "orthodox feminine employments," and was temperamental, fitfully clever, and unpredictable in a "will-o'-the-wisp" fashion. Lord David Cecil further describes her, of course without reference to Scott's heroines:

> Slight, agile, and ethereal, with a wide-eyed wilful little face, and curly short hair, she still looked a child; like something less substantial even,— "the Sprite," people called her, "the Fairy Queen, Ariel." Her fresh lisping voice . . . was a child's voice.[16]

---

[16] Lord David Cecil, "The Young Melbourne" (1939) in *Melbourne*, London 1955, p. 48. For "the Fairy Queen's spell," see pp. 49, 65. An old Highland woman reported that Byron as a boy was attended by a greenclad maid who combined the flowing hair, beauty, and agility of Fenella with the ubiquity and prescience of the White Lady in *The Monastery*. James Grant, *The Mysteries of All Nations*, Leith 1880, pp. 197–8.

Wayward and spoiled, this sexual medley of arrested and premature development, this transvestite and perhaps suppressed Lesbian, was born to tantalise jaded and special appetites. Annot Lyle in *A Legend of Montrose*, bred among men, feels no feminine timidity. "The fairy queen of song and minstrelsy," she is twice described as the lightest, most beautiful little fairy that ever danced by moonlight. Though nearly eighteen, she seems to be four years younger. Her diminutive stature "gave her the appearance of extreme youth. . . . Her figure, hands, and feet, were formed upon a model of exquisite symmetry with the size and lightness of her person, so that Titania herself could scarce have found a more fitting representative." Yet she appeals to apparently full-blooded men.

The mysterious Fenella, or Zarah, in *Peveril of the Peak*, is "a most beautiful miniature" in face and body, "exquisitely well formed in all her limbs," darker than most maidens and with hair that descends almost to her ankles. This sometimes irascible and vindictive changeling, or "Elfin Queen," floats from parapets like gossamer and springs up stairs like a kid. Trained as a rope-dancer and acrobat, "she is like a fairy who trips it in moonlight." Though her figure is actually "almost infantine," she allures the Duke of Buckingham in an Oriental veil which "induced the imagination even to enhance the charms it shaded"; then she escapes from his amorousness by a window some fourteen feet above the ground. Through Fenella, Scott affirms and yet denies sex. The girl is both "yon black-eyed houri of the Mahometan paradise" and a Rosicrucian sylphid, both a sexually appealing "Moorish sorceress" and a sexless "little fairy." Of course, delicate Alice Bridgenorth is the real heroine of *Peveril*, not Fenella, whom she resembles in having an exquisite, "sylphlike form . . . not, as yet, sufficiently rounded in the outlines to produce the perfection of female beauty." Both love the hero, one with ladylike restraint, the other with emotional abandon. Cultivated and natural, they complement each other and present together something like the whole of young womanhood.

Scott has other techniques for disclosing the double nature of woman. In *The Abbot*, he takes his time before explaining Catherine Seyton's duplicity. Her "excellent shape" is "rather that of a Hebe than of a Sylph," bordering "perhaps on *embonpoint*." Forgetting himself later on, the novelist describes "the nymph" as having a "light and lovely form" like that of "sylph" or "fairy." When in man's attire, "this singular female" is a regular "Will o' the Wisp," resembling "a masculine virago and termagant" by her insolence and cruelty. After hinting at the domineering, male elements in female character, Scott extricates himself by revealing that Catherine's *alter ego* is actually her twin brother Henry. Young Seyton, it should be noted, sometimes assumes "a female dress."

Anne of Geierstein is also ambiguous. As a maiden, her "matchless form" is "something above the common size," her limbs are "well-formed and active," and her step is "firm and yet light." "Without being in the slightest degree masculine," her figure is like that of the wise and chaste Minerva rather than the stately matron, Juno, or the yielding paramour, Venus. But in Anne's double-ganger aspect, her body seems as light and almost as translucent as a cloud. As a mortal, Anne is like Diana the chaste huntress, the winsome and convincing Diana Vernon, who rides boldly in *Rob Roy*, consorts mostly with men, and confesses to Frank Osbaldistone, "I belong, in habits of thinking and acting, rather to your sex . . . than to my own." Anne also moves sexlessly in the company of men without losing her fascination, and she is also poised between the insipidity of Scott's ladies and the dangerously exercised freedom of his fallen women. By portraying daring in the unawakened, Scott combines safety features with seductiveness. As a supernatural, this daughter of "a wizard," grand-daughter of "a will-of-wisp," and great-grand-daughter of a Persian sorcerer borrows traits from Scott's tomboy type, his immature and underweight paragons of agility, in order to warn and to protect. Her two natures, familiar and awesome, permit her to be both playfellow-sweetheart and mother-wife, woman in almost all her relationship to man. In innocent companionship, her physique is recognised, but in the maturer attachment, it is distanced and etherealised. Anne is Scott's secular image of a warmly beautiful, yet remote virgin mother. This ambivalent quality is possessed by all the heroines whom Scott portrays with a certain fervour.

Perhaps, the most unusual of Scott's Egerias is Rose Flammock, Eveline Berenger's "wise maiden and monitress" in *The Betrothed*. She is at first described as having "almost infantine features" and the "form and figure . . . of a girl who has scarce emerged from childhood." She develops into the "pure and white" protectress who, lovely, blue-eyed, and fair-haired, "with half-veiled bosom and dishevelled locks, flitted through her vision," waking her mistress from a dream of the frightful spirit, Vanda of the Red Finger, by covering her face with tears and kisses "in a passion of affection."

When she is guarding a hero, an Egeria is more restrained in expressing affection though not in bestowing counsel. She takes on maternal characteristics in relation to the feckless hero, and a sexual taboo is set up, at least for a time, by her apparent physical immaturity. But in *Redgauntlet* Green

Mantle[17] is withheld from Darsie when she turns out to be his sister;[18] his complementary, down-to-earth *persona*, Alan, wins her instead. The feminine Egeria may be contrasted with the forbidding, arbitrary, somewhat masculine mother image of the sibyl. Thus the ductile Roland Graeme of *The Abbot* is advised by his beloved Catherine and by his mysterious grandmother, Magdalen. Because of her function, Scott may represent his Egeria as having more intellectual than physical loveliness. Catharine Glover is "made of better clay" than "earthly, coarse, ferocious" mankind, her beauty being "of that kind which we connect more with the mind than with the person." Yet she does attract the love of Lowland smith and Highland chief, as well as the twice foiled lust of a prince. After all, she is Perth's fairest maid in the flesh.

Alice Lee of *Woodstock* is another spiritual-intellectual-physical beauty. Partly modelled on Anne Scott, who never married, she is perhaps a father's ideal of an innocent, resourceful daughter. She has "a slight and sylphlike form, with a person so delicately made, and so beautiful in countenance," that the earth seems too gross for such an aerial creature. As a girl, she has enacted "an elfin page, or a fairy, or an enchanted princess" in her cousin Markham's games. She is conscious of reluctant blooming. When love does come, it is purer, freer from violence or jealousy, than the passion of those who have not been brought up together. "Such love as I have to bestow" is not that of romance or song, but she is sufficiently awakened to marry and to have children. The sexual plot, if such it may be called, is developed as parallel and contrast to the story of Henry II's mistress, Fair Rosamond, who was poisoned at Woodstock by the jealous Queen Eleanor. On Scott's own theory that certain settings call for appropriate action, the disguised Charles II, who first sees Alice at Rosamond's Well, tries to seduce her. Since Alice is not to be a second Rosamond, Scott has echoes of *Comus* in which Charles's sophistry about the privilege of kings and Alice's rebuttal are Miltonic. With aristocratic Alice, the attempted rape is verbal and Markham's duel with Charles is interrupted. But when plebeian Phoebe Mayflower is encountered at Rosamond's Well, Joseph Tomkins urges the privilege of saints and advances from verbal to active attempt at rape. Phoebe flees and Tomkins

---

[17] Note that the Green Lady is a supernatural tutelary spirit who is known in the Highlands as the green-clad maiden (*Maighdeann Uaine*) or as wan and green-clad (*Glaistig Uaine*). McNeill, *The Silver Bough*, I. 115. She is, of course, sexually unapproachable.

[18] Eveline Berenger, recognised by "her green mantle," is kept from Damian for years in tortured abstinence, while the ironic report circulates that they know each other *par amours*. Their longing is in contrast to the indulgence of Dame Gillian, who is as gay and amoral a cuckolder as the Wife of Bath.

is slain by her sweetheart, Joceline Joliffe. The gamut of sex from intellectual Alice to lively Phoebe to indulgent Rosamond is sounded, with the shriller notes of passion diminished by time.

In *Kenilworth*, Amy Robsart inspires three kinds of love, romantic, wedded, and sensual. Tressilian is described as "languishing after a shadow which has lost all the gaiety of its colouring" and has become a "dream by night and . . . vision by day." His beloved Amy is "like a phantom," a paler, thinner being than when, a virgin, she "possessed the form and hue of a wood-nymph, with the beauty of a sylph." All this may seem pretty and meaningless, but sexual substance is not wanting. When the Earl of Leicester and his countess retire for the night, "all was silent in the castle." Soon after, content is read back into the relationship by the bailiff's guess at the reason for Leicester's looking "somewhat pale. I warrant him he hath spent the whole night in perusing our memorial. . . . See if the Earl hath not knocked the marrow out of it in twenty-four hours!" Richard Varney speaks to the Earl of his looking "babies in the eyes of *his* fair wife" and, Iago-fashion, lusts after his master's soft, hazel-eyed, red and white "pretty piece of painted Eve's flesh." The atmosphere is thickened by allusions to Janet Foster, pretty Cicely, the purchase of virtue, and the "damned pander" Varney sounding his quailpipe "to wile wantons into his nets." In this context, Amy is more full-bodied and sexually identifiable than in the author's or Tressilian's direct references to her.

Both Amy Robsart and Lucy Ashton are studies in weakness which is uncomplicated by sexual sin. Undisciplined in her reading, the Bride of Lammermoor secretly delights in tales of unearthly horror, constant ardour, and adventure until the wand of enchantment at last conjures up nightmare beings that cannot be dispelled. To control her daughter's will, Lady Ashton places the impressionable girl in the charge of Ailsie Gourlay, whose stories grow in terror as she narrows "her magic circle around the devoted victim on whose spirit she practised." The witch concentrates on omens, interpretation of dreams, and the fate looming over Ravenswood until Lucy's health, temper, and mind are imperilled. Superstitiousness in a heroine who lacks countervailing willpower, like Lucy Ashton or Clara Mowbray, may help to destroy her. No sceptic is needed here, for it is impossible to doubt Ailsie's evil power or Lucy's tragic passivity.

When weakness leads to sexual sin, Scott is usually too careless, too embarrassed, or too indignant to represent degeneration of character or punishment from within. Instead, the same upright man who refused to attend the funeral of his immoral brother Daniel sentences erring womankind to retribution from without, at times with the illusory terror of spirits, or turns remorse into insanity that resembles Biblical possession by the Devil. The pattern is crudely set by Alice in Scott's early poem, "Frederick and Alice." She mourns over "honour flown" and is drastically punished. Melodrama reappears in the justice meted out to Clara Mowbray, Zilia de Monçada, and Effie Deans. Of these Effie is especially interesting because she bears the trade-mark of Scott's innocents. The Lily of St Leonard's has a "sylph-like" or "nymph-like form." But the secret comes out when she attracts, and responds to, Robertson. By making it distinctive and exotic, supernatural terms enhance sex.[19]

Scott's physical prognosis for young women seems to have been that a maiden who is slight, almost sexless, though beautifully proportioned, will mature to perfection, whereas a maiden who is seductive in contours will be overblown in womanhood. In *Count Robert of Paris*, Scott contrasts "the charming beauties of the Saxon virgin, and the more ripened charms of her mother." The linnet-like virgin, Bertha, is also a foil to the Amazonian beauty, Countess Brenhilda. Underprivileged girls are likely to bloom and go to seed early. At sixteen, Hob the Miller's daughter Mysie in *The Monastery* is an agile, graceful "Hebe" with an "energetic arm ... possessing more than female strength." Hers is a "full and round, and firm and fair" form which may become "coarse and masculine" later in life, "the common fault of Scottish beauty."[19a] Scott rescues some of his heroines from this fleshly fate by making them undersized and even anaemic. Unlike Mysie, the pale and well-born Mary Avenel, visionary child of Halloween, has a "fair but fragile form" which seems to link "the Spirit of Avenel" more with "the immaterial than the substantial world." "The fine, delicate, fragile form of Lucy Ashton" also comes from a brittle mould. There is a suggestion of decadence in all this, as there is in the appeal of consumptives to the Pre-Raphaelites. To express this quality of refinement, Scott depends somewhat superficially on fairies and elemental spirits.

The heroines of the first Waverley Novels are tragedy queens, polite and passive maidens, or formal and sententious ladies. Even after his success with the charming tomboy, Diana Vernon, Scott falls back on the earlier stereotypes, but he also attempts portraits of weak and erring, weak and doomed, moral and superstitious, protective, exotic, and intellectual

---

[19] Brenda Troil has "a fairy form" and is a "more fairy-formed siren."
[19a] Effie Deans has a "Hebe countenance" and "a shape, which time, perhaps, might be expected to render too robust, the frequent objection to Scottish beauty," and she matures to "rather above the middle size, beautifully made, though something *embonpoint*."

heroines. And he conceives of a being with mature and immature, sexual and sexless, boyish and feminine, maternal, protective, and maidenly traits. For aid in characterisation and in half-articulate exploration, he turns to witchcraft, demonology, ghost-lore, Rosicrucian tenets, and the German double-ganger. The evocation is more generally effective than has been critically conceded, but insight and clarity too often yield to artifice.

The supernatural has a bearing as well on Scott's historical and pseudo-historical characters. The demonologist, James VI and I, and the star-governed Louis XI illustrate the greatness and the paltriness of monarchs, a complex theme which appealed to Sir Walter. In his Introduction to *Quentin Durward* of 1831, he characterises the French King as one who "almost seems an incarnation of the devil himself, permitted to do his utmost to corrupt our ideas of honour."[20] His "excessive superstition" is due to irreligious actions whose consequences he tries to escape by means of formulae, penance, and bribes. The barber, Oliver the Devil, realising that "his master had superstition in a large proportion to his want of religion," steers his course accordingly, as does the royal astrologer, Martius Galeotti. But Louis is not unaware of his wily servant's cynicism toward the starry science and religion, nor does his searching mind remain consistently under a planetary spell. In this interpretation, Scott owes more to Nathaniel Wraxall's *Memoirs of the Kings of France* (1777)[21] than to his apparent authority, Philippe de Comines, who declares that his master "seemed a Prince woorthier to govern the whole world than one realme alone."[22] Similar court tensions and conflicts in *Kenilworth*, arising from the Machiavellian ruthlessness of a superior, the Earl of Leicester, who is in turn dominated by the mean cunning and astral dupery of his own para-sites, have already been explored.

The Talisman introduces a chivalrous king who is not superstitious. As Richard Coeur de Lion rather brusquely announces to the Hakim (Saladin in disguise), he is no believer in the stars or observer of idle omens and ceremonies. This he repeats to the Hermit of Engaddi, for astrology is "heathen science," neither practised by Christians nor countenanced by wise men. To the same hermit, who is "like enough to those spirits which

---

[20] In the Introduction of 1828 to the second series of *Chronicles of the Canongate*, Scott describes "the fierce fanatic Ruthven" as re-enacting the murder of David Rizzio with "writhen features . . . like those of a corpse tenanted by a demon."

[21] Orville W. Mosher, *Louis XI . . . in History and in Literature*, Toulouse 1925, p. 231.

[22] *The History of Comines*, Anglicised by Thomas Danett, 1596, London 1897, II. 115. Cp. Charles Whibley's Introduction, I. xxx: "For the misappreciation of modern times Sir Walter Scott is largely responsible."

walk in dry places," the king errant boasts, "Richard fears no hobgoblins." Such scepticism helps to characterise a ruler who, resenting the assumption of any power superior to military skill and courage, puts his trust in these high human endowments. The evocation of wilfulness and vaulting self-confidence through the Lion Hearted's attitude toward nebulous restraining powers is not enough, however, to make his incredulity convincing.

Sir Kenneth of the Couchant Leopard is somewhat nearer the twelfth-century mark when he fearlessly accepts Saladin's declaration of devil ancestry, for "tales of magic and necromancy were the learning of the period." Even the human gnome, Nectabanus, awes the Prince Royal of Scotland, who is "superior in no respect to the ideas and manners of his time."[23] This is an interesting concession for Scott to make. No matter what the period of his story and the likely susceptibility of the hero, the novelist usually puts him forward as a standard of values for the reader, who may learn through him how far it is safe to pursue the unreal. With the King zealous in that mission, Sir Kenneth may be his normal self and only suggest incidentally the medieval golden mean between the extremes of Richard and Saladin.

With the exception of Saladin, leaders who combine power and superstition tend to be neurotic, guilt-laden, or excessively ambitious. In *Ivanhoe*, the Grand Master of the Templars has striven like a medieval Balfour of Burley "with devils embodied and disembodied." He is determined to cleanse his order of magic and heresy, and avoids women as snares of the Ancient Enemy. With this cast of mind, he sees possession and demonic spells in such phenomena as silence and sexual attraction. His most frequent exclamation is, "Semper Leo percutiatur [or *feriatur*—his vocabulary is not limited]!" Inasmuch as Rebecca's trial on a charge of witchcraft is managed by the Grand Master, his brand of superstition affects the plot centrally.

Although the high and mighty do not always conform to the gradation of superstition, which increases in the Waverley population as rank decreases, the exceptions characteristically fall into aristocratic rather than folk error. Superstitiousness is more frequently assigned to the ignorant or learning-choked (pedantic) than to the well-educated, to disturbed than to self-possessed persons, to the unstable than to the established segments of society, and consequently to turbulent than to peaceful eras. The richer seedbeds of superstition are the relatively propertyless and the

---

[23] Similarly, the hero of *The Fortunes of Nigel*, living in an age "when a certain degree of superstition was inculcated as a point of religious faith," is not free from dread of the unknown.

socially faceless; the shallow-rooted political ways of life, commonwealth and anti-monarchic; and such parallels in religious rebellion as the Independent and Covenanting. Rationality almost always accompanies the values which Scott approves.

NATIONAL AND CULTURAL HISTORY

In these value-judgments Scott proceeds from individual to group portraits and takes on the responsibilities of a culture historian. The difference between the two kinds of portrayal may be suggested by two men in *The Heart of Midlothian* and *Old Mortality*. The novelist uses demonology as an external equivalent of Robertson's and Burley's inner reality. Yet Robertson the individual does little more than exemplify a passage in Scott's review of Richard Cumberland's novel, *John de Lancaster*, "We must recollect that there are incredibilities in the moral as well as physical world."[24] Within the honest, simple, shallow, graphic ethical box constructed for him, the warning marionette is more lively than lifelike. In contrast, demonology helps Burley emerge as a convincing fanatic, unique and at the same time representative of Covenanters in diabolically highlighted conflict with Royalists. When he reveals the influence of an age on the individual or embodies the age in its leaders and fashioners, Scott gains in sureness of touch and judgment. The explicit moralist of individual lives becomes absorbed in individuals as part of larger movements.

The role of national and cultural historian, the greatest of his fictional capacities, was consciously assumed by Scott in *Chronicles of the Canongate*, whose object was "to throw some light on the manners of Scotland as they were, and to contrast them, occasionally, with those of the present day." Events then become not only curious in themselves but interesting "as chapters in the history of the human race." As he explained eight years earlier, the unearthly is introduced as part and parcel of the life of the past, though not necessarily of the unbelieving present:

> Some curious particulars respecting that time . . . are mixed with that measure of the wild and wonderful which belongs to the period . . . but which I do not in the least object to the reader's treating with disbelief.[25]

Viewed in this light, single constituents, whether scenic, narrative, psychological, historical, or legendary, should not be judged by themselves.

[24] Quoted in *Letters*, II. 176, n. 1.
[25] Introduction to the first edition of *A Legend of Montrose* (1819).

They relate to each other through tension, contrast, or harmony. Thus Vanda, Fenella, and the White Lady are functional because they belong to the legendry of Wales, the Isle of Man, and Scotland. Any failure is due to their creator, who gave them contradictory duties (Vanda is both "avenging fiend" and "good genius") or destroyed balance in some way (the White Lady is divided in allegiance to family tradition and to plot). Even in his last novel, *Castle Dangerous*, if the fitfully inspired novelist had introduced enough interdependent elements in his picture of the early fourteenth century, the search for Thomas the Rhymer's manuscripts would have had adequate cultural bearing instead of floating in a void.

So much for the intention. Accomplishment is more significant. "Wandering Willie's Tale" has most often been considered as a short story *per se*. As such, it is Scott's most concentrated and telling venture into the supernatural. There is an interpretation to suit every reader: Steenie was drunk, dreaming, lying, or actually in Hell; Redgauntlet was a phantom, a devil, an illusion, or a damned soul; Major Weir did all the things that seemed supernatural; or Wandering Willie was just telling another story. Yet the tale bears its full freight of horror, humour, fantasy, irony, reason and unreason, as does the artistically similar exploit of Tam o' Shanter.

"Wandering Willie's Tale" is no mere diversion in a novel whose tightly intertwined *identity* and *strife* plots get little help from the uncanny except for symbolic birthmarks. In developing its father-son theme, *Redgauntlet* asks two questions, one personal, Who is—or will be—Darsie's father? and the other national, Who is the true father of his country? Alan Fairford has a formal but loving father. His very dear friend, Darsie Latimer, not knowing who his parent is, seeks a father. As surrogates, Saunders Fairford, the Quaker Joshua Geddes, and a long unidentified uncle, the Laird of Redgauntlet, are inadequate. It is Willie Steenson for whom Darsie develops a filial feeling. And it is the wandering fiddler who offers the story of his gudesire Steenie's dreadful time after encountering a stranger on horseback (the Devil) as "a lesson" to heedless Darsie not to take up with "a stranger traveller . . . in an uncouth land" (the mysterious Redgauntlet, also on horseback). In its warnings, devilish company kept, temptation to dangerous allegiance (diabolical or Jacobite), and escape, the tale reflects, emphasizes, and foreshadows the meaning of the longer narrative. It also reveals the temperamental, legendary, and political background of the house of Redgauntlet, as well as its violence. This violence is now concentrated in the Laird who, instead of loving his nephew, wishes to consecrate him to the Jacobite cause, as he once sacrificed Darsie's father. Part of this study of fathers, lost fathers, and surrogates is a contrast between two fathers of their country, the Young Pretender and would-be king, "Father Buonaventure," whose wilfulness and self-indulgence bring on failure, and General Campbell, magnanimous representative of the Hanoverian king of Britain. It is in this large context that Scott masterfully fits an episode, "Wandering Willie's Tale," which helps to illuminate the history and culture of the past.

ACHIEVEMENT

When the supernatural appears in the Waverley Novels, it is either extrinsic or intrinsic. If extrinsic, it is superfluous, distracting, or merely decorative. If intrinsic, it helps to define the setting of "localized Romance," advances the plot by precipitating, complicating, or resolving action, interprets character, exists—though infrequently—for its own sake, provides the local colour of beliefs, or stresses the forces of history. When Scott's imagination glows, a just balance is struck between sympathy and objective understanding, as with witchcraft in *The Bride of Lammermoor*, demonology in "Wandering Willie's Tale," and omens in "The Highland Widow" and "The Two Drovers."

The novelist's not always consistent attitude toward phenomena is that of eighteenth-century rationalism, an attitude which has its drawbacks. It hampers the straightforward presentation in which Scott can be most effective, and it induces a self-consciousness which, along with the uncongenial influence of Gothic and German tales, too often reduces grotesque and humour-leavened terror to clumsy fabrication.

But Scott rarely intends the weird merely to startle or to entertain. Instead, he avails himself of materials appropriate to time, place, and people in order to convey a sense of the past. Although the Age of Hume may not raise him to Burns's level in witchcraft, to James Hogg's in demonology, or to Neil Gunn's in second sight, it does sustain him in a more massive achievement. In long and short Scottish narratives, Sir Walter encompasses the great range of native superstitious belief and sharpens understanding of a tumultuous national past through its legendary fears.

CHAPTER VI

SCOTT'S CONTEMPORARIES

1. JAMES HOGG

A TRADITION-STEEPED parent may school a child in native lore. The assurance of the fireside, of familiar objects and a loving face, contrasts with the powers of darkness outside which are brought fearfully close by the narrator—but not too close for enjoyment. Juxtaposed, the everyday and the unearthly sharpen each other. Thus, before formal literary standards affect him, the child is given an example of racy, brief, idiomatic story-telling.

"Many traditions" were passed on to James Hogg (1770–1835) by his father, Robert Hogg, and the narrative powers of his mother, Margaret Laidlaw, can best be suggested by his later personification of "Superstition." That lady could renew the seer's vision, people the green with elves and fairies, make ghosts walk and witches mount the midnight sky, until the boy would

> All breathless stand, unknowing what to fear;
> Or panting deep beneath his co'erlet lie.

Having grown up fearful of the haunted churchyard, the suicide's grave, and the spot where harper or pedlar was slain, Hogg understood the conditioning of a boy by imaginative terror. In "Duncan Campbell," a boy is so "terribly harassed" by a slain piper's ghost that he has a fever and recovers to leave the place but not the fear behind. After talking about "the Piper of Dewar, the Maid of Plora, or the Pedlar of Thirlestane Mill," Duncan and a friend draw the bedclothes over their heads "till nearly suffocated."[1] They love fairies and brownies, distrust water-kelpies, hate but do not tremble at the Devil, and are petrified by anything ghostly.

Elsewhere, Hogg rejoices that at least two "well attested . . . modern incidents" of abduction by fairies are still talked about and that "the belief in wraiths, ghaists, and bogles is little or nothing abated." And in another

[1] In *The Queen's Wake*, a warrior bard is so seared by a tale of spectral revenge heard at "his nurse's knee" that he quakes ever after at bush or stone when "wandering in the gloom alone."

mood, he laments that prayers, psalms, religious persecution, and a cold, mocking day have put the fairies to flight. "All these light unbodied forms are fled, | Or good or evil, save the ghost alone" ("Superstition"). Through his mother's family, Hogg had a proprietary interest in fairies, for his great-grandfather, Will Laidlaw, was the last Ettrick man to commune with the fairies. But in his account of "Will o' Phaup," as in "The Origin of the Fairies," he gives substance to his confession of adding "thousands of *lees*" to marvellous subjects ("Nature's Magic Lantern"). Perhaps the greatest *lee* of all is that these creatures of mingled virtue and blame, spirit and flame, Heaven and Hell, "body and passion fell," are mostly carefree and benevolent. Despite his boast to Scott of being "the king o' the mountain and fairy school... a far higher ane nor yours [of chivalry],"[2] Hogg does much to banish the fairies by stripping them of their robust malice and leaving a *Midsummer Night's Dream* residue of "the most delightful little spirits that ever haunted the Scottish dells" in their innocuous and "tiny moonlight forms."

Through his father's family, the Ettrick Shepherd reached back to a Witch of Fauldshope whose contest with Michael Scott he found sadly garbled by Walter Scott in a note to *The Lay of the Last Minstrel*. A sympathetic descendant, Hogg achieves a complex understanding of witchcraft, of its pagan roots, its real existence, and the mixed nature of its votaries, good and evil, ludicrous and tragic. The Ettrick witches were "extremely whimsical and diverting" in their rumoured transformations into hares and partridges or fearful in their blasting of sheep and cattle. Hogg recalls the counter-charm to livestock-impairment—a barred door, a mysterious seething of the animal's milk, and an incantation. The witch, irresistibly drawn to the cottage, was "cut above the breath" and allowed to flee, yelling.[3] Before they are destroyed by Colin's guardian spirits, the chief warlock and witch of "The Witches of Traquair" are carefully motivated in their frenzied evil. Disappointment and ill usage produce the warlock, and the witch, having grown too old for youthful hope and pleasure, turns "to an intercourse with the unseen powers, as affording an excitement of a higher and more terrible nature."[4] The "old witch-wife" of "A Story of Good Queen Bess" dresses like a Scott sibyl "in an antique and fantastic mode" and, like Galt's Spaewife, has compensatory powers:

[2] Hogg, *Domestic Manners of Sir Walter Scott* [=*Domestic Manners*], Stirling 1909, p. 94.
[3] In a note to "The Pedlar," however, Hogg calls this counter-charm a "weak and superstitious notion" of illiterate countrymen, who also crush eggshells to destroy the witches' sailing vessels.
[4] Mad, gloating pride of power finds a voice in Hogg's poem, "A Witch's Chant."

Wha kens what she may hae suffered i' this wicked world!... her losses may hae injured her reason... an' that's the way how she sees intil hidden mysteries an' events. For it is weel kend that when God bereaves o' ae sense, he always supplies another, and that aften of a deeper and mair incomprehensible nature.

In "The Hunt of Eildon," a witch-mark is found on innocent Pery, who is almost convinced of her guilt and brought to confession by inquisitors. Miraculously, she is saved from "the superstition of the times" and from the stake. And in the poem "Superstition," Hogg defends harmless beldames—"sorely crazed" by age and poverty—whose "feeble senses were abused | By gleesome demon." The true wonder will ever be the Inquisitor who "could the wretches make | Believe these things all real, and swear them at the stake." Whether it is loss of youth, a defect, the Devil's cajolery, or the Inquisitor's sophistry which twists her, Hogg is indulgent to almost every witch except the reputation-sapping modern hag. She makes him wish that the "old times" of the demonologist, James VI and I, might return.

Hogg's finest evocation of witchcraft is a ballad, "The Witch of Fife," which is founded on an old tradition. To the queries of her "guid auld man," a witch-wife replies that she has left her hearth to dance to the reed-pipe of a boneless and bloodless "wee wee man," to voyage to Norway and fly to Lapland, to drink deep and then sleep in a warlock's arms. The old fellow objects to her infidelity to God and him, and thinks the whole venture far from practical, "Quhat guid was that to thee?" But when he learns that the last flight was to the Bishop's wine-cellar in Carlisle, he eavesdrops until he hears the formula which will put him in orbit. Getting too drunk to return with his party, he is tortured until the blood—or claret—runs out before being perched on lighted faggots. When his wife descends with a red cap and a potent word, he evades shackles and flames and laughs as he vanishes in the sky. Humour, concrete detail, and rushing movement carry the reader triumphantly along.

"Kilmeny," another tradition-inspired poem in *The Queen's Wake* (1813), is like a companion piece to "The Witch of Fife." Together, they represent extremes of womanhood, one innocent and contemplative, the other shameless and instinctive. Hogg responds ideally to one, sensuously and emotionally to the other. In the same way, Hogg the writer wants his work to be free from anything "injurious to the cause of religion, of virtue, or of good manners,"[5] and Hogg the man is puzzled by the approach of

---

[5] The confusion of morality and aesthetics by Burns's critics may have been a warning to Hogg to go cautiously.

two strangers, "I was afraid they were come to look after me with an accusation regarding some of the lasses." Man's responses to the two natures of woman are combined in a song, "The Witch o' Fife," which almost transforms the ballad witch into Keats's nightingale:

> Away, thou bonnie witch o' Fife,
>   On foam of the air to heave an' flit,
> An' little reck thou of a poet's life,
>   For he sees thee yet, he sees thee yet!

The "Bonny Kilmeny" of the poem goes up the glen, which Hogg elsewhere associates with sensuality and danger. She falls asleep and wakes in a lovely, luminous, sinless realm. "A virgin in her prime," she is preserved from "the snares of men . . . sin or death" as a pattern to "the land of the spirits" of "what a woman may be!" But the fairy magic and beauty begin to fade as Hogg moralises, drifts through "the land of thought," and unrolls episodes of violent history preceding a time of "love and harmony." It is a commentary on the poet's two visions of woman that he sustains the mood in "The Witch of Fife" and lets it diffuse after the wonderful opening of "Kilmeny."

In these contrasting pieces, Hogg's feeling for tradition is deep and varied. His sense of history and of the prevalence of superstition in the past is less sure. The reign of James IV (1488–1513) was "the very time that fairies, brownies, and witches were at the rifest in Scotland" ("Mary Burnet"). The degree of superstitiousness in 1645 is incomprehensible to the modern mind: "People lived and breathed in a world of spirits, witches, warlocks, and necromancers of all descriptions, so that it was amazing how they escaped a day with life and reason" ("The Adventures of Colonel Peter Aston"). The presence of Catholics complicated the problem. Although the "auld papist beggar" in "Mr. Adamson of Laverhope" denies that he is "the vera deevil himsel," he admits that "it is a sublimer thing . . . to be a deil" than a Roman Catholic among Calvinists. And the Devil in the gaberlunzie's likeness carries off a harsh landlord's soul. In "The Witches of Traquair," Hell is said to find Popery "a very convenient and profitable sort of religion" and real warlocks and witches its fittest instruments. Young Colin is brought up sinfully among "Papists and witches,"[6] and he is not free from their machinations until he becomes religious and understands that, in the light of original sin,

---

[6] "A Strange Secret" includes a dream in which unearthly birds or hill spirits "or mayhap whole flocks of Papists trying feats of witchcraft" are shot.

iniquity can engender and breed "in *his* heart as fast as maggots on tainted carrion."

Sincere religion has a reassuring correlation with superstition. Because the most religious country people of his own day are invariably the firmest believers in supernatural agency, Hogg concludes that the times of the Rev. Thomas Boston (d. 1732), "an age singular . . . for devotion, would readily be as much so for superstition" (note on "The Pedlar"). In "The Bridal of Polmood," Anna vindicates her belief in ghosts as an assurance that God and Providence cope with guilt and defend innocence. A shepherd in "The Wool-Gatherer" puts his faith in "a' the apparitions that warn o' death, that save life, an' that discover guilt," and lets the "lightheaded" countryfolk take fright at "the gomral fantastic bogles an' spirits." Despite his delight in "vulgar superstitions," Hogg more often agrees with this moral selectivity. And the proper language for supernatural beings is, of course, Scots. As a character protests in "The Hunt of Eildon," "That tale winna tell in English."

Hogg's characters often distinguish between supernatural beings that are pagan, anti-Christian, amoral, or immoral, and those that are channels of divine mercy and vengeance. Riding on a good errand through "the very country of the ghosts and fairies," a man fears none "save the devil and the water-kelpie" ("The Wool-Gatherer"). Although she does not fear evil spirits in general, because "they hae nae power" over the good, a servant in *The Brownie of Bodsbeck* (1818) would rather not meet a bogle "an' me a' my lane." A maid ventures into a haunted glen confident that "neither ghaist, nor man, nor beast" can harm a virgin ("The Spirit of the Glen"). But if such a maid is over rash, a spirit, a guardian angel, or the Fairy Queen may be there to aid. When the enemy is man, that "defacer of all good," he is likely to come to a bad end, as in "Tibby Hyslop's Dream."

If a maiden is injured, she may take matters into her own hands. The jilted woman of "The Mysterious Bride" manages to lure her betrayer, his son, and his grandson, "the last of his race," to their death at the spot where she was slain. A demon lover *par excellence*, the bride returns for three generations until success and proper burial lay her ghost. Thus "wicked people . . . have got a lesson on divine justice written to them in lines of blood." The psychically more complex maiden of "Mary Burnet" is also transformed from a victim into a ruthless and seductive spirit. Although Mary lies at home in the body, agonising and weeping, her likeness, whether mermaid, fairy, or "beastly sensitive spirit," answers the invocation of a libertine who thrice wishes that "some witch or fairy" will draw her to him in spite of her scruples. Mary later disappears, and the "flagitious young man," riding to an assignation with a strange lady who resembles her, falls to his death in an abyss.[7] The author complacently adds, "What a beautiful moral may be extracted from this fairy tale?" Ghostly justice is always, of course, superior to the bungling human variety, as in "The Wife of Lochmaben."[8]

According to the gardener in "Welldean Hall," ghosts are not lightly summoned but appear "only when all natural means are cut off, either of discovering guilt and blood, or of saving life." A ghost punishes a seducer and murderer or discovers murder and stolen money in two poems, "Young Kennedy" and "The Pedlar." There is further elaboration in "The Cameronian Preacher's Tale" when a ghost foreshadows its murderer's death and the murderer's ghost later effects restitution of money and religious burial of its victim. The narrator's problem is how to achieve variety in a repetitive pattern. His solution is to allow the first ghost only to be heard when it calls the murderer into a tavern garden and the second ghost to be seen and heard. The motive of the slain man's spirit is revenge; that of the slayer is "some assuagement of misery." Both ghost-seers, the first a guilty and the second an innocent man, must die, "for he who converses with a spirit, a spirit shall he soon become."

A less conventional use of ghosts—and of wraiths—is to discover family tension and affection. In "The Adventures of Basil Lee," a man left on the Island of Lewis becomes "like one half-crazed about spirits." Hearing of a "miserable old shrivelled creature" who conjures her son to appear at dead of night, he goes to look on at a wild rite and to behold the youth in death-wrappings talking with his mother. After the woman expires, her body rises in bed and stretches its arms toward the son's ghost, which is seated once more beside the hearth.

Wraiths are just as active. Hogg variously defines the wraith as a guardian angel which warns of danger to its ward, a good or bad spirit which appears immediately before a death to conduct the soul to its proper abode, or a person showing himself immediately after his death to whatever acquaintance is next to die. "And that's the true doctrine o' wraiths . . . and we should a' profit by it" ("Tibby Johnson's Wraith"). Hogg's best wraiths belong to yet another category, that of the living torn from their bodies by the urgency of giving or seeking help.

[7] In "Nancy Chisholm," a father's rather than a lover's cruelty forces an angel out and lets a Devil in: "She had a desire that the Evil One would appear in person that she might enter into a formal contract to do evil."

[8] In this story, a court refuses to accept ghost evidence at second hand. The incident also appears in *Demonology*, p. 357.

In "The Laird of Cassway," a beldame's wraith warns the Laird of his sons' intended duel over her niece. Then she convoys his wraith some 200 miles in time to prevent fratricide. The disembodiment is so consuming that the father dies. The wraith of a young woman in "The Fords of Callum" tries to draw her father to the Fords. Timorous, self-centred, and bigoted, Walter interprets this "singular warning" as "some heavy judgment" for sin or backsliding and does not go. A second time, Annie is heard tapping at the window and crying, "Mither, are ye waukin? . . . Is Wat Douglas away to the Fords o' Callum? . . . Oh! lack-a-day! Then it is ower late now!" "A mile or twae" from home, the couple see a body "lying athraw," but they do not cross the burn to it, in terror and suspense, until a man joins them. Then they recognise the "pale corpse" of Annie, "her bosom still warm" though she has been "dead some hours." Walter returns to his bed and dies a fortnight later.

Like the ballad, "Edward," "The Fords of Callum" has compression, simple, moving diction, and power of suggestion. The righteous father turns from the wraith of his "queer mysterious" daughter. When the wraith comes back hours later, it calls out to the mother and refers to the father as Wat Douglas. This rankles in Wat, "*Your* daughter say, Janet, for you hear I'm denied." The poignancy of the futile visits and the sense of constraint, yearning, and rejection are heightened by the father's fear and the couple's hesitancy in approaching the body. By not solving the murder, Hogg keeps attention on the sadness of constricted love.

In dreams and visions, strange knowledge may come to mortals or a troubled spirit may go questing. A dream in "A Tale of the Martyrs" leads a widow to the body of her husband, who has been shot by Bloody Claverse. And in "Wat Pringle o' the Yair," a vision after the Battle of Philiphaugh (1645) shows a lady her lord—headless. In delirium, she speaks unfamiliar words, lays her head on an imaginary block, and dies. Through "sympathetic feeling" she has foreseen her spouse's fate, repeated his last speech, and died at the instant of his beheading. In her is concentrated the profound suffering of a war-scarred land.

It may be difficult to distinguish between dream-content and fantastic reality. In "George Dobson's Expedition to Hell," a coachman unwittingly drives a recently drowned gentleman and his son to Hell, from which Dobson is released only on a promise to return for good the very next night. Although his body has lain in bed all this time, "the marks of the porter's fingers" on his throat, news of the drowning, and the sight of certain lawyers at the gate of Hell suggest that his spirit has been abroad.

Toward midnight, Dobson dies in bed while seeming to urge his horses to the infernal appointment.[9]

The coachman opens up a possibility which the exuberant Shepherd seldom permits himself to contemplate, that life is ruled by mysterious forces which are unrelated to morality. Hogg's usual cosmos is a peasant one in which little justice may be expected from organised religion and less from organised society. Moral balance is precariously kept by omens and supernatural beings which are more pagan than Christian. Heaven is a nebulous place, and Hell is the arsenal of iniquity.

Despite his intention—like Burns—to put the Devil in his place, Hogg grants him a sinister pervasiveness. Witch women in "The Hunt of Eildon" confess that the mysterious old knight seduces both sexes by his power of transformation into vigorous manhood and entrancing womanhood. His face has been seen "a thousand times" at court, and he has scarcely ever been from the King's side "since you were first laid in your cradle." Unwilling to pursue this novel insight further, the author has "a reverend old friar" who is an expert in "diablery and exorcism" sprinkle holy water on the knight and turn him into a conventionally "furious fiend."

Another tale of the Devil's work on earth is "The Brownie of the Black Haggs." Descended from "a wicked and degenerate race" which has "reached the utmost bounds o' earthly wickedness" in her, Lady Wheelhope is inhumanly cruel to Covenanters and inferiors until she meets her match in a new servant. With his aged face and puerile form, Merodach seems a mongrel, a kelpie, a brownie, a wizard, a fairy, and a fiend. Attempting to kill him, the lady stabs her own son. Tormentor and tormented become so bound to each other that the mistress gives her servant-master "such a look as one fiend would cast on another." Full of love and hate, desire and disgust, she follows Merodach and cannot be beaten off. At last, she is tormented to death.[10] Interwoven in this short story are local lore, masochism and sadism, sin and retribution, natural and supernatural evil.

Literary tradition is both followed and flaunted in Hogg's masterpiece, *The Private Memoirs and Confessions of a Justified Sinner* (anonymously

[9] Other dreams, serving a moral purpose, reveal that an accused man is no thief or murderer ("Adam Scott") and that a lewd employee will be punished ("Tibby Hyslop's Dream").

[10] The mystery of antipathy-and-attachment is briefly explored in "Daft Jock Amos." "The Marvellous Doctor" plays up sado-masochism in a contest between two discoverers of attachment elixirs; the defeated Spanish professor would rather die than leave the English proficient, who lashes and humiliates him.

published in 1824). As demonology wielded in religious controversy, it is reminiscent of Covenanting writers, but it is also close to Burns's "Holy Willie's Prayer" in turning the tables on orthodoxy. As a study of pride going before a fall, it is like an awful travesty of the Miltonic fall, with a protagonist who is mean, not magnificent, and therefore uncomfortably akin to the reader. As a brother-contrast, it is in the long line of descent from Cain and Abel to Blifil and Tom Jones, or to Joseph and Charles Surface; but Hogg's Cain and Abel are strangely one.

This is indeed the central originality of the novel, that the conflicts between individuals are simultaneously taking place within Wringhim. Consequently, the tensions between the half-brothers, George Colwan and Robert Wringhim, and between Wringhim and his devil-mentor, Gil-Martin, are expressed in terms of doubles, of affinities and antipathies. Wringhim, the younger brother, a by-blow of Calvinist fanatics, impresses different people as a "hellish-looking student," "a fiend" clothed in flesh and blood, and the "brunstane thief." The Devil is reported to be often by his side, even entering into him. At first sight, Gil-Martin strikes him as "the same being as myself!" He cannot shake off the mysterious stranger, because they are "incorporated together—identified with one another." Gil-Martin admits that they are "amalgamated, as it were, and consociated": "I feel as if I were the same person. Our essences are one, our bodies and spirits being united." Yet Wringhim acquires a "second self" which "appears in *his* likeness" and performs those acts of lust, greed, and murderous hate which he subconsciously wills. Gil-Martin assures him that this is the lot of mankind, "We are all subjected to two distinct natures in the same person."

In a distemper, Wringhim senses that he is "two people," his brother and Gil-Martin, and is at the same time separate from them. The three merge, draw apart, and exchange places in an intricate pattern. Gil-Martin haunts that "devilish-looking youth," Wringhim, "like *his* shadow," and his victim in turn attends his elder brother "as constantly as his shadow." Colwan thinks himself haunted by "some horrid demon . . . that had assumed the features of his brother" or, as he later conceives, by "some evil genius in the shape of his brother, as well as by that dark and mysterious wretch himself." Wringhim's intuition of Colwan's thoughts and movements is "like the attendance of a demon on some devoted being that had sold himself to destruction." He is also like an evil genius to Gil-Martin, drawing him "as by magnetism."

The remaining transformation, of Colwan into Wringhim's Devil, follows inevitably. Wringhim suffers from "the constant and unnatural persuasion that I was my brother," and to one observer the two seem the same. After Wringhim kills his brother, Gil-Martin grows more and more like Colwan in "figure, air, and features." According to Wringhim, this "extraordinary likeness to my late brother" is one "which misfortune and despair tended only to heighten." Thus Gil-Martin, in his final vengeful aggressions against Wringhim, is like the ghost of Colwan tormenting his murderer. Throughout these transpositions, Wringhim is the psychic focus. His brother and Gil-Martin, the Devil, exist tangentially in order to bring out aspects of his nature.

André Gide has praised "the figurative portrayal of states of subjective consciousness" in *Justified Sinner*. Except for the conclusion, he says, the Devil's actions are "always psychologically explicable, without having recourse to the supernatural." Indeed, the Devil presents "the exteriorized development of our own desires, of our pride, of our most secret thoughts" and indulgences.[11] The demonological framework of the narrative, how-ever, is more complex and important than Gide seems to suspect.

After his first meeting with Gil-Martin, Wringhim seems transformed, and his father, believing that both "calling and election" have been con-firmed and revealed, sets aside "a day of solemn thanksgiving" during which paternal hands are laid on Robert's head, "I dedicate him unto Thee, soul, body, and spirit." Soon after, in exchange for Gil-Martin's "solemn assurance, and bond of blood," against all human harm, Wringhim vows obedience. Following an ironic dedication, "the self-justified bigot" accepts the Devil's compact. He is persuaded to run his brother through the body and to shoot an old divine who, resisting the Devil's creed of Calvinism, preaches that morality and good works, not grace, are the true pathway to Heaven. When Gil-Martin closes in on his victim, horses, sensing the diabolical, mill about in panic terror. There is a noise of con-tention between Gil-Martin and a pack of vulgar fiends over sovereign rights in Wringhim. To escape pursuit and to destroy his *alter ego*, Wring-him enters into a suicide pact with Gil-Martin and hangs himself with a brittle hay rope. Two figures are reportedly seen going round and round the hay-rick. Thus is Wringhim received into Hell, his soul forfeit; the body of the "religious maniac" is thrust into a suicide's grave.[12]

Like the ballad-makers, Hogg slips almost imperceptibly from the

[11] Gide's Introduction to Hogg, *Private Memoirs and Confessions of a Justified Sinner*, London 1947, pp. xii, xv. Cp. Heinrich Heine, *Doktor Faust*, tr. Basil Ashmore, London 1952, p. 19: "The devils, when conjured ... answered ... Faust ... 'We always appear in the form of your most secret thoughts.'"

[12] On acknowledging the story in 1828, Hogg changed the title to *The Suicide's Grave*. A revision, published in 1837, was called *The Confessions of a Fanatic*.

familiar to the unfamiliar. His novel has three parts: "Editor's Narrative,"
which combines realism and transitional Devil similes; "Private Memoirs,"
which moves through demonology to psychological subtlety; and Editor's
gleanings (untitled), which is realistic once more and—in demonology—
conventional. Whereas the supernatural is the core of many a ballad, it is
in Hogg's masterpiece a corridor leading to the ultimate strangeness, that
the individual is both tempter and tempted. As evil wells up from within,
the city of Mansoul, to use Bunyan's phrase, does not fall to besiegers but
to a fifth column. The irony is heightened without sacrifice of universality
by the choice of a Calvinist as the protagonist who prides himself on his
knowledge of original sin and salvation. Because his interpretation of the
Devil as a man is less familiar than the Devil as corruptor of man, Hogg
advances from the supernatural convention to the human anomaly.

The supernatural in Hogg's fiction as a whole is disturbingly real when
it is made to convey the intensity, refractoriness, and mystery of existence,
its love, grief, frustration, and evil. His basic technique is that of Petronius
Arbiter, of Blind Harry, and of the ballad,—the juxtaposing in simple
language of the horrible, the grotesque, the particular, and the common.[13]
While the supernatural is being tied to reality by naturalness and humour,
its weirdness is preserved by a subtle indeterminateness. This is often true
when Hogg is embodying profound feeling or working within the restraints of living tradition. When he yields to an uncontrolled rush of
fancy, or manufactures episodes in an inadequately realised historical time,
he tends to be trivial, repetitive, and involved. In a remark to Scott,
Hogg reveals an awareness of his strength and weakness: "When my tale
is traditionary . . . I . . . see my way before me . . . but in all prose works
of imagination, knowing little of the world, I sail on without star or
compass."

Scott's "good taste, and judgment" were generally depended on as
Hogg's compass "in everything regarding literature." Thus the Great
Unknown gave advice on accuracy in the "historical tales" and found fault
with the "extravagance in demonology" of *The Three Perils of Man; or
War, Women, and Witchcraft* (1822). In *The Siege of Roxburgh*, a version
which was posthumously published in 1837, Hogg deleted the wild and
digressive adventures of a party sent to consult Master Michael Scott in his
enchanted tower at Aikwood. And in poetry, Scott communicated
enthusiasm for "our ancient ballads" to the Shepherd and later persuaded

---

[13] Louis Simpson is right in his analysis and praise, but he is mistaken in supposing that
Hogg's method is unique, "a peculiar secret of his fiction." *James Hogg: A Critical Study*,
Edinburgh and London 1962, pp. 121–2, 159, 202.

him to revise the ending of "The Witch of Fife," so that the old man might escape incineration at the stake. The whiplash close of the first and second editions, however, is rich in irony, as the would-be warlock of Fife unexpectedly pays for his "lawless greide." In calling attention to the effects of Hogg's not being "master of *his* own capabilities," his lack of structure and revision, his rambling and crudity, Scott was helpful.[14]

Some harm may have been done to Hogg by Scott's stressing the truth of history as far more important than the truth of popular tradition. Indeed, Louis Simpson asserts that Scott warped Hogg out of his true bent.[15] That there was friction and a sense of being overshadowed is revealed by the lesser known author's frankness about the low boiling-point of his "peasant blood." Besides the pettish year during which the Shepherd would not speak to the Laird of Abbotsford, Hogg reveals himself in scattered autobiographical comments as Scott's rival and—occasionally—his superior in literature. Not only could the ballad imitations in *Minstrelsy of the Scottish Border* be improved, but Hogg's "mountain and fairy school" was "far higher" than Scott's "school of chivalry."[16] Hogg resentfully called to mind the general opinion of *The Brownie of Bodsbeck* as an imitation of *Old Mortality*. Had Blackwood only published the *Brownie* when it was ready for the press, the Author of Waverley would have seemed the imitator. But no, Hogg had to injure his story in order to remove the more obvious similarities to *Old Mortality*. "A better instance could not be given of the good luck attached to one person, and the bad luck which attended the efforts of another."[17]

2. JOHN GALT

John Galt (1779–1839) admitted that his *Ringan Gilhaize; or the Covenanters* (1823) "was certainly suggested by Sir Walter Scott's *Old Mortality*, in which I thought he treated the defenders of the Presbyterian Church with too much levity," and that the "radical defect" of *The Spaewife* (1823)

---

[14] *Domestic Manners*, pp. 57, 61, 69–71, 78, 89, 101–02; also see pp. 75–7, 85, and *The Works of the Ettrick Shepherd*, ed. Thomas Thomson, London 1874, II. 459.

[15] Simpson, *James Hogg*, pp. 41–3, 64.

[16] *Domestic Manners*, pp. 71, 93–5; *Works*, II. 24, 446, 453.

[17] Hogg, "Autobiography" in *Works*, II. 456. In this discussion of Hogg, "The Bridal of Polmood," "A Story of Good Queen Bess," "The Laird of Wineholm," "Julia M'Kenzie," and *The Brownie of Bodsbeck* have received little or no attention because the unearthly turns out to be either a trick or a mistake. For further bibliographical references and a somewhat different treatment of Hogg and Scott, see C. O. Parsons, "Scott's Fellow Demonologists," *M.L.Q.*, IV (1943), 476–9.

was its too great resemblance to "the compositions of Sir Walter Scott, with whom I never placed myself consciously in any rivalry."[18] Nevertheless, there was a one-sided rivalry in which Galt felt himself thwarted by the demon of his destiny and the older man befriended by his guardian angel. Whether it was the Scottish historical ballad, a long narrative poem with three "weird sisters," or a Scottish novel, Galt had the idea first but Scott set the fashion by getting into print ahead of him. "What a cursed fellow that Walter Scott has been, to drive me out of my original line."[19]

Galt's resentment against his Nemesis comes out in his first novel, *The Majolo* (1816). When the Sardinian unaccountably turns up in Edinburgh, he notices the "singularity" of Scott's "bee-hive" skull but not "the poet's feet," and finds his translation of Bürger's "Lenora" very dull.[20] This draws ready comment from the narrator. Instead of letting his work rest entirely on "its own merits," Scott insures success "by dedications to public and popular characters," so that his vogue is probably due as much to patrons and literary friends as to his "own talents." After all, Edinburgh is a good place "for a mediocre genius . . . to obtain distinction." Eight years later, on the appearance of *Redgauntlet*, Galt added a chapter entitled "Redgauntlet" to *Rothelan* (1824). The *Black Book of Abbotsford* is whimsically blamed for a recent, "very inaccurate and imperfect account" of a birthmark being formed "in the moment of parturition." The correct version, which is more in keeping with "the philosophy of occult sympathies," is that Sir Alberick Redgauntlet's lady was in her fifth month when she heard of the "impress of the horse's-hoof on the brow of her beloved first-born." After brooding on his death, she gave birth to a marked child.[21]

But Galt was subdued by Scott's magnanimity, as was Byron after writing "English Bards and Scotch Reviewers." The unequal feud probably ended about July 1826 when *The Omen* "was reviewed by Sir Walter

---

[18] *The Literary Life, and Miscellanies of John Galt* [= *Literary Life*], Edinburgh and London 1834, I. 254, 262. Galt would also seem to have been influenced in *Sir Andrew Wylie, The Entail*, and other novels by Scott's susceptible-sceptical heroes and the effect of their education, sectarian demonology, fulfilled curses, and sibyls. "The Howdie: an Autobiography," possibly drawing on Scott's source, Hoffmann, duplicates the opening action of *The Surgeon's Daughter*. Left unfinished, it was first published in 1923.

[19] *Literary Life*, I. 49, and a letter to [William Blackwood], 30 Jan. 1821, in Erik Frykman, *John Galt's Scottish Stories 1820–1823*, Uppsala 1959, p. 32. Frykman also quotes Galt's assertion to R. P. Gillies "that his literary resources were far greater in extent than those of Sir Walter Scott or any other contemporary" (p. 40).

[20] Bürger, that "man of genius," inspired Galt to translate "Lenora" and "The Lass of Fair Wone," ballads of a demon lover and a gibbeted infanticide. See Galt, *The Bachelor's Wife*, Edinburgh 1824, pp. 356–72.

[21] *Rothelan*, Edinburgh 1824, II. 102–10. Scott's overuse of "mysterious castles and turretry" seems to be intended in I. 280–1.

Scott in Blackwood's Magazine, and with, in my opinion, a commendable degree of approbation, and facts stated corroborative of incidents that were pure metaphysical inventions."[22] In Galt's final judgment, the demon of destiny yields half the ground: Although Scott's poetry is overrated, "in romance, he towers into unapproachable excellence."[23]

Galt is set apart from Scott and Hogg by his religion, a moody, fanciful, resigned West of Scotland Calvinism which excludes responsibility for failure. "I . . . profess myself openly a predestinarian," subject to "the law of necessity, philosophical fatality."[24] He believed in "the unchangeable nature and purposes of the Deity" expressing themselves systematically and not through the "temporary meddling and uncertainty in the universe" which is known as particular providence. What is permitted by Providence is an occasional glimpse of the plan, granted chiefly to persons of morbid and abnormal psychic or sensory development. Because men lack free will, any such revelation may heighten suspense in a Galt story but it cannot change action.

> Men and gods vainly struggle to free themselves from the adamantine bonds of destiny. The oracle, or the omen which declares the impending evil, affords no method of averting it. All insight into futurity proves a curse to those on whom the power descends. We hear the warning which we cannot obey.[25]

Providence may be personified as the demon of destiny. Although Elspeth in *Southennan* (1830) is a spaewife, a changeling, and a goblin who walks "like something mis-shapen and unblest," she is also a perverse turnkey of destiny. Both defective and acid keen, she has a second-sighted vision of a mouldy-fingered "demon thing, holding outspread a winding-sheet, spotted with many a blob of blood." Such "demons of fate" are harbingers of evil turns of fortune in Rizzio's life. Remembering a childhood dream of ancestors who died violently, Mary Queen of Scots exclaims, "Oh, I am as one amid the spectres of slaughtered kings." Forebears have been blasted by "the demon of her race," who now sweeps her along "in the stream of fate." Though heavily disguised, heredity is fate.

[22] *Literary Life*, I. 270. Some readers took the anonymous novelette to be Scott's work.
[23] *The Autobiography of John Galt*, London 1833, II. 211. There is a reference to "that mighty master" in Galt, *The Bachelor's Wife*, p. 69. Unlike Galt, William Godwin as a novelist never freed himself from the oppression of Scott's success.
[24] "Fatalism, and Particular Providence," ch. 33, *Literary Life*, I. 283–91 (cp. I. 59–60). Galt rejected all determinists who left God out, such as "atheistical astrologers" and impious craniologists. Galt, *Life of Cardinal Wolsey*, 3rd edn, London 1846, p. 426; *Stories of the Study*, London 1833, III. 175–7.
[25] Galt, *The Bachelor's Wife*, p. 70 (see also pp. 67–76).

The demon is more individualised in *Bogle Corbet; or, The Emigrants* (1831). As an acquaintance says of Eric Pullicate, "That shrewd man thinks he is lord of your ascendant," and Bogle agrees that his "evil genius" and "that pawkie get of Belzeebub" are one and the same. Whereas Eric's "occult influence" bodes ill for the Corbets, Bogle's coming presages good for the Pullicates. After erecting this psychic scheme and pursuing it for a time, Galt drops the idea of adversely intertwined destinies and ships Bogle off to Canada—out of harm's way. In *Eben Erskine; or, The Traveller* (1833), a tutor expounds his doctrine "that a demon of destiny was attached to every individual in the world, sometimes in the shape of a friend, but oftener as an adversary." His pupil, Father Paul, interiorises the idea, as Hogg does in *Justified Sinner*: "The demon of a man's destiny may be in himself" or may be a "mysterious stranger" who is one's double.[26]

Galt returns to the subject in such poems as "The Tower of Destiny" and "The Demon of Destiny." Although hope may deny it, "a stalwart demon" bruises drugs for every mortal "in Fate's dread mortar." While a conflict is still going on between ineffectual good angels and the Satan-commissioned "Demon of his fate," Salome longs for fame and fortune, responds to pride and ambition, and aspires "to improve mankind." Because his ambition exceeds his capacity, he is frustrated, and frustrated men "become the victims of phantastical notions." Still under the illusion that he has the free will to control fate, he dies.[27]

Five years before his own death, Galt sums up his personal account: "Against many faults and blemishes many cares should be placed, disappointments, ill-requited struggles, and misfortunes of no common kind, with the depressing feeling, in calamitous circumstances, of how much I stood in the need of heartening from a friend." In various passages, he speaks of his lonely, unfriended, unpatronised state in London; his extreme sensitivity; his "inordinate ambition"; his "love of fame" and distinction as a "ruling passion"; his attempts to improve Canada, alleviate distress in Britain, and affect "the destinies of nations"; his "hope to have sufficient philosophy to embrace *his* destiny without fear" if horizons close in; his reward, "contumely and poverty; perhaps, also, incurable

---

[26] In most of his stories, however, Hogg shares the belief in a particular providence of the dwarfish and resourceful nail-maker in Galt, *Lawrie Todd; or, The Settlers in the Woods* (1830). Galt does not agree with Lawrie "that the lidless eye of Providence is ever fixed on mortal beings with a fearful vigilance to anticipate the attacks of incomprehensible evil." *Literary Life*, I. 292.

[27] *Literary Life*, II. 102–05; *The Demon of Destiny; and Other Poems*, Greenock 1839. The conflict between Nature and the Demon of Destiny is elsewhere explored by Galt: "Upon fatality and the tenet of conflicting power, popular mythology is wholly founded." Galt, *The Bachelor's Wife*, p. 70.

disease," culminating in eleven paralytic strokes and withered limbs; "the querulousness of a disappointed man"; and predestinarian "resignation."[28] While retaining the self-exculpating "phantastical notions" of his protagonist in "The Demon of Destiny," Galt abandons the illusion of responsible volition.

Other aspects of destiny, such as extra-sensory perception, the seer, and the victim, are considered in *The Majolo* (1816), *The Spaewife* (1823), and *The Omen* (1825). As a traveller in the Levant, Galt made notes on ghosts, witches, omens, "second hearing" (aural foreknowledge), the invisible *Miri* that has charge of a child's destiny, and "the most interesting of all the unexplained magnetisms of our species," human attraction and repulsion.[29] His first novel was "calculated to illustrate the mystical feelings connected with our sympathies and antipathies," as in the discovery of a poisoner by "some indescribable antipathy."[30] Just as a body ammonia given off by a corpse may induce a sleeper in an adjoining room to dream of being "in an unwholesome sepulchre," so a "moral ammonia" may account for presentiments. Man is endowed "with more senses than he is aware of," and each sense has multiple powers. Thus Highland second sight is "one of the *seven* senses of the human species" possessed by everyone "in some degree."[31] It reveals links in the adamantine "chain of destiny," as do dreams, omens, and prophecies. Because "Fate is Providence," our role "in the universal system of the world" is inescapable.

The Spaewife concentrates on the glimpses of fate vouchsafed to man, on his inability to change the pattern, and on the frail vessel of communication. Galt associates sensory acumen with primitive faculties and lack of balance.[32] Thus he makes his spaewife, Anniple of Dunblane, a "Ta'en-awa," a changeling made of a benweed (ragwort) "and left in the stead o' the weaver's wife's bairn. . . . But the fairies have nae power to put heavenly souls intil their effigies, which is the cause, folks say, that I have a want of some o' the seven senses." An orphan full of eloquent self-pity, growing up without sister, brother, or playmate and "hated by all living things," she weeps and longs for the stolen mortal to die among the

[28] *Literary Life*, I. 56–8, 216, 249, 292, 354, 357–8. Cp. Galt's remark on adversity and superstition in *Life of Cardinal Wolsey*, p. 192.

[29] Galt, *Voyages and Travels, in the Years 1809, 1810, and 1811*, London 1812, pp. iv, 225, etc.; *Letters from the Levant*, London 1813, pp. 168–80.

[30] *Literary Life*, I. 181–2.

[31] A short version of *The Majolo* has the title, "The Physiognomist; A Biographical Tale of the Seven Senses," *Rothelan*, III. 121–98.

[32] The God's fools of George MacDonald fit this pattern, as do Scott's sibyls, although the latter tend to have illusory rather than real powers. The increase of insight with the loss of external vision in Homer, Tiresias, Milton's Samson Agonistes, and Milton himself is a more cultivated formulation.

fairies, so that the changeling may "lie on the loan what I am, a weed to be trampled on." Sentimentalising over human oddities does not begin with George MacDonald or with the "Kailyard School" of the late nineteenth century; the indulgence goes back at least to John Galt.

Anniple is remarkable in other ways. She is a more complicated hybrid than Scott's White Lady, being a seer and a prophet, a mind-reader and a fortune-teller, a vengeful plotter, a rescuer, a protectress, a changeling, a brownie, and a witch with animal familiars ("Nobody thrives that does ill to Anniple of Dunblane"). Yet, despite her multiple supernaturalism, her persistent ubiquity, her frequent second-sighted visions, her prophecies to all and sundry, Galt pours so much energy into the Ta'en-awa that she is the most convincing character in *The Spaewife*.[33]

The text of the plot is the legendary warning of the Erse "suthsayer" to James I not to cross the Firth of Forth, the King's wilfulness, and his assassination at Perth. Anniple's warning is tied with a second-sighted vision of James's "eight-and-twenty bloody wounds—I see them all, and the hands that bear the knives." She sees but cannot prevent—or cause— disaster to the doomed King or to the Earl of Athol, whom she hates for his niggardliness. There is rude power in her forecast that the Earl will wear a crown. The king-of-traitors does at last wear a red-hot crown. The nobleman is in turn the demon of the spaewife's destiny, "I ne'er forgather with Lord Athol himself, but some dule or damage ever befalls me."

Attention shifts in *The Omen* from the spokesman of fate to the one who attends. The "occult and inscrutable intelligence" between moon and tides seems to be like the "apocalyptical admonitions from heaven" that reveal "parts of the providential machinery" to "other faculties of perception than those of the corporeal senses." The protagonist is equipped with an "inward sense" which is responsive to such "influences from futurity," and his dreams are like "the unsleeping soul's attempt to reason meta-phorically."[34] Morbidly passive, he is "predestined" to suffer—and does. The author, aware of "the brevity that befits a tale of a single feeling," limits himself to 160 pages in which omens are heaped up, the mood is heavy and unrelieved, and narrative lines are left dangling. Yet Galt achieves a gloomy strength through unflawed unity of tone which is appropriate to a destiny-constricted life.

Galt is most deeply concerned with the supernatural as an embodiment

[33] Less convincing is the Negress, Yaninah, who traces "hieroglyphical figures on the sand" in Galt, "The Horoscope," *Stories of the Study*, III. 178–97.
[34] The same conception of dreams appears in Galt's earlier story, "Deucalion of Kentucky," *The Steamboat* (B.E.M., 1821, and book form, 1822).

of his predestinarian vision. But the novelist is also interested in Gothic character, action, and setting, in ghosts, demons, and witches, and in the humour of credulity. As a young man, he was "prodigiously affected" by Mrs Radcliffe's *Mysteries of Udolpho* and *The Italian*.[35] His own Gothicism was to be of the order of Mrs Radcliffe, of "Monk" Lewis and the German horror school, and of such parodies as Jane Austen's *Northanger Abbey*. In *The Earthquake* (1820), the natural violence of the Messina earthquake serves as a background to human violence. The secret tribunal, Byronic Castagnello, "naturally vicious" Count Corneli, and minor demonic characters push evil to the edge of vampirism.

The association of marriage and death fascinates Galt. After frightening away a sexton who is whittling a garnet ring from the Lady of Limmerton's wedding finger, the wise woman of *The Spaewife* removes the ring and the corpse, sleeps in the coffin, and dreams of coiling worms. What is variously described in *The Omen* as the "ancestral curse" and the "spectre of the past" is a mother's adultery. The son's dreams mingle a mother-bride's "cany fingers of a skeleton" with "weddings and funerals . . . and banquets at which the dead sat in their cerements." The "entombment" of his uncle takes place on the very day he is prevented at the altar from marrying his half-sister.[36] Queen Mary's wedding in *Southennan* is related through "prophetic fears" to Chatelard's execution, and the hero marries at the very time that "a dreadful cry" intimates Rizzio's murder.

Whenever a German is introduced, Galt calls up the appropriate associations. Thus an old Göttingen Illuminatus in *Rothelan* tells a story of a noble's selling his soul to a demon for revenge. And Bremen in *Stanley Buxton; or, The Schoolfellows* (1832) has a confused tale of a dream which leads to the discovery of a shining skeleton and a murderer. After the tired Gothic tale of "The Rosicrucians" in *Eben Erskine*, dictated from a sickbed, the influence of Bürger, "the father of our taste for German literature," lapses.[37] As a character remarks to Troven in *The Stolen Child* (1833), "We grow less credulous as we grow old, and meet also with fewer miracles."

The most successful resort to the Gothic, however, is in a poem, "The Ferry House: A Scottish Tale of Halloween," which combines horror and burlesque in the manner of Burns. A public-house-keeper's wife,

[35] *Literary Life*, I. 24–5.
[36] On incest as "a regular feature of novels," see J. M. S. Tompkins, *The Popular Novel in England 1770–1800*, London 1932, pp. 65–6.
[37] *Literary Life*, I. 24; Galt, *The Bachelor's Wife*, chs. 31, 42, "German Genius" and "Bürger the German Poet." Galt was "very strongly excited" by Schiller's *The Robbers*. Like Scott, he was unresponsive to *Faust* and preferred Goethe in his lesser dimension.

Auld Janet, lies a corpse with "a plate of salt . . . on her breast." Once she has been put in a coffin, her wraith comes out of a drawer, tears off the shroud, and calls "the mort" to join a dance of great folk and criminals. An invitation of "the shadowy bridegroom" to take part is so startling that the narrator wakes from his grisly dream.[38]

Whenever the Gothic is too much for him, Galt rebels. *Sir Andrew Wylie, of that Ilk* (1822) has both the mysterious Monimia and a genuine Udolpho, "yon old warlock tower . . . darkened with the shadow of past time," which ought to be stocked with Radcliffian romances. From this incidental satire, Galt turns in *Stanley Buxton* to farcical take-off. Jacintha Rosedale's night in a "Udolphian" chamber is perturbed by an apparitional dress, a strayed owl, and "a stranger, with a helmet of towering plumes, like that of [Walpole's Castle of] Otranto," which is found to be a tree.

Throughout his fiction Galt is responsive to atmosphere of place. The settings of *The Majolo* are Radcliffian. A "poetical superstition" of presage and melancholy is evoked in the Sardinian by "the genius of the place" of "a vast monastic pile." The "dismal island" of Maddalena induces "a kind of superstitious dread . . . truly awful," a sympathetic horror which brings strange dreams, as if from "some malignant devil in the air." A girl is murdered there. In *Southennan*, Rizzio is sensitive to a castle courtyard's "dreamy and apparitional" aspect "suggesting dim reminiscences of ghastly visitants from crypts and cloisters." Despite their monotony, such details as silence, gloom, shrubs "in winding-sheets of hoar-frost," clouds and a foreboding moon make the atmosphere of *The Omen* more telling than its plot. In *The Steamboat* (1822), the "Deucalion of Kentucky" is awakened by a classicist who "ascribed living powers" to woods, streams, and rocks. He vainly begs his father not to sink a well lest there be "something unhallowed in disturbing the ancient channel of these holy waters." A buried lake is released in flood, and only the New World animist survives. Conventionally gloomy setting and misplaced classicism yield to analysis in *Rothelan*, with the revelation that there are crucial times "when the mind discovers a mystical similitude between the appearance of external nature and the aspect of its own destinies." These correspondences are most likely to be sensed in spring and autumn and in the obscurity of dawn or twilight. Galt's real sensitivity to place is too often obscured, especially in hasty work, by melodrama and convention.[39]

---

[38] *Literary Life*, II. 124–33.
[39] See Frykman, *John Galt's Scottish Stories*, pp. 133–4, for setting in *Sir Andrew Wylie* and *The Entail*.

In Galt's treatment of alchemy and astrology, omens, ghosts, wraiths, demonology, and witchcraft, there is the same alternation between convention and originality. Mystical studies so absorbed him as a young man that he became a very great "reader of alchymical books," which convinced him that gold could be made, though unprofitably. He was also "most learned in astrology."[40] He found much rationality in the two sciences, despite "the theory of nativities" and "the cabalistic technical jargon" of "ignorant pretenders."[41] The self-made hero of *The Majolo*, who resembles Galt in several respects, meets alchemists, conceives "some foundation in nature for the principles of the art," and resolves to master the subject frankly and properly. The promise is hardly kept. In both *The Spaewife* and *Rothelan*, there is brief mention of the star of one's destiny which changes intensity as one's good or evil genius predominates. The "good and simple" schoolmaster of *The Last of the Lairds* (1826) believes in the "astrological reciprocity between the course of moral actions and celestial signs." "The Rosicrucians" reveals alchemical quackery. And that is all.

"Strange intimations by auguries and signs," Gothic, gruesome, and Roman, abound in *Southennan, The Omen,* and a chapter of *Rothelan* entitled "Omens." Although they create an atmosphere of apprehension and doom, they do not deter a single character from his "unhappy destiny." Instead, by paralysing the will, these "signs and omens . . . portents and prodigies" emphasise the futility of struggle.

Providence seems less likely to permit a ghost to return to earth after death than to let a wraith, or psychic double, try to establish communion at the moment of death. Galt shares the Majolo's dim view. Having nothing but "the testimony of others," he cannot believe in ghosts. In *Ringan Gilhaize*, living people are mistaken for ghosts, and in *The Earthquake*, a "terrific phantom," on investigation, turns out to be a dying person walking at night. The treatment of an illusory wraith in *Southennan* is less perfunctory. Rizzio is rumoured to "gang . . . like a ghaist at uncanny hours in the King's Park." When the Italian courtier disappears in the moonlight, Southennan exclaims, "in the low hollow voice of fear": "Is it his wraith!" Rizzio's wraithlikeness foreshadows the moment when his spirit will be released from his body by assassins. Every step which brings a character nearer to his fate is ominous.

Because he believes that there is much "stupidity involved in the popular allegory of Satan,"[42] Galt conveys his predestinarian ideas

---

[40] *Literary Life*, I. 61, 64.
[41] Galt, *Life of Cardinal Wolsey*, pp. 425–8.   [42] Galt, *The Bachelor's Wife*, p. 75

through the Demon of Destiny rather than the Devil. His phrasing may be humorously picturesque, as in "The devil ding a dirk through my tongue ... but words trintle from it that should be better guided" (*Bogle Corbet*), but his demonology is basically conventional. Religious and political differences sharpen tempers and distort judgment, so that factions in *Ringan Gilhaize, The Member* (1832), *The Radical* (1833), and "The Lutherans"[43] associate the Devil with their foes. The device has less variety and power than it does in Scott's *Old Mortality*, but it serves its purpose.

The novelist comes to witchcraft with ideas of his own. Former law-makers were wrong in assuming any power in witchcraft or magic as such but right in punishing witches and wizards as exercisers of an "un-blest predominance ... over the timid and the credulous." The witch law was a deterrent to old-fashioned "malignancy of disposition" and could be such to modern ascendancy or "evil jurisdiction"; therefore, it "ought not to have been abolished, but rendered more philosophical."[44] "The Sibyl of Norwood," according to the author, illustrates his "opinion of the species of delinquency which was formerly punished as witchcraft, and which, by the abrogation of the statutes against it, may now be prac-tised with impunity." In this short story, "grim Moll, a gipsy woman ... of a large stalwart form," thrice works on the fears of a young gardener in order to get money. But the dupe, whose "superstitious temperament made him shy and diffident," withers away and dies. At the assizes, after accepting the hag's admission of deceit to relieve her wants, the judge finds that she is setting an evil example. The jury promptly finds Moll guilty and sentences her to death.[45]

When Galt is not riding his hobbies or falling back on supernatural conventions, he may be amused by the weird. With such exceptions as Providence, sympathy and antipathy, and the demon of destiny, the humorous and ironic approach is most used during the years of his

[43] Galt, *Stories of the Study* (1833), I. 7–314; II. 1–161.

[44] "Witchcraft," ch. 12 of Galt, *The Bachelor's Wife*, pp. 119–27; *Literary Life*, I. 68–9. In Dryden's "An Essay of Dramatic Poesy" (3rd edn, 1693), Lisideius says that an ineffective satirist "ought to be punished for the malice of the action, as our witches are justly hanged, because they think themselves to be such; and suffer deservedly for believing they did mischief, because they meant it."

[45] *Literary Life*, II. 266–82. George MacDonald suggests that, to attract worship, ruthlessly proud and domineering women "use means as deserving of the fire as any witchcraft." *What's Mine's Mine*, London 1886, II. 103. Galt intimately knew a gentleman who was subject to another. Had the "demon of his fate" both recognised and used his psychic power, "he would have been what the law considered as a wizard." Some support is given to "the gossipry about the influence of the evil eye, and the good and bad luck of certain visitors" by "this mystic potentiality." *Literary Life*, I. 69–70.

greatest creativity, 1820–6. Work in Canada in 1825 and again in 1826–9, his recall and imprisonment for debt, took Galt from literature, to which he returned for income but seldom with the buoyancy to laugh at superstition. In 1820, he pokes fun at omens in *Glenfell; or, Macdonalds and Campbells*. When a bridesmaid's wig and bonnet are blown off, "it would be an ill omen" for the groom to turn back to help. However, the bridesmaid's marriage to Colonel Rupee demonstrates that "*dirt bodes luck*." Intense and light-hearted in turn, *The Steamboat* is full of surprises. "The Wraith" is a skeleton which appears to a ten-year-old girl at the time of a death. The impressiveness of her "waff o' the second sight" is then punctured by the narrator's memory of seeing "a tall white figure" which resolved itself into boiler vapour. And in "King Charles and the Witches," a Scottish minister tells the monarch about Renfrewshire witches who assume "the shape of cats and mawkins [hares]." To break the witch-animal charm against lead and powder, he once shared his silver sleeve-buttons with a skilled hunter. They both fired and brought down—"just a fine fat hare." Command of witch-lore, rapid narration, evocative phrasing, and slyness of tone make this surprise ending crack like a whip.[46] Galt is less successful when he tries to revive the trick in *Ringan Gilhaize*. Lieutenant Swaby is paid back by "a lanerly [lonely] widow bent with age and poortith" for seeking "a cast of her skill" on the minister's daughter. What awaits his pleasure in bed on Halloween is a black ram that butts like the Evil One.[47]

Galt recaptures his skill as humour changes to drama, pathos, and humour again in "The Chief; or, The Gael and the Sassenach" (1833). When ignorant and superstitious Roderick M'Goul becomes chief of the Clan Jamphrey, he assumes "the gentlemanly quality of free-thinking." One squally night, he tries to "hoot, toot" his housekeeper's account of presages, a coffin-shaped splinter, a black hen's disarrayed feather, and such-like. As the sea roars through the night, the mood changes. A ship is wrecked, lives are lost, and cupidity is grotesquely aroused.[48]

The best novels have been reserved for discussion by themselves. It is characteristic of the realistic tales, *The Ayrshire Legatees; or, The Pringle Family*, and *Annals of the Parish; or, The Chronicle of Dalmailing* (both 1821), that the allusions to witchcraft are brief and amusing. As an ambling

[46] Other stories in *The Steamboat* shift from fearful to farcical ("The Wig and the Black Cat") or from levity on a cat's ominously "freaking about" to seriousness ("The Hurricane").

[47] Allan Ramsay is less pedestrian in Mause's similar discomfiture of Bauldy in *The Gentle Shepherd*, II. 3; IV. 1. Cp. Mak the sheep-stealer's ruse in the medieval *Second Shepherd's Play*.

[48] First collected in Galt, *The Howdie and Other Tales*, ed. William Roughead, Edinburgh and London, 1923, pp. 113–70.

survey of parish life from 1760 to 1810, *Annals* has a little demonological humour about a yird [earth] toad found in a stone and short, non-humorous incidents of second sight, a dream, and a wraith. The last shows "a far-seeing discernment in the spirit, that reaches beyond the scope of our incarnate senses."

According to the account in the *Autobiography* and the *Literary Life*, a publisher had Galt expand *Sir Andrew Wylie* in order to include marvels. Thus the three volumes encompass a fatalistic bond of sympathy, a dream truly signifying a death, and gipsies. When a Meg-Merrilies-style gipsy "ancestress" alarms the hero, he cutely belittles her pretensions, "Hooly, hooly, lucky, come down out of the clouds, and set by your broomstick." Despite suspected sources of information in fortune-telling and trickery in boosting Andrew into Parliament, the sibyl still remains "no canny." After all, the author slyly comments, she believes in her skill, and a venerable faith need not be rudely shaken.

The same mixture of humour and superstition is found in *The Entail; or, The Lairds of Grippy* (1823). Names suggest as much: Maudge *Dobbie* (a household goblin) is a servant who has "a rich stock of goblin lore and romantic stories," and Elspeth *Freet* (an omen) is a midwife who thinks Watty a *ta'en-awa* (a changeling). Within an action whose human emotions are centred on hunger for land, the overwrought and sickly Highland-woman, Mrs Gertrude Eadie, has another kind of hunger. A foil to the intense worldliness of the Lairds of Grippy, she moans among the graves of her lost children, voices an Ossianic grief, and longs for freedom from earthly affections so that she may join "the spirits of *her* fathers." No wonder that she has mystic anticipations, dreams dreams, sees a wraith, and is proud of the ancestral gift of second sight. As she drifts into lunacy, her character is rich in the contrasting colours of humour, drama, mystery, burlesque, and Kailyard pathos. She is presented with more restraint than Galt's melodramatic Spaewife.[49]

A number of Galt's characters display a certain duplicity of attitude toward the supernatural. For instance, the Countess of Athol discloses "with what sorceries, horoscopes, and divinations, he [the Earl] was wont to question destiny concerning his fortunes,—and yet none mocked more at the tales of legendary oracles" (*The Spaewife*). Galt himself has multiple reactions. He is reportorial or analytical in non-fictional works and in fiction sensational, conventional, humorous and ironic, or absorbed and

---

[49] *The Last of the Lairds* (1826) has incidental humour concerning astrology, demonology, ghosts, sorcery, dreams, omens, prophecy, and a spaewife. Belief, not involvement, is chiefly indicated. *The Provost* (1822) is free from the supernatural.

exploratory. The flatness of contrivance in potboilers and historical novels may be unpredictably relieved at any moment. Note the tired author manufacturing narration and then waking to life at the end of an episode in *Southennan*. In a "hollow and superstitious voice," Chatelard, the sentenced prisoner, tells Rizzio to remember him when a dagger ends his life, " 'Go! I see gouts of blood already on thy vest! Fated man! depart! leave me!' " Affected by the Gaul's second sight, the Italian turns and beholds "a tall figure wrapped as it were in a shroud. 'Your time is come!' said the jailer."

When the novelist earnestly gropes his way in psychically tendentious narratives, as in *The Majolo*, he subordinates plot and character to "calculated" illustration. The defence is later advanced in the *Autobiography* that several of his efforts should be called "theoretical histories of society" rather than novels. Thus the story is "a vehicle of instruction, or philosophy teaching, by example, parables, in which the moral was more valuable than the incidents were impressive." While warping the narrative by exposition, Galt still fails to be clear in his formulation; the result is diffuse and dull. The irony of Galt's very real concern with psychic phenomena as partial unveilings of Providence is that, when he tries to plumb his own intuitions, he loses artistic control.

Although Galt is convinced that we are less subject to supernatural agency from without than to "occult sympathy" from within, he is most successful when he treats the partly external superstitions in which he only half believes. Then he combines realism, scepticism, humour, and conviction.

CHAPTER VII

THE SUPERNATURAL IN FICTION AFTER SCOTT

SIX novelists will have to represent the range of the supernatural in a century of Scottish fiction: George MacDonald (1824–1905), Margaret Oliphant (1828–97), Robert Louis Stevenson (1850–94), John Buchan (1875–1940), Neil Gunn (1891–), and Eric Linklater (1899–). Comment will be summary.

1. GEORGE MACDONALD

Like Galt, MacDonald is more interested in psychic phenomena than in the wonderful creatures of folklore; and, like Hogg, he moralises the supernatural. His fairy-tales sketch a mythology of evil in which the victory of good becomes less convincing as the series moves toward the nightmarish sadism and vampirism of *Lilith* (1895). The most powerful figure in this mythology is a kind of Kali, or devouring female, who fittingly appears as a lycanthrope in one short story, "The Gray Wolf." The menace, which is usually that of a bewildering natural and supernatural world, comes from the accursed past in a novelette, *The Portent* (1864).

The characters in the full-length narratives are mostly gropers who come to the light eventually, sceptics who spread dry rot, and didacts who instruct by word and deed. Mammon and the Devil in man do battle with God's fools and the gropers, and dreams give depth and complexity to the struggle by revealing hidden states of consciousness. The two Devils whom MacDonald fears most are Pride, absorption in self, and Mammon, lust for possessions. Rationalists, who invariably hate superstition, demonstrate that the Enemy is "the worship of one's own will" and that "the universal self is *the* devil." In *What's Mine's Mine* (1886), Lowland greed and modern, rational values are opposed to Highland virtue and primitive, intuitive values. And in *The Elect Lady* (1888), a miser who dies fettered by "his mammon-besotted imagination" is contrasted with a spiritual hero who is so mature that "there were no demons riding the whirlwinds of his soul." MacDonald's more convincing heroes, those of *The Marquis of Lossie* (1877) and *Castle Warlock* (1882), for instance, have a streak of the demonic.

God's fool is a defective with special endowments. This intuitive innocent may range in age from an eight-year-old girl in *Guild Court* (1868) to a seventy-year-old foundling in "The Wow o' Rivven" (1864). Whether he is an idiot or just an anatomical oddity, he is likely to have "all the divine senses of the half-witted." The best of MacDonald's menagerie of children and the childlike is the dumb hero of *Sir Gibbie* (1879). A creature "from some other and nobler world" or "the verra deevil himsel'," he tests mankind by eliciting kindness or inhumanity. When he comes into his own, Gibbie acquires title, property, and a genteel wife. MacDonald is often tempted into the moral ambivalence of rewarding his selfless heroes with rank, estate, or good marriage.

Dreams tend to be morally ambivalent as well. The hero of *Wilfrid Cumbermede* (1872) has an active dream-life. He loses his sword, follows a long-loved maiden, Athanasia or death, into a catacomb-like passage, sees an almost identical woman, Mary, folded in ice, beholds horror, not beauty, when a shining veil is lifted. Wilfrid's inhibition, though complicated by homosexuality, is relaxed by the suicide of his friend, Mary's brother, and by the death of Mary's husband.

The dreams of *Castle Warlock* convey acquisitive rather than sexual intention. The search for a great-granduncle's walled-up fortune makes Cosmo the field on which a dubious battle is fought between the dead pirate and the youth's unselfish father. Cosmo's waking thoughts are of love, honour, and service, but his many dreams are of possession. The Laird of Warlock's prayer is greatly needed, "O my God, latna the sunshiny Mammon creep intil my Cosmo's hert an' mak a' mirk." As in *Wilfrid Cumbermede*, MacDonald does not seem to realise how much of the contradiction of life and of his own nature he has exposed in fictional dreams.

Throughout, MacDonald prefers a "wild" story because "one can put so much more" into it[1] and startle both readers and characters out of their blind burrows. A didactic mystic, he believes that the golden mean between gullibility and scepticism is a wise credulity, and that imagination is the guide. The novels which result may be read for their story, their doctrine, or their revelation of the tensions and temporary resolutions of the author's spirit. To all these, dreams and devils contribute complexity and power.[2]

[1] Greville MacDonald, *George MacDonald and his Wife*, 2nd edn, London 1924, p. 468.
[2] For the anti-Calvinist, theological novels, which I have not discussed, see Robert L. Wolff, *The Golden Key: A Study of the Fiction of George MacDonald*, New Haven, Conn. 1961, pp. 180–265.

2. MARGARET OLIPHANT

In the reign of Queen Victoria, both novelists and mediums protested against the cold comfort of formal religion. In *séances* the "Great Wizard of the North," Daniel Dunglas Home (1833–86), brought assurance that the world of the departed had pretty much the same work and play, the same dwellings, farms, cities, flora and fauna, as this world. There were no stern sentences of purgation and no penitential fires. Home's boast was that, in one decade, spiritualism had converted more people to belief in immortality and angel communion than all the Christian sects had.[3] Yet George MacDonald and Mrs Oliphant looked on Home as an insensitive fellow who tried to turn spirit into matter.

The life of Margaret Oliphant was one long lesson in the responsibility of women and the fecklessness of men, until she came to feel "like the sufferers in Dante."[4] Out of concern over the death, bankruptcy, and moral decay of weak male relatives came her deeply personal creed of benevolent non-intervention by the Deity, of earthly frailty and post-mortal rehabilitation. Although human beings possess free will, they cannot exercise it to protect, elevate, or change "those who are most dear."[5] The strong are thus doomed to be ineffectual spectators of men's tragic blunders. After death, men usually go to Purgatory, where sloth, pride, and selfishness can be cleansed from their natures. They are not likely to return as ghosts, and those who reach Heaven will be tender and true. But these conjectures still left the after-life in shadow. In fiction which was written "not from the head but from the heart," it was possible to be more decisive.[6]

The first and the best of Mrs Oliphant's stories of the seen and the unseen, *A Beleaguered City* (1880), poignantly relates the garrisoning of Semur by "those who knew the meaning of life, being dead." But, failing to communicate the meaning, the Immortals withdraw their forces after three days, and the city returns to worldliness once more. Vagueness and sentimentality mar *A Little Pilgrim in the Unseen* (1882), in which a woman who is too scant of stature to be loved goes to Heaven and renders service to newcomers. "The Lady's Walk" (1882–3)[7] shows a spinster's

[3] D. D. Home, *Incidents in My Life*, 5th edn, New York 1864, p. 98.

[4] Mrs M. O. W. Oliphant, *The Autobiography and Letters of Mrs. M. O. W. Oliphant*, ed. Mrs Harry Coghill, New York 1899, p. 80.

[5] Oliphant, "The Fancies of a Believer," *B.E.M.*, CLVII (1895), 237–55.

[6] Mrs Oliphant, *The Autobiography and Letters of Mrs. M. O. W. Oliphant*, pp. 93, 412, 427.

[7] *Longman's Magazine*, I (Dec. 1882 and Jan. 1883), 229–52, 341–64 (book form, 1897). Although "The Open Door," "Our Lady Mary," "The Portrait," and "The Library Window," 1882–96, have been collected as *Stories of the Seen and the Unseen*, they are ghost stories and do not belong in this special category.

compulsive mothering in rivalry with an ancestral ghost's longing to be the family Providence. The ghost learns its lesson and retires; the mortal goes on sapping the will of her orphan brothers through over-protection. *The Land of Darkness, The Little Pilgrim in the Seen and Unseen*, and *On the Dark Mountains* (all in 1888) use narration to describe Heaven and a place of probation, with increasing emphasis on justice and self-help: "The Father hinders them not, nor helps them: but leaves them." The final narrative of the series, *The Land of Suspense* (1897), is perhaps the most subjective. To a land where the heels of the dead are cooled until Judgment Day comes a young man [Cyril Oliphant] who has always found his mother forgiving when he took the easy way. On the death of his younger brother, the heedless youth realises that his mother is finally alone on earth and prays selflessly for her. The mood is one of crystalline sincerity, and the narrative style is Biblical.[8]

Three months after the death of its frequent contributor, *Blackwood's* summed up her literary account. Mrs Oliphant's "excursions into the supernatural" seem to leave behind "an indescribable sense of futility."[9] With this comment the unseen author could hardly have agreed, for her excursions were undertaken in order to establish "the communion of sorrowful souls" in which "one puts out one's hand" to the desolate.[10] The supernatural had been her means of formulating human problems and working them out in terms of an after-life which offers some chance of a solution. Her vision of man's plight, of mortal weakness, lights up *A Beleaguered City* with flashes of irony and truth. It is dimmed in later stories by wishful imagining and the pathos of the anaemic little pilgrim, and it is renewed by the integrity of grief in *The Land of Suspense*.

3. ROBERT LOUIS STEVENSON

In her stories, Stevenson's "nurse and second mother," Alison Cunningham, communicated not so much a distant rumour as a present sense of the Black Man. Once conjured up, "the b'acky man" slipped into the boy's "high-strung religious ecstasies and terrors" and nightmares. Grown familiar, the Devil almost pleased, and Louis, years later, tried to summon him with a formula[11] and planned with his wife a nest of "crawlers,"

---

[8] *B.E.M.*, CLXI (1897), 131–57. Stephen Gwynn calls the story "a mother's vision of the punishment meted to her firstborn son." *Saints & Sinners*, London 1929, p. 255.
[9] "Mrs Oliphant as a Novelist," *B.E.M.*, CLXII (Sep. 1897), 316.
[10] Mrs Oliphant, *The Autobiography and Letters of Mrs. M. O. W. Oliphant*, p. 430.
[11] Rosaline Masson, *The Life of Robert Louis Stevenson*, 2nd edn, Edinburgh and London 1924, pp. 37–8.

The Black Man and Other Tales, "all supernatural . . . all ghastly."[12]

My comment on Stevenson's fiction will be limited to a few appearances of the Devil and of evil. In "Thrawn Janet" (1881), the servant of the minister, Murdock Soulis, is given the water test of a witch, rescued, and persuaded to renounce "the de'il before them a'." After her apostasy, she appears thrawn-necked and ghastly (palsied, her employer says), and soon hangs herself. Then she begins to walk, and her "unholy footstep" puts the minister to flight. Stevenson was later to feel that he had "coarsened" Soulis by terrifying him into belief in witchcraft, that the story lacked universality, and that he himself perhaps brooded unwholesomely "on the evil in the world and man."[13]

What "Thrawn Janet" most lacks is moral vision. It is doubtful whether Stevenson, in writing the short story, was concerned with good and evil at all. He almost chortles with delight over its frightening him to death; after he read it to his wife, they "crept down the stairs clinging hand in hand like two scared children."[14] The agent of the minister's conversion from unconvincing rationalism to equally unconvincing credulousness is a woman who is so monstrous and mindless that she can function only on the most primitive plane of evil. When she dies for renouncing Satan, narrative interest shifts from the persecuted witch to the persecuted minister, who presents a moral anomaly, as the name Soulis hints, in becoming hardened and soulless through knowledge and experience. As a tale that aims at effect rather than significance, "Thrawn Janet" is a *tour de force*, stark, fleet, and sinuous.[15]

That "fine bogey tale," *The Strange Case of Dr. Jekyll and Mr. Hyde* (1886), also makes much of the picturesqueness and melodrama of evil but neglects its profounder meaning. Jekyll confesses himself in Calvinistic terms "the chief of sinners . . . sold a slave to my original sin," and Hyde, the more confident half of his dual nature, boasts of "a new province of knowledge and new avenues to fame and power . . . laid open." Yet the knowledge and power are ultimately trivial, and sin wells up in a moral vacuum. The best that the moronic delinquent can do is to get a thrill from chance brutality such as trampling on a girl or beating an old man to death in the street. He is no Robert Wringhim, no Scottish Faust or Satan. There is

---

[12] *The Letters of Robert Louis Stevenson,* new edn, ed. Sidney Colvin, New York 1911, II. 5, 36–7.

[13] "Note for 'The Merry Men,' " *The Works of Robert Louis Stevenson,* Tusitala Edn, London 1924, VIII. xv–xvi; Stevenson's *Letters,* II. 359.

[14] Stevenson's *Letters,* II, 37, and Mrs Stevenson's "Prefatory Note," Stevenson's *Works,* VIII. xii–xiii.

[15] For Stevenson's indebtedness to Sinclair, see C. O. Parsons, "Stevenson's Use of Witchcraft Cases in 'Thrawn Janet,' " *Studies in Philology,* XLIII (1946), 551–71.

more perception in *The Master of Ballantrae* (1889), with the evil and the good distinguished in two brothers who, through their mutual tensions, partially exchange moral traits. The complex villain was to his creator "all I know of the devil . . . an INCUBUS," fascinating and repellent.[16]

When Stevenson voyaged to the South Pacific, he found that the Devil had been there before him. Night after night on Fakarava, he swapped Scottish legends for the Governor's "stories of Tahiti and the Paumotus, always of a supernatural character."[17] Whether it comes from this interchange or not, "The Isle of Voices" is full of wizards, magic, and devilry, signifying nothing. Another tale in *Island Nights' Entertainment* (1893) is "The Beach of Falesá." To dispose of a competitor, Case uses taboo, the evil eye, and island fear of devils and spirits. The rival trader enters the bush, destroys bogus idols and a devil shrine, and stabs Case, thereby freeing natives from the *Tiapolo*, or Christian Devil, who has commanded the *aitus*, or island devils. Although the islanders' subjection and the white man's growing wariness of pig-men and demon-women are brought in, a comparison of "The Beach of Falesá" with Joseph Conrad's *Heart of Darkness* (1902) makes Stevenson's picture of the contamination of one culture by another seem superficial. The narrative surface is wonderfully varied, but natives react like Scottish peasants, and the moral, that greed is the root of evil, is uninspired. Once again, Stevenson masters the trappings of evil without penetrating to its core. His supernatural exoticism, however, prepares the way for later work by John Buchan[18] and Eric Linklater.

4. JOHN BUCHAN

Brought up in "a noted household for fairy tales," John Buchan listened to his father's "great collection" of ballads and stories and to his evocation of the Scottish past as "a design in snow and ink, one long contest between villains of admitted villainy and honest men." Just as the suspicion grew on Stevenson that "man is but a devil weakly fettered by some generous beliefs and impositions," so Buchan came to feel that human beings

---

[16] David Daiches, *Robert Louis Stevenson*, Norfolk, Conn. 1947, pp. 77–8, 81. Demonology is skilfully used in "Black Andie's Tale of Tod Lapraik," (*Catriona* 1892–3), to bring out a warlock's hate and his joy in evil.

[17] Mrs Stevenson in Stevenson's *Works*, XIII. xiv.

[18] An example would be Stevenson's heightening of suspense in "The Pavilion on the Links" (1880) by an association of the diabolical and the foreign. The mysterious *carbonari* who attack and burn the pavilion are "all the devils in Italy . . . all hell upon us."

combine "both heavenly and hellish elements."[19] When the hellish elements predominate in an individual or a part of the world, conspiracy may marshal the energies of evil against civilisation.

This menace is the major theme of Buchan's fiction, which transforms the sensationally exploited masterminds and secret bands of Gothic and Romantic novelists into warnings to a world in jeopardy. In *The Half-Hearted, Prester John,* and *Salute to Adventurers,* 1900–15, the arch-plotter is a racial or cultural half-breed or else a renegade, stirring up natives in India, Africa, and North America. The First World War inspires Buchan to bring the threat closer home in *The Thirty-Nine Steps, Greenmantle,* and *The Power-House,* 1915–6. Post-war degeneracy, with Bolshevism as the "nursery of crime" which employs "the special devil that dwells in each country," is represented in *Huntingtower* (1922). The dark psyche of traitors to humanity is analysed in a man without a country who has been warped by his father, "an embittered genius" (*The Courts of the Morning,* 1929), in a man who becomes an "incarnate devil" after being broken by the army (*The Free Fishers,* 1934), and in men of "rootless, marginal mind" (*The Island of Sheep,* 1936). Buchan's most fascinating villain is brilliant, handsome, possibly mad Dominick Medina in *The Three Hostages* (1924). Some ancestral maladjustment, accumulating into a capacity for universal hate, makes this mixed blood practice "all the diabolic lore of the ages," so that he may turn the world back from "ethical codes" to "ancient devil-worship" and "mysteries of the spirit" which he can manipulate.

Buchan is absorbed by the phenomenon of induced atavism. Strange creeds and powers may be exuded by an apparently dead past. Different short stories in *The Watcher by the Threshold* (1902) bring back a "hoary Evil which is older than the stars," a "horrible primitive survival" of Pict-brownies, secret and "abominable rites" which involve warlocks, witches, and the Devil as a black dog, and a girl who perilously awakens the fears once due to Proserpina, "the Queen of Hell." "Basilissa," the last narrative, was amplified into a novel, *The Dancing Floor,* in 1926. Blaming Koré (the Maiden) for a cruel winter, crop failure, disease, and death of children, Greek islanders desert Christianity and long to sacrifice her "in order that the Ancient Ones may appear and bless the people." Koré in turn feels that she must atone for her father, who has abandoned himself to lust,

[19] Buchan, *Memory Hold-the-Door*, London 1940, pp. 4–7, 78, 248–9; *The Novel and the Fairy Tale*, English Association Pamphlet, 79 (1931), p. 11. Cp. Mrs Weir's artless "view of history" in Stevenson, *Weir of Hermiston*, "a design in snow and ink; upon the one side, tender innocents . . . upon the other, the persecutors . . . a suffering Christ, a raging Beelzebub."

sadism, and "researches in devilry." Respect for Greek myth and culture makes Buchan represent the "surge of daemonic energy out of the deeps of the past" as somehow good until corrupted and misapprehended by the superstitious present.

A modern may be swept off his feet by repeating some vestigial ritual or frequenting an unhallowed place. Thus a man of mixed Saxon and Jewish blood is compelled by the "subtle and evil mystery" of a South African grove to the worship of the "old goddess of the East" ("The Grove of Ashtaroth," in *The Moon Endureth*, 1912). In *Witch Wood* (1927), Buchan's favourite among his novels, a seventeenth-century Scottish minister stumbles on "horrible mysteries of heathendom" performed by half-naked celebrants to "witch-music as horrid as a moan of terror." In a contest with his chief elder, who is the leader of the coven, the minister wins no support from his Presbytery and is himself charged with meeting a green-gowned fairy in the Black, or Witch, Wood. In its Calvinistic ironies and moral tensions, its substitution of the Devil and the elder for conspiratorial villains, and its animistic setting, from which both good and evil flow,[20] *Witch Wood* sharply focuses Buchan's powers.

Whenever science can throw any light on elusive operations, Buchan turns to it. In *The Gap in the Curtain* (1932), a Scandinavian mathematical physicist of "demonic power" of mind and spell-like persuasiveness gets seven Englishmen to diet, take a drug, and look into the future. The scientist dies during the experiment, which seems to be futile, harmful, almost wicked. A helpful look into the past is provided in *The Long Traverse* (1941), so that a boy may have ancestral roots in what Buchan considers a tragically rootless world.[21]

In his fiction John Buchan is too often induced by hasty composition and desire for moral clarity to oversimplify character. Thus his narrative case is at times trivialised by champions of civilisation who resemble oversize Rover Boys and by apostles of chaos who lean to stereotype and melodrama. His more perceptive work, however, reveals that good men may be restive and lawless, as in *John Macnab* (1925), and that a "dark angel" may even reform, as in *A Prince of the Captivity* (1933). The impression of evil in men of atrocious resources and cunning, though better conveyed in individuals than in hateful groups, is genuine and in-

[20] In *The Blanket of the Dark* (1931), good comes from old superstitions. A "little old witch-wife" uses "white and unhurtful magic."

[21] For a man's terror of "those eerie shifting corridors of Space," see "Space" in *The Moon Endureth*, and for places of psychic darkness and denial of life (setting as part of the struggle between civilisation and chaos), see "Skule Skerry" in *The Runagates Club* (1928).

sistent. This impression is strengthened by settings which seem to vibrate with peril, suspense, or "the pathos of lost things."[22]

5. NEIL GUNN

A contrast between "the stolidly obvious and . . . the dream-like unknown" appears in Neil M. Gunn's first novel, *The Grey Coast* (1926), and runs through most of his fiction. When the mundane becomes unbearable, a sensitive character may long to be absorbed by "elemental forces," by the "uttermost essence" of things. After destroying his identity, he may be lured on to physical extinction by a death wish.[23] He is given a tangible antagonist in *The Lost Glen* (1932). The glen is an emblem of the visionary ideal, pure and primal, lost in a time of ambition and materialism which is embodied in a human incubus who abuses the Highlands. The hero strangles him and rows out to his own death in unquiet waters.

In *Butcher's Broom* (1934), an early cause of Highland degradation is shown to be the eviction of crofters to make way for profitable sheepwalks. When the villages die, there are voices on the wind and "spirits wandering in the night, the disembodied dead." Gunn reaches back in allusions to changelings, fairies, witches, and spells to more "ancient heathen superstitions" which recall through water kelpies and the Nameless Ones the gross beginnings of life and, perhaps, an epoch before light or creation. Dark and deep, therefore, is the culture which is so monstrously uprooted. Dark Mairi of the Shore, who is mythic like the procreative, all-nourishing "black earth mother," is central to this tale of Highland doom. In the end, even this repository of a knowledge which has been sadly impoverished by time and misuse is killed by sheep-dogs (selfish progress).

Both the earth mother and the earth spirit of Gunn's earlier stories reappear in *The Serpent* (1943). Almost everyone has "a sense of the marvellous, of a pagan forbidden country, of divination and second sight and ghosts, of a door behind them that might open." It is in this "vast and cunning lore of tradition" that the spaewife, Margad, specialises. Another core of pre-Christian experience is the Serpent, a kind of "earth spirit" which is woman, wisdom, and eternity, the source, way, and end of life.

---

[22] Further discussion may be found in Howard Swiggett's Introduction to Buchan, *Mountain Meadow* (1941) and in Gertrude Himmelfarb, "John Buchan," *Encounter*, vx (1960), 46–53.

[23] "Half-Light" and "Hidden Doors" in *Hidden Doors* (1929). The title of the first short story refers to the "tenuous half-light" of the present dimmed by the heroic past.

When the adder stings the philosopher, he becomes one with this older comprehension. Still another earth mother is Mad Mairag in *The Drinking Well* (1946), a shattered vessel of ageless wisdom. "The dead come out of the land and speak to her."

The seer's exercise of ancient powers is more confined than the earth mother's. Gunn's fullest treatment is in *Second Sight* (1940). A Highland stalker's vision of a "phantom funeral" with four men "carrying a dead body" in a shroud annoys a scoffing rationalist. One who "disintegrates—without integrating," he wants generally to discredit "our primitive appetite for wonders"[24] and particularly to ridicule the stalker's gift. Acting like a fey man, he brings on his own dimly foreseen death. The stalker, demonically endowed and unworthy, is at once a more complex and more convincing study. Failing to do justice to second sight in the discussions and actions of his principal characters, Gunn brings in three extra persons to deliver carefully-wrought discourses on the supernatural. One of them conjectures that ghosts, dreams, prophecy, and second sight are now so fragmentary that, even in the Highlands, last refuge of the psychic, they reveal spirit in decline.

From spiritual decay Gunn turns to the maturing boy in three novels. The sea lore and land beliefs of *The Silver Darlings* (1941) are "part of the core and quick of life," and religion is remote. The boy grows up under these influences and, on becoming engaged, undergoes a kind of *rite de passage* by lying on the knoll of the haunted House of Peace and then creeping into a circle of low flat stones: "Life had come for him." The eight-year-old boy of *Young Art and Old Hector* (1942) is instructed by an octogenarian to tread cautiously so as not to offend "the old dark ones." Living in two worlds, "his own and the one beyond," he creates fables and grows in subtlety and imagination. The shaping of his spirit by folk wisdom is vindicated in the sequel, *The Green Isle of the Great Deep* (1944), when Art tumbles into an other-world of forbidden fruit and regimentation. There he rebels against rigidity, and his mentor, Hector, upholds intuition against sterile intellection. Superstition and fancy underpin such values as freedom and sensitivity.

The past is explored in *The Well at the World's End* (1951). A professor of ancient history induces "the illusion of the races flowing up and round you and vanishing away," the Gaels, the Picts, and the megalithic folk. But a ghost trick played by Highlanders on Lowland workers makes him think of a darker past. When one of the victims seems fatally shocked,

---

[24] When he shoots a superstitiously venerated stag, he seems to be imitating the arid sceptic who kills the "live symbol" stag in MacDonald, *What's Mine's Mine*.

a ghost-maker, believing the harm done by a real "evil left behind from old happenings" (clan hatred and stabbing), returns to the haunted cottage to take the evil on himself.

Still another part of the "realm of extra-sensory perceptions and kinetic forces" is considered in *The Other Landscape* (1954). A husband and his dead wife are drawn by the intensity of their love to a tragic and beautiful borderland of "wordless communion" until the husband crosses over to the other landscape.

Although he possesses greater sensitivity than James Macpherson and a firmer grasp of reality than Fiona Macleod, Gunn is a fosterling—however rebellious—of Ossian and the Celtic twilight. Full acceptance of his heritage has resulted in inferior work, and tension between that heritage and his resistance to its sentimental and vague excesses has contributed to his best work. His sharpness of observation and a certain diffuseness of feeling at times pull in opposite directions. Insight tends to shift from word and deed, the substance of narration, to reflexion which may become so involved as to be self-cancelling. The over-subtlety of a novel like *Sun Circle* (1933) suggests a resort to fiction not because it is entirely congenial to Gunn's great talent but because it is the dominant literary mode of communication.

What he seeks to convey through this imperfect medium is that man's well-being depends on a sentience and wisdom which flow silently from long-neglected sources. Human life accumulates through time as experience rather than as history or knowledge. This experience mingles with "the secrecies and sensitiveness" of the blood to give man dignity and understanding and, perhaps, to bring back the "lost green world." This is not so much Scott's or Stevenson's sense of the past as a special, neo-pagan sensing of the past through individual and racial intuition.

In Gunn's novels, the preference of old intuition to new rationality is likely to be regressive, involving schizophrenia and the death wish, when expressed in terms of the earth spirit. When symbolised by the earth mother, it has a mindless benevolence. But, as tradition that environs and sustains the present, it renews lapsed sensitivity and is potentially constructive. The supernatural emphasises the values by which Neil Gunn would have men live.

6. ERIC LINKLATER

An Orcadian, Eric Linklater began reading Icelandic sagas as a boy. As a man, he came to believe that a study of "the superstitions and the sagas of the forefathers" is a proper background of authorship and of the Scottish Renaissance.[25] He introduces the superstitions in his first novel, *White-maa's Saga* (1929). Once the setting of primeval sun-worship, a stone circle on a lonely moor between two lochs worries Norsemen until they cut a cross on the master stone. Centuries later, when the Christian talisman is razed from the Viking Stone by lightning, fears revive and the Peerie Folk (fairies) dance among the megaliths. Lambs are sacrificed at the Stone until Daft Sammy is discovered in his grotesque dance and oblation, and a new cross is incised. Under the seemingly firm crust of the present lie the shifting strata of time.

The real and the fantastic, as well as the humour of the horrible, re-appear in Linklater's "imitation of a saga," *The Men of Ness* (1932). Far more interesting than royal spectres that resent the plundering of their burial place is the ghost of jealous Geira. She rides the roof, cracks the rafters with her heels, and fights like a troll. When she is slain and her body burned, the ashes are covered with boulders. In his idea of a ghost as a substantial corpse returned to life and in his stark, swift narration, Linklater is close to the saga.[25a]

Memory of the dark eyes and "wrinkled yellow face" of his grand-mother and her reputation as a witch who ill-wished her rivals[26] finds place in *Magnus Merriman* (1934). Magnus's tale of an ancestress who was an Orkney witch inspires his mistress, whom he has playfully called a witch, to begin a story which love-making interrupts. Then Frieda goes on to tell how she saw a corpse with "queer torn marks on her arms and breast." In Pennsylvania Dutch lore, if coffin or burial is unfit, a witch has power to tear the body "to bits with her teeth." Magnus thinks no more of sex that night. As Linklater tangles his fingers in the reader's nerve-threads and tugs, he is more effective with exotic vampirism than with native ill-wishing.

The setting moves north of Orkney to the Shetland Islands in *The Dark of Summer* (1956). A wartime search for spies brings the hero to "the ghost of Roger Casement," Mungo Wishart, who anticipates discovery by killing himself. Then the traitor's ghost seems to beat on "the door of the bridal chamber" to deny fulfilment to the living. The twisting of Wishart's psyche is revealed in natural and supernatural terms. The latter refer to the

[25] Linklater, *The Man on My Back*, London 1941, pp. 227–8.

[25a] The saga that most influenced *The Men of Ness* was probably *The Story of Grettir the Strong*. See the translation of Magnússon and Morris, new edn, London 1900, pp. 95–111, 162–4; Linklater, *The Ultimate Viking*, New York 1956, pp. 206–10, 213, and—for *White-maa's Saga*—p. 18.

[26] Linklater, *The Man on My Back*, pp. 3–4, 8.

grýla of the *huldufólk*, familiar spirits, and men who change shape into baleful seals,[27] as he has changed into a despiser of his own land and people.

A West Highland coastal town is the scene of *Laxdale Hall* (1951), which takes up one of Buchan's themes, "Atavism is a kittle thing to play with" (*A Prince of the Captivity*). The community prepares a summer production of Euripides' *Bacchae*, in which Pentheus, an arbitrary rationalist, is torn to pieces by frenzied Bacchanals. Samuel Pettigrew, the modern counterpart of Pentheus, wants to attract Highlanders to his factory in Drumliedubbs and is almost fatally mobbed by the local women. Perhaps, a Pettigrew strain appears in the author in his incidental debunking of second sight. After having "the sight" of his father at the bed foot, Willy John Watt meets the next steamer from Glasgow with his hearse. But no body or coffin is unloaded, only "a smart new perambulator" for Mrs Watt, who is expecting again. This is "the latest failure of Willy John's supernatural gift."

During a "walkabout year" in 1951–2, Linklater went as far afield as Papua, where "the power of the sorcerer had not been extirpated," and New Guinea, which had lately emerged "from primeval sleep, from sorcery and cannibalism."[28] That sorcery is used in *The Faithful Ally* (1954). After Samarai's promise of an aerial cargo and freedom for the natives, a sacrificial boy is hanged, revived on the third day, perched on the sorcerer's left thigh "like a ventriloquist's dummy," and rubbed and kneaded into a ghastly semi-animation. At last, "a hoarse murmur from his sagging lips" conveys "the wisdom of the dead" to the squatting elders. Everyone who can touches the marvellous boy "on the head and the genitals." In the fighting, both the sorcerer who wants to be "a great king" and his puerile instrument are killed. But the horror and a residuum of inexplicable power remain.

Imitation of the saga has taught Linklater that a strong action can bear a weight of wild, disgusting, comic, and poignant detail. With firmness and restraint, he has applied the lesson to Orcadian lore, which he has brought into the main stream of Scottish fiction, and to non-Norse matter, such as Papuan sorcery. His humour enables him to lighten his touch, to relieve pressure when it becomes too insistent, and to hint rather than

[27] For humour, satire, and steadily mounting credibility in the presentation of "the unique and solitary example of a sophisticated seal-man," see the title story of Linklater, *Sealskin Trousers and Other Stories*, London 1947.

[28] Linklater, *A Year of Space: A Chapter in Autobiography*, New York 1953, pp. 225, 237, 263–4. For material probably used by Linklater, see Lewis Lett, *Sir Hubert Murray of Papua*, London and Sydney 1949, pp. 71–4, 98, 106–7, 110, 175–6, 234–5, 248–51. *Samarai* is the name of an island.

propose rational explanations.[29] An islander, he is certainly not in any line of descent from Macpherson, George MacDonald, or Fiona Macleod, Highland writers who sentimentalise, moralise, or etherialise the supernatural. Rather, he approaches the robust Lowland tradition which produced "Tam o' Shanter" and "Wandering Willie's Tale."

[29] A recent instance is the tempered use of demonology to portray Samson through contemporary eyes. Linklater, *Husband of Delilah* (1962).

BIBLIOGRAPHY

I. MANUSCRIPTS AND TYPESCRIPTS

Unless otherwise stated, all items in the following list are MSS.

Abbotsford MSS. N.L.S.

ANON. Sir Walter Scott and his Contemporaries. 2 vols. Anonymous life. Forster Collection, the Victoria and Albert Museum, London.

BALLANTYNE, JOHN. Private Diary 1819–21. Morgan Library, New York City.

BOATRIGHT, MODY C. Scott's use of the Supernatural in the Waverley Novels. Ph.D. dissertation in TS. (1932). University of Texas.

British Soldier: or, Life's Campaign, The. Play (1804). Larpent Collection in Henry E. Huntington Library.

ELLIS, GEORGE. Letters from George Ellis Esq. ((to Scott)). N.L.S.

LOCKHART, J. G. Letters to J.G.L. 10 vols. N.L.S.

OCHOJSKI, PAUL M. Walter Scott and Germany. Ph.D. dissertation in TS. (1960). Columbia University.

SCOTT, SIR WALTER.

——. Letters to W.S., 1796–1831, acquired by Hugh Walpole. N.L.S.

——. Letters to W.S. E.U.L.

——. The Tapestried Chamber. B.M. IV. HP. 13.

SIBBALD, SIR ROBERT. MS. Collections. N.L.S.

STROUT, ALAN L. Scottish Superstition in the Waverley Novels. M.A. essay in TS. (1920). University of Chicago.

TRAIN, JOSEPH. Letters of Joseph Train (and others) to Scott, 1810–31. N.L.S.

WALPOLE, HUGH. See SCOTT, SIR WALTER.

WILKIE, THOMAS. Old Scots Songs . . . Roxburghshire, Berwickshire & Selkirkshire . . . A.D. 1814–15. N.L.S.

II. PERIODICALS

Atlas, The.

Beauties of all the Magazines selected for the Year 1762, The.

Blackwood's Edinburgh Magazine.

Caledonian Mercury, The.

Chambers's Edinburgh Journal.

Edinburgh Magazine, The.

Edinburgh Monthly Review, The.

Edinburgh Review, The.

Foreign Quarterly Review, The.

Gentleman's Magazine, The.

Keepsake for 1829, The, ed. F. M. Reynolds. London ((1828)).

London Christian Instructor, The.

London Magazine, The.

Monthly Review, The.

Notes and Queries.

Quarterly Review, The.

Retrospective Review, The.

Sale-Room, The (1817).

Scotsman, The.

Spectator, The.

III. REFERENCE BOOKS

BLACK, GEORGE F. *A Gypsy Bibliography.* London 1914.

——. *A List of Works relating to Scotland.* New York 1916.

BREWER, E. COBHAM. *Reader's Handbook.* London 1902.

——. *Brewer's Dictionary of Phrase & Fable.* 6th edn. London 1962.

Chambers's Encyclopaedia. 10 vols., new edn. London and Edinburgh 1895.

COCHRANE, JOHN G. *Catalogue of the Library at Abbotsford.* Maitland Club, VOL. XLV. Edinburgh 1838.

COLLIN DE PLANCY, JACQUES. *Dictionnaire Infernal.* 2nd edn, 4 vols. Paris 1825–6. Supplemented in "Les Sciences Occultes," *Crapouillot*, No. 18 (1952), 2–27.

CORSON, JAMES C. *A Bibliography of Sir Walter Scott . . . 1797–1940.* Edinburgh 1943. Supplemented in *University of Edinburgh Journal*, XVIII (1955–6), 23–32, 104–13.

DOUGLAS, SIR ROBERT. *The Scots Peerage*, ed. Sir James B. Paul. 9 vols. Edinburgh 1904–1914.

DONALD, JAMES. See HENDERSON, ANDREW.

Faclair Gaidhlig: a Gaelic Dictionary. 3 vols. Herne Bay 1902.

GROSE, FRANCIS. *A Provincial Glossary.* London 1811.

HENDERSON, ANDREW. *Scottish Proverbs.* New edn., ed. James Donald. Glasgow 1881.

HOWLAND, ARTHUR C. See LEA, HENRY C.

JOHNSTON, JAMES B. *Place-Names of Scotland.* London 1934.

LANG, THEO, ed. *The King's Scotland.* London 1951.

——. *The Queen's Scotland.* In progress, 7 vols. London 1952–. . . .

Larousse Encyclopedia of Mythology, tr. Aldington and Ames. New York 1960.

LEA, HENRY C. *Materials Toward A History of Witchcraft*, ed. Arthur C. Howland. 3 vols. New York 1957. (1st publ. 1939).

LEACH, MARIA, ed. *Funk & Wagnalls Standard Dictionary of Folklore.* 2 vols. New York 1949–50.

MACNEILL, F. MARIAN. *The Silver Bough.* 4 vols. Glasgow 1957–64.

MACTAGGART, JOHN. *The Scottish Gallovidian Encyclopedia.* London 1824.

MORGAN, B. Q. *A Critical Bibliography of German Literature in English Translation.* Palo Alto 1938.

——, and A. R. HOHLFELD. *German Literature in British Magazines 1750–1860.* Madison 1949.

RADFORD, EDWIN, and MONA A. *Encyclopaedia of Superstitions.* New York 1949.

ROBBINS, ROSSELL H. *The Encyclopedia of Witchcraft and Demonology.* New York [1959].

SPENCE, LEWIS. *An Encyclopaedia of Occultism.* New York [1959].

THOMPSON, STITH. *Motif-Index of Folk-Literature.* 6 vols, rev. edn. Bloomington 1955–8.

IV. OTHER BOOKS AND ARTICLES

AARNE, ANTTI. "The Types of the Folk-Tale," tr. Stith Thompson. *Folklore Fellows Communications.* XXV. no. 74. Helsinki 1928.

Account of Some Imaginary Apparitions, An. Stirling 1801.

ADDISON, JOSEPH. *The Dramatic Works.* Glasgow 1750.

——. *The Spectator,* ed. G. A. Aitken. 8 vols. London 1898.

ALDERSON, JOHN. *An Essay on Apparitions.* Hull 1811.

ALISON, SIR ARCHIBALD. *Lives of Lord Castlereagh and Sir Charles Stewart.* 3 vols. Edinburgh and London 1861.

ALLAN, GEORGE. *Life of Sir Walter Scott.* Philadelphia 1835.

ALLARDYCE, ALEXANDER. See SHARPE, CHARLES K.

AMOURS, F. J. ed. *Scottish Alliterative Poems,* S.T.S. Edinburgh and London 1897.

ANDREW OF WYNTOUN. *The Original Chronicle of Andrew of Wyntoun,* ed. F. J. Amours. S.T.S., 6 vols. Edinburgh 1903–14.

ANDREWS, WILLIAM. "The Lee Penny." *The Reliquary.* XVI (1875–6), 87–9.

Antidote to Superstition, An. Dunbar n.d.

ARGYLL, ARCHIBALD, EARL OF. *Letters from Archibald, Earl of Argyll, to John, Duke of Lauderdale,* ed. C. K. Sharpe. Bannatyne Club, VOL. XXXIII. Edinburgh 1829.

ARMSTRONG, JOHN. *Miscellanies.* 2 vols. London 1770.

ARNOT, HUGO. *A Collection and Abridgement of Celebrated Criminal Trials in Scotland.* Glasgow 1812.

AUBREY, JOHN. *Remaines of Gentilisme and Judaisme,* ed. James Britten. London 1881.

——. *Miscellanies upon Various Subjects.* 5th edn. London 1890.

——. *Brief Lives,* ed. Andrew Clark. 2 vols. Oxford 1898.

BACON, ROGER. *The Famous History of Fryar Bacon.* London 1766.

BAGEHOT, WALTER. *The Works and Life of Walter Bagehot,* ed. Mrs Russell Barrington. 10 vols. London 1915.

BAILLIE, JOANNA. *Dramas.* 3 vols. London 1836.

——. *Dramatic and Poetical Works.* 2nd edn. London 1853.

BAKER, ERNEST A. *The History of the English Novel.* 10 vols. London 1924–39.

BARBOUR, JOHN. *Bruce,* ed. Walter W. Skeat. S.T.S. 2 vols. Edinburgh and London 1894.

BARHAM, RICHARD H. *The Ingoldsby Legends,* ed. R. H. D. Barham. 2 vols. London 1870.

BARHAM, R. H. D., *The Life and Letters of the Rev. Richard Harris Barham.* 2 vols. London 1870.

BARING, MRS HENRY. See WINDHAM, WILLIAM.

BARNARD, P. M. *Catalogue*, Tunbridge Wells 1916.

BARRINGTON, MRS RUSSELL. See BAGEHOT, WALTER.

BARTLETT, ALFRED D. *An Historical and Descriptive Account of Cumnor Place, Berks.* Oxford and London 1850.

BATHO, EDITH C. "Sir Walter Scott and the Sagas." *M.L.R.* XXIV (1929), 409–15.

BAXTER, RICHARD. *The Certainty of the World of Spirits.* London 1691.

BEATTIE, JAMES. *The Minstrel . . . Book the First.* London 1771.

——. *The Minstrel . . . The Second Book.* London 1774.

——. *Essays.* 3rd edn. London 1779.

BEERS, HENRY A. *A History of English Romanticism in the Nineteenth Century.* New York 1901.

BERNARD, JOHN. *Retrospections of the Stage.* 2 vols. London 1830.

BLACK, GEORGE F. "Scottish Charms and Amulets." *Proceedings* of the Society of Antiquaries of Scotland. XXVII (1893), 433–526.

——, ed. *Some Unpublished Scottish Witchcraft Trials.* New York 1941.

BLACKSTONE, SIR WILLIAM. *Commentaries on the Laws of England.* 4 vols. Oxford 1765–8.

BLAIR, ROBERT. *The Poetical Works of Robert Blair.* London 1794.

BLISS, D. P., ed. *Border Ballads.* London 1925.

BLISS, PHILIP. See WOOD, ANTHONY À.

BOADEN, JAMES. *The Secret Tribunal: A Play.* London 1795.

BOATRIGHT, MODY C. "Witchcraft in the Novels of Sir Walter Scott." *University of Texas Studies in English.* XIII (1933), 95–112.

——. "Demonology in the Novels of Sir Walter Scott." *University of Texas Studies in English.* XIV (1934), 75–88.

——. "Scott's Theory and Practice concerning the Use of the Supernatural in Prose Fiction in relation to the Chronology of the Waverley Novels." *P.M.L.A.* L (1935), 235–261.

Book of Scotish Pasquils. 1568–1715, A. Edinburgh 1868.

Book of Scottish Pasquils &c., A. Edinburgh 1827.

BORROW, GEORGE. *The Bible in Spain.* 3 vols. London 1843.

BOS, KLAAS. *Religious Creeds and Philosophies as Represented by Characters in Sir Walter Scott's Works and Biography.* Amsterdam 1932.

BOULTON, RICHARD. *A Compleat History of Magick, Sorcery and Witchcraft.* 2 vols. London 1715–16.

BOWD, JAMES and JAMES SKENE. "Letter . . . to . . . Scott" on cattle and witchcraft. *Archaeologia Scotica.* III (1831), 300–01.

BOWER, EDMUND. *Doctor Lamb Revived, or Witchcraft Condemned in Anne Bodenham.* London 1653.

BRAND, JOHN. *Popular Antiquities of Great Britain,* ed. W. C. Hazlitt. 3 vols. London 1870.

BRANDES, GEORGE. *Main Currents in Nineteenth Century Literature.* New York 1923.

BREWER, J. N. "Oxfordshire." *The Beauties of England and Wales.* XII, PT II. London 1813.

BREWER, WILMON. *Shakespeare's Influence on Sir Walter Scott.* Boston 1925.

BREWSTER, SIR DAVID. *Letters on Natural Magic addressed to Sir Walter Scott.* London 1832.

BRITTEN, JAMES. See AUBREY, JOHN.

BRÖKER, CARL. *Scotts "Anne of Geierstein."* Kiel 1927.

BRUCE, J. DOUGLAS, ed. *Le Morte Arthur.* E.E.T.S. London 1903.

BRYDGES, SIR SAMUEL EGERTON. *The Ruminator.* 2 vols. London 1813.

BUCHAN, JAMES W., ed. *A History of Peeblesshire.* 3 vols. Glasgow 1925–7.

BUCHAN, JOHN. Novels and stories: *The Half-Hearted* (1900); *The Watcher by the Threshold* (1902); *Prestor John* (1910); *The Moon Endureth* (1912); *Salute to Adventurers* (1915), *The Thirty-Nine Steps* (1915); *Greenmantle* (1916); *The Power-House* (1916); *Huntingtower* (1922); *The Three Hostages* (1924); *John Macnab* (1925); *The Dancing Floor* (1926); *Witch Wood* (1927); *The Runagates Club* (1928); *The Courts of the Morning* (1929); *The Blanket of the Dark* (1931); *The Gap in the Curtain* (1932); *A Prince of the Captivity* (1933); *The Free Fishers* (1934); *The Island of Sheep* (1936); *The Long Traverse* (1941); *Mountain Meadow* (1941).

——. *The Novel and the Fairy Tale.* English Association Pamphlet 79 (1931).

——. *Sir Walter Scott.* London 1932.

——. *Memory Hold-the-Door.* London 1940. (American title, *Pilgrim's Way*).

——. *Montrose.* London 1949 (1st edn, 1928).

BUCHANAN, GEORGE. *The History of Scotland.* London 1690 and 1722.

BURKE, SIR JOHN B. *Vicissitudes of Families.* 2 vols. London 1869.

BURNS, ROBERT. *The Letters of Robert Burns,* ed. J. Delancey Ferguson. 2 vols. Oxford 1931.

——. *The Poetical Works of Robert Burns,* ed. J. Logie Robertson. London 1960.

BURNS, REV. ROBERT. See WODROW, ROBERT.

BUTLER, R. F. "Maria Edgeworth and Sir Walter Scott." *Review of English Studies.* N.S. IX (1958), 23–40.

BURTON, J. H. See CARLYLE, ALEXANDER.

CAGLIOSTRO. *The Life of Joseph Balsamo, commonly called Count Cagliostro.* London 1791.

CALDERWOOD, DAVID. *The History of the Kirk of Scotland,* ed. Thomas Thomson. Wodrow Society, 8 vols. Edinburgh 1842–9.

CAMERON, ISABEL. *A Highland Chapbook.* Stirling 1928.

CAMPBELL, JOHN F. *Popular Tales of the West Highlands Orally Collected.* 4 vols. Edinburgh 1860–2.

CAMPBELL, JOHN G. *Witchcraft & Second Sight in the Highlands and Islands of Scotland.* Glasgow 1902.

CARLISLE, WILLIAM. *An Essay on Evil Spirits: or, Reasons to Prove their Existence.* 2nd edn. London 1825.

CARLYLE, ALEXANDER. *Autobiography of the Rev. Dr. Alexander Carlyle,* ed. J. H. Burton. Edinburgh 1860.

CARLYLE, THOMAS. *German Romance.* 4 vols. Edinburgh 1827.

——. *The Works of Thomas Carlyle,* ed. H. D. Traill. Centenary Edition 30 vols., London 1896–9.

CARSWELL, DONALD. *Sir Walter: A Four-Part Study in Biography.* London 1930.

CARSWELL, JOHN. *The Prospector: Being the Life and Times of Rudolf Erich Raspe.* London 1950.

CASTLEREAGH, VISCOUNT. *Memoirs and Correspondence of Viscount Castlereagh,* ed. Charles Vane, Marquess of Londonderry. 12 vols. London 1848–53.

CECIL, LORD DAVID. *Sir Walter Scott.* London 1933.

——. *Melbourne.* London 1955.

CHAMBERS, ROBERT. *Illustrations of the Author of Waverley.* 2nd edn. Edinburgh 1825.

——. *Traditions of Edinburgh.* 2 vols. Edinburgh 1825.

——. "Life of Sir Walter Scott." *Chambers's Edinburgh Journal.* 1 (supplement of 6 Oct. 1832), 1–12.

——. *Domestic Annals of Scotland.* 2 vols. Edinburgh 1858.

——. *The Book of Days.* 2 vols. Edinburgh 1862–4.

——. *Popular Rhymes of Scotland.* New edn. London and Edinburgh 1870.

CHAMBERS, WILLIAM. *The Life and Anecdotes of the Black Dwarf.* Edinburgh 1820.

——. *Exploits, Curious Anecdotes, and Sketches of the most remarkable Scottish Gypsies.* 3rd edn. Edinburgh 1823.

CHARLES, R. H., ed. *The Apocrypha and Pseudepigrapha of the Old Testament in English.* 2 vols. Oxford 1913.

CHILD, FRANCIS J. *The English and Scottish Popular Ballads.* 5 vols. Boston 1882–98.

CHRISTIANSEN, R. TH. "Scotsmen and Norsemen." *Scottish Studies.* 1 (1957), 15–37.

CHURCHILL, CHARLES. *The Ghost.* London 1762.

CLARK, ANDREW. See AUBREY, JOHN.

CLARK, W. FORDYCE. *The Shetland Sketch Book.* Edinburgh 1930.

CLARKE, ADAM. *Memoirs of the Wesley Family.* New York 1824.

——. *An Account of the Religious and Literary Life of Adam Clarke.* New York 1837.

CLEAVER, R. S. "Sir Walter Scott and Mrs. Veal's Ghost." *Nineteenth Century.* XXXVII (1895), 271–2.

COCLÈS, BARTHÉLEMY. *Le Compendion et brief Enseignement de Physiognomie et Chiromancie.* Paris 1546.

CODY, F. G. See LESLIE, JOHN.

COGHILL, MRS HARRY. See OLIPHANT, MARGARET.

COLERIDGE, SAMUEL T. *The Friend,* ed. H. N. Coleridge. 4th edn. London 1844.

——. *Coleridge's Miscellaneous Criticism,* ed, T. M. Raysor. Cambridge, Mass. 1936.

COLLINS, WILLIAM. *The Poetical Works of James Beattie . . . and William Collins.* London 1823.

COLVIN, SIDNEY. See STEVENSON, ROBERT LOUIS.

COMINES, PHILIPPE DE. *The History of Comines,* tr. Thomas Danett in 1596, ed. Charles Whibley. 2 vols. London 1897.

COMNENA, ANNA. *The Alexiad,* tr. Elizabeth Dawes. London 1928.

CONSTABLE, THOMAS. *Archibald Constable and his Literary Correspondents.* 3 vols. Edinburgh 1873.

COOK and WEDDERBURN. See RUSKIN, JOHN.

COOPER, THOMAS. *The Poetical Works of Thomas Cooper.* London 1877.

CORSON, JAMES C. "Verses on the Death of Scott." *N. & Q.* CLXXVII (1939) 417–19.
——. See GELL, SIR WILLIAM.

COULTON, G. G. *The Medieval Village.* Cambridge 1925.

CRAIG, DAVID. *Scottish Literature and the Scottish People 1680–1830.* London 1961.

CRAIG-BROWN, THOMAS. *The History of Selkirkshire.* 2 vols. Edinburgh 1886.

CRAIGIE, W. A., ed. *The Maitland Folio Manuscript.* S.T.S., 2 vols. Edinburgh and London 1919–27.

CRAWFORD, THOMAS. *Burns: A Study of the Poems and Songs.* Edinburgh and London 1960.

CRAWFURD, GEORGE. *The History of the Shire of Renfrew.* Paisley 1782.

CROCKETT, WILLIAM S. *The Scott Country.* 6th edn. London 1930.
——. *The Scott Originals,* 3rd. edn. Edinburgh 1932.

CROKER, T. CROFTON. *Researches in the South of Ireland.* London 1824.

CROMEK, R. H. *Remains of Nithsdale and Galloway Song.* London 1810 and Paisley 1880.

CROWE, CATHERINE. *The Night Side of Nature.* 2 vols. London 1848.
——. *Ghosts and Family Legends.* London 1859.

CUNNINGHAM, ALLAN. *Traditional Tales of the English and Scottish Peasantry.* 2 vols. London 1822.
——. *Sir Michael Scott.* 3 vols. London 1828.
——, ed. "Abbotsford." *The Anniversary: or, Poetry and Prose for* MDCCCXXIX. pp. 81–100. London 1829 ((1828)).

CURNOCK, NEHEMIAH. See WESLEY, REV. JOHN.

DAICHES, DAVID. *Robert Louis Stevenson.* Norfolk, Conn. 1947.
——. "Scott's *Redgauntlet.*" *From Jane Austen to Joseph Conrad,* edd. Rathburn and Steinmann. Pp. 46–59. Minneapolis 1958.

DALGLEISH, WILLIAM. "Memoirs of William Dalgleish, butler to Sir Walter Scott," ed. G. E. Mitton. *The Cornhill Magazine.* 3rd series, LXX (1931), 738–54; LXXI (1931), 75–93, 213–31.

DALYELL, JOHN G. *The Darker Superstitions of Scotland.* Edinburgh 1834 and Glasgow 1835.

DANEAU, LAMBERT. *A Dialogue of Witches,* tr. R. W. London 1575.

DAVIDSON, THOMAS. *Rowan Tree and Red Thread.* Edinburgh and London 1949.

DAVIE, DONALD, *The Heyday of Sir Walter Scott.* London 1961.

DAVY, JOHN. *Memoirs of the Life of Sir Humphry Davy, Bart.* 2 vols. London 1836.

DEBES, LUCAS J. *A Description of the Islands and Inhabitants of Foeroe,* Anglicised by John Sterpin. London 1676.

DEE, JOHN. *A True & Faithful Relation of What passed for many Years Between D^r. John Dee . . . and Some Spirits.* Preface by Meric Casaubon. London 1659.

DEFOE, DANIEL. *A General History of the Pyrates.* 2nd edn. London 1724.
——. *The Novels and Miscellaneous Works of Daniel DeFoe.* 20 vols. Oxford 1840–1.

DELABORDE, LÉON. "Magie Orientale." *Revue des deux Mondes.* 2nd series, III (1833), 332–343.

DENHAM, MICHAEL A. *The Denham Tracts,* ed. James Hardy for Folk-lore Society. XXIX, XXXV (1892–5).

DEVONSHIRE, GEORGIANA DUCHESS OF. *The Sylph*. 2 vols. London 1779.

DOBRÉE, BONAMY, ed. *From Anne to Victoria*. New York 1937.

DODDRIDGE, PHILIP. *The Most Remarkable Passages in the Life of the Honourable Colonel James Gardiner*. Falkirk 1805. Scott's copy of this chapbook, Edinburgh 1747.

DOUGLAS, DAVID. See SCOTT, SIR WALTER.

DOUGLAS, GAVIN. *The Poetical Works of Gavin Douglas*, ed. John Small. 4 vols. Edinburgh and London 1874.

DOUGLAS, SIR GEORGE, ed. *The Book of Scottish Poetry*. London 1911.

DOUGLAS, RONALD M. *The Scots Book*. New York 1935.

DOWDEN, EDWARD. See TRELAWNY, EDWARD J.

DRAGE, WILLIAM. *Daimonomageia*. London 1665.

DUNBAR, WILLIAM. *Poems*, ed. James Kinsley. Oxford 1958.

ECHARD, LAURENCE. *The History of England*. 3 vols. London 1707–18.

EVANS, JOAN. *Magical Jewels of the Middle Ages and the Renaissance*. Oxford 1922.

FANSHAWE, ANNE. *Memoirs of Lady Fanshawe*, ed. N. H. Nicolas. London 1829.

FARMER, HUGH. *An Essay on the Demoniacs of the New Testament*. 2nd edn. London 1805.

FARRELL, WALTER. *A Companion to the Summa*. 4 vols. New York 1938–42.

FEA, ALLAN. *The Real Captain Cleveland*. London 1912.

FENN, W. W. *Woven in Darkness. A Medley of Stories, Essays, and Dreamwork*. 2 vols. London 1885.

FERGUSON, J. DeLANCEY. See BURNS, ROBERT.

FERGUSSON, ALEXANDER. *The Laird of Lag*. Edinburgh 1886.

FERGUSSON, ROBERT. *The Poems of Robert Fergusson*, ed. Matthew P. McDiarmid. S.T.S., 2 vols. Edinburgh and London 1954–6.

——. See SMITH, SYDNEY G.

FERRIAR, JOHN. *An Essay towards a Theory of Apparitions*. London 1813.

FINLAYSON, MALCOLM J., ed. *An Anthology of Carrick*. Kilmarnock 1925.

FISHER, P. F. "Providence, Fate, and the Historical Imagination in Scott's *The Heart of Midlothian*." *Nineteenth-Century Fiction*. X (1955), 99–114.

Folk Lore. Choice Notes from "Notes and Queries." London 1859.

FORBES, SIR WILLIAM. *An Account of the Life and Writings of James Beattie*. 2nd edn. Edinburgh 1807.

FORSYTH, J. S. *Demonologia*. London 1831.

FORSYTHE, R. S. "Two Debts of Scott to *Le Morte d'Arthur*." *Modern Language Notes*. XXVII (1912), 51–2.

FRASER, ALEXANDER. *Northern Folk-Lore on Wells and Water*. Inverness 1878.

FRASER, JAMES. *Major Fraser's Manuscript*, ed. Alexander Fergusson. 2 vols. Edinburgh 1889.

——. *Chronicles of the Frasers*, ed. William Mackay. Edinburgh 1905.

FRASER, WILLIAM C. "Oral tradition about Sir Walter Scott." *Transactions of the Hawick Archaeological Society*. Session 1932, pp. 26–33.

FRAZER, SIR JAMES G. *The Golden Bough: A Study in Magic and Religion*, abridged edn. New York 1958. *The New Golden Bough*, ed. Theodor H. Gaster. New York 1959.

FREEMAN, DAVID. "Sir Walter Scott's Villains." *The Dublin Review*. CXCV (1934), 305–16.

FRERE, W. H., ed. *Visitation Articles and Injunctions of the Period of the Reformation*. Alcuin Club Collections, VOL. XIV. London 1910.

FREYE, WALTER. *The Influence of "Gothic" Literature on Sir Walter Scott*. Rostock 1902.

FROISSART, JEAN. *The Chronicle of Froissart*, tr. Lord Berners, ed. W. P. Ker. 6 vols. London 1901–03.

FRYKMAN, ERIK. *John Galt's Scottish Stories 1820–1823*. Uppsala 1959.

GACHET D'ARTIGNY, ANTOINE. *Nouveaux Mémoires d'Histoire, de Critique et de Littérature*. 7 vols. Paris 1749–56.

GALL, RICHARD. *Poems and Songs*. Edinburgh 1819.

GALT, JOHN. *Voyages and Travels, in the Years 1809, 1810, and 1811*. London 1812.

——. *Letters from the Levant*. London 1813.

——. Novels and stories: *The Majolo*, 2 vols. (1816); *The Earthquake*, 3 vols. (1820); *Glenfell* (1820); *The Ayrshire Legatees* (1821); *The Steamboat* (1822); *The Spaewife*, 3 vols. (1823); *Rothelan*, 3 vols. (1824); *The Omen* (1825–Postscript, 1826); *Lawrie Todd*, 3 vols. (1830); *Southennan*, 3 vols. (1830); *Bogle Corbet*, 3 vols. (1831); *Stanley Buxton*, 3 vols. (1832); *The Member* (1832); *The Radical* (1833); *Eben Erskine*, 3 vols. (1833); *The Stolen Child* (1833); *Stories of the Study*, 3 vols. (1833); *The Howdie and Other Tales* (1923).

——. *The Bachelor's Wife*. Edinburgh 1824.

——. *The Autobiography of John Galt*. 2 vols. London 1833.

——. *The Literary Life and Miscellanies of John Galt*. 3 vols. Edinburgh and London 1834.

——. *The Demon of Destiny; and Other Poems*. Greenock 1839.

——. *Life of Cardinal Wolsey*. 3rd edn. London 1846.

——. *The Works of John Galt*, edd. Meldrum and Roughead. 10 vols. Edinburgh 1936.

GARDINER, JAMES. *The Life of the Honourable Col. James Gardiner*. Greenock 1812.

GASPEY, THOMAS. *The Witch-Finder; or, the Wisdom of Our Ancestors*. 3 vols. London 1824.

GELL, SIR WILLIAM. *Reminiscences of Sir Walter Scott's Residence in Italy, 1832*, ed. James C. Corson. London 1957.

Ghost Stories. London 1823.

GILLIES, ROBERT P. *Recollections of Sir Walter Scott, Bart*. London 1837.

——. *Memoirs of a Literary Veteran*. 3 vols. London 1851.

GLANVIL, JOSEPH. *Saducismus Triumphatus; Or Full and Plain Evidence concerning Witches*. London 1681.

GLEIG, GEORGE. See STOCKHOUSE, THOMAS.

GODWIN, WILLIAM. *St. Leon: A Tale of the Sixteenth Century*. 4 vols. London 1799.

GOETHE, J. W. VON. *Conversations with Eckermann*. New York 1901.

——. *Claudine von Villa Bella: Goethes erste Lottedichtung*, ed. Willy Krogmann. Berlin 1937.

GOODALL, WALTER. See John of Fordun.

GORDON, ROBERT C. "*The Bride of Lammermoor:* A Novel of Tory Pessimism." *Nineteenth-Century Fiction.* XII (1957), 110–24.

GOTTSCHALK, FRIEDRICH. *Die Sagen und Volksmärchen der Deutschen.* Halle 1814.

GRADY, SISTER ROSE M. *The Sources of Scott's Eight Long Poems* (thesis abstract). Urbana 1934.

GRAHAM, PATRICK. *Sketches of Perthshire.* 2nd edn. Edinburgh 1812.

GRANT, ANNE M. *Essays on Superstitions of the Highlanders in Scotland.* London 1811.

——. *Memoir and Correspondence of Mrs. Grant of Laggan,* ed. J. P. Grant. 3 vols. London 1844.

GRANT, DOUGLAS. See SCOTT, SIR WALTER.

GRANT, SIR FRANCIS. *A True Narrative of the Sufferings and Relief of a Young Girle.* Edinburgh 1698. Printed as *Sadducismus Debellatus.* London 1698.

GRANT, JAMES. *The Captain of the Guard.* Oxford 1910.

GRANT, JAMES, Archaeologist. *The Mysteries of All Nations.* Leith ((1880)).

GRAY, M. M., ed. *Scottish Poetry from Barbour to James VI.* London 1935.

GRAY, W. FORBES. *Scott in Sunshine & Shadow.* London 1931.

——. "Friends of Sir Walter: Unpublished Letters." *Cornhill Magazine.* 3rd series. LXXIII (1932), 257–65.

GREGOR, WALTER. "Guardian Spirits of Wells and Lochs." *Folk-Lore.* III (1892), 67–73.

GRETTIR THE STRONG. *The Story of Grettir the Strong,* tr. Magnússon and Morris. New edn. London 1900.

GRIERSON, SIR HERBERT. *Sir Walter Scott, Bart.* New York 1938.

——, ed. *Sir Walter Scott To-day.* London 1932.

——. See SCOTT, SIR WALTER.

GRIERSON OF LAG, SIR ROBERT. *An Elegy in Memory of . . . Sir Robert Grierson of Lag.* 5th edn. n.p. 1753.

GRILLOT DE GIVRY, ÉMILE A. *Witchcraft Magic & Alchemy,* tr. J. Courtenay Locke. New York ((1954)).

GRIMM, JACOB and WILHELM. *Deutsche Sagen.* 2 vols. Berlin 1911.

GUNN, ALEXANDER. See TIMBS, JOHN.

GUNN, NEIL M. Novels and stories: *The Grey Coast* (1926); *Hidden Doors* (1929); *The Last Glen* (1932); *Sun Circle* (1933); *Butcher's Broom* (1934); *Second Sight* (1940); *The Silver Darlings* (1941); *Young Art and Old Hector* (1942); *The Serpent* (1943); *The Green Isle of the Great Deep* (1944); *The Drinking Well* (1946); *The Well at the World's End* (1951); *The Other Landscape* (1954).

GUNTHER, JOHN. *Inside Asia.* New York and London 1939.

GWYNN, STEPHEN. *Saints & Scholars.* London 1929.

——. *Mungo Park.* London 1934.

HAMER, DOUGLAS. See LINDSAY, SIR DAVID.

HARDY, JAMES. See DENHAM, MICHAEL A.

HAMILTON, W. R. "Notes on a Roman Villa on the Coast of Naples." *Transactions* of the Royal Society of Literature. III, Pt. I (1839), 108–13.

"Hampshire Ghost Story, A." *G.M.* CCXXXIII (1872), 547–59, 666–78.

HARDWICK, CHARLES. *Traditions, Superstitions, and Folk-Lore*. Manchester 1872.

HARSNET, SAMUEL. *A Declaration of Egregious Popish Impostures*. London 1603.

HARTSTONGE, MATTHEW W. *The Eve of All-Hallows*. 3 vols. London 1825.

HAWTHORNE, NATHANIEL. *The Complete Writings*, ed. H. E. Scudder. 22 vols. Boston and New York 1900.

——. *The English Notebooks*, ed. Randall Stewart. New York 1941.

HAYDON, B. R. *The Autobiography and Memoirs of Benjamin Robert Haydon (1786–1846)*, edd. Tom Taylor and Aldous Huxley. 2 vols. London 1926.

HAZLITT, WILLIAM. *Conversations of James Northcote, R.A.*, ed. Edmund Gosse. London 1894.

HEINE, HEINRICH. *Doktor Faustus*, tr. Basil Ashmore. London 1952.

HENDERSON, GEORGE. "The Proverbs and Popular Sayings of Berwickshire." *History of the Berwickshire Naturalists' Club*. I (1834), 119–23.

HENDERSON, THOMAS. See SCOTT, SIR WALTER.

HENDERSON, WILLIAM. *Notes on the Folk-lore of the Northern Counties of England and the Borders*. 2nd edn. London 1879.

HENRY THE MINSTREL. *The History . . . of the Renowned Sir William Wallace*, modernised by William Hamilton of Gilbertfield. Edinburgh 1812.

HENRYSON, ROBERT. *The Poems and Fables of Robert Henryson*, ed. H. Harvey Wood. 2nd edn. Edinburgh and London 1958.

HEYWOOD, THOMAS. *The Hierarchie of the Blessed Angells*. London 1635.

HIBBERT, SAMUEL. *A Description of the Shetland Islands*. Edinburgh 1822.

——. *Sketches of the Philosophy of Apparitions*. Edinburgh 1824.

"HIBERNICUS." "Scott and Homer." *N. & Q.* CLXXIII (1937), 171.

HILLHOUSE, JAMES T. *The Waverley Novels and their Critics*. Minneapolis 1936.

HIMMELFARB, GERTRUDE. "John Buchan." *Encounter*. XV (1960), 46–53.

HOFMANN, GEORG. *Entstehungsgeschichte von Sir Walter Scotts 'Marmion.'* Königsberg 1913.

HOGG, DAVID. *Life of Allan Cunningham*. Dumfries 1875.

HOGG, JAMES. *The Mountain Bard*. Edinburgh 1807.

——. *The Spy*. Edinburgh 1811.

——. *The Brownie of Bodsbeck*. 2 vols. Edinburgh 1818.

——. *The Three Perils of Man; or, War, Women and Witchcraft*. 3 vols. London 1822.

——. *The Works of the Ettrick Shepherd*, ed. Thomas Thomson. 2 vols. London 1874.

——. *Domestic Manners of Sir Walter Scott*. With a memoir of Hogg by J. E. H. Thomson. Stirling 1909.

——. *The Private Memoirs and Confessions of a Justified Sinner*. Introduction by André Gide. London 1947.

HOLTHAUSEN, F. and MAX F. MANN. "Die Geschichte von Martin Waldeck in W. Scotts *The Antiquary*." *Beiblatt zur Anglia*. XXIX (1918), 280–3, 375–6.

HOME, DANIEL D. *Incidents in My Life*. 5th edn. New York 1864.

HOME, J. A. See STUART, LADY LOUISA.

HONE, WILLIAM. *Buonapartephobia.* 10th edn. London 1820.

——. *The Every-Day Book.* 2 vols. London 1826-7.

HOWIE, JOHN. *The Judgment and Justice of God Exemplified.* Glasgow 1782.

HOWITT, WILLIAM. "Visits to Remarkable Places. Glammis Castle." *Howitt's Journal.* II (1847), 121-3.

HOYLAND, JOHN. *A Historical Survey of the Customs . . . of the Gypsies.* York 1816.

HUGHES, MARY ANN. *Letters and Recollections of Sir Walter Scott,* ed. H. G. Hutchinson. London 1904.

HUME, DAVID. *The History of England.* New edn., 6 vols. New York 1879.

HUTCHINSON, H. G. See HUGHES, MARY ANN.

INGRAM, J. H. *The Haunted Homes and Family Traditions of Great Britain.* London 1929.

IRVING, WASHINGTON. *Abbotsford and Newstead Abbey.* Philadelphia 1835.

——. *The Complete Writings of Washington Irving.* National edn., 21 vols. New York 1905.

JAMES, G. P. R. *Darnley; or, The Field of the Cloth of Gold.* London 1910.

JARVIS, T. M. *Accredited Ghost Stories.* London 1823.

JEFFREY, ALEXANDER. *The History and Antiquities of Roxburghshire and Adjacent Districts.* 2nd edn., 4 vols. Edinburgh 1855-64.

JENKINS, HERBERT. *The Life of George Borrow.* New York 1924.

JENNINGS, HARGRAVE. *The Rosicrucians: Their Rites and Mysteries.* 7th edn. London n.d.

JOHN OF FORDUN. *Scotichronicon,* ed. Walter Goodall. 2 vols. Edinburgh 1759.

JOHNSON, R. B. See STUART, LADY LOUISA.

JOSEPHUS, FLAVIUS. *Josephus,* tr. H. St. J. Thackeray. 7 vols., Loeb Classical Library. London and New York 1926-43.

KEIGHTLEY, THOMAS. *The Fairy Mythology.* 2 vols. London 1833.

KENNEDY, PATRICK. *Legendary Fictions of the Irish Celts.* London 1866.

KER, W. P. See FROISSART, JEAN.

KINLOCH, GEORGE R., ed. *Ancient Scottish Ballads.* London 1827.

KINSLEY, JAMES, ed. *Scottish Poetry: A Critical Study.* London 1955.

——. See DUNBAR, WILLIAM.

KIRK, ROBERT. *Secret Commonwealth,* 1691. Reprinted as *An Essay of the Nature and Actions of the Subterranean . . . Invisible People . . . .* Edinburgh 1815: ed. Andrew Lang, London 1893.

KIRKTON, JAMES. *The Secret and True History of the Church of Scotland,* ed. C. K. Sharpe. Edinburgh 1817.

KITTREDGE, GEORGE L. "English Witchcraft and James the First." *Studies . . . Presented to Crawford Howell Toy.* New York 1912.

——. *Witchcraft in Old and New England.* Cambridge, Mass. 1929.

KOTHEN, BERTEL. *Quellenuntersuchung zu Walter Scotts Romanen "The Monastery" und "The Abbot."* Weimar 1931.

KRAPPE, A. H. *The Science of Folk-Lore.* New York 1930.

KROEBER, KARL. *Romantic Narrative Art.* Madison 1960

KROGMANN, WILLY. See GOETHE J. W. VON.

L., G. G. "Shelley and Scott." *N. & Q.* CLXXI (1936), 60.

LAING, DAVID. *Select Remains of the Ancient Popular and Romance Poetry of Scotland*, ed. John Small. 2nd edn. Edinburgh and London 1885.

LAING, MALCOLM. See MACPHERSON, JAMES.

"The Laird of Redgauntlet." *Macmillan's Magazine.* LIV (1886), 116–24.

LAKE, J. W. "Memoir of Sir Walter Scott." *The Poetical Works of Sir Walter Scott.* Philadelphia 1836.

LAMB, CHARLES. *The Complete Works of Charles Lamb*, ed. R. H. Shepherd. London 1892.

LAMBERT, M. and J. T. HILLHOUSE. "The Scott Letters in the Huntington Library." *Huntington Library Quarterly.* II (1939), 319–52.

LA MOTTE FOUQUÉ, F. H. K. DE. *Undine*, tr. George Soane. London 1818.

LANE, EDWARD W. *An Account of the Manners and Customs of the Modern Egyptians*, ed. E. S. Poole. 5th edn., 2 vols. London 1871.

LANG, ANDREW. "An Unpublished Work of Scott." *Scribner's Magazine.* XIV (1893), 733–48.

——. See SCOTT, SIR WALTER.

——. *Cock Lane and Commen-Sense.* New edn. London 1894.

——. *The Life and Letters of John Gibson Lockhart.* 2 vols. London 1897.

——. *Alfred Tennyson.* New York 1901.

LANGHORNE, JOHN. *Genius and Valour: A Scotch Pastoral.* 2nd edn. London 1764.

LAW, ROBERT. *Memorialls*, ed. C. K. Sharpe. Edinburgh 1819.

LEA, HENRY C. *A History of the Inquisition of the Middle Ages.* 3 vols. New York 1911.

LECKY, W. E. H. *History of the Rise and Influence of the Spirit of Rationalism in Europe.* 2 vols. New York 1866.

LEE, REV. FREDERICK. *The Other World.* 2 vols. London 1875.

LELAND, CHARLES G. *Gypsy Sorcery and Fortune Telling.* London 1891.

LESLIE, CHARLES R. *Autobiographical Recollections*, ed. Tom Taylor. Boston 1860.

LESLIE, JOHN. *The Historie of Scotland*, ed. E. G. Cody. S.T.S., 4 vols. Edinburgh and London 1888–95.

LETT, LEWIS. *Sir Hubert Murray of Papua.* London and Sydney 1949.

LEWIS, MATTHEW G. *Tales of Wonder.* 2nd edn. London 1801.

——. *The Isle of Devils.* London 1912.

LEYDEN, JOHN. *The Poetical Works of Dr John Leyden.* London and Edinburgh 1875.

——. *Journal of a Tour in the Highlands and Western Islands of Scotland in 1800*, ed. James Sinton. Edinburgh and London 1903.

LIEDER, PAUL R. "Scott and Scandinavian Literature." *Smith College Studies in Modern Languages.* II. 1 (1920), 8–57.

LILLY, WILLIAM. *The Lives of those eminent Antiquaries Elias Ashmole, Esquire, and Mr. William Lilly.* London 1774.

——. *William Lilly's History of His Life and Times, from the Year 1602 to 1681.* London 1822.

——. *An Introduction to Astrology*, from Lilly's *Christian Astrology* of 1647. London 1887.

LINDSAY, SIR DAVID. *The Works of Sir David Lindsay*, ed. Douglas Hamer. S.T.S., 4 vols. Edinburgh and London 1931–6.

LINKLATER, ERIC. Novels and Stories: *White-maa's Saga* (1929); *The Men of Ness* (1932); *Magnus Merriman* (1934); *Sealskin Trousers and Other Stories* (1947); *Laxdale Hall* (1951); *The Faithful Ally* (1954); *The Dark of Summer* (1956); *Husband of Delilah* (1962).

——. *The Man on My Back*. London 1941.

——. *A Year of Space: A Chapter in Autobiography*. New York 1953.

——. *The Ultimate Viking*. New York 1956.

"LLWYVEIN." "The Subtleties of Scott's Names." *The Knickerbocker*. XLVIII (1856), 111–19.

LOCKHART, JOHN G. *Peter's Letters to his Kinsfolk*. New York 1820.

——. *Memoirs of the Life of Sir Walter Scott, Bart*. 7 vols. Edinburgh 1837–8.

LOGAN, JOHN. *Poems*. London 1781.

LONDONDERRY, MARQUESS OF. See CASTLEREAGH, VISCOUNT.

LONGMAN, E. D. and S. LOCH. *Pins and Pincushions*. London 1911.

LYNSKEY, WINIFRED. "The Drama of the Elect and the Reprobate in Scott's *Heart of Midlothian*," *Boston University Studies in English*, IV (1960), 39–48.

McCOMAS, HENRY C. *Ghosts I have Talked With*. Baltimore 1935.

McDIARMID, MATTHEW P. See FERGUSSON, ROBERT.

MacDONALD OF INVERLOCKY, ARCHIBALD. *The Second-Sighted Highlander*. London 1715.

MacDONALD, GEORGE. Novels: *Adela Cathcart*. 3 vols. (1864); *Guild Court*. 3 vols. (1868); *Wilfrid Cumbermede*. 3 vols. (1872); *The Marquis of Lossie*. 3 vols. (1877); *Sir Gibbie*. 3 vols. (1879); *Castle Warlock*. 3 vols. (1882); *What's Mine's Mine*. 3 vols. (1886); *The Elect Lady* (1888); *Lilith* (1895).

——. *Works of Fancy and Imagination*. 10 vols. London 1871; new edn., 1905–11.

MacDONALD, GREVILLE. *George MacDonald and his Wife*. 2nd edn. London 1924.

MACFARLANE, WALTER. *Geographical Collections relating to Scotland*, ed. Sir Arthur Mitchell. Scottish History Society, 3 vols. Edinburgh 1906–08.

MACGREGOR, ALEXANDER. *Highland Superstitions*. 5th edn. Stirling 1937.

MACINTOSH, WILLIAM. *Scott and Goethe*. Glasgow 1925.

MACKAY, CHARLES. *Forty Years' Recollections . . . from 1830 to 1870*. 2 vols. London 1877.

——. *Extraordinary Popular Delusions and the Madness of Crowds*. New York 1960.

McKAY, J. G. "The Deer-Cult and the Deer-Goddess Cult of the Ancient Caledonians." *Folk-Lore*. XLIII (1932), 144–74.

MacKAY, WILLIAM. See FRASER, JAMES.

MacKELLAR, MARY, tr. "The Tale of the 'Bodach Glas.'" *The Celtic Magazine*. XII (1887), 12–16, 57, 106–07.

MACKENZIE, AGNES M. *An Historical Survey of Scottish Literature to 1714*. London 1933.

MACKENZIE, ALEXANDER. *The Prophecies of the Brahan Seer*. Stirling 1899.

MACKENZIE, DONALD A. *Scottish Folk-Lore and Folk Life*. London 1935.

MACKENZIE, SIR GEORGE. *The Laws and Customes of Scotland in Matters Criminal*. Edinburgh 1678.

MACKENZIE, HENRY. *The Works of Henry Mackenzie.* 8 vols. Edinburgh 1808.

MACKINLAY, JAMES M. *Folklore of Scottish Lochs and Springs.* Glasgow 1893.

MACKNIGHT, JAMES. *The Truth of the Gospel History Shewed.* London 1763.

MACLEOD, R. C., ed. *The Book of Dunvegan.* 2 vols. Aberdeen 1938–9.

MACMANUS, FRANCIS. *Boccaccio.* London 1947.

McNEILL, GEORGE P., ed. *Sir Tristrem.* S.T.S., VOL. VIII. Edinburgh 1886.

MACPHERSON, JAMES. *The Poems of Ossian,* ed. Malcolm Laing. 2 vols. Edinburgh 1805.

MALLET, DAVID. *The Excursion.* London 1728.

MALLET, PAUL H. *Northern Antiquities,* tr. Thomas Percy. 2 vols. London 1770.

MALORY, SIR THOMAS. *Le Morte Darthur,* ed. H. Oskar Sommer. 3 vols. London 1889–1891.

MARSHALL, EDWARD. *The Early History of Woodstock Manor.* Oxford and London 1873.
——. *A Supplement to the History of Woodstock Manor.* Oxford and London 1874.

MARTIN, MARTIN. *A Description of the Western Islands of Scotland.* London 1703.

MASSON, ROSALINE. *The Life of Robert Louis Stevenson.* 2nd edn. Edinburgh 1924.

MATHEWS, ANNE. *Memoirs of Charles Mathews, Comedian.* 4 vols. London 1838–9.

MATTHEWS, GEORGE K. *Abbotsford and Sir Walter Scott.* 2nd edn. London 1854.

MATURIN, CHARLES R. *The Milesian Chief.* 4 vols. London 1812.

MAXWELL-SCOTT, MARY M. "Gabions of Abbotsford." *Harper's New Monthly Magazine.* LXXVIII (1889), 778–88.
——. *Abbotsford.* London 1893.
——. "Sir Walter Scott on his 'Gabions.'" *The Nineteenth Century and After.* LVIII (1905), 621–33.

MAYHOFF, KARL. See PLINY THE ELDER.

MAYNE (or MAINE), JOHN. *Two Scots Poems.* Glasgow 1783.

MEDWIN, THOMAS. *Journal of the Conversations of Lord Byron.* New York 1824.

MEINHOLD, WILLIAM. *Sidonia the Sorceress,* tr. Lady Wilde. 2 vols. London 1894.

MELDRUM and ROUGHEAD. See GALT, JOHN.

MENNIE, DUNCAN M. "Sir Walter Scott's Unpublished Translations of German Plays." *M.L.R.* XXXIII (1938), 234–9.

MICKLE, WILLIAM J. *Poems, and a Tragedy.* London 1794.

MILLAR, JOHN, ed. *From Authentic Documents. A History of the Witches of Renfrewshire.* Paisley 1809. Enlarged in new edn., Paisley 1877.

MITCHELL, SIR ARTHUR. See MACFARLANE, WALTER.

MITTON, G. E. See DALGLEISH, WILLIAM.

Miscellanea Scotica. 4 vols. Glasgow 1818–20.

MOIR, GEORGE. *Magic and Witchcraft.* London 1852. First publ. in *F.Q.R.* of 1830.

MONCRIEF, JOHN. *The Poor Man's Physician.* 3rd edn. Edinburgh 1731.

MONTFAUCON DE VILLARS, NICOLAS DE. *The Count of Gabalis . . . the Rosicrucian Doctrine of Spirits.* London 1714.

MONTGOMERIE, WILLIAM. *New Judgments: Robert Burns.* Glasgow 1947.

MOORE, JOHN R. "Scott's *Antiquary* and Defoe's *History of Apparitions.*" *Modern Language Notes*. LIX (1944), 550–1.

MOORE, THOMAS. *Memoirs, Journal, and Correspondence of Thomas Moore*, ed. Lord John Russell. 8 vols. London 1853–6.

——. *The Life, Letters and Journals of Lord Byron*. New edn. London 1920.

MORE, HENRY. *An Antidote to Atheism*. 2nd edn., "corrected and enlarged." London 1655.

MORGAN, LADY. *The Book of the Boudoir*. 2 vols. New York 1829.

MORRISON, JOHN. "Random Reminiscences of Sir Walter Scott. . . ." *Tait's Edinburgh Magazine*. X (1843), 569–78, 626–8, 780–6; XI (1844), 15–19.

MOSHER, ORVILLE W. *Louis XI King of France as he appears in History and in Literature*. Toulouse 1925.

Most Strange and Dreadful Apparition of several Spirits & Visions . . . July, 1680, at the House of Mr. John Thomas . . . London, A. n.p. 1680.

MUKHOPADHAYA, HARENDRAKUMAR. *The Supernatural in Scott*. Calcutta 1917.

MURRAY, J. A. H. See THOMAS OF ERCELDOUNE.

MURRAY, MARGARET. *The Witch-Cult in Western Europe*. Oxford 1921.

NAIDEN, JAMES R. *The Sphera of George Buchanan (1506–1582)*, repr. ((1952)).

NAPIER, MARK. *Memorials and Letters illustrative . . . of John Graham of Claverhouse.* . . . 3 vols. Edinburgh 1859–62.

NASHE, THOMAS. *The Unfortunate Traveller*, ed. John Berryman. New York 1960.

NAUBERT, C. B. E. *Alf von Deulman*, tr. A. E. Booth. London 1790 and 1794.

——. *Herman of Unna*, tr. anon. 2nd edn., 3 vols. London 1794.

NAYLER, B. S. *A Memoir of the Life and Writings of Walter Scott; the Wizzard of the North*. Amsterdam 1833.

NEILSON, GEORGE. "*Huchown of the Awle Ryale*" *the Alliterative Poet*. Glasgow 1902.

Newes from Scotland, Declaring the Damnable Life of Dr. Fian, a Notable Sorcerer. London 1591: rep. 1816 & 1924.

NEWNHAM, WILLIAM. *Essay on Superstition*. London 1830.

NICOLAS, N. H. See FANSHAWE, ANNE.

NICHOLS, J. G. ed. *Narratives of the Days of the Reformation*. Camden Society, LXXVII. London 1859.

NICHOLSON, WILLIAM. *Poetical Works*. 3rd edn. Castle-Douglas 1878.

NICOLL, ALLARDYCE. *A History of Early Nineteenth Century Drama*. Cambridge 1930.

NICOLSON, HAROLD. *Sainte-Beuve*. Garden City, N.Y. ((1956)).

NODIER, CHARLES. *Œuvres de Charles Nodier*. 12 vols. Paris 1832–7.

NOTESTEIN, WALLACE. *A History of Witchcraft in England from 1558 to 1718*. Washington 1911.

NUTT, ALFRED. "Notes on the 'Bodach Glas.'" *The Celtic Magazine*. XII (1887), 106.

O'DONNELL, ELLIOTT. *Scottish Ghost Stories*. London 1911.

——. *The Banshee*. London and Edinburgh [1920].

OLIPHANT, MARGARET. Novels and stories: *A Beleaguered City* (1880); *A Little Pilgrim in the Unseen* (1882); *The Lady's Walk* (1882–3); *The Land of Darkness, along with* some *Further Chapters in the Experiences of the Little Pilgrim* (1888); *The Land of Suspense* (1897).

——. "The Fancies of a Believer." *B.E.M.* CLVII (1895), 237–55.

——. "Mrs Oliphant as a Novelist." *B.E.M.* CLXII (1897), 305–19.

——. *The Autobiography and Letters of Mrs. M. O. W. Oliphant*, ed. Mrs Harry Coghill. New York 1899.

OVID. *The Fasti of Ovid*, tr. Sir James Frazer. 5 vols. London 1929.

P., W. *The History of Witches and Wizards*. London ((?1700)).

PALGRAVE, FRANCIS T. See SCOTT, SIR WALTER.

PARACELSUS. *Four Treatises of . . . Paracelsus*, tr. Henry E. Sigerist and others. Baltimore 1941.

PARK, MUNGO. *Journal of a Mission to the Interior of Africa, in the Year 1805*, with Addenda, ed. John Whishaw. 2nd edn. London 1815.

PARSONS, C. O. "Scott's Experiences in Haunted Chambers." *Modern Philology.* XXX (1932), 103–5.

——. "Anecdotal Background of Rab Tull's Dream." *Scottish Notes and Queries.* 3rd series, XI (1933), 162–3.

——. "Association of the White Lady with Wells." *Folk-Lore.* XLIV (1933), 295–305.

——. "Demonological Background of 'Donnerhugel's Narrative' and 'Wandering Willie's Tale.' " *Studies in Philology.* XXX (1933), 604–17.

——. "Manuscript of Scott's *Letters on Demonology and Witchcraft*." *N. & Q.* CLXIV (1933) 276–7.

——. "Two Notes on Scott." *N. & Q.* CLXIV (1933), 75–7.

——. "Character Names in the Waverley Novels." *P.M.L.A.* XLIX (1934), 276–94.

——. "Scott's Translation of Bürger's 'Das Lied von Treue.' " *Journal of English and Germanic Philology.* XXXIII (1934), 240–9.

——. "Journalistic Anecdotage about Scott." *N. & Q.* CLXXXIII (1942), 339–40.

——. "Scott's *Letters on Demonology and Witchcraft*: Outside Contributors." *N. & Q.* CLXXXII (1942), 156–8, 173–4.

——. "The Bodach Glas in *Waverley*." *N. & Q.* CLXXXIV (1943), 95–7.

——. "The Dalrymple Legend in *The Bride of Lammermoor*." *Review of English Studies.* XIX (1943), 51–8.

——. "The Interest of Scott's Public in the Supernatural." *N. & Q.* CLXXXV (1943), 92–100.

——. "Minor Spirits and Superstitions in the Waverley Novels." *N. & Q.* CLXXXIV (1943), 358–63; CLXXXV (1943), 4–9.

——. "The Original of the Black Dwarf." *Studies in Philogy.* XL (1943), 567–75.

——. "Scott's Fellow Demonologists." *M.L.Q.* IV (1943), 473–93.

——. "Sir John Sinclair's Raspe and Scott's Dousterswivel." *N. & Q.* CLXXXIV (1943), 63–66.

——. "Walter Scott in Pandemonium." *M.L.R.* XXXVIII (1943), 244–9.

——. "The Deaths of Glossin and Hatteraick in *Guy Mannering*." *Philological Quarterly.* XXIV (1945), 169–74.

——. "The Supernatural in Scott's Poetry." *N. & Q.* CLXXXVIII (1945), 2–8, 30–3, 76–7, 98–101.

——. "Stevenson's Use of Witchcraft Cases in 'Thrawn Janet.'" *Studies in Philology.* XLIII (1946), 551–71.

——. "Ghost-Stories before Defoe." *N. & Q.* CCI (1956), 293–8.

——. "Scott's Prior Version of 'The Tapestried Chamber.'" *N. & Q.* CCVII (1962), 417–20.

PARTINGTON, WILFRED. *Sir Walter's Post-Bag.* London 1932.

——, ed. *The Private Letter-Books of Sir Walter Scott.* London 1930.

PATERSON, JAMES. *A Belief in Witchcraft Unsupported by Scripture.* Aberdeen 1815.

PATTERSON, JOHN. *Memoir of Joseph Train . . . the Antiquarian Correspondent of Sir Walter Scott.* Glasgow 1857.

PAULDING, JAMES K. *The Lay of the Scottish Fiddle.* London 1814 (1st edn, 1813).

PEACOCK, THOMAS L. *Nightmare Abbey.* London 1818.

PENNANT, THOMAS. *A Tour in Scotland; 1769.* Chester 1771: 4th edn., London 1776.

PENNECUIK, ALEXANDER. *A Compleat Collection of all the Poems.* Edinburgh ((1750?)).

——, and others. *A Collection of Scots Poems on Several Occasions.* Edinburgh 1769.

PETRONIUS. *The Satyricon of Petronius,* tr. William Arrowsmith. Ann Arbor, Mich. 1959.

PHILLIPS, FORBES and R. T. HOPKINS. *War and the Weird.* London 1916.

PICHOT, AMÉDÉE. "Trois Jours chez Sir Walter Scott." *Revue de Paris.* XXX (1831), 129–44.

PLINY THE ELDER. *C. Plini Secundi Naturalis Historiae Libri XXXVII,* ed. Karl Mayhoff. 6 vols. Leipzig 1870–98.

PLOT, ROBERT. *The Natural History of Oxford-shire.* 2nd edn. Oxford 1705.

PLUMPTRE, JAMES. *Four Discourses on Subjects relating to the Amusement of the Stage.* Cambridge 1809.

PLUTARCH. LIVES, tr. Bernadotte Perrin. 11 vols., Loeb Classical Library. London and New York 1914–26.

POLIDORI, JOHN W. *Ernestus Berchtold.* London 1819.

POOLE, E. S. See LANE, EDWARD W.

POTOCKI, COUNT JAN. *The Saragossa Manuscript,* tr. Elisabeth Abbott. New York 1960.

POTTLE, FREDERICK A. "The Power of Memory in Boswell and Scott." *Essays on the Eighteenth Century Presented to David Nichol Smith.* Oxford 1945.

PRAZ, MARIO. *The Romantic Agony,* tr. Angus Davidson. London 1933.

PRITCHETT, V. S. *The Living Novel.* New York 1947.

RAMESEY, WILLIAM. *Vox Stellarum. Or, The Voice of the Starres.* London 1652.

RAMSAY, ALLAN. *The Works of Allan Ramsay,* ed. Martin and Oliver. S.T.S., 2 vols. Edinburgh and London 1951–3.

RATHBURN and STEINMANN. See DAICHES, DAVID.

Relation of the Diabolical Practices of above Twenty Wizards and Witches . . . of Renfrew . . . 1697, A. London ((1697)).

REMY, NICHOLAS. *Nicolai Remigii Daemonolatreiae Libri Tres.* Lyons 1595: tr. Montague Summers, *Demonolatry.* London 1930.

RICHARDSON, M. A. *The Borderer's Table Book.* 8 vols. Newcastle-upon-Tyne 1846.

RITCHIE, LEITCH. *Scott and Scotland.* London 1835.

RITCHIE, W. TOD, ed. *The Bannatyne Manuscript*. S.T.S., 4 vols. Edinburgh and London 1928–34.

ROBERTSON, J. LOGIE. See BURNS, ROBERT.

——. See THOMSON, JAMES.

ROGERS, CHARLES. *Genealogical Memoirs of the Family of Sir Walter Scott*. London 1877.

ROSS, ALEXANDER. *The Fortunate Shepherdess*. Aberdeen 1768: 2nd edn., *Helenore, or the Fortunate Shepherdess*. Aberdeen 1778.

RUFF, WILLIAM. "Walter Scott and The Erl-King." *Englische Studien*. LXIX (1934), 106–08.

RUSKIN, JOHN. *The Works of John Ruskin*, edd. Cook and Wedderburn, 39 vols. London 1903–12.

RUSSELL, LORD JOHN. See THOMAS MOORE.

RUSSELL and NAPIER. See SPOTTISWOOD, JOHN.

SAMPSON, WILLIAM. *The Vow Breaker. Or, the Faire Maide of Clifton*. London 1636.

Satan's Warehouse Door; or Water Willie's New Mode of Purifying his Hands. Glasgow 1808.

SCHEFFER, JOHANN. *Joannis Schefferi von Strassburg Lappland*. Frankfurt am Main 1675.

SCHOTT, GASPAR. *P. Gasparis Schotti . . . Physica Curiosa, sive Mirabilia Naturae et Artis*. 2 vols. Würzburg 1667.

SCHUMACHER, DOUGLAS F. *Der Volksaberglaube in den Waverley Novels*. Göttingen 1935.

SCOT, REGINALD. *The Discoverie of Witchcraft*, ed. Montague Summers. London 1930.

SCOT, CAPTAIN WALTER. *A True History . . . of the Right Honourable Name of Scot*. 3rd edn. Hawick 1786.

SCOTT, SIR WALTER. *Goetz of Berlichingen, With the Iron Hand*, Goethe, tr. Walter Scott. London 1799.

——. Review of Ossian. *The Edinburgh Review*. VI (1805), 429–62.

——, ed. "*The Somers Tracts*" *A Collection of Scarce and Valuable Tracts*. 2nd edn., 13 vols. London 1809–15.

——. Review of Maturin's *Fatal Revenge*. Q.R. III (1810), 339–47.

——, ed. *Secret History of the Court of James the First*. 2 vols. Edinburgh 1811.

——, ed. *Sir Tristrem*. 3rd edn. Edinburgh 1811.

——. *The Border Antiquities of England and Scotland*. 2 vols. London 1814–17.

——. Review of "Culloden Papers." Q.R. XIV (1815–16), 283–333.

——. *Paul's Letters to His Kinsfolk*. Edinburgh 1816.

——, and WILLIAM ERSKINE. Review of *Tales of My Landlord*. 3rd edn. Q.R. XVI (1817), 430–80. Repr. in *Famous Reviews*, ed. R. Brimley Johnson, pp. 309–28. London 1914.

——. "Story of an Apparition." B.E.M. III (1818), 705–07.

——, ed. *Chronological Notes of Scottish Affairs, from 1680 till 1701 . . . from the Diary of Lord Fountainhall*. Edinburgh 1822.

——. Review of Galt's *The Omen*. B.E.M., XX (1826), 52–9.

——. *The Life of Napoleon Buonaparte*. 3 vols. Philadelphia 1827.

——. "On the Supernatural in Fictitious Composition; and particularly on the Works of . . . Hoffman." F.Q.R. I (1827), 60–98.

——. *Anne of Geierstein.* 3 vols. Edinburgh 1829. Interleaved copy, with Scott's corrections, in Harvard College Library.

——. *The History of Scotland.* 2 vols. London 1830; Philadelphia 1830.

——. *Letters on Demonology and Witchcraft, Addressed to J. G. Lockhart, Esq.* London 1830. Reviewed in the *Athenaeum, Atlas, Court Journal, Eclectic Review, Fraser's Magazine, Monthly Review, Spectator, Tatler,* G.M., etc.

——. *The Miscellaneous Prose Works of Sir Walter Scott.* 30 vols. Edinburgh 1834–71.

——. *The Miscellaneous Works of Sir Walter Scott.* Edinburgh 1836.

——. *Lives of Eminent Novelists and Dramatists.* New edn. London and New York 1887.

——. *The Journal of Sir Walter Scott,* ed. David Douglas. 2 vols. Edinburgh 1890.

——. Waverley Novels. Border Edition, ed. Andrew Lang. 48 vols. London 1892–4. Also Waverley Novels, "Macmillan's Illustrated Pocket Scott," ed. Andrew Lang, 25 vols. London 1905.

——. *Familiar Letters of Sir Walter Scott.* 2 vols. Boston and New York 1894.

——. *Minstrelsy of the Scottish Border,* ed. Thomas F. Henderson. 4 vols. Edinburgh 1902: ed. Thomas Henderson, New York ((1931)).

——. *The Poetical Works,* ed. Francis T. Palgrave. London 1923.

——. *Tales of a Grandfather; being Stories taken from Scottish History.* 3 vols. London and Glasgow 1923.

——. *The Letters of Sir Walter Scott,* ed. H. J. C. Grierson. 12 vols. London 1932–7.

——. *Short Stories.* Introduction by Lord David Cecil. London 1934.

——. *The Correspondence of Sir Walter Scott and Charles Robert Maturin,* edd. Ratchford and McCarthy. Austin, Texas 1937.

——. *Private Letters of the Seventeenth Century,* ed. Douglas Grant. Oxford 1947.

——. *The Journal of Sir Walter Scott,* ed. J. G. Tait. Edinburgh 1950.

——. *Rob Roy.* Introduction by Edgar Johnson. Boston ((1956)).

Second Book of Scottish Pasquils &c., A. Edinburgh 1828.

SEMPILL, ROBERT. *The Sempill Ballates,* ed. T. G. Stevenson. Edinburgh 1872.

SHAKESPEARE, WILLIAM. *The Yale Shakespeare,* edd. Wilbur L. Cross and Tucker Brooke. 40 vols. New Haven 1918–28.

SHARP, GRANVILLE. *The Case of Saul, shewing that his disorder was a real Spiritual Possession.* London 1807.

SHARPE, CHARLES K. Introduction to Law's *Memorialls* (1819).

——. *A Historical Account of the Belief in Witchcraft in Scotland.* London 1884.

——. *Letters from and to Charles Kirkpatrick Sharpe,* ed. Alexander Allardyce. 2 vols. Edinburgh and London 1888.

——. See ARGYLL, ARCHIBALD EARL OF.

——. See LAW, ROBERT.

SILONE, IGNAZIO. *Bread and Wine,* tr. David and Mosbacher. New York and London 1937.

SIMON, EDITH. *The Piebald Standard: A Biography of the Knights Templars.* Boston and Toronto ((1959)).

SIMOND, LOUIS. *Switzerland.* 2 vols. Boston 1822.

SIMPSON, J. Y. "Notes on Some Scottish Magical Charm-Stones, or Curing Stones *Proceedings* of the Society of Antiquaries of Scotland. IV (1863), 211–24.

z

SIMPSON, LOUIS. *James Hogg: A Critical Study*. Edinburgh and London 1962.

SIMSON, WALTER. "Anecdotes of the Fife Gipsies." *B.E.M.* II (1817), 282–5, 523–8; III (1818), 14–18, 393–8.

——. *A History of the Gypsies*, ed. James Simson. London 1865.

SINCLAIR, GEORGE. *Satan's Invisible World Discovered*, ed. T. G. Stevenson. Edinburgh 1871: 1st edn. in Abbotsford Library has MS notes and letter, Edinburgh 1685.

SINTON, JAMES. See LEYDEN, JOHN.

SITWELL, SACHEVERELL. *Poltergeists*. New York 1959.

SKENE, JAMES. "Some Account of a Subterraneous Structure in Swabia, supposed to have been connected with . . . the Secret Tribunal" (1824), *Archaeologia Scotica*, III, Pt. I (1828), in *Transactions* of the Society of Antiquaries of Scotland. III (1831) 17–39.

——. *Memories of Sir Walter Scott*, ed. Basil Thomson. London 1909.

SKENE, WILLIAM F. *Celtic Scotland*. 2nd edn., 3 vols. Edinburgh 1886–90.

——, ed. *Chronicles of the Picts . . . Scots, and Other Early Memorials of Scottish History*. Edinburgh 1867.

SMALL, JOHN. See DOUGLAS, GAVIN.

SMART, J. S. *James Macpherson*. London 1905.

SMITH, EDWIN W. and A. M. DALE. *The Ila-speaking Peoples of Northern Rhodesia*. 2 vols. London 1920.

SMITH, G. GREGORY. *Scottish Literature*. London 1919.

SMITH, HORACE. *Brambletye House; or, Cavaliers and Roundheads*. 3rd edn., 3 vols. London 1826.

SMITH, JOHN. "The Geology and Romance of the Rhymer's Glen." *Transactions* of the Hawick Archaeological Society. Session 1931, pp. 36–9.

SMITH, SYDNEY G., ed. *Robert Fergusson 1750–1774: Essays by Various Hands*. Edinburgh 1952.

SMITH, WALTER. *The Poetical Works*. London 1906: 1st edn., 1902.

SOMMER, H. OSKAR. See MALORY, SIR THOMAS.

"Spectre Dog of Peel Castle, The. The 'Manthe Dhoo' of 'Peveril of the Peak.' " *Borderland*. I (1894), 472–5.

SPEIRS, JOHN. *The Scots Literary Tradition*. 2nd edn. London 1962.

SPENCE, LEWIS. *Second Sight: Its History and Origins*. London 1951.

SPENCE, RHODA, ed. *The Scottish Companion*. Edinburgh 1955.

SPIESS, CHRISTIAN H. *Das Petermänchen*. Prague and Leipzig 1793. Translated as *The Dwarf of Westerbourg*. 2 vols. London 1827.

Spirit of Partridge; or, the Astrologer's Pocket Companion, and General Magazine, The. London 1825.

SPOTTISWOOD, JOHN. *The History of the Church of Scotland*, edd. Russell and Napier, Spottiswood Society. 3 vols. Edinburgh 1847–51.

SPRENGER, JAKOB, and HEINRICH KRÄMER. *Malleus Maleficarum*, tr. Montague Summers. London 1928.

STAAKE, PAUL. *A Critical Introduction to Sir Walter Scott's Lay of the Last Minstrel*. Meerane 1888.

STACKHOUSE, THOMAS. *A History of the Holy Bible*, ed. George Gleig. 3 vols. London 1817.

STANHOPE, LADY HESTER. *Memoirs of the Lady Hester Stanhope*, ed. C. L. Meryon. 3 vols. London 1845.

Statutes: Revised Edition, The. 18 vols. London 1870–85.

STEPHEN, SIR LESLIE. *History of English Thought in the Eighteenth Century.* 3rd edn., 2 vols. New York 1927.

STEVENSON, ROBERT LOUIS. *Edinburgh Picturesque Notes.* New edn. London 1889.

——. "Scott's Voyage in the Lighthouse Yacht." *Scribner's Magazine.* XIV (1893), 492–502.

——. *The Letters of Robert Louis Stevenson*, ed. Sidney Colvin. New edn., 4 vols. New York 1911.

——. *The Works of Robert Louis Stevenson.* Tusitala Edition, 35 vols. London 1923–4.

STEVENSON, T. G. See SINCLAIR, GEORGE.

——. See SEMPILL, ROBERT.

STOKOE, F. W. *German Influence in the English Romantic Period 1788–1818.* Cambridge 1926.

Storys of the Bewitched Fiddler, Perilous Situation, and John Hetherington's Dream. Glasgow n.d.

STREATFEILD, REV. THOMAS. *The Bridal of Armagnac, a Tragedy.* London 1823.

STUART, LADY LOUISA. *Lady Louisa Stuart: Selections from Her Manuscripts,* ed. J. A. Home. Edinburgh 1899.

——. *Letters of Lady Louisa Stuart to Miss Louisa Clinton,* ed. J. A. Home. Edinburgh 1901.

——. *Letters of Lady Louisa Stuart to Miss Louisa Clinton,* ed. J. A. Home. 2nd series. Edinburgh 1903.

——. *The Letters of Lady Louisa Stuart,* ed. R. B. Johnson. London 1926.

SUMMERS, MONTAGUE, ed. *The Supernatural Omnibus.* London 1931.

——. *The Gothic Quest: A History of the Gothic Novel.* London ((1938)).

——. *The History of Witchcraft and Demonology.* 2nd edn. New York ((1956)).

SURTEES, ROBERT. *The History and Antiquities of the County Palatine of Durham.* 4 vols. London 1816–40.

TAILLEPIED, NOEL. *A Treatise of Spirits,* tr. Montague Summers. London ((1933)).

TAIT, J. G. See SCOTT, SIR WALTER.

TATE, GEORGE, "Notes on the Geology of the Eildon Hills." *History of the Berwickshire Naturalists' Club.* V (1868), 4–6.

TAYLOR, JOHN. *The Caledonian Comet.* London 1810.

TAYLOR, JOSEPH. *Apparitions.* 2nd edn., enlarged. London 1815.

TAYLOR, SISTER M. EUSTACE. *William Julius Mickle (1734–1788): A Critical Study.* Washington 1937.

TAYLOR, TOM. See LESLIE, CHARLES R.

THOMAS OF ERCELDOUNE. *The Romance and Prophecies of Thomas of Erceldoune,* ed. J. A. H. Murray. E.E.T.S., VOL. LXI. London 1875.

THOMSON, BASIL. See SKENE, JAMES.

THOMSON, JAMES. *The Complete Poetical Works of James Thomson*, ed. J. Logie Robertson. London 1908.

THOMSON, THOMAS. See CALDERWOOD, DAVID.

TICKNOR, GEORGE. *Life, Letters, and Journals of George Ticknor*. 2 vols. Boston and New York 1909.

TIMBS, JOHN. *Ancestral Stories and Traditions of Great Families*. London 1869.
——. *Abbeys, Castles, and Ancient Halls of England and Wales*. ed. Alexander Gunn. 2nd edn., 3 vols. London 1872.

TOMPKINS, J. M. S. *The Popular Novel in England 1770–1800*. London 1932.

TORFAEUS, THORMODUS. *Universi Septentrionis Antiquitates*. Copenhagen 1705.

TRAILL, H. D. See CARLYLE, THOMAS.

TRAIN, JOSEPH. *Strains of the Mountain Muse*. Edinburgh 1814.
——. *An Historical and Statistical Account of the Isle of Man*. 2 vols. Douglas 1845.

TRELAWNY, EDWARD J. *Recollections of the Last Days of Shelley and Byron*, ed. Edward Dowden. London 1906.

The Trial of Joseph Powell, the Fortune-Teller . . . 1807. London 1808.

True and Faithful Narrative of Oliver Cromwell's compact with the Devil for seven years. 2nd edn. London 1720.

True and Genuine Copy of the Last Speech . . . of Nicol Muschet of Boghall, A. (?) Edinburgh (?) 1725.

The Tryal of Thomas Colley. 2nd edn. London ((?1751)).

TURNER, WILLIAM. *A Compleat History of the Most Remarkable Providences . . . in this Present Age*. London 1697.

VANE, CHARLES. See CASTLEREAGH, VISCOUNT.

VERNER, GERALD, ed. *Prince of Darkness*. London 1946.

Visits from the World of Spirits. Glasgow n.d.

WAITE, ARTHUR E. *The Brotherhood of the Rosy Cross*. London 1924.

WALDRON, GEORGE. *A Description of the Isle of Man*, ed. William Harrison. Douglas 1865.

WALKER, CLEMENT. *The Compleat History of Independency*. 4 pts. London 1660–1.

WALKER, PATRICK. *Biographia Presbyteriana*. 2 vols. Edinburgh 1827.

WALPOLE, HORACE. *The Castle of Otranto; a Gothic Story*. Introduction by Scott. Edinburgh 1811.

WARNER, RICHARD. *Illustrations, Critical, Historical, Biographical, and Miscellaneous, of Novels by the Author of Waverley*. 3 vols. London 1824.

WATSON, WILLIAM J. *The History of the Celtic Place-Names of Scotland*. Edinburgh and London 1926.

WEBSTER, JOHN. *The Displaying of Supposed Witchcraft*. London 1677.

WELSH, ALEXANDER. *The Hero of the Waverley Novels*. New Haven 1963.

WESLEY, REV. JOHN. *The Journal of the Rev. John Wesley*, ed. Nehemiah Curnock. London 1909.

WEST, ROBERT H. *The Invisible World: A Study of Pneumatology in Elizabethan Drama*. Athens, Georgia 1939.

WHISHAW, JOHN. See PARK, MUNGO.

WHITE, HENRY A. *Sir Walter Scott's Novels on the Stage*. New Haven 1927.

WILKIE, JAMES. *Bygone Fife*. Edinburgh and London 1931.

WILSON, JOHN. *Noctes Ambrosianae*. 4 vols. Edinburgh 1855.

WIMBERLY, LOWRY C. *Folklore in the English and Scottish Ballads*. New York 1959.

WINDHAM, WILLIAM. *The Diary of the Right Hon. William Windham 1784–1810*, ed. Mrs Henry Baring. London 1866.

WISHART, GEORGE. *Memoirs of the most renowned James Graham, Marquis of Montrose*. Edinburgh 1819.

WITTIG, KURT. *The Scottish Tradition in Literature*. Edinburgh 1958.

WODROW, ROBERT. *The History of the Sufferings of the Church of Scotland*, ed. Robert Burns. 4 vols. Glasgow 1830–5.

——. *Analecta*. Maitland Club, 4 vols. Glasgow 1842–3.

WOLFF, JOSEPH. *Journal of the Rev. Joseph Wolff*. London 1839.

WOLFF, ROBERT L. *The Golden Key: A Study of the Fiction of George MacDonald*. New Haven, Conn. 1961.

WOLTMANN, KAROLINE VON. *Neue Volkssager der Böhmen*. Halberstadt 1821. "Der weisse Frau," pp. 1–118, was translated by C. L. Lyttelton as *The White Lady*. London 1844.

WOOD, ANTHONY À. *Athenae Oxonienses*, ed. Philip Bliss. 5 vols. London 1813–20.

WOOD, H. HARVEY. See HENRYSON, ROBERT.

YEATS, WILLIAM B. Works, separately titled, 6 vols. New York 1924–30.

YONGE, CHARLES D. *Life of Sir Walter Scott*. London 1888.

GENERAL INDEX

alchemy: Galt on, in *The Majolo*, 305; and in *The Rosicrucians*, 305; Scott on, in *Anne of Geierstein*, 229; and in *Kenilworth*, 89.

amulets: as charms against fairies, 169; and against witchcraft, 135–6; in *Ivanhoe*, 149.

animal magnetism: 8.

antipathy: Galt on, 301, 306; Scott on, 93.

antiquarian: 33, 46, 178; Mrs Hughes as, 207; Scott as, 48, 66, 85, 105, 173, 186, 238, 262; and in *The Antiquary*, 118; and in astrological studies, 86; and in *Chronicles of the Canongate*, 283–5; and in *Peveril of the Peak*, 77; and in *The Pirate*, 85, 223, 252; and in projected *Demonology*, 13; and in reading, 68; and in Waverley Novels, 95; Train as, 136, 151.

astrology: Barbour on, 17, 18; Comnena on, 91; Galt on, 305, 308; Henryson on, 21; Lilly on, 94; Scott on, 17, 73, 86, 88–9, 91–3, 164; and in *The Abbot*, 83; and in *Anne of Geierstein*, 229; and in *The Antiquary*, 94; and in *The Bride of Lammermoor*, 144; and in *Guy Mannering*, 73, 81, 82, 87, 89, 91, 221, 266, 273–4; and in *Kenilworth*, 89–90, 133, 198, 281; and in *The Pirate*, 83–4; and in *Quentin Durward*, 89–90, 200, 239–40, 265, 281; and in *The Talisman*, 17, 89, 90–1, 225, 237, 268, 281. See also Nativity, theory of.

atavism: Buchan on, 316, 322; Linklater on, 322.

augury: 248; Galt on, 305; Macpherson on, 43; Scott on, 235, 251.

aural foreknowledge: 301.

ballads: 47, 51, 58, 113, 178; Buchan's knowledge of, 315; fairies in, 40; German, Scott's interest in, 53, 66, 93,

204; ghosts in, 113; Hogg as author of, 288, 289, 292, 295–6; Scott as author of, 49, 52, 53, 55, 61; and as collector of, 57, 136; and as editor of, 49, 57; and as imitator of, 57, 297; and as narrator of, 111; and as reader of, 40, 49; and as translator of, 51, 153; Scott's use of techniques of, in *The Black Dwarf*, 99; and in *The Bride of Lammermoor*, 41; and in *The Lady of the Lake*, 61; and in *The Shepherd's Tale*, 54; and in the Waverley Novels, 68; supernatural in, 40, 55, 295–6; witchcraft in, 40.

banshee: 61, 74, 76, 77, 160, 161, 163, 171.

bahr-geist: 19, 77, 273.

bier-right: 230, 231, 268.

birthmark: 252, 284, 298.

bogles: 96, 128; in *The Black Dwarf*, 126, 256; in *The Bride of Lammermoor*, 256; in *The Brownie of Bodsbeck*, 290; in *St Ronan's Well*, 256; in *Rob Roy*, 132, 191; in "The Wool-Gatherers," 290; relation of to duergar, 258; and to "racketing-devil," 256.

brownie: 6, 32, 128; Collins on, 39; definition of by Scott, 255; Galt on, 302; Hogg on, 255, 286, 289, 293; in *The Fortunes of Nigel*, 119; in *The Heart of Midlothian*, 256; in *The Lay of the Last Minstrel*, 58, 59; in *The Monastery*, 161; in *Rob Roy*, 132, 255–256; in "The Shepherd's Tale," 54; in *The Watcher by the Threshold*, 316.

cabalism: 93, 180; Galt on, 305; in *Kenilworth*, 199; in "My Aunt Margaret's Mirror," 219.

changeling: 28, 134, 170–2, 176; in *Peveril of the Peak*, 76, 163, 171, 276; in

INDEX OF AUTHORS AND TITLES